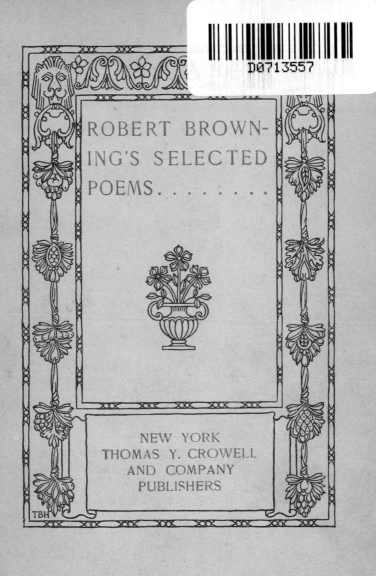

ROBERT BROWN-
ING'S SELECTED
POEMS. . . . .

NEW YORK
THOMAS Y. CROWELL
AND COMPANY
PUBLISHERS

TBH

POEMS

OF

ROBERT BROWNING

From the Author's Revised Text of 1889

HIS OWN SELECTIONS

WITH ADDITIONS FROM HIS LATEST WORKS

EDITED WITH BIOGRAPHICAL AND CRITICAL
NOTES AND INTRODUCTIONS

BY

CHARLOTTE PORTER AND HELEN A. CLARKE

EDITORS OF "POET LORE"

———•◦❀◦•———

NEW YORK
THOMAS Y. CROWELL & CO.
PUBLISHERS

In the present selection from my poetry, there is an attempt to escape from the embarrassment of appearing to pronounce upon what myself may consider the best of it. I adopt another principle; and by simply stringing together certain pieces on the thread of an imaginary personality, I present them in succession, rather as the natural development of a particular experience than because I account them the most noteworthy portion of my work. Such an attempt was made in the volume of selections from the poetry of Elizabeth Barrett Browning: to which — in outward uniformity, at least — my own would venture to become a companion.

A few years ago, had such an opportunity presented itself, I might have been tempted to say a word in reply to the objections my poetry was used to encounter. Time has kindly co-operated with my disinclination to write the poetry and the criticism besides. The readers I am at last privileged to expect, meet me fully half-way; and if, from the fitting stand-point, they must still "censure me in their wisdom," they have previously "awakened their senses that they may the better judge." Nor do I apprehend any more charges of being wilfully obscure, unconscientiously careless, or perversely harsh. Having hitherto done my utmost in the art to which my life is a devotion, I cannot engage to increase the effort; but I conceive that there may be helpful light, as well as re-assuring warmth, in the attention and sympathy I gratefully acknowledge.

R. B.

London, May 14, 1872.

CONTENTS.

	PAGE
EDITOR'S PREFACE	ix
BIOGRAPHICAL INTRODUCTION	xi
CRITICAL INTRODUCTION	xxv
My Star	1
A Face	1
My Last Duchess	2
Song from "Pippa Passes"	3
Cristina	4
Count Gismond	5
Eurydice to Orpheus	9
The Glove	9
Song	14
A Serenade at the Villa	14
Youth and Art	16
The Flight of the Duchess	19
Song from "Pippa Passes"	39
"How they brought the Good News from Ghent to Aix"	39
Song from "Paracelsus"	41
Through the Metidja to Abd-el-Kadr	42
Incident of the French Camp	43
The Lost Leader	44
In a Gondola	45
A Lovers' Quarrel	51
Earth's Immortalities	56
The Last Ride together	56
Mesmerism	59
By the Fireside	64
Any Wife to Any Husband	72
In a Year	76
Song from "James Lee"	79
A Woman's Last Word	79
Meeting at Night	81
Parting at Morning	81
Women and Roses	81
Misconceptions	83
A Pretty Woman	83
A Light Woman	86
Love in a Life	88
Life in a Love	88
The Laboratory	89
Gold Hair: A Story of Pornic	91
The Statue and the Bust	96
Love among the Ruins	103
Time's Revenges	105
Waring	107
Home Thoughts from Abroad	113
The Italian in England	113
The Englishman in Italy	117

	PAGE
Up at a Villa — Down in the City	120
Pictor Ignotus	123
Fra Lippo Lippi	124
Andrea del Sarto	133
The Bishop orders his Tomb at Saint Praxed's Church	138
A Toccata of Galuppi's	141
How it strikes a Contemporary	143
Protus	146
Master Hugues of Saxe-Gotha	147
Abt Vogler	152
Two in the Campagna	155
"De Gustibus——"	157
The Guardian-Angel	158
Evelyn Hope	160
Memorabilia	162
Apparent Failure	162
Prospice	164
"Childe Roland to the Dark Tower came"	165
A Grammarian's Funeral	171
Cleon	174
Instans Tyrannus	182
An Epistle containing the Strange Medical Experience of Karshish, the Arab Physician	184
Caliban upon Setebos ; or, Natural Theology in the Island	191
Saul	198
Rabbi Ben Ezra	207
Epilogue	213
A Wall	217
Apparitions	218
Natural Magic	218
Magical Nature	219
Garden Fancies	219
In Three Days	223
The Lost Mistress	224
One Way of Love	225
Rudel to the Lady of Tripoli	225
Numpholeptos	226
Appearances	230
The Worst of it	230
Too Late	234
Bifurcation	237
A Likeness	238
May and Death	240
A Forgiveness	241
Cenciaja	251

CONTENTS.

	PAGE
Porphyria's Lover	257
Filippo Baldinucci on the Privilege of Burial	259
Soliloquy of the Spanish Cloister	272
The Heretic's Tragedy	275
Holy-Cross Day	278
Amphibian	282
St. Martin's Summer	285
James Lee's Wife	288
Respectability	300
Dis Aliter Visum; or, Le Byron de Nos Jours	301
Confessions	306
The Householder	307
Tray	308
Cavalier Tunes	310
Before	312
After	314
Hervé Riel	314
In a Balcony	318
Old Pictures in Florence	339
Bishop Blougram's Apology	347
Mr. Sludge, "The Medium"	369
The Boy and the Angel	403
A Death in the Desert	406
Fears and Scruples	421
Artemis Prologizes	422
Pheidippides	425
The Patriot	428

	PAGE
Popularity	429
Pisgah Sights. 1	432
Pisgah Sights. 2	433
Pisgah Sights. 3	434
At the "Mermaid"	435
House	439
Shop	441
A Tale	444
Additional Selections from Browning's Latest Works, 1880–1889	448
Echetlos	448
Touch him ne'er so Lightly	449
Wanting is — What?	449
Never the Time and the Place	450
Round us the Wild Creatures	450
Ask not One Least Word of Praise	451
Epilogue to "Ferishtah's Fancies"	451
The Names	452
Why I am a Liberal	452
Prologue to "Asolando"	453
Rosny	454
Poetics	455
Summum Bonum	455
Muckle-Mouth Meg	455
Epilogue to "Asolando"	456
Notes	459
Bibliography	504
Index to Poems	509
Index to First Lines	511

EDITORS' PREFACE.

———◦◦◦———

BROWNING'S own selections from his works supply the general reader, or the student who intends further complete study, with the most coherent representative short survey or initial presentation of his whole complex and voluminous genius.

The poet has made his selections cover the entire range of his work from 1833 to 1879; the present editors, not presuming to go back over any part of the field from which he has garnered, have added from his later publications a choice handful of short poems, mainly lyrical, beginning with the second series of 'Dramatic Idyls,' 1880, and closing with the final volume, 'Asolando,' 1889, which was published in London on the day of Browning's death in Venice.

Care has been taken to give with accuracy Browning's own latest revised text of 1888, 1889; also, to make the Introduction and Notes rich in small space. In making the æsthetic part of the Notes, the aim has been neither to paraphrase, nor to give comment about the poems, but to epitomize the gist of each one, or, at most, where the poem demanded such treatment, to summarize its leading traits and show its outcome. Such a procedure seemed especially appropriate to this volume which Browning intended should offer the public a representative view of his poetic domain, and the editors hope this part of their work will especially commend itself. They believe the Notes will also be found to shed light on many allusions not before explained.

Finally, they desire to acknowledge with cordial gratitude their indebtedness to the work of their predecessors, especially to Mrs. Orr, Professor Hiram Corson, Mr. George Willis Cooke, Dr. Edward Berdoe, Dr. W. J. Rolfe, and Miss Hersey for help in allusions; and to Mrs. Orr, Mr. William Sharpe, Mr. Edmund Gosse, and Mr. W. G. Kingsland, from whom the materials for the biographical sketch were drawn; also to the Boston Browning Society, whose collection of first editions was consulted in compiling the bibliography.

BOSTON, *May* 20, 1896.

BIOGRAPHICAL INTRODUCTION.

"A peep through my window, if folk prefer;
But, please you, no foot over threshold of mine." — 'HOUSE.'

WHEN some depreciator of the familiar declared that "Only in Italy is there any romance left," Browning replied, "Ah! well, I should like to include poor old Camberwell," and "poor old Camberwell," where Robert Browning was born, May 7, 1812, offered no meagre nurture for the fancy of a child gifted with the ardor that greatens and glorifies the real.

Nature still garlanded this suburban part of London with bowery spaces breathing peace. The view of the region from Herne Hill over softly wreathing distances of domestic wood "was, before railroads came, entirely lovely," Ruskin says. He writes of "the tops of twenty square miles of politely inhabited groves," of bloom of lilac and laburnum and of almond-blossoms, intermingling suggestions of the wealth of fruit-trees in enclosed gardens, and companioning all this with the furze, birch, oak, and bramble of the Norwood hills, and the open fields of Dulwich "animate with cow and buttercup."

Nature was ready to beckon the young poet to dreams and solitude, and, too close to need to vie with her, the great city was at hand to make her power intimately felt. From a height crowned by three large elms, Browning, as a lad, used to enjoy the picturesqueness of his "poor old Camberwell." Its heart of romance was centred for him in the sight of the vast city lying to the westward. His memory singled out one such visit as peculiarly significant, the first one on which he beheld teeming London by night, and heard the vague confusion of her collective voice beneath the silence of the stars.

Within the home into which he was born, equally well-poised conditions befriended him, fostering the development of his emotional and intellectual nature. His mother was once described by Carlyle as "the true type of a Scottish gentlewoman." Browning himself used to say of her "with tremulous emotion," according to his friend, Mrs. Orr, "she was a divine woman." Her gentle, deeply religious nature evidently derived its evangelical tendency from her mother, also Scotch; while from her father, William Wiedemann, ship-owner, a Hamburg German, settled in Dundee, who was an accomplished draughtsman and musician, she seems to have derived the liking and facility for music which was one of the characteristic bents of the poet. To this Scotch-German descent on his mother's side the metaphysical quality of his mind is accountable, concerning which Harriet Martineau is recorded as having said to him, "You have no need to study German thought, your mind is German enough already." The peculiarly tender affection his mother called out in him seems to have been at once proof and enhancement of the mystical, emotional, and impressible side of his disposition; and these traits were founded on an organic inheritance from her of "what he called a nervousness of nature," which his father could not have bequeathed to him.

Exuberant vitality, insatiable intellectual curiosity and capacity, the characteristics of Robert Browning the elder, were the heritage of his son, but raised in him to a more effective power, through their transmutation, perhaps, as Mrs. Orr suggests, in the more sensitive physique and temperament inherited from his mother. Of his father, Browning wrote that his "Powers, natural and acquired, would easily have made him a notable man, had he known what vanity or ambition or the love of money or social influence meant." He had refused to stay on his mother's sugar plantation at St. Kitt's in the West Indies, losing the fortune to be achieved there, because of his detestation of slavery, and the office he filled in the Bank of England was never close enough to his liking to induce him to rise in it so far as his father had risen; but it enabled him to indulge his tastes for many books and a few pictures and to secure for his son, as that son said shortly before his death, "all the ease and comfort that a literary man needs to do good work."

One of the poet's own early recollections gives a picture that epitomizes the joint influence of his happy parentage. It depicts the child "sitting on his father's knees in the library, listening with enthralled attention to the tale of Troy, with marvellous illustrations among the glowing coals in the fireplace; with, below all, the vaguely heard accompaniment — from the neighboring room where Mrs. Browning sat 'in her chief happiness, her hour of darkness and solitude and music' — of a wild Gaelic lament."

His father's brain was itself a library, stored with literary antiquities, which, his son used to say, made him seem to have known Paracelsus, Faustus, and even Talmudic personages personally, and his heart was so young and buoyant that his lore, instead of isolating him from his boy and girl, made him their most entertaining companion.

It is not surprising that under such circumstances the ordinary schooling was too puerile for young Robert's wide-awake wits. He was so energetic in mind and body that he was sent to a day-school near by for peace' sake at an early age, and sent back again, for peace' sake, too, because his proficiency made the mammas complain that Mrs. —— was neglecting her other pupils for the sake of bringing on Master Browning. Home teaching followed. Also home amusement, which included the keeping of a variety of pets, — owls, monkeys, magpies, hedgehogs, an eagle, a toad, and two snakes. If any further proof is needed of the hospitable warmth of his youthful heart, an entry in his diary at the age of seven or eight may serve — " married two wives this morning." This referred, of course, to an imaginary appropriation of two girls he had just seen in church.

Later he entered the school of the Misses Ready and passed thence to their brother's school, staying there till he was fourteen, but his contempt for the petty and formal learning which is the best accorded many children, was marked, and perfectly natural to a boy who delighted to plunge in the deeper knowledge his father's book-crammed house opened generously to him.

In the list, given by Mrs. Orr, of books early attractive to him, were a seventeenth edition of Quarles's 'Emblems'; first editions of ' Robinson Crusoe,' and Milton; the original pamphlet, ' Killing no Murder ' (1559) which Carlyle borrowed for his ' Cromwell'; an early edition of the ' Bees ' by the Bernard Mandeville, with whom he was destined later to hold a ' Parleying' of his own: rare old Bibles; Voltaire; a wide range of English poetry; the Greek and Elizabethan dramatists.

His father's profound love of poetry was essentially classic, and his marked aptitude in rhyming followed the models of Pope, but Browning's early poet was Byron, and all his sympathies were warmly romantic. His verse-making, which began before he could write, resulted at twelve in a volume of short poems, presumably Byronic, which he gracefully entitled ' Incondita.'

He wanted, in vain, to find a publisher for this, and soon afterwards destroyed it, but not before his mother had shown it to Miss Flower, and she, to her sister, Sarah Flower, and to Mr. Fox, and the budding poet had thus gained the attention of three genuine friends.

Shortly after this, the Byronic star which had shed its somewhat lurid influence over the first ebullitions of his genius, was forever banished by the appearance of a new star within his field of vision. Incredible as it may seem to the present generation, he had never heard

of Shelley, and if it had not been for a happy chance, an important in-
fluence in the early shaping of his poetic faculties might have been
postponed until too late to furnish its quickening impulse.

One day in passing a book-stall, he happened to see advertised in a
box of second-hand wares a little book, ' Mr. Shelley's Atheistical
Poems : ' very scarce.   Though the little second-hand volume was
only a miserable pirated edition, by its means such entrancing glimpses
of an unsuspected world were revealed to the boy that he longed to
possess more of Shelley. His mother, accordingly, sallied forth in search
of Shelley's poems, which, after many tribulations, she at length found at
C. and J. Ollier's of Vere Street.   She brought away not only nearly all
of Shelley in first editions (the ' Cenci ' excepted), but three volumes
of Keats, whom she was assured would interest anybody who liked
Shelley.   Browning, himself, used to recall how, at the end of this
eventful day, two nightingales, one in the laburnum at the end of his
father's garden, and one in a copper beech in the next garden, sang in
emulation of the poets whose music had laid its subtile spell upon him.
While Keats was duly appreciated, it was Shelley who appealed most
to Browning, and although it was some years before any poetic mani-
festation of Shelley's influence was to work itself out, he, with youthful
ardor, at once adopted the crude attitude taken by Shelley in his
immature work ' Queen Mab,' became a professing atheist, and even
went so far as to practise vegetarianism, of which, however, he was soon
cured because of its unpleasant effect on his eyesight.   Of his atheism
Mrs. Orr says, " His mind was not so constituted that such doubt fast-
ened itself upon it ; nor did he ever in after life speak of this period of
negation except as an access of boyish folly, with which his mature self
could have no concern.   The return to religious belief did not shake
his faith in his new prophet.   It only made him willing to admit that
he had misread him.   This period of Browning's life remained, never-
theless, one of rebellion and unrest, to which many circumstances may
have contributed besides the influence of one mind."

With the exception of the poetic awakening just recorded, Brown-
ing's youthful life is uneventful.

By his father's decision his education was continued at home with
instruction in dancing, riding, boxing, fencing; in French with a tutor
for two years ; and in music with John Relfe for theory, and a Mr. Abel,
pupil of Moscheles, for execution, doubtless supplemented with contin-
uous browsing among the rare books in his father's library.   At eighteen
he attended a Greek class at the London University for a term or two
and with this his formal education ceased.   It was while at the uni-
versity that his final choice of poetry as his future profession was made.

That he had a bent in other artistic directions as well as that of poetry is witnessed by his own confession written on the fly-leaf of a first edition of 'Pauline' now treasured in the South Kensington Museum. "'Pauline' written in pursuance of a foolish plan I forget, or have no wish to remember; involving the assumption of several distinct characters: the world was never to guess that such an opera, such a comedy, such a speech proceeded from the same notable person."

Some idea had been entertained of the possibility of Robert's qualifying himself for the bar, but Mr. Browning was entirely too much in sympathy with his son's interests to put any obstacles in the way of his choice, and did everything in his power to help him in establishing himself in his poetical career. When the decision was made, Browning's first step was to read and digest the whole of Johnson's Dictionary.

During these years of preparation his consciousness of his own latent powers, together with youthful immaturity, made him, from all accounts, a somewhat obstreperous personage. Mrs. Orr says that his mother was much distressed at his impatience and aggressiveness. "He set the judgments of those about him at defiance, and gratuitously proclaimed himself everything that he was and some things that he was not." It is probable, as his sister suggests, that the life of Camberwell, in spite of the dear home to which he was much attached, and a small coterie of congenial friends, including his cousins, the Silverthornes, and Alfred Domett, did not afford sufficient scope for the expansion of his eager intelligence.

In 1833 appeared the first flowering of his genius in 'Pauline,' for the publication of which his aunt, Mrs. Silverthorne, furnished the money. It was printed with no name affixed, by Saunders and Otley.

The influence of Shelley breathes through this poem; not only is it immanent in the music of the verse, but in its general atmosphere, while one of its finest climaxes is the apostrophe to Shelley beginning, "Sun-treader, life and light be thine forever!" These influences, however, are commingled with elements of striking originality indicating, in spite of some crudities of construction, that here was a new force in the poetic world. Not many recognized it at the time. Among those who did was his former friend, Mr. Fox, then editor of the *Monthly Repository*, who gave 'Pauline' a sympathetic review in his magazine. Later, another article praising it was printed in the same magazine. This and one or two other inadequate notices ended its early literary history, and thus was unassumingly planted the first seed of one of the most splendid poetical growths the world has seen. How completely 'Pauline' was forgotten is shown by the anecdote told of Rossetti's coming across it in the British Museum twenty years later, and guess-

have had a long run had it not been for difficulties which arose in the theatre management.

If Shelley was the paramount influence of his youthful years, from the time of his Italian journey in 1838, Italy became an influence which was henceforth to exert its magic over his work. He liked to call Italy his university. In 'Sordello' he had already chosen an Italian subject, and his journey was undertaken partly with the idea of gaining personal experience of the scenes wherein the tragedy of Sordello's soul was enacted.

It was published in 1840, and except for a notice in the *Eclectic Review*, and the appreciation of a few friends, was ignored. A world not over sensitive to the beauties of his previous work, could hardly be expected to welcome enthusiastically a poem so complex in its historical setting and so full of philosophy. Even the keenest intellects approach this poem with the feeling that they are about to attack a problem; for in spite of undoubted power and many beauties, it must be confessed that the luxuriance of the poet's mental force often unduly overbalances his sense of artistic proportion. Evidently the world was frightened. The little breeze, with which Browning's career began, instead of developing as it normally should into a strong wind of universal recognition, died out, and for twenty years nothing he could do seemed to win for him his just deserts, though his very next poem, 'Pippa Passes,' showed him already a consummate master of his forces both on the artistic side and in the special realm which he chose, the development of the soul.

'Pippa Passes,' 'King Victor and King Charles,' and 'The Return of the Druses' lay in his desk for some time without a publisher. He finally arranged with Edward Moxon to bring them out in pamphlet form, using cheap type, each issue to consist of a sixteen-page form, printed in double columns. This was the beginning of the now celebrated series, 'Bells and Pomegranates.' They were issued from 1841 to 1846, and included all the dramas and a number of short poems.

The only one of these poems with a story other than literary, is 'The Blot in the 'Scutcheon,' written for Macready, and performed at Drury Lane, on February 11, 1843. A favorite weapon in the hands of the Philistines has been the often reiterated statement that the performance was a failure. A letter from Browning to Mr. Hill, editor of the *Daily News*, at the time of the revival of 'The Blot' by Lawrence Barrett in 1884, drawn out by the same old falsehood, gives the truth in regard to the matter, and should silence once for all the ubiquitous Philistines.

"Macready received and accepted the play, while he was engaged at the Haymarket, and retained it for Drury Lane, of which I was ignorant that he was about to become the manager: he accepted it at the instigation of nobody. . . . When the Drury Lane season began, Macready informed me that he would act the play when he had brought out two others, — 'The Patrician's Daughter' and 'Plighted Troth.' Having done so, he wrote to me that the former had been unsuccessful in money-drawing, and the latter had 'smashed his arrangements altogether': but he would still produce my play. In my ignorance of certain symptoms better understood by Macready's professional acquaintances — I had no notion that it was a proper thing, in such a case, to release him from his promise; on the contrary, I should have fancied that such a proposal was offensive. Soon after, Macready begged that I would call on him: he said the play had been read to the actors the day before, 'and laughed at from beginning to end'; on my speaking my mind about this, he explained that the reading had been done by the prompter, a grotesque person with a red nose and wooden leg, ill at ease in the love scenes, and that he would himself make amends by reading the play next morning, — which he did, and very adequately, — but apprised me that in consequence of the state of his mind, harassed by business and various troubles, the principal character must be taken by Mr. Phelps; and again I failed to understand, . . . that to allow at Macready's theatre any other than Macready to play the principal part in a new piece was suicidal, and really believed I was meeting his exigencies by accepting the substitute. At the rehearsal, Macready announced that Mr. Phelps was ill, and that he himself would read the part: on the third rehearsal, Mr. Phelps appeared for the first time . . . while Macready more than read, rehearsed the part. The next morning Mr. Phelps waylaid me to say . . . that Macready would play Tresham on the ground that himself, Phelps, was unable to do so. . . . He added that he could not expect me to waive such an advantage, — but that if I were prepared to waive it, 'he would take ether, sit up all night, and have the words in his memory by next day.' I bade him follow me to the green-room, and hear what I decided upon — which was that as Macready had given him the part, he should keep it: this was on a Thursday; he rehearsed on Friday and Saturday, — the play being acted the same evening, — *of the fifth day after the 'reading' by Macready.* Macready at once wished to reduce the importance of the play . . . tried to leave out so much of the text, that I baffled him by getting it printed in four and twenty hours, by Moxon's assistance. He wanted me to call it 'The Sister!' — and I have before me . . . the stage-acting copy, with two lines of his own insertion to avoid the tragical ending — Tresham was to announce his intention of going into a monastery! all this, to keep up the belief that Macready, and Macready alone, could produce a veritable 'tragedy' unproduced before. Not a shilling was spent on scenery or dresses. If your critic considers this treatment of the play an instance of 'the failure of powerful and experienced actors' to insure its success, — I can only say that my own opinion was shown by at once breaking off a friendship . . . which had a right to be plainly and simply told that the play I had contributed as a proof of it would, through a change of circumstances, no longer be to my friend's advantage. . . . Only recently, . . . when the extent of his pecuniary embarrassments at that time was made known, could I in a measure understand his motives — less than ever understand why he so strangely disguised them. If 'applause,' means success, the play thus maimed and maltreated was successful enough; it 'made way' for Macready's own Benefit and the theatre closed a fortnight after."

Browning's second visit to Italy took place in the autumn of 1844, from which he returned to meet with the supreme spiritual influence of his life. 'Lady Geraldine's Courtship' had just been published, and Browning expressing his enthusiasm for it to Mr. Kenyon, a dear friend of his and a cousin of Miss Barrett's, the latter immediately suggested that Browning should write and tell her of his delight in it. The correspondence soon developed into a meeting which was at first refused by Miss Barrett in a few self-depreciative words, "There is nothing to see in me, nothing to hear in me, I am a weed fit for the ground and darkness."

Mr. Browning's fate was sealed at the first meeting, we are told, but Miss Barrett, conscious of the obstacle offered by her ill-health, was not easily won, and only consented, at last, with the proviso that their marriage should depend upon improvement in her health.

Though the new joy in her life seemed to give her fresh strength, her doctor told her, in the summer of 1846, that her only hope of recovery depended upon her spending the coming winter in Italy. Her father having absolutely refused to hear of such a course, she was persuaded to consent to a private marriage with Mr. Browning, which took place on September 12, 1846, at St. Pancras Church. A week later they started for Italy. Mrs. Orr writes: —

"In the late afternoon or evening of September 19, Mrs. Browning, attended by her maid and her dog, stole away from her father's house. The family were at dinner, at which meal she was not in the habit of joining them; her sisters, Henrietta and Arabel, had been throughout in the secret of her attachment and in full sympathy with it; in the case of the servants she was also sure of friendly connivance. There was no difficulty in her escape, but that created by the dog, which might be expected to bark its consciousness of the unusual situation. She took him into her confidence. She said, 'O Flush, if you make a sound, I am lost.' And Flush understood, as what good dog would not, and crept after his mistress in silence."

Mr. Barrett never forgave her and never saw her again. The surprise and consternation of Mr. Browning's family was soon transformed into love for Mrs. Browning, while Mr. Kenyon, who had not been told because, as Mrs. Browning said, she did not wish to implicate any one in the deception she was obliged to practise against her father, was overjoyed at the result of his kindly offices in bringing the two poets together.

After a journey full of suffering for Mrs. Browning and the tenderest devotion on the part of Mr. Browning, they halted at Pisa, memorable as the spot where Mrs. Browning presented her husband with the matchless 'Sonnets from the Portuguese.' Mrs. Browning's health improved greatly in the genial climate. The whole of their married life, with the exception of occasional summers in England and two winters in Paris, was spent in Italy, and what that married life was in its harmonious blending of two unusually congenial souls we have abundant evidence in the glimpses obtained from Mrs. Browning's letters, and the recollections of it in the minds of their many friends.

In the summer of 1847 they established themselves in Florence in the Casa Guidi. It became practically their Italian home, varied by sojourns in Ancona, at the baths of Lucca, Venice, and winters in Rome in 1854 and 1859.

In Florence, March 9, 1849, their son was born, and to Mrs. Browning's life, especially, was added one more element of intense happiness. Mrs. Orr thinks that in Pompilia in 'The Ring and the Book,' is reflected the maternal joy as Browning saw it revealed in Mrs. Browning's relation to her son. A shadow was at the same time cast over Browning's life by the death of his mother, who died just as the news was received of the birth of her grandchild. Mrs. Browning, writing to a friend, said, "My husband has been in the greatest anguish. . . . He has loved his mother as such passionate natures only can love, and I never saw a man so bowed down in an extremity of sorrow, — never."

The first effect of Browning's marriage seems to have been to put his muse to sleep. Up to 1850 the only events in his literary career were the performance of 'The Blot' at Sadler's Wells in 1848, and the issue of a collected edition of his works in 1849. In 1850, in Florence, he wrote 'Christmas Eve' and 'Easter Day,' and in Paris, 1857, the 'Essay on Shelley' to be prefixed to twenty-five letters of Shelley's, that afterwards turned out to be spurious.

The fifty poems in 'Men and Women' complete the record of Browning's work during his wife's life. They appeared in 1855, and reflect very directly new sources of inspiration which had come into his life with his marriage.

Though Mr. and Mrs. Browning led a comparatively quiet life, they gathered around them, wherever they were, a distinguished circle of friends. In the early days at Florence, they much enjoyed the society of Margaret Fuller Ossoli. Joseph Milsand and George Sand — the first a cherished friend, the last simply an acquaintance — connect themselves with their life in Paris, while in London and Rome all the bright particular stars of the time circled about them, some of whom were the Storys, the Hawthornes, the Carlyles, the Kemble sisters, Cardinal Manning, Sir Frederick Leighton, Rossetti, Val Princeps, and Landor.

Mrs. Browning's death at dawn, on the 29th of June, 1861, cut short the golden period of these Italian days. Even in his bereavement he had cause to be poignantly happy. For he had watched beside his wife on that last night, and she, weak, though suffering little and without presentiment of the end which even to him seemed not so imminent, had given him, as he wrote, — "what my heart will keep till I see her again and longer, — the most perfect expression of her love to me within my whole knowledge of her." He added, "I shall grow still, I hope, but my root is taken and remains." He left Florence never to return. His settling in London that winter was a result of his wife's death, destined to bring him into closer touch with an English public which was to like him yet. The change was dictated by his care for his son's education, whose well-being he considered a trust from his wife.

In 1862, he wrote from Biarritz of 'Pen's' enjoyment of his holidays, adding, "for me I have got on by having a great read at Euripides besides attending to my own matters, my new poem that is about to be and of which the whole is pretty well in my head — the Roman murder story." But the Roman murder story was long in taking shape as 'The Ring and the Book.' It had been conceived in one of his last June evenings at Casa Guidi, but the rude break in his life made by Mrs. Browning's death remains marked in the record of this work's incubation. During the next years spent in London, with holidays in Brittany, work went steadily on, first for the three-volume collected edition of 1863 of his works, and then for 'Dramatis Personæ,' published in the year following, before 'The Ring and the Book' came out at last, in 1868. With the appearance of this, and the six-volume edition of his works, the poet began to reap the abundant fruits of a slow but solidly-founded fame.

It was not until 1871, however, that the "great read at Euripides" showed its significance in 'Balaustion's Adventure' and four years later again, in 'Aristophanes' Apology,' rounding out thus his original criticism of Greek life and literature and especially affecting 'Euripides the human,' whom his wife had been earliest to deliver from blundering censure.

While in the midst of this prosperous scheme of work he wrote: "I feel such comfort and delight in doing the best I can with my own object of life, poetry, — which, I think, I never could have seen the good of before, — that it shows me I have taken the root I did take well. I hope to do much more — and that the flower of it will be put into Her hand somehow."

His father had died in Paris in 1866, at the age of eighty-five. Brother and sister, now each left alone, lived together thenceforth a life of tranquil uneventfulness, alternating between London and the Continent — a life rich in pleasant acquaintances and warm friendships and increasingly full of invitations and honors of all sorts for the poet. Supreme among the friendships was that with Miss Anne Egerton Smith. Music was the special bond of sympathy between her and Browning, and while they were both in London no important concert lacked their appreciation. Miss Browning, her brother, and Miss Smith spent also four successive summers together, the fourth at Salève, near Geneva, where Miss Smith's sudden death was the occasion of Browning's poem on immortality, 'La Saisiaz.' Among the honors the poet received were the organization of the London Browning Society in 1881, degrees from Oxford and from Cambridge, and nominations for the Rectorship of Glasgow University and for that of St. Andrews. The latter was a unanimous nomination from the students, and as an evidence of the younger generation's esteem of his poetic influence was more than commonly gratifying to Browning, although he declined this and all other such overtures.

His activities during the remainder of his days, his social and friendly life in London and later in Venice, were habitually cheerful and genial. He sedulously cultivated happiness. This was indeed the consistent result of the fact to which those who knew him best bear witness, that he held the great lyric love of his life as sacred, and cherished it as a religion. Those who know the whole body of his work most intimately will be readiest to corroborate this on subtler evidence; for only on the hypothesis of a unique revelation of the significance of a supreme human love from whose large sureness smaller dramatic exemplifications of love in life derive their vitality can the varied overplay of his art and the deep sufficiency of his religious reconciliation of Power and Love be adequately understood. As he himself once said, the romance of his life was in his own soul. To this perhaps the bibliography of his works will ever provide the most accurate outline map.

After the issue of his Greek pieces, the most noticeable new features of his remaining work may be summed up as idyllic and lyric. A new picturesqueness interpenetrated his dramatic pieces, as if he were dowered with a fresh pleasure in eyesight. This was shown in the 'Dramatic Idyls.' A new purity intensified his lyrical faculty. This is shown in the lyrics in 'Ferishtah's Fancies' and in 'Asolando.'

To his whole achieved work add the brief final record of his contentment in his son's marriage in 1887, his removal to the house he bought in De Vere Gardens, the gradual weakening of his robust health in his last years, his painless death in Venice in his son's Palazzo Rezzonico on the very day, December 12, 1889, of the issue of 'Asolando' in London, his burial in Westminster Abbey in Poets' Corner, December 31, and the story of Robert Browning's earthly life is told.

CHARLOTTE PORTER.
HELEN A. CLARKE.

May 20, 1896.

CRITICAL INTRODUCTION.

> " What were life
> Did soul stand still therein, forego her strife
> Through the ambiguous Present to the goal
> Of some all-reconciling Future?"
> — 'PARLEYINGS: WITH GERARD DE LAIRESSE.'

WHAT principle guided Browning in making the present Selections from his poetry? On this interesting question there is no other light than the hint he gives in his preface, that he had strung together certain pieces "on the thread of an imaginary personality," and the internal evidence which the poems themselves offer of their susceptibility to an inter-relationship of this sort.

'My Star,' striking a preluding note of love, seems to usher in poems broadly capable of being grouped together on the score of their expressing, in a fresh way, indicative of a youthful attitude toward life, various phases of love, — either as sensation or as observed or recorded experience. Poems follow of a more active sort, adventurous and partisan in spirit, — the 'Good News,' the 'Lost Leader,' and others, which belong to the outlook of manhood; and these pass again, in subject, into the groove of love, but from the standpoint, now, of the stress and trial belonging to maturer life and thought. Larger themes succeed, related to national characteristics and history, to art, to music, to religion, and, finally, the summing up of life's meanings natural to ripe vision. The second series of Selections, made by Browning eight years later, follows, in general, a similar line of evolving thought and experience.

If it be granted that some such natural development of a typical experience, *not* personal to Browning, underlies these Selections, the clue it supplies for a brief critical consideration of the poet's distinctive traits, as shown throughout his work and representatively in this volume, is peculiarly trustworthy and appropriate because it is the poet's own clue. He disclaimed a selection based on an assumption of judgment as to what was best; he made a selection based upon motive

The poetic motive informing Browning's work is, in one word, aspiration, which moulds and develops the varied and complex personalities of the humanity he depicts, as the persistent energy of the scientist, holding its never-wearying way, gives to the world of phenomena its infinite array of shows and shapes. Aspiration — a reaching on and upwards — is the primal energy underneath that law which we call progress. Through aspiration, ideals — social, religious, artistic — are formed; and through it ideals perish, as it breaks away from them to seek more complete realizations of truth. Aspiration, therefore, has its negative as well as its positive side. While it ever urges the human soul to love and achievement, through its very persistence the soul learns that the perfect flowering of its rare imaginings is not possible of attainment in this life.

Assurance of the ultimate fulfilment of the ideal is one of the forms in which Browning unfolds the workings of this life principle, well illustrated in 'Abt Vogler,' who has implicit faith in his own intuitions of a final harmony; or in those poems where the crowning of aspiration in a supreme earthly love flashes upon the understanding a clear vision of infinite love. But by far the larger number of poems discloses the underlying force at work in ways more subtle and obscure, through the conflict of good and evil, of lower with higher ideals, either as emphasized in great social movements, in the struggle between individuals, or in struggles fought out on the battle-ground within every human soul.

With a motive so all-inclusive, the whole panorama of human life, with its loves and hates, its strivings and failures, its half-reasonings and beguiling sophistries, is material ready at hand for illustration. Browning, inspired with a democratic inclusiveness, allowed his choice in subject-matter to range through fields both new and old, unploughed by any poet before him. Progress, to be imaged forth in its entirety, must be interpreted, not only through the individual soul, but through the collective soul of the human race; wherefore many phases of civilization and many attitudes of mind must be detailed for service. There is no choosing a subject, as a Tennyson might, on the ground that it will best point the moral of a preconceived theory of life; on the contrary, every such theory is bound to be of interest as one of the phenomena exhibited by the transcending principle.

From first to last Browning portrayed life either developing or at some crucial moment, the outcome of past development, or the determinative influence for future growth or decay.

His interest in the phenomena of life as a whole, freed him from the trammels of any literary cult. He steps out from under the yoke of the classicist, where only gods and heroes have leave to breathe; and, equally, from that of the romanticist, where kings and persons of quality alone flourish. Wherever he found latent possibilities of character, which might be made to expand under the glare of his brilliant imagination, whether in hero, king, or knave, that being he chose to set before his readers as a living individuality to show whereof he was made, either through his own ruminations or through the force of circumstances.

Upon examination it will be found that the sources, many and various, of Browning's subject-matter are broadly divisible into subjects derived from history, from personal experience or biography, from true incidents, popular legend, the classics, and from his own fertile imagination. Of these, history proper furnishes the smallest proportion. 'Strafford' and 'King Victor and King Charles' are his only historical dramas, and with 'Sordello,' and a few stray short poems, based on historical incidents, exhaust his drafts upon history. Several more have a historical setting with fictitious plot and characters, such as the 'Return of the Druses' and 'Luria'; and still more have a historical atmosphere in which think and move creatures of his own fancy, such as 'My Last Duchess,' 'Count Gismond,' 'In A Gondola.' His most important work, 'The Ring and the Book,' is founded on the true story of a Roman murder case. Others of his longer poems, developed from real occurrences, are 'The Inn Album,' 'Red Cotton Night-Cap Country,' 'Ivàn Ivànovitch,' and some shorter poems. The individual living to develop the mind stuff of the world rather than the individual playing a part in action, attracted Browning, and we find a large percentage of his subjects — between twenty and thirty poems — to be dramatic presentations of characters not distinguished for their part in the history of action, but who have played a part more or less prominent in the history of thought or art. Such are 'Paracelsus,' 'Saul,' 'Abt Vogler,' 'Fra Lippo Lippi.' Sometimes they appear in the disguise of a name not their own, as in 'Bishop Blougram,' for whom Cardinal Wiseman sat, 'Prince Hohenstiel-Schwangau' — Napoleon, Mr. Sludge — Home, the 'Spiritualist.' 'The Pied Piper,' and 'The Story of Pornic,' are familiar examples of legendary subjects. Greece is drawn upon in the translation from the Greek of 'Agamemnon,' to which must be added 'Balaustion's Adventure' and 'Aristophanes' Apology,' both of which contain transcripts from Euripides; also 'Echetlos,' 'Pheidippides,' 'Artemis Prologizes,' and 'Ixion.' There should furthermore be mentioned a few poems which grew out of suggestions furnished by poetry, music, and art, as 'Cenciaja,' 'A Toccata of Galuppi's,' 'The Guardian Angel.' And last, out of the pure stuff of imagination, have been fashioned some of his most lifelike characters. Sometimes, as

already stated, they move in an actual historical environment, some-
times merely in an atmosphere of history, and sometimes, detached
from time and place, is pictured a human soul struggling with a passion
universal to mankind.

This vast range of material is not by any means chosen at random
by the poet. There are several centres of human thought, around
which the genius of Browning plays with exceptional power. Such,
for example, are the ideas symbolized in human love and service, in
art, and in the Incarnation.

Clustering about the instinct of human love, gathers thickest a maze
of poems bearing witness to the force, sweetness, and versatility of
Browning's treatment of the purely personal emotions. The scope
sweeps from primitive to consummate types, as if none conceivable
were to be tabooed; and if not all are represented, the intention
towards all is evidently hospitable. Yet the unifying current is clear
through all differentiations, because it is based on the vital fact of the
psychical origin of the emotion of love as desire, and capable, therefore,
of a never-ending tendency to impel and energize the powers and re-
veal the highest potency of each individual soul. The conditions under
which it acts may be favorable or not, the outgoing love may be satis-
fied or not, by eliciting and enjoying love in return; in any case, the
test is equally good to make a soul declare itself — "to wit, by its
fruit, the thing it does," and thus, through living out its own life, to
recruit both the general plan of the race and its own individual possi-
bilities.

This psychical value, of which the commonest instinct towards love,
in any and every human creature, is capable, relates all men to each
other, and, pointing out the implicit use of each to each, permits none
to be scorned as having no part in the scheme, nor any to be denied
the vision of some dim descried glory "ever on before." It consti-
tutes a revelation to every man of the Infinite, incarnate within his
own grasp and proof, — a miracle, only to be felt, differing in this from
any attempt to achieve the Absolute through act or deed or any product
of effort outside oneself, one instant of human consciousness enabling
the laying hold on eternity.

In these Selections are poems that represent the instinct of love astir
in modes that foster the transmutation of desire into force, no matter
what obstacles beset it; or that chill and obstruct its saving rule although
its way be smooth. The merely selfish expression of the common in-
stinct is depicted in 'The Laboratory' and 'My Last Duchess'; the
unselfish, in 'One Way of Love.' Its seeing faculty appears in 'Cris-
tina,' and 'The Last Ride Together'; but its eyes are sealed until too

late in 'The Confessional' and in Constance in 'In a Balcony.' It finds itself expressed in a conventionalized way in 'Numpholeptos'; in a realistic way in 'Poetics.' It is revealed in 'Count Gismond' as rudimentary; as ripe in 'By the Fireside.' It is stifled in 'Bifurcation,' 'The Statue and the Bust,' 'Youth and Art,' 'Dîs Aliter Visum'; it is self-baffled in 'A Forgiveness,' and 'In a Balcony'; but has sway despite Death in 'Prospice,' and 'Never the Time and the Place.' All these separate ways of love are glimpses at parts of human experience, which, since they can be correlated, illumine the course of growth latent for any soul in a crisis of emotion. Other poems still, exemplify this by correlating various stages of development occurring in the experience of one person, the original manifestation of love adding to itself a new psychical value, as in 'James Lee's Wife.'

Taken as a whole, Browning's broad and vital representations of love reveal the related values of different phases of personal experience and of each personal experience to every other; and, also, the bearing of each and all such experiences on human progress and on an ecstatic consciousness of the Infinite.

In the manifestations of human energy commonly called social, corresponding orbits of relative values are brought to light by Browning through his reconstruction from life itself of numerous varying types of work and consequent service to humanity at large. The range exemplified includes the exercise of his art by a Fra Lippo Lippi, an Abt Vogler, or a Cleon, the devotion to his study of a Grammarian or the public achievement of a Pheidippides, a Hervé Riel, a Pym, a Strafford, or a Luria. Browning shows a consciousness of the special influence of certain historic periods of civic enthusiasm on the development of social ideals. The grim righteousness of Pym's London, the glories of Athens and of Florence, are fitly celebrated. And in the whole pioneer period which sowed the seed and set the shape of much that is not yet ripe for fulfilment in modern civilization — in the period of the Italian Renaissance, Browning's imaginative conception found frame and flesh. In 'Sordello' he descried the incipient democratic tendencies of that period, anticipating the conclusions of its special historians : of Burckhardt, who characterized it as " the awakening of the individual in love with his own possibilities "; of Vernon Lee, who describes it as " the movement for mediæval democratic progress "; of Symonds, who speaks of it as " the persistent effort after liberty of the unconquerable soul of man." Browning embodies it, in the period that prepared the way for the Renaissance, in the consciousness of his hero, the warrior-poet Sordello, as the dawn and struggle for supremacy of the democratic ideal.

About the Renaissance crystallized an important group of Browning's art poems, nearly all of which appear in this volume.

' Pictor Ignotus ' shows us the personality of the typical, often unknown monastic painter of the Renaissance period, the nature of his beautiful but cold art, and the conditions of servitude to ecclesiastical beliefs and ideals which shaped both personality and art. Fra Lippo exhibits the irresistible tendency of the art impulse to expand beyond bounds either of the church or of set laws of art and finding beauty wheresoever in life it chooses to turn the light of its gaze. The Bishop who ordered his tomb at St. Praxed's, stands for somewhat more than the typical art-patronizing priest, whose connoisseurship, strong in death, serves his vanity, worldliness, and envy. He gathers up in his person the pagan survivals, the normal grossness, the assumption of authority, which were the ecclesiastical and aristocratic clogs that dragged back the forward-tending and freedom-seeking Renaissance movement. ' Old Pictures in Florence ' shows more explicitly the relation to historic periods of various new art impulses working themselves out in schools ; the indebtedness of each to each ; and the onflowing movement belonging to all collectively. At the same time is emphasized the supreme importance to the world of assimilating the work of the pioneering artists, from whom their successors derive vitality. There is also no mistaking the expression in favor of free democratic conditions which conduce to " art's best birth." So, throughout these poems, manifesting Browning's universal enthusiasm for all varieties of art, the relativity and unity of all art expression is shown to be perfectly reconcilable with the independent worth of the special exponent of the art of his time ; and the development both of art and the artist is shown to be dependent on the free play and unresting aspiration of his powers.

Not less sympathetic is Browning's understanding of art as wrought out in music, though in his musical poems the historical atmosphere is not so prominent as it is in the art poems. They dwell upon the different attitudes taken toward music as the result of differences in temperament, rather than upon any distinct phases of musical growth. His chief musicians, — David, Abt Vogler, Hugues, and the organist who performs his mountainous fugues, Galuppi and the man who plays his toccata, the husband in ' Fifine at the Fair,' and the musical critic of ' Charles Avison,' — all see different possibilities in music. David is more the poet than the musician since, when he reaches his highest point of inspiration, he throws his harp aside and depends entirely upon language for his effect. He uses music primarily as an awakener — through the familiarity of the tunes, he sings to Saul — of long-forgotten memories, along with which comes the renewal of early emotions, — an effect of music often observed and used to good purpose in arousing soldiers to patriotism, through melodies that awaken memories of home and childhood. David, casting aside his harp, when filled with the intense desire of adequate expression, is the exact antipode of the husband in 'Fifine at the Fair,' who feels that the most complete expression is only possible by means of music. This opinion, however, is somewhat discounted by the character of the man, sophistical as he often is in his arguments. When he finds himself pushed for logical reasons for his moral conduct, he falls back upon music, by means of which he could make all plain to his wife if she only understood its language. His dependence upon music as a revealer of the truth is based on the ground that it gives form to feeling, and is equivalent to his founding his arguments on feeling. That to reflect moods of feeling is among the highest offices of music is doubtless true, but to formulate theories of moral conduct upon this fact is sophistical in the highest degree, for the all-sufficient reason that music may reflect a mood the opposite of aspiring. The critic in 'Charles Avison' recognizes to the full the limitations of music. Though it gives form to feeling, with the passage of time the form becomes obsolete, and the feeling once expressed is no longer discernible through it. An understanding of its mood can then be gained only by recourse to the historical sense, reconstructing the time that gave it birth, and by this means obtaining a glimpse of the mood that inspired it. Thus, music furnishes to Browning another illustration of the relativity of art form, of its failure — as of every effort of man — to touch perfection, though, none the less, the record of man's effort to give adequate expression to his aspirations.

'A Toccata of Galuppi' furnishes a fine illustration of the exercise of the historical sense on the part of the person who plays the toccata in conjuring up a lifelike picture of the pleasure-loving Venice, whose heartlessness re-lives for him in the dreary harmonies of Galuppi's music. The organist in 'Master Hugues' is not blessed with any such historical sense, and he is therefore incapable of penetrating within the outer crust of the fugue. On the other hand, the fugue, as well as the toccata, are both examples of music which is less the outcome of aspiration than an intellectual playing with forms for form's sake, and as such furnish a warrant for the delicious humor which Browning expends on them.

In 'Abt Vogler,' Browning has represented music from the point of view of the man who has, so to speak, fathomed the heart of the mystery. He has none of the misgivings of the critic. Like the man in 'Fifine,' he, too, regards music as the most complete means of expression; but it is more to him than the mere reflection of earthly emotions, — it is the incarnation of the wish of his soul to be in touch with the Infinite. His purer spirit feels the revelation in the inspired effort to image in entirely beautiful form the strivings upward of the soul, and in a form, moreover, which is itself evolved out of the soul. Aspiration becomes, as it were, flesh and blood; is not indirectly expressed by means of symbols as in the arts of painting and poetry. So much is the form identified with the spirit in the Abbé's mind, that he thinks of his music winging its way up to God, an eternal good, to take its place in the completed round of everlasting beauty. He, indeed, is just the needed supplement to the critic, in 'Charles Avison,' who perhaps is not sufficiently alive to the fact that a new beauty does not necessarily exclude the old.

Though the importance of these poems is chiefly due to their bringing out the various functions which music may perform for different individuals, there is a historical element of considerable interest. David's use of music is quite in keeping with an age that had not altogether learned to regard music other than as a handmaid to poetry. In Hugues, there is certainly pictured the revolt against the over-learned amplifications indulged in by the old contrapuntal writers, which was triumphantly led by Palestrina. An epoch of musical decay breathes through the 'Toccata,' which belongs to the period of the decline of the Italian influence in music, justly following upon a wornout inspiration, to give place to the glories of the pre-eminent German school; while Abt Vogler is fired with the enthusiasm of a period when music, its shackles of the past rent asunder, had in the romantic school entered upon a long triumphant march of development.

Browning's portraits of poets and poems illustrating in diverse ways various principles of poetic art naturally ally themselves to the groups of poems on the fine arts just considered. His early devotion to Shelley, expressed in 'Pauline,' was succeeded in 'Paracelsus' by an imaginary representation of a poet, Aprile, who, like Shelley, was the impersonation of spiritual love and ardor. In 'Sordello' this fervent poetic type again appears, which yearns to bury itself in what it worships. It is now contrasted with a new self-centred type of poet which holds its own consciousness aloof from its dreams, yet finds no dream or function of life without as good a counterpart within itself. The distinction here made between what is called the subjective poet, such a one as Shelley, and the objective or dramatic poet, such a one as Shakespeare, recurs in his prose essay on Shelley, and some variety of one or the other or hoped-for blending of both types animates all his impersonations of poets. Eglamor in 'Sordello' is a half-ripe bardling of the Shelley order. In

· The Glove' Ronsard and Marot are incidentally characterized and contrasted to the advantage of the poet more deeply versed in lore and life. Keats appears in 'Popularity,' as a poet dowering the world and many imitators with a beauty never seen before. Shelley again has a tribute of personal love in 'Memorabilia.' Euripides and Aristophanes owe to Browning, in 'Balaustion's Adventure' and 'Aristophanes' Apology,' the deepest appreciation and soundest criticism they have ever received at any one man's hands. Shakespeare is directly defended in 'At the Mermaid' from charges of pessimism, derision of women, and uneasy ambition to figure in court life — charges more or less involved in some modern conceptions of him based on an autobiographical reading of the Sonnets and Plays. The sonnet theory is again directly combated in 'House;' and 'Shop' may perhaps be taken as falling in with these two. Both 'At the Mermaid' and 'House' rest on a conception of Shakespeare as belonging altogether to the objective type of poet. And the Shakespeare Sonnet, 'The Names,' is in accord with a view which accepts him as supreme dramatic creator.

In the verses beginning 'Touch him ne'er so lightly,' Browning sings the way of pain and obstacle through which pass the master poets who sum up great epochs of national life — such a poet as Dante — and who transmute the bitterness of sorrow into the splendor of song.

In 'Transcendentalism' and 'How it Strikes a Contemporary' are celebrated the vitality of the poet's gift, the keenness of the poet's sight, the warmth and humanity of his heart and office.

Expressions concerning the philosophy of the poet's art and self-development are to be found in 'Sordello,' 'The Ring and the Book' and other of his most profound works. The simple poems on poetic art given in this volume, are like the whole range of his work on this subject, in placing the poet somewhat less within the influence of the historic times to which he is related, than the artist or even the musician. The poet's fortune is read aright in his intimate and loving kinships with humanity, his clear outsight and deep insight upon the springs of life and progress, in the dependency of his artistic power on his truth to his own highest energies and aspiration.

The most exalted ideal towards which the human soul aspires is that of divine love, and this, as symbolized in the idea of the Incarnation, Browning has presented from every side. Even in so humble a thinker as Caliban, the germ of religious aspiration is discernible in his conception of a God above Setebos who, if not very positive in his possession of good qualities, is at least negative so far as bad ones are concerned.

This volume is rich in poems which revolve about this central idea. In David, the intensity of his human love exalts his conception of God

from that of power into that of love, and with prophetic vision he sees
the future attainment of a religious ideal in which love like unto human
love shall have a place. What a powerful force this longing is in the
human mind is again illustrated in Cleon, the cultured Greek who, de-
spite his broad sympathies and deep appreciation of all forms of beauty,
feels that life is not capable of affording a realization of joy such as the
soul sees. Like Saul, an immortality of deed has no attractions for him ;
it is the assurance of a continuing personality that he wants. Karshish,
the Arab, too, is haunted by the idea of a God who is love ; but neither
in him nor in Cleon has the aspiration reached such a point that they
are enabled to conceive of the ideal as actual, though living at the time
of Christ. In ' The Death in the Desert,' is presented the portrait of
one who has seen the ideal incarnate.

Other phases of doubt and faith are pictured as affected by more
sophisticated stages of culture. While Cleon and Karshish belong to
a phase of development wherein the mind has not fully grasped the
possibilities of such a conception, a Bishop Blougram's doubts grow
out of the uncertainties of the nature of proof. Far from being sure,
like David, that the incarnation will become a veritable truth, he can
only hope that it may have been true, and resolve to act as if he be-
lieved it were. Still another phase of doubt is shown in ' Ferishtah's
Fancies,' where the belief in an actual incarnation is scouted by an
Oriental as preposterous.

The assurance of divine love does not come to all of Browning's
characters through a belief in external revelation. For instance, in
the Epilogue to the first series of Selections, in the present volume,
and in ' Fears and Scruples,' it is through the experiencing of human
love alone, reaching out toward God, which carries the conviction that
there must be a God of love to receive it, though he may never have
manifested himself in the flesh. In 'Ferishtah's Fancies,' again, Fer-
ishtah, who sternly reprimands the unbeliever already mentioned, seems
to regard the ideal of an actual incarnation as a human conception,
but, nevertheless, doing duty as a symbol of the Divine, and thus help-
ing men to approach the Infinite.

In giving a sketch of the general motive and content of Browning's
work, we have treated it as essentially dramatic. It is to be noted,
however, that he has carried his observations of the realities of life into
regions never approached by any other poet, — that is, into the thoughts
and motives of humanity, the very sources of world movements, — with
the result that we do not see his characters in action so much as in the
intellectual fermentation, which is the concomitant of action. This fact,
namely, that his imagination invests the subjective side of man's life

with vitality, sets up a certain spiritual kinship between the poet and his characters, and justifies the search for a philosophy which may be styled Browning's own; yet, that any such search must be conducted with the utmost discretion is evidenced by the existence of many diversities in opinion upon this subject. It is dangerous to regard each poem as a mask from behind which Browning in his own person peeps forth; for the more one studies his creations, the more the peculiar individualisms of their natures assert themselves, and the more the poet retires into the background. Even admitting that there are certain religious and philosophical ideas upon which many of his *dramatis personæ* dwell, each one presents them from his own point of view, and in a form of expression suited to the particular character and circumstance. Moreover, the ever-recurring idea in new modes of expression is absolutely true to the life of thought in the world. It is no more surprising that David, Rabbi Ben Ezra, the husband in 'Fifine at the Fair,' and Paracelsus should have some points of philosophy in common, than that the wits of Plato, Buddha, Herbert Spencer, and the North American Indians should occasionally jump together. We have seen how he discriminates against no form of doubt or faith by allowing every shade of opinion to be presented from the standpoint of one who holds it. This is external evidence of his friendliness toward all forms of effort that indicate a search for the truth. With which particular phase of truth the poet, himself, is to be identified, it would be difficult to discover, but it is not so impossible to deduce general principles; not only from the fact that aspiration is plainly the informing spirit of his work, but because from time to time this informing spirit forces itself to the surface in an expression avowedly the poet's own. From such expressions, of which the third division of the 'Epilogue' in the present volume, 'Reverie' in 'Asolando,' passages in 'Paracelsus,' 'Sordello,' and 'Ferishtah's Fancies,' are examples, together with the whole trend of his work, his philosophy, broadly speaking, may be described as based upon the revelation of divine love in every human being, through experience of love reaching out toward an object which shall completely satisfy aspiration. The partial manifestations of love include the feeling of gratitude awakened through the enjoyment of benefits received, like that felt by Ferishtah when he eats a cherry for breakfast; the creative impulse, yearning to all-express itself in art; love seeking its human complement; and love seeking expression in service to humanity. Moral failure, resulting in evil; intellectual failure, resulting in ignorance, are simply the necessary means for the further development of the soul, and the continuance of the law of progress. While the revelation of God is thus entirely subjective, his conception of God is both subjective and objective. Looking forth upon the world, he sees Power and Law exemplified; looking within himself, he sees Power and Law manifested as Love. God, then, must be both Power and Love, as Rabbi Ben Ezra discovered, and with this dramatic expression may be paralleled the subjective expression of the same conclusion in 'Reverie,' — the poet's last piece of profound philosophizing.

The faculty for twofold gaze within and without, on which Browning's reconciliation of Power and Love is built, has enabled him to effect a like reconciliation between Power in Art — the ability to appropriate and project into form large swaths of fresh and living material — and Love in Art — the ardor to charge and energize the whole with spiritual attractiveness and meaning.

The analytic tendency, for which he is often censured, does not control, it subserves a much more noticeable faculty for synthesis — for seeing and reproducing wholes.

Another unusually happy balance of capabilities distinguishes Browning. The moral interests which weight his work with significance are lightened with an over-play of humor — a product of his double vision. With what genial facility he enters, for example, into Baldinucci's simple old man's nature, and lends the poet-wit to the exquisite clumsiness of his joke against the Jews; and then again, with what easy-going, wide-sweeping sympathy he enters into the complex course of law and custom which turns the laugh on Baldinucci, after all. So, in this, as in many another such dramatic picture of poor old human nature, the moral lesson is itself made dramatic.

Lend Browning but a little consideration, and the opulence of his effects will convince you that these twofold counter-poised faculties have found way in the sort of art which embodies them, because that alone was large enough to befit them. Lyric, idyl, tale, fantasy, or philosophic imagining, are enclosed in the all-embracing dramatic frame.

His artistic invention, moreover, working within the dramatic sphere, expended itself in perfecting a poetical form peculiarly his own, — the monologue.

His monologues range from expressions of mood as simple as in the song, 'Nay, but you, who do not love her,' to those in which not only the complex feelings of the speaker are expressed, but complete pictures of a second and sometimes a third character are given; or even groups of characters as in 'Fra Lippo Lippi,' where the curious, alert, Florentine guards are not all portrayed with equal clearness, but are all made to emerge effectively in a picturesque knot, showing here a hang-dog face, and there a twinkling eye, or a brawny arm elbowing a neighbor. By dexterous weaving in of allusions, flashes of light are turned upon events and feelings of the past, so adding harmonious depths to the general effect.

His diction is noticeable in that he uses a large proportion of Saxon words, and, by so doing, gives a lifelike naturalness to his speech, especially in his shorter poems, in which his characters do not talk as if they were confined within metrical limits, but seemingly as if the unstilted ways of daily life were open to them. Yet in all this apparently natural flow of words, there is a harmony of rhythm, a recurring stress of rhyme, and a condensation of thought that produces an effect of consummate art, frequently enhanced by a subtle symbolism underlying the words. How simple in its mere external form is the little poem, 'Appearances.' Two momentary scenes, a few words to each, yet there have been laid bare the worldly, ambitious heart of one person and the true heart of another, disappointed by the shattering of his idol; and under all, symbolically, a universal truth.

The obscurity with which Browning has been taxed so often is largely due to this monologue form. It is apt to be confusing at first, mainly because nothing like it has been met with before. The mind must be on the alert to catch the power of every word, to see its individual force and its relational force. Nothing, neither a scene nor an event, is described outright. Only in the course of the talk, references to events and scenes are made a part of the very warp and woof of the poem, and woven in with such skilfulness by the poet that the entire scene or event may be reconstructed by those who have eyes to see.

A harmonizing of imagery and of rhythm and even rhyme with the subject in hand is a marked characteristic of Browning's verse.

In the poems 'Meeting at Night' and 'Parting at Morning,' the wave motion of the sea is indicated in the form, not only by the arrangement of the rhymes to form a climax by bringing a couplet in the middle of the stanza like the crest of the wave, but the thought, also, gathers to a climax midway in the stanzas, and subsides toward their close.

In 'Pheidippides' the measure is a mixture of dactyls and spondees, original with the poet, with a pause at the end of each line, which reflects the firm-set eager purpose of the patriotic Greek runner and the breath-obstructed rhythm of his bounding flight.

In 'James Lee's Wife,' the metre is changed in each lyric to chime in with the changing mood dictating each one; and the imagery is in general chosen to mate every aspect of the thought dominating each mood. For example, in the second section, called 'By the Fireside,' the fire of shipwreck wood is the metaphor made to yield the mood of the brooding wife a mould which takes the cast of every sudden turn and cranny of her ill-foreboding reverie.

In the grotesque, frequently double rhymes, and the rough rhythm of 'The Flight of the Duchess,' the bluff, blunt manner of the huntsman who tells the story is conveyed. The subtle change that passes over the spirit of the tale as the rhythm falls tranquilly, with pure rhymes, now, into the dreamy chant of the gypsy, is the more effective for the colloquial swing, stop, and start of the forester's gruff-voiced diction.

As in his choice of poems for this volume Browning says he had an imaginary personality in mind to guide him, so it may be said that he has had always in mind imaginary personalities, in various guises and manifold circumstances, to guide him in fashioning his style. The marked traits of his art are keyed to attune with the theme and motive they interpret.

As an artist Browning disclaimed the nice selection and employment of a style in itself beautiful. As an artist, none the less, he chose to create in every given case a style fitly proportioned to the design, finding in that dramatic relating of style and motive a more vital beauty.

CHARLOTTE PORTER.
HELEN A. CLARKE.

MAY 25, 1896.

ROBERT BROWNING'S POEMS.

MY STAR.

irregular stress

ALL that I know
   Of a certain star
Is, it can throw
  (Like the angled spar)
Now a dart of red,
  Now a dart of blue;
Till my friends have said
  They would fain see, too,

interwoven

My star that dartles the red and the blue!
Then it stops like a bird; like a flower, hangs furled: **10**
  They must solace themselves with the Saturn above it.
What matter to me if their star is a world?
  Mine has opened its soul to me; therefore I love it.

five stress iambic

A FACE.

IF one could have that little head of hers
  Painted upon a background of pale gold,
Such as the Tuscan's early art prefers!
No shade encroaching on the matchless mould
Of those two lips, which should be opening soft
In the pure profile; not as when she laughs,
For that spoils all: but rather as if aloft
Yon hyacinth, she loves so, leaned its staff's
Burthen of honey-coloured buds, to kiss
And capture 'twixt the lips apart for this.
Then her lithe neck, three fingers might surround,   **10**
How it should waver, on the pale gold ground,
Up to the fruit-shaped, perfect chin it lifts!
I know, Correggio loves to mass, in rifts
Of heaven, his angel faces, orb on orb
Breaking its outline, burning shades absorb:

interwoven

double couplet

But these are only massed there, I should think,
Waiting to see some wonder momently
Grow out, stand full, fade slow against the sky,
(That 's the pale ground you 'd see this sweet face by)   20
All heaven, meanwhile, condensed into one eye
Which fears to lose the wonder, should it wink.

MY LAST DUCHESS.

FERRARA.

THAT 'S my last Duchess painted on the wall,
    Looking as if she were alive.   I call
That piece a wonder, now : Frà Pandolf's hands
Worked busily a day, and there she stands.
Will 't please you sit and look at her?   I said
"Frà Pandolf" by design : for never read
Strangers like you that pictured countenance,
The depth and passion of its earnest glance,
But to myself they turned (since none puts by
The curtain I have drawn for you, but I)   10
And seemed as they would ask me, if they durst,
How such a glance came there ; so, not the first
Are you to turn and ask thus.   Sir, 't was not
Her husband's presence only, called that spot
Of joy into the Duchess' cheek : perhaps
Frà Pandolf chanced to say " Her mantle laps
Over my lady's wrist too much," or " Paint
Must never hope to reproduce the faint
Half-flush that dies along her throat : " such stuff
Was courtesy, she thought, and cause enough   20
For calling up that spot of joy.   She had
A heart — how shall I say? — too soon made glad,
Too easily impressed ; she liked whate'er
She looked on, and her looks went everywhere.
Sir, 't was all one ! My favour at her breast,
The dropping of the daylight in the West,
The bough of cherries some officious fool
Broke in the orchard for her, the white mule
She rode with round the terrace — all and each
Would draw from her alike the approving speech,   30
Or blush, at least.   She thanked men, — good! but thanked
Somehow — I know not how — as if she ranked
My gift of a nine-hundred-years-old name
With anybody's gift.   Who 'd stoop to blame

BROWNING AT 77 (1889).

This sort of trifling?   Even had you skill
In speech — (which I have not) — to make your will
Quite clear to such an one, and say, " Just this
Or that in you disgusts me ; here you miss,
Or there exceed the mark " — and if she let
Herself be lessoned so, nor plainly set   40
Her wits to yours, forsooth, and made excuse,
— E'en then would be some stooping ; and I choose
Never to stoop.   Oh sir, she smiled, no doubt,
Whene'er I passed her ; but who passed without
Much the same smile?   This grew ; I gave commands ;
Then all smiles stopped together.   There she stands
As if alive.   Will 't please you rise?   We 'll meet
The company below, then.   I repeat,
The Count your master's known munificence
Is ample warrant that no just pretence   50
Of mine for dowry will be disallowed ;
Though his fair daughter's self, as I avowed
At starting, is my object.   Nay, we 'll go
Together down, sir.   Notice Neptune, though,
Taming a sea-horse, thought a rarity,
Which Claus of Innsbruck cast in bronze for me!

SONG FROM "PIPPA PASSES."

I.

GIVE her but a least excuse to love me !
    When — where —
How — can this arm establish her above me,
    If fortune fixed her as my lady there,
There already, to eternally reprove me ?
    (" Hist ! " — said Kate the queen ;
But " Oh," cried the maiden, binding her tresses,
    " 'T is only a page that carols unseen,
Crumbling your hounds their messes ! ")

II.

Is she wronged? — To the rescue of her honour,   10
    My heart!
Is she poor? — What costs it to be styled a donor?
    Merely an earth to cleave, a sea to part.
But that fortune should have thrust all this upon her!
    (" Nay, list ! " — bade Kate the queen ;
And still cried the maiden, binding her tresses,
    " 'T is only a page that carols unseen,
Fitting your hawks their jesses ! ")

CRISTINA.

I.

SHE should never have looked at me if she meant I should not love
    her !
There are plenty . . . men, you call such, I suppose . . . she may discover
All her soul to, if she pleases, and yet leave much as she found them :
But I 'm not so, and she knew it when she fixed me, glancing round
    them.

II.

What ? To fix me thus meant nothing? But I can't tell (there 's my
    weakness)
What her look said ! — no vile cant, sure, about " need to strew the
    bleakness
Of some lone shore with its pearl-seed, that the sea feels " — no
    " strange yearning
That such souls have, most to lavish where there 's chance of least
    returning."

III.

Oh, we 're sunk enough here, God knows ! but not quite so sunk that
    moments,
Sure tho' seldom, are denied us, when the spirit's true endowments   10
Stand out plainly from its false ones, and apprise it if pursuing
Or the right way or the wrong way, to its triumph or undoing.

IV.

There are flashes struck from midnights, there are fire-flames noondays
    kindle,
Whereby piled-up honours perish, whereby swollen ambitions dwindle,
While just this or that poor impulse, which for once had play unstifled,
Seems the sole work of a life-time that away the rest have trifled.

V.

Doubt you if, in some such moment, as she fixed me, she felt clearly,
Ages past the soul existed, here an age 't is resting merely,
And hence fleets again for ages, while the true end, sole and single,
It stops here for is, this love-way, with some other soul to mingle?   20

VI.

Else it loses what it lived for, and eternally must lose it ;
Better ends may be in prospect, deeper blisses (if you choose it),
But this life's end and this love-bliss have been lost here. Doubt you
    whether
This she felt as, looking at me, mine and her souls rushed together?

VII.

Oh, observe !   Of course, next moment, the world's honours, in derision,
Trampled out the light for ever.   Never fear but there's provision
Of the devil's to quench knowledge, lest we walk the earth in rapture !
— Making those who catch God's secret, just so much more prize their
   capture !

VIII.

Such am I : the secret 's mine now !   She has lost me, I have gained
   her ;
Her soul 's mine : and thus, grown perfect, I shall pass my life's re-
   mainder.   30
Life will just hold out the proving both our powers, alone and blended :
And then, come next life quickly !   This world's use will have been
   ended.

COUNT GISMOND.

AIX IN PROVENCE.

I.

CHRIST God who savest man, save most
  Of men Count Gismond who saved me !
Count Gauthier, when he chose his post,
  Chose time and place and company
To suit it ; when he struck at length
My honour, 't was with all his strength.

II.

And doubtlessly, ere he could draw
  All points to one, he must have schemed !
That miserable morning saw
  Few half so happy as I seemed,   10
While being dressed in queen's array
To give our tourney prize away.

III.

I thought they loved me, did me grace
  To please themselves ; 't was all their deed ;
God makes, or fair or foul, our face ;
  If showing mine so caused to bleed
My cousins' hearts, they should have dropped
A word, and straight the play had stopped.

IV.

They, too, so beauteous!   Each a queen
    By virtue of her brow and breast;   20
Not needing to be crowned, I mean,
    As I do.   E'en when I was dressed,
Had either of them spoke, instead
Of glancing sideways with still head!

V.

But no : they let me laugh, and sing
    My birthday song quite through, adjust
The last rose in my garland, fling
    A last look on the mirror, trust
My arms to each an arm of theirs,
And so descend the castle-stairs —   30

VI.

And come out on the morning troop
    Of merry friends who kissed my cheek,
And called me queen, and made me stoop
    Under the canopy — (a streak
That pierced it, of the outside sun,
Powdered with gold its gloom's soft dun) —

VII.

And they could let me take my state
    And foolish throne amid applause
Of all come there to celebrate
    My queen's-day — Oh I think the cause   40
Of much was, they forgot no crowd
Makes up for parents in their shroud!

VIII.

However that be, all eyes were bent
    Upon me, when my cousins cast
Theirs down; 't was time I should present
    The victor's crown, but . . . there, 't will last
No long time . . . the old mist again
Blinds me as then it did.   How vain!

IX.

See! Gismond 's at the gate, in talk
    With his two boys: I can proceed.   50

Well, at that moment, who should stalk
   Forth boldly — to my face, indeed —
But Gauthier ? and he thundered "Stay !"
And all stayed.   "Bring no crowns, I say !

X.

"Bring torches !   Wind the penance-sheet
   About her !   Let her shun the chaste,
Or lay herself before their feet !
   Shall she, whose body I embraced
A night long, queen it in the day ?
For honour's sake no crowns, I say !"   60

XI.

I ?   What I answered ?   As I live,
   I never fancied such a thing
As answer possible to give.
   What says the body when they spring
Some monstrous torture-engine's whole
Strength on it ?   No more says the soul.

XII.

Till out strode Gismond ; then I knew
   That I was saved.   I never met
His face before, but, at first view,
   I felt quite sure that God had set   70
Himself to Satan : who would spend
A minute's mistrust on the end ?

XIII.

He strode to Gauthier, in his throat
   Gave him the lie, then struck his mouth
With one back-handed blow that wrote
   In blood men's verdict there.   North, South,
East, West, I looked.   The lie was dead,
And damned, and truth stood up instead.

XIV.

This glads me most, that I enjoyed
   The heart of the joy, with my content   80
In watching Gismond unalloyed
   By any doubt of the event :
God took that on him — I was bid
Watch Gismond for my part : I did.

XV.

Did I not watch him while he let
  His armourer just brace his greaves,
Rivet his hauberk, on the fret
  The while ! His foot . . . my memory leaves
No least stamp out, nor how anon
He pulled his ringing gauntlets on.   90

XVI.

And e'en before the trumpet's sound
  Was finished, prone lay the false knight,
Prone as his lie, upon the ground :
  Gismond flew at him, used no sleight
O' the sword, but open-breasted drove,
Cleaving till out the truth he clove.

XVII.

Which done, he dragged him to my feet
  And said, " Here die, but end thy breath
In full confession, lest thou fleet
  From my first, to God's second death !   100
Say, hast thou lied ? " And, " I have lied
To God and her," he said, and died.

XVIII.

Then Gismond, kneeling to me, asked
  —What safe my heart holds, though no word
Could I repeat now, if I tasked
  My powers for ever, to a third
Dear even as you are.   Pass the rest
Until I sank upon his breast.

XIX.

Over my head his arm he flung
  Against the world ; and scarce I felt   110
His sword (that dripped by me and swung)
  A little shifted in its belt :
For he began to say the while
How South our home lay many a mile.

XX.

So, 'mid the shouting multitude
  We two walked forth to never more

Return.   My cousins have pursued
   Their life, untroubled as before
I vexed them.   Gauthier's dwelling-place
God lighten !   May his soul find grace !   120

XXI.

Our elder boy has got the clear
   Great brow ; tho' when his brother's black
Full eye shows scorn, it . . . Gismond here ?
   And have you brought my tercel back ?
I was just telling Adela
How many birds it struck since May.

EURYDICE TO ORPHEUS.

A PICTURE BY FREDERICK LEIGHTON, R.A.

BUT give them me, the mouth, the eyes, the brow !
  Let them once more absorb me !   One look now
Will lap me round for ever, not to pass
Out of its light, though darkness lie beyond :
Hold me but safe again within the bond
  Of one immortal look !   All woe that was,
Forgotten, and all terror that may be,
Defied, — no past is mine, no future : look at me !

THE GLOVE.

(PETER RONSARD *loquitur.*)

" HEIGHO!" yawned one day King Francis,
   " Distance all value enhances !
When a man 's busy, why, leisure
Strikes him as wonderful pleasure :
'Faith, and at leisure once is he ?
Straightway he wants to be busy.
Here we 've got peace ; and aghast I 'm
Caught thinking war the true pastime.
Is there a reason in metre ?
Give us your speech, master Peter ! "   10
I who, if mortal dare say so,

Ne'er am at loss with my Naso,
"Sire," I replied, "joys prove cloudlets:
Men are the merest Ixions" —
Here the King whistled aloud, " Let 's
. . . Heigho . . . go look at our lions ! "
Such are the sorrowful chances
If you talk fine to King Francis.

And so, to the courtyard proceeding,
Our company, Francis was leading,   20
Increased by new followers tenfold
Before he arrived at the penfold;
Lords, ladies, like clouds which bedizen
At sunset the western horizon.
And Sir De Lorge pressed 'mid the foremost
With the dame he professed to adore most.
Oh, what a face !   One by fits eyed
Her, and the horrible pitside;
For the penfold surrounded a hollow
Which led where the eye scarce dared follow,   30
And shelved to the chamber secluded
Where Bluebeard, the great lion, brooded.
The King hailed his keeper, an Arab
As glossy and black as a scarab,
And bade him make sport and at once stir
Up and out of his den the old monster.
They opened a hole in the wire-work
Across it, and dropped there a firework,
And fled : one's heart's beating redoubled;
A pause, while the pit's mouth was troubled,   40
The blackness and silence so utter,
By the firework's slow sparkling and sputter;
Then earth in a sudden contortion
Gave out to our gaze her abortion.
Such a brute !   Were I friend Clement Marot
(Whose experience of nature's but narrow,
And whose faculties move in no small mist
When he versifies David the Psalmist)
I should study that brute to describe you
Illum Juda Leonem de Tribu.   50
One's whole blood grew curdling and creepy
To see the black mane, vast and heapy,
The tail in the air stiff and straining,
The wide eyes, nor waxing nor waning,
As over the barrier which bounded
His platform, and us who surrounded
The barrier, they reached and they rested
On space that might stand him in best stead:

For who knew, he thought, what the amazement,
The eruption of clatter and blaze meant,   60
And if, in this minute of wonder,
No outlet, 'mid lightning and thunder,
Lay broad, and, his shackles all shivered,
The lion at last was delivered?
Ay, that was the open sky o'erhead!
And you saw by the flash on his forehead,
By the hope in those eyes wide and steady,
He was leagues in the desert already,
Driving the flocks up the mountain,
Or catlike couched hard by the fountain   70
To waylay the date-gathering negress:
So guarded he entrance or egress.
"How he stands!" quoth the King: "we may well swear,
(No novice, we 've won our spurs elsewhere
And so can afford the confession,)
We exercise wholesome discretion
In keeping aloof from his threshold;
Once hold you, those jaws want no fresh hold,
Their first would too pleasantly purloin
The visitor's brisket or sirloin: 80
But who 's he would prove so fool-hardy?
Not the best man of Marignan, pardie!"

The sentence no sooner was uttered,
Than over the rails a glove fluttered,
Fell close to the lion, and rested:
The dame 't was, who flung it and jested
With life so, De Lorge had been wooing
For months past; he sat there pursuing
His suit, weighing out with nonchalance
Fine speeches like gold from a balance.   90

Sound the trumpet, no true knight 's a tarrier!
De Lorge made one leap at the barrier,
Walked straight to the glove, — while the lion
Ne'er moved, kept his far-reaching eye on
The palm-tree-edged desert-spring's sapphire,
And the musky oiled skin of the Kaffir, —
Picked it up, and as calmly retreated,
Leaped back where the lady was seated
And full in the face of its owner
Flung the glove.

                    "Your heart's queen, you dethrone her?   100
So should I!"— cried the King — "'t was mere vanity,
Not love, set that task to humanity!"

Lords and ladies alike turned with loathing
From such a proved wolf in sheep's clothing.

Not so, I ; for I caught an expression
In her brow's undisturbed self-possession
Amid the Court's scoffing and merriment, —
As if from no pleasing experiment
She rose, yet of pain not much heedful
So long as the process was needful, —   110
As if she had tried, in a crucible,
To what "speeches like gold" were reducible,
And, finding the finest prove copper,
Felt the smoke in her face was but proper ;
To know what she had *not* to trust to,
Was worth all the ashes and dust too.
She went out 'mid hooting and laughter ;
Clement Marot stayed ; I followed after,
And asked, as a grace, what it all meant?
If she wished not the rash deed's recalment?   120
" For I " — so I spoke — " am a poet :
Human nature — behoves that I know it ! "

She told me, " Too long had I heard
Of the deed proved alone by the word :
For my love — what De Lorge would not dare !
With my scorn — what De Lorge could compare !
And the endless descriptions of death
He would brave when my lip formed a breath,
I must reckon as braved, or, of course,
Doubt his word — and moreover, perforce,   130
For such gifts as no lady could spurn,
Must offer my love in return.
When I looked on your lion, it brought
All the dangers at once to my thought,
Encountered by all sorts of men,
Before he was lodged in his den, —
From the poor slave whose club or bare hands
Dug the trap, set the snare on the sands,
With no King and no Court to applaud,
By no shame, should he shrink, overawed,   140
Yet to capture the creature made shift,
That his rude boys might laugh at the gift,
— To the page who last leaped o'er the fence
Of the pit, on no greater pretence
Than to get back the bonnet he dropped,
Lest his pay for a week should be stopped.
So, wiser I judged it to make
One trial what ' death for my sake '

Really meant, while the power was yet mine,
Than to wait until time should define 150
Such a phrase not so simply as I,
Who took it to mean just 'to die.'
The blow a glove gives is but weak :
Does the mark yet discolour my cheek?
But when the heart suffers a blow,
Will the pain pass so soon, do you know?"

I looked, as away she was sweeping,
And saw a youth eagerly keeping
As close as he dared to the doorway.
No doubt that a noble should more weigh 160
His life than befits a plebeian ;
And yet, had our brute been Nemean —
(I judge by a certain calm fervour
The youth stepped with, forward to serve her)
— He 'd have scarce thought you did him the worst turn
If you whispered, " Friend, what you 'd get, first earn ! "
And when, shortly after, she carried
Her shame from the Court, and they married,
To that marriage some happiness, maugre
The voice of the Court, I dared augur.

For De Lorge, he made women with men vie,
Those in wonder and praise, these in envy ;
And, in short, stood so plain a head taller
That he wooed and won . . . how do you call her?
The beauty, that rose in the sequel
To the King's love, who loved her a week well.
And 't was noticed he never would honour
De Lorge (who looked daggers upon her)
With the easy commission of stretching
His legs in the service, and fetching 180
His wife, from her chamber, those straying
Sad gloves she was always mislaying,
While the King took the closet to chat in, —
But of course this adventure came pat in.
And never the King told the story,
How bringing a glove brought such glory,
But the wife smiled — " His nerves are grown firmer :
Mine he brings now and utters no murmur."

Venienti occurrite morbo !
With which moral I drop my theorbo. 190

SONG.

I.

NAY but you, who do not love her,
  Is she not pure gold, my mistress?
Holds earth aught — speak truth — above her?
  Aught like this tress, see, and this tress,
And this last fairest tress of all,
So fair, see, ere I let it fall?

II.

Because, you spend your lives in praising;
  To praise, you search the wide world over:
Then why not witness, calmly gazing,
  If earth holds aught — speak truth — above her?   10
Above this tress, and this, I touch
But cannot praise, I love so much!

A SERENADE AT THE VILLA.

I.

THAT was I, you heard last night,
  When there rose no moon at all,
Nor, to pierce the strained and tight
  Tent of heaven, a planet small:
Life was dead, and so was light.

II.

Not a twinkle from the fly,
  Not a glimmer from the worm;
When the crickets stopped their cry,
  When the owls forbore a term,
You heard music; that was I.   10

III.

Earth turned in her sleep with pain,
  Sultrily suspired for proof:
In at heaven and out again,
  Lightning! — where it broke the roof,
Bloodlike, some few drops of rain.

IV.

What they could my words expressed,
　O my love, my all, my one!
Singing helped the verses best,
　And when singing's best was done,
To my lute I left the rest.　　　　20

V.

So wore night; the East was gray,
　White the broad-faced hemlock flowers:
There would be another day;
　Ere its first of heavy hours
Found me, I had passed away.

VI.

What became of all the hopes,
　Words and song and lute as well?
Say, this struck you: "When life gropes
　Feebly for the path where fell
Light last on the evening slopes, —　　30

VII.

"One friend in that path shall be,
　To secure my step from wrong;
One to count night day for me,
　Patient through the watches long,
Serving most with none to see."

VIII.

Never say — as something bodes —
　"So, the worst has yet a worse!
When life halts 'neath double loads,
　Better the task-master's curse
Than such music on the roads!　　　40

IX.

"When no moon succeeds the sun,
　Nor can pierce the midnight's tent
Any star, the smallest one,
　While some drops, where lightning rent,
Show the final storm begun —

X.

"When the fire-fly hides its spot,
  When the garden-voices fail
In the darkness thick and hot, —
  Shall another voice avail,
That shape be where these are not?   50

XI.

" Has some plague a longer lease,
  Proffering its help uncouth?
Can't one even die in peace?
  As one shuts one's eyes on youth,
Is that face the last one sees?"

XII.

Oh how dark your villa was,
  Windows fast and obdurate!
How the garden grudged me grass
  Where I stood — the iron gate
Ground its teeth to let me pass!   60

YOUTH AND ART.

I.

IT once might have been, once only:
  We lodged in a street together,
You, a sparrow on the housetop lonely,
  I, a lone she-bird of his feather.

II.

Your trade was with sticks and clay,
  You thumbed, thrust, patted and polished,
Then laughed "They will see, some day,
  Smith made, and Gibson demolished."

III.

My business was song, song, song;
  I chirped, cheeped, trilled and twittered,   10
"Kate Brown 's on the boards ere long,
  And Grisi's existence embittered!"

IV.

I earned no more by a warble
    Than you by a sketch in plaster;
You wanted a piece of marble,
    I needed a music-master.

V.

We studied hard in our styles,
    Chipped each at a crust like Hindoos,
For air, looked out on the tiles,
    For fun, watched each other's windows.   20

VI.

You lounged, like a boy of the South,
    Cap and blouse — nay, a bit of beard too;
Or you got it, rubbing your mouth
    With fingers the clay adhered to.

VII.

And I — soon managed to find
    Weak points in the flower-fence facing,
Was forced to put up a blind
    And be safe in my corset-lacing.

VIII.

No harm ! It was not my fault
    If you never turned your eye's tail up   30
As I shook upon E *in alt*,
    Or ran the chromatic scale up :

IX.

For spring bade the sparrows pair,
    And the boys and girls gave guesses,
And stalls in our street looked rare
    With bulrush and watercresses.

X.

Why did not you pinch a flower
    In a pellet of clay and fling it?
Why did not I put a power
    Of thanks in a look, or sing it?   40

C

XI.

I did look, sharp as a lynx,
   (And yet the memory rankles)
When models arrived, some minx
   Tripped up stairs, she and her ankles.

XII.

But I think I gave you as good !
   "That foreign fellow, — who can know
How she pays, in a playful mood,
   For his tuning her that piano?"

XIII.

Could you say so, and never say
   "Suppose we join hands and fortunes,   50
And I fetch her from over the way,
   Her, piano, and long tunes and short tunes?"

XIV.

No, no : you would not be rash,
   Nor I rasher and something over;
You 've to settle yet Gibson's hash,
   And Grisi yet lives in clover.

XV.

But you meet the Prince at the Board,
   I 'm queen myself at *bals-parés*,
I 've married a rich old lord,
   And you 're dubbed knight and an R.**A.**   60

XVI.

Each life unfulfilled, you see ;
   It hangs still, patchy and scrappy :
We have not sighed deep, laughed free,
   Starved, feasted, despaired, — been happy.

XVII.

And nobody calls you a dunce,
   And people suppose me clever ;
This could but have happened once,
   And we missed it, lost it for ever.

THE FLIGHT OF THE DUCHESS.

I.

YOU 'RE my friend :
        I was the man the Duke spoke to ;
I helped the Duchess to cast off his yoke, too ;
So, here 's the tale from beginning to end,
My friend !

II.

Ours is a great wild country :
If you climb to our castle's top,
I don't see where your eye can stop ;
For when you 've passed the corn-field country,
Where vineyards leave off, flocks are packed,   10
And sheep-range leads to cattle-tract,
And cattle-tract to open-chase,
And open-chase to the very base
Of the mountain where, at a funeral pace,
Round about, solemn and slow,
One by one, row after row,
Up and up the pine-trees go,
So, like black priests up, and so
Down the other side again
To another greater, wilder country,   20
That 's one vast red drear burnt-up plain,
Branched through and through with many a vein
Whence iron 's dug, and copper 's dealt ;
Look right, look left, look straight before,—
Beneath they mine, above they smelt,
Copper-ore and iron-ore,
And forge and furnace mould and melt,
And so on, more and ever more,
Till at the last, for a bounding belt,
Comes the salt sand hoar of the great sea-shore,   30
— And the whole is our Duke's country.

III.

I was born the day this present Duke was —
(And O, says the song, ere I was old !)
In the castle where the other Duke was —
(When I was happy and young, not old !)
I in the kennel, he in the bower :
We are of like age to an hour.
My father was huntsman in that day ;

Who has not heard my father say
That, when a boar was brought to bay,   40
Three times, four times out of five,
With his huntspear he'd contrive
To get the killing-place transfixed,
And pin him true, both eyes betwixt?
And that's why the old Duke would rather
He lost a salt-pit than my father,
And loved to have him ever in call;
That's why my father stood in the hall
When the old Duke brought his infant out
To show the people, and while they passed   50
The wondrous bantling round about,
Was first to start at the outside blast
As the Kaiser's courier blew his horn,
Just a month after the babe was born.
"And," quoth the Kaiser's courier, "since
The Duke has got an heir, our Prince
Needs the Duke's self at his side:"
The Duke looked down and seemed to wince,
But he thought of wars o'er the world wide,
Castles a-fire, men on their march,   60
The toppling tower, the crashing arch;
And up he looked, and awhile he eyed
The row of crests and shields and banners
Of all achievements after all manners,
And "ay," said the Duke with a surly pride.
The more was his comfort when he died
At next year's end, in a velvet suit,
With a gilt glove on his hand, his foot
In a silken shoe for a leather boot,
Petticoated like a herald,   70
In a chamber next to an ante-room,
Where he breathed the breath of page and groom,
What he called stink, and they, perfume:
— They should have set him on red Berold
Mad with pride, like fire to manage!
They should have got his cheek fresh tannage
Such a day as to-day in the merry sunshine!
Had they stuck on his fist a rough-foot merlin!
(Hark, the wind's on the heath at its game!
Oh for a noble falcon-lanner   80
To flap each broad wing like a banner,
And turn in the wind, and dance like flame!)
Had they broached a white-beer cask from Berlin
— Or if you incline to prescribe mere wine
Put to his lips, when they saw him pine,
A cup of our own Moldavia fine,

Cotnar for instance, green as May sorrel
And ropy with sweet, — we shall not quarrel.

IV.

So, at home, the sick tall yellow Duchess
Was left with the infant in her clutches,   90
She being the daughter of God knows who:
And now was the time to revisit her tribe.
Abroad and afar they went, the two,
And let our people rail and gibe
At the empty hall and extinguished fire,
As loud as we liked, but ever in vain,
Till after long years we had our desire,
And back came the Duke and his mother again.

V.

And he came back the pertest little ape
That ever affronted human shape;   100
Full of his travel, struck at himself.
You 'd say, he despised our bluff old ways?
— Not he !   For in Paris they told the elf
Our rough North land was the Land of Lays,
The one good thing left in evil days;
Since the Mid-Age was the Heroic Time,
And only in wild nooks like ours
Could you taste of it yet as in its prime,
And see true castles with proper towers,
Young-hearted women, old-minded men,   110
And manners now as manners were then.
So, all that the old Dukes had been, without knowing it,
This Duke would fain know he was, without being it;
'T was not for the joy's self, but the joy of his showing it,
Nor for the pride's self, but the pride of our seeing it,
He revived all usages thoroughly worn-out,
The souls of them fumed-forth, the hearts of them torn-out:
And chief in the chase his neck he perilled,
On a lathy horse, all legs and length,
With blood for bone, all speed, no strength;   120
— They should have set him on red Berold
With the red eye slow consuming in fire,
And the thin stiff ear like an abbey spire!

VI.

Well, such as he was, he must marry, we heard:
And out of a convent, at the word,

Came the lady, in time of spring.
— Oh, old thoughts they cling, they cling!
That day, I know, with a dozen oaths
I clad myself in thick hunting-clothes
Fit for the chase of urochs or buffle   130
In winter-time when you need to muffle.
But the Duke had a mind we should cut a figure,
And so we saw the lady arrive :
My friend, I have seen a white crane bigger!
She was the smallest lady alive,
Made in a piece of nature's madness,
Too small, almost, for the life and gladness
That over-filled her, as some hive
Out of the bears' reach on the high trees
Is crowded with its safe merry bees :   140
In truth, she was not hard to please!
Up she looked, down she looked, round at the mead,
Straight at the castle, that 's best indeed
To look at from outside the walls :
As for us, styled the "serfs and thralls,"
She as much thanked me as if she had said it,
(With her eyes, do you understand?)
Because I patted her horse while I led it ;
And Max, who rode on her other hand,
Said, no bird flew past but she inquired   150
What its true name was, nor ever seemed tired —
If that was an eagle she saw hover,
And the green and gray bird on the field was the plover.
When suddenly appeared the Duke :
And as down she sprung, the small foot pointed
On to my hand, — as with a rebuke,
And as if his backbone were not jointed,
The Duke stepped rather aside than forward
And welcomed her with his grandest smile ;
And, mind you, his mother all the while   160
Chilled in the rear, like a wind to Nor'ward ;
And up, like a weary yawn, with its pullies
Went, in a shriek, the rusty portcullis ;
And, like a glad sky the north-wind sullies,
The lady's face stopped its play,
As if her first hair had grown gray ;
For such things must begin some one day.

VII.

In a day or two she was well again :
As who should say, "You labour in vain!
This is all a jest against God, who meant   170

I should ever be, as I am, content
And glad in his sight; therefore, glad I will be."
So, smiling as at first went she.

VIII.

She was active, stirring, all fire —
Could not rest, could not tire —
To a stone she might have given life!
(I myself loved once, in my day)
— For a shepherd's, miner's, huntsman's wife,
(I had a wife, I know what I say)
Never in all the world such an one!   180
And here was plenty to be done,
And she that could do it, great or small,
She was to do nothing at all.
There was already this man in his post,
This in his station, and that in his office,
And the Duke's plan admitted a wife, at most,
To meet his eye with the other trophies.
Now outside the hall, now in it,
To sit thus, stand thus, see and be seen,
At the proper place in the proper minute,   190
And die away the life between.
And it was amusing enough, each infraction
Of rule — (but for after-sadness that came)
To hear the consummate self-satisfaction
With which the young Duke and the old dame
Would let her advise, and criticise,
And, being a fool, instruct the wise,
And, child-like, parcel out praise or blame.
They bore it all in complacent guise,
As though an artificer, after contriving   200
A wheel-work image as if it were living,
Should find with delight it could motion to strike him!
So found the Duke, and his mother like him:
The lady hardly got a rebuff —
That had not been contemptuous enough,
With his cursed smirk, as he nodded applause,
And kept off the old mother-cat's claws.

IX.

So, the little lady grew silent and thin,
  Paling and ever paling,
As the way is with a hid chagrin;   210
  And the Duke perceived that she was ailing,
And said in his heart, "'T is done to spite me,

But I shall find in my power to right me ! "
Don't swear, friend!   The old one, many a year,
Is in hell, and the Duke's self . . . you shall hear.

X.

Well, early in autumn, at first winter-warning,
When the stag had to break with his foot, of a morning
A drinking-hole out of the fresh tender ice,
That covered the pond till the sun, in a trice,
Loosening it, let out a ripple of gold,   220
And another, and faster and faster,
Till, dimpling to blindness, the wide water rolled, —
Then it so chanced that the Duke our master
Asked himself what were the pleasures in season,
And found, since the calendar bade him be hearty,
He should do the Middle Age no treason
In resolving on a hunting-party.
Always provided, old books showed the way of it !
What meant old poets by their strictures ?
And when old poets had said their say of it,   230
How taught old painters in their pictures?
We must revert to the proper channels,
Workings in tapestry, paintings on panels,
And gather up woodcraft's authentic traditions.
Here was food for our various ambitions,
As on each case, exactly stated —
To encourage your dog, now, the properest chirrup,
Or best prayer to St. Hubert on mounting your stirrup —
We of the household took thought and debated.
Blessed was he whose back ached with the jerkin   240
His sire was wont to do forest-work in ;
Blesseder he who nobly sunk " ohs "
And " ahs " while he tugged on his grandsire's trunk-hose ;
What signified hats if they had no rims on,
Each slouching before and behind like the scallop,
And able to serve at sea for a shallop,
Loaded with lacquer and looped with crimson?
So that the deer now, to make a short rhyme on 't,
What with our Venerers, Prickers and Verderers,
Might hope for real hunters at length and not murderers,   250
And oh the Duke's tailor, he had a hot time on 't!

XI.

Now you must know that when the first dizziness
Of flap-hats and buff-coats and jack-boots subsided,
The Duke put this question, " The Duke's part provided

Had not the Duchess some share in the business ? "
For out of the mouth of two or three witnesses
Did he establish all fit-or-unfitnesses :
And, after much laying of heads together,
Somebody's cap got a notable feather
By the announcement with proper unction   260
That he had discovered the lady's function ;
Since ancient authors gave this tenet,
"When horns wind a mort and the deer is at siege,
Let the dame of the castle prick forth on her jennet,
And with water to wash the hands of her liege
In a clean ewer with a fair toweling,
Let her preside at the disemboweling."
Now, my friend, if you had so little religion
As to catch a hawk, some falcon-lanner,
And thrust her broad wings like a banner   270
Into a coop for a vulgar pigeon ;
And if day by day and week by week
You cut her claws, and sealed her eyes,
And clipped her wings, and tied her beak,
Would it cause you any great surprise
If, when you decided to give her an airing,
You found she needed a little preparing ?
— I say, should you be such a curmudgeon,
If she clung to the perch, as to take it in dudgeon ?
Yet when the Duke to his lady signified,   280
Just a day before, as he judged most dignified,
In what a pleasure she was to participate, —
And, instead of leaping wide in flashes,
Her eyes just lifted their long lashes,
As if pressed by fatigue even he could not dissipate,
And duly acknowledged the Duke's forethought,
But spoke of her health, if her health were worth aught,
Of the weight by day and the watch by night,
And much wrong now that used to be right,
So, thanking him, declined the hunting, —   290
Was conduct ever more affronting ?
With all the ceremony settled —
With the towel ready, and the sewer
Polishing up his oldest ewer,
And the jennet pitched upon, a piebald,
Black-barred, cream-coated and pink eye-balled, —
No wonder if the Duke was nettled !
And when she persisted nevertheless, —
Well, I suppose here 's the time to confess
That there ran half round our lady's chamber   300
A balcony none of the hardest to clamber ;
And that Jacynth the tire-woman, ready in waiting,

Stayed in call outside, what need of relating?
And since Jacynth was like a June rose, why, a fervent
Adorer of Jacynth of course was your servant;
And if she had the habit to peep through the casement,
How could I keep at any vast distance?
And so, as I say, on the lady's persistence,
The Duke, dumb stricken with amazement,
Stood for a while in a sultry smother,   310
And then, with a smile that partook of the awful,
Turned her over to his yellow mother
To learn what was held decorous and lawful;
And the mother smelt blood with a cat-like instinct,
As her cheek quick whitened thro' all its quince-tint.
Oh, but the lady heard the whole truth at once!
What meant she? — Who was she? — Her duty and station,
The wisdom of age and the folly of youth, at once,
Its decent regard and its fitting relation —
In brief, my friend, set all the devils in hell free   320
And turn them out to carouse in a belfry
And treat the priests to a fifty-part canon,
And then you may guess how that tongue of hers ran on!
Well, somehow or other it ended at last,
And, licking her whiskers, out she passed;
And after her, — making (he hoped) a face
Like Emperor Nero or Sultan Saladin,
Stalked the Duke's self with the austere grace
Of ancient hero or modern paladin,
From door to staircase — oh such a solemn   330
Unbending of the vertebral column!

XII.

However, at sunrise our company mustered;
And here was the huntsman bidding unkennel,
And there 'neath his bonnet the pricker blustered,
With feather dank as a bough of wet fennel;
For the court-yard walls were filled with fog
You might have cut as an axe chops a log —
Like so much wool for colour and bulkiness;
And out rode the Duke in a perfect sulkiness,
Since, before breakfast, a man feels but queasily,   340
And a sinking at the lower abdomen
Begins the day with indifferent omen.
And lo, as he looked around uneasily,
The sun ploughed the fog up and drove it asunder,
This way and that, from the valley under;
And, looking through the court-yard arch,
Down in the valley, what should meet him

But a troop of Gipsies on their march?
No doubt with the annual gifts to greet him.

XIII.

Now, in your land, Gipsies reach you, only   350
After reaching all lands beside;
North they go, South they go, trooping or lonely,
And still, as they travel far and wide,
Catch they and keep now a trace here, a trace there,
That puts you in mind of a place here, a place there.
But with us, I believe they rise out of the ground,
And nowhere else, I take it, are found
With the earth-tint yet so freshly embrowned;
Born, no doubt, like insects which breed on
The very fruit they are meant to feed on.   360
For the earth — not a use to which they don't turn it,
The ore that grows in the mountain's womb,
Or the sand in the pits like a honeycomb,
They sift and soften it, bake it and burn it —
Whether they weld you, for instance, a snaffle
With side-bars never a brute can baffle;
Or a lock that 's a puzzle of wards within wards;
Or, if your colt's forefoot inclines to curve inwards,
Horseshoes they hammer which turn on a swivel
And won't allow the hoof to shrivel.   370
Then they cast bells like the shell of the winkle
That keep a stout heart in the ram with their tinkle;
But the sand — they pinch and pound it like otters;
Commend me to Gipsy glass-makers and potters!
Glasses they 'll blow you, crystal-clear,
Where just a faint cloud of rose shall appear,
As if in pure water you dropped and let die
A bruised black-blooded mulberry;
And that other sort, their crowning pride,
With long white threads distinct inside,   380
Like the lake-flower's fibrous roots which dangle
Loose such a length and never tangle,
Where the bold sword-lily cuts the clear waters,
And the cup-lily couches with all the white daughters:
Such are the works they put their hand to,
The uses they turn and twist iron and sand to.
And these made the troop, which our Duke saw sally
Toward his castle from out of the valley,
Men and women, like new-hatched spiders,
Come out with the morning to greet our riders.   390
And up they wound till they reached the ditch,
Whereat all stopped save one, a witch

That I knew, as she hobbled from the group,
By her gait directly and her stoop,
I, whom Jacynth was used to importune
To let that same witch tell us our fortune.
The oldest Gipsy then above ground;
And, sure as the autumn season came round,
She paid us a visit for profit or pastime,
And every time, as she swore, for the last time.   400
And presently she was seen to sidle
Up to the Duke till she touched his bridle,
So that the horse of a sudden reared up
As under its nose the old witch peered up
With her worn-out eyes, or rather eye-holes
Of no use now but to gather brine,
And began a kind of level whine
Such as they used to sing to their viols
When their ditties they go grinding
Up and down with nobody minding.   410
And then, as of old, at the end of the humming
Her usual presents were forthcoming
— A dog-whistle blowing the fiercest of trebles,
(Just a sea-shore stone holding a dozen fine pebbles,
Or a porcelain mouth-piece to screw on a pipe-end, —
And so she awaited her annual stipend.
But this time, the Duke would scarcely vouchsafe
A word in reply; and in vain she felt
With twitching fingers at her belt
For the purse of sleek pine-martin pelt,   420
Ready to put what he gave in her pouch safe, —
Till, either to quicken his apprehension,
Or possibly with an after-intention,
She was come, she said, to pay her duty
To the new Duchess, the youthful beauty.
No sooner had she named his lady,
Than a shine lit up the face so shady,
And its smirk returned with a novel meaning:
For it struck him, the babe just wanted weaning;
If one gave her a taste of what life was and sorrow   430
She, foolish to-day, would be wiser to-morrow;
And who so fit a teacher of trouble
As this sordid crone bent well-nigh double?
So, glancing at her wolf-skin vesture,
(If such it was, for they grow so hirsute
That their own fleece serves for natural fur-suit)
He was contrasting, 't was plain from his gesture,
The life of the lady so flower-like and delicate
With the loathsome squalor of this helicat.
I, in brief, was the man the Duke beckoned   440

From out of the throng : and while I drew near
He told the crone — as I since have reckoned
By the way he bent and spoke into her ear
With circumspection and mystery —
The main of the lady's history,
Her frowardness and ingratitude ;
And for all the crone's submissive attitude
I could see round her mouth the loose plaits tightening,
And her brow with assenting intelligence brightening,
As though she engaged with hearty goodwill   450
Whatever he now might enjoin to fulfil,
And promised the lady a thorough frightening.
And so, just giving her a glimpse
Of a purse, with the air of a man who imps
The wing of the hawk that shall fetch the hernshaw,
He bade me take the Gipsy mother
And set her telling some story or other
Of hill or dale, oak-wood or fernshaw,
To wile away a weary hour
For the lady left alone in her bower,   460
Whose mind and body craved exertion
And yet shrank from all better diversion.

XIV.

Then clapping heel to his horse, the mere curveter,
Out rode the Duke, and after his hollo
Horses and hounds swept, huntsman and servitor,
And back I turned and bade the crone follow.
And what makes me confident what's to be told you
Had all along been of this crone's devising,
Is, that, on looking round sharply, behold you,
There was a novelty quick as surprising :   470
For first, she had shot up a full head in stature,
And her step kept pace with mine nor faltered,
As if age had foregone its usurpature,
And the ignoble mien was wholly altered,
And the face looked quite of another nature.
And the change reached too, whatever the change meant,
Her shaggy wolf-skin cloak's arrangement :
For where its tatters hung loose like sedges,
Gold coins were glittering on the edges,
Like the band-roll strung with tomans   480
Which proves the veil a Persian woman's :
And under her brow, like a snail's horns newly
Come out as after the rain he paces,
Two unmistakable eye-points duly
Live and aware looked out of their places.

So, we went and found Jacynth at the entry
Of the lady's chamber standing sentry.
I told the command and produced my companion,
And Jacynth rejoiced to admit any one,
For since last night, by the same token,   490
Not a single word had the lady spoken.
They went in both to the presence together,
While I in the balcony watched the weather.

XV.

And now, what took place at the very first of all,
I cannot tell, as I never could learn it:
Jacynth constantly wished a curse to fall
On that little head of hers and burn it
If she knew how she came to drop so soundly
Asleep of a sudden, and there continue
The whole time sleeping as profoundly   500
As one of the boars my father would pin you
'Twixt the eyes where life holds garrison,
— Jacynth, forgive me the comparison!
But where I begin my own narration
Is a little after I took my station
To breathe the fresh air from the balcony,
And, having in those days a falcon eye,
To follow the hunt thro' the open country,
From where the bushes thinlier crested
The hillocks, to a plain where 's not one tree.   510
When, in a moment, my ear was arrested
By — was it singing, or was it saying,
Or a strange musical instrument playing
In the chamber? — and to be certain
I pushed the lattice, pulled the curtain,
And there lay Jacynth asleep,
Yet as if a watch she tried to keep,
In a rosy sleep along the floor
With her head against the door;
While in the midst, on the seat of state,   520
Was a queen — the Gipsy woman late,
With head and face downbent
On the lady's head and face intent:
For, coiled at her feet like a child at ease,
The lady sat between her knees,
And o'er them the lady's clasped hands met,
And on those hands her chin was set,
And her upturned face met the face of the crone
Wherein the eyes had grown and grown
As if she could double and quadruple   530

At pleasure the play of either pupil
— Very like, by her hands' slow fanning,
As up and down like a gor-crow's flappers
They moved to measure, or like bell-clappers.
I said, "Is it blessing, is it banning,
Do they applaud you or burlesque you —
Those hands and fingers with no flesh on?"
But, just as I thought to spring in to the rescue,
At once I was stopped by the lady's expression:
For it was life her eyes were drinking   540
From the crone's wide pair above unwinking,
— Life's pure fire, received without shrinking,
Into the heart and breast whose heaving
Told you no single drop they were leaving,
— Life, that filling her, passed redundant
Into her very hair, back swerving
Over each shoulder, loose and abundant,
As her head thrown back showed the white throat curving;
And the very tresses shared in the pleasure,
Moving to the mystic measure,   550
Bounding as the bosom bounded.
I stopped short, more and more confounded,
As still her cheeks burned and eyes glistened,
As she listened and she listened.
When all at once a hand detained me,
The selfsame contagion gained me,
And I kept time to the wondrous chime,
Making out words and prose and rhyme,
Till it seemed that the music furled
Its wings like a task fulfilled, and dropped   560
From under the words it first had propped,
And left them midway in the world.
Word took word as hand takes hand,
I could hear at last, and understand;
And when I held the unbroken thread,
The Gipsy said: —

"And so at last we find my tribe,
And so I set thee in the midst,
And to one and all of them describe
What thou saidst and what thou didst,   570
Our long and terrible journey through,
And all thou art ready to say and do
In the trials that remain.
I trace them the vein and the other vein
That meet on thy brow and part again
Making our rapid mystic mark;
And I bid my people prove and probe

Each eye's profound and glorious globe
Till they detect the kindred spark
In those depths so dear and dark,   580
Like the spots that snap and burst and flee,
Circling over the midnight sea.
And on that round young cheek of thine
I make them recognise the tinge,
As when of the costly scarlet wine
They drip so much as will impinge
And spread in a thinnest scale afloat
One thick gold drop from the olive's coat
Over a silver plate whose sheen
Still thro' the mixture shall be seen.   590
For so I prove thee, to one and all,
Fit, when my people ope their breast,
To see the sign, and hear the call,
And take the vow, and stand the test
Which adds one more child to the rest —
When the breast is bare and the arms are wide,
And the world is left outside.
For there is probation to decree,
And many and long must the trials be
Thou shalt victoriously endure,   600
If that brow is true and those eyes are sure.
Like a jewel-finder's fierce assay
Of the prize he dug from its mountain-tomb, —
Let once the vindicating ray
Leap out amid the anxious gloom,
And steel and fire have done their part,
And the prize falls on its finder's heart :
So, trial after trial past,
Wilt thou fall at the very last
Breathless, half in trance   610
With the thrill of the great deliverance,
Into our arms for evermore ;
And thou shalt know, those arms once curled
About thee, what we knew before,
How love is the only good in the world.
Henceforth be loved as heart can love,
Or brain devise, or hand approve!
Stand up, look below,
It is our life at thy feet we throw
To step with into light and joy ;   620
Not a power of life but we employ
To satisfy thy nature's want.
Art thou the tree that props the plant,
Or the climbing plant that seeks the tree —
Canst thou help us, must we help thee?

If any two creatures grew into one,
They would do more than the world has done;
Though each apart were never so weak,
Ye vainly through the world should seek
For the knowledge and the might   630
Which in such union grew their right:
So, to approach at least that end,
And blend, — as much as may be, blend
Thee with us or us with thee, —
As climbing plant or propping tree,
Shall some one deck thee over and down,
Up and about, with blossoms and leaves?
Fix his heart's fruit for thy garland-crown,
Cling with his soul as the gourd-vine cleaves
Die on thy boughs and disappear   640
While not a leaf of thine is sere?
Or is the other fate in store,
And art thou fitted to adore,
To give thy wondrous self away,
And take a stronger nature's sway?
I foresee and could foretell
Thy future portion, sure and well:
But those passionate eyes speak true, speak true.
Let them say what thou shalt do!
Only be sure thy daily life,   650
In its peace or in its strife,
Never shall be unobserved;
We pursue thy whole career,
And hope for it, or doubt, or fear, —
Lo, hast thou kept thy path or swerved,
We are beside thee in all thy ways,
With our blame, with our praise,
Our shame to feel, our pride to show,
Glad, angry — but indifferent, no!
Whether it be thy lot to go,   660
For the good of us all, where the haters meet
In the crowded city's horrible street;
Or thou step alone through the morass
Where never sound yet was
Save the dry quick clap of the stork's bill,
For the air is still, and the water still,
When the blue breast of the dipping coot
Dives under, and all is mute.
So, at the last shall come old age,
Decrepit as befits that stage;   670
How else wouldst thou retire apart
With the hoarded memories of thy heart,
And gather all to the very least

D

Of the fragments of life's earlier feast,
Let fall through eagerness to find
The crowning dainties yet behind?
Ponder on the entire past
Laid together thus at last,
When the twilight helps to fuse
The first fresh with the faded hues,   680
And the outline of the whole,
As round eve's shades their framework roll,
Grandly fronts for once thy soul!
And then as, 'mid the dark, a gleam
Of yet another morning breaks,
And like the hand which ends a dream,
Death, with the might of his sunbeam,
Touches the flesh and the soul awakes,
Then — "
           Ay, then indeed something would happen!
But what ?   For here her voice changed like a bird's ;   690
There grew more of the music and less of the words ;
Had Jacynth only been by me to clap pen
To paper and put you down every syllable
With those clever clerkly fingers,
All I 've forgotten as well as what lingers
In this old brain of mine that 's but ill able
To give you even this poor version
Of the speech I spoil, as it were, with stammering
— More fault of those who had the hammering
Of prosody into me and syntax,   700
And did it, not with hobnails but tintacks !
But to return from this excursion, —
Just, do you mark, when the song was sweetest,
The peace most deep and the charm completest,
There came, shall I say, a snap —
And the charm vanished!
And my sense returned, so strangely banished,
And, starting as from a nap,
I knew the crone was bewitching my lady,
With Jacynth asleep ; and but one spring made I   710
Down from the casement, round to the portal, —
Another minute and I had entered, —
When the door opened, and more than mortal
Stood, with a face where to my mind centred
All beauties I ever saw or shall see,
The Duchess : I stopped as if struck by palsy.
She was so different, happy and beautiful,
I felt at once that all was best,
And that I had nothing to do, for the rest,
But wait her commands, obey and be dutiful.   720

Not that, in fact, there was any commanding;
I saw the glory of her eye,
And the brow's height and the breast's expanding,
And I was hers to live or to die.
As for finding what she wanted,
You know God Almighty granted
Such little signs should serve wild creatures
To tell one another all their desires,
So that each knows what his friend requires,
And does its bidding without teachers.   730
I preceded her; the crone
Followed silent and alone;
I spoke to her, but she merely jabbered
In the old style; both her eyes had slunk
Back to their pits; her stature shrunk;
In short, the soul in its body sunk
Like a blade sent home to its scabbard.
We descended, I preceding;
Crossed the court with nobody heeding;
All the world was at the chase,   740
The court-yard like a desert-place,
The stable emptied of its small fry;
I saddled myself the very palfrey
I remember patting while it carried her,
The day she arrived and the Duke married her.
And, do you know, though it 's easy deceiving
Oneself in such matters, I can't help believing
The lady had not forgotten it either,
And knew the poor devil so much beneath her
Would have been only too glad, for her service,   750
To dance on hot ploughshares like a Turk dervise,
But, unable to pay proper duty where owing it,
Was reduced to that pitiful method of showing it:
For though the moment I began setting
His saddle on my own nag of Berold's begetting,
(Not that I meant to be obtrusive)
She stopped me, while his rug was shifting,
By a single rapid finger's lifting,
And, with a gesture kind but conclusive,
And a little shake of the head, refused me, —   76c
I say, although she never used me,
Yet when she was mounted, the Gipsy behind her,
And I ventured to remind her,
I suppose with a voice of less steadiness
Than usual, for my feeling exceeded me,
— Something to the effect that I was in readiness
Whenever God should please she needed me, —
Then, do you know, her face looked down on me

With a look that placed a crown on me,
And she felt in her bosom, — mark, her bosom —   770
And, as a flower-tree drops its blossom,
Dropped me . . . ah, had it been a purse
Of silver, my friend, or gold that's worse,
Why, you see, as soon as I found myself
So understood, — that a true heart so may gain
Such a reward, — I should have gone home again,
Kissed Jacynth, and soberly drowned myself!
It was a little plait of hair
Such as friends in a convent make
To wear, each for the other's sake, —   780
This, see, which at my breast I wear,
Ever did (rather to Jacynth's grudgment),
And ever shall, till the Day of Judgment.
And then, — and then, — to cut short, — this is idle,
These are feelings it is not good to foster, —
I pushed the gate wide, she shook the bridle,
And the palfrey bounded, — and so we lost her.

XVI.

When the liquor's out why clink the cannikin?
I did think to describe you the panic in
The redoubtable breast of our master the mannikin,   790
And what was the pitch of his mother's yellowness,
How she turned as a shark to snap the spare-rib
Clean off, sailors say, from a pearl-diving Carib,
When she heard, what she called the flight of the feloness
— But it seems such child's play,
What they said and did with the lady away!
And to dance on, when we 've lost the music,
Always made me — and no doubt makes you — sick.
Nay, to my mind, the world's face looked so stern
As that sweet form disappeared through the postern,   800
She that kept it in constant good humour,
It ought to have stopped; there seemed nothing to do more.
But the world thought otherwise and went on,
And my head's one that its spite was spent on:
Thirty years are fled since that morning,
And with them all my head's adorning.
Nor did the old Duchess die outright,
As you expect, of suppressed spite,
The natural end of every adder
Not suffered to empty its poison-bladder: 810
But she and her son agreed, I take it,
That no one should touch on the story to wake it,
For the wound in the Duke's pride rankled fiery;

So, they made no search and small inquiry:
And when fresh Gipsies have paid us a visit, I 've
Noticed the couple were never inquisitive,
But told them they 're folks the Duke don't want here,
And bade them make haste and cross the frontier.
Brief, the Duchess was gone and the Duke was glad of it,
And the old one was in the young one's stead,   820
And took, in her place, the household's head,
And a blessed time the household had of it!
And were I not, as a man may say, cautious
How I trench, more than needs, on the nauseous,
I could favour you with sundry touches
Of the paint-smutches with which the Duchess
Heightened the mellowness of her cheek's yellowness
(To get on faster) until at last her
Cheek grew to be one master-plaster
Of mucus and fucus from mere use of ceruse: 830
In short, she grew from scalp to udder
Just the object to make you shudder.

XVII.

You 're my friend —
What a thing friendship is, world without end!
How it gives the heart and soul a stir-up
As if somebody broached you a glorious runlet,
And poured out, all lovelily, sparklingly, sunlit,
Our green Moldavia, the streaky syrup,
Cotnar as old as the time of the Druids —
Friendship may match with that monarch of fluids;   840
Each supples a dry brain, fills you its ins-and-outs,
Gives your life's hour-glass a shake when the thin sand doubts
Whether to run on or stop short, and guarantees
Age is not all made of stark sloth and arrant ease.
I have seen my little lady once more,
Jacynth, the Gipsy, Berold, and the rest of it,
For to me spoke the Duke, as I told you before;
I always wanted to make a clean breast of it:
And now it is made — why, my heart's blood, that went trickle,
Trickle, but anon, in such muddy driblets,   850
Is pumped up brisk now, through the main ventricle,
And genially floats me about the giblets.
I 'll tell you what I intend to do:
I must see this fellow his sad life through —
He is our Duke, after all,
And I, as he says, but a serf and thrall.
My father was born here, and I inherit
His fame, a chain he bound his son with;

Could I pay in a lump I should prefer it,
But there 's no mine to blow up and get done with :   860
So, I must stay till the end of the chapter.
For, as to our middle-age-manners-adapter,
Be it a thing to be glad on or sorry on,
Some day or other, his head in a morion
And breast in a hauberk, his heels he 'll kick up,
Slain by an onslaught fierce of hiccup.
And then, when red doth the sword of our Duke rust,
And its leathern sheath lie o'ergrown with a blue crust,
Then I shall scrape together my earnings ;
For, you see, in the churchyard Jacynth reposes,   870
And our children all went the way of the roses ;
It 's a long lane that knows no turnings.
One needs but little tackle to travel in ;
So, just one stout cloak shall I indue :
And for a staff, what beats the javelin
With which his boars my father pinned you?
And then, for a purpose you shall hear presently,
Taking some Cotnar, a tight plump skinful,
I shall go journeying, who but I, pleasantly !
Sorrow is vain and despondency sinful.   880
What 's a man's age?   He must hurry more, that 's all ;
Cram in a day, what his youth took a year to hold :
When we mind labour, then only, we 're too old —
What age had Methusalem when he begat Saul?
And at last, as its haven some buffeted ship sees,
(Come all the way from the north-parts with sperm oil)
I hope to get safely out of the turmoil
And arrive one day at the land of the Gipsies,
And find my lady, or hear the last news of her
From some old thief and son of Lucifer,   890
His forehead chapleted green with wreathy hop,
Sunburned all over like an Æthiop.
And when my Cotnar begins to operate
And the tongue of the rogue to run at a proper rate,
And our wine-skin, tight once, shows each flaccid dent,
I shall drop in with — as if by accident —
" You never knew then, how it all ended,
What fortune good or bad attended
The little lady your Queen befriended? "
— And when that 's told me, what 's remaining?   900
This world 's too hard for my explaining.
The same wise judge of matters equine
Who still preferred some slim four-year-old
To the big-boned stock of mighty Berold,
And, for strong Cotnar, drank French weak wine,
He also must be such a lady's scorner !

Smooth Jacob still robs homely Esau :
Now up, now down, the world's one see-saw.
— So, I shall find out some snug corner
Under a hedge, like Orson the wood-knight,   910
Turn myself round and bid the world good night ;
And sleep a sound sleep till the trumpet's blowing
Wakes me (unless priests cheat us laymen)
To a world where will be no further throwing
Pearls before swine that can't value them.   Amen!

SONG FROM "PIPPA PASSES."

THE year 's at the spring,
    And day 's at the morn ;
Morning 's at seven ;
The hill-side 's dew-pearled ;
The lark 's on the wing ;
The snail 's on the thorn ;
God 's in His heaven —
All 's right with the world !

"HOW THEY BROUGHT THE GOOD NEWS FROM GHENT TO AIX."

[16—.]

I.

I SPRANG to the stirrup, and Joris, and he ;
    I galloped, Dirck galloped, we galloped all three ;
"Good speed ! " cried the watch, as the gate-bolts undrew ;
"Speed ! " echoed the wall to us galloping through ;
Behind shut the postern, the lights sank to rest,
And into the midnight we galloped abreast.

II.

Not a word to each other ; we kept the great pace
Neck by neck, stride by stride, never changing our place ;
I turned in my saddle and made its girths tight,
Then shortened each stirrup, and set the pique right,   10
Rebuckled the cheek-strap, chained slacker the bit,
Nor galloped less steadily Roland a whit.

III.

'T was moonset at starting; but while we drew neaɪ
Lokeren, the cocks crew and twilight dawned clear;
At Boom, a great yellow star came out to see;
At Düffeld, 't was morning as plain as could be;
And from Mecheln church-steeple we heard the half-chime,
So, Joris broke silence with, "Yet there is time!"

IV.

At Aershot, up leaped of a sudden the sun,
And against him the cattle stood black every one, **20**
To stare thro' the mist at us galloping past,
And I saw my stout galloper Roland at last,
With resolute shoulders, each butting away
The haze, as some bluff river headland its spray:

V.

And his low head and crest, just one sharp ear bent back
For my voice, and the other pricked out on his track;
And one eye's black intelligence,— ever that glance
O'er its white edge at me, his own master, askance!
And the thick heavy spume-flakes which aye and anon
His fierce lips shook upwards in galloping on. **30**

VI.

By Hasselt, Dirck groaned; and cried Joris "Stay spur!
Your Roos galloped bravely, the fault 's not in her,
We 'll remember at Aix"— for one heard the quick wheeze
Of her chest, saw the stretched neck and staggering knees,
And sunk tail, and horrible heave of the flank,
As down on her haunches she shuddered and sank.

VII.

So, we were left galloping, Joris and I,
Past Looz and past Tongres, no cloud in the sky;
The broad sun above laughed a pitiless laugh,
'Neath our feet broke the brittle bright stubble like chaff; **40**
Till over by Dalhem a dome-spire sprang white,
And "Gallop," gasped Joris, "for Aix is in sight!"

VIII.

"How they 'll greet us !"— and all in a moment his roan
Rolled neck and croup over, lay dead as a stone;

And there was my Roland to bear the whole weight .
Of the news which alone could save Aix from her fate,
With his nostrils like pits full of blood to the brim,
And with circles of red for his eye-sockets' rim.

IX.

Then I cast loose my buff-coat, each holster let fall,
Shook off both my jack-boots, let go belt and all,   50
Stood up in the stirrup, leaned, patted his ear,
Called my Roland his pet-name, my horse without peer;
Clapped my hands, laughed and sang, any noise, bad or good,
Till at length into Aix Roland galloped and stood.

X.

And all I remember is, — friends flocking round
As I sat with his head 'twixt my knees on the ground;
And no voice but was praising this Roland of mine,
As I poured down his throat our last measure of wine,
Which (the burgesses voted by common consent)
Was no more than his due who brought good news from Ghent.   60

* * *

SONG FROM "PARACELSUS."

I.

HEAP cassia, sandal-buds and stripes
   Of labdanum, and aloe-balls,
Smeared with dull nard an Indian wipes
   From out her hair: such balsam falls
   Down sea-side mountain pedestals,
From tree-tops where tired winds are fain,
Spent with the vast and howling main,
To treasure half their island gain.

II.

And strew faint sweetness from some old
   Egyptian's fine worm-eaten shroud   10
Which breaks to dust when once unrolled;
   Or shredded perfume, like a cloud
   From closet long to quiet vowed,
With mothed and dropping arras hung,
Mouldering her lute and books among,
As when a queen, long dead, was young.

THROUGH THE METIDJA TO ABD-EL-KADR.

1842.

I.

A S I ride, as I ride,
   With a full heart for my guide,
So its tide rocks my side,
As I ride, as I ride,
That, as I were double-eyed,
He, in whom our Tribes confide,
Is descried, ways untried,
As I ride, as I ride.

II.

As I ride, as I ride
To our Chief and his Allied,   10
Who dares chide my heart's pride
As I ride, as I ride?
Or are witnesses denied —
Through the desert waste and wide
Do I glide unespied
As I ride, as I ride?

III.

As I ride, as I ride,
When an inner voice has cried,
The sands slide, nor abide
(As I ride, as I ride)   20
O'er each visioned homicide
That came vaunting (has he lied?)
To reside — where he died,
As I ride, as I ride.

IV.

As I ride, as I ride,
Ne'er has spur my swift horse plied,
Yet his hide, streaked and pied,
As I ride, as I ride,
Shows where sweat has sprung and dried,
— Zebra-footed, ostrich-thighed —   30
How has vied stride with stride
As I ride, as I ride!

V.

As I ride, as I ride,
Could I loose what Fate has tied,
Ere I pried, she should hide
(As I ride, as I ride)
All that 's meant me — satisfied
When the Prophet and the Bride
Stop veins I 'd have subside
As I ride, as I ride!   40

INCIDENT OF THE FRENCH CAMP.

eight line stanza
interwoven rhyme
alternate 4 & 3 stress

I.

YOU know, we French stormed Ratisbon:
    A mile or so away
On a little mound, Napoleon
    Stood on our storming-day;
With neck out-thrust, you fancy how,
    Legs wide, arms locked behind,
As if to balance the prone brow
    Oppressive with its mind.

II.

Just as perhaps he mused " My plans
    That soar, to earth may fall,   10
Let once my army-leader Lannes
    Waver at yonder wall " —
Out 'twixt the battery-smokes there flew
    A rider, bound on bound
Full-galloping; nor bridle drew
    Until he reached the mound.

III.

Then off there flung in smiling joy,
    And held himself erect
By just his horse's mane, a boy:
    You hardly could suspect —   20
(So tight he kept his lips compressed,
    Scarce any blood came through)
You looked twice ere you saw his breast
    Was all but shot in two.

IV.

"Well," cried he, "Emperor, by God's grace
  We 've got you Ratisbon!
The Marshal 's in the market-place,
  And you 'll be there anon
To see your flag-bird flap his vans
  Where I, to heart's desire,   30
Perched him!" The chief's eye flashed; his plans
  Soared up again like fire.

V.

The chief's eye flashed; but presently √
  Softened itself, as sheathes
A film the mother-eagle's eye ×
  When her bruised eaglet breathes.
"You 're wounded!" "Nay," the soldier's pride
  Touched to the quick, he said:
"I 'm killed, Sire!" And his chief beside,
  Smiling the boy fell dead.   40

THE LOST LEADER.

I.

JUST for a handful of silver he left us,
  Just for a riband to stick in his coat—
Found the one gift of which fortune bereft us,
  Lost all the others, she lets us devote;
They, with the gold to give, doled him out silver,
  So much was theirs who so little allowed:
How all our copper had gone for his service!
  Rags—were they purple, his heart had been proud!
We that had loved him so, followed him, honoured him,
  Lived in his mild and magnificent eye.   10
Learned his great language, caught his clear accents,
  Made him our pattern to live and to die!
Shakespeare was of us, Milton was for us,
  Burns, Shelley, were with us,—they watch from their graves!
He alone breaks from the van and the freemen,
  He alone sinks to the rear and the slaves!

II.

We shall march prospering,—not thro' his presence;
  Songs may inspirit us,—not from his lyre;

Deeds will be done, — while he boasts his quiescence,
  Still bidding crouch whom the rest bade aspire: 20
Blot out his name, then, record one lost soul more,
  One task more declined, one more footpath untrod,
One more devil's-triumph and sorrow for angels,
  One wrong more to man, one more insult to God!
Life's night begins: let him never come back to us!
  There would be doubt, hesitation and pain,
Forced praise on our part — the glimmer of twilight,
  Never glad confident morning again!
Best fight on well, for we taught him — strike gallantly,
  Menace our heart ere we master his own;   30
Then let him receive the new knowledge and wait us,
  Pardoned in heaven, the first by the throne!

IN A GONDOLA.

He sings.

I SEND my heart up to thee, all my heart
  In this my singing.
For the stars help me, and the sea bears part;
  The very night is clinging
Closer to Venice' streets to leave one space
  Above me, whence thy face
May light my joyous heart to thee its dwelling-place.

She speaks.

Say after me, and try to say
My very words, as if each word
Came from you of your own accord,   10
In your own voice, in your own way:
"This woman's heart and soul and brain
Are mine as much as this gold chain
She bids me wear; which " (say again)
"I choose to make by cherishing
A precious thing, or choose to fling
Over the boat-side, ring by ring."
And yet once more say . . . no word more!
Since words are only words.   Give o'er!

Unless you call me, all the same,   20
Familiarly by my pet name,
Which if the Three should hear you call,
And me reply to, would proclaim

At once our secret to them all.
Ask of me, too, command me, blame —
Do, break down the partition-wall
'Twixt us, the daylight world beholds
Curtained in dusk and splendid folds!
What's left but — all of me to take?
I am the Three's: prevent them, slake 30
Your thirst! 'T is said, the Arab sage
In practising with gems, can loose
Their subtle spirit in his cruce
And leave but ashes: so, sweet mage,
Leave them my ashes when thy use
Sucks out my soul, thy heritage!

He sings.

I.

Past we glide, and past, and past!
 What's that poor Agnese doing
Where they make the shutters fast?
 Gray Zanobi's just a-wooing 40
To his couch the purchased bride:
 Past we glide!

II.

Past we glide, and past, and past!
 Why's the Pucci Palace flaring
Like a beacon to the blast?
 Guests by hundreds, not one caring
If the dear host's neck were wried:
 Past we glide!

She sings.

I.

The moth's kiss, first!
Kiss me as if you made believe
You were not sure, this eve, 50
How my face, your flower, had pursed
Its petals up; so, here and there
You brush it, till I grow aware
Who wants me, and wide ope I burst.

II.

The bee's kiss, now!
Kiss me as if you entered gay

My heart at some noonday, —
A bud that dares not disallow
The claim, so all is rendered up, 60
And passively its shattered cup
Over your head to sleep I bow.

He sings.

I.

What are we two?
I am a Jew,
And carry thee, farther than friends can pursue,
To a feast of our tribe;
Where they need thee to bribe
The devil that blasts them unless he imbibe
Thy . . . Scatter the vision for ever! And now,
As of old, I am I, thou art thou! 70

II.

Say again, what we are?
The sprite of a star,
I lure thee above where the destinies bar
My plumes their full play
Till a ruddier ray
Than my pale one announce there is withering away
Some . . . Scatter the vision for ever! And now,
As of old, I am I, thou art thou!

He muses.

Oh, which were best, to roam or rest?
The land's lap or the water's breast? 80
To sleep on yellow millet-sheaves,
Or swim in lucid shallows just
Eluding water-lily leaves,
An inch from Death's black fingers, thrust
To lock you, whom release he must;
Which life were best on Summer eves?

He speaks, musing.

Lie back: could thought of mine improve you?
From this shoulder let there spring
A wing; from this, another wing;
Wings, not legs and feet, shall move you! 90
Snow-white must they spring, to blend
With your flesh, but I intend

They shall deepen to the end,
Broader, into burning gold,
Till both wings crescent-wise enfold
Your perfect self, from 'neath your feet
To o'er your head, where, lo, they meet
As if a million sword-blades hurled
Defiance from you to the world !

Rescue me thou, the only real !   100
And scare away this mad ideal
That came, nor motions to depart !
Thanks ! Now, stay ever as thou art !

Still he muses.

I.

What if the Three should catch at last
Thy serenader? While there 's cast
Paul's cloak about my head, and fast
Gian pinions me, Himself has past
His stylet through my back ; I reel ;
And . . . is it thou I feel?

II.

They trail me, these three godless knaves,   110
Past every church that saints and saves,
Nor stop till, where the cold sea raves
By Lido's wet accursed graves,
They scoop mine, roll me to its brink,
And . . . on thy breast I sink!

She replies, musing.

I.

Dip your arm o'er the boat side, elbow-deep,
As I do : thus : were death so unlike sleep,
Caught this way? Death 's to fear from flame or steel,
Or poison doubtless ; but from water — feel!

II.

Go find the bottom! Would you stay me? There!   120
Now pluck a great blade of that ribbon-grass
To plait in where the foolish jewel was,
I flung away : since you have praised my hair,
'T is proper to be choice in what I wear.

He speaks.

Row home? must we row home?   Too surely
Know I where its front's demurely
Over the Guidecca piled;
Window just with window mating,
Door on door exactly waiting,
All's the set face of a child :   130
But behind it, where's a trace
Of the staidness and reserve,
And formal lines without a curve,
In the same child's playing-face?
No two windows look one way
O'er the small sea-water thread
Below them.   Ah, the autumn day
I, passing, saw you overhead!
First, out a cloud of curtain blew,
Then a sweet cry, and last came you —   140
To catch your lory that must needs
Escape just then, of all times then,
To peck a tall plant's fleecy seeds
And make me happiest of men.
I scarce could breathe to see you reach
So far back o'er the balcony,
To catch him ere he climbed too high
Above you in the Smyrna peach,
That quick the round smooth cord of gold,
This coiled hair on your head, unrolled,   150
Fell down you like a gorgeous snake
The Roman girls were wont, of old,
When Rome there was, for coolness' sake
To let lie curling o'er their bosoms.
Dear lory, may his beak retain
Ever its delicate rose stain,
As if the wounded lotus-blossoms
Had marked their thief to know again!

Stay longer yet, for others' sake
Than mine!   What should your chamber do?   160
— With all its rarities that ache
In silence while day lasts, but wake
At night-time and their life renew,
Suspended just to pleasure you
Who brought against their will together
These objects, and, while day lasts, weave
Around them such a magic tether
That dumb they look : your harp, believe
With all the sensitive tight strings

E

Which dare not speak, now to itself   . 170
Breathes slumberously, as if some elf
Went in and out the chords, his wings
Make murmur, wheresoe'er they graze,
As an angel may, between the maze
Of midnight palace-pillars, on
And on, to sow God's plagues, have gone
Through guilty glorious Babylon.
And while such murmurs flow, the nymph
Bends o'er the harp-top from her shell
As the dry limpet for the lymph   180
Come with a tune he knows so well.
And how your statues' hearts must swell !
And how your pictures must descend
To see each other, friend with friend !
Oh, could you take them by surprise,
You'd find Schidone's eager Duke
Doing the quaintest courtesies
To that prim saint by Haste-thee-Luke!
And, deeper into her rock den,
Bold Castelfranco's Magdalen   190
You'd find retreated from the ken
Of that robed counsel-keeping Ser —
As if the Tizian thinks of her,
And is not, rather, gravely bent
On seeing for himself what toys
Are these, his progeny invent,
What litter now the board employs
Whereon he signed a document
That got him murdered!   Each enjoys
Its night so well, you cannot break   200
The sport up : so, indeed must make
More stay with me, for others' sake.

She speaks.

I.

To-morrow, if a harp-string, say,
Is used to tie the jasmine back
That overfloods my room with sweets,
Contrive your Zorzi somehow meets
My Zanze!   If the ribbon's black,
The Three are watching : keep away!

II.

Your gondola — let Zorzi wreathe
A mesh of water-weeds about   210

Its prow, as if he unaware
Had struck some quay or bridge-foot stair!
That I may throw a paper out
As you and he go underneath.

There 's Zanze's vigilant taper; safe are we.
Only one minute more to-night with me?
Resume your past self of a month ago!
Be you the bashful gallant, I will be
The lady with the colder breast than snow.
Now bow you, as becomes, nor touch my hand   220
More than I touch yours when I step to land,
And say, "All thanks, Siora!" —
                                        Heart to heart
And lips to lips!   Yet once more, ere we part,
Clasp me and make me thine, as mine thou art!

He is surprised, and stabbed.

It was ordained to be so, sweet! — and best
Comes now, beneath thine eyes, upon thy breast.
Still kiss me!   Care not for the cowards!   Care
Only to put aside thy beauteous hair
My blood will hurt!   The Three, I do not scorn
To death, because they never lived: but I   230
Have lived indeed, and so — (yet one more kiss) — can die!

A LOVERS' QUARREL.

I.

OH, what a dawn of day!
    How the March sun feels like May!
        All is blue again
        After last night's rain,
And the South dries the hawthorn-spray.
        Only, my Love 's away!
I 'd as lief that the blue were gray.

II.

Runnels, which rillets swell,
Must be dancing down the dell,
        With a foaming head   10
        On the beryl bed
Paven smooth as a hermit's cell:
        Each with a tale to tell,
Could my Love but attend as well.

III.

Dearest, three months ago!
When we lived blocked-up with snow, —
  When the wind would edge
  In and in his wedge,
In, as far as the point could go —
  Not to our ingle, though,   20
Where we loved each the other so!

IV.

Laughs with so little cause!
We devised games out of straws.
  We would try and trace
  One another's face
In the ash, as an artist draws;
  Free on each other's flaws,
How we chattered like two church daws!

V.

What's in the " Times "? —a scold
At the Emperor deep and cold;   30
  He has taken a bride
  To his gruesome side,
That's as fair as himself is bold:
  There they sit ermine-stoled,
And she powders her hair with gold.

VI.

Fancy the Pampas' sheen!
Miles and miles of gold and green
  Where the sunflowers blow
  In a solid glow,
And — to break now and then the screen — 40
  Black neck and eyeballs keen,
Up a wild horse leaps between!

VII.

Try, will our table turn?
Lay your hands there light, and yearn
  Till the yearning slips
  Thro' the finger-tips
In a fire which a few discern,
  And a very few feel burn,
And the rest, they may live and learn!

VIII.

Then we would up and pace,   50
For a change, about the place,
  Each with arm o'er neck:
  'T is our quarter-deck,
We are seamen in woeful case.
  Help in the ocean-space!
Or, if no help, we 'll embrace.

IX.

See, how she looks now, dressed
In a sledging-cap and vest!
  'T is a huge fur cloak —
  Like a reindeer's yoke   60
Falls the lappet along the breast:
  Sleeves for her arms to rest,
Or to hang, as my Love likes best.

X.

Teach me to flirt a fan
As the Spanish ladies can,
  Or I tint your lip
  With a burnt stick's tip
And you turn into such a man!
  Just the two spots that span
Half the bill of the young male swan.   70

XI.

Dearest, three months ago,
When the mesmerizer Snow
  With his hand's first sweep
  Put the earth to sleep,
'T was a time when the heart could show
  All — how was earth to know,
Neath the mute hand's to-and-fro?

XII.

Dearest, three months ago,
When we loved each other so,
  Lived and loved the same   80
  Till an evening came
When a shaft from the devil's bow
  Pierced to our ingle-glow,
And the friends were friend and foe!

XIII.

Not from the heart beneath —
'T was a bubble born of breath,
    Neither sneer nor vaunt,
    Nor reproach nor taunt.
See a word, how it severeth !
    Oh, power of life and death   90
In the tongue, as the Preacher saith !

XIV.

Woman, and will you cast
For a word, quite off at last
    Me, your own, your You, —
    Since, as truth is true,
I was You all the happy past —
    Me do you leave aghast
With the memories We amassed ?

XV.

Love, if you knew the light
That your soul casts in my sight,   100
    How I look to you
    For the pure and true,
And the beauteous and the right, —
    Bear with a moment's spite
When a mere mote threats the white !

XVI.

What of a hasty word ?
Is the fleshly heart not stirred
    By a worm's pin-prick
    Where its roots are quick ?
See the eye, by a fly's foot blurred —   110
    Ear, when a straw is heard
Scratch the brain's coat of curd !

XVII.

Foul be the world or fair
More or less, how can I care ?
    'T is the world the same
    For my praise or blame,
And endurance is easy there.
    Wrong in the one thing rare —
Oh, it is hard to bear !

XVIII.

Here 's the spring back or close,   120
When the almond-blossom blows ;
 We shall have the word
 In a minor third
There is none but the cuckoo knows :
 Heaps of the guelder-rose !
I must bear with it, I suppose.

XIX.

Could but November come,
Were the noisy birds struck dumb
 At the warning slash
 Of his driver's-lash —   130
I would laugh like the valiant Thumb
 Facing the castle glum
And the giant's fee-faw-fum !

XX.

Then, were the world well-stripped
Of the gear wherein equipped
 We can stand apart,
 Heart dispense with heart
In the sun, with the flowers unnipped, —
 Oh, the world's hangings ripped,
We were both in a bare-walled crypt !   140

XXI.

Each in the crypt would cry
" But one freezes here ! and why ?
 When a heart, as chill,
 At my own would thrill
Back to life, and its fires out-fly ?
 Heart, shall we live or die ?
The rest . . . settle by-and-by ! "

XXII.

So, she 'd efface the score,
And forgive me as before.
 It is twelve o'clock :   150
 I shall hear her knock
In the worst of a storm's uproar :
 I shall pull her through the door,
I shall have her for evermore !

EARTH'S IMMORTALITIES.

FAME.

SEE, as the prettiest graves will do in time,
    Our poet's wants the freshness of its prime;
Spite of the sexton's browsing horse, the sods
Have struggled through its binding osier rods;
Headstone and half-sunk footstone lean awry,
Wanting the brick-work promised by-and-by;
How the minute gray lichens, plate o'er plate,
Have softened down the crisp-cut name and date

LOVE.

So, the year's done with!
    (*Love me for ever!*)   10
All March begun with,
    April's endeavour;
May-wreaths that bound me
    June needs must sever;
Now snows fall round me,
    Quenching June's fever —
    (*Love me for ever!*)

———◦✦◦———

THE LAST RIDE TOGETHER

I.

I SAID — Then, dearest, since 't is so,
    Since now at length my fate I know,
Since nothing all my love avails,
Since all, my life seemed meant for, fails,
    Since this was written and needs must be —
My whole heart rises up to bless
Your name in pride and thankfulness!
Take back the hope you gave, — I claim
Only a memory of the same,
— And this beside, if you will not blame,   10
    Your leave for one more last ride with me.

II.

My mistress bent that brow of hers;
Those deep dark eyes where pride demurs

When pity would be softening through,
Fixed me a breathing-while or two
   With life or death in the balance : right!
The blood replenished me again ;
My last thought was at least not vain :
I and my mistress, side by side
Shall be together, breathe and ride,   20
So, one day more am I deified.
   Who knows but the world may end to-night?

III.

Hush! if you saw some western cloud
All billowy-bosomed, over-bowed
By many benedictions — sun's
And moon's and evening star's at once —
   And so, you, looking and loving best,
Conscious grew, your passion drew
Cloud, sunset, moonrise, star-shine too,
Down on you, near and yet more near,   30
Till flesh must fade for heaven was here! —
Thus leant she and lingered — joy and fear!
   Thus lay she a moment on my breast.

IV.

Then we began to ride. My soul
Smoothed itself out, a long-cramped scroll
Freshening and fluttering in the wind.
Past hopes already lay behind.
   What need to strive with a life awry?
Had I said that, had I done this,
So might I gain, so might I miss.
Might she have loved me? just as well   40
She might have hated, who can tell!
Where had I been now if the worst befell?
   And here we are riding, she and I.

V.

Fail I alone, in words and deeds?
Why, all men strive and who succeeds?
We rode ; it seemed my spirit flew,
Saw other regions, cities new,
   As the world rushed by on either side.
I thought, — All labour, yet no less   50
Bear up beneath their unsuccess.
Look at the end of work, contrast
The petty done, the undone vast,

This present of theirs with the hopeful past!
  I hoped she would love me; here we ride.

VI.

What hand and brain went ever paired?
What heart alike conceived and dared?
What act proved all its thought had been?
What will but felt the fleshly screen?
  We ride and I see her bosom heave.   60
There 's many a crown for who can reach.
Ten lines, a statesman's life in each!
The flag stuck on a heap of bones,
A soldier's doing! what atones?
They scratch his name on the Abbey-stones.
  My riding is better, by their leave.

VII.

What does it all mean, poet?   Well,
Your brains beat into rhythm, you tell
What we felt only; you expressed
You hold things beautiful the best,   70
  And pace them in rhyme so, side by side.
'T is something, nay 't is much: but then,
Have you yourself what 's best for men?
Are you — poor, sick, old ere your time —
Nearer one whit your own sublime
Than we who never have turned a rhyme?
  Sing, riding 's a joy!   For me, I ride.

VIII.

And you, great sculptor — so, you gave
A score of years to Art, her slave,
And that 's your Venus, whence we turn   80
To yonder girl that fords the burn!
  You acquiesce, and shall I repine?
What, man of music, you grown gray
With notes and nothing else to say,
Is this your sole praise from a friend,
"Greatly his opera's strains intend,
But in music we know how fashions end!"
  I gave my youth; but we ride, in fine.

IX.

Who knows what 's fit for us?   Had fate
Proposed bliss here should sublimate   90

My being — had I signed the bond —
Still one must lead some life beyond,
    Have a bliss to die with, dim-descried.
This foot once planted on the goal,
This glory-garland round my soul,
Could I descry such?   Try and test!
I sink back shuddering from the quest.
Earth being so good, would heaven seem best?
    Now, heaven and she are beyond this ride.

x.

And yet — she has not spoke so long!   100
What if heaven be that, fair and strong
At life's best, with our eyes upturned
Whither life's flower is first discerned,
    We, fixed so, ever should so abide?
What if we still ride on, we two,
With life for ever old yet new,
Changed not in kind but in degree,
The instant made eternity, —
And heaven just prove that I and she
    Ride, ride together, for ever ride?   110

MESMERISM.

I.

ALL I believed is true!
    I am able yet
    All I want, to get
By a method as strange as new:
Dare I trust the same to you?

II.

If at night, when doors are shut,
    And the wood-worm picks,
    And the death-watch ticks,
And the bar has a flag of smut,
And a cat 's in the water-butt —   10

III.

And the socket floats and flares,
    And the house-beams groan,
    And a foot unknown

Is surmised on the garret-stairs,
And the locks slip unawares —

IV.

And the spider, to serve his ends,
   By a sudden thread,
   Arms and legs outspread,
On the table's midst descends,
Comes to find, God knows what friends! —   20

V.

If since eve drew in, I say,
   I have sat and brought
   (So to speak) my thought
To bear on the woman away,
Till I felt my hair turn gray —

VI.

Till I seemed to have and hold,
   In the vacancy
   'Twixt the wall and me
From the hair-plait's chestnut-gold
To the foot in its muslin fold —   30

VII.

Have and hold, then and there,
   Her, from head to foot,
   Breathing and mute,
Passive and yet aware,
In the grasp of my steady stare —

VIII.

Hold and have, there and then,
   All her body and soul
   That completes my whole,
All that women add to men,
In the clutch of my steady ken —   40

IX.

Having and holding, till
   I imprint her fast
   On the void at last
As the sun does whom he will
By the calotypist's skill —

X.

Then, — if my heart's strength serve,
   And thro' all and each
   Of the veils I reach
To her soul and never swerve,
Knitting an iron nerve —   50

XI.

Command her soul to advance
   And inform the shape
   Which has made escape
And before my countenance
Answers me glance for glance —

XII.

I, still with a gesture fit
   Of my hands that best
   Do my soul's behest,
Pointing the power from it,
While myself do steadfast sit —   60

XIII.

Steadfast and still the same
   On my object bent,
   While the hands give vent
To my ardour and my aim
And break into very flame —

XIV.

Then I reach, I must believe,
   Not her soul in vain,
   For to me again
It reaches, and past retrieve
Is wound in the toils I weave;   70

XV.

And must follow as I require,
   As befits a thrall,
   Bringing flesh and all,
Essence and earth-attire,
To the source of the tractile fire:

XVI.

Till the house called hers, not mine,
   With a growing weight
   Seems to suffocate
If she break not its leaden line
And escape from its close confine.   80

XVII.

Out of doors into the night !
   On to the maze
   Of the wild wood-ways,
Not turning to left nor right
From the pathway, blind with sight —

XVIII.

Making thro' rain and wind
   O'er the broken shrubs,
   'Twixt the stems and stubs,
With a still, composed, strong mind,
Not a care for the world behind —   90

XIX.

Swifter and still more swift,
   As the crowding peace
   Doth to joy increase
In the wide blind eyes uplift
Thro' the darkness and the drift!

XX.

While I — to the shape, I too
   Feel my soul dilate :
   Not a whit abate,
And relax not a gesture due,
As I see my belief come true.   100

XXI.

For, there ! have I drawn or no
   Life to that lip?
   Do my fingers dip
In a flame which again they throw
On the cheek that breaks a-glow?

XXII.

Ha! was the hair so first?
    What, unfilleted,
    Made alive, and spread
Thro' the void with a rich outburst,
Chestnut gold-interspersed?   110

XXIII.

Like the doors of a casket-shrine,
    See, on either side,
    Her two arms divide
Till the heart betwixt makes sign,
Take me, for I am thine?

XXIV.

" Now — now " — the door is heard!
    Hark, the stairs! and near —
    Nearer — and here —
" Now ! " and, at call the third,
She enters without a word.   120

XXV.

On doth she march and on
    To the fancied shape;
    It is, past escape,
Herself, now: the dream is done
And the shadow and she are one.

XXVI.

First, I will pray.   Do Thou
    That ownest the soul,
    Yet wilt grant control
To another, nor disallow
For a time, restrain me now !   130

XXVII.

I admonish me while I may,
    Not to squander guilt,
    Since require Thou wilt
At my hand its price one day!
What the price is, who can say?

BY THE FIRESIDE.

I.

HOW well I know what I mean to do
　　When the long dark autumn evenings come:
And where, my soul, is thy pleasant hue?
　　With the music of all thy voices, dumb
In life's November too!

II.

I shall be found by the fire, suppose,
　　O'er a great wise book, as beseemeth age;
While the shutters flap as the cross-wind blows,
　　And I turn the page, and I turn the page,
Not verse now, only prose!   10

III.

Till the young ones whisper, finger on lip,
　　"There he is at it, deep in Greek:
Now then, or never, out we slip
　　To cut from the hazels by the creek
A mainmast for our ship!"

IV.

I shall be at it indeed, my friends!
　　Greek puts already on either side
Such a branch-work forth as soon extends
　　To a vista opening far and wide,
And I pass out where it ends.   20

V.

The outside-frame, like your hazel-trees —
　　But the inside-archway widens fast,
And a rarer sort succeeds to these,
　　And we slope to Italy at last
And youth, by green degrees.

VI.

I follow wherever I am led,
　　Knowing so well the leader's hand:
Oh woman-country, wooed not wed,
　　Loved all the more by earth's male-lands,
Laid to their hearts instead!   30

VII.

Look at the ruined chapel again
    Half-way up in the Alpine gorge!
Is that a tower, I point you plain,
    Or is it a mill, or an iron-forge
Breaks solitude in vain?

VIII.

A turn, and we stand in the heart of things;
    The woods are round us, heaped and dim;
From slab to slab how it slips and springs,
    The thread of water single and slim,
Thro' the ravage some torrent brings!   40

IX.

Does it feed the little lake below?
    That speck of white just on its marge
Is Pella; see, in the evening-glow,
    How sharp the silver spear-heads charge
When Alp meets heaven in snow!

X.

On our other side is the straight-up rock;
    And a path is kept 'twixt the gorge and it
By boulder-stones where lichens mock
    The marks on a moth, and small ferns fit
Their teeth to the polished block.   50

XI.

Oh the sense of the yellow mountain-flowers,
    And thorny balls, each three in one,
The chestnuts throw on our path in showers!
    For the drop of the woodland fruit's begun,
These early November hours,

XII.

That crimson the creeper's leaf across
    Like a splash of blood, intense, abrupt,
O'er a shield else gold from rim to boss,
    And lay it for show on the fairy-cupped
Elf-needled mat of moss,   60

F

XIII.

By the rose-flesh mushrooms, undivulged
  Last evening — nay, in to-day's first dew
Yon sudden coral nipple bulged,
  Where a freaked fawn-coloured flaky crew
Of toad-stools peep indulged.

XIV.

And yonder, at foot of the fronting ridge
  That takes the turn to a range beyond,
Is the chapel reached by the one-arched bridge,
  Where the water is stopped in a stagnant pond
Danced over by the midge.   70

XV.

The chapel and bridge are of stone alike,
  Blackish-gray and mostly wet;
Cut hemp-stalks steep in the narrow dyke.
  See here again, how the lichens fret
And the roots of the ivy strike!

XVI.

Poor little place, where its one priest comes
  On a festa-day, if he comes at all,
To the dozen folk from their scattered homes,
  Gathered within that precinct small
By the dozen ways one roams —   80

XVII.

To drop from the charcoal-burners' huts,
  Or climb from the hemp-dresser's low shed,
Leave the grange where the woodman stores his nuts,
  Or the wattled cote where the fowlers spread
Their gear on the rock's bare juts.

XVIII.

It has some pretension too, this front,
  With its bit of fresco half-moon-wise
Set over the porch, Art's early wont:
  'T is John in the Desert, I surmise,
But has borne the weather's brunt —   90

XIX.

Not from the fault of the builder, though,
　For a pent-house properly projects
Where three carved beams make a certain show,
　Dating — good thought of our architect's —
Five, six, nine, he lets you know.

XX.

And all day long a bird sings there,
　And a stray sheep drinks at the pond at times ;
The place is silent and aware ;
　It has had its scenes, its joys and crimes,
But that is its own affair.　　　　　　　　100

XXI.

My perfect wife, my Leonor,
　Oh heart, my own, oh eyes, mine too,
Whom else could I dare look backward for,
　With whom besides should I dare pursue
The path gray heads abhor?

XXII.

For it leads to a crag's sheer edge with them ;
　Youth, flowery all the way, there stops —
Not they ; age threatens and they contemn,
　Till they reach the gulf wherein youth drops,
One inch from life's safe hem !　　　　　　110

XXIII.

With me, youth led . . . I will speak now,
　No longer watch you as you sit
Reading by firelight, that great brow
　And the spirit-small hand propping it,
Mutely, my heart knows how —

XXIV.

When, if I think but deep enough,
　You are wont to answer, prompt as rhyme ;
And you, too, find without rebuff
　Response your soul seeks many a time,
Piercing its fine flesh-stuff.　　　　　　120

XXV.

My own, confirm me ! If I tread
  This path back, is it not in pride
To think how little I dreamed it led
  To an age so blest that, by its side,
Youth seems the waste instead?

XXVI.

My own, see where the years conduct!
  At first, 't was something our two souls
Should mix as mists do ; each is sucked
  In each now : on, the new stream rolls,
Whatever rocks obstruct.   130

XXVII.

Think, when our one soul understands
  The great Word which makes all things new,
When earth breaks up and heaven expands,
  How will the change strike me and you
In the house not made with hands?

XXVIII.

Oh I must feel your brain prompt mine,
  Your heart anticipate my heart,
You must be just before, in fine,
  See and make me see, for your part,
New depths of the divine !   140

XXIX.

But who could have expected this
  When we two drew together first
Just for the obvious human bliss,
  To satisfy life's daily thirst
With a thing men seldom miss?

XXX.

Come back with me to the first of all,
  Let us lean and love it over again,
Let us now forget and now recall,
  Break the rosary in a pearly rain,
And gather what we let fall !   150

XXXI.

What did I say? — that a small bird sings
    All day long, save when a brown pair
Of hawks from the wood float with wide wings
    Strained to a bell: 'gainst noon-day glare
You count the streaks and rings.

XXXII.

But at afternoon or almost eve
    'T is better; then the silence grows
To that degree, you half believe
    It must get rid of what it knows,
Its bosom does so heave.   160

XXXIII.

Hither we walked then, side by side,
    Arm in arm and cheek to cheek,
And still I questioned or replied,
    While my heart, convulsed to really speak,
Lay choking in its pride.

XXXIV.

Silent the crumbling bridge we cross,
    And pity and praise the chapel sweet,
And care about the fresco's loss,
    And wish for our souls a like retreat,
And wonder at the moss.   170

XXXV.

Stoop and kneel on the settle under,
    Look through the window's grated square:
Nothing to see! For fear of plunder,
    The cross is down and the altar bare,
As if thieves don't fear thunder.

XXXVI.

We stoop and look in through the grate,
    See the little porch and rustic door,
Read duly the dead builder's date;
    Then cross the bridge that we crossed before,
Take the path again — but wait!   180

XXXVII.

Oh moment one and infinite!
 The water slips o'er stock and stone;
The West is tender, hardly bright:
 How gray at once is the evening grown —
One star, its chrysolite!

XXXVIII.

We two stood there with never a third,
 But each by each, as each knew well:
The sights we saw and the sounds we heard,
 The lights and the shades made up a spell
Till the trouble grew and stirred.   190

XXXIX.

Oh, the little more, and how much it is!
 And the little less, and what worlds away!
How a sound shall quicken content to bliss,
 Or a breath suspend the blood's best play,
And life be a proof of this!

XL.

Had she willed it, still had stood the screen
 So slight, so sure, 'twixt my love and her:
I could fix her face with a guard between,
 And find her soul as when friends confer,
Friends — lovers that might have been.   200

XLI.

For my heart had a touch of the woodland time,
 Wanting to sleep now over its best.
Shake the whole tree in the summer-prime,
 But bring to the last leaf no such test!
"Hold the last fast!" runs the rhyme.

XLII.

For a chance to make your little much,
 To gain a lover and lose a friend,
Venture the tree and a myriad such,
 When nothing you mar but the year can mend:
But a last leaf — fear to touch!   210

XLIII.

Yet should it unfasten itself and fall
   Eddying down till it find your face
At some slight wind — best chance of all !
   Be your heart henceforth its dwelling-place
You trembled to forestall !

XLIV.

Worth how well, those dark gray eyes,
   That hair so dark and dear, how worth
That a man should strive and agonize,
   And taste a veriest hell on earth
For the hope of such a prize!   220

XLV.

You might have turned and tried a man,
   Set him a space to weary and wear,
And prove which suited more your plan,
   His best of hope or his worst despair,
Yet end as he began.

XLVI.

But you spared me this, like the heart you are,
   And filled my empty heart at a word.
If two lives join, there is oft a scar,
   They are one and one, with a shadowy third;
One near one is too far.   230

XLVII.

A moment after, and hands unseen
   Were hanging the night around us fast;
But we knew that a bar was broken between
   Life and life : we were mixed at last
In spite of the mortal screen.

XLVIII.

The forests had done it; there they stood;
   We caught for a moment the powers at play:
They had mingled us so, for once and good,
   Their work was done — we might go or stay,
They relapsed to their ancient mood.   240

XLIX.

How the world is made for each of us!
    How all we perceive and know in it
Tends to some moment's product thus,
    When a soul declares itself — to wit,
By its fruit, the thing it does!

L.

Be hate that fruit or love that fruit,
    It forwards the general deed of man:
And each of the Many helps to recruit
    The life of the race by a general plan;
Each living his own, to boot.   250

LI.

I am named and known by that moment's feat;
    There took my station and degree;
So grew my own small life complete,
    As nature obtained her best of me —
One born to love you, sweet!

LII.

And to watch you sink by the fireside now
    Back again, as you mutely sit
Musing by firelight, that great brow
    And the spirit-small hand propping it,
Yonder, my heart knows how!   260

LIII.

So, earth has gained by one man the more,
    And the gain of earth must be heaven's gain too;
And the whole is well worth thinking o'er
    When autumn comes: which I mean to do
One day, as I said before.

—◦◦—

ANY WIFE TO ANY HUSBAND.

I.

MY love, this is the bitterest, that thou —
    Who art all truth, and who dost love me now
As thine eyes say, as thy voice breaks to say —
Shouldst love so truly, and couldst love me still

A whole long life through, had but love its will,
  Would death that leads me from thee brook delay.

II.

I have but to be by thee, and thy hand
Will never let mine go, nor heart withstand
  The beating of my heart to reach its place.
When shall I look for thee and feel thee gone?   10
When cry for the old comfort and find none?
  Never, I know! Thy soul is in thy face.

III.

Oh, I should fade — 't is willed so!   Might I save,
Gladly I would, whatever beauty gave
  Joy to thy sense, for that was precious too.
It is not to be granted.   But the soul
Whence the love comes, all ravage leaves that whole;
  Vainly the flesh fades; soul makes all things new.

IV.

It would not be because my eye grew dim
Thou couldst not find the love there, thanks to Him   20
  Who never is dishonoured in the spark
He gave us from his fire of fires, and bade
Remember whence it sprang, nor be afraid
  While that burns on, tho' all the rest grow dark.

V.

So, how thou wouldst be perfect, white and clean
Outside as inside, soul and soul's demesne
  Alike, this body given to show it by!
Oh, three-parts thro' the worst of life's abyss,
What plaudits from the next world after this,
  Couldst thou repeat a stroke and gain the sky!   30

VI.

And is it not the bitterer to think
That, disengage our hands and thou wilt sink
  Altho' thy love was love in very deed?
I know that nature!   Pass a festive day,
Thou dost not throw its relic-flower away
  Nor bid its music's loitering echo speed.

VII.

Thou let'st the stranger's glove lie where it fell;
If old things remain old things all is well,
    For thou art grateful as becomes man best:
And hadst thou only heard me play one tune,   40
Or viewed me from a window, not so soon
    With thee would such things fade as with the rest.

VIII.

I seem to see! We meet and part; 't is brief;
The book I opened keeps a folded leaf,
    The very chair I sat on, breaks the rank;
That is a portrait of me on the wall —
Three lines, my face comes at so slight a call:
    And for all this, one little hour to thank!

IX.

But now, because the hour thro' years was fixed,
Because our inmost beings met and mixed,
    Because thou once hast loved me — wilt thou dare   50
Say to thy soul and Who may list beside,
" Therefore she is immortally my bride;
    Chance cannot change my love, nor time impair.

X.

" So, what if in the dusk of life that 's left,
I, a tired traveller of my sun bereft,
    Look from my path when, mimicking the same,
The fire-fly glimpses past me, come and gone?
— Where was it till the sunset? where anon
    It will be at the sunrise! What 's to blame? "   60

XI.

Is it so helpful to thee? Canst thou take
The mimic up, nor, for the true thing's sake,
    Put gently by such efforts at a beam?
Is the remainder of the way so long,
Thou need'st the little solace, thou the strong?
    Watch out thy watch, let weak ones doze and dream.

XII.

— Ah, but the fresher faces! " Is it true,"
Thou 'lt ask, " some eyes are beautiful and new?
    Some hair, — how can one choose but grasp such wealth?

And if a man would press his lips to lips 70
Fresh as the wilding hedge-rose-cup there slips
   The dew-drop out of, must it be by stealth?

XIII.

"It cannot change the love still kept for Her,
More than if such a picture I prefer
   Passing a day with, to a room's bare side:
The painted form takes nothing she possessed,
Yet, while the Titian's Venus lies at rest,
   A man looks. Once more, what is there to chide?"

XIV.

So must I see, from where I sit and watch,
My own self sell myself, my hand attach 80
   Its warrant to the very thefts from me —
Thy singleness of soul that made me proud,
Thy purity of heart I loved aloud,
   Thy man's-truth I was bold to bid God see!

XV.

Love so, then, if thou wilt! Give all thou canst
Away to the new faces — disentranced,
   (Say it and think it) obdurate no more:
Re-issue looks and words from the old mint,
Pass them afresh, no matter whose the print,
   Image and superscription once they bore! 90

XVI.

Re-coin thyself and give it them to spend, —
It all comes to the same thing at the end,
   Since mine thou wast, mine art, and mine shalt be,
Faithful or faithless: sealing up the sum
Or lavish of my treasure, thou must come
   Back to the heart's place here I keep for thee!

XVII.

Only, why should it be with stain at all?
Why must I, 'twixt the leaves of coronal,
   Put any kiss of pardon on thy brow?
Why need the other women know so much, 100
And talk together, "Such the look and such
   The smile he used to love with, then as now!"

XVIII.

Might I die last and show thee!   Should I find
Such hardship in the few years left behind,
    If free to take and light my lamp, and go
Into thy tomb, and shut the door and sit,
Seeing thy face on those four sides of it
    The better that they are so blank, I know!

XIX.

Why, time was what I wanted, to turn o'er
Within my mind each look, get more and more   110
    By heart each word, too much to learn at first;
And join thee all the fitter for the pause
'Neath the low door-way's lintel.   That were cause
    For lingering, though thou calledst, if I durst!

XX.

And yet thou art the nobler of us two:
What dare I dream of, that thou canst not do,
    Outstripping my ten small steps with one stride?
I 'll say then, here 's a trial and a task;
Is it to bear? — if easy, I 'll not ask:
    Tho' love fail, I can trust on in thy pride.   120

XXI.

Pride? — when those eyes forestall the life behind
The death I have to go through! — when I find,
    Now that I want thy help most, all of thee!
What did I fear?   Thy love shall hold me fast
Until the little minute's sleep is past
    And I wake saved. — And yet it will not be!

IN A YEAR.

I.

NEVER any more,
    While I live,
Need I hope to see his face
    As before.
Once his love grown chill,
    Mine may strive:
Bitterly we re-embrace,
    Single still.

II.

Was it something said,
   Something done,
Vexed him? was it touch of hand,
   Turn of head?
Strange! that very way
   Love begun:
I as little understand
   Love's decay.

III.

When I sewed or drew,
   I recall
How he looked as if I sung,
   — Sweetly too.
If I spoke a word,
   First of all
Up his cheek the colour sprung,
   Then he heard.

IV.

Sitting by my side,
   At my feet,
So he breathed but air I breathed,
   Satisfied!
I, too, at love's brim
   Touched the sweet:
I would die if death bequeathed
   Sweet to him.

V.

" Speak, I love thee best! "
   He exclaimed:
" Let thy love my own foretell! "
   I confessed:
" Clasp my heart on thine
   Now unblamed,
Since upon thy soul as well
   Hangeth mine! "

VI.

Was it wrong to own,
   Being truth?
Why should all the giving prove
   His alone?

I had wealth and ease,
  Beauty, youth :
Since my lover gave me love,
  I gave these.

VII.

That was all I meant,
  — To be just,
And the passion I had raised,
  To content.
Since he chose to change
  Gold for dust,
If I gave him what he praised
  Was it strange?

VIII.

Would he loved me yet,
  On and on,
While I found some way undreamed
  — Paid my debt!   60
Gave more life and more,
  Till all gone,
He should smile " She never seemed
  Mine before.

IX.

" What, she felt the while,
  Must I think?
Love 's so different with us men!"
  He should smile :
" Dying for my sake —
  White and pink!   70
Can't we touch these bubbles then
  But they break? "

X.

Dear, the pang is brief,
  Do thy part,
Have thy pleasure!   How perplexed
  Grows belief!
Well, this cold clay clod
  Was man's heart :
Crumble it, and what comes next?
  Is it God?   80

SONG FROM "JAMES LEE'S WIFE."

I.

OH, good gigantic smile o' the brown old earth,
      This autumn morning! How he sets his bones
To bask i' the sun, and thrusts out knees and feet
For the ripple to run over in its mirth:
      Listening the while, where on the heap of stones
The white breast of the sea-lark twitters sweet.

II.

That is the doctrine, simple, ancient, true;
      Such is life's trial, as old earth smiles and knows.
If you loved only what were worth your love,
Love were clear gain, and wholly well for you.
      Make the low nature better by your throes!   10
Give earth yourself, go up for gain above!

———◆———

A WOMAN'S LAST WORD.

I.

LET 'S contend no more, Love,
      Strive nor weep:
All be as before, Love,
      —Only sleep!

II.

What so wild as words are?
      I and thou
In debate, as birds are,
      Hawk on bough!

III.

See the creature stalking
      While we speak!
Hush and hide the talking,   10
      Cheek on cheek.

IV.

What so false as truth is,
  False to thee?
Where the serpent's tooth is,
  Shun the tree —

V.

Where the apple reddens,
  Never pry —
Lest we lose our Edens,
  Eve and I.   20

VI.

Be a god and hold me
  With a charm!
Be a man and fold me
  With thine arm!

VII.

Teach me, only teach, Love!
  As I ought
I will speak thy speech, Love,
  Think thy thought —

VIII.

Meet, if thou require it,
  Both demands,   30
Laying flesh and spirit
  In thy hands.

IX.

That shall be to-morrow,
  Not to-night:
I must bury sorrow
  Out of sight:

X.

— Must a little weep, Love,
  (Foolish me!)
And so fall asleep, Love,
  Loved by thee.   40

MEETING AT NIGHT.

I.

THE gray sea and the long black land;
   And the yellow half-moon large and low;
And the startled little waves that leap
In fiery ringlets from their sleep,
As I gain the cove with pushing prow,
And quench its speed i' the slushy sand.

II.

Then a mile of warm sea-scented beach;
Three fields to cross till a farm appears;
A tap at the pane, the quick sharp scratch
And blue spurt of a lighted match,   10
And a voice less loud, thro' its joys and fears,
Than the two hearts beating each to each!

PARTING AT MORNING.

ROUND the cape of a sudden came the sea,
   And the sun looked over the mountain's rim:
And straight was a path of gold for him,
And the need of a world of men for me.

WOMEN AND ROSES.

I.

I DREAM of a red-rose tree.
   And which of its roses three
Is the dearest rose to me?

II.

Round and round, like a dance of snow
In a dazzling drift, as its guardians, go
Floating the women faded for ages,
Sculptured in stone, on the poet's pages.
Then follow women fresh and gay,
Living and loving and loved to-day.

G

Last, in the rear, flee the multitude of maidens,
Beauties yet unborn.   And all, to one cadence,
They circle their rose on my rose tree.

III.

Dear rose, thy term is reached,
Thy leaf hangs loose and bleached:
Bees pass it unimpeached.

IV.

Stay then, stoop, since I cannot climb,
You, great shapes of the antique time,
How shall I fix you, fire you, freeze you,
Break my heart at your feet to please you?
Oh, to possess and be possessed!   20
Hearts that beat 'neath each pallid breast!
Once but of love, the poesy, the passion,
Drink but once and die! — In vain, the same fashion,
They circle their rose on my rose tree.

V.

Dear rose, thy joy's undimmed:
Thy cup is ruby-rimmed,
Thy cup's heart nectar-brimmed.

VI.

Deep, as drops from a statue's plinth
The bee sucked in by the hyacinth,
So will I bury me while burning,   30
Quench like him at a plunge my yearning,
Eyes in your eyes, lips on your lips!
Fold me fast where the cincture slips,
Prison all my soul in eternities of pleasure,
Girdle me for once!   But no — the old measure,
They circle their rose on my rose tree.

VII.

Dear rose without a thorn,
Thy bud 's the babe unborn:
First streak of a new morn.

VIII.

Wings, lend wings for the cold, the clear!   40
What is far conquers what is near.

Roses will bloom nor want beholders,
Sprung from the dust where our flesh moulders,
What shall arrive with the cycle's change?
A novel grace and a beauty strange.
I will make an Eve, be the Artist that began her,
Shaped her to his mind! — Alas! in like manner
They circle their rose on my rose tree.

MISCONCEPTIONS.

I.

THIS is a spray the Bird clung to,
   Making it blossom with pleasure,
Ere the high tree-top she sprung to,
   Fit for her nest and her treasure.
   Oh, what a hope beyond measure
Was the poor spray's, which the flying feet hung to, —
So to be singled out, built in, and sung to!

II.

This is a heart the Queen leant on,
   Thrilled in a minute erratic,
Ere the true bosom she bent on,
   Meet for love's regal dalmatic.
   Oh, what a fancy ecstatic
Was the poor heart's, ere the wanderer went on, —
Love to be saved for it, proffered to, spent on!

A PRETTY WOMAN.

I.

THAT fawn-skin-dappled hair of hers,
   And the blue eye
   Dear and dewy,
And that infantine fresh air of hers!

II.

To think men cannot take you, Sweet,
   And enfold you,
   Ay, and hold you,
And so keep you what they make you, Sweet!

III.

You like us for a glance, you know —
    For a word's sake   10
    Or a sword's sake:
All's the same, whate'er the chance, you know.

IV.

And in turn we make you ours, we say —
    You and youth too,
    Eyes and mouth too,
All the face composed of flowers, we say.

V.

All's our own, to make the most of, Sweet —
    Sing and say for,   •
    Watch and pray for,
Keep a secret or go boast of, Sweet!   20

VI.

But for loving, why, you would not, Sweet,
    Tho' we prayed you,
    Paid you, brayed you
In a mortar — for you could not, Sweet!

VII.

So, we leave the sweet face fondly there,
    Be its beauty
    Its sole duty!
Let all hope of grace beyond, lie there!

VIII.

And while the face lies quiet there,
    Who shall wonder   30
    That I ponder
A conclusion?   I will try it there.

IX.

As, — why must one, for the love foregone
    Scout mere liking?
    Thunder-striking
Earth, — the heaven, we looked above for, gone!

X.

Why, with beauty, needs there money be,
    Love with liking?
    Crush the fly-king
In his gauze, because no honey-bee?   40

XI.

May not liking be so simple-sweet,
    If love grew there
    'T would undo there
All that breaks the cheek to dimples sweet?

XII.

Is the creature too imperfect, say?
    Would you mend it
    And so end it?
Since not all addition perfects aye!

XIII.

Or is it of its kind, perhaps,
    Just perfection —   50
    Whence, rejection
Of a grace not to its mind, perhaps?

XIV.

Shall we burn up, tread that face at once
    Into tinder,
    And so hinder
Sparks from kindling all the place at once?

XV.

Or else kiss away one's soul on her?
    Your love-fancies!
    — A sick man sees
Truer, when his hot eyes roll on her!   60

XVI.

Thus the craftsman thinks to grace the rose, —
    Plucks a mould-flower
    For his gold flower,
Uses fine things that efface the rose.

XVII.

Rosy rubies make its cup more rose,
    Precious metals
    Ape the petals, —
Last, some old king locks it up, morose!

XVIII.

Then how grace a rose? I know a way!
    Leave it, rather.
    Must you gather?
Smell, kiss, wear it — at last, throw away.

70

———◦◦———

A LIGHT WOMAN.

I.

SO far as our story approaches the end,
    Which do you pity the most of us three? —
My friend, or the mistress of my friend
    With her wanton eyes, or me?

II.

My friend was already too good to lose.
    And seemed in the way of improvement yet,
When she crossed his path with her hunting-noose
    And over him drew her net.

III.

When I saw him tangled in her toils,
    A shame, said I, if she adds just him
To her nine-and-ninety other spoils,
    The hundredth for a whim!

10

IV.

And before my friend be wholly hers,
    How easy to prove to him, I said,
An eagle 's the game her pride prefers,
    Tho' she snaps at a wren instead!

V.

So, I gave her eyes my own eyes to take,
    My hand sought hers as in earnest need,

And round she turned for my noble sake,
   And gave me herself indeed!   20

VI.

The eagle am I, with my fame in the world,
   The wren is he, with his maiden face.
— You look away and your lip is curled ?
   Patience, a moment's space!

VII.

For see, my friend goes shaking and white,
   He eyes me as the basilisk:
I have turned, it appears, his day to night,
   Eclipsing his sun's disk.

VIII.

And I did it, he thinks, as a very thief:
   " Tho' I love her — that, he comprehends —   30
One should master one's passions, (love, in chief)
   And be loyal to one's friends ! "

IX.

And she, — she lies in my hand as tame
   As a pear late basking over a wall ;
Just a touch to try, and off it came ;
   'T is mine, — can I let it fall ?

X.

With no mind to eat it, that 's the worst !
   Were it thrown in the road, would the case assist ?
'T was quenching a dozen blue-flies' thirst
   When I gave its stalk a twist.   40

XI.

And I, — what I seem to my friend, you see ;
   What I soon shall seem to his love, you guess :
What I seem to myself, do you ask of me?
   No hero, I confess.

XII.

'T is an awkward thing to play with souls,
   And matter enough to save one's own :
Yet think of my friend, and the burning coals
   He played with for bits of stone !

XIII.

One likes to show the truth for the truth;
  That the woman was light is very true: **50**
But suppose she says, — Never mind that youth
  What wrong have I done to you?

XIV.

Well, any how, here the story stays,
  So far at least as I understand;
And, Robert Browning, you writer of plays,
  Here's a subject made to your hand!

———◦◦———

LOVE IN A LIFE.

I.

ROOM after room,
  I hunt the house through
We inhabit together.
Heart, fear nothing, for, heart, thou shalt find her —
Next time, herself! — not the trouble behind her
Left in the curtain, the couch's perfume!
As she brushed it, the cornice-wreath blossomed anew;
Yon looking-glass gleamed at the wave of her feather.

II.

Yet the day wears,
And door succeeds door; **10**
I try the fresh fortune —
Range the wide house from the wing to the centre.
Still the same chance! she goes out as I enter.
Spend my whole day in the quest, — who cares?
But 't is twilight, you see, — with such suites to explore,
Such closets to search, such alcoves to importune!

———◦◦———

LIFE IN A LOVE.

ESCAPE me?
  Never —
Beloved!
While I am I, and you are you,

So long as the world contains us both,
  Me the loving and you the loth,
While the one eludes, must the other pursue.
My life is a fault at last, I fear:
  It seems too much like a fate, indeed!
  Though I do my best I shall scarce succeed.   10
But what if I fail of my purpose here?
It is but to keep the nerves at strain,
  To dry one's eyes and laugh at a fall,
And baffled, get up and begin again,—
  So the chace takes up one's life, that's all.
While, look but once from your farthest bound
  At me so deep in the dust and dark,
No sooner the old hope goes to ground
  Than a new one, straight to the self-same mark,
I shape me—   20
Ever
Removed!

THE LABORATORY.

ANCIEN RÉGIME.

I.

NOW that I, tying thy glass mask tightly,
  May gaze thro' these faint smokes curling whitely,
As thou pliest thy trade in this devil's-smithy—
Which is the poison to poison her, prithee?

II.

He is with her, and they know that I know
Where they are, what they do: they believe my tears flow
While they laugh, laugh at me, at me fled to the drear
Empty church, to pray God in, for them!—I am here.

III.

Grind away, moisten and mash up thy paste,
Pound at thy powder,—I am not in haste!   10
Better sit thus and observe thy strange things,
Than go where men wait me, and dance at the King's.

IV.

That in the mortar—you call it a gum?
Ah, the brave tree whence such gold oozings come!

And yonder soft phial, the exquisite blue,
Sure to taste sweetly, — is that poison too?

v.

Had I but all of them, thee and thy treasures,
What a wild crowd of invisible pleasures!
To carry pure death in an earring, a casket,
A signet, a fan-mount, a filigree basket!   20

vi.

Soon, at the King's, a mere lozenge to give
And Pauline should have just thirty minutes to live!
But to light a pastile, and Elise, with her head
And her breast and her arms and her hands, should drop dead!

vii.

Quick — is it finished? The colour 's too grim!
Why not soft like the phial's, enticing and dim?
Let it brighten her drink, let her turn it and stir,
And try it and taste, ere she fix and prefer!

viii.

What a drop! She 's not little, no minion like me!
That 's why she ensnared him: this never will free   30
The soul from those masculine eyes, — say, "No!"
To that pulse's magnificent come-and-go.

ix.

For only last night, as they whispered, I brought
My own eyes to bear on her so, that I thought
Could I keep them one half minute fixed, she would fall
Shrivelled; she fell not; yet this does it all!

x.

Not that I bid you spare her the pain;
Let death be felt and the proof remain:
Brand, burn up, bite into its grace —
He is sure to remember her dying face!   40

xi.

Is it done? Take my mask off! Nay, be not morose;
It kills her, and this prevents seeing it close:
The delicate droplet, my whole fortune's fee!
If it hurts her, beside, can it ever hurt me?

XII.

Now, take all my jewels, gorge gold to your fill,
You may kiss me, old man, on my mouth if you will!
But brush this dust off me, lest horror it brings
Ere I know it — next moment I dance at the King's!

GOLD HAIR:

A STORY OF PORNIC.

I.

OH, the beautiful girl, too white,
  Who lived at Pornic down by the sea,
Just where the sea and the Loire unite!
  And a boasted name in Brittany
She bore, which I will not write.

II.

Too white, for the flower of life is red;
  Her flesh was the soft seraphic screen
Of a soul that is meant (her parents said)
  To just see earth, and hardly be seen,
And blossom in heaven instead.   10

III.

Yet earth saw one thing, one how fair!
  One grace that grew to its full on earth:
Smiles might be sparse on her cheek so spare
  And her waist want half a girdle's girth,
But she had her great gold hair.

IV.

Hair, such a wonder of flix and floss,
  Freshness and fragrance — floods of it, too!
Gold, did I say? Nay, gold's mere dross:
  Here, Life smiled, "Think what I meant to do!"
And Love sighed, "Fancy my loss!"   20

V.

So, when she died, it was scarce more strange
  Than that, when delicate evening dies,
And you follow its spent sun's pallid range,

There 's a shoot of colour startles the skies
  With sudden, violent change, —

VI.

That, while the breath was nearly to seek,
  As they put the little cross to her lips,
She changed ; a spot came out on her cheek,
  A spark from her eye in mid-eclipse,
And she broke forth, " I must speak ! "   30

VII.

" Not my hair ! " made the girl her moan —
  " All the rest is gone or to go ;
But the last, last grace, my all, my own,
  Let it stay in the grave, that the ghosts may know!
Leave my poor gold hair alone! "

VIII.

The passion thus vented, dead lay she :
  Her parents sobbed their worst on that,
All friends joined in, nor observed degree :
  For indeed the hair was to wonder at,
As it spread — not flowing free,   40

IX.

But curled around her brow, like a crown,
  And coiled beside her cheeks, like a cap,
And calmed about her neck — ay, down
  To her breast, pressed flat, without a gap
I' the gold, it reached her gown.

X.

All kissed that face, like a silver wedge
  Mid the yellow wealth, nor disturbed its hair :
E'en the priest allowed death's privilege,
  As he planted the crucifix with care
On her breast, 'twixt edge and edge.   50

XI.

And thus was she buried, inviolate
  Of body and soul, in the very space
By the altar ; keeping saintly state
  In Pornic church, for her pride of race,
Pure life and piteous fate.

XII.

And in after-time would your fresh tear fall,
    Though your mouth might twitch with a dubious smile,
As they told you of gold, both robe and pall,
    How she prayed them leave it alone awhile,
So it never was touched at all.   60

XIII.

Years flew; this legend grew at last
    The life of the lady; all she had done,
All been, in the memories fading fast
    Of lover and friend, was summed in one
Sentence survivors passed: —

XIV.

To wit, she was meant for heaven, not earth;
    Had turned an angel before the time:
Yet, since she was mortal, in such dearth
    Of frailty, all you could count a crime
Was — she knew her gold hair's worth.   70

XV.

At little pleasant Pornic church,
    It chanced, the pavement wanted repair,
Was taken to pieces: left in the lurch,
    A certain sacred space lay bare,
And the boys began research.

XVI.

'T was the space where our sires would lay a saint,
    A benefactor, — a bishop, suppose,
A baron with armour-adornments quaint,
    Dame with chased ring and jewelled rose,
Things sanctity saves from taint;   80

XVII.

So we come to find them in after-days
    When the corpse is presumed to have done with gauds
Of use to the living, in many ways:
    For the boys get pelf, and the town applauds,
And the church deserves the praise.

GOLD HAIR.

XVIII.

They grubbed with a will: and at length — *O cor
    Humanum, pectora cæca*, and the rest! —
They found — no gaud they were prying for,
    No ring, no rose, but — who would have guessed? —
A double Louis-d'or!   90

XIX.

Here was a case for the priest: he heard,
    Marked, inwardly digested, laid
Finger on nose, smiled, " There 's a bird
    Chirps in my ear: " then, " Bring a spade,
Dig deeper! " — he gave the word.

XX.

And lo, when they came to the coffin-lid,
    Or rotten planks which composed it once,
Why, there lay the girl's skull wedged amid
    A mint of money, it served for the nonce
To hold in its hair-heaps hid!   100

XXI.

Hid there?   Why?   Could the girl be wont
    (She the stainless soul) to treasure up
Money, earth's trash and heaven's affront?
    Had a spider found out the communion-cup,
Was a toad in the christening-font?

XXII.

Truth is truth: too true it was.
    Gold!   She hoarded and hugged it first,
Longed for it, leaned o'er it, loved it — alas —
    Till the humour grew to a head and burst,
And she cried, at the final pass, —   110

XXIII.

" Talk not of God, my heart is stone!
    Nor lover nor friend — be gold for both!
Gold I lack; and, my all, my own,
    It shall hide in my hair.   I scarce die loth
If they let my hair alone ! "

XXIV.

Louis-d'or, some six times five,
    And duly double, every piece.
Now, do you see? With the priest to shrive,
    With parents preventing her soul's release
By kisses that kept alive, —   120

XXV.

With heaven's gold gates about to ope,
    With friends' praise, gold-like, lingering still,
An instinct had bidden the girl's hand grope
    For gold, the true sort — " Gold in heaven, if you will ;
But I keep earth's too, I hope."

XXVI.

Enough! The priest took the grave's grim yield :
    The parents, they eyed that price of sin
As if *thirty pieces* lay revealed
    On the place *to bury strangers in*,
The hideous Potter's Field.   130

XXVII.

But the priest bethought him : " ' Milk that 's spilt '
    — You know the adage! Watch and pray !
Saints tumble to earth with so slight a tilt !
    It would build a new altar ; that, we may ! "
And the altar therewith was built.

XXVIII.

Why I deliver this horrible verse?
    As the text of a sermon, which now I preach :
Evil or good may be better or worse
    In the human heart, but the mixture of each
Is a marvel and a curse.   140

XXIX.

The candid incline to surmise of late
    That the Christian faith proves false, I find ;
For our Essays-and-Reviews' debate
    Begins to tell on the public mind,
And Colenso's words have weight :

XXX.

I still, to suppose it true, for my part,
  See reasons and reasons; this, to begin:
'T is the faith that launched point-blank her dart
  At the head of a lie — taught Original Sin,
The Corruption of Man's Heart.   150

———◦◦———

THE STATUE AND THE BUST.

THERE 'S a palace in Florence, the world knows well,
    And a statue watches it from the square,
And this story of both do our townsmen tell.

Ages ago, a lady there,
At the farthest window facing the East
Asked, "Who rides by with the royal air?"

The bridesmaids' prattle around her ceased;
She leaned forth, one on either hand;
They saw how the blush of the bride increased —

They felt by its beats her heart expand —   10
As one at each ear and both in a breath
Whispered, "The Great Duke Ferdinand."

That self-same instant, underneath,
The Duke rode past in his idle way,
Empty and fine like a swordless sheath.

Gay he rode, with a friend as gay,
Till he threw his head back — "Who is she?"
— "A bride the Riccardi brings home to-day."

Hair in heaps lay heavily
Over a pale brow spirit-pure —   20
Carved like the heart of the coal-black tree,

Crisped like a war-steed's encolure —
And vainly sought to dissemble her eyes
Of the blackest black our eyes endure.

And lo, a blade for a knight's emprise
Filled the fine empty sheath of a man, —
The Duke grew straightway brave and wise.

He looked at her, as a lover can;
She looked at him, as one who awakes:
The Past was a sleep, and her life began. 30

Now, love so ordered for both their sakes,
A feast was held, that self-same night,
In the pile which the mighty shadow makes.

(For Via Larga is three parts light,
But the palace overshadows one,
Because of a crime which may God requite!

To Florence and God the wrong was done,
Thro' the first republic's murder there
By Cosimo and his cursed son.)

The Duke (with the statue's face in the square) 40
Turned, in the midst of his multitude,
At the bright approach of the bridal pair.

Face to face the lovers stood
A single minute and no more,
While the bridegroom bent as a man subdued —

Bowed till his bonnet brushed the floor —
For the Duke on the lady a kiss conferred,
As the courtly custom was of yore.

In a minute can lovers exchange a word?
If a word did pass, which I do not think, 50
Only one out of the thousand heard.

That was the bridegroom.   At day's brink
He and his bride were alone at last
In a bed-chamber by a taper's blink.

Calmly he said that her lot was cast,
That the door she had passed was shut on her
Till the final catafalk repassed.

The world meanwhile, its noise and stir,
Thro' a certain window facing the East,
She could watch like a convent's chronicler. 60

Since passing the door might lead to a feast,
And a feast might lead to so much beside,
He, of many evils, chose the least.

H

"Freely I choose too," said the bride:
"Your window and its world suffice,"
Replied the tongue, while the heart replied —

"If I spend the night with that devil twice,
May his window serve as my loop of hell
Whence a damned soul looks on paradise!

"I fly to the Duke who loves me well,   70
Sit by his side and laugh at sorrow
Ere I count another ave-bell.

"'T is only the coat of a page to borrow,
And tie my hair in a horse-boy's trim,
And I save my soul — but not to-morrow "—

(She checked herself and her eye grew dim)
"My father tarries to bless my state:
I must keep it one day more for him.

"Is one day more so long to wait?
Moreover the Duke rides past, I know;   80
We shall see each other, sure as fate."

She turned on her side and slept.   Just so!
So we resolve on a thing, and sleep:
So did the lady, ages ago.

That night the Duke said, "Dear or cheap
As the cost of this cup of bliss may prove
To body or soul, I will drain it deep."

And on the morrow, bold with love,
He beckoned the bridegroom (close on call,
As his duty bade, by the Duke's alcove)   90

And smiled "'T was a very funeral,
Your lady will think, this feast of ours, —
A shame to efface, whate'er befall!

"What if we break from the Arno bowers,
And try if Petraja, cool and green,
Cure last night's fault with this morning's flowers?"

The bridegroom, not a thought to be seen
On his steady brow and quiet mouth,
Said, "Too much favour for me so mean!

"But, alas! my lady leaves the South;   100
Each wind that comes from the Apennine
Is a menace to her tender youth:

"Nor a way exists, the wise opine,
If she quits her palace twice this year,
To avert the flower of life's decline."

Quoth the Duke, "A sage and a kindly fear.
Moreover Petraja is cold this spring:
Be our feast to-night as usual here!"

And then to himself — "Which night shall bring
Thy bride to her lover's embraces, fool —   110
Or I am the fool, and thou art the king!

"Yet my passion must wait a night, nor cool
For to-night the Envoy arrives from France
Whose heart I unlock with thyself, my tool.

"I need thee still and might miss perchance.
To-day is not wholly lost, beside,
With its hope of my lady's countenance:

"For I ride — what should I do but ride?
And, passing her palace, if I list,
May glance at its window — well betide!"   120

So said, so done: nor the lady missed
One ray that broke from the ardent brow,
Nor a curl of the lips where the spirit kissed.

Be sure that each renewed the vow,
No morrow's sun should arise and set
And leave them then as it left them now.

But next day passed, and next day yet,
With still fresh cause to wait one day more
Ere each leaped over the parapet.

And still, as love's brief morning wore,   130
With a gentle start, half smile, half sigh,
They found love not as it seemed before.

They thought it would work infallibly,
But not in despite of heaven and earth:
The rose would blow when the storm passed by.

Meantime they could profit, in winter's dearth,
By store of fruits that supplant the rose:
The world and its ways have a certain worth:

And to press a point while these oppose
Were simple policy; better wait: 140
We lose no friends and we gain no foes.

Meantime, worse fates than a lover's fate,
Who daily may ride and pass and look
Where his lady watches behind the grate!

And she — she watched the square like a book
Holding one picture and only one,
Which daily to find she undertook:

When the picture was reached the book was done,
And she turned from the picture at night to scheme
Of tearing it out for herself next sun.   150

So weeks grew months, years; gleam by gleam
The glory dropped from their youth and love,
And both perceived they had dreamed a dream;

Which hovered as dreams do, still above:
But who can take a dream for a truth?
Oh, hide our eyes from the next remove!

One day as the lady saw her youth
Depart, and the silver thread that streaked
Her hair, and, worn by the serpent's tooth,

The brow so puckered, the chin so peaked, —   160
And wondered who the woman was,
Hollow-eyed and haggard-cheeked,

Fronting her silent in the glass —
" Summon here," she suddenly said,
" Before the rest of my old self pass,

" Him, the Carver, a hand to aid,
Who fashions the clay no love will change,
And fixes a beauty never to fade.

" Let Robbia's craft so apt and strange
Arrest the remains of young and fair,   170
And rivet them while the seasons range.

"Make me a face on the window there,
Waiting as ever, mute the while,
My love to pass below in the square!

"And let me think that it may beguile
Dreary days which the dead must spend
Down in their darkness under the aisle,

"To say, 'What matters it at the end?
I did no more while my heart was warm
Than does that image, my pale-faced friend.'   180

"Where is the use of the lip's red charm,
The heaven of hair, the pride of the brow,
And the blood that blues the inside arm —

"Unless we turn, as the soul knows how,
The earthly gift to an end divine?
A lady of clay is as good, I trow."

But long ere Robbia's cornice, fine,
With flowers and fruits which leaves enlace,
Was set where now is the empty shrine —

(And, leaning out of a bright blue space,   190
As a ghost might lean from a chink of sky,
The passionate pale lady's face —

Eyeing ever, with earnest eye
And quick-turned neck at its breathless stretch,
Some one who ever is passing by —)

The Duke had sighed like the simplest wretch
In Florence, "Youth — my dream escapes!
Will its record stay?" and he bade them fetch

Some subtle moulder of brazen shapes —
"Can the soul, the will, die out of a man   200
Ere his body find the grave that gapes?

"John of Douay shall effect my plan,
Set me on horseback here aloft,
Alive, as the crafty sculptor can,

"In the very square I have crossed so oft:
That men may admire, when future suns
Shall touch the eyes to a purpose soft,

"While the mouth and the brow stay brave in bronze —
Admire and say, ' When he was alive
How he would take his pleasure once ! '   210

" And it shall go hard but I contrive
To listen the while, and laugh in my tomb
At idleness which aspires to strive."

So ! While these wait the trump of doom,
How do their spirits pass, I wonder,
Nights and days in the narrow room ?

Still, I suppose, they sit and ponder
What a gift life was, ages ago,
Six steps out of the chapel yonder.

Only they see not God, I know,   220
Nor all that chivalry of his,
The soldier-saints who, row on row,

Burn upward each to his point of bliss —
Since, the end of life being manifest,
He had burned his way thro' the world to this.

I hear you reproach, " But delay was best,
For their end was a crime." — Oh, a crime will do
As well, I reply, to serve for a test,

As a virtue golden through and through,
Sufficient to vindicate itself   230
And prove its worth at a moment's view !

Must a game be played for the sake of pelf ?
Where a button goes, 't were an epigram
To offer the stamp of the very Guelph.

The true has no value beyond the sham :
As well the counter as coin, I submit,
When your table 's a hat, and your prize, a dram.

Stake your counter as boldly every whit,
Venture as warily, use the same skill,
Do your best, whether winning or losing it,   240

If you choose to play! — is my principle.
Let a man contend to the uttermost
For his life's set prize, be it what it will.

The counter our lovers staked was lost
As surely as if it were lawful coin:
And the sin I impute to each frustrate ghost

Is, the unlit lamp and the ungirt loin,
Tho' the end in sight was a vice, I say.
You of the virtue (we issue join)
How strive you ? *De te, fabula!* 250

—•◦•—

LOVE AMONG THE RUINS.

I.

WHERE the quiet-coloured end of evening smiles,
        Miles and miles
On the solitary pastures where our sheep
        Half-asleep
Tinkle homeward thro' the twilight, stray or stop
        As they crop —
Was the site once of a city great and gay,
        (So they say)
Of our country's very capital, its prince
        Ages since
Held his court in, gathered councils, wielding far
        Peace or war.   10

II.

Now, — the country does not even boast a tree,
        As you see,
To distinguish slopes of verdure, certain rills
        From the hills
Intersect and give a name to, (else they run
        Into one)
Where the domed and daring palace shot its spires
        Up like fires
O'er the hundred-gated circuit of a wall
        Bounding all,   20
Made of marble, men might march on nor be pressed,
        Twelve abreast.

III.

And such plenty and perfection, see, of grass
    Never was !
Such a carpet as, this summer-time, o'erspreads
    And embeds
Every vestige of the city, guessed alone,
    Stock or stone —   30
Where a multitude of men breathed joy and woe
    Long ago ;
Lust of glory pricked their hearts up, dread of shame
    Struck them tame ;
And that glory and that shame alike, the gold
    Bought and sold.

IV.

Now, — the single little turret that remains
    On the plains,
By the caper overrooted, by the gourd
    Overscored,   40
While the patching houseleek's head of blossom winks
    Thro' the chinks —
Marks the basement whence a tower in ancient time
    Sprang sublime,
And a burning ring, all round, the chariots traced
    As they raced,
And the monarch and his minions and his dames
    Viewed the games.

V.

And I know — while thus the quiet-coloured eve
    Smiles to leave   50
To their folding, all our many tinkling fleece
    In such peace,
And the slopes and rills in undistinguished gray
    Melt away —
That a girl with eager eyes and yellow hair
    Waits me there
In the turret whence the charioteers caught soul
    For the goal,
When the king looked, where she looks now, breathless, dumb
    Till I come.   60

VI.

But he looked upon the city, every side,
    Far and wide,

All the mountains topped with temples, all the glades'
    Colonnades,
All the causeys, bridges, aqueducts, — and then,
    All the men!
When I do come, she will speak not, she will stand,
    Either hand
On my shoulder, give her eyes the first embrace
    Of my face,   70
Ere we rush, ere we extinguish sight and speech
    Each on each.

VII.

In one year they sent a million fighters forth
    South and North,
And they built their gods a brazen pillar high
    As the sky,
Yet reserved a thousand chariots in full force —
    Gold, of course.
Oh heart! oh blood that freezes, blood that burns!
    Earth's returns   80
For whole centuries of folly, noise and sin!
    Shut them in,
With their triumphs and their glories and the rest!
    Love is best.

TIME'S REVENGES.

I'VE a Friend, over the sea;
  I like him, but he loves me.
It all grew out of the books I write;
They find such favour in his sight
That he slaughters you with savage looks
Because you don't admire my books.
He does himself though, — and if some vein
Were to snap to-night in this heavy brain,
To-morrow month, if I lived to try,
Round should I just turn quietly,   10
Or out of the bedclothes stretch my hand
Till I found him, come from his foreign land
To be my nurse in this poor place,
And make my broth and wash my face
And light my fire and, all the while,
Bear with his old good-humoured smile
That I told him " Better have kept away
Than come and kill me, night and day,
With, worse than fever throbs and shoots,

The creaking of his clumsy boots."   20
I am as sure that this he would do,
As that Saint Paul's is striking two.
And I think I rather . . . woe is me!
— Yes, rather would see him than not see
If lifting a hand could seat him there
Before me in the empty chair
To-night, when my head aches indeed,
And I can neither think nor read
Nor make these purple fingers hold
The pen; this garret's freezing cold!   30

And I 've a Lady — there he wakes,
The laughing fiend and prince of snakes
Within m-, at her name, to pray
Fate send some creature in the way
Of my love for her, to be down-torn,
Upthrust and outward-borne,
So I might prove myself that sea
Of passion whi-h I needs must be!
Call my thoughts false and my fancies quaint
And my style infirm and its figures faint,   40
All the critics say, and more blame yet,
And not one angry word you get.
But, please you, wonder I would put
My cheek beneath that lady's foot
Rather than trample under mine
The laurels of the Florentine,
And you shall see how the devil spends
A fire God gave for other ends!
I tell you, I stride up and down
This garret, crowned with love's best crown,   50
And feasted with love's perfect feast,
To think I kill for her, at least,
Body and soul and peace and fame,
Alike youth's end and manhood's aim,
— So is my spirit, as flesh with sin,
Filled full, eaten out and in
With the face of her, the eyes of her,
The lips, the little chin, the stir
Of shadow round her mouth; and she
— I 'll tell you, — calmly would decree   60
That I should roast at a slow fire,
If that would compass her desire
And make her one whom they invite
To the famous ball to-morrow night.

There may be heaven; there must be hell;
Meantime, there is our earth here — well!

WARING.

I.

I.

WHAT'S become of Waring
   Since he gave us all the slip,
Chose land-travel or seafaring,
Boots and chest or staff and scrip,
Rather than pace up and down
Any longer London town?

II.

Who'd have guessed it from his lip
Or his brow's accustomed bearing,
On the night he thus took ship
Or started landward? — little caring   10
For us, it seems, who supped together
(Friends of his too, I remember)
And walked home thro' the merry weather,
The snowiest in all December.
I left his arm that night myself
For what's-his-name's, the new prose-poet
Who wrote the book there on the shelf —
How, forsooth, was I to know it
If Waring meant to glide away
Like a ghost at break of day?   20
Never looked he half so gay!

III.

He was prouder than the devil:
How he must have cursed our revel!
Ay and many other meetings,
Indoor visits, outdoor greetings,
As up and down he paced this London,
With no work done, but great works undone,
Where scarce twenty knew his name.
Why not, then, have earlier spoken,
Written, bustled? Who's to blame   30
If your silence kept unbroken?
" True, but there were sundry jottings,
Stray-leaves, fragments, blurrs and blottings,
Certain first steps were achieved
Already which " — (is that your meaning?)
" Had well borne out whoe'er believed

In more to come!" But who goes gleaning
Hedge-side chance-blades, while full-sheaved
Stand cornfields by him? Pride, o'erweening
Pride alone, puts forth such claims   40
O'er the day's distinguished names.

IV.

Meantime, how much I loved him,
I find out now I 've lost him.
I who cared not if I moved him,
Who could so carelessly accost him,
Henceforth never shall get free
Of his ghostly company,
His eyes that just a little wink
As deep I go into the merit
Of this and that distinguished spirit —   50
His cheeks' raised colour, soon to sink,
As long I dwell on some stupendous
And tremendous (Heaven defend us!)
Monstr'-inform'-ingens-horrend-ous
Demoniaco-seraphic
Penman's latest piece of graphic.
Nay, my very wrist grows warm
With his dragging weight of arm.
E'en so, swimmingly appears,
Thro' one's after-supper musings,   60
Some lost lady of old years
With her beauteous vain endeavour
And goodness unrepaid as ever;
The face, accustomed to refusings,
We, puppies that we were . . . Oh never
Surely, nice of conscience, scrupled
Being aught like false, forsooth, to?
Telling aught but honest truth to?
What a sin, had we centupled
Its possessor's grace and sweetness!   70
No! she heard in its completeness
Truth, for truth 's a weighty matter
And truth, at issue, we can't flatter!
Well, 't is done with; she 's exempt
From damning us thro' such a sally;
And so she glides, as down a valley,
Taking up with her contempt,
Past our reach; and in, the flowers
Shut her unregarded hours.

V.

Oh, could I have him back once more,   80
This Waring, but one half-day more!

Back, with the quiet face of yore,
So hungry for acknowledgment
Like mine!   I 'd fool him to his bent.
Feed, should not he, to heart's content?
I 'd say, " To only have conceived,
Planned your great works, apart from progress,
Surpasses little works achieved! "
I 'd lie so, I should be believed.
I 'd make such havoc of the claims   90
Of the day's distinguished names
To feast him with, as feasts an ogress
Her feverish sharp-toothed gold-crowned child !
Or as one feasts a creature rarely
Captured here, unreconciled
To capture ; and completely gives
Its pettish humours license, barely
Requiring that it lives.

VI.

Ichabod, Ichabod,
The glory is departed!   100
Travels Waring East away?
Who, of knowledge, by hearsay,
Reports a man upstarted
Somewhere as a god,
Hordes grown European-hearted,
Millions of the wild made tame
On a sudden at his fame?
In Vishnu-land what Avatar?
Or who in Moscow, toward the Tsar,
With the demurest of footfalls   110
Over the Kremlin's pavement bright
With serpentine and syenite,
Steps, with five other Generals
That simultaneously take snuff,
For each to have pretext enough
And kerchiefwise unfold his sash
Which, softness' self, is yet the stuff
To hold fast where a steel chain snaps,
And leave the grand white neck no gash?
Waring in Moscow, to those rough   120
Cold northern natures borne perhaps,
Like the lambwhite maiden dear
From the circle of mute kings
Unable to repress the tear,
Each as his sceptre down he flings,
To Dian's fane at Taurica,
Where now a captive priestess, she alway

Mingles her tender grave Hellenic speech
With theirs, tuned to the hailstone-beaten beach
As pours some pigeon, from the myrrhy lands　　　130
Rapt by the whirlblast to fierce Scythian strands
Where breed the swallows, her melodious cry
Amid their barbarous twitter!
In Russia?　Never!　Spain were fitter!
Ay, most likely 't is in Spain
That we and Waring meet again
Now, while he turns down that cool narrow lane
Into the blackness, out of grave Madrid
All fire and shine, abrupt as when there 's slid
Its stiff gold blazing pall　　　　　　　140
From some black coffin-lid.
Or, best of all,
I love to think
The leaving us was just a feint;
Back here to London did he slink,
And now works on without a wink
Of sleep, and we are on the brink
Of something great in fresco-paint:
Some garret's ceiling, walls and floor,
Up and down and o'er and o'er　　　　　150
He splashes, as none splashed before
Since great Caldara Polidore.
Or Music means this land of ours
Some favour yet, to pity won
By Purcell from his Rosy Bowers,—
"Give me my so-long promised son,
Let Waring end what I begun!"
Then down he creeps and out he steals,
Only when the night conceals
His face;　in Kent 't is cherry-time,　　　160
Or hops are picking: or at prime
Of March he wanders as, too happy,
Years ago when he was young,
Some mild eve when woods grew sappy
And the early moths had sprung
To life from many a trembling sheath
Woven the warm boughs beneath;
While small birds said to themselves
What should soon be actual song,
And young gnats, by tens and twelves　　　170
Made as if they were the throng
That crowd around and carry aloft
The sound they have nursed, so sweet and pure
Out of a myriad noises soft,
Into a tone that can endure

Amid the noise of a July noon
When all God's creatures crave their boon,
All at once, and all in tune,
And get it, happy as Waring then,
Having first within his ken   180
What a man might do with men:
And far too glad, in the even-glow,
To mix with the world he meant to take
Into his hand, he told you, so —
And out of it his world to make,
To contract and to expand
As he shut or oped his hand.
Oh Waring, what 's to really be?
A clear stage and a crowd to see!
Some Garrick, say, out shall not he   190
The heart of Hamlet's mystery pluck?
Or, where most unclean beasts are rife,
Some Junius — am I right? — shall tuck
His sleeve, and forth with flaying-knife!
Some Chatterton shall have the luck
Of calling Rowley into life!
Someone shall somehow run a muck
With this old world, for want of strife
Sound asleep.   Contrive, contrive
To rouse us, Waring!   Who 's alive?   200
Our men scarce seem in earnest now.
Distinguished names! but 't is, somehow,
As if they played at being names
Still more distinguished, like the games
Of children.   Turn our sport to earnest
With a visage of the sternest!
Bring the real times back, confessed
Still better than our very best!

II.

I.

"WHEN I last saw Waring . . ."
(How all turned to him who spoke!   210
You saw Waring ?   Truth or joke?
In land-travel or seafaring ?)

II.

" We were sailing by Triest
Where a day or two we harboured:
A sunset was in the West,
When, looking over the vessel's side,

One of our company espied
A sudden speck to larboard.
And as a sea-duck flies and swims
At once, so came the light craft up,   220
With its sole lateen sail that trims
And turns (the water round its rims
Dancing, as round a sinking cup)
And by us like a fish it curled,
And drew itself up close beside,
Its great sail on the instant furled,
And o'er its thwarts a shrill voice cried,
(A neck as bronzed as a Lascar's)
'Buy wine of us, you English Brig?
Or fruit, tobacco and cigars?   230
A pilot for you to Triest?
Without one, look you ne'er so big,
They 'll never let you up the bay!
We natives should know best.'
I turned, and ' Just those fellows' way,'
Our captain said, ' the 'long-shore thieves
Are laughing at us in their sleeves.'

III.

" In truth, the boy leaned laughing back;
And one, half-hidden by his side
Under the furled sail, soon I spied,   240
With great grass hat and kerchief black,
Who looked up with his kingly throat,
Said somewhat, while the other shook
His hair back from his eyes to look
Their longest at us; then the boat,
I know not how, turned sharply round,
Laying her whole side on the sea
As a leaping fish does; from the lee
Into the weather, cut somehow
Her sparkling path beneath our bow,   250
And so went off, as with a bound,
Into the rosy and golden half
O' the sky, to overtake the sun
And reach the shore, like the sea-calf
Its singing cave; yet I caught one
Glance ere away the boat quite passed,
And neither time nor toil could mar
Those features: so I saw the last
Of Waring!" — You?   Oh, never star
Was lost here but it rose afar!   260
Look East where whole new thousands are!
In Vishnu-land what Avatar?

HOME THOUGHTS FROM ABROAD.

I.

OH, to be in England now that April's there,
      And whoever wakes in England sees, some morning, unaware,
That the lowest boughs and the brushwood sheaf
Round the elm-tree bole are in tiny leaf,
While the chaffinch sings on the orchard bough
In England — now!
And after April, when May follows
And the white-throat builds, and all the swallows!
Hark, where my blossomed pear-tree in the hedge
Leans to the field and scatters on the clover   10
Blossoms and dewdrops — at the bent spray's edge —
That 's the wise thrush : he sings each song twice over
Lest you should think he never could recapture
The first fine careless rapture!
And, tho' the fields look rough with hoary dew,
All will be gay when noontide wakes anew
The buttercups, the little children's dower
— Far brighter than this gaudy melon-flower!

THE ITALIAN IN ENGLAND.

THAT second time they hunted me
      From hill to plain, from shore to sea,
And Austria, hounding far and wide
Her blood-hounds thro' the country-side,
Breathed hot an instant on my trace, —
I made, six days, a hiding-place
Of that dry green old aqueduct
Where I and Charles, when boys, have plucked
The fire-flies from the roof above,
Bright creeping thro' the moss they love :   10
— How long it seems since Charles was lost!
Six days the soldiers crossed and crossed
The country in my very sight ;
And when that peril ceased at night,
The sky broke out in red dismay
With signal-fires.   Well, there I lay
Close covered o'er in my recess,
Up to the neck in ferns and cress,
Thinking on Metternich our friend,
And Charles's miserable end,   20

I

And much beside, two days; the third,
Hunger o'ercame me when I heard
The peasants from the village go
To work among the maize: you know,
With us in Lombardy, they bring
Provisions packed on mules, a string,
With little bells that cheer their task,
And casks, and boughs on every cask
To keep the sun's heat from the wine;
These I let pass in jingling line;   30
And, close on them, dear noisy crew,
The peasants from the village, too;
For at the very rear would troop
Their wives and sisters in a group
To help, I knew.   When these had passed,
I threw my glove to strike the last,
Taking the chance: she did not start,
Much less cry out, but stooped apart,
One instant rapidly glanced round,
And saw me beckon from the ground.   40
A wild bush grows and hides my crypt;
She picked my glove up while she stripped
A branch off, then rejoined the rest
With that; my glove lay in her breast:
Then I drew breath; they disappeared:
It was for Italy I feared.

An hour, and she returned alone
Exactly where my glove was thrown.
Meanwhile came many thoughts: on me
Rested the hopes of Italy.   50
I had devised a certain tale
Which, when 't was told her, could not fail
Persuade a peasant of its truth;
I meant to call a freak of youth
This hiding, and give hopes of pay,
And no temptation to betray.
But when I saw that woman's face,
Its calm simplicity of grace,
Our Italy's own attitude
In which she walked thus far, and stood,   60
Planting each naked foot so firm,
To crush the snake and spare the worm —
At first sight of her eyes, I said,
" I am that man upon whose head
They fix the price, because I hate
The Austrians over us; the State
Will give you gold — oh, gold so much! —

If you betray me to their clutch,
And be your death, for aught I know,
If once they find you saved their foe.   70
Now, you must bring me food and drink,
And also paper, pen and ink,
And carry safe what I shall write
To Padua, which you 'll reach at night
Before the duomo shuts ; go in,
And wait till Tenebræ begin ;
Walk to the third confessional,
Between the pillar and the wall,
And kneeling whisper, *Whence comes peace ?*
Say it a second time, then cease ;   80
And if the voice inside returns,
*From Christ and Freedom; what concerns
The cause of Peace ?* — for answer, slip
My letter where you placed your lip ;
Then come back happy we have done
Our mother service — I, the son,
As you the daughter of our land! "

Three mornings more, she took her stand
In the same place, with the same eyes :
I was no surer of sun-rise   90
Than of her coming. We conferred
Of her own prospects, and I heard
She had a lover — stout and tall,
She said — then let her eyelids fall,
" He could do much " — as if some doubt
Entered her heart, — then, passing out,
" She could not speak for others, who
Had other thoughts ; herself she knew : "
And so she brought me drink and food.
After four days, the scouts pursued   100
Another path ; at last arrived
The help my Paduan friends contrived
To furnish me : she brought the news.
For the first time I could not choose
But kiss her hand, and lay my own
Upon her head — " This faith was shown
To Italy, our mother ; she
Uses my hand and blesses thee."
She followed down to the sea-shore ;
I left and never saw her more.   110

How very long since I have thought
Concerning — much less wished for — aught
Beside the good of Italy.

For which I live and mean to die!
I never was in love; and since
Charles proved false, what shall now convince
My inmost heart I have a friend?
However, if I pleased to spend
Real wishes on myself — say, three —
I know at least what one should be.   120
I would grasp Metternich until
I felt his red wet throat distil
In blood thro' these two hands.   And next,
— Nor much for that am I perplexed —
Charles, perjured traitor, for his part,
Should die slow of a broken heart
Under his new employers.   Last
— Ah, there, what should I wish?   For fast
Do I grow old and out of strength.
If I resolved to seek at length   130
My father's house again, how scared
They all would look, and unprepared!
My brothers live in Austria's pay
— Disowned me long ago, men say;
And all my early mates who used
To praise me so — perhaps induced
More than one early step of mine —
Are turning wise: while some opine
"Freedom grows license," some suspect
"Haste breeds delay," and recollect   140
They always said, such premature
Beginnings never could endure!
So, with a sullen "All's for best,"
The land seems settling to its rest.
I think then, I should wish to stand
This evening in that dear, lost land,
Over the sea the thousand miles,
And know if yet that woman smiles
With the calm smile; some little farm
She lives in there, no doubt: what harm   150
If I sat on the door-side bench,
And while her spindle made a trench
Fantastically in the dust,
Inquired of all her fortunes — just
Her children's ages and their names,
And what may be the husband's aims
For each of them.   I'd talk this out,
And sit there, for an hour about,
Then kiss her hand once more, and lay
Mine on her head, and go my way.   160

    So much for idle wishing — how
It steals the time!   To business now.

THE ENGLISHMAN IN ITALY.

PIANO DI SORRENTO.

FORTÙ, Fortù, my beloved one, sit here by my side,
  On my knees put up both little feet ! I was sure, if I tried,
I could make you laugh spite of Scirocco. Now, open your eyes,
Let me keep you amused, till he vanish in black from the skies,
With telling my memories over, as you tell your beads ;
All the Plain saw me gather, I garland — the flowers or the weeds.
Time for rain ! for your long hot dry Autumn had networked with
  brown
The white skin of each grape on the bunches, marked like a quail's
  crown,
Those creatures you make such account of, whose heads, — speckled
  white
Over brown like a great spider's back, as I told you last night, — 10
Your mother bites off for her supper. Red-ripe as could be,
Pomegranates were chapping and splitting in halves on the tree.
And betwixt the loose walls of great flintstone, or in the thick dust
On the path, or straight out of the rock-side, wherever could thrust
Some burnt sprig of bold hardy rock-flower its yellow face up,
For the prize were great butterflies fighting, some five for one cup.
So, I guessed, ere I got up this morning, what change was in store,
By the quick rustle-down of the quail-nets which woke me before
I could open my shutter, made fast with a bough and a stone,
And look thro' the twisted dead vine-twigs, sole lattice that 's
  known. 20
Quick and sharp rang the rings down the net-poles, while, busy
  beneath,
Your priest and his brother tugged at them, the rain in their teeth.
And out upon all the flat house-roofs, where split figs lay drying,
The girls took the frails under cover : nor use seemed in trying
To get out the boats and go fishing, for, under the cliff,
Fierce the black water frothed o'er the blind-rock. No seeing our skiff
Arrive about noon from Amalfi ! — our fisher arrive,
And pitch down his basket before us, all trembling alive
With pink and gray jellies, your sea-fruit ; you touch the strange
  lumps,
And mouths gape there, eyes open, all manner of horns and of humps, 30
Which only the fisher looks grave at, while round him like imps
Cling screaming the children as naked and brown as his shrimps ;
Himself too as bare to the middle — you see round his neck
The string and its brass coin suspended, that saves him from wreck.
But to-day not a boat reached Salerno : so back, to a man,
Came our friends, with whose help in the vineyards grape-harvest
  began.

In the vat, halfway up in our house-side, like blood the juice spins,
While your brother all bare-legged is dancing till breathless he grins
Dead-beaten in effort on effort to keep the grapes under,
Since still, when he seems all but master, in pours the fresh plunder   40
From girls who keep coming and going with basket on shoulder,
And eyes shut against the rain's driving; your girls that are older, —
For under the hedges of aloe, and where, on its bed
Of the orchard's black mould, the love-apple lies pulpy and red,
All the young ones are kneeling and filling their laps with the snails
Tempted out by this first rainy weather, — your best of regales,
As to-night will be proved to my sorrow, when, supping in state,
We shall feast our grape-gleaners (two dozen, three over one plate)
With lasagne so tempting to swallow in slippery ropes,
And gourds fried in great purple slices, that colour of popes.   50
Meantime, see the grape bunch they 've brought you: the rain-water
    slips
O'er the heavy blue bloom on each globe which the wasp to your lips
Still follows with fretful persistence. Nay, taste, while awake,
This half of a curd-white smooth cheese-ball that peels, flake by flake,
Like an onion, each smoother and whiter: next, sip this weak wine
From the thin green glass flask, with its stopper, a leaf of the vine;
And end with the prickly-pear's red flesh that leaves thro' its juice
The stony black seeds on your pearl-teeth.

                              Scirocco is loose!
Hark, the quick, whistling pelt of the olives which, thick in one's track,
Tempt the stranger to pick up and bite them, tho' not yet half black! 60
How the old twisted olive trunks shudder, the medlars let fall
Their hard fruit, and the brittle great fig-trees snap off, figs and all,
For here comes the whole of the tempest! no refuge, but creep
Back again to my side and my shoulder, and listen or sleep.

O how will your country show next week, when all the vine-boughs
Have been stripped of their foliage to pasture the mules and the cows?
Last eve, I rode over the mountains; your brother, my guide,
Soon left me, to feast on the myrtles that offered, each side,
Their fruit-balls, black, glossy, and luscious, — or strip from the sorbs
A treasure, or, rosy and wondrous, those hairy gold orbs!   70
But my mule picked his sure sober path out, just stopping to neigh
When he recognized down in the valley his mates on their way
With the faggots and barrels of water.   And soon we emerged
From the plain where the woods could scarce follow; and still, as we
    urged
Our way, the woods wondered, and left us, as up still we trudged,
Tho' the wild path grew wilder each instant, and place was e'en
    grudged
'Mid the rock-chasms and piles of loose stones like the loose broken
    teeth

Of some monster which climbed there to die, from the ocean beneath —
Place was grudged to the silver-gray fume-weed that clung to the path,
And dark rosemary ever a-dying, that, 'spite the wind's wrath,   80
So loves the salt rock's face to seaward, and lentisks as stanch
To the stone where they root and bear berries: and . . . what shows
    a branch
Coral-coloured, transparent, with circlets of pale seagreen leaves;
Over all trod my mule with the caution of gleaners o'er sheaves.
Still, foot after foot like a lady, till, round after round,
He climbed to the top of Calvano: and God's own profound
Was above me, and round me the mountains, and under, the sea,
And within me my heart to bear witness what was and shall be.
Oh, heaven and the terrible crystal! no rampart excludes
Your eye from the life to be lived in the blue solitudes.   90
Oh, those mountains, their infinite movement! still moving with you;
For, ever some new head and breast of them thrusts into view
To observe the intruder; you see it if quickly you turn
And, before they escape you, surprise them. They grudge you should
    learn
How the soft plains they look on, lean over and love (they pretend)
— Cower beneath them, the flat sea-pine crouches, the wild fruit-trees
    bend,
E'en the myrtle-leaves curl, shrink and shut: all is silent and grave:
'T is a sensual and timorous beauty, — how fair! but a slave.
So, I turned to the sea; and there slumbered, as greenly as ever,
Those isles of the siren, your Galli. No ages can sever   100
The Three, nor enable their sister to join them, — halfway
On the voyage, she looked at Ulysses — no farther to-day!
Tho' the small one, just launched in the wave, watches breast-high and
    steady
From under the rock her bold sister, swum halfway already.
Fortù, shall we sail there together, and see, from the sides,
Quite new rocks show their faces, new haunts where the siren abides?
Shall we sail round and round them, close over the rocks, tho' unseen,
That ruffle the gray glassy water to glorious green?
Then scramble from splinter to splinter, reach land, and explore,
On the largest, the strange square black turret with never a door,   110
Just a loop to admit the quick lizards; then, stand there and hear
The birds' quiet singing, that tells us what life is, so clear?
— The secret they sang to Ulysses when, ages ago,
He heard and he knew this life's secret I hear and I know.

Ah, see! The sun breaks o'er Calvano; he strikes the great gloom
And flutters it o'er the mount's summit in airy gold fume.
All is over. Look out, see the gipsy, our tinker and smith,
Has arrived, set up bellows and forge, and down-squatted forthwith
To his hammering under the wall there; one eye keeps aloof
The urchins that itch to be putting his jews'-harps to proof,   120

While the other, thro' locks of curled wire, is watching how sleek
Shines the hog, come to share in the windfall. — Chew, abbot's own
    cheek!
All is over. Wake up and come out now, and down let us go,
And see the fine things got in order at church for the show
Of the Sacrament, set forth this evening. To-morrow's the Feast
Of the Rosary's Virgin, by no means of Virgins the least,
As you'll hear in the off-hand discourse which (all nature, no art)
The Dominican brother, these three weeks, was getting by heart.
Not a pillar nor post but is dizened with red and blue papers;
All the roof waves with ribbons, each altar a-blaze with long tapers. 130
But the great masterpiece is the scaffold rigged glorious to hold
All the fiddlers and fifers and drummers and trumpeters bold
Not afraid of Bellini nor Auber, who, when the priest's hoarse,
Will strike us up something that's brisk for the feast's second course.
And then will the flaxen-wigged Image be carried in pomp
Thro' the plain, while, in gallant procession, the priests mean to stomp.
All round the glad church lie old bottles with gunpowder stopped,
Which will be, when the Image re-enters, religiously popped.
And at night from the crest of Calvano great bonfires will hang:
On the plain will the trumpets join chorus, and more poppers bang. 140
At all events, come — to the garden as far as the wall;
See me tap with a hoe on the plaster, till out there shall fall
A scorpion with wide angry nippers!

                — "Such trifles!" you say?
Fortù, in my England at home, men meet gravely to-day
And debate, if abolishing Corn-laws be righteous and wise!
— If 't were proper, Scirocco should vanish in black from the skies!

UP AT A VILLA — DOWN IN THE CITY.

(AS DISTINGUISHED BY AN ITALIAN PERSON OF QUALITY.)

I.

HAD I but plenty of money, money enough and to spare,
   The house for me, no doubt, were a house in the city-square;
Ah, such a life, such a life, as one leads at the window there!

II.

Something to see, by Bacchus, something to hear, at least!
There, the whole day long, one's life is a perfect feast;
While up at a villa one lives, I maintain it, no more than a beast.

III.

Well now, look at our villa! stuck like the horn of a bull
Just on a mountain edge as bare as the creature's skull,
Save a mere shag of a bush with hardly a leaf to pull!
— I scratch my own, sometimes, to see if the hair 's turned wool.   10

IV.

But the city, oh the city — the square with the houses!   Why?
They are stone-faced, white as a curd, there 's something to take the eye!
Houses in four straight lines, not a single front awry;
You watch who crosses and gossips, who saunters, who hurries by;
Green blinds, as a matter of course, to draw when the sun gets high;
And the shops with fanciful signs which are painted properly.

V.

What of a villa?   Tho' winter be over in March by rights,
'T is May perhaps ere the snow shall have withered well off the heights:
You 've the brown ploughed land before, where the oxen steam and
        wheeze,
And the hills over-smoked behind by the faint gray olive-trees.   20

VI.

Is it better in May, I ask you ?   You 've summer all at once;
In a day he leaps complete with a few strong April suns.
'Mid the sharp short emerald wheat, scarce risen three fingers well,
The wild tulip, at end of its tube, blows out its great red bell
Like a thin clear bubble of blood, for the children to pick and sell.

VII.

Is it ever hot in the square ?   There 's a fountain to spout and splash!
In the shade it sings and springs; in the shine such foam-bows flash
On the horses with curling fish-tails, that prance and paddle and pash
Round the lady atop in her conch — fifty gazers do not abash,
Tho' all that she wears is some weeds round her waist in a sort of sash. 30

VIII.

All the year long at the villa, nothing to see though you linger,
Except yon cypress that points like death's lean lifted forefinger.
Some think fireflies pretty, when they mix i' the corn and mingle,
Or thrid the stinking hemp till the stalks of it seem a-tingle.
Late August or early September, the stunning cicala is shrill,

And the bees keep their tiresome whine round the resinous firs on the hill.
Enough of the seasons,—I spare you the months of the fever and chill.

IX.

Ere you open your eyes in the city, the blessed church-bells begin:
No sooner the bells leave off than the diligence rattles in:
You get the pick of the news, and it costs you never a pin.   40
By and by there's the traveling doctor gives pills, lets blood, draws teeth;
Or the Pulcinello-trumpet breaks up the market beneath.
At the post-office such a scene-picture — the new play, piping hot!
And a notice how, only this morning, three liberal thieves were shot.
Above it, behold the Archbishop's most fatherly of rebukes,
And beneath, with his crown and his lion, some little new law of the Duke's!
Or a sonnet with flowery marge, to the Reverend Don So-and-so
Who is Dante, Boccaccio, Petrarca, St. Jerome and Cicero,
"And moreover," (the sonnet goes rhyming,) "the skirts of St. Paul has reached,
Having preached us those six Lent-lectures more unctuous than ever he preached."   50
Noon strikes,—here sweeps the procession! our Lady borne smiling and smart,
With a pink gauze gown all spangles, and seven swords stuck in her heart!
Bang-whang-whang goes the drum, *tootle-te-tootle* the fife;
No keeping one's haunches still: it's the greatest pleasure in life.

X.

But bless you, it's dear — it's dear! fowls, wine, at double the rate.
They have clapped a new tax upon salt, and what oil pays passing the gate
It's a horror to think of.   And so, the villa for me, not the city!
Beggars can scarcely be choosers: but still — ah, the pity, the pity!
Look, two and two go the priests, then the monks with cowls and sandals,
And the penitents dressed in white shirts, a-holding the yellow candles;   60
One, he carries a flag up straight, and another a cross with handles,
And the Duke's guard brings up the rear, for the better prevention of scandals:
Bang-whang-whang goes the drum, *tootle-te-tootle* the fife.
Oh, a day in the city-square, there is no such pleasure in life!

PICTOR IGNOTUS.

FLORENCE, 15—.

I COULD have painted pictures like that youth's
  Ye praise so.   How my soul springs up !   No bar
Stayed me — ah, thought which saddens while it soothes!
  — Never did fate forbid me, star by star,
To outburst on your night, with all my gift
  Of fires from God : nor would my flesh have shrunk
From seconding my soul, with eyes uplift
  And wide to heaven, or, straight like thunder, sunk
To the centre, of an instant ; or around
  Turned calmly and inquisitive, to scan   10
The license and the limit, space and bound,
  Allowed to truth made visible in man.
And, like that youth ye praise so, all I saw,
  Over the canvas could my hand have flung,
Each face obedient to its passion's law,
  Each passion clear proclaimed without a tongue;
Whether Hope rose at once in all the blood,
  A-tiptoe for the blessing of embrace,
Or Rapture drooped the eyes, as when her brood
  Pull down the nesting dove's heart to its place ;   20
Or Confidence lit swift the forehead up,
  And locked the mouth fast, like a castle braved, —
O human faces, hath it spilt, my cup?
  What did ye give me that I have not saved?
Nor will I say I have not dreamed (how well!)
  Of going — I, in each new picture, — forth,
As, making new hearts beat and bosoms swell,
  To Pope or Kaiser, East, West, South, or North,
Bound for the calmly satisfied great State,
  Or glad aspiring little burgh, it went,   30
Flowers cast upon the car which bore the freight,
  Thro' old streets named afresh from the event,
Till it reached home, where learned age should greet
  My face, and youth, the star not yet distinct
Above his hair, lie learning at my feet! —
  Oh, thus to live, I and my picture, linked
With love about, and praise, till life should end,
  And then not go to heaven, but linger here,
Here on my earth, earth's every man my friend,
  The thought grew frightful, 't was so wildly dear !   40
But a voice changed it.   Glimpses of such sights
  Have scared me, like the revels thro' a door
Of some strange house of idols at its rites!

This world seemed not the world it was before.
Mixed with my loving trusting ones, there trooped
. . . Who summoned those cold faces that begun
To press on me and judge me? Tho' I stooped
  Shrinking, as from the soldiery a nun,
They drew me forth, and spite of me . . enough!
  These buy and sell our pictures, take and give,   50
Count them for garniture and household-stuff,
  And where they live needs must our pictures live
And see their faces, listen to their prate,
  Partakers of their daily pettiness,
Discussed of, — " This I love, or this I hate
  This likes me more, and this affects me less!"
Wherefore I chose my portion.   If at whiles
  My heart sinks, as monotonous I paint
These endless cloisters and eternal aisles
  With the same series, Virgin, Babe, and Saint,   60
With the same cold calm beautiful regard, —
  At least no merchant traffics in my heart ;
The sanctuary's gloom at least shall ward
  Vain tongues from where my pictures stand apart :
Only prayer breaks the silence of the shrine
  While, blackening in the daily candle-smoke,
They moulder on the damp wall's travertine,
  'Mid echoes the light footstep never woke.
So, die my pictures! surely, gently die!
  O youth, men praise so, — holds their praise its worth ?   70
Blown harshly, keeps the trump its golden cry?
  Tastes sweet the water with such specks of earth?

FRA LIPPO LIPPI.

I AM poor brother Lippo, by your leave !
  You need not clap your torches to my face.
Zooks, what 's to blame? you think you see a monk!
What, 't is past midnight, and you go the rounds,
And here you catch me at an alley's end
Where sportive ladies leave their doors ajar?
The Carmine 's my cloister : hunt it up,
Do, — harry out, if you must show your zeal,
Whatever rat, there, haps on his wrong hole,
And nip each softling of a wee white mouse,   10
Weke, weke, that 's crept to keep him company!
Aha, you know your betters?   Then, you 'll take
Your hand away that 's fiddling on my throat,

And please to know me likewise.   Who am I?
Why, one, sir, who is lodging with a friend
Three streets off—he 's a certain . . . how d' ye call?
Master—a . . . Cosimo of the Medici,
I' the house that caps the corner.   Boh! you were best!
Remember and tell me, the day you 're hanged,
How you affected such a gullet's-gripe!   20
But you, sir, it concerns you that your knaves
Pick up a manner nor discredit you:
Zooks, are we pilchards, that they sweep the streets
And count fair prize what comes into their net?
He 's Judas to a tittle, that man is!
Just such a face!   Why, sir, you make amends.
Lord, I 'm not angry!   Bid your hangdogs go
Drink out this quarter-florin to the health
Of the munificent House that harbours me
(And many more beside, lads! more beside!)   30
And all 's come square again.   I 'd like his face—
His, elbowing on his comrade in the door
With the pike and lantern,—for the slave that holds
John Baptist's head a-dangle by the hair
With one hand ("Look you, now," as who should say)
And his weapon in the other, yet unwiped!
It 's not your chance to have a bit of chalk,
A wood-coal or the like? or you should see!
Yes, I 'm the painter, since you style me so.
What, brother Lippo's doings, up and down,   40
You know them, and they take you? like enough!
I saw the proper twinkle in your eye—
'Tell you, I liked your looks at very first.
Let 's sit and set things straight now, hip to haunch.
Here 's spring come, and the nights one makes up bands
To roam the town and sing out carnival,
And I 've been three weeks shut within my mew,
A-painting for the great man, saints and saints
And saints again.   I could not paint all night—
Ouf!   I leaned out of window for fresh air.   50
There came a hurry of feet and little feet,
A sweep of lute-strings, laughs, and whifts of song,
Flower o' the broom,
Take away love, and our earth is a tomb!
Flower o' the quince,
I let Lisa go, and what good in life since?
Flower o' the thyme—and so on.   Round they went.
Scarce had they turned the corner when a titter
Like the skipping of rabbits by moonlight,—three slim shapes,
And a face that looked up . . zooks, sir, flesh and blood,   60
That 's all I 'm made of!   Into shreds it went,

Curtain and counterpane and coverlet,
All the bed-furniture — a dozen knots,
There was a ladder!   Down I let myself,
Hands and feet, scrambling somehow, and so dropped,
And after them.   I came up with the fun
Hard by Saint Laurence, hail fellow, well met, —
Flower o' the rose,
If I 've been merry, what matter who knows?
And so, as I was stealing back again,   70
To get to bed and have a bit of sleep
Ere I rise up to-morrow and go work
On Jerome knocking at his poor old breast
With his great round stone to subdue the flesh,
You snap me of the sudden.   Ah, I see!
Tho' your eye twinkles still, you shake your head —
Mine 's shaved — a monk, you say — the sting 's in that!
If Master Cosimo announced himself,
Mum 's the word naturally ; but a monk!
Come, what am I a beast for? tell us, now!   80
I was a baby when my mother died
And father died and left me in the street.
I starved there, God knows how, a year or two
On fig-skins, melon-parings, rinds and shucks,
Refuse and rubbish.   One fine frosty day,
My stomach being empty as your hat,
The wind doubled me up and down I went.
Old Aunt Lapaccia trussed me with one hand,
(Its fellow was a stinger as I knew)
And so along the wall, over the bridge,   90
By the straight cut to the convent.   Six words there,
While I stood munching my first bread that month :
" So, boy, you 're minded," quoth the good fat father
Wiping his own mouth, 't was refection-time, —
" To quit this very miserable world ?
Will you renounce " . . . " the mouthful of bread? "
        thought I ;
By no means!   Brief, they made a monk of me ;
I did renounce the world, its pride and greed,
Palace, farm, villa, shop and banking-house,
Trash, such as these poor devils of Medici   100
Have given their hearts to — all at eight years old.
Well, sir, I found in time, you may be sure,
'T was not for nothing — the good bellyful,
The warm serge and the rope that goes all round,
And day-long blessed idleness beside!
" Let 's see what the urchin 's fit for " — that came next.
Not overmuch their way, I must confess.
Such a to-do!   They tried me with their books :

Lord, they 'd have taught me Latin in pure waste!
Flower o' the clove,   110
All the Latin I construe is, " amo " I love !
But, mind you, when a boy starves in the streets
Eight years together, as my fortune was,
Watching folk's faces to know who will fling
The bit of half-stripped grape-bunch he desires,
And who will curse or kick him for his pains,—
Which gentleman processional and fine,
Holding a candle to the Sacrament,
Will wink and let him lift a plate and catch
The droppings of the wax to sell again,   120
Or holla for the Eight and have him whipped,—
How say I?—nay, which dog bites, which lets drop
His bone from the heap of offal in the street,—
Why, soul and sense of him grow sharp alike,
He learns the look of things, and none the less
For admonition from the hunger-pinch.
I had a store of such remarks, be sure,
Which, after I found leisure, turned to use :
I drew men's faces on my copy-books,
Scrawled them within the antiphonary's marge,   130
Joined legs and arms to the long music-notes,
Found eyes and nose and chin for A's and B's
And made a string of pictures of the world
Betwixt the ins and outs of verb and noun,
On the wall, the bench, the door.   The monks looked
     black.
"Nay," quoth the Prior, " turn him out, d' ye say?
In no wise.   Lose a crow and catch a lark.
What if at last we get our man of parts,
We Carmelites, like those Camaldolese
And Preaching Friars, to do our church up fine   140
And put the front on it that ought to be!"
And hereupon he bade me daub away.
Thank you! my head being crammed, the walls a blank,
Never was such prompt disemburdening.
First every sort of monk, the black and white,
I drew them, fat and lean : then, folk at church,
From good old gossips waiting to confess
Their cribs of barrel-droppings, candle-ends,—
To the breathless fellow at the altar-foot,
Fresh from his murder, safe and sitting there   150
With the little children round him in a row
Of admiration, half for his beard, and half
For that white anger of his victim's son
Shaking a fist at him with one fierce arm,
Signing himself with the other because of Christ

(Whose sad face on the cross sees only this
After the passion of a thousand years)
Till some poor girl, her apron o'er her head,
(Which the intense eyes looked through) came at eve
On tiptoe, said a word, dropped in a loaf,   160
Her pair of ear-rings and a bunch of flowers
(The brute took growling) prayed, and so was gone.
I painted all, then cried, "'T is ask and have;
Choose, for more 's ready!" — laid the ladder flat,
And showed my covered bit of cloister-wall.
The monks closed in a circle and praised loud
Till checked, taught what to see and not to see,
Being simple bodies, — "That's the very man!
Look at the boy who stoops to pat the dog!
That woman's like the Prior's niece who comes   170
To care about his asthma: it's the life!"
But there my triumph's straw-fire flared and funked;
Their betters took their turn to see and say:
The Prior and the learned pulled a face
And stopped all that in no time. "How! what's here?
Quite from the mark of painting, bless us all!
Faces, arms, legs and bodies like the true
As much as pea and pea! it's devil's game!
Your business is not to catch men with show,
With homage to the perishable clay,   180
But lift them over it, ignore it all,
Make them forget there's such a thing as flesh.
Your business is to paint the souls of men —
Man's soul, and it's a fire, smoke . . no, it's not . .
It's vapour done up like a new-born babe —
(In that shape when you die it leaves your mouth)
It's . . well, what matters talking, it's the soul!
Give us no more of body than shows soul!
Here's Giotto, with his Saint a-praising God,
That sets us praising, — why not stop with him?   190
Why put all thoughts of praise out of our head
With wonder at lines, colours, and what not?
Paint the soul, never mind the legs and arms!
Rub all out, try at it a second time!
Oh, that white smallish female with the breasts,
She's just my niece . . . Herodias, I would say, —
Who went and danced, and got men's heads cut off!
Have it all out!" Now, is this sense, I ask?
A fine way to paint soul, by painting body
So ill, the eye can't stop there, must go further   200
And can't fare worse! Thus, yellow does for white
When what you put for yellow 's simply black,
And any sort of meaning looks intense

When all beside itself means and looks naught.
Why can't a painter lift each foot in turn,
Left foot and right foot, go a double step,
Make his flesh liker and his soul more like,
Both in their order? Take the prettiest face,
The Prior's niece . . . patron-saint — is it so pretty
You can't discover if it means hope, fear,   210
Sorrow or joy? won't beauty go with these?
Suppose I've made her eyes all right and blue,
Can't I take breath and try to add life's flash,
And then add soul and heighten them threefold?
Or say there's beauty with no soul at all —
(I never saw it — put the case the same —)
If you get simple beauty and naught else,
You get about the best thing God invents :
That's somewhat : and you'll find the soul you have missed,
Within yourself, when you return him thanks.   220
"Rub all out!" Well, well, there's my life, in short,
And so the thing has gone on ever since.
I'm grown a man no doubt, I've broken bounds :
You should not take a fellow eight years old
And make him swear to never kiss the girls.
I'm my own master, paint now as I please —
Having a friend, you see, in the Corner-house!
Lord, it's fast holding by the rings in front —
Those great rings serve more purposes than just
To plant a flag in, or tie up a horse!   230
And yet the old schooling sticks, the old grave eyes
Are peeping o'er my shoulder as I work,
The heads shake still — "It's art's decline, my son!
You're not of the true painters, great and old ;
Brother Angelico's the man, you'll find ;
Brother Lorenzo stands his single peer :
Fag on at flesh, you'll never make the third!"
Flower o' the pine,
You keep your mistr . . . manners, and I'll stick to mine!
I'm not the third, then : bless us, they must know!   240
Don't you think they're the likeliest to know,
They with their Latin? So, I swallow my rage,
Clench my teeth, suck my lips in tight, and paint
To please them — sometimes do, and sometimes don't ;
For, doing most, there's pretty sure to come
A turn, some warm eve finds me at my saints —
A laugh, a cry, the business of the world —
(*Flower o' the peach,*
Death for us all, and his own life for each!)
And my whole soul revolves, the cup runs over,   250
The world and life's too big to pass for a dream,

K

And I do these wild things in sheer despite,
And play the fooleries you catch me at,
In pure rage!   The old mill-horse, out at grass
After hard years, throws up his stiff heels so,
Altho' the miller does not preach to him
The only good of grass is to make chaff.
What would men have?   Do they like grass or no —
May they or may n't they? all I want 's the thing
Settled for ever one way.   As it is,   260
You tell too many lies and hurt yourself:
You don't like what you only like too much,
You do like what, if given you at your word,
You find abundantly detestable.
For me, I think I speak as I was taught:
I always see the garden, and God there
A-making man's wife: and, my lesson learned,
The value and significance of flesh,
I can't unlearn ten minutes afterwards.

    You understand me: I 'm a beast, I know.   270
But see, now — why, I see as certainly
As that the morning-star 's about to shine,
What will hap some day.   We 've a youngster here
Comes to our convent, studies what I do,
Slouches and stares and lets no atom drop:
His name is Guidi — he 'll not mind the monks —
They call him Hulking Tom, he lets them talk —
He picks my practice up — he 'll paint apace,
I hope so — tho' I never live so long,
I know what 's sure to follow.   You be judge!   280
You speak no Latin more than I, belike;
However, you 're my man, you 've seen the world
— The beauty and the wonder and the power,
The shapes of things, their colours, lights and shades,
Changes, surprises, — and God made it all!
— For what?   Do you feel thankful, ay or no,
For this fair town's face, yonder river's line,
The mountain round it and the sky above,
Much more the figures of man, woman, child,
These are the frame to?   What 's it all about?   290
To be passed over, despised? or dwelt upon,
Wondered at? oh, this last of course! — you say.
But why not do as well as say, — paint these
Just as they are, careless what comes of it?
God's works — paint any one, and count it crime
To let a truth slip.   Don't object, "His works
Are here already; nature is complete:
Suppose you reproduce her — (which you can't)

There 's no advantage! you must beat her, then."
For, don't you mark? we 're made so that we love   300
First when we see them painted, things we have passed
Perhaps a hundred times nor cared to see;
And so they are better, painted — better to us,
Which is the same thing.   Art was given for that;
God uses us to help each other so,
Lending our minds out.   Have you noticed, now,
Your cullion's hanging face?   A bit of chalk,
And trust me but you should, though!   How much more
If I drew higher things with the same truth!
That were to take the Prior's pulpit-place,   310
Interpret God to all of you!   Oh, oh,
It makes me mad to see what men shall do
And we in our graves!   This world 's no blot for us
Nor blank; it means intensely, and means good:
To find its meaning is my meat and drink.
"Ay, but you don't so instigate to prayer!"
Strikes in the Prior: " when your meaning 's plain
It does not say to folk — remember matins,
Or, mind you fast next Friday!"   Why, for this
What need of art at all?   A skull and bones,   320
Two bits of stick nailed cross-wise, or, what 's best,
A bell to chime the hour with, does as well.
I painted a Saint Laurence six months since
At Prato, splashed the fresco in fine style:
" How looks my painting, now the scaffold 's down?"
I ask a brother: " Hugely," he returns —
" Already not one phiz of your three slaves
Who turn the Deacon off his toasted side,
But 's scratched and prodded to our heart's content,
The pious people have so eased their own   330
With coming to say prayers there in a rage:
We get on fast to see the bricks beneath.
Expect another job this time next year,
For pity and religion grow i' the crowd —
Your painting serves its purpose!"   Hang the fools!

— That is — you 'll not mistake an idle word
Spoke in a huff by a poor monk, Got wot,
Tasting the air this spicy night which turns
The unaccustomed head like Chianti wine!
Oh, the church knows! don't misreport me, now!   340
It 's natural a poor monk out of bounds
Should have his apt word to excuse himself:
And hearken how I plot to make amends.
I have bethought me : I shall paint a piece
. . . There 's for you!   Give me six months, then go, see

Something in Sant' Ambrogio's! Bless the nuns!
They want a cast o' my office. I shall paint
God in the midst, Madonna and her babe,
Ringed by a bowery flowery angel-brood,
Lilies and vestments and white faces, sweet　　　　　　350
As puff on puff of grated orris-root
When ladies crowd to church at midsummer.
And then i' the front, of course a saint or two —
Saint John, because he saves the Florentines,
Saint Ambrose, who puts down in black and white
The convent's friends and gives them a long day,
And Job, I must have him there past mistake,
The man of Uz (and Us without the z,
Painters who need his patience). Well, all these
Secured at their devotion, up shall come　　　　　　360
Out of a corner when you least expect,
As one by a dark stair into a great light,
Music and talking, who but Lippo! I! —
Mazed, motionless and moon-struck — I'm the man!
Back I shrink — what is this I see and hear?
I, caught up with my monk's things by mistake,
My old serge gown and rope that goes all round,
I, in this presence, this pure company!
Where's a hole, where's a corner for escape?
Then steps a sweet angelic slip of a thing　　　　　　370
Forward, puts out a soft palm — "Not so fast!"
— Addresses the celestial presence, "nay —
He made you and devised you, after all,
Tho' he's none of you! Could Saint John there, draw —
His camel-hair make up a painting-brush?
We come to brother Lippo for all that,
Iste perfecit opus!" So, all smile —
I shuffle sideways with my blushing face
Under the cover of a hundred wings
Thrown like a spread of kirtles when you're gay　　　　　　380
And play hot cockles, all the doors being shut,
Till, wholly unexpected, in there pops
The hothead husband! Thus I scuttle off
To some safe bench behind, not letting go
The palm of her, the little lily thing
That spoke the good word for me in the nick,
Like the Prior's niece . . . Saint Lucy, I would say.
And so all's saved for me, and for the church
A pretty picture gained. Go, six months hence!
Your hand, sir, and good bye: no lights, no lights!　　　　　　390
The street's hushed, and I know my own way back,
Don't fear me! There's the gray beginning. Zooks!

ANDREA DEL SARTO.

(CALLED "THE FAULTLESS PAINTER.")

BUT do not let us quarrel any more,
  No, my Lucrezia! bear with me for once:
Sit down and all shall happen as you wish.
You turn your face, but does it bring your heart?
I 'll work then for your friend's friend, never fear,
Treat his own subject after his own way,
Fix his own time, accept too his own price,
And shut the money into this small hand
When next it takes mine. Will it? tenderly?
Oh, I 'll content him, — but to-morrow, Love!   10
I often am much wearier than you think,
This evening more than usual: and it seems
As if — forgive now — should you let me sit
Here by the window, with your hand in mine,
And look a half-hour forth on Fiesole,
Both of one mind, as married people use,
Quietly, quietly the evening through,
I might get up to-morrow to my work
Cheerful and fresh as ever. Let us try.
To-morrow, how you shall be glad for this!   20
Your soft hand is a woman of itself,
And mine the man's bared breast she curls inside.
Don't count the time lost, neither; you must serve
For each of the five pictures we require:
It saves a model. So! keep looking so —
My serpentining beauty, rounds on rounds!
— How could you ever prick those perfect ears,
Even to put the pearl there! oh, so sweet —
My face, my moon, my everybody's moon,
Which everybody looks on and calls his,   30
And, I suppose, is looked on by in turn,
While she looks — no one's: very dear, no less.
You smile? why, there 's my picture ready made,
There 's what we painters call our harmony!
A common grayness silvers everything, —
All in a twilight, you and I alike
— You, at the point of your first pride in me
(That 's gone, you know) — but I, at every point;
My youth, my hope, my art, being all toned down
To yonder sober pleasant Fiesole.   40
There 's the bell clinking from the chapel-top;
That length of convent-wall across the way
Holds the trees safer, huddled more inside;

The last monk leaves the garden; days decrease,
And autumn grows, autumn in everything.
Eh? the whole seems to fall into a shape,
As if I saw alike my work and self
And all that I was born to be and do,
A twilight-piece.   Love, we are in God's hand.
How strange now, looks the life he makes us lead;   50
So free we seem, so fettered fast we are!
I feel he laid the fetter: let it lie!
This chamber for example — turn your head –
All that 's behind us!   You don't understand
Nor care to understand about my art,
But you can hear at least when people speak:
And that cartoon, the second from the door
— It is the thing, Love! so such things should be —
Behold Madonna! — I am bold to say.
I can do with my pencil what I know,   60
What I see, what at bottom of my heart
I wish for, if I ever wish so deep —
Do easily, too — when I say, perfectly,
I do not boast, perhaps: yourself are judge,
Who listened to the Legate's talk last week;
And just as much they used to say in France.
At any rate 't is easy, all of it!
No sketches first, no studies, that 's long past:
I do what many dream of, all their lives,
— Dream? strive to do, and agonize to do,   70
And fail in doing.   I could count twenty such
On twice your fingers, and not leave this town,
Who strive — you don't know how the others strive
To paint a little thing like that you smeared
Carelessly passing with your robes afloat, —
Yet do much less, so much less, Someone says,
(I know his name, no matter) — so much less!
Well, less is more, Lucrezia: I am judged.
There burns a truer light of God in them,
In their vexed beating stuffed and stopped-up brain,   80
Heart, or whate'er else, than goes on to prompt
This low-pulsed forthright craftsman's hand of mine.
Their works drop groundward, but themselves, I know,
Reach many a time a heaven that 's shut to me,
Enter and take their place there sure enough,
Tho' they come back and cannot tell the world.
My works are nearer heaven, but I sit here.
The sudden blood of these men! at a word —
Praise them, it boils, or blame them, it boils too.
I, painting from myself and to myself,   90
Know what I do, am unmoved by men's blame

Or their praise either.   Somebody remarks
Morello's outline there is wrongly traced,
His hue mistaken ; what of that ? or else,
Rightly traced and well ordered ; what of that?
Speak as they please, what does the mountain care?
Ah, but a man's reach should exceed his grasp,
Or what 's a heaven for?   All is silver-gray,
Placid and perfect with my art : the worse!
I know both what I want and what might gain,   100
And yet how profitless to know, to sigh
" Had I been two, another and myself,
Our head would have o'erlooked the world! " No doubt.
Yonder 's a work now, of that famous youth
The Urbinate who died five years ago.
('T is copied, George Vasari sent it me.)
Well, I can fancy how he did it all,
Pouring his soul, with kings and popes to see,
Reaching, that heaven might so replenish him,
Above and thro' his art — for it gives way ;   110
That arm is wrongly put — and there again —
A fault to pardon in the drawing's lines,
Its body, so to speak : its soul is right,
He means right — that, a child may understand.
Still, what an arm! and I could alter it :
But all the play, the insight and the stretch —
Out of me, out of me!   And wherefore out?
Had you enjoined them on me, given me soul,
We might have risen to Rafael, I and you!
Nay, Love, you did give all I asked, I think —   120
More than I merit, yes, by many times.
But had you — oh, with the same perfect brow,
And perfect eyes, and more than perfect mouth,
And the low voice my soul hears, as a bird
The fowler's pipe, and follows to the snare —
Had you, with these the same, but brought a mind!
Some women do so.   Had the mouth there urged
" God and the glory! never care for gain.
The present by the future, what is that?
Live for fame, side by side with Agnolo!   130
Rafael is waiting : up to God, all three! "
I might have done it for you.   So it seems :
Perhaps not.   All is as God over-rules.
Beside, incentives come from the soul's self;
The rest avail not.   Why do I need you?
What wife had Rafael, or has Agnolo?
In this world, who can do a thing, will not ;
And who would do it, can not, I perceive :
Yet the will 's somewhat — somewhat, too, the power

And thus we half-men struggle.   At the end,   140
God, I conclude, compensates, punishes.
'T is safer for me, if the award be strict,
That I am something underrated here,
Poor this long while, despised, to speak the truth.
I dared not, do you know, leave home all day,
For fear of chancing on the Paris lords.
The best is when they pass and look aside;
But they speak sometimes; I must bear it all.
Well may they speak!   That Francis, that first time,
And that long festal year at Fontainebleau!   150
I surely then could sometimes leave the ground,
Put on the glory, Rafael's daily wear,
In that humane great monarch's golden look, —
One finger in his beard or twisted curl
Over his mouth's good mark that made the smile,
One arm about my shoulder, round my neck,
The jingle of his gold chain in my ear,
I painting proudly with his breath on me,
All his court round him, seeing with his eyes,
Such frank French eyes, and such a fire of souls   160
Profuse, my hand kept plying by those hearts, —
And, best of all, this, this, this face beyond,
This in the background, waiting on my work,
To crown the issue with a last reward!
A good time, was it not, my kingly days?
And had you not grown restless . . . but I know —
'T is done and past; 't was right, my instinct said;
Too live the life grew, golden and not gray:
And I 'm the weak-eyed bat no sun should tempt
Out of the grange whose four walls make his world.   170
How could it end in any other way?
You called me, and I came home to your heart.
The triumph was — to reach and stay there; since
I reached it ere the triumph, what is lost?
Let my hands frame your face in your hair's gold,
You beautiful Lucrezia that are mine!
"Rafael did this, Andrea painted that;
The Roman's is the better when you pray,
But still the other's Virgin was his wife — "
Men will excuse me.   I am glad to judge   180
Both pictures in your presence; clearer grows
My better fortune, I resolve to think.
For, do you know, Lucrezia, as God lives,
Said one day Agnolo, his very self,
To Rafael . . . I have known it all these years . . .
(When the young man was flaming out his thoughts
Upon a palace-wall for Rome to see,

Too lifted up in heart because of it)
"Friend, there's a certain sorry little scrub
Goes up and down our Florence, none cares how,   190
Who, were he set to plan and execute
As you are, pricked on by your popes and kings,
Would bring the sweat into that brow of yours!"
To Rafael's! — And indeed the arm is wrong.
I hardly dare . . . yet, only you to see,
Give the chalk here — quick, thus the line should go!
Ay, but the soul! he's Rafael! rub it out!
Still, all I care for, if he spoke the truth,
(What he? why, who but Michel Agnolo?
Do you forget already words like those?)   200
If really there was such a chance so lost, —
Is, whether you're — not grateful — but more pleased.
Well, let me think so. And you smile indeed!
This hour has been an hour! Another smile?
If you would sit thus by me every night
I should work better, do you comprehend?
I mean that I should earn more, give you more.
See, it is settled dusk now; there's a star;
Morello's gone, the watch-lights show the wall,
The cue-owls speak the name we call them by.   210
Come from the window, love, — come in, at last,
Inside the melancholy little house
We built to be so gay with. God is just.
King Francis may forgive me: oft at nights
When I look up from painting, eyes tired out,
The walls become illumined, brick from brick
Distinct, instead of mortar, fierce bright gold,
That gold of his I did cement them with!
Let us but love each other. Must you go?
That Cousin here again? he waits outside?   220
Must see you — you, and not with me? Those loans?
More gaming debts to pay? you smiled for that?
Well, let smiles buy me! have you more to spend?
While hand and eye and something of a heart
Are left me, work's my ware, and what's it worth?
I'll pay my fancy. Only let me sit
The gray remainder of the evening out,
Idle, you call it, and muse perfectly
How I could paint, were I but back in France,
One picture, just one more — the Virgin's face,   230
Not yours this time! I want you at my side
To hear them — that is, Michel Agnolo —
Judge all I do and tell you of its worth.
Will you? To-morrow, satisfy your friend.
I take the subjects for his corridor,

Finish the portrait out of hand — there, there,
And throw him in another thing or two
If he demurs; the whole should prove enough
To pay for this same Cousin's freak.   Beside,
What 's better and what 's all I care about,   240
Get you the thirteen scudi for the ruff !
Love, does that please you?   Ah, but what does he,
The Cousin! what does he to please you more?

    I am grown peaceful as old age to-night.
I regret little, I would change still less.
Since there my past life lies, why alter it?
The very wrong to Francis! — it is true
I took his coin, was tempted and complied,
And built this house and sinned, and all is said.
My father and my mother died of want.   250
Well, had I riches of my own? you see
How one gets rich!   Let each one bear his lot.
They were born poor, lived poor, and poor they died:
And I have laboured somewhat in my time
And not been paid profusely.   Some good son
Paint my two hundred pictures — let him try!
No doubt, there 's something strikes a balance.   Yes,
You loved me quite enough, it seems to-night.
This must suffice me here.   What would one have?
In heaven, perhaps, new chances, one more chance —   260
Four great walls in the New Jerusalem,
Meted on each side by the angel's reed,
For Leonard, Rafael, Agnolo and me
To cover — the three first without a wife,
While I have mine!   So — still they overcome
Because there 's still Lucrezia, — as I choose.

    Again the Cousin's whistle!   Go, my Love.

———◦———

THE BISHOP ORDERS HIS TOMB AT SAINT PRAXED'S CHURCH.

ROME, 15—.

VANITY, saith the preacher, vanity!
   Draw round my bed : is Anselm keeping back?
Nephews — sons mine . . . ah God, I know not!   Well —
She, men would have to be your mother once,
Old Gandolf envied me, so fair she was!

What 's done is done, and she is dead beside,
Dead long ago, and I am Bishop since,
And as she died so must we die ourselves,
And thence ye may perceive the world 's a dream.
Life, how and what is it?   As here I lie   10
In this state-chamber, dying by degrees,
Hours and long hours in the dead night, I ask
"Do I live, am I dead?"   Peace, peace seems all.
Saint Praxed's ever was the church for peace ;
And so, about this tomb of mine.   I fought
With tooth and nail to save my niche, ye know :
— Old Gandolf cozened me, despite my care ;
Shrewd was that snatch from out the corner South
He graced his carrion with, God curse the same !
Yet still my niche is not so cramped but thence   20
One sees the pulpit o' the epistle-side,
And somewhat of the choir, those silent seats,
And up into the aery dome where live
The angels, and a sunbeam 's sure to lurk :
And I shall fill my slab of basalt there,
And 'neath my tabernacle take my rest,
With those nine columns round me, two and two,
The odd one at my feet where Anselm stands :
Peach-blossom marble all, the rare, the ripe
As fresh-poured red wine of a mighty pulse.   30
— Old Gandolf with his paltry onion-stone,
Put me where I may look at him !   True peach,
Rosy and flawless : how I earned the prize !
Draw close : that conflagration of my church
— What then ?   So much was saved if aught were missed !
My sons, ye would not be my death ?   Go dig
The white-grape vineyard where the oil-press stood,
Drop water gently till the surface sink,
And if ye find . . . Ah God, I know not, I ! . . .
Bedded in store of rotten fig-leaves soft,   40
And corded up in a tight olive-frail,
Some lump, ah God, of *lapis lazuli*,
Big as a Jew's head cut off at the nape,
Blue as a vein o'er the Madonna's breast . . .
Sons, all have I bequeathed you, villas, all,
That brave Frascati villa with its bath,
So, let the blue lump poise between my knees,
Like God the Father's globe on both his hands
Ye worship in the Jesu Church so gay,
For Gandolf shall not choose but see and burst !   50
Swift as a weaver's shuttle fleet our years :
Man goeth to the grave, and where is he ?
Did I say, basalt for my slab, sons ?   Black —

'T was ever antique-black I meant!   How else
Shall ye contrast my frieze to come beneath?
The bas-relief in bronze ye promised me,
Those Pans and Nymphs ye wot of, and perchance
Some tripod, thyrsus, with a vase or so,
The Saviour at his sermon on the mount,
Saint Praxed in a glory, and one Pan   60
Ready to twitch the Nymph's last garment off,
And Moses with the tables . . . but I know
Ye mark me not!   What do they whisper thee,
Child of my bowels, Anselm?   Ah, ye hope
To revel down my villas while I gasp
Bricked o'er with beggar's mouldy travertine
Which Gandolf from his tomb-top chuckles at!
Nay, boys, ye love me — all of jasper, then!
'T is jasper ye stand pledged to, lest I grieve
My bath must needs be left behind, alas!   70
One block, pure green as a pistachio-nut,
There 's plenty jasper somewhere in the world —
And have I not Saint Praxed's ear to pray
Horses for ye, and brown Greek manuscripts,
And mistresses with great smooth marbly limbs?
— That 's if ye carve my epitaph aright,
Choice Latin, picked phrase, Tully's every word,
No gaudy ware like Gandolf's second line —
Tully, my masters?   Ulpian serves his need!
And then how I shall lie thro' centuries,   80
And hear the blessed mutter of the mass,
And see God made and eaten all day long,
And feel the steady candle-flame, and taste
Good strong thick stupefying incense-smoke!
For as I lie here, hours of the dead night,
Dying in state and by such slow degrees,
I fold my arms as if they clasped a crook,
And stretch my feet forth straight as stone can point,
And let the bedclothes, for a mortcloth, drop
Into great laps and folds of sculptor's-work: 90
And as yon tapers dwindle, and strange thoughts
Grow, with a certain humming in my ears,
About the life before I lived this life,
And this life too, popes, cardinals and priests,
Saint Praxed at his sermon on the mount,
Your tall pale mother with her talking eyes,
And new-found agate urns as fresh as day,
And marble's language, Latin pure, discreet,
— Aha, ELUCESCEBAT quoth our friend?
No Tully, said I, Ulpian at the best!   100
Evil and brief hath been my pilgrimage.

All *lapis*, all, sons! Else I give the Pope
My villas! Will ye ever eat my heart?
Ever your eyes were as a lizard's quick,
They glitter like your mother's for my soul,
Or ye would heighten my impoverished frieze.
Piece out its starved design, and fill my vase
With grapes, and add a vizor and a Term,
And to the tripod ye would tie a lynx
That in his struggle throws the thyrsus down, 110
To comfort me on my entablature
Whereon I am to lie till I must ask
"Do I live, am I dead?" There, leave me, there!
For ye have stabbed me with ingratitude
To death — ye wish it — God, ye wish it! Stone —
Gritstone, a-crumble! Clammy squares which sweat
As if the corpse they keep were oozing through —
And no more *lapis* to delight the world!
Well, go! I bless ye. Fewer tapers there,
But in a row: and, going, turn your backs 120
— Ay, like departing altar-ministrants,
And leave me in my church, the church for peace
That I may watch at leisure if he leers —
Old Gandolf at me, from his onion-stone,
As still he envied me, so fair she was!

A TOCCATA OF GALUPPI'S.

I.

OH Galuppi, Baldassaro, this is very sad to find!
 I can hardly misconceive you; it would prove me deaf and blind;
But altho' I take your meaning, 't is with such a heavy mind!

II.

Here you come with your old music, and here 's all the good it brings.
What, they lived once thus at Venice where the merchants were the
  kings,
Where St. Mark's is, where the Doges used to wed the sea with rings?

III.

Ay, because the sea 's the street there; and 't is arched by . . .
  what you call
 . . . Shylock's bridge with houses on it, where they kept the
  carnival:
I was never out of England — it 's as if I saw it all.

IV.

Did young people take their pleasure when the sea was warm in
　　May?　　　　　　　　　　　　　　　　　　　　　　　　10
Balls and masks begun at midnight, burning ever to mid-day,
When they made up fresh adventures for the morrow, do you say?

V.

Was a lady such a lady, cheeks so round and lips so red,—
On her neck the small face buoyant, like a bell-flower on its bed,
O'er the breast's superb abundance where a man might base his head?

VI.

Well, and it was graceful of them: they'd break talk off and afford
— She, to bite her mask's black velvet— he, to finger on his sword,
While you sat and played Toccatas, stately at the clavichord?

VII.

What? Those lesser thirds so plaintive, sixths diminished, sigh on
　　sigh,
Told them something? Those suspensions, those solutions — "Must
　　we die?"　　　　　　　　　　　　　　　　　　　　　　20
Those commiserating sevenths — "Life might last! we can but try!"

VIII.

"Were you happy?"—"Yes."—"And are you still as happy?"—
　　"Yes. And you?"
— "Then, more kisses!"—"Did *I* stop them, when a million seemed
　　so few?"
Hark, the dominant's persistence till it must be answered to!

IX.

So, an octave struck the answer. Oh, they praised you, I dare say!
"Brave Galuppi! that was music! good alike at grave and gay!
I can always leave off talking when I hear a master play!"

X.

Then they left you for their pleasure: till in due time, one by one,
Some with lives that came to nothing, some with deeds as well undone,
Death stepped tacitly and took them where they never see the
　　sun.　　　　　　　　　　　　　　　　　　　　　　　　30

XI.

But when I sit down to reason, think to take my stand nor swerve,
While I triumph o'er a secret wrung from nature's close reserve,
In you come with your cold music till I creep thro' every nerve.

XII.

Yes, you, like a ghostly cricket, creaking where a house was burned:
" Dust and ashes, dead and done with, Venice spent what Venice
    earned.
The soul, doubtless, is immortal — where a soul can be discerned.

XIII.

" Yours for instance: you know physics, something of geology,
Mathematics are your pastime; souls shall rise in their degree;
Butterflies may dread extinction, — you 'll not die, it can not be !

XIV.

" As for Venice and her people, merely born to bloom and drop,   40
Here on earth they bore their fruitage, mirth and folly were the crop:
What of soul was left, I wonder, when the kissing had to stop?

XV.

" Dust and ashes!"   So you creak it, and I want the heart to scold.
Dear dead women, with such hair, too — what 's become of all the
    gold
Used to hang and brush their bosoms?   I feel chilly and grown old.

HOW IT STRIKES A CONTEMPORARY

I ONLY knew one poet in my life:
And this, or something like it, was his way.

  You saw go up and down Valladolid,
A man of mark, to know next time you saw.
His very serviceable suit of black
Was courtly once and conscientious still,
And many might have worn it, tho' none did:
The cloak, that somewhat shone and showed the threads,
Had purpose, and the ruff, significance.
He walked, and tapped the pavement with his cane,   ·   10
Scenting the world, looking it full in face,

An old dog, bald and blindish, at his heels.
They turned up, now, the alley by the church,
That leads no whither ; now, they breathed themselves
On the main promenade just at the wrong time :
You 'd come upon his scrutinizing hat,
Making a peaked shade blacker than itself
Against the single window spared some house
Intact yet with its mouldered Moorish work, —
Or else surprise the ferrel of his stick   20
Trying the mortar's temper 'tween the chinks
Of some new shop a-building, French and fine.
He stood and watched the cobbler at his trade,
The man who slices lemons into drink,
The coffee-roaster's brazier, and the boys
That volunteer to help him turn its winch.
He glanced o'er books on stalls with half an eye,
And fly-leaf ballads on the vendor's string,
And broad-edge bold-print posters by the wall.
He took such cognizance of men and things,   30
If any beat a horse, you felt he saw ;
If any cursed a woman, he took note ;
Yet stared at nobody, — you stared at him,
And found, less to your pleasure than surprise,
He seemed to know you and expect as much.
So, next time that a neighbour's tongue was loosed,
It marked the shameful and notorious fact
We had among us, not so much a spy
As a recording chief-inquisitor,
The town's true master if the town but knew !   40
We merely kept a governor for form,
While this man walked about and took account
Of all thought, said and acted, then went home,
And wrote it fully to our Lord the King
Who has an itch to know things, he knows why,
And reads them in his bed-room of a night.
Oh, you might smile ! there wanted not a touch,
A tang of . . . well, it was not wholly ease
As back into your mind the man's look came.
Stricken in years a little — such a brow   50
His eyes had to live under ! — clear as flint
On either side the formidable nose
Curved, cut and coloured like an eagle's claw.
Had he to do with A's surprising fate ?
When altogether old B disappeared
And young C got his mistress, — was 't our friend,
His letter to the King, that did it all ?
What paid the bloodless man for so much pains ?
Our Lord the King has favourites manifold,

And shifts his ministry some once a month; 60
Our city gets new governors at whiles, —
But never word or sign, that I could hear,
Notified to this man about the streets,
The King's approval of those letters conned
The last thing duly at the dead of night.
Did the man love his office? Frowned our Lord,
Exhorting when none heard — " Beseech me not!
Too far above my people, — beneath me!
I set the watch, — how should the people know?
Forget them, keep me all the more in mind!" 70
Was some such understanding 'twixt the two?

I found no truth in one report at least —
That if you tracked him to his home, down lanes
Beyond the Jewry, and as clean to pace,
You found he ate his supper in a room
Blazing with lights, four Titians on the wall,
And twenty naked girls to change his plate!
Poor man, he lived another kind of life
In that new stuccoed third house by the bridge,
Fresh-painted, rather smart than otherwise! 80
The whole street might o'erlook him as he sat,
Leg crossing leg, one foot on the dog's back,
Playing a decent cribbage with his maid
(Jacynth, you 're sure her name was) o'er the cheese
And fruit, three red halves of starved winter-pears,
Or treat of radishes in April. Nine,
Ten, struck the church clock, straight to bed went he.

My father, like the man of sense he was,
Would point him out to me a dozen times;
" St — St," he 'd whisper, " the Corregidor!" 90
I had been used to think that personage
Was one with lacquered breeches, lustrous belt,
And feathers like a forest in his hat,
Who blew a trumpet and proclaimed the news,
Announced the bull-fights, gave each church its turn,
And memorized the miracle in vogue!
He had a great observance from us boys;
We were in error; that was not the man.

I 'd like now, yet had haply been afraid,
To have just looked, when this man came to die, 100
And seen who lined the clean gay garret sides,
And stood about the neat low truckle-bed,
With the heavenly manner of relieving guard.

L

Here had been, mark, the general-in-chief,
Thro' a whole campaign of the world's life and death,
Doing the King's work all the dim day long,
In his old coat and up to knees in mud,
Smoked like a herring, dining on a crust, —
And, now the day was won, relieved at once!
No further show or need for that old coat,   110
You are sure, for one thing!   Bless us, all the while
How sprucely we are dressed out, you and I!
A second, and the angels alter that.
Well, I could never write a verse, — could you?
Let 's to the Prado and make the most of time.

—•◦•—

PROTUS.

A MONG these latter busts we count by scores,
Half-emperors and quarter-emperors,
Each with his bay-leaf fillet, loose-thonged vest,
Loric and low-browed Gorgon on the breast, —
One loves a baby face, with violets there,
Violets instead of laurel in the hair,
As those were all the little locks could bear.

Now read here, " Protus ends a period
Of empery beginning with a god ;
Born in the porphyry chamber at Byzant,   10
Queens by his cradle, proud and ministrant :
And if he quickened breath there, 't would like fire
Pantingly thro' the dim vast realm transpire.
A fame that he was missing, spread afar :
The world from its four corners rose in war,
Till he was borne out on a balcony
To pacify the world when it should see.
The captains ranged before him, one, his hand
Made baby points at, gained the chief command.
And day by day more beautiful he grew   20
In shape, all said, in feature and in hue,
While young Greek sculptors gazing on the child
Became with old Greek sculpture reconciled.
Already sages laboured to condense
In easy tomes a life's experience :
And artists took grave counsel to impart
In one breath and one hand-sweep, all their art,
To make his graces prompt as blossoming
Of plentifully-watered palms in spring :

Since well beseems it, whoso mounts the throne, 30
For beauty, knowledge, strength, should stand alone,
And mortals love the letters of his name."

—Stop! Have you turned two pages? Still the same.
New reign, same date. The scribe goes on to say
How that same year, on such a month and day,
"John the Pannonian, groundedly believed
A blacksmith's bastard, whose hard hand reprieved
The Empire from its fate the year before, —
Came, had a mind to take the crown, and wore
The same for six years (during which the Huns 40
Kept off their fingers from us), till his sons
Put something in his liquor"—and so forth.
Then a new reign. Stay—"Take at its just worth "
(Subjoins an annotator) "what I give
As hearsay. Some think, John let Protus live
And slip away. 'T is said, he reached man's age
At some blind northern court; made, first a page,
Then tutor to the children; last, of use
About the hunting stables. I deduce
He wrote the little tract 'On worming dogs,' 50
Whereof the name in sundry catalogues
Is extant yet. A Protus of the race
Is rumoured to have died a monk in Thrace, —
And, if the same, he reached senility."

Here 's John the Smith's rough-hammered head. Great eye,
Gross jaw and griped lips do what granite can
To give you the crown-grasper. What a man!

———◆———

MASTER HUGUES OF SAXE-GOTHA.

I.

HIST, but a word, fair and soft!
Forth and be judged, Master Hugues!
Answer the question I 've put you so oft:
    What do you mean by your mountainous fugues?
See, we 're alone in the loft, —

II.

I, the poor organist here,
    Hugues, the composer of note,

Dead though, and done with, this many a year:
  Let 's have a colloquy, something to quote,
Make the world prick up its ear!   10

III.

See, the church empties apace:
  Fast they extinguish the lights.
Hallo there, sacristan! Five minutes' grace!
  Here 's a crank pedal wants setting to rights,
Balks one of holding the base.

IV.

See, our huge house of the sounds,
  Hushing its hundreds at once,
Bids the last loiterer back to his bounds!
  — O you may challenge them, not a response
Get the church-saints on their rounds!   20

V.

(Saints go their rounds, who shall doubt?
  — March, with the moon to admire,
Up nave, down chancel, turn transept about,
  Supervise all betwixt pavement and spire,
Put rats and mice to the rout —

VI.

Aloys and Jurien and Just —
  Order things back to their place,
Have a sharp eye lest the candlesticks rust,
  Rub the church-plate, darn the sacrament-lace,
Clear the desk-velvet of dust.)   30

VII.

Here 's your book, younger folks shelve!
  Played I not off-hand and runningly,
Just now, your masterpiece, hard number twelve?
  Here 's what should strike, could one handle it cunningly:
Help 'he axe, give it a helve!

VIII.

Page after page as I played,
  Every bar's rest, where one wipes
Sweat from one's brow, I looked up and surveyed,
  O'er my three claviers, yon forest of pipes
Whence you still peeped in the shade.   40

IX.

Sure you were wishful to speak?
　You, with brow ruled like a score,
Yes, and eyes buried in pits on each cheek,
　Like two great breves, as they wrote them of yore,
Each side that bar, your straight beak!

X.

Sure you said — " Good, the mere notes!
　Still, couldst thou take my intent,
Know what procured me our Company's votes —
　A master were lauded and sciolists shent,
Parted the sheep from the goats!"

50

XI.

Well then, speak up, never flinch!
　Quick, ere my candle 's a snuff
— Burnt, do you see? to its uttermost inch —
　I believe in you, but that 's not enough:
Give my conviction a clinch!

XII.

First you deliver your phrase
　— Nothing propound, that I see,
Fit in itself for much blame or much praise —
　Answered no less, where no answer needs be:
Off start the Two on their ways.

60

XIII.

Straight must a Third interpose,
　Volunteer needlessly help;
In strikes a Fourth, a Fifth thrusts in his nose,
　So the cry 's open, the kennel 's a-yelp,
Argument 's hot to the close.

XIV.

One dissertates, he is candid;
　Two must discept, — has distinguished
Three helps the couple, if ever yet man did;
　Four protests; Five makes a dart at the thing wished:
Back to One, goes the case bandied.

70

XV.

One says his say with a difference;
　More of expounding, explaining!

All now is wrangle, abuse and vociferance;
  Now there 's a truce, all 's subdued, self-restraining:
Five, though, stands out all the stiffer hence.

XVI.

One is incisive, corrosive;
  Two retorts, nettled, curt, crepitant;
Three makes rejoinder, expansive, explosive;
  Four overbears them all, strident and strepitant:
Five . . O Danaides, O Sieve!   80

XVII.

Now, they ply axes and crowbars;
  Now, they prick pins at a tissue
Fine as a skein of the casuist Escobar's
  Worked on the bone of a lie.   To what issue?
Where is our gain at the Two-bars?

XVIII.

Est fuga, volvitur rota.
  On we drift: where looms the dim port?
One, Two, Three, Four, Five, contribute their quota;
  Something is gained, if one caught but the import —
Show it us, Hugues of Saxe-Gotha!   90

XIX.

What with affirming, denying,
  Holding, risposting, subjoining,
All 's like . . . . it 's like . . . . for an instance I 'm
    trying . . .
  There! See our roof, its gilt moulding and groining
Under those spider-webs lying!

XX.

So your fugue broadens and thickens,
  Greatens and deepens and lengthens,
Till we exclaim — "But where 's music, the dickens?
  Blot ye the gold, while your spider-web strengthens
— Blacked to the stoutest of tickens?"   100

XXI.

I for man's effort am zealous:
  Prove me such censure unfounded!

Seems it surprising a lover grows jealous —
  Hopes 't was for something, his organ pipes sounded
Tiring three boys at the bellows?

XXII.

Is it your moral of Life?
  Such a web, simple and subtle,
Weave we on earth here in impotent strife,
  Backward and forward each throwing his shuttle,
Death ending all with a knife?   110

XXIII.

Over our heads truth and nature —
  Still our life's zigzags and dodges,
Ins and outs, weaving a new legislature —
  God's gold just shining its last where that lodges,
Palled beneath man's usurpature.

XXIV.

So we o'ershroud stars and roses,
  Cherub and trophy and garland ;
Nothings grow something which quietly closes
  Heaven's earnest eye : not a glimpse of the far land
Gets thro' our comments and glozes.   120

XXV.

Ah but traditions, inventions,
  (Say we and make up a visage)
So many men with such various intentions,
  Down the past ages, must know more than this age!
Leave we the web its dimensions!

XXVI.

Who thinks Hugues wrote for the deaf,
  Proved a mere mountain in labour?
Better submit ; try again ; what 's the clef?
  'Faith, 't is no trifle for pipe and for tabor —
Four flats, the minor in F.   130

XXVII.

Friend, your fugue taxes the finger :
  Learning it once, who would lose it?
Yet all the while a misgiving will linger,
  Truth 's golden o'er us altho' we refuse it —
Nature, thro' cobwebs we string her.

XXVIII.

Hugues! I advise *meâ pœnâ*
   (Counterpoint glares like a Gorgon)
Bid One, Two, Three, Four, Five, clear the arena!
   Say the word, straight I unstop the full-organ,
Blare out the *mode Palestrina*.   140

XXIX.

While in the roof, if I 'm right there,
   . . . Lo you, the wick in the socket!
Hallo, you sacristan, show us a light there!
   Down it dips, gone like a rocket.
What, you want, do you, to come unawares,
Sweeping the church up for first morning-prayers,
And find a poor devil has ended his cares
At the foot of your rotten-runged rat-riddled stairs?
   Do I carry the moon in my pocket?

ABT VOGLER.

(AFTER HE HAS BEEN EXTEMPORIZING UPON THE MUSICAL INSTRUMENT OF HIS INVENTION.)

I.

WOULD that the structure brave, the manifold music I build,
   Bidding my organ obey, calling its keys to their work,
Claiming each slave of the sound, at a touch, as when Solomon willed
   Armies of angels that soar, legions of demons that lurk,
Man, brute, reptile, fly, — alien of end and of aim,
   Adverse, each from the other heaven-high, hell-deep removed, —
Should rush into sight at once as he named the ineffable Name,
   And pile him a palace straight, to pleasure the princess he loved!

II.

Would it might tarry like his, the beautiful building of mine,
   This which my keys in a crowd pressed and importuned to raise! 10
Ah, one and all, how they helped, would dispart now and now combine,
   Zealous to hasten the work, heighten their master his praise!
And one would bury his brow with a blind plunge down to hell,
   Burrow awhile and build, broad on the roots of things,
Then up again swim into sight, having based me my palace well,
   Founded it, fearless of flame, flat on the nether springs.

III.

And another would mount and march, like the excellent minion he
   was,
    Ay, another and yet another, one crowd but with many a crest,
Raising my rampired walls of gold as transparent as glass,
    Eager to do and die, yield each his place to the rest: 20
For higher still and higher (as a runner tips with fire,
    When a great illumination surprises a festal night—
Outlining round and round Rome's dome from space to spire)
    Up, the pinnacled glory reached, and the pride of my soul was in
    sight.

IV.

In sight? Not half! for it seemed, it was certain, to match man's
    birth,
    Nature in turn conceived, obeying an impulse as I ;
And the emulous heaven yearned down, made effort to reach the
  earth,
    As the earth had done her best, in my passion, to scale the sky:
Novel splendours burst forth, grew familiar and dwelt with mine,
    Not a point nor peak but found and fixed its wandering star ;   30
Meteor-moons, balls of blaze: and they did not pale nor pine,
    For earth had attained to heaven, there was no more near nor far.

V.

Nay more ; for there wanted not who walked in the glare and glow,
    Presences plain in the place ; or, fresh from the Protoplast,
Furnished for ages to come, when a kindlier wind should blow,
    Lured now to begin and live, in a house to their liking at last ;
Or else the wonderful Dead who have passed thro' the body and
  gone,
    But were back once more to breathe in an old world worth their
    new :
What never had been, was now ; what was, as it shall be anon ;
    And what is, — shall I say, matched both? for I was made per-
    fect too.   40

VI.

All thro' my keys that gave their sounds to a wish of my soul,
    All thro' my soul that praised as its wish flowed visibly forth,
All thro' music and me ! For think, had I painted the whole,
    Why, there it had stood, to see, nor the process so wonder-worth :
Had I written the same, made verse — still, effect proceeds from
  cause,
    Ye know why the forms are fair, ye hear how the tale is told ;
It is all triumphant art, but art in obedience to laws,
    Painter and poet are proud, in the artist-list enrolled : —

VII.

But here is the finger of God, a flash of the will that can,
   Existent behind all laws, that made them, and, lo, they are!   50
And I know not if, save in this, such gift be allowed to man,
   That out of three sounds he frame, not a fourth sound, but a star.
Consider it well: each tone of our scale in itself is naught;
   It is everywhere in the world — loud, soft, and all is said:
Give it to me to use! I mix it with two in my thought,
   And, there! Ye have heard and seen: consider and bow the head!

VIII.

Well, it is gone at last, the palace of music I reared;
   Gone! and the good tears start, the praises that come too slow;
For one is assured at first, one scarce can say that he feared,
   That he even gave it a thought, the gone thing was to go.   60
Never to be again! But many more of the kind
   As good, nay, better perchance: is this your comfort to me?
To me, who must be saved because I cling with my mind
   To the same, same self, same love, same God: ay, what was, shall be.

IX.

Therefore to whom turn I but to Thee, the ineffable Name?
   Builder and maker, thou, of houses not made with hands!
What, have fear of change from thee who art ever the same?
   Doubt that thy power can fill the heart that thy power expands?
There shall never be one lost good! What was, shall live as before;
   The evil is null, is naught, is silence implying sound;   70
What was good, shall be good, with, for evil, so much good more;
   On the earth the broken arcs; in the heaven, a perfect round.

X.

All we have willed or hoped or dreamed of good shall exist;
   Not its semblance, but itself; no beauty, nor good, nor power
Whose voice has gone forth, but each survives for the melodist,
   When eternity affirms the conception of an hour.
The high that proved too high, the heroic for earth too hard,
   The passion that left the ground to lose itself in the sky,
Are music sent up to God by the lover and the bard;
   Enough that he heard it once: we shall hear it by-and-by.   80

XI.

And what is our failure here but a triumph's evidence
   For the fulness of the days? Have we withered or agonized?
Why else was the pause prolonged but that singing might issue thence?
   Why rushed the discords in but that harmony should be prized?

Sorrow is hard to bear, and doubt is slow to clear,
    Each sufferer says his say, his scheme of the weal and woe:
But God has a few of us whom he whispers in the ear;
    The rest may reason and welcome; 't is we musicians know.

XII.

Well, it is earth with me; silence resumes her reign:
    I will be patient and proud, and soberly acquiesce.   90
Give me the keys. I feel for the common chord again,
    Sliding by semitones, till I sink to the minor, — yes,
And I blunt it into a ninth, and I stand on alien ground,
    Surveying awhile the heights I rolled from into the deep:
Which, hark, I have dared and done, for my resting-place is found,
    The C Major of this life: so, now I will try to sleep.

TWO IN THE CAMPAGNA.

I.

I WONDER do you feel to-day
    As I have felt since, hand in hand,
We sat down on the grass, to stray
    In spirit better thro' the land,
This morn of Rome and May?

II.

For me, I touched a thought, I know,
    Has tantalized me many times,
(Like turns of thread the spiders throw
    Mocking across our path) for rhymes
To catch at and let go.   10

III.

Help me to hold it! First it left
    The yellowing fennel, run to seed
There, branching from the brickwork's cleft,
    Some old tomb's ruin: yonder weed
Took up the floating weft,

IV.

Where one small orange cup amassed
    Five beetles, — blind and green they grope

Among the honey-meal : and last,
   Everywhere on the grassy slope,
I traced it.   Hold it fast!   20

V.

The champaign with its endless fleece
   Of feathery grasses everywhere!
Silence and passion, joy and peace,
   An everlasting wash of air —
Rome's ghost since her decease.

VI.

Such life here, thro' such lengths of hours,
   Such miracles performed in play,
Such primal naked forms of flowers,
   Such letting nature have her way
While heaven looks from its towers!   30

VII.

How say you?   Let us, O my dove,
   Let us be unashamed of soul,
As earth lies bare to heaven above!
   How is it under our control
To love or not to love?

VIII.

I would that you were all to me,
   You that are just so much, no more.
Nor yours nor mine, nor slave nor free!
   Where does the fault lie?   What the core
O' the wound, since wound must be?   40

IX.

I would I could adopt your will,
   See with your eyes, and set my heart
Beating by yours, and drink my fill
   At your soul's springs, — your part my part
In life, for good and ill.

X.

No.   I yearn upward, touch you close,
   Then stand away.   I kiss your cheek,
Catch your soul's warmth, — I pluck the rose
   And love it more than tongue can speak —
Then the good minute goes.

XI.

Already how am I so far
　　Out of that minute? Must I go
Still like the thistle-ball, no bar,
　　Onward, whenever light winds blow,
Fixed by no friendly star?

XII.

Just when I seemed about to learn!
　　Where is the thread now? Off again.
The old trick! Only I discern —
　　Infinite passion, and the pain
Of finite hearts that yearn.

60

"DE GUSTIBUS—"

I.

YOUR ghost will walk, you lover of trees,
　　(If our loves remain)
　　　In an English lane,
By a cornfield-side a-flutter with poppies.
Hark, those two in the hazel coppice —
A boy and a girl, if the good fates please,
　　Making love, say, —
　　　The happier they!
Draw yourself up from the light of the moon,
And let them pass, as they will too soon,
　　With the beanflower's boon,
　　And the blackbird's tune,
　　And May, and June!

10

II.

What I love best in all the world
Is a castle, precipice-encurled,
In a gash of the wind-grieved Apennine.
Or look for me, old fellow of mine,
(If I get my head from out the mouth
O' the grave, and loose my spirit's bands,
And come again to the land of lands) —
In a sea-side house to the farther South,
Where the baked cicala dies of drouth,
And one sharp tree — 'tis a cypress — stands,
By the many hundred years red-rusted,

20

Rough iron-spiked, ripe fruit-o'ercrusted
My sentinel to guard the sands
To the water's edge.   For, what expands
Before the house, but the great opaque
Blue breadth of sea without a break?
While, in the house, for ever crumbles   30
Some fragment of the frescoed walls,
From blisters where a scorpion sprawls.
A girl bare-footed brings, and tumbles
Down on the pavement, green-flesh melons,
And says there 's news to-day — the king
Was shot at, touched in the liver-wing,
Goes with his Bourbon arm in a sling:
— She hopes they have not caught the felons.
Italy, my Italy!
Queen Mary's saying serves for me —   40
        (When fortune's malice
        Lost her, Calais)
Open my heart and you will see
Graved inside of it, " Italy."
Such lovers old are I and she:
So it always was, so shall ever be!

------◦◦------

THE GUARDIAN-ANGEL.

A PICTURE AT FANO.

I.

D EAR and great Angel, wouldst thou only leave
        That child, when thou hast done with him, for me!
Let me sit all the day here, that when eve
    Shall find performed thy special ministry,
And time come for departure, thou, suspending
Thy flight, mayst see another child for tending,
    Another still to quiet and retrieve.

II.

Then I shall feel thee step one step, no more,
    From where thou standest now, to where I gaze.
— And suddenly my head is covered o'er   10
    With those wings, white above the child who prays
Now on that tomb — and I shall feel thee guarding
Me, out of all the world ; for me, discarding
    Yon heaven thy home, that waits and opes its door.

III.

I would not look up thither past thy head
   Because the door opes, like that child, I know,
For I should have thy gracious face instead,
   Thou bird of God! And wilt thou bend me low
Like him, and lay, like his, my hands together,
And lift them up to pray, and gently tether   20
   Me, as thy lamb there, with thy garment's spread?

IV.

If this was ever granted, I would rest
   My head beneath thine, while thy healing hands
Close-covered both my eyes beside thy breast,
   Pressing the brain which too much thought expands,
Back to its proper size again, and smoothing
Distortion down till every nerve had soothing,
   And all lay quiet, happy and suppressed.

V.

How soon all worldly wrong would be repaired!
   I think how I should view the earth and skies   30
And sea, when once again my brow was bared
   After thy healing, with such different eyes.
O world, as God has made it! All is beauty:
And knowing this is love, and love is duty.
   What further may be sought for or declared?

VI.

Guercino drew this angel I saw teach
   (Alfred, dear friend!) — that little child to pray,
Holding the little hands up, each to each
   Pressed gently, — with his own head turned away
Over the earth where so much lay before him   40
Of work to do, tho' heaven was opening o'er him,
   And he was left at Fano by the beach.

VII.

We were at Fano, and three times we went
   To sit and see him in his chapel there,
And drink his beauty to our soul's content
   — My angel with me too: and since I care
For dear Guercino's fame (to which in power
And glory comes this picture for a dower,
   Fraught with a pathos so magnificent) —

VIII.

And since he did not work thus earnestly   50
    At all times, and has else endured some wrong —
I took one thought his picture struck from me,
    And spread it out, translating it to song.
My love is here.   Where are you, dear old friend?
How rolls the Wairoa at your world's far end?
    This is Ancona, yonder is the sea.

EVELYN HOPE.

I.

BEAUTIFUL Evelyn Hope is dead!
    Sit and watch by her side an hour.
That is her book-shelf, this her bed;
    She plucked that piece of geranium-flower,
Beginning to die too, in the glass;
    Little has yet been changed, I think:
The shutters are shut, no light may pass
    Save two long rays thro' the hinge's chink.

II.

Sixteen years old when she died!
    Perhaps she had scarcely heard my name;   10
It was not her time to love; beside,
    Her life had many a hope and aim,
Duties enough and little cares,
    And now was quiet, now astir,
Till God's hand beckoned unawares, —
    And the sweet white brow is all of her.

III.

Is it too late then, Evelyn Hope?
    What, your soul was pure and true,
The good stars met in your horoscope,
    Made you of spirit, fire and dew —   20
And, just because I was thrice as old
    And our paths in the world diverged so wide,
Each was naught to each, must I be told?
    We were fellow mortals, naught beside?

IV.

No, indeed! for God above
    Is great to grant, as mighty to make,

And creates the love to reward the love :
    I claim you still, for my own love's sake!
Delayed it may be for more lives yet,
    Thro' worlds I shall traverse, not a few :   30
Much is to learn, much to forget
    Ere the time be come for taking you.

V.

But the time will come, at last it will,
    When, Evelyn Hope, what meant (I shall say)
In the lower earth, in the years long still,
    That body and soul so pure and gay?
Why your hair was amber, I shall divine,
    And your mouth of your own geranium's red—
And what you would do with me, in fine,
    In the new life come in the old one's stead.   40

VI.

I have lived (I shall say) so much since then,
    Given up myself so many times,
Gained me the gains of various men,
    Ransacked the ages, spoiled the climes ;
Yet one thing, one, in my soul's full scope,
    Either I missed or itself missed me :
And I want and find you, Evelyn Hope!
    What is the issue? let us see!

VII.

I loved you, Evelyn, all the while!
    My heart seemed full as it could hold ;   50
There was place and to spare for the frank young
        smile,
    And the red young mouth, and the hair's young
        gold.
So hush, — I will give you this leaf to keep :
    See, I shut it inside the sweet cold hand!
There, that is our secret : go to sleep!
    You will wake, and remember, and understand

M

MEMORABILIA.

I.

AH, did you once see Shelley plain,
    And did he stop and speak to you
And did you speak to him again?
    How strange it seems and new!

II.

But you were living before that,
    And also you are living after;
And the memory I started at —
    My starting moves your laughter!

III.

I crossed a moor, with a name of its own
    And a certain use in the world, no doubt,   10
Yet a hand's-breadth of it shines alone
    'Mid the blank miles round about:

IV.

For there I picked up on the heather
    And there I put inside my breast
A moulted feather, an eagle-feather!
    Well, I forget the rest.

———

APPARENT FAILURE.

" We shall soon lose a celebrated building."
                                    Paris Newspaper.

I.

NO, for I 'll save it!   Seven years since,
    I passed thro' Paris, stopped a day
To see the baptism of your Prince;
    Saw, made my bow, and went my way:
Walking the heat and headache off,
    I took the Seine-side, you surmise,
Thought of the Congress, Gortschakoff,
    Cavour's appeal and Buol's replies,
So sauntered till — what met my eyes?

II.

Only the Doric little Morgue!   10
   The dead-house where you show your drowned :
Petrarch's Vaucluse makes proud the Sorgue,
   Your Morgue has made the Seine renowned.
One pays one's debt in such a case ;
   I plucked up heart and entered, — stalked,
Keeping a tolerable face
   Compared with some whose cheeks were chalked :
Let them!   No Briton 's to be balked!

III.

First came the silent gazers ; next,
   A screen of glass, we 're thankful for ;   20
Last, the sight's self, the sermon's text,
   The three men who did most abhor
Their life in Paris yesterday,
   So killed themselves : and now, enthroned
Each on his copper couch, they lay
   Fronting me, waiting to be owned.
I thought, and think, their sin 's atoned.

IV.

Poor men, God made, and all for that!
   The reverence struck me ; o'er each head
Religiously was hung its hat,   30
   Each coat dripped by the owner's bed,
Sacred from touch : each had his berth,
   His bounds, his proper place of rest,
Who last night tenanted on earth
   Some arch, where twelve such slept abreast, —
Unless the plain asphalt seemed best.

V.

How did it happen, my poor boy?
   You wanted to be Buonaparte
And have the Tuileries for toy,
   And could not, so it broke your heart?   40
You, old one by his side, I judge,
   Were, red as blood, a socialist,
A leveller!   Does the Empire grudge
   You 've gained what no Republic missed?
Be quiet, and unclench your fist!

VI.

And this — why, he was red in vain,
   Or black, — poor fellow that is blue!

What fancy was it, turned your brain?
    Oh, women were the prize for you!
Money gets women, cards and dice   50
    Get money, and ill-luck gets just
The copper couch and one clear nice
    Cool squirt of water o'er your bust,
The right thing to extinguish lust!

VII.

It's wiser being good than bad;
    It's safer being meek than fierce:
It's fitter being sane than mad.
    My own hope is, a sun will pierce
The thickest cloud earth ever stretched;
    That, after Last, returns the First,
Tho' a wide compass round be fetched;
    That what began best, can't end worst,
    Nor what God blessed once, prove accurst.

———◆———

PROSPICE.

FEAR death? — to feel the fog in my throat,
    The mist in my face,
When the snows begin, and the blasts denote
    I am nearing the place,
The power of the night, the press of the storm,
    The post of the foe;
Where he stands, the Arch Fear in a visible form,
    Yet the strong man must go:
For the journey is done and the summit attained,
    And the barriers fall,   10
Tho' a battle 's to fight ere the guerdon be gained,
    The reward of it all.
I was ever a fighter, so — one fight more,
    The best and the last!
I would hate that death bandaged my eyes, and forbore,
    And bade me creep past.
No! let me taste the whole of it, fare like my peers
    The heroes of old,
Bear the brunt, in a minute pay glad life's arrears
    Of pain, darkness and cold.   20
For sudden the worst turns the best to the brave,
    The black minute 's at end,
And the elements' rage, the fiend-voices that rave,

Shall dwindle, shall blend,
Shall change, shall become first a peace out of pain,
   Then a light, then thy breast,
O thou soul of my soul!   I shall clasp thee again,
   And with God be the rest!

———◦◦———

"CHILDE ROLAND TO THE DARK TOWER CAME."

(See Edgar's song in "LEAR.")

I.

MY first thought was, he lied in every word,
   That hoary cripple, with malicious eye
   Askance to watch the working of his lie
On mine, and mouth scarce able to afford
Suppression of the glee, that pursed and scored
   Its edge, at one more victim gained thereby.

II.

What else should he be set for, with his staff?
   What, save to waylay with his lies, ensnare
   All travelers who might find him posted there,
And ask the road?   I guessed what skull-like laugh   10
Would break, what crutch 'gin write my epitaph
   For pastime in the dusty thoroughfare,

III.

If at his counsel I should turn aside
   Into that ominous tract which, all agree,
   Hides the Dark Tower.   Yet acquiescingly
I did turn as he pointed : neither pride
Nor hope rekindling at the end descried,
   So much as gladness that some end might be.

IV.

For, what with my whole world-wide wandering,
   What with my search drawn out thro' years, my hope   20
   Dwindled into a ghost not fit to cope
With that obstreperous joy success would bring, —
I hardly tried now to rebuke the spring
   My heart made, finding failure in its scope.

v.

As when a sick man very near to death
  Seems dead indeed, and feels begin and end
  The tears and takes the farewell of each friend,
And hears one bid the other go, draw breath
Freelier outside, (" since all is o'er," he saith,
  " And the blow fallen no grieving can amend ; ")   30

vi.

While some discuss if near the other graves
  Be room enough for this, and when a day
  Suits best for carrying the corpse away,
With care about the banners, scarves and staves :
And still the man hears all, and only craves
  He may not shame such tender love and stay.

vii.

Thus, I had so long suffered in this quest,
  Heard failure prophesied so oft, been writ
  So many times among " The Band " — to wit,
The knights who to the Dark Tower's search addressed   40
Their steps — that just to fail as they, seemed best,
  And all the doubt was now — should I be fit?

viii

So, quiet as despair, I turned from him,
  That hateful cripple, out of his highway
  Into the path he pointed.   All the day
Had been a dreary one at best, and dim
Was settling to its close, yet shot one grim
  Red leer to see the plain catch its estray.

ix.

For mark! no sooner was I fairly found
  Pledged to the plain, after a pace or two,   50
  Than, pausing to throw backward a last view
O'er the safe road, 't was gone ; gray plain all round :
Nothing but plain to the horizon's bound.
  I might go on ; naught else remained to do.

x.

So, on I went.   I think I never saw
  Such starved ignoble nature ; nothing throve :

For flowers — as well expect a cedar grove!
But cockle, spurge, according to their law
Might propagate their kind, with none to awe,
    You 'd think ; a burr had been a treasure trove.   60

XI.

No! penury, inertness and grimace,
    In some strange sort, were the land's portion.   "See
    Or shut your eyes," said Nature peevishly,
"It nothing skills : I can not help my case :
'T is the Last Judgment's fire must cure this place,
    Calcine its clods and set my prisoners free."

XII.

If there pushed any ragged thistle-stalk
    Above its mates, the head was chopped ; the bents
    Were jealous else.   What made those holes and rents
In the dock's harsh swarth leaves, bruised as to balk   70
All hope of greenness ? 't is a brute must walk
    Pashing their life out, with a brute's intents.

XIII.

As for the grass, it grew as scant as hair
    In leprosy ; thin dry blades pricked the mud
    Which underneath looked kneaded up with blood.
One stiff blind horse, his every bone a-stare,
Stood stupefied, however he came there :
    Thrust out past service from the devil's stud!

XIV.

Alive? he might be dead for aught I know,
    With that red gaunt and colloped neck a-strain,   80
    And shut eyes underneath the rusty mane ;
Seldom went such grotesqueness with such woe ;
I never saw a brute I hated so ;
    He must be wicked to deserve such pain.

XV.

I shut my eyes and turned them on my heart.
    As a man calls for wine before he fights,
    I asked one draught of earlier, happier sights,
Ere fitly I could hope to play my part.
Think first, fight afterwards — the soldier's art :
    One taste of the old time sets all to rights.   90

XVI.

Not it ! I fancied Cuthbert's reddening face
   Beneath its garniture of curly gold,
   Dear fellow, till I almost felt him fold
An arm in mine to fix me to the place,
That way he used.   Alas, one night's disgrace!
   Out went my heart's new fire and left it cold.

XVII.

Giles then, the soul of honour — there he stands .
   Frank as ten years ago when knighted first.
   What honest man should dare (he said) he durst.
Good — but the scene shifts — faugh! what hangman
      hands   100
Pin to his breast a parchment?   His own bands
   Read it.   Poor traitor, spit upon and curst!

XVIII.

Better this present than a past like that;
   Back therefore to my darkening path again!
   No sound, no sight as far as eye could strain.
Will the night send a howlet or a bat?
I asked : when something on the dismal flat
   Came to arrest my thoughts and change their train.

XIX.

A sudden little river crossed my path
   As unexpected as a serpent comes.   110
   No sluggish tide congenial to the glooms ;
This, as it frothed by, might have been a bath
For the fiend's glowing hoof — to see the wrath
   Of its black eddy bespate with flakes and spumes

XX.

So petty yet so spiteful!   All along,
   Low scrubby alders kneeled down over it ;
   Drenched willows flung them headlong in a fit
Of mute despair, a suicidal throng :
The river which had done them all the wrong,
   Whate'er that was, rolled by, deterred no whit.   120

XXI.

Which, while I forded, — good saints, how I feared
   To set my foot upon a dead man's cheek,
   Each step, or feel the spear I thrust to seek

For hollows, tangled in his hair or beard!
— It may have been a water-rat I speared,
   But, ugh! it sounded like a baby's shriek.

XXII.

Glad was I when I reached the other bank.
   Now for a better country. Vain presage!
   Who were the strugglers, what war did they wage
Whose savage trample thus could pad the dank   130
Soil to a plash? Toads in a poisoned tank,
   Or wild cats in a red-hot iron cage —

XXIII.

The fight must so have seemed in that fell cirque.
   What penned them there, with all the plain to choose?
   No foot-print leading to that horrid mews,
None out of it. Mad brewage set to work
Their brains, no doubt, like galley-slaves the Turk
   Pits for his pastime, Christians against Jews.

XXIV.

And more than that — a furlong on — why, there!
   What bad use was that engine for, that wheel,   140
   Or brake, not wheel — that harrow fit to reel
Men's bodies out like silk? with all the air
Of Tophet's tool, on earth left unaware,
   Or brought to sharpen its rusty teeth of steel.

XXV.

Then came a bit of stubbed ground, once a wood,
   Next a marsh, it would seem, and now mere earth
   Desperate and done with; (so a fool finds mirth,
Makes a thing and then mars it, till his mood
Changes and off he goes!) within a rood —
   Bog, clay, and rubble, sand and stark black dearth.   150

XXVI.

Now blotches rankling, coloured gay and grim,
   Now patches where some leanness of the soil's
   Broke into moss or substances like boils;
Then came some palsied oak, a cleft in him
Like a distorted mouth that splits its rim
   Gaping at death, and dies while it recoils.

XXVII.

And just as far as ever from the end,
    Naught in the distance but the evening, naught
    To point my footstep further!   At the thought,
A great black bird, Apollyon's bosom-friend,   160
Sailed past, nor beat his wide wing dragon-penned
    That brushed my cap — perchance the guide I sought.

XXVIII.

For, looking up, aware I somehow grew,
    'Spite of the dusk, the plain had given place
    All round to mountains — with such name to grace
Mere ugly heights and heaps now stolen in view.
How thus they had surprised me, — solve it, you!
    How to get from them was no clearer case.

XXIX.

Yet half I seemed to recognize some trick
    Of mischief happened to me, God knows when —   170
    In a bad dream perhaps.   Here ended, then,
Progress this way.   When, in the very nick
Of giving up, one time more, came a click
    As when a trap shuts — you 're inside the den.

XXX.

Burningly it came on me all at once.
    This was the place! those two hills on the right,
    Crouched like two bulls locked horn in horn in fight,
While, to the left, a tall scalped mountain . . . Dunce,
Dotard, a-dozing at the very nonce,
    After a life spent training for the sight!   180

XXXI.

What in the midst lay but the Tower itself?
    The round squat turret, blind as the fool's heart,
    Built of brown stone, without a counterpart
In the whole world.   The tempest's mocking elf
Points to the shipman thus the unseen shelf
    He strikes on, only when the timbers start.

XXXII.

Not see? because of night perhaps? — why, day
    Came back again for that! before it left,
    The dying sunset kindled thro' a cleft:

The hills, like giants at a hunting, lay,   190
Chin upon hand, to see the game at bay, —
    " Now stab and end the creature — to the heft! "

XXXIII.

Not hear? when noise was everywhere! it tolled
    Increasing like a bell.   Names in my ears
    Of all the lost adventurers my peers, —
How such a one was strong, and such was bold,
And such was fortunate, yet each of old
    Lost, lost! one moment knelled the woe of years.

XXXIV.

There they stood, ranged along the hill-sides, met
    To view the last of me, a living frame   200
    For one more picture! in a sheet of flame
I saw them and I knew them all.   And yet
Dauntless the slug-horn to my lips I set,
    And blew *" Childe Roland to the Dark Tower came."*

———•◦•———

A GRAMMARIAN'S FUNERAL.

SHORTLY AFTER THE REVIVAL OF LEARNING IN EUROPE.

LET us begin and carry up this corpse,
        Singing together.
Leave we the common crofts, the vulgar thorpes,
        Each in its tether
Sleeping safe on the bosom of the plain,
        Cared-for till cock-crow :
Look out if yonder be not day again
        Rimming the rock-row!
That 's the appropriate country ; there, man's thought,
        Rarer, intenser,   10
Self-gathered for an outbreak, as it ought,
        Chafes in the censer.
Leave we the unlettered plain its herd and crop ;
        Seek we sepulture
On a tall mountain, cited to the top,
        Crowded with culture!
All the peaks soar, but one the rest excels ;
        Clouds overcome it ;
No! yonder sparkle is the citadel's

Circling its summit.   20
Thither our path lies; wind we up the heights:
    Wait ye the warning?
Our low life was the level's and the night's:
    He's for the morning.
Step to a tune, square chests, erect each head,
    'Ware the beholders!
This is our master, famous calm and dead,
    Borne on our shoulders.

Sleep, crop and herd! sleep, darkling thorpe and croft
    Safe from the weather!   30
He, whom we convoy to his grave aloft,
    Singing together,
He was a man born with thy face and throat,
    Lyric Apollo!
Long he lived nameless: how should spring take note
    Winter would follow?
Till lo, the little touch, and youth was gone!
    Cramped and diminished,
Moaned he, "New measures, other feet anon!
    My dance is finished?"   40
No, that's the world's way; (keep the mountain-side,
    Make for the city!)
He knew the signal, and stepped on with pride
    Over men's pity;
Left play for work, and grappled with the world
    Bent on escaping:
"What's in the scroll," quoth he, "thou keepest furled?
    Show me their shaping,
Theirs who most studied man, the bard and sage, —
    Give!" — So, he gowned him,   50
Straight got by heart that book to its last page:
    Learned, we found him.
Yea, but we found him bald too, eyes like lead,
    Accents uncertain:
"Time to taste life," another would have said,
    "Up with the curtain!"
This man said rather, " Actual life comes next?
    Patience a moment!
Grant I have mastered learning's crabbed text,
    Still there's the comment.   60
Let me know all!   Prate not of most or least,
    Painful or easy!
Even to the crumbs I'd fain eat up the feast,
    Ay, nor feel queasy."
Oh, such a life as he resolved to live,
    When he had learned it,

When he had gathered all books had to give!
    Sooner, he spurned it.
Image the whole, then execute the parts—
    Fancy the fabric   70
Quite, ere you build, ere steel strike fire from quartz,
    Ere mortar dab brick!

(Here 's the town-gate reached ; there 's the market-place
    Gaping before us.)
● Yea, this in him was the peculiar grace
    (Hearten our chorus!)
That before living he 'd learn how to live —
    No end to learning:
Earn the means first — God surely will contrive
    Use for our earning.   80
Others mistrust and say, " But time escapes!
    Live now or never!"
He said, " What 's time? Leave Now for dogs and apes!
    Man has Forever."
Back to his book then: deeper drooped his head:
    Calculus racked him:
Leaden before, his eyes grew dross of lead:
    Tussis attacked him.
" Now, master, take a little rest!" — not he!
    (Caution redoubled!   90
Step two abreast, the way winds narrowly!)
    Not a whit troubled,
Back to his studies, fresher than at first,
    Fierce as a dragon
He (soul-hydroptic with a sacred thirst)
    Sucked at the flagon.
Oh, if we draw a circle premature,
    Heedless of far gain,
Greedy for quick returns of profit, sure
    Bad is our bargain!   100
Was it not great? did not he throw on God
    (He loves the burthen) —
God's task to make the heavenly period
    Perfect the earthen?
Did not he magnify the mind, show clear
    Just what it all meant?
He would not discount life, as fools do here,
    Paid by instalment.
He ventured neck or nothing — heaven's success
    Found, or earth's failure :   110
" Wilt thou trust death or not?" He answered " Yes!
    Hence with life's pale lure! "
That low man seeks a little thing to do,

> Sees it and does it :
> This high man, with a great thing to pursue,
> > Dies ere he knows it.
> That low man goes on adding one to one,
> > His hundred 's soon hit :
> This high man, aiming at a million,
> > Misses an unit. 120
> That, has the world here — should he need the next,
> > Let the world mind him!
> This, throws himself on God, and unperplexed
> > Seeking shall find him.
> So, with the throttling hands of death at strife,
> > Ground he at grammar ;
> Still, thro' the rattle, parts of speech were rife :
> > While he could stammer
> He settled *Hoti's* business — let it be ! —
> > Properly based *Oun* — 130
> Gave us the doctrine of the enclitic *De*,
> > Dead from the waist down.
> Well, here 's the platform, here 's the proper place :
> > Hail to your purlieus,
> All ye highfliers of the feathered race,
> > Swallows and curlews!
> Here 's the top-peak ; the multitude below
> > Live, for they can, there :
> This man decided not to Live but Know —
> > Bury this man there? 140
> Here — here 's his place, where meteors shoot, clouds form,
> > Lightnings are loosened,
> Stars come and go! Let joy break with the storm,
> > Peace let the dew send!
> Lofty designs must close in like effects :
> > Loftily lying,
> Leave him — still loftier than the world suspects,
> > Living and dying.

CLEON.

" As certain also of your own poets have said " —

CLEON the poet, (from the sprinkled isles,
Lily on lily, that o'erlace the sea,
And laugh their pride when the light wave lisps " Greece ") —
To Protus in his Tyranny : much health!

They give thy letter to me, even now:
I read and seem as if I heard thee speak.
The master of thy galley still unlades
Gift after gift; they block my court at last
And pile themselves along its portico
Royal with sunset, like a thought of thee;   10
And one white she-slave, from the group dispersed
Of black and white slaves, (like the chequer-work
Pavement, at once my nation's work and gift,
Now covered with this settle-down of doves)
One lyric woman, in her crocus vest
Woven of sea-wools, with her two white hands
Commends to me the strainer and the cup
Thy lip hath bettered ere it blesses mine.

Well-counselled, king, in thy munificence!
For so shall men remark, in such an act   20
Of love for him whose song gives life its joy,
Thy recognition of the use of life:
Nor call thy spirit barely adequate
To help on life in straight ways, broad enough
For vulgar souls, by ruling and the rest.
Thou, in the daily building of thy tower, —
Whether in fierce and sudden spasms of toil,
Or thro' dim lulls of unapparent growth,
Or when the general work, 'mid good acclaim,
Climbed with the eye to cheer the architect, —   30
Didst ne'er engage in work for mere work's sake:
Hadst ever in thy heart the luring hope
Of some eventual rest a-top of it,
Whence, all the tumult of the building hushed,
Thou first of men mightst look out to the East:
The vulgar saw thy tower, thou sawest the sun.
For this, I promise on thy festival
To pour libation, looking o'er the sea,
Making this slave narrate thy fortunes, speak
Thy great words and describe thy royal face —   40
Wishing thee wholly where Zeus lives the most,
Within the eventual element of calm.

Thy letter's first requirement meets me here.
It is as thou hast heard: in one short life
I, Cleon, have effected all those things
Thou wonderingly dost enumerate.
That epos on thy hundred plates of gold
Is mine, and also mine the little chant
So sure to rise from every fishing bark
When, lights at prow, the seamen haul their net.   50

The image of the sun-god on the phare,
Men turn from the sun's self to see, is mine;
The Pœcile, o'er-storied its whole length,
As thou didst hear, with painting, is mine too.
I know the true proportions of a man
And woman also, not observed before;
And I have written three books on the soul,
Proving absurd all written hitherto,
And putting us to ignorance again.
For music, — why, I have combined the moods,   60
Inventing one.   In brief, all arts are mine;
Thus much the people know and recognize,
Throughout our seventeen islands.   Marvel not!
We of these latter days, with greater mind
Than our forerunners, since more composite,
Look not so great, beside their simple way,
To a judge who only sees one way at once,
One mind-point and no other at a time, —
Compares the small part of a man of us
With some whole man of the heroic age,   70
Great in his way — not ours, nor meant for ours;
And ours is greater, had we skill to know:
For, what we call this life of men on earth,
This sequence of the soul's achievements here,
Being, as I find much reason to conceive,
Intended to be viewed eventually
As a great whole, not analyzed to parts,
But each part having reference to all, —
How shall a certain part, pronounced complete,
Endure effacement by another part?   80
Was the thing done? — then, what 's to do again?
See, in the chequered pavement opposite,
Suppose the artist made a perfect rhomb,
And next a lozenge, then a trapezoid —
He did not overlay them, superimpose
The new upon the old and blot it out,
But laid them on a level in his work,
Making at last a picture; there it lies.
So first the perfect separate forms were made,
The portions of mankind; and after, so,   90
Occurred the combination of the same.
For where had been a progress, otherwise?
Mankind, made up of all the single men, —
In such a synthesis the labour ends.
Now mark me ! those divine men of old time
Have reached, thou sayest well, each at one point
The outside verge that rounds our faculty;
And where they reached, who can do more than reach?

It takes but little water just to touch
At some one point the inside of a sphere. 100
And, as we turn the sphere, touch all the rest
In due succession: but the finer air
Which not so palpably nor obviously,
Though no less universally, can touch
The whole circumference of that emptied sphere,
Fills it more fully than the water did;
Holds thrice the weight of water in itself
Resolved into a subtler element.
And yet the vulgar call the sphere first full
Up to the visible height—and after, void; 110
Not knowing air's more hidden properties.
And thus our soul, misknown, cries out to Zeus
To vindicate his purpose in our life:
Why stay we on the earth unless to grow?
Long since, I imaged, wrote the fiction out,
That he or other god descended here
And, once for all, showed simultaneously
What, in its nature, never can be shown
Piecemeal or in succession: showed, I say,
The worth both absolute and relative 120
Of all his children from the birth of time,
His instruments for all appointed work.
I now go on to image,—might we hear
The judgment which should give the due to each,
Show where the labour lay and where the ease,
And prove Zeus' self, the latent everywhere!
This is a dream:—but no dream, let us hope,
That years and days, the summers and the springs,
Follow each other with unwaning powers.
The grapes which dye thy wine, are richer far 130
Thro' culture, than the wild wealth of the rock;
The suave plum than the savage-tasted drupe;
The pastured honey-bee drops choicer sweet;
The flowers turn double, and the leaves turn flowers;
That young and tender crescent moon, thy slave,
Sleeping above her robe as buoyed by clouds,
Refines upon the women of my youth.
What, and the soul alone deteriorates?
I have not chanted verse like Homer, no—
Nor swept string like Terpander, no—nor carved 140
And painted men like Phidias and his friend:
I am not great as they are, point by point.
But I have entered into sympathy
With these four, running these into one soul,
Who, separate, ignored each other's art.
Say, is it nothing that I know them all?

N

The wild flower was the larger; I have dashed
Rose-blood upon its petals, pricked its cup's
Honey with wine, and driven its seed to fruit,
And show a better flower if not so large: 150
I stand myself.   Refer this to the gods
Whose gift alone it is! which, shall I dare
(All pride apart) upon the absurd pretext
That such a gift by chance lay in my hand,
Discourse of lightly or depreciate?
It might have fallen to another's hand: what then?
I pass too surely: let at least truth stay!

And next, of what thou followest on to ask.
This being with me as I declare, O king,
My works in all these varicoloured kinds,   160
So done by me, accepted so by men —
Thou askest, if (my soul thus in men's hearts)
I must not be accounted to attain
The very crown and proper end of life ?
Inquiring thence how, now life closeth up,
I face death with success in my right hand:
Whether I fear death less than dost thyself
The fortunate of men?   "For" (writest thou)
"Thou leavest much behind, while I leave naught.
Thy life stays in the poems men shall sing,   170
The pictures men shall study; while my life,
Complete and whole now in its power and joy,
Dies altogether with my brain and arm,
Is lost indeed; since, what survives myself?
The brazen statue to o'erlook my grave,
Set on the promontory which I named.
And that — some supple courtier of my heir
Shall use its robed and sceptred arm, perhaps
To fix the rope to, which best drags it down.
I go then: triumph thou, who dost not go !"   180

Nay, thou art worthy of hearing my whole mind.
Is this apparent, when thou turn'st to muse
Upon the scheme of earth and man in chief,
That admiration grows as knowledge grows?
That imperfection means perfection hid,
Reserved in part, to grace the after-time?
If, in the morning of philosophy,
Ere aught had been recorded, nay perceived,
Thou, with the light now in thee, couldst have looked
On all earth's tenantry, from worm to bird,   190
Ere man, her last, appeared upon the stage —
Thou wouldst have seen them perfect, and deduced

The perfectness of others yet unseen.
Conceding which, — had Zeus then questioned thee
" Shall I go on a step, improve on this,
Do more for visible creatures than is done?"
Thou wouldst have answered, " Ay, by making each
Grow conscious in himself — by that alone.
All 's perfect else : the shell sucks fast the rock,
The fish strikes thro' the sea, the snake both swims   200
And slides, forth range the beasts, the birds take flight,
Till life's mechanics can no further go —
And all this joy in natural life is put
Like fire from off thy finger into each,
So exquisitely perfect is the same.
But 't is pure fire, and they mere matter are :
It has them, not they it ; and so I choose
For man, thy last premeditated work
(If I might add a glory to the scheme)
That a third thing should stand apart from both,   210
A quality arise within his soul,
Which, intro-active, made to supervise
And feel the force it has, may view itself,
And so be happy." Man might live at first
The animal life : but is there nothing more?
In due time, let him critically learn
How he lives ; and, the more he gets to know
Of his own life's adaptabilities,
The more joy-giving will his life become.
Thus man, who hath this quality, is best.   220

But thou, king, hadst more reasonably said :
" Let progress end at once, — man make no step
Beyond the natural man, the better beast,
Using his senses, not the sense of sense!"
In man there 's failure, only since he left
The lower and inconscious forms of life.
We called it an advance, the rendering plain
Man's spirit might grow conscious of man's life,
And, by new lore so added to the old,
Take each step higher over the brute's head.   230
This grew the only life, the pleasure-house,
Watch-tower and treasure-fortress of the soul,
Which whole surrounding flats of natural life
Seemed only fit to yield subsistence to ;
A tower that crowns a country. But alas,
The soul now climbs it just to perish there!
For thence we have discovered ('t is no dream —
We know this, which we had not else perceived)
That there 's a world of capability

For joy spread round about us, meant for us,   240
Inviting us ; and still the soul craves all,
And still the flesh replies, " Take no jot more
Than ere thou clombst the tower to look abroad!
Nay, so much less as that fatigue has brought
Deduction to it."   We struggle, fain to enlarge
Our bounded physical recipiency,
Increase our power, supply fresh oil to life,
Repair the waste of age and sickness : no,
It skills not! life 's inadequate to joy,
As the soul sees joy, tempting life to take.   250
They praise a fountain in my garden here
Wherein a Naiad sends the water-bow
Thin from her tube ; she smiles to see it rise.
What if I told her, it is just a thread
From that great river which the hills shut up,
And mock her with my leave to take the same?
The artificer has given her one small tube
Past power to widen or exchange — what boots
To know she might spout oceans if she could?
She can not lift beyond her first thin thread :   260
And so a man can use but a man's joy
While he sees God's.   Is it, for Zeus to boast
" See, man, how happy I live, and despair —
That I may be still happier — for thy use!"
If this were so, we could not thank our lord,
As hearts beat on to doing : 't is not so —
Malice it is not.   Is it carelessness?
Still, no.   If care — where is the sign?   I ask,
And get no answer, and agree in sum,
O king, with thy profound discouragement,   270
Who seest the wider but to sigh the more.
Most progress is most failure : thou sayest well.

    The last point now : — thou dost except a case —
Holding joy not impossible to one
With artist-gifts — to such a man as I
Who leave behind me living works indeed ;
For, such a poem, such a painting lives.
What? dost thou verily trip upon a word,
Confound the accurate view of what joy is
(Caught somewhat clearer by my eyes than thine)   280
With feeling joy? confound the knowing how
And showing how to live (my faculty)
With actually living? — Otherwise
Where is the artist's vantage o'er the king?
Because in my great epos I display
How divers men young, strong, fair, wise, can act —

Is this as tho' I acted? if I paint,
Carve the young Phœbus, am I therefore young?
Methinks I 'm older that I bowed myself
The many years of pain that taught me art!   290
Indeed, to know is something, and to prove
How all this beauty might be enjoyed, is more:
But, knowing naught, to enjoy is something too.
Yon rower, with the moulded muscles there,
Lowering the sail, is nearer it than I.
I can write love-odes: thy fair slave 's an ode.
I get to sing of love, when grown too gray
For being beloved: she turns to that young man,
The muscles all a-ripple on his back.
I know the joy of kingship: well, thou art king!   300
" But," sayest thou — (and I marvel, I repeat,
To find thee trip on such a mere word) "what
Thou writest, paintest, stays; that does not die:
Sappho survives, because we sing her songs,
And Æschylus, because we read his plays!"
Why, if they live still, let them come and take
Thy slave in my despite, drink from thy cup,
Speak in my place.   Thou diest while I survive?
Say rather that my fate is deadlier still,
In this, that every day my sense of joy   310
Grows more acute, my soul (intensified
By power and insight) more enlarged, more keen;
While every day my hairs fall more and more,
My hand shakes, and the heavy years increase —
The horror quickening still from year to year,
The consummation coming past escape,
When I shall know most, and yet least enjoy —
When all my works wherein I prove my worth,
Being present still to mock me in men's mouths,
Alive still, in the praise of such as thou,   320
I, I the feeling, thinking, acting man,
The man who loved his life so over-much,
Sleep in my urn.   It is so horrible,
I dare at times imagine to my need
Some future state revealed to us by Zeus,
Unlimited in capability
For joy, as this is in desire for joy,
— To seek which, the joy-hunger forces us:
That, stung by straitness of our life, made strait
On purpose to make prized the life at large —   330
Freed by the throbbing impulse we call death,
We burst there as the worm into the fly,
Who, while a worm still, wants his wings.   But no!
Zeus has not yet revealed it; and alas,
He must have done so, were it possible!

Live long and happy, and in that thought die,
Glad for what was!   Farewell.   And for the rest,
I cannot tell thy messenger aright
Where to deliver what he bears of thine
To one called Paulus; we have heard his fame   340
Indeed, if Christus be not one with him —
I know not, nor am troubled much to know.
Thou canst not think a mere barbarian Jew
As Paulus proves to be, one circumcised,
Hath access to a secret shut from us?
Thou wrongest our philosophy, O king,
In stooping to inquire of such an one,
As if his answer could impose at all!
He writeth, doth he? well, and he may write.
Oh, the Jew findeth scholars! certain slaves   350
Who touched on this same isle, preached him and Christ;
And (as I gathered from a bystander)
Their doctrine could be held by no sane man.

INSTANS TYRANNUS.

I.

OF the million or two, more or less,
      I rule and possess,
One man, for some cause undefined,
Was least to my mind.

II.

I struck him, he grovelled of course —
For, what was his force?
I pinned him to earth with my weight
And persistence of hate;
And he lay, would not moan, would not curse,
As his lot might be worse.   10

III.

"Were the object less mean, would he stand
At the swing of my hand!
For obscurity helps him, and blots
The hole where he squats."
So, I set my five wits on the stretch
To inveigle the wretch.
All in vain!   Gold and jewels I threw,

Still he couched there perdue;
I tempted his blood and his flesh.
Hid in roses my mesh,
Choicest cates and the flagon 's best spilth: 20
Still he kept to his filth.

IV.

Had he kith now or kin, were access
To his heart, did I press:
Just a son or a mother to seize!
No such booty as these.
Were it simply a friend to pursue
'Mid my million or two,
Who could pay me, in person or pelf,
What he owes me himself!   30
No: I could not but smile thro' my chafe:
For the fellow lay safe
As his mates do, the midge and the nit,
— Thro' minuteness, to wit.

V.

Then a humour more great took its place
At the thought of his face:
The droop, the low cares of the mouth,
The trouble uncouth
Twixt the brows, all that air one is fain
To put out of its pain.   40
And, "no!" I admonished myself,
"Is one mocked by an elf,
Is one baffled by toad or by rat?
The gravamen 's in that!
How the lion, who crouches to suit
His back to my foot,
Would admire that I stand in debate!
But the small turns the great
If it vexes you, — that is the thing!
Toad or rat vex the king?   50
Tho' I waste half my realm to unearth
Toad or rat, 't is well worth!"

VI.

So, I soberly laid my last plan
To extinguish the man.
Round his creep-hole, with never a break
Ran my fires for his sake;
Overhead, did my thunder combine

With my under-ground mine:
Till I looked from my labour **content**
To enjoy the event.   60

VII.

When sudden . . . how think ye, the end?
Did I say " without friend?"
Say rather, from marge to blue marge
The whole sky grew his targe
With the sun's self for visible boss,
While an Arm ran across
Which the earth heaved beneath like a breast
Where the wretch was safe prest!
Do you see!   Just my vengeance complete,
The man sprang to his feet,   70
Stood erect, caught at God's skirts, and prayed!
— So, *I* was afraid!

AN EPISTLE.

CONTAINING THE STRANGE MEDICAL EXPERIENCE OF KARSHISH, THE ARAB PHYSICIAN.

KARSHISH, the picker-up of learning's crumbs,
   The not-incurious in God's handiwork
(This man's-flesh he hath admirably made,
Blown like a bubble, kneaded like a paste,
To coop up and keep down on earth a space
That puff of vapour from his mouth, man's soul)
— To Abib, all-sagacious in our art,
Breeder in me of what poor skill I boast,
Like me inquisitive how pricks and cracks
Befall the flesh thro' too much stress and strain,   10
Whereby the wily vapour fain would slip
Back and rejoin its source before the term, —
And aptest in contrivance (under God)
To baffle it by deftly stopping such : —
The vagrant Scholar to his Sage at home
Sends greeting (health and knowledge, fame with peace)
Three samples of true snake-stone — rarer still,
One of the other sort, the melon-shaped,
(But fitter, pounded fine, for charms than drugs)
And writeth now the twenty-second time.   20

My journeyings were brought to Jericho:
Thus I resume. Who studious in our art
Shall count a little labour unrepaid?
I have shed sweat enough, left flesh and bone
On many a flinty furlong of this land.
Also, the country-side is all on fire
With rumours of a marching hitherward:
Some say Vespasian cometh, some, his son.
A black lynx snarled and pricked a tufted ear:
Lust of my blood inflamed his yellow balls: 30
I cried and threw my staff and he was gone.
Twice have the robbers stripped and beaten me,
And once a town declared me for a spy;
But at the end, I reach Jerusalem,
Since this poor covert where I pass the night,
This Bethany, lies scarce the distance thence
A man with plague-sores at the third degree
Runs till he drops down dead. Thou laughest here!
'Sooth, it elates me, thus reposed and safe,
To void the stuffing of my travel-scrip   40
And share with thee whatever Jewry yields.
A viscid choler is observable
In tertians, I was nearly bold to say;
And falling-sickness hath a happier cure
Than our school wots of: there's a spider here
Weaves no web, watches on the ledge of tombs,
Sprinkled with mottles on an ash-gray back;
Take five and drop them . . . but who knows his mind
The Syrian run-a-gate I trust this to?
His service payeth me a sublimate   50
Blown up his nose to help the ailing eye.
Best wait: I reach Jerusalem at morn,
There set in order my experiences,
Gather what most deserves, and give thee all—
Or I might add, Judæa's gum-tragacanth
Scales off in purer flakes, shines clearer-grained,
Cracks 'twixt the pestle and the porphyry,
In fine exceeds our produce. Scalp-disease
Confounds me, crossing so with leprosy:
Thou hadst admired one sort I gained at Zoar—   60
But zeal outruns discretion. Here I end.

Yet stay! my Syrian blinketh gratefully,
Protesteth his devotion is my price —
Suppose I write what harms not, tho' he steal?
I half resolve to tell thee, yet I blush,
What set me off a-writing first of all.
An itch I had, a sting to write, a tang!

For, be it this town's barrenness — or else
The Man had something in the look of him —
His case has struck me far more than 't is worth.   70
So, pardon if — (lest presently I lose,
In the great press of novelty at hand,
The care and pains this somehow stole from me)
I bid thee take the thing while fresh in mind,
Almost in sight — for, wilt thou have the truth?
The very man is gone from me but now,
Whose ailment is the subject of discourse.
Thus then, and let thy better wit help all!

    'T is but a case of mania: subinduced
By epilepsy, at the turning-point   80
Of trance prolonged unduly some three days
When, by the exhibition of some drug
Or spell, exorcisation, stroke of art
Unknown to me and which 't were well to know,
The evil thing, out-breaking all at once,
Left the man whole and sound of body indeed, —
But, flinging (so to speak) life's gates too wide,
Making a clear house of it too suddenly,
The first conceit that entered might inscribe
Whatever it was minded on the wall   90
So plainly at that vantage, as it were,
(First come, first served) that nothing subsequent
Attaineth to erase those fancy-scrawls
The just-returned and new-established soul
Hath gotten now so thoroughly by heart
That henceforth she will read or these or none.
And first — the man's own firm conviction rests
That he was dead (in fact they buried him)
— That he was dead and then restored to life
By a Nazarene physician of his tribe: 100
— 'Sayeth, the same bade "Rise," and he did rise.
"Such cases are diurnal," thou wilt cry.
Not so this figment! — not, that such a fume,
Instead of giving way to time and health,
Should eat itself into the life of life,
As saffron tingeth flesh, blood, bones, and all!
For see, how he takes up the after-life.
The man — it is one Lazarus a Jew,
Sanguine, proportioned, fifty years of age,
The body's habit wholly laudable,   110
As much, indeed, beyond the common health
As he were made and put aside to show.
Think, could we penetrate by any drug
And bathe the wearied soul and worried flesh,

And bring it clear and fair, by three days' sleep!
Whence has the man the balm that brightens all?
This grown man eyes the world now like a child.
Some elders of his tribe, I should premise,
Led in their friend, obedient as a sheep,
To bear my inquisition.   While they spoke,   120
Now sharply, now with sorrow, — told the case, —
He listened not except I spoke to him,
But folded his two hands and let them talk,
Watching the flies that buzzed: and yet no fool.
And that's a sample how his years must go.
Look if a beggar, in fixed middle-life,
Should find a treasure, — can he use the same
With straitened habits and with tastes starved small,
And take at once to his impoverished brain
The sudden element that changes things,   130
That sets the undreamed-of rapture at his hand,
And puts the cheap old joy in the scorned dust?
Is he not such an one as moves to mirth —
Warily parsimonious, when no need,
Wasteful as drunkenness at undue times?
All prudent counsel as to what befits
The golden mean, is lost on such an one:
The man's fantastic will is the man's law.
So here — we call the treasure knowledge, say,
Increased beyond the fleshly faculty —   140
Heaven opened to a soul while yet on earth,
Earth forced on a soul's use while seeing heaven:
The man is witless of the size, the sum,
The value in proportion of all things,
Or whether it be little or be much.
Discourse to him of prodigious armaments
Assembled to besiege his city now,
And of the passing of a mule with gourds —
'T is one!   Then take it on the other side,
Speak of some trifling fact, — he will gaze rapt   150
With stupor at its very littleness,
(Far as I see) as if in that indeed
He caught prodigious import, whole results;
And so will turn to us the bystanders
In ever the same stupor (note this point)
That we too see not with his opened eyes.
Wonder and doubt come wrongly into play,
Preposterously, at cross purposes.
Should his child sicken unto death, — why, look
For scarce abatement of his cheerfulness,   160
Or pretermission of the daily craft!
While a word, gesture, glance from that same child

At play or in the school or laid asleep,
Will startle him to an agony of fear,
Exasperation, just as like.   Demand
The reason why — "'t is but a word," object —
" A gesture " — he regards thee as our lord
Who lived there in the pyramid alone,
Looked at us (dost thou mind?) when, being young,
We both would unadvisedly recite   170
Some charm's beginning, from that book of his,
Able to bid the sun throb wide and burst
All into stars, as suns grown old are wont.
Thou and the child have each a veil alike
Thrown o'er your heads, from under which ye both
Stretch your blind hands and trifle with a match
Over a mine of Greek fire, did ye know!
He holds on firmly to some thread of life —
(It is the life to lead perforcedly)
Which runs across some vast distracting orb   180
Of glory on either side that meagre thread,
Which, conscious of, he must not enter yet —
The spiritual life around the earthly life :
The law of that is known to him as this,
His heart and brain move there, his feet stay here.
So is the man perplext with impulses
Sudden to start off crosswise, not straight on,
Proclaiming what is right and wrong across,
And not along, this black thread thro' the blaze —
" It should be " balked by " here it can not be."   190
And oft the man's soul springs into his face
As if he saw again and heard again
His sage that bade him " Rise " and he did rise.
Something, a word, a tick o' the blood within
Admonishes : then back he sinks at once
To ashes, who was very fire before,
In sedulous recurrence to his trade
Whereby he earneth him the daily bread ;
And studiously the humbler for that pride,
Professedly the faultier that he knows   200
God's secret, while he holds the thread of life.
Indeed the especial marking of the man
Is prone submission to the heavenly will —
Seeing it, what it is, and why it is.
'Sayeth, he will wait patient to the last
For that same death which must restore his being
To equilibrium, body loosening soul
Divorced even now by premature full growth :
He will live, nay, it pleaseth him to live
So long as God please, and just how God please.   210

He even seeketh not to please God more
(Which meaneth, otherwise) than as God please.
Hence, I perceive not he affects to preach
The doctrine of his sect whate'er it be,
Make proselytes as madmen thirst to do:
How can he give his neighbour the real ground,
His own conviction? Ardent as he is —
Call his great truth a lie, why, still the old
" Be it as God please " reassureth him.
I probed the sore as thy disciple should: 220
" How, beast," said I, " this stolid carelessness
Sufficeth thee, when Rome is on her march
To stamp out like a little spark thy town,
Thy tribe, thy crazy tale and thee at once?"
He merely looked with his large eyes on me.
The man is apathetic, you deduce?
Contrariwise, he loves both old and young,
Able and weak, affects the very brutes
And birds — how say I? flowers of the field —
As a wise workman recognizes tools   230
In a master's workshop, loving what they make.
Thus is the man as harmless as a lamb:
Only impatient, let him do his best,
At ignorance and carelessness and sin —
An indignation which is promptly curbed:
As when in certain travel I have feigned
To be an ignoramus in our art
According to some preconceived design,
And happed to hear the land's practitioners
Steeped in conceit sublimed by ignorance,   240
Prattle fantastically on disease,
Its cause and cure — and I must hold my peace!

Thou wilt object — Why have I not ere this
Sought out the sage himself, the Nazarene
Who wrought this cure, inquiring at the source,
Conferring with the frankness that befits?
Alas! it grieveth me, the learned leech
Perished in a tumult many years ago,
Accused, — our learning's fate, — of wizardry,
Rebellion, to the setting up a rule   250
And creed prodigious as described to me.
His death, which happened when the earthquake fell
(Prefiguring, as soon appeared, the loss
To occult learning in our lord the sage
Who lived there in the pyramid alone)
Was wrought by the mad people — that's their wont!
On vain recourse, as I conjecture it,

To his tried virtue, for miraculous help —
How could he stop the earthquake?   That 's their way!
The other imputations must be lies :   260
But take one, tho' I loathe to give it thee,
In mere respect for any good man's fame.
(And after all, our patient Lazarus
Is stark mad ; should we count on what he says?
Perhaps not : tho' in writing to a leech
'T is well to keep back nothing of a case.)
This man so cured regards the curer, then,
As — God forgive me! who but God himself,
Creator and sustainer of the world,
That came and dwelt in flesh on it awhile.   270
—'Sayeth that such an one was born and lived,
Taught, healed the sick, broke bread at his own house,
Then died, with Lazarus by, for aught I know,
And yet was . . . what I said nor choose repeat,
And must have so avouched himself, in fact,
In hearing of this very Lazarus
Who saith — but why all this of what he saith?
Why write of trivial matters, things of price
Calling at every moment for remark?
I noticed on the margin of a pool   280
Blue-flowering borage, the Aleppo sort,
Aboundeth, very nitrous.   It is strange!

Thy pardon for this long and tedious case,
Which, now that I review it, needs must seem
Unduly dwelt on, prolixly set forth!
Nor I myself discern in what is writ
Good cause for the peculiar interest
And awe indeed this man has touched me with.
Perhaps the journey's end, the weariness
Had wrought upon me first.   I met him thus :   290
I crossed a ridge of short sharp broken hills
Like an old lion's cheek teeth.   Out there came
A moon made like a face with certain spots
Multiform, manifold and menacing :
Then a wind rose behind me.   So we met
In this old sleepy town at unaware,
The man and I.   I send thee what is writ.
Regard it as a chance, a matter risked
To this ambiguous Syrian : he may lose,
Or steal, or give it thee with equal good.   300
Jerusalem's repose shall make amends
For time this letter wastes, thy time and mine ;
Till when, once more thy pardon and farewell!

The very God! think, Abib; dost thou think?
So, the All-Great, were the All-Loving too —
So, thro' the thunder comes a human voice
Saying, " O heart I made, a heart beats here!
Face, my hands fashioned, see it in myself!
Thou hast no power nor mayst conceive of mine:
But love I gave thee, with myself to love,   310
And thou must love me who have died for thee!"
The madman saith He said so: it is strange.

————•◦•————

CALIBAN UPON SETEBOS;

OR,

NATURAL THEOLOGY IN THE ISLAND.

" Thou thoughtest that I was altogether such a one as thyself."

['WILL sprawl, now that the heat of day is best,
     Flat on his belly in the pit's much mire,
With elbows wide, fists clenched to prop his chin,
And, while he kicks both feet in the cool slush,
And feels about his spine small eft-things course,
Run in and out each arm, and make him laugh:
And while above his head a pompion-plant,
Coating the cave-top as a brow its eye,
Creeps down to touch and tickle hair and beard,
And now a flower drops with a bee inside,   10
And now a fruit to snap at, catch and crunch, —
He looks out o'er yon sea which sunbeams cross
And recross till they weave a spider-web,
(Meshes of fire, some great fish breaks at times)
And talks to his own self, howe'er he please,
Touching that other, whom his dam called God.
Because to talk about Him, vexes — ha,
Could He but know! and time to vex is now,
When talk is safer than in winter-time.
Moreover Prosper and Miranda sleep   20
In confidence he drudges at their task,
And it is good to cheat the pair, and gibe,
Letting the rank tongue blossom into speech.]

    Setebos, Setebos, and Setebos!
'Thinketh, He dwelleth i' the cold o' the moon.

'Thinketh He made it, with the sun to match,
But not the stars; the stars came otherwise;

Only made clouds, winds, meteors, such as that:
Also this isle, what lives and grows thereon,
And snaky sea which rounds and ends the same.   30

'Thinketh, it came of being ill at ease:
He hated that He can not change His cold,
Nor cure its ache.   'Hath spied an icy fish
That longed to 'scape the rock-stream where she lived,
And thaw herself within the lukewarm brine
O' the lazy sea her stream thrusts far amid,
A crystal spike 'twixt two warm walls of wave;
Only, she ever sickened, found repulse
At the other kind of water, not her life,
(Green-dense and dim-delicious, bred o' the sun)   40
Flounced back from bliss she was not born to breathe,
And in her old bounds buried her despair,
Hating and loving warmth alike: so He.

'Thinketh, He made thereat the sun, this isle,
Trees and the fowls here, beast and creeping thing.
Yon otter, sleek-wet, black, lithe as a leech;
Yon auk, one fire-eye in a ball of foam,
That floats and feeds; a certain badger brown,
He hath watched hunt with that slant white-wedge eye
By moonlight; and the pie with the long tongue   50
That pricks deep into oakwarts for a worm,
And says a plain word when she finds her prize,
But will not eat the ants; the ants themselves
That build a wall of seeds and settled stalks
About their hole — He made all these and more,
Made all we see, and us, in spite: how else?
He could not, Himself, make a second self
To be His mate: as well have made Himself:
He would not make what He mislikes or slights,
An eyesore to Him, or not worth His pains;   60
But did, in envy, listlessness or sport,
Make what Himself would fain, in a manner, be —
Weaker in most points, stronger in a few,
Worthy, and yet mere playthings all the while,
Things He admires and mocks too, — that is it!
Because, so brave, so better tho' they be,
It nothing skills if He begin to plague.
Look now, I melt a gourd-fruit into mash,
Add honeycomb and pods, I have perceived,
Which bite like finches when they bill and kiss, —   70
Then, when froth rises bladdery, drink up all,
Quick, quick, till maggots scamper thro' my brain;
Last, throw me on my back i' the seeded thyme,

And wanton, wishing I were born a bird.
Put case, unable to be what I wish,
I yet could make a live bird out of clay:
Would not I take clay, pinch my Caliban
Able to fly? — for, there, see, he hath wings,
And great comb like the hoopoe's to admire,
And there, a sting to do his foes offence,   80
There, and I will that he begin to live,
Fly to yon rock-top, nip me off the horns
Of grigs high up that make the merry din,
Saucy thro' their veined wings, and mind me not.
In which feat, if his leg snapped, brittle clay,
And he lay stupid-like, — why, I should laugh;
And if he, spying me, should fall to weep,
Beseech me to be good, repair his wrong,
Bid his poor leg smart less or grow again, —
Well, as the chance were, this might take or else   90
Not take my fancy: I might hear his cry,
And give the mankin three sound legs for one,
Or pluck the other off, leave him like an egg,
And lessoned he was mine and merely clay.
Were this no pleasure, lying in the thyme,
Drinking the mash, with brain become alive,
Making and marring clay at will? So He.

'Thinketh, such shows nor right nor wrong in Him
Nor kind, nor cruel: He is strong and Lord.
'Am strong myself compared to yonder crabs   100
That march now from the mountain to the sea;
'Let twenty pass, and stone the twenty-first,
Loving not, hating not, just choosing so.
'Say, the first straggler that boasts purple spots
Shall join the file, one pincer twisted off;
'Say, this bruised fellow shall receive a worm,
And two worms he whose nippers end in red:
As it likes me each time, I do: so He.

Well then, 'supposeth He is good i' the main,
Placable if His mind and ways were guessed,   110
But rougher than His handiwork, be sure!
Oh, He hath made things worthier than Himself,
And envieth that, so helped, such things do more
Than He who made them! What consoles but this?
That they, unless thro' Him, do naught at all,
And must submit: what other use in things?
'Hath cut a pipe of pithless elder-joint
That, blown through, gives exact the scream o' the jay
When from her wing you twitch the feathers blue:

o

Sound this, and little birds that hate the jay   120
Flock within stone's throw, glad their foe is hurt:
Put case such pipe could prattle and boast forsooth
"I catch the birds, I am the crafty thing,
I make the cry my maker can not make
With his great round mouth; he must blow thro' mine!"
Would not I smash it with my foot? So He.

But wherefore rough, why cold and ill at ease?
Aha, that is a question! Ask, for that,
What knows, — the something over Setebos
That made Him, or He, may be, found and fought,   130
Worsted, drove off and did to nothing, perchance.
There may be something quiet o'er His head,
Out of His reach, that feels nor joy nor grief,
Since both derive from weakness in some way.
I joy because the quails come; would not joy
Could I bring quails here when I have a mind:
This Quiet, all it hath a mind to, doth.
'Esteemeth stars the outposts of its couch,
But never spends much thought nor care that way.
It may look up, work up, — the worse for those   140
It works on! 'Careth but for Setebos
The many-handed as a cuttle-fish,
Who, making Himself feared thro' what He does,
Looks up, first, and perceives he can not soar
To what is quiet and hath happy life;
Next looks down here, and out of very spite
Makes this a bauble-world to ape yon real,
These good things to match those as hips do grapes.
'T is solace making baubles, ay, and sport.
Himself peeped late, eyed Prosper at his books   150
Careless and lofty, lord now of the isle:
Vexed, 'stitched a book of broad leaves, arrow-shaped,
Wrote thereon, he knows what, prodigious words;
Has peeled a wand and called it by a name;
Weareth at whiles for an enchanter's robe
The eyed skin of a supple oncelot;
And hath an ounce sleeker than youngling mole,
A four-legged serpent he makes cower and couch,
Now snarl, now hold its breath and mind his eye,
And saith she is Miranda and my wife: 160
'Keeps for his Ariel a tall pouch-bill crane
He bids go wade for fish and straight disgorge;
Also a sea-beast, lumpish, which he snared,
Blinded the eyes of, and brought somewhat tame,
And split its toe-webs, and now pens the drudge
In a hole o' the rock, and calls him Caliban;

A bitter heart that bides its time and bites.
'Plays thus at being Prosper in a way,
Taketh his mirth with make-believes: so He.

His dam held that the Quiet made all things   170
Which Setebos vexed only: 'holds not so.
Who made them weak, meant weakness He might vex.
Had He meant other, while His hand was in,
Why not make horny eyes no thorn could prick,
Or plate my scalp with bone against the snow,
Or overscale my flesh 'neath joint and joint,
Like an orc's armour?   Ay,—so spoil His sport!
He is the One now: only He doth all.

' Saith, He may like, perchance, what profits Him.
Ay, himself loves what does him good; but why?   180
'Gets good no otherwise.   This blinded beast
Loves whoso places flesh-meat on his nose,
But, had he eyes, would want no help, but hate
Or love, just as it liked him: He hath eyes.
Also it pleaseth Setebos to work,
Use all His hands, and exercise much craft,
By no means for the love of what is worked.
'Tasteth, himself, no finer good i' the world
When all goes right, in this safe summer-time,
And he wants little, hungers, aches not much,   190
Than trying what to do with wit and strength.
'Falls to make something: 'piled yon pile of turfs,
And squared and stuck there squares of soft white chalk,
And, with a fish-tooth, scratched a moon on each,
And set up endwise certain spikes of tree,
And crowned the whole with a sloth's skull a-top,
Found dead i' the woods, too hard for one to kill.
No use at all i' the work, for work's sole sake;
'Shall some day knock it down again: so He.

'Saith He is terrible: watch His feats in proof!   200
One hurricane will spoil six good months' hope.
He hath a spite against me, that I know.
Just as He favours Prosper, who knows why?
So it is, all the same, as well I find.
'Wove wattles half the winter, fenced them firm
With stone and stake to stop she-tortoises
Crawling to lay their eggs here: well, one wave,
Feeling the foot of Him upon its neck,
Gaped as a snake does, lolled out its large tongue,
And licked the whole labour flat: so much for spite!   210
'Saw a ball flame down late (yonder it lies)

Where, half an hour before, I slept i' the shade:
Often they scatter sparkles: there is force!
'Dug up a newt He may have envied once
And turned to stone, shut up inside a stone.
Please Him and hinder this?— What Prosper does?
Aha, if he would tell me how.   Not He!
There is the sport: discover how or die!
All need not die, for of the things o' the isle
Some flee afar, some dive, some run up trees;   220
Those at His mercy,— why, they please Him most
When . . . when . . . well, never try the same way twice!
Repeat what act has pleased, He may grow wroth.
You must not know His ways, and play Him off,
Sure of the issue.   'Doth the like himself:
'Spareth a squirrel that it nothing fears
But steals the nut from underneath my thumb,
And when I threat, bites stoutly in defence:
'Spareth an urchin that contrariwise,
Curls up into a ball, pretending death   230
For fright at my approach: the two ways please.
But what would move my choler more than this,
That either creature counted on its life
To-morrow, next day and all days to come,
Saying forsooth in the inmost of its heart,
" Because he did so yesterday with me,
And otherwise with such another brute,
So must he do henceforth and always."   Ay?
'Would teach the reasoning couple what " must " means!
'Doth as he likes, or wherefore Lord?   So He.   240

'Conceiveth all things will continue thus,
And we shall have to live in fear of Him
So long as He lives, keeps His strength: no change,
If He have done His best, make no new world
To please Him more, so leave off watching this,—
If He surprise not even the Quiet's self
Some strange day,— or, suppose, grow into it
As grubs grow butterflies: else, here are we,
And there is He, and nowhere help at all.

'Believeth with the life the pain shall stop.   250
His dam held different, that after death
He both plagued enemies and feasted friends:
Idly!   He doth His worst in this our life,
Giving just respite lest we die thro' pain,
Saving last pain for worst,— with which, an end.
Meanwhile, the best way to escape His ire
Is, not to seem too happy.   'Sees, himself,

Yonder two flies, with purple films and pink,
Bask on the pompion-bell above : kills both.
'Sees two black painful beetles roll their ball 260
On head and tail as if to save their lives :
'Moves them the stick away they strive to clear.

Even so, 'would have Him misconceive, suppose
This Caliban strives hard and ails no less,
And always, above all else, envies Him ;
Wherefore he mainly dances on dark nights,
Moans in the sun, gets under holes to laugh,
And never speaks his mind save housed as now :
Outside, 'groans, curses. If He caught me here,
O'erheard this speech, and asked "What chucklest at?" 270
'Would, to appease Him, cut a finger off,
Or of my three kid yearlings burn the best,
Or let the toothsome apples rot on tree,
Or push my tame beast for the orc to taste :
While myself lit a fire, and made a song
And sung it, *"What I hate, be consecrate*
To celebrate Thee and Thy state, no mate
For Thee ; what see for envy in poor me ?"
Hoping the while, since evils sometimes mend,
Warts rub away and sores are cured with slime, 280
That some strange day, will either the Quiet catch
And conquer Setebos, or likelier He
Decrepit may doze, doze, as good as die.

[What, what? A curtain o'er the world at once!
Crickets stop hissing ; not a bird — or, yes,
There scuds His raven that hath told Him all!
It was fool's play, this prattling! Ha! The wind
Shoulders the pillared dust, death's house o' the move,
And fast invading fires begin! White blaze —
A tree's head snaps — and there, there, there, there, there, 290
His thunder follows! Fool to gibe at Him!
Lo! 'Lieth flat and loveth Setebos!
'Maketh his teeth meet thro' his upper lip,
Will let those quails fly, will not eat this month
One little mess of whelks, so he may 'scape!]

SAUL.

I.

SAID Abner, "At last thou art come!   Ere I tell, ere thou speak,
      Kiss my cheek, wish me well!"   Then I wished it, and did kiss
      his cheek.
And he, "Since the King, O my friend, for thy countenance sent,
Neither drunken nor eaten have we; nor until from his tent
Thou return with the joyful assurance the King liveth yet,
Shall our lip with the honey be bright, with the water be wet.
For out of the black mid-tent's silence, a space of three days,
Not a sound hath escaped to thy servants, of prayer nor of praise,
To betoken that Saul and the Spirit have ended their strife,
And that, faint in his triumph, the monarch sinks back upon life.   10

II.

"Yet now my heart leaps, O beloved!   God's child with his dew
On thy gracious gold hair, and those lilies still living and blue
Just broken to twine round thy harp-strings, as if no wild heat
Were now raging to torture the desert!"

III.

                        Then I, as was meet,
Knelt down to the God of my fathers, and rose on my feet,
And ran o'er the sand burnt to powder.   The tent was unlooped;
I pulled up the spear that obstructed, and under I stooped;
Hands and knees on the slippery grass-patch, all withered and gone,
That extends to the second enclosure, I groped my way on
Till I felt where the foldskirts fly open.   Then once more I prayed, 20
And opened the foldskirts and entered, and was not afraid
But spoke, "Here is David, thy servant!"   And no voice replied.
At the first I saw naught but the blackness; but soon I descried
A something more black than the blackness — the vast, the upright
Main prop which sustains the pavilion: and slow into sight
Grew a figure against it, gigantic and blackest of all.
Then a sunbeam, that burst thro' the tent roof, showed Saul.

IV.

He stood as erect as that tent-prop, both arms stretched out wide
On the great cross-support in the centre, that goes to each side;
He relaxed not a muscle, but hung there as, caught in his pangs   30
And waiting his change, the king serpent all heavily hangs,
Far away from his kind, in the pine, till deliverance come
With the spring-time, — so agonized Saul, drear and stark, blind and
      dumb.

V.

Then I tuned my harp,—took off the lilies we twine round its chords
Lest they snap 'neath the stress of the noontide—those sunbeams like
    swords!
And I first played the tune all our sheep know, as, one after one,
So docile they come to the pen-door till folding be done.
They are white and untorn by the bushes, for lo, they have fed
Where the long grasses stifle the water within the stream's bed;
And now one after one seeks its lodging, as star follows star   40
Into eve and the blue far above us,—so blue and so far!

VI.

—Then the tune, for which quails on the cornland will each leave his
    mate
To fly after the player; then, what makes the crickets elate
Till for boldness they fight one another: and then, what has weight
To set the quick jerboa a-musing outside his sand house—
There are none such as he for a wonder, half bird and half mouse!
God made all the creatures and gave them our love and our fear,
To give sign, we and they are his children, one family here.

VII.

Then I played the help-tune of our reapers, their wine-song, when hand
Grasps at hand, eye lights eye in good friendship, and great hearts
    expand   50
And grow one in the sense of this world's life.—And then, the last
    song
When the dead man is praised on his journey—"Bear, bear him along
With his few faults shut up like dead flowerets! Are balm-seeds not
    here
To console us? The land has none left such as he on the bier.
"Oh, would we might keep thee, my brother!"—And then, the glad
    chaunt
Of the marriage,—first go the young maidens, next, she whom we
    vaunt
As the beauty, the pride of our dwelling.—And then, the great march
Wherein man runs to man to assist him and buttress an arch
Naught can break; who shall harm them, our friends?—Then, the
    chorus intoned
As the Levites go up to the altar in glory enthroned.   60
But I stopped here: for here in the darkness Saul groaned.

VIII.

And I paused, held my breath in such silence, and listened apart;
And the tent shook, for mighty Saul shuddered: and sparkles 'gan
    dart

From the jewels that woke in his turban, at once with a start
All its lordly male-sapphires, and rubies courageous at heart.
So the head: but the body still moved not, still hung there erect.
And I bent once again to my playing, pursued it unchecked,
As I sang,—

IX.

      "Oh, our manhood's prime vigour!   No spirit feels waste,
Not a muscle is stopped in its playing nor sinew unbraced.
Oh, the wild joys of living! the leaping from rock up to rock,   70
The strong rending of boughs from the fir-tree, the cool silver shock
Of the plunge in a pool's living water, the hunt of the bear,
And the sultriness showing the lion is couched in his lair.
And the meal, the rich dates yellowed over with gold dust divine,
And the locust-flesh steeped in the pitcher, the full draught of wine,
And the sleep in the dried river-channel where bulrushes tell
That the water was wont to go warbling so softly and well.
How good is man's life, the mere living! how fit to employ
All the heart and the soul and the senses for ever in joy!
Hast thou loved the white locks of thy father, whose sword thou didst
      guard   80
When he trusted thee forth with the armies, for glorious reward?
Didst thou see the thin hands of thy mother, held up as men sung
The low song of the nearly departed, and hear her faint tongue
Joining in while it could to the witness, 'Let one more attest,
I have lived, seen God's hand thro' a lifetime, and all was for best!'
Then they sung thro' their tears in strong triumph, not much, but the
      rest.
And thy brothers, the help and the contest, the working whence grew
Such result as, from seething grape-bundles, the spirit strained true:
And the friends of thy boyhood — that boyhood of wonder and hope,
Present promise and wealth of the future beyond the eye's scope, — 90
Till lo, thou art grown to a monarch; a people is thine:
And all gifts, which the world offers singly, on one head combine!
On one head, all the beauty and strength, love and rage (like the throe
That, a-work in the rock, helps its labour and lets the gold go)
High ambition and deeds which surpass it, fame crowning them, — all
Brought to blaze on the head of one creature — King Saul!"

X.

And lo, with that leap of my spirit, — heart, hand, harp and voice,
Each lifting Saul's name out of sorrow, each bidding rejoice
Saul's fame in the light it was made for — as when, dare I say,
The Lord's army, in rapture of service, strains thro' its array,   100
And upsoareth the cherubim-chariot — "Saul!" cried I, and stopped,
And waited the thing that should follow. Then Saul, who hung
      propped

By the tent's cross-support in the centre, was struck by his name.
Have ye seen when Spring's arrowy summons goes right to the aim,
And some mountain, the last to withstand her, that held (he alone,
While the vale laughed in freedom and flowers) on a broad bust of
    stone
A year's snow bound about for a breastplate, — leaves grasp of the
    sheet?
Fold on fold all at once it crowds thunderously down to his feet,
And there fronts you, stark, black, but alive yet, your mountain of old,
With his rents, the successive bequeathings of ages untold :   110
Yea, each harm got in fighting your battles, each furrow and scar
Of his head thrust 'twixt you and the tempest — all hail, there they
    are!
— Now again to be softened with verdure, again hold the nest
Of the dove, tempt the goat and its young to the green on his crest
For their food in the ardours of summer.   One long shudder thrilled
All the tent till the very air tingled, then sank and was stilled
At the King's self left standing before me, released and aware.
What was gone, what remained?   All to traverse 'twixt hope and
    despair.
Death was past, life not come : so he waited.   Awhile his right hand
Held the brow, helped the eyes left too vacant, forthwith to remand   120
To their place what new objects should enter : 't was Saul as before.
I looked up, and dared gaze at those eyes, nor was hurt any more
Than by slow pallid sunsets in autumn, ye watch from the shore,
At their sad level gaze o'er the ocean — a sun's slow decline
Over hills which, resolved in stern silence, o'erlap and entwine
Base with base to knit strength more intensely : so, arm folded arm
O'er the chest whose slow heavings subsided.

XI.

                    What spell or what charm,
(For, awhile there was trouble within me) what next should I urge
To sustain him where song had restored him ?   Song filled to the
    verge
His cup with the wine of this life, pressing all that it yields   130
Of mere fruitage, the strength and the beauty : beyond, on what fields,
Glean a vintage more potent and perfect to brighten the eye,
And bring blood to the lip, and commend them the cup they put by ?
He saith, " It is good ; " still he drinks not : he lets me praise life,
Gives assent, yet would die for his own part.

XII.

                  Then fancies grew rife
Which had come long ago on the pasture, when round me the sheep
Fed in silence — above, the one eagle wheeled slow as in sleep ;

And I lay in my hollow and mused on the world that might lie
'Neath his ken, tho' I saw but the strip 'twixt the hill and the sky:
And I laughed — " Since my days are ordained to be passed with my
    flocks, 140
Let me people at least, with my fancies, the plains and the rocks,
Dream the life I am never to mix with, and image the show
Of mankind as they live in those fashions I hardly shall know!
Schemes of life, its best rules and right uses, the courage that gains,
And the prudence that keeps what men strive for ! " And now these
    old trains
Of vague thought came again; I grew surer; so, once more the string
Of my harp made response to my spirit, as thus —

XIII.

                           " Yea, my King,"
I began — " thou dost well in rejecting mere comforts that spring
From the mere mortal life held in common by man and by brute:
In our flesh grows the branch of this life, in our soul it bears fruit. 150
Thou hast marked the slow rise of the tree, — how its stem trembled
    first
Till it passed the kid's lip, the stag's antler; then safely outburst
The fan-branches all round; and thou mindest when these too, in
    turn
Broke a-bloom and the palm-tree seemed perfect: yet more was to
    learn,
E'en the good that comes in with the palm-fruit. Our dates shall we
    slight,
When their juice brings a cure for all sorrow? or care for the plight
Of the palm's self whose slow growth produced them? Not so! stem
    and branch
Shall decay, nor be known in their place, while the palm-wine shall
    staunch
Every wound of man's spirit in winter. I pour thee such wine.
Leave the flesh to the fate it was fit for! the spirit be thine! 160
By the spirit, when age shall o'ercome thee, thou still shalt enjoy
More indeed, than at first when, inconscious, the life of a boy.
Crush that life, and behold its wine running! Each deed thou hast
    done
Dies, revives, goes to work in the world; until e'en as the sun
Looking down on the earth, tho' clouds spoil him, tho' tempests efface,
Can find nothing his own deed produced not, must everywhere trace
The results of his past summer-prime, — so, each ray of thy will,
Every flash of thy passion and prowess, long over, shall thrill
Thy whole people, the countless, with ardour, till they too give forth
A like cheer to their sons: who in turn, fill the South and the
    North 170
With the radiance thy deed was the germ of. Carouse in the past!

But the license of age has its limit; thou diest at last.
As the lion when age dims his eyeball, the rose at her height,
So with man — so his power and his beauty for ever take flight.
No! Again a long draught of my soul-wine! Look forth o'er the
    years!
Thou hast done now with eyes for the actual; begin with the seer's!
Is Saul dead? In the depth of the vale make his tomb — bid arise
A gray mountain of marble heaped four-square, till, built to the skies,
Let it mark where the great First King slumbers: whose fame would
    ye know?
Up above see the rock's naked face, where the record shall go   180
In great characters cut by the scribe, — Such was Saul, so he did;
With the sages directing the work, by the populace chid, —
For not half, they 'll affirm, is comprised there! Which fault to amend,
In the grove with his kind grows the cedar, whereon they shall spend
(See, in tablets 't is level before them) their praise, and record
With the gold of the graver, Saul's story, — the statesman's great
    word
Side by side with the poet's sweet comment.   The river 's a-wave
With smooth paper-reeds grazing each other when prophet-winds
    rave:
So the pen gives unborn generations their due and their part
In thy being! Then, first of the mighty, thank God that thou
    art!"   190

XIV.

And behold while I sang . . . but O Thou who didst grant me that
    day,
And before it not seldom has granted thy help to essay,
Carry on and complete an adventure, — my shield and my sword
In that act where my soul was thy servant, thy word was my word, —
Still be with me, who then at the summit of human endeavour
And scaling the highest, man's thought could, gazed hopeless as ever
On the new stretch of heaven above me — till, mighty to save,
Just one lift of thy hand cleared that distance — God's throne from
    man's grave!
Let me tell out my tale to its ending — my voice to my heart
Which can scarce dare believe in what marvels last night I took part, 200
As this morning I gather the fragments, alone with my sheep,
And still fear lest the terrible glory evanish like sleep !
For I wake in the gray dewy covert, while Hebron upheaves
The dawn struggling with night on his shoulder, and Kidron retrieves
Slow the damage of yesterday's sunshine.

XV.

                I say then, — my song
While I sang thus, assuring the monarch, and, ever more strong,

Made a proffer of good to console him — he slowly resumed
His old motions and habitudes kingly.   The right hand replumed
His black locks to their wonted composure, adjusted the swathes
Of his turban, and see — the huge sweat that his countenance bathes, 210
He wipes off with the robe ; and he girds now his loins as of yore,
And feels slow for the armlets of price, with the clasp set before.
He is Saul, ye remember in glory, — ere error had bent
The broad brow from the daily communion ; and still, tho' much
    spent
Be the life and the bearing that front you, the same, God did choose,
To receive what a man may waste, desecrate, never quite lose.
So sank he along by the tent-prop, till, stayed by the pile
Of his armour and war-cloak and garments, he leaned there awhile,
And sat out my singing, — one arm round the tent-prop, to raise
His bent head, and the other hung slack — till I touched on the
    praise   220
I foresaw from all men in all time, to the man patient there ;
And thus ended, the harp falling forward.   Then first I was 'ware
That he sat, as I say, with my head just above his vast knees
Which were thrust out on each side around me, like oak roots which
    please
To encircle a lamb when it slumbers.   I looked up to know
If the best I could do had brought solace : he spoke not, but slow
Lifted up the hand slack at his side, till he laid it with care
Soft and grave, but in mild settled will, on my brow : thro' my hair
The large fingers were pushed, and he bent back my head, with kind
    power —
All my face back, intent to peruse it, as men do a flower.   230
Thus held he me there with his great eyes that scrutinized mine —
And oh, all my heart how it loved him! but where was the sign?
I yearned — " Could I help thee, my father, inventing a bliss,
I would add, to that life of the past, both the future and this ;
I would give thee new life altogether, as good, ages hence,
As this moment, — had love but the warrant, love's heart to dispense! "

XVI.

Then the truth came upon me.   No harp more — no song more! out-
    broke —

XVII.

" I have gone the whole round of creation : I saw and I spoke ;
I, a work of God's hand for that purpose, received in my brain
And proncunced on the rest of his handwork — returned him again 240
His creation's approval or censure : I spoke as I saw,
Reported, as man may of God's work — all 's love, yet all 's law.
Now I lay down the judgeship he lent me.   Each faculty tasked

To perceive him has gained an abyss, where a dewdrop was asked.
Have I knowledge? confounded it shrivels at Wisdom laid bare.
Have I forethought? how purblind, how blank, to the Infinite Care!
Do I task any faculty highest, to image success?
I but open my eyes, — and perfection, no more and no less,
In the kind I imagined, full-fronts me, and God is seen God
In the star, in the stone, in the flesh, in the soul and the clod.   250
And thus looking within and around me, I ever renew
(With that stoop of the soul which in bending upraises it too)
The submission of man's nothing-perfect to God's all-complete,
As by each new obeisance in spirit, I climb to his feet.
Yet with all this abounding experience, this deity known,
I shall dare to discover some province, some gift of my own.
There 's a faculty pleasant to exercise, hard to hoodwink,
I am fain to keep still in abeyance, (I laugh as I think)
Lest, insisting to claim and parade in it, wot ye, I worst
E'en the Giver in one gift. — Behold, I could love if I durst!   260
But I sink the pretension as fearing a man may o'ertake
God's own speed in the one way of love : I abstain for love's sake.
— What, my soul? see thus far and no farther? when doors great
      and small,
Nine-and-ninety flew ope at our touch, should the hundredth appal?
In the least things have faith, yet distrust in the greatest of all?
Do I find love so full in my nature, God's ultimate gift,
That I doubt his own love can compete with it? Here, the parts
      shift?
Here, the creature surpass the creator, — the end, what began?
Would I fain in my impotent yearning do all for this man,
And dare doubt he alone shall not help him, who yet alone can?   270
Would it ever have entered my mind, the bare will, much less power,
To bestow on this Saul what I sang of, the marvellous dower
Of the life he was gifted and filled with? to make such a soul,
Such a body, and then such an earth for insphering the whole?
And doth it not enter my mind (as my warm tears attest),
These good things being given, to go on, and give one more, the
      best?
Ay, to save and redeem and restore him, maintain at the height
This perfection, — succeed with life's dayspring, death's minute of
      night?
Interpose at the difficult minute, snatch Saul the mistake,
Saul the failure, the ruin he seems now, — and bid him awake   280
From the dream, the probation, the prelude, to find himself set
Clear and safe in new light and new life, — a new harmony yet
To be run, and continued, and ended — who knows? — or endure!
The man taught enough by life's dream, of the rest to make sure ;
By the pain-throb, triumphantly winning intensified bliss,
And the next world's reward and repose, by the struggles in this.

XVIII.

"I believe it! 'T is thou, God, that givest, 't is I who receive:
In the first is the last, in thy will is my power to believe.
All 's one gift: thou canst grant it moreover, as prompt to my prayer,
As I breathe out this breath, as I open these arms to the air.   290
From thy will, stream the worlds, life and nature, thy dread Sabaoth:
I will? — the mere atoms despise me! Why am I not loth
To look that, even that in the face too? Why is it I dare
Think but lightly of such impuissance? What stops my despair?
This; — 't is not what man Does which exalts him, but what man
          Would do!
See the King — I would help him, but cannot, the wishes fall through.
Could I wrestle to raise him from sorrow, grow poor to enrich,
To fill up his life, starve my own out, I would — knowing which,
I know that my service is perfect. Oh, speak thro' me now!
Would I suffer for him that I love? So wouldst thou — so wilt thou! 300
So shall crown thee the topmost, ineffablest, uttermost crown —
And thy love fill infinitude wholly, nor leave up nor down
One spot for the creature to stand in! It is by no breath,
Turn of eye, wave of hand, that salvation joins issue with death!
As thy love is discovered almighty, almighty be proved
Thy power, that exists with and for it, of being Beloved!
He who did most, shall bear most; the strongest shall stand the most
          weak.
'T is the weakness in strength, that I cry for! my flesh, that I seek
In the Godhead! I seek and I find it. O Saul, it shall be
A Face like my face that receives thee; a Man like to me,   310
Thou shalt love and be loved by, for ever: a Hand like this hand
Shall throw open the gates of new life to thee! See the Christ stand!"

XIX.

I know not too well how I found my way home in the night.
There were witnesses, cohorts about me, to left and to right,
Angels, powers, the unuttered, unseen, the alive, the aware:
I repressed, I got thro' them as hardly, as strugglingly there,
As a runner beset by the populace famished for news —
Life or death. The whole earth was awakened, hell loosed with her
          crews;
And the stars of night beat with emotion, and tingled and shot
Out in fire the strong pain of pent knowledge: but I fainted not,   320
For the Hand still impelled me at once and supported, suppressed
All the tumult, and quenched it with quiet, and holy behest,
Till the rapture was shut in itself, and the earth sank to rest.
Anon at the dawn, all that trouble had withered from earth —
Not so much, but I saw it die out in the day's tender birth;
In the gathered intensity brought to the gray of the hills;
In the shuddering forests' held breath; in the sudden wind-thrills;

In the startled wild beasts that bore off, each with eye sidling still,
Tho' averted with wonder and dread; in the birds stiff and chill
That rose heavily as I approached them, made stupid with awe: 330
E'en the serpent that slid away silent — he felt the new law.
The same stared in the white humid faces upturned by the flowers;
The same worked in the heart of the cedar and moved the vine-
   bowers:
And the little brooks witnessing murmured, persistent and low,
With their obstinate, all but hushed voices — " E'en so, it is so!"

RABBI BEN EZRA.

I.

GROW old along with me!
   The best is yet to be,
The last of life, for which the first was made:
Our times are in His hand
Who saith " A whole I planned,
Youth shows but half; trust God: see all, nor be afraid!"

II.

Not that, amassing flowers,
Youth sighed "Which rose make ours,
Which lily leave and then as best recall!"
Not that, admiring stars,   10
It yearned " Nor Jove, nor Mars;
Mine be some figured flame which blends, transcends them all!"

III.

Not for such hopes and fears
Annulling youth's brief years,
Do I remonstrate: folly wide the mark!
Rather I prize the doubt
Low kinds exist without,
Finished and finite clods, untroubled by a spark.

IV.

Poor vaunt of life indeed,
Were man but formed to feed   20
On joy, to solely seek and find and feast:
Such feasting ended, then
As sure an end to men;
Irks care the crop-full bird? Frets doubt the maw-crammed beast?

v.

Rejoice we are allied
To That which doth provide
And not partake, effect and not receive!
A spark disturbs our clod;
Nearer we hold of God
Who gives, than of His tribes that take, I must believe.   30

VI.

Then, welcome each rebuff
That turns earth's smoothness rough,
Each sting that bids nor sit nor stand but go!
Be our joys three-parts pain!
Strive, and hold cheap the strain;
Learn, nor account the pang; dare, never grudge the throe!

VII.

For thence,— a paradox
Which comforts while it mocks,—
Shall life succeed in that it seems to fail:
What I aspired to be,   40
And was not, comforts me:
A brute I might have been, but would not sink i' the scale.

VIII.

What is he but a brute
Whose flesh has soul to suit,
Whose spirit works lest arms and legs want play?
To man, propose this test—
Thy body at its best,
How far can that project thy soul on its lone way?

IX.

Yet gifts should prove their use:
I own the Past profuse   50
Of power each side, perfection every turn:
Eyes, ears took in their dole,
Brain treasured up the whole;
Should not the heart beat once "How good to live and learn?"

X.

Not once beat "Praise be Thine!
I see the whole design,
I, who saw power, see now love perfect too:
Perfect I call Thy plan:

Thanks that I was a man!
Maker, remake, complete, — I trust what Thou shalt do!"   60

XI.

For pleasant is this flesh;
Our soul, in its rose-mesh
Pulled ever to the earth, still yearns for rest:
Would we some prize might hold
To match those manifold
Possessions of the brute, — gain most, as we did best!

XII.

Let us not always say
"Spite of this flesh to-day
I strove, made head, gained ground upon the whole!"
As the bird wings and sings,   70
Let us cry "All good things
Are ours, nor soul helps flesh more, now, than flesh helps soul!"

XIII.

Therefore I summon age
To grant youth's heritage,
Life's struggle having so far reached its term:
Thence shall I pass, approved
A man, for aye removed
From the developed brute; a God tho' in the germ.

XIV.

And I shall thereupon
Take rest, ere I be gone   80
Once more on my adventure brave and new:
Fearless and unperplexed,
When I wage battle next,
What weapons to select, what armour to indue.

XV.

Youth ended, I shall try
My gain or loss thereby;
Leave the fire ashes, what survives is gold:
And I shall weigh the same,
Give life its praise or blame:
Young, all lay in dispute; I shall know, being old.   90

XVI.

For, note when evening shuts,
A certain moment cuts

P

The deed off, calls the glory from the gray:
A whisper from the west
Shoots — "Add this to the rest,
Take it and try its worth: here dies another day."

XVII.

So, still within this life,
Tho' lifted o'er its strife,
Let me discern, compare, pronounce at last,
"This rage was right i' the main,   100
That acquiescence vain:
The Future I may face now I have proved the Past."

XVIII.

For more is not reserved
To man, with soul just nerved
To act to-morrow what he learns to-day:
Here, work enough to watch
The Master work, and catch
Hints of the proper craft, tricks of the tool's true play.

XIX.

As it was better, youth
Should strive, thro' acts uncouth,   110
Toward making, than repose on aught found made:
So, better, age, exempt
From strife, should know, than tempt
Further.   Thou waitedst age: wait death nor be afraid!

XX.

Enough now, if the Right
And Good and Infinite
Be named here, as thou callest thy hand thine own,
With knowledge absolute,
Subject to no dispute
From fools that crowded youth, nor let thee feel alone.   120

XXI.

Be there, for once and all,
Severed great minds from small,
Announced to each his station in the Past!
Was I, the world arraigned,
Were they, my soul disdained,
Right?   Let age speak the truth and give us peace at last!

XXII.

Now, who shall arbitrate?
Ten men love what I hate,
Shun what I follow, slight what I receive;
Ten, who in ears and eyes   130
Match me: we all surmise,
They, this thing, and I, that: whom shall my soul believe?

XXIII.

Not on the vulgar mass
Called " work," must sentence pass,
Things done, that took the eye and had the price;
O'er which, from level stand,
The low world laid its hand,
Found straightway to its mind, could value in a trice:

XXIV.

But all, the world's coarse thumb
And finger failed to plumb,   140
So passed in making up the main account:
All instincts immature,
All purposes unsure,
That weighed not as his work, yet swelled the man's amount:

XXV.

Thoughts hardly to be packed
Into a narrow act,
Fancies that broke thro' language and escaped:
All I could never be,
All, men ignored in me,
This, I was worth to God, whose wheel the pitcher shaped.   150

XXVI.

Ay, note that Potter's wheel,
That metaphor! and feel
Why time spins fast, why passive lies our clay,—
Thou, to whom fools propound,
When the wine makes its round,
" Since life fleets, all is change; the Past gone, seize to-day!"

XXVII.

Fool! All that is, at all,
Lasts ever, past recall;
Earth changes, but thy soul and God stand sure:
What entered into thee,   160

That was, is, and shall be :
Time's wheel runs back or stops : Potter and clay endure.

XXVIII.

He fixed thee mid this dance
Of plastic circumstance,
This Present, thou, forsooth, wouldst fain arrest :
Machinery just meant
To give thy soul its bent,
Try thee and turn thee forth, sufficiently impressed.

XXIX.

What tho' the earlier grooves
Which ran the laughing loves   170
Around thy base, no longer pause and press?
What tho' about thy rim,
Scull-things in order grim
Grow out, in graver mood, obey the sterner stress?

XXX.

Look not thou down but up!
To uses of a cup,
The festal board, lamp's flash and trumpet's peal,
The new wine's foaming flow,
The Master's lips a-glow!
Thou, heaven's consummate cup, what needst thou with
          earth's wheel?   180

XXXI.

But I need, now as then,
Thee, God, who mouldest men!
And since, not even while the whirl was worst,
Did I, — to the wheel of life
With shapes and colours rife,
Bound dizzily, — mistake my end, to slake Thy thirst :

XXXII.

So, take and use Thy work,
Amend what flaws may lurk,
What strain o' the stuff, what warpings past the aim!
My times be in Thy hand!   190
Perfect the cup as planned!
Let age approve of youth, and death complete the same!

EPILOGUE.

FIRST SPEAKER, *as David.*

I.

ON the first of the Feast of Feasts,
   The Dedication Day,
When the Levites joined the Priests
   At the Altar in robed array,
Gave signal to sound and say, —

II.

When the thousands, rear and van,
   Swarming with one accord,
Became as a single man
   (Look, gesture, thought and word)
In praising and thanking the Lord, —   10

III.

When the singers lift up their voice,
   And the trumpets made endeavour,
Sounding, " In God rejoice! "
   Saying, " In Him rejoice
Whose mercy endureth for ever! " —

IV.

Then the Temple filled with a cloud,
   Even the House of the Lord :
Porch bent and pillar bowed :
   For the presence of the Lord,
In the glory of His cloud,
   Had filled the House of the Lord.   20

SECOND SPEAKER, *as Renan.*

Gone now! All gone across the dark so far,
  Sharpening fast, shuddering ever, shutting still,
Dwindling into the distance, dies that star
  Which came, stood, opened once! We gazed our fill
With upturned faces on as real a Face
  That, stooping from grave music and mild fire,
Took in our homage, made a visible place
  Thro' many a depth of glory, gyre on gyre,
For the dim human tribute. Was this true?
  Could man indeed avail, mere praise of his,   30

To help by rapture God's own rapture too,
  Thrill with a heart's red tinge that pure pale bliss?
Why did it end?   Who failed to beat the breast,
  And shriek, and throw the arms protesting wide,
When a first shadow showed the star addressed
  Itself to motion, and on either side
The rims contracted as the rays retired;
  The music, like a fountain's sickening pulse,
Subsided on itself; awhile transpired
  Some vestige of a Face no pangs convulse,   40
No prayers retard; then even this was gone,
  Lost in the night at last.   We, lone and left
Silent thro' centuries, ever and anon
  Venture to probe again the vault bereft
Of all now save the lesser lights, a mist
  Of multitudinous points, yet suns, men say —
And this leaps ruby, this lurks amethyst,
  But where may hide what came and loved our clay?
How shall the sage detect in yon expanse
  The star which chose to stoop and stay for us? 50
Unroll the records!   Hailed ye such advance
  Indeed, and did your hope evanish thus?
Watchers of twilight, is the worst averred?
  We shall not look up, know ourselves are seen,
Speak, and be sure that we again are heard,
  Acting or suffering, have the disk's serene
Reflect our life, absorb an earthly flame,
  Nor doubt that, were mankind inert and numb,
Its core had never crimsoned all the same,
  Nor, missing ours, its music fallen dumb?   60
Oh, dread succession to a dizzy post,
  Sad sway of sceptre whose mere touch appals,
Ghastly dethronement, cursed by those the most
  On whose repugnant brow the crown next falls!

Third Speaker.

I.

Witless alike of will and way divine,
How heaven's high with earth's low should intertwine!
Friends, I have seen thro' your eyes: now use mine!

II.

Take the least man of all mankind, as I;
Look at his head and heart, find how and why
He differs from his fellows utterly: 70

III.

Then, like me, watch when nature by degrees
Grows alive round him, as in Arctic seas
(They said of old) the instinctive water flees

IV.

Toward some elected point of central rock,
As tho', for its sake only, roamed the flock
Of waves about the waste : awhile they mock

V.

With radiance caught for the occasion, — hues
Of blackest hell now, now such reds and blues
As only heaven could fitly interfuse, —

VI.

The mimic monarch of the whirlpool, king   80
O' the current for a minute : then they wring
Up by the roots and oversweep the thing,

VII.

And hasten off, to play again elsewhere
The same part, choose another peak as bare,
They find and flatter, feast and finish there.

VIII.

When you see what I tell you, — nature dance
About each man of us, retire, advance,
As tho' the pageant's end were to enhance

IX.

His worth, and — once the life, his product, gained —
Roll away elsewhere, keep the strife sustained,   90
And show thus real, a thing the North but feigned, —

X.

When you acknowledge that one world could do
All the diverse work, old yet ever new,
Divide us, each from other, me from you, —

XI.

Why, where 's the need of Temple, when the walls
O' the world are that?   What use of swells and falls
From Levites' choir, Priests' cries, and trumpet-calls?

XII.

That one Face, far from vanish, rather grows,
Or decomposes but to recompose,
Become my universe that feels and knows!   100

A WALL.

I.

O THE old wall here! How I could pass
    Life in a long midsummer day,
My feet confined to a plot of grass,
    My eyes from a wall not once away!

II.

And lush and lithe do the creepers clothe
    Yon wall I watch, with a wealth of green:
Its bald red bricks draped, nothing loth,
    In lappets of tangle they laugh between.

III.

Now, what is it makes pulsate the robe?
    Why tremble the sprays? What life o'erbrims   10
The body, — the house, no eye can probe, —
    Divined as, beneath a robe, the limbs?

IV.

And there again! But my heart may guess
    Who tripped behind; and she sang perhaps:
So, the old wall throbbed, and its life's excess
    Died out and away in the leafy wraps.

V.

Wall upon wall are between us: life
    And song should away from heart to heart!
I — prison-bird, with a ruddy strife
    At breast, and a lip whence storm-notes start —   20

VI.

Hold on, hope hard in the subtle thing
    That's spirit: tho' cloistered fast, soar free;
Account as wood, brick, stone, this ring
    Of the rueful neighbours, and — forth to thee!

APPARITIONS.

I.

SUCH a starved bank of moss
   Till, that May-morn,
Blue ran the flash across:
   Violets were born!

II.

Sky — what a scowl of cloud
   Till, near and far,
Ray on ray split the shroud:
   Splendid, a star!

III.

World — how it walled about
   Life with disgrace   10
Till God's own smile came **out**:
   That was thy face!

NATURAL MAGIC.

I.

ALL I can say is — I saw it!
   The room was as bare as your hand.
I locked in the swarth little lady, — I swear,
From the head to the foot of her — well, quite as bare!
"No Nautch shall cheat me," said I, " taking my stand
At this bolt which I draw!" And this bolt — I withdraw it,
And there laughs the lady, not bare, but embowered
With — who knows what verdure, o'erfruited, o'erflowered?
Impossible! Only — I saw it!

II.

All I can sing is — I feel it!   10
This life was as blank as that room;
I let you pass in here. Precaution, indeed?
Walls, ceiling and floor, — not a chance for a weed!
Wide opens the entrance: where 's cold now, where's gloom?
No May to sow seed here, no June to reveal it,

Behold you enshrined in these blooms of your bringing,
These fruits of your bearing — nay, birds of your winging!
A fairy-tale!   Only — I feel it!

MAGICAL NATURE.

I.

FLOWER — I never fancied, jewel — I profess you!
   Bright I see and soft I feel the outside of a flower.
Save but glow inside and — jewel, I should guess you,
   Dim to sight and rough to touch : the glory is the dower.

II.

You, forsooth, a flower?   Nay, my love, a jewel —
   Jewel at no mercy of a moment in your prime!
Time may fray the flower-face : kind be time or cruel,
   Jewel, from each facet, flash your laugh at time!

GARDEN FANCIES.

I. THE FLOWER'S NAME.

I.

HERE 'S the garden she walked across,
   Arm in my arm, such a short while since :
Hark, now I push its wicket, the moss
   Hinders the hinges and makes them wince!
She must have reached this shrub ere she turned,
   As back with that murmur the wicket swung ;
For she laid the poor snail, my chance foot spurned,
   To feed and forget it the leaves among.

II.

Down this side of the gravel-walk
   She went while her robe's edge brushed the box :   10
And here she paused in her gracious talk
   To point me a moth on the milk-white phlox.
Roses, ranged in valiant row,
   I will never think that she passed you by!
She loves you noble roses, I know ;
   But yonder, see, where the rock-plants lie!

III.

This flower she stopped at, finger on lip,
    Stooped over, in doubt, as settling its claim;
Till she gave me, with pride to make no slip,
    Its soft meandering Spanish name.   20
What a name! Was it love or praise?
    Speech half-asleep or song half-awake?
I must learn Spanish, one of these days,
    Only for that slow sweet name's sake.

IV.

Roses, if I live and do well,
    I may bring her, one of these days,
To fix you fast with as fine a spell,
    Fit you each with his Spanish phrase.
But do not detain me now; for she lingers
    There, like sunshine over the ground,   30
And ever I see her soft white fingers
    Searching after the bud she found.

V.

Flower, you Spaniard, look that you grow not,
    Stay as you are and be loved for ever!
Bud, if I kiss you 't is that you blow not:
    Mind, the shut pink mouth opens never!
For while it pouts, her fingers wrestle,
    Twinkling the audacious leaves between,
Till round they turn and down they nestle;
    Is not the dear mark still to be seen?   40

VI.

Where I find her not, beauties vanish;
    Whither I follow her, beauties flee;
Is there no method to tell her in Spanish
    June 's twice June since she breathed it with me?
Come, bud, show me the least of her traces,
    Treasure my lady's lightest footfall!
— Ah, you may flout and turn up your faces —
    Roses, you are not so fair after all!

II. SIBRANDUS SCHAFNABURGENSIS.

I.

Plague take all your pedants, say I!
  He who wrote what I hold in my hand,
Centuries back was so good as to die,
  Leaving this rubbish to cumber the land;
This, that was a book in its time,
  Printed on paper and bound in leather,
Last month in the white of a matin-prime
  Just when the birds sang all together.—

II.

Into the garden I brought it to read,
  And under the arbute and laurustine   **10**
Read it, so help me grace in my need,
  From title-page to closing line.
Chapter on chapter did I count,
  As a curious traveler counts Stonehenge;
Added up the mortal amount,
  And then proceeded to my revenge.

III.

Yonder 's a plum-tree with a crevice
  An owl would build in, were he but sage;
For a lap of moss, like a fine pont-levis
  In a castle of the Middle Age,   **20**
Joins to a lip of gum, pure amber;
  When he 'd be private, there might he spend
Hours alone in his lady's chamber:
  Into this crevice I dropped our friend.

IV.

Splash, went he, as under he ducked,
  — At the bottom, I knew, rain-drippings stagnate;
Next, a handful of blossoms I plucked
  To bury him with, my bookshelf's magnate;
Then I went in-doors, brought out a loaf,
  Half a cheese, and a bottle of Chablis;   **30**
Lay on the grass and forgot the oaf
  Over a jolly chapter of Rabelais.

V.

Now, this morning, betwixt the moss
  And gum that locked our friend in limbo,

A spider had spun his web across,
 And sat in the midst with arms akimbo:
So, I took pity, for learning's sake,
 And, *de profundis, accentibus lætis,*
Cantate! quoth I, as I got a rake;
 And up I fished his delectable treatise.   40

VI.

Here you have it, dry in the sun,
 With all the binding all of a blister,
And great blue spots where the ink has run,
 And reddish streaks that wink and glister
O'er the page so beautifully yellow:
 Oh, well have the droppings played their tricks!
Did he guess how toadstools grow, this fellow?
 Here's one stuck in his chapter six!

VII.

How did he like it when the live creatures
 Tickled and toused and browsed him all over, 50
And worm, slug, eft, with serious features,
 Came in, each one, for his right of trover?
— When the water-beetle with great blind deaf face
 Made of her eggs the stately deposit,
And the newt borrowed just so much of the preface
 As tiled in the top of his black wife's closet?

VIII.

All that life and fun and romping,
 All that frisking and twisting and coupling,
While slowly our poor friend's leaves were swamping
 And clasps were cracking and covers suppling! 60
As if you had carried sour John Knox
 To the play-house at Paris, Vienna or Munich,
Fastened him into a front-row box,
 And danced off the ballet with trousers and tunic.

IX.

Come, old martyr! What, torment enough is it?
 Back to my room shall you take your sweet self.
Good-bye, mother-beetle; husband-eft, *sufficit!*
 See the snug niche I have made on my shelf!
A's book shall prop you up, B's shall cover you,
 Here's C to be grave with, or D to be gay, 70
And with E on each side, and F right over you,
 Dry-rot at ease till the Judgment-day!

IN THREE DAYS.

I.

SO, I shall see her in three days
   And just one night, but nights are short,
Then two long hours, and that is morn.
See how I come, unchanged, unworn!
Feel, where my life broke off from thine
How fresh the splinters keep and fine, —
Only a touch and we combine!

II.

Too long, this time of year, the days!
But nights, at least the nights are short.
As night shows where her one moon is,   10
A hand's-breadth of pure light and bliss,
So life's night gives my lady birth
And my eyes hold her!   What is worth
The rest of heaven, the rest of earth?

III.

O loaded curls, release your store
Of warmth and scent, as once before
The tingling hair did, lights and darks
Outbreaking into fairy sparks,
When under curl and curl I pried
After the warmth and scent inside,   20
Thro' lights and darks how manifold —
The dark inspired, the light controlled,
As early Art embrowns the gold!

IV.

What great fear, should one say, " Three days,
That change the world might change as well
Your fortune ; and if joy delays,
Be happy that no worse befell ! "
What small fear, if another says,
" Three days and one short night beside
May throw no shadow on your ways ;
But years must teem with change untried,   30
With chance not easily defied,
With an end somewhere undescried."
No fear ! — or, if a fear be born

This minute, it dies out in scorn.
Fear? I shall see her in three days
And one night, now the nights are short,
Then just two hours, and that is morn!

THE LOST MISTRESS.

I.

ALL 'S over, then: does truth sound bitter
As one at first believes?
Hark, 't is the sparrows' good-night twitter
About your cottage eaves!

II.

And the leaf-buds on the vine are woolly,
I noticed that, to-day;
One day more bursts them open fully:
You know the red turns gray.

III.

To-morrow we meet the same then, dearest?
May I take your hand in mine?
Mere friends are we, — well, friends the merest
Keep much that I resign:

10

IV.

For each glance of the eye so bright and black,
Tho' I keep with heart's endeavour, —
Your voice, when you wish the snowdrops back,
Tho' it stay in my soul for ever! —

V.

Yet I will but say what mere friends say,
Or only a thought stronger;
I will hold your hand but as long as all may,
Or so very little longer!

ONE WAY OF LOVE.

I.

ALL June I bound the rose in sheaves.
　　Now, rose by rose, I strip the leaves
And strew them where Pauline may pass.
She will not turn aside?　Alas!
Let them lie.　Suppose they die?
The chance was they might take her eye.

II.

How many a month I strove to suit
These stubborn fingers to the lute!
To-day I venture all I know.
She will not hear my music?　So!　　　　　10
Break the string; fold music's wing:
Suppose Pauline had bade me sing!

III.

My whole life long I learned to love.
This hour my utmost art I prove
And speak my passion — heaven or hell?
She will not give me heaven?　'T is well!
Lose who may — I still can say,
Those who win heaven, blest are they!

RUDEL TO THE LADY OF TRIPOLI.

I.

I KNOW a Mount, the gracious Sun perceives
　　First, when he visits, last, too, when he leaves
The world; and, vainly favoured, it repays
The day-long glory of his steadfast gaze
By no change of its large calm front of snow.
And, underneath the Mount, a Flower I know,
He can not have perceived, that changes ever
At his approach; and, in the lost endeavour
To live his life, has parted, one by one,
With all a flower's true graces, for the grace　　　　　10
Of being but a foolish mimic sun,
With ray-like florets round a disk-like face.

Q

Men nobly call by many a name the Mount
As over many a land of theirs its large
Calm front of snow like a triumphal targe
Is reared, and still with old names, fresh names vie,
Each to its proper praise and own account:
Men call the Flower, the Sunflower, sportively.

II.

Oh, Angel of the East, one, one gold look
Across the waters to this twilight nook,   20
— The far sad waters, Angel, to this nook!

III.

Dear Pilgrim, art thou for the East indeed?
Go! — saying ever as thou dost proceed,
That I, French Rudel, choose for my device
A sunflower outspread like a sacrifice
Before its idol.   See!   These inexpert
And hurried fingers could not fail to hurt
The woven picture; 't is a woman's skill
Indeed; but nothing baffled me, so, ill
Or well, the work is finished.   Say, men feed   30
On songs I sing, and therefore bask the bees
On my flower's breast as on a platform broad:
But, as the flower's concern is not for these
But solely for the sun, so men applaud
In vain this Rudel, he not looking here
But to the East — the East!   Go, say this, Pilgrim dear!

———◦◦◦———

NUMPHOLEPTOS.

STILL you stand, still you listen, still you smile!
   Still melts your moonbeam thro' me, white awhile,
Softening, sweetening, till sweet and soft
Increase so round this heart of mine, that oft
I could believe your moonbeam-smile has past
The pallid limit lies, transformed at last
To sunlight and salvation — warms the soul
It sweetens, softens!   Would you pass that goal,
Gain love's birth at the limit's happier verge,
And, where an iridescence lurks, but urge   10
The hesitating pallor on to prime
Of dawn' — true blood-streaked, sun-warmth, action-time,

By heart-pulse ripened to a ruddy glow
Of gold above my clay — I scarce should know
From gold's self, thus suffused! For gold means love.
What means the sad slow silver smile above
My clay but pity, pardon? — at the best,
But acquiescence that I take my rest,
Contented to be clay, while in your heaven
The sun reserves love for the Spirit-Seven   20
Companioning God's throne they lamp before,
— Leaves earth a mute waste only wandered o'er
By that pale soft sweet disempassioned moon
Which smiles me slow forgiveness! Such the boon
I beg? Nay, dear, submit to this — just this
Supreme endeavour! As my lips now kiss
Your feet, my arms convulse your shrouding robe,
My eyes acquainted with the dust, dare probe
Your eyes above for — what, if born, would blind
Mine with redundant bliss, as flash may find   30
The inert nerve, sting awake the palsied limb,
Bid with life's ecstacy sense overbrim
And suck back death in the resurging joy —
Love, the love whole and sole without alloy!

Vainly! The promise withers! I employ
Lips, arms, eyes, pray the prayer which finds the word,
Make the appeal which must be felt, not heard,
And none the more is changed your calm regard:
Rather, its sweet and soft grow harsh and hard —
Forbearance, then repulsion, then disdain.   40
Avert the rest! I rise, see! — make, again
Once more, the old departure for some track
Untried yet thro' a world which brings me back
Ever thus fruitlessly to find your feet,
To fix your eyes, to pray the soft and sweet
Which smile there — take from his new pilgrimage
Your outcast, once your inmate, and assuage
With love — not placid pardon now — his thirst
For a mere drop from out the ocean erst
He drank at! Well, the quest shall be renewed.   50
Fear nothing! Tho' I linger, unembued
With any drop, my lips thus close. I go!
So did I leave you, I have found you so,
And doubtlessly, if fated to return,
So shall my pleading persevere and earn
Pardon — not love — in that same smile, I learn,
And lose the meaning of, to learn once more,
Vainly!

What fairy track do I explore?
What magic hall return to, like the gem
Centuply-angled o'er a diadem?   60
You dwell there, hearted; from your midmost home
Rays forth — thro' that fantastic world I roam
Ever — from centre to circumference,
Shaft upon coloured shaft: this crimsons thence,
That purples out its precinct thro' the waste.
Surely I had your sanction when I faced,
Fared forth upon that untried yellow ray
Whence I retrack my steps? They end to-day
Where they began, before your feet, beneath
Your eyes, your smile: the blade is shut in sheath,   70
Fire quenched in flint; irradiation, late
Triumphant thro' the distance, finds its fate,
Merged in your blank pure soul, alike the source
And tomb of that prismatic glow: divorce
Absolute, all-conclusive! Forth I fared,
Treading the lambent flamelet: little cared
If now its flickering took the topaz tint,
If now my dull-caked path gave sulphury hint
Of subterranean rage — no stay nor stint
To yellow, since you sanctioned that I bathe,   80
Burnish me, soul and body, swim and swathe
In yellow license. Here I reek suffused
With crocus, saffron, orange, as I used
With scarlet, purple, every dye o' the bow
Born of the storm-cloud. As before, you show
Scarce recognition, no approval, some
Mistrust, more wonder at a man become
Monstrous in garb, nay — flesh disguised as well,
Thro' his adventure. Whatsoe'er befell,
I followed, wheresoe'er it wound, that vein   90
You authorized should leave your whiteness, stain
Earth's sombre stretch beyond your midmost place
Of vantage, — trode that tinct whereof the trace
On garb and flesh repel you! Yes, I plead
Your own permission — your command, indeed,
That who would worthily retain the love
Must share the knowledge shrined those eyes above,
Go boldly on adventure, break thro' bounds
O' the quintessential whiteness that surrounds
Your feet, obtain experience of each tinge   100
That bickers forth to broaden out, impinge
Plainer his foot its pathway all distinct
From every other. Ah, the wonder, linked
With fear, as exploration manifests
What agency it was first tipped the crests

Of unnamed wildflower, soon protruding grew
Portentous 'mid the sands, as when his hue
Betrays him and the burrowing snake gleams through ;
Till, last . . but why parade more shame and pain?
Are not the proofs upon me?   Here again   110
I pass into your presence, I receive
Your smile of pity, pardon, and I leave . . .
No, not this last of times I leave you, mute,
Submitted to my penance, so my foot
May yet again adventure, tread, from source
To issue, one more ray of rays which course
Each other, at your bidding, from the sphere
Silver and sweet, their birthplace, down that drear
Dark of the world, — you promise shall return
Your pilgrim jewelled as with drops o' the urn   120
The rainbow paints from, and no smatch at all
Of ghastliness at edge of some cloud-pall
Heaven cowers before, as earth awaits the fall
O' the bolt and flash of doom.   Who trusts your word
Tries the adventure : and returns — absurd
As frightful — in that sulphur-steeped disguise
Mocking the priestly cloth-of-gold, sole prize
The arch-heretic was wont to bear away
Until he reached the burning.   No, I say :
No fresh adventure!   No more seeking love   130
At end of toil, and finding, calm above
My passion, the old statuesque regard,
The sad petrific smile!

                        O you — less hard
And hateful than mistaken and obtuse
Unreason of a she-intelligence!
You very woman with the pert pretence
To match the male achievement!   Like enough!
Ay, you were easy victors, did the rough
Straightway efface itself to smooth, the gruff
Grind down and grow a whisper, — did man's truth   140
Subdue, for sake of chivalry and ruth,
Its rapier-edge to suit the bulrush-spear
Womanly falsehood fights with!   O that ear
All fact pricks rudely, that thrice-superfine
Feminity of sense, with right divine
To waive all process, take result stain-free
From out the very muck wherein . . .
                                    Ah me!
The true slave's querulous outbreak!   All the rest
Be resignation!   Forth at your behest

I fare.   Who knows but this — the crimson-quest —   150
May deepen to a sunrise, not decay
To that cold sad sweet smile? — which I obey.

———◆◆———

APPEARANCES.

I.

A ND so you found that poor room dull,
    Dark, hardly to your taste, my Dear?
Its features seemed unbeautiful :
    But this I know — 't was there, not here,
You plighted troth to me, the word
Which — ask that poor room how it heard!

II.

And this rich room obtains your praise
    Unqualified, — so bright, so fair,
So all whereat perfection stays?
    Ay, but remember — here, not there,   10
The other word was spoken!   Ask
This rich room how you dropped the mask!

———◆◆———

THE WORST OF IT.

I.

W OULD it were I had been false, not you!
    I that am nothing, not you that are all :
I, never the worse for a touch or two
    On my speckled hide ; not you, the pride
Of the day, my swan, that a first fleck's fall
    On her wonder of white must unswan, undo!

II.

I had dipped in life's struggle and, out again,
    Bore specks of it here, there, easy to see,
When I found my swan and the cure was plain ;
    The dull turned bright as I caught your white   10
On my bosom : you saved me — saved in vain
    If you ruined yourself, and all thro' me!

III.

Yes, all thro' the speckled beast that I am,
  Who taught you to stoop; you gave me yourself,
And bound your soul by the vows that damn:
  Since on better thought you break, as you ought,
Vows — words, no angel set down, some elf
  Mistook, — for an oath, an epigram!

IV.

Yes, might I judge you, here were my heart,
  And a hundred its like, to treat as you pleased!   20
I choose to be yours, for my proper part,
  Yours, leave or take, or mar me or make;
If I acquiesce, why should you be teased
  With the conscience-prick and the memory-smart?

V.

But what will God say? Oh, my Sweet,
  Think, and be sorry you did this thing!
Tho' earth were unworthy to feel your feet,
  There's a heaven above may deserve your love:
Should you forfeit heaven for a snapt gold ring
  And a promise broke, were it just or meet?   30

VI.

And I to have tempted you! I, who tried
  Your soul, no doubt, till it sank! Unwise,
I loved and was lowly, loved and aspired,
  Loved, grieving or glad, till I made you mad
And you meant to have hated and despised —
  Whereas, you deceived me nor inquired!

VII.

She, ruined? How? No heaven for her?
  Crowns to give, and none for the brow
That looked like marble and smelt like myrrh?
  Shall the robe be worn, and the palm-branch borne,   40
And she go graceless, she graced now
  Beyond all saints, as themselves aver?

VIII.

Hardly! That must be understood!
  The earth is your place of penance, then;

And what will it prove?   I desire your good,
    But, plot as I may, I can find no way•
How a blow should fall, such as falls on men,
    Nor prove too much for your womanhood.

IX.

It will come, I suspect, at the end of life,
    When you walk alone, and review the past ;   50
And I, who so long shall have done with strife,
    And journeyed my stage and earned my wage
And retired as was right, — I am called at last
    When the devil stabs you, to lend the knife.

X.

He stabs for the minute of trivial wrong,
    Nor the other hours are able to save,
The happy, that lasted my whole life long :
    For a promise broke, not for first words spoke,
The true, the only, that turn my grave
    To a blaze of joy and a crash of song.   60

XI.

Witness beforehand!   Off I trip
    On a safe path gay thro' the flowers you flung :
My very name made great by your lip,
    And my heart a-glow with the good I know
Of a perfect year when we both were young,
    And I tasted the angels' fellowship.

XII.

And witness, moreover . . . Ah, but wait !
    I spy the loop whence an arrow shoots!
It may be for yourself, when you meditate,
    That you grieve — for slain ruth, murdered truth :   70
" Tho' falsehood escape in the end, what boots?
    How truth would have triumphed!" — you sigh too late.

XIII.

Ay, who would have triumphed like you, I say !
    Well, it is lost now ; well, you must bear,
Abide and grow fit for a better day :
    You should hardly grudge, could I be your judge!
But hush!   For you, can be no despair :
    There 's amends : 't is a secret : hope and pray!

XIV.

For I was true at least — oh, true enough!
 And, Dear, truth is not as good as it seems! 80
Commend me to conscience!   Idle stuff !
 Much help is in mine, as I mope and pine,
And skulk thro' day, and scowl in my dreams
 At my swan's obtaining the crow's rebuff.

XV.

Men tell me of truth now — "False!" I cry :
 Of beauty — "A mask, friend!   Look beneath!"
We take our own method, the devil and I,
 With pleasant and fair and wise and rare :
And the best we wish to what lives, is — death ;
 Which even in wishing, perhaps we lie! 90

XVI.

Far better commit a fault and have done —
 As you, Dear! — for ever ; and choose the pure,
And look where the healing waters run,
 And strive and strain to be good again,
And a place in the other world ensure,
 All glass and gold, with God for its sun.

XVII.

Misery!   What shall I say or do ?
 I can not advise, or, at least, persuade.
Most like, you are glad you deceived me — rue
 No whit of the wrong : you endured too long, 100
Have done no evil and want no aid,
 Will live the old life out and chance the new.

XVIII.

And your sentence is written all the same,
 And I can do nothing, — pray, perhaps :
But somehow the world pursues its game, —
 If I pray, if I curse, — for better or worse :
And my faith is torn to a thousand scraps,
 And my heart feels ice while my words breathe flame.

XIX.

Dear, I look from my hiding-place.
 Are you still so fair?   Have you still the eyes? 110
Be happy!   Add but the other grace,
 Be good!   Why want what the angels vaunt?
I knew you once : but in Paradise,
 If we meet, I will pass nor turn my face.

TOO LATE.

I.

HERE was I with my arm and heart
    And brain, all yours for a word, a want
Put into a look — just a look, your part, —
    While mine, to repay it . . . vainest vaunt,
Were the woman, that 's dead, alive to hear,
    Had her lover, that 's lost, love's proof to show!
But I can not show it ; you can not speak
    From the churchyard neither, miles removed,
Tho' I feel by a pulse within my cheek,
    Which stabs and stops, that the woman I loved   10
Needs help in her grave and finds none near,
    Wants warmth from the heart which sends it — so!

II.

Did I speak once angrily, all the drear days
    You lived, you woman I loved so well,
Who married the other?   Blame or praise,
    Where was the use then?   Time would tell,
And the end declare what man for you,
    What woman for me was the choice of God.
But, Edith dead! no doubting more!
    I used to sit and look at my life   20
As it rippled and ran till, right before,
    A great stone stopped it : oh, the strife
Of waves at the stone some devil threw
    In my life's midcurrent, thwarting God!

III.

But either I thought, " They may churn and chide
    Awhile, — my waves which came for their joy
And found this horrible stone full-tide :
    Yet I see just a thread escape, deploy
Thro' the evening-country, silent and safe,
    And it suffers no more till it finds the sea."   30
Or else I would think, " Perhaps some night
    When new things happen, a meteor-ball
May slip thro' the sky in a line of light,
    And earth breathe hard, and landmarks fall,
And my waves no longer champ nor chafe,
    Since a stone will have rolled from its place : let be! "

IV.

But, dead! All 's done with : wait who may,
  Watch and wear and wonder who will.
Oh, my whole life that ends to-day!
  Oh, my soul's sentence, sounding still,   40
" The woman is dead, that was none of his ;
  And the man, that was none of hers may go!"
There 's only the past left: worry that!
  Wreak, like a bull, on the empty coat,
Rage, its late wearer is laughing at!
  Tear the collar to rags, having missed his throat ;
Strike stupidly on — " This, this and this,
  Where I would that a bosom received the blow!"

V.

I ought to have done more : once my speech,
  And once your answer, and there, the end,   50
And Edith was henceforth out of reach!
  Why, men do more to deserve a friend,
Be rid of a foe, get rich, grow wise,
  Nor, folding their arms, stare fate in the face.
Why, better even have burst like a thief
  And borne you away to a rock for us two,
In a moment's horror, bright, bloody and brief,
  Then changed to myself again — " I slew
Myself in that moment ; a ruffian lies
  Somewhere : your slave, see, born in his place!"   60

VI.

What did the other do? You be judge!
  Look at us, Edith! Here are we both!
Give him his six whole years : I grudge
  None of the life with you, nay, loathe
Myself that I grudged his start in advance
  Of me who could overtake and pass.
But, as if he loved you! No, not he,
  Nor anyone else in the world, 't is plain :
Who ever heard that another, free
  As I, young, prosperous, sound and sane,   70
Poured life out, proffered it — " Half a glance
  Of those eyes of yours and I drop the glass!"

VII.

Handsome, were you? 'T is more than they held,
  More than they said ; I was 'ware and watched :

I was the 'scapegrace, this rat belled
  The cat, this fool got his whiskers scratched:
The others? No head that was turned, no heart
  Broken, my lady, assure yourself!
Each soon made his mind up; so and so
  Married a dancer, such and such   80
Stole his friend's wife, stagnated slow,
  Or maundered, unable to do as much,
And muttered of peace where he had no part:
  While, hid in the closet, laid on the shelf, —

VIII.

On the whole, you were let alone, I think!
  So, you looked to the other, who acquiesced;
My rival, the proud man, — prize your pink
  Of poets! A poet he was! I 've guessed:
He rhymed you his rubbish nobody read,
  Loved you and doved you — did not I laugh!   90
There was a prize! But we both were tried.
  Oh, heart of mine, marked broad with her mark,
Tekel, found wanting, set aside,
  Scorned! See, I bleed these tears in the dark
Till comfort come and the last be bled:
  He? He is tagging your epitaph.

IX.

If it would only come over again!
  — Time to be patient with me, and probe
This heart till you punctured the proper vein,
  Just to learn what blood is: twitch the robe   100
From that blank lay-figure your fancy draped,
  Prick the leathern heart till the — verses spirt!
And late it was easy; late, you walked
  Where a friend might meet you; Edith's name
Arose to one's lip if one laughed or talked;
  If I heard good news, you heard the same;
When I woke, I knew that your breath escaped;
  I could bide my time, keep alive, alert.

X.

And alive I shall keep and long, you will see!
  I knew a man, was kicked like a dog   110
From gutter to cesspool; what cared he
  So long as he picked from the filth his prog?
He saw youth, beauty and genius die.

And jollily lived to his hundredth year.
But I will live otherwise : none of such life!
    At once I begin as I mean to end.
Go on with the world, get gold in its strife,
    Give your spouse the slip and betray your friend!
There are two who decline, a woman and I,
    And enjoy our death in the darkness here.   120

XI.

I liked that way you had with your curls
    Wound to a ball in a net behind :
Your cheek was chaste as a quaker-girl's
    And your mouth — there was never, to my mind,
Such a funny mouth, for it would not shut ;
    And the dented chin too — what a chin!
There were certain ways when you spoke, some words
    That you know you never could pronounce :
You were thin, however ; like a bird's
    Your hand seemed — some would say, the pounce   130
Of a scaly-footed hawk — all but!
    The world was right when it called you thin.

XII.

But I turn my back on the world : I take
    Your hand, and kneel, and lay to my lips.
Bid me live, Edith! Let me slake
    Thirst at your presence! Fear no slips!
'T is your slave shall pay, while his soul endures,
    Full due, love's whole debt, *summum jus*.
My queen shall have high observance, planned
    Courtship made perfect, no least line   140
Crossed without warrant. There you stand,
    Warm too, and white too : would this wine
Had washed all over that body of yours,
    Ere I drank it, and you down with it, thus!

BIFURCATION.

WE were two lovers ; let me lie by her,
        My tomb beside her tomb. On hers inscribe —
"I loved him ; but my reason bade prefer
Duty to love, reject the tempter's bribe
Of rose and lily when each path diverged,

And either I must pace to life's far end
As love should lead me, or, as duty urged,
Plod the worn causeway arm in arm with friend.
So, truth turned falsehood: 'How I loathe a flower,
How prize the pavement!' still caressed his ear —   10
The deafish friend's — thro' life's day, hour by hour,
As he laughed (coughing) 'Ay, it would appear!'
But deep within my heart of hearts there hid
Ever the confidence, amends for all,
That heaven repairs what wrong earth's journey did,
When love from life-long exile comes at call.
Duty and love, one broad way, were the best —
Who doubts?   But one or other was to choose.
I chose the darkling half, and wait the rest
In that new world where light and darkness fuse."   20

Inscribe on mine — "I loved her: love's track lay
O'er sand and pebble, as all travelers know.
Duty led thro' a smiling country, gay
With greensward where the rose and lily blow.
'Our roads are diverse: farewell, love!' said she:
''T is duty I abide by: homely sward
And not the rock-rough picturesque for me!
Above, where both roads join, I wait reward.
Be you as constant to the path whereon
I leave you planted!'   But man needs must move,   30
Keep moving — whither, when the star is gone
Whereby he steps secure nor strays from love?
No stone but I was tripped by, stumbling-block
But brought me to confusion.   Where I fell,
There I lay flat, if moss disguised the rock:
Thence, if flint pierced, I rose and cried 'All 's well!
Duty be mine to tread in that high sphere
Where love from duty ne'er disparts, I trust,
And two halves make that whole, whereof — since here
One must suffice a man — why, this one must!' "   40

Inscribe each tomb thus: then, some sage acquaint
The simple — which holds sinner, which holds saint!

<hr />

A LIKENESS.

SOME people hang portraits up
In a room where they dine or sup:
And the wife clinks tea-things under,

And her cousin, he stirs his cup,
Asks, "Who was the lady, I wonder?"
" 'T is a daub John bought at a sale,"
Quoth the wife, — looks black as thunder:
"What a shade beneath her nose!
Snuff-taking, I suppose, — "
Adds the cousin, while John's corns ail.   10

Or else, there 's no wife in the case,
But the portrait 's queen of the place,
Alone mid the other spoils
Of youth, — masks, gloves and foils,
And pipe-sticks, rose, cherry-tree, jasmine,
And the long whip, the tandem-lasher,
And the cast from a fist, ("not, alas! mine,
But my master's, the Tipton Slasher ")
And the cards where pistol-balls mark ace,
And a satin shoe used for cigar-case,   20
And the chamois-horns ("shot in the Chablais ")
And prints — Rarey drumming on Cruiser,
And Sayers, our champion, the bruiser,
And the little edition of Rabelais:
Where a friend, with both hands in his pockets
May saunter up close to examine it,
And remark a good deal of Jane Lamb in it,
"But the eyes are half out of their sockets;
That hair 's not so bad, where the gloss is,
But they 've made the girl's nose a proboscis: 30
Jane Lamb, that we danced with at Vichy!
What, is not she Jane?   Then, who is she?"

All that I own is a print,
An etching, a mezzotint;
'T is a study, a fancy, a fiction,
Yet a fact (take my conviction)
Because it has more than a hint
Of a certain face, I never
Saw elsewhere touch or trace of
In women I 've seen the face of: 40
Just an etching, and, so far, clever.

I keep my prints, an imbroglio,
Fifty in one portfolio.
When somebody tries my claret,
We turn round chairs to the fire,
Chirp over days in a garret,
Chuckle o'er increase of salary,
Taste the good fruits of our leisure,

Talk about pencil and lyre,
And the National Portrait Gallery: 50
Then I exhibit my treasure.
After we 've turned over twenty,
And the debt of wonder my crony owes
Is paid to my Marc Antonios,
He stops me — "*Festina lentè!*
What 's that sweet thing there, the etching?"
How my waistcoat-strings want stretching,
How my cheeks grow red as tomatoes,
How my heart leaps!   But hearts, after leaps, ache.

"By the by, you must take, for a keepsake,   60
That other, you praised, of Volpato's."
The fool! would he try a flight further and say —
He never saw, never before to-day,
What was able to take his breath away,
A face to lose youth for, to occupy age
With the dream of, meet death with, — why, I 'll not engage
But that, half in a rapture and half in a rage,
I should toss him the thing's self — " 'T is only a duplicate,
A thing of no value!   Take it, I supplicate!"

MAY AND DEATH.

I.

I WISH that when you died last May,
  Charles, there had died along with you
Three parts of spring's delightful things;
  Ay, and, for me, the fourth part too.

II.

A foolish thought, and worse, perhaps!
  There must be many a pair of friends
Who, arm in arm, deserve the warm
  Moon-births and the long evening-ends.

III.

So, for their sake, be May still May!
  Let their new time, as mine of old,   10
Do all it did for me: I bid
  Sweet sights and sounds throng manifold.

IV.

Only, one little sight, one plant,
　Woods have in May, that starts up green
Save a sole streak which, so to speak,
　Is spring's blood, spilt its leaves between, —

V.

That, they might spare ; a certain wood
　Might miss the plant ; their loss were small :
But I, — whene'er the leaf grows there,
　Its drop comes from my heart, that 's all.　　20

A FORGIVENESS.

I AM indeed the personage you know.
　As for my wife, — what happened long ago —
You have a right to question me, as I
Am bound to answer.
　　　　　　("Son, a fit reply!"
The monk half spoke, half ground thro' his clenched teeth,
At the confession-grate I knelt beneath.)

Thus then all happened, Father!　Power and place
I had as still I have.　I ran life's race,
With the whole world to see, as only strains
His strength some athlete whose prodigious gains　　10
Of good appal him : happy to excess, —
Work freely done should balance happiness
Fully enjoyed ; and, since beneath my roof
Housed she who made home heaven, in heaven's behoof
I went forth every day, and all day long
Worked for the world.　Look, how the labourer's song
Cheers him!　Thus sang my soul, at each sharp throe
Of labouring flesh and blood — "She loves me so!"

One day, perhaps such song so knit the nerve
That work grew play and vanished.　"I deserve　　20
Haply my heaven an hour before the time!"
I laughed, as silverly the clockhouse-chime
Surprised me passing thro' the postern-gate
— Not the main entry where the menials wait
And wonder why the world's affairs allow

R

The master sudden leisure.   That was how
I took the private garden-way for once.

Forth from the alcove, I saw start, ensconce
Himself behind the porphyry vase, a man.

My fancies in the natural order ran: 30
" A spy, — perhaps a foe in ambuscade, —
A thief, — more like, a sweetheart of some maid
Who pitched on the alcove for tryst perhaps."

" Stand there! "   I bid.

                        Whereat my man but wraps
His face the closelier with uplifted arm
Whereon the cloak lies, strikes in blind alarm
This and that pedestal as, — stretch and stoop, —
Now in, now out of sight, he thrids the group
Of statues, marble god and goddess ranged
Each side the pathway, till the gate 's exchanged   40
For safety: one step thence, the street, you know!

Thus far I followed with my gaze.   Then, slow,
Near on admiringly, I breathed again,
And — back to that last fancy of the train —
" A danger risked for hope of just a word
With — which of all my nest may be the bird
This poacher covets for her plumage, pray?
Carmen?   Juana?   Carmen seems too gay
For such adventure, while Juana 's grave
— Would scorn the folly.   I applaud the knave!   50
He had the eye, could single from my brood
His proper fledgeling ! "

                        As I turned, there stood
In face of me, my wife stone-still stone-white.
Whether one bound had brought her, — at first sight
Of what she judged the encounter, sure to be
Next moment, of the venturous man and me, —
Brought her to clutch and keep me from my prey:
Whether impelled because her death no day
Could come so absolutely opportune
As now at joy's height, like a year in June   60
Stayed at the fall of its first ripened rose;
Or whether hungry for my hate — who knows? —
Eager to end an irksome lie, and taste
Our tingling true relation, hate embraced
By hate one naked moment: — anyhow

There stone-still stone-white stood my wife, but now
The woman who made heaven within my house.
Ay, she who faced me was my very spouse
As well as love — you are to recollect !

" Stay ! " she said.   " Keep at least one soul unspecked   70
With crime, that 's spotless hitherto — your own !
Kill me who court the blessing, who alone
Was, am and shall be guilty, first to last !
The man lay helpless in the toils I cast
About him, helpless as the statue there
Against that strangling bell-flower's bondage : tear
Away and tread to dust the parasite,
But do the passive marble no despite !
I love him as I hate you.   Kill me !   Strike
At one blow both infinitudes alike   80
Out of existence — hate and love !   Whence love?
That 's safe inside my heart, nor will remove
For any searching of your steel, I think.
Whence hate?   The secret lay on lip, at brink
Of speech, in one fierce tremble to escape,
At every form wherein your love took shape,
At each new provocation of your kiss,
Kill me ! "

> We went in.

> > > Next day after this,
I felt as if the speech might come.   I spoke —
Easily, after all.

> > " The lifted cloak   90
Was screen sufficient : I concern myself
Hardly with laying hands on who for pelf —
Whate'er the ignoble kind — may prowl and brave
Cuffing and kicking proper to a knave
Detected by my household's vigilance.
Enough of such !   As for my love-romance —
I, like our good Hidalgo, rub my eyes
And wake and wonder how the film could rise
Which changed for me a barber's basin straight
Into — Mambrino's helm?   I hesitate   100
Nowise to say — God's sacramental cup !
Why should I blame the brass which, burnished up,
Will blaze, to all but me, as good as gold?
To me — a warning I was overbold
In judging metals.   The Hidalgo waked
Only to die, if I remember, — staked

His life upon the basin's worth, and lost:
While I confess torpidity at most
In here and there a limb; but, lame and halt,
Still should I work on, still repair my fault   110
Ere I took rest in death, — no fear at all!
Now, work — no word before the curtain fall!"

The "curtain"? That of death on life, I meant:
My "word" permissible in death's event,
Would be — truth, soul to soul; for, otherwise,
Day by day, three years long, there had to rise
And, night by night, to fall upon our stage —
Ours, doomed to public play by heritage —
Another curtain, when the world, perforce
Our critical assembly, in due course   120
Came and went, witnessing, gave praise or blame
To art-mimetic. It had spoiled the game
If, suffered to set foot behind our scene,
The world had witnessed how stage-king and queen,
Gallant and lady, but a minute since
Enarming each the other, would evince
No sign of recognition as they took
His way and her way to whatever nook
Waited them in the darkness either side
Of that bright stage where lately groom and bride   130
Had fired the audience to a frenzy-fit
Of sympathetic rapture — every whit
Earned as the curtain fell on her and me,
— Actors. Three whole years, nothing was to see
But calm and concord: where a speech was due
There came the speech; when smiles were wanted too
Smiles were as ready. In a place like mine,
Where foreign and domestic cares combine,
There 's audience every day and all day long;
But finally the last of the whole throng   140
Who linger lets one see his back. For her —
Why, liberty and liking: I aver,
Liking and liberty! For me — I breathed,
Let my face rest from every wrinkle wreathed
Smile-like about the mouth, unlearned my task
Of personation till next day bade mask,
And quietly betook me from that world
To the real world, not pageant: there unfurled
In work, its wings, my soul, the fretted power.
Three years I worked, each minute of each hour   150
Not claimed by acting: — work I may dispense
With talk about, since work in evidence,
Perhaps in history; who knows or cares?

After three years, this way, all unawares,
Our acting ended.   She and I, at close
Of a loud night-feast, led, between two rows
Of bending male and female loyalty,
Our lord the king down staircase, while, held high
At arm's length did the twisted tapers' flare
Herald his passage from our palace where   160
Such visiting left glory evermore.
Again the ascent in public, till at door
As we two stood by the saloon — now blank
And disencumbered of its guests — there sank
A whisper in my ear, so low and yet
So unmistakable !

          " I half forget
The chamber you repair to, and I want
Occasion for one short word — if you grant
That grace — within a certain room you called
Our '*Study*,' for you wrote there while I scrawled   170
Some paper full of faces for my sport.
That room I can remember.   Just one short
Word with you there, for the remembrance' sake !"

" Follow me thither !" I replied.

                  We break
The gloom a little, as with guiding lamp
I lead the way, leave warmth and cheer, by damp
Blind disused serpentining ways afar
From where the habitable chambers are, —
Ascend, descend stairs tunneled thro' the stone, —
Always in silence, — till I reach the lone   180
Chamber sepulchred for my very own
Out of the palace-quarry.   When a boy,
Here was my fortress, stronghold from annoy,
Proof-positive of ownership ; in youth
I garnered up my gleanings here — uncouth
But precious relics of vain hopes, vain fears ;
Finally, this became in after years
My closet of entrenchment to withstand
Invasion of the foe on every hand —
The multifarious herd in bower and hall,   190
State-room, — rooms whatsoe'er the style, which call
On masters to be mindful that, before
Men, they must look like men and something more.
Here, — when our lord the king's bestowment ceased
To deck me on the day that, golden-fleeced,
I touched ambition's height, — 't was here, released

From glory (always symboled by a chain !)
No sooner was I privileged to gain
My secret domicile than glad I flung
That last toy on the table — gazed where hung   200
On hook my father's gift, the arquebus —
And asked myself " Shall I envisage thus
The new prize and the old prize, when I reach
Another year's experience ? — own that each
Equaled advantage — sportsman's — statesman's tool ?
That brought me down an eagle, this — a fool ! "

Into which room on entry, I set down
The lamp, and turning saw whose rustled gown
Had told me my wife followed, pace for pace.
Each of us looked the other in the face.   210
She spoke.   " Since I could die now . . . "

                                        (To explain
Why that first struck me, know — not once again
Since the adventure at the porphyry's edge
Three years before, which sundered like a wedge
Her soul from mine, — tho' daily, smile to smile,
We stood before the public, — all the while
Not once had I distinguished, in that face
I paid observance to, the faintest trace
Of feature more than requisite for eyes
To do their duty by and recognize :   220
So did I force mine to obey my will
And pry no further.   There exists such skill, —
Those know who need it.   What physician shrinks
From needful contact with a corpse ?   He drinks
No plague so long as thirst for knowledge, — not
An idler impulse, — prompts inquiry.   What,
And will you disbelieve in power to bid
Our spirit back to bounds, as tho' we chid
A child from scrutiny that 's just and right
In manhood ?   Sense, not soul, accomplished sight,   230
Reported daily she it was — not how
Nor why a change had come to cheek and brow.)

" Since I could die now of the truth concealed,
Yet dare not, must not die, — so seems revealed
The Virgin's mind to me, — for death means peace,
Wherein no lawful part have I, whose lease
Of life and punishment the truth avowed
May haply lengthen, — let me push the shroud
Away, that steals to muffle ere is just
My penance-fire in snow !   I dare — I must   240

Live, by avowal of the truth — this truth —
I loved you !   Thanks for the fresh serpent's tooth
That, by a prompt new pang more exquisite
Than all preceding torture, proves me right !
I loved you yet I lost you !   May I go
Burn to the ashes, now my shame you know?"

I think there never was such — how express? —
Horror coquetting with voluptuousness,
As in those arms of Eastern workmanship —
Yataghan, kandjar, things that rend and rip,   250
Gash rough, slash smooth, help hate so many ways,
Yet ever keep a beauty that betrays
Love still at work with the artificer
Throughout his quaint devising.   Why prefer,
Except for love's sake, that a blade should writhe
And bicker like a flame? — now play the scythe
As if some broad neck tempted, — now contract
And needle off into a fineness lacked
For just that puncture which the heart demands?
Then, such adornment !   Wherefore need our hands   260
Enclose not ivory alone, nor gold
Roughened for use, but jewels?   Nay, behold !
Fancy my favourite — which I seem to grasp
While I describe the luxury.   No asp
Is diapered more delicate round throat
Than this below the handle !   These denote
— These mazy lines meandering, to end
Only in flesh they open — what intend
They else but water-purlings — pale contrast
With the life-crimson where they blend at last?   270
And mark the handle's dim pellucid green,
Carved, the hard jadestone, as you pinch a bean,
Into a sort of parrot-bird !   He pecks
A grape-bunch; his two eyes are ruby-specks
Pure from the mine : seen this way, — glassy blank,
But turn them, — lo the inmost fire, that shrank
From sparkling, sends a red dart right to aim !
Why did I choose such toys?   Perhaps the game
Of peaceful men is warlike, just as men
War-wearied get amusement from that pen   280
And paper we grow sick of — statesfolk tired
Of merely (when such measures are required)
Dealing out doom to people by three words,
A signature and seal : we play with swords
Suggestive of quick process.   That is how
I came to like the toys described you now,
Store of which glittered on the walls and strewed

The table, even, while my wife pursued
Her purpose to its ending.   "Now you know
This shame, my three years' torture, let me go, —   290
Burn to the very ashes!   You — I lost,
Yet you — I loved !"

                              The thing I pity most
In men is — action prompted by surprise
Of anger: men? nay, bulls — whose onset lies
At instance of the firework and the goad !
Once the foe prostrate, — trampling once bestowed, —
Prompt follows placability, regret,
Atonement.   Trust me, blood-warmth never yet
Betokened strong will !   As no leap of pulse
Pricked me, that first time, so did none convulse   300
My veins at this occasion for resolve.
Had that devolved which did not then devolve
Upon me, I had done — what now to do
Was quietly apparent.

                              "Tell me who
The man was, crouching by the porphyry vase !"

"No, never !   All was folly in his case,
All guilt in mine.   I tempted, he complied."

"And yet you loved me?"

                              "Loved you.   Double-dyed
In folly and in guilt, I thought you gave
Your heart and soul away from me to slave   310
At statecraft.   Since my right in you seemed lost,
I stung myself to teach you, to your cost,
What you rejected could be prized beyond
Life, heaven, by the first fool I threw a fond
Look on, a fatal word to."

                              "And you still
Love me ?   Do I conjecture well or ill? "

"Conjecture — well or ill !   I had three years
To spend in learning you."

                              "We both are peers
In knowledge, therefore : since three years are spent
Ere thus much of yourself *I* learn — who went   320
Back to the house, that day, and brought my mind
To bear upon your action: uncombined

Motive from motive, till the dross, deprived
Of every purer particle, survived
At last in native simple hideousness,
Utter contemptibility, nor less
Nor more.   Contemptibility — exempt
How could I, from its proper due — contempt?
I have too much despised you to divert
My life from its set course by help or hurt   330
Of your all-despicable life — perturb
The calm I work in, by — men's mouths to curb,
Which at such news were clamorous enough —
Men's eyes to shut before my broidered stuff
With the huge hole there, my emblazoned wall
Blank where a scutcheon hung, — by, worse than all,
Each day's procession, my paraded life
Robbed and impoverished thro' the wanting wife
— Now that my life (which means — my work) was grown
Riches indeed!   Once, just this worth alone   340
Seemed work to have, that profit gained thereby
Of good and praise would — how rewardingly! —
Fall at your feet, — a crown I hoped to cast
Before your love, my love should crown at last.
No love remaining to cast crown before,
My love stopped work now : but contempt the more
Impelled me task as ever head and hand,
Because the very fiends weave ropes of sand
Rather than taste pure hell in idleness.
Therefore I kept my memory down by stress   350
Of daily work I had no mind to stay
For the world's wonder at the wife away.
Oh, it was easy all of it, believe,
For I despised you !   But your words retrieve
Importantly the past.   No hate assumed
The mask of love at any time !   There gloomed
A moment when love took hate's semblance, urged
By causes you declare ; but love's self purged
Away a fancied wrong I did both loves
— Yours and my own ; by no hate's help, it proves   36c
Purgation was attempted.   Then, you rise
High by how many a grade !   I did despise —
I do but hate you.   Let hate's punishment
Replace contempt's!   First step to which ascent —
Write down your own words I re-utter you !
'I loved my husband and I hated — who
He was, I took up as my first chance, mere
Mud-ball to fling and make love foul with !'   Here
Lies paper !"

"Would my blood for ink suffice!"

"It may : this minion from a land of spice,   370
Silk, feather — every bird of jeweled breast —
This poignard's beauty, ne'er so lightly prest
Above your heart there.". . .
                              "Thus ?"
                                        "It flows, I see.
Dip there the point and write!"
                                "Dictate to me!
Nay, I remember."

                    And she wrote the words.
I read them.   Then — "Since love, in you, affords
License for hate, in me, to quench (I say)
Contempt — why, hate itself has passed away
In vengeance — foreign to contempt.   Depart
Peacefully to that death which Eastern art   380
Imbued this weapon with, if tales be true !
Love will succeed to hate.   I pardon you —
Dead in our chamber !"

                        True as truth the tale.
She died ere morning ; then, I saw how pale
Her cheek was ere it wore day's paint-disguise,
And what a hollow darkened 'neath her eyes,
Now that I used my own.   She sleeps, as erst
Beloved, in this your church : ay, yours !

                                        Immersed
In thought so deeply, Father ?   Sad, perhaps?
For whose sake, hers or mine or his who wraps   390
— Still plain I seem to see ! — about his head
The idle cloak, — about his heart (instead
Of cuirass) some fond hope he may elude
My vengeance in the cloister's solitude?
Hardly, I think !   As little helped his brow
The cloak then, Father — as your grate helps now !

CENCIAJA.

Ogni cencio vuol entrare in bucato. —Italian Proverb.

MAY I print, Shelley, how it came to pass
That when your Beatrice seemed — by lapse
Of many a long month since her sentence fell —
Assured of pardon for the parricide, —
By intercession of staunch friends, or say,
By certain pricks of conscience in the Pope,
Conniver at Francesco Cenci's guilt, —
Suddenly all things changed and Clement grew
" Stern," as you state, " nor to be moved nor bent,
But said these three words coldly ' *She must die;* '   10
Subjoining ' *Pardon?   Paolo Santa Croce*
Murdered his mother also yestereve,
And he is fled: she shall not flee, at least! ' "
— So, to the letter, sentence was fulfilled ?
Shelley, may I condense verbosity
That lies before me, into some few words
Of English, and illustrate your superb
Achievement by a rescued anecdote,
No great things, only new and true beside?
As if some mere familiar of a house   20
Should venture to accost the group at gaze
Before its Titian, famed the wide world through,
And supplement such pictured masterpiece
By whisper " Searching in the archives here,
I found the reason of the Lady's fate,
And how by accident it came to pass
She wears the halo and displays the palm:
Who, haply, else had never suffered — no,
Nor graced our gallery, by consequence."
Who loved the work would like the little news: 30
Who lauds your poem lends an ear to me
Relating how the penalty was paid
By one Marchese dell' Oriolo, called
Onofrio Santa Croce otherwise,
For his complicity in matricide
With Paolo his own brother, — he whose crime
And flight induced " those three words — She must die."
Thus I unroll you then the manuscript.

" God's justice " — (of the multiplicity
Of such communications extant still,   40
Recording, each, injustice done by God
In person of his Vicar-upon-earth,

Scarce one but leads off to the self-same tune) —
"God's justice, tardy tho' it prove perchance,
Rests never on the track until it reach
Delinquency.   In proof I cite the case
Of Paolo Santa Croce."

      Many times
The youngster, — having been importunate
That Marchesine Costanza, who remained
His widowed mother, should supplant the heir   50
Her elder son, and substitute himself
In sole possession of her faculty, —
And meeting just as often with rebuff, —
Blinded by so exorbitant a lust
Of gold, the youngster straightway tasked his wits,
Casting about to kill the lady — thus.

He first, to cover his iniquity,
Writes to Onofrio Santa Croce, then
Authoritative lord, acquainting him
Their mother was contamination — wrought   60
Like hell-fire in the beauty of their House
By dissoluteness and abandonment
Of soul and body to impure delight.
Moreover, since she suffered from disease,
Those symptoms which her death made manifest
Hydroptic, he affirmed were fruits of sin
About to bring confusion and disgrace
Upon the ancient lineage and high fame
O' the family, when published.   Duty-bound,
He asked his brother — what a son should do?   70

Which when Marchese dell' Oriolo heard
By letter, being absent at his land
Oriolo, he made answer, this, no more :
"It must behove a son, — things haply so, —
To act as honour prompts a cavalier
And son, perform his duty to all three,
Mother and brothers " — here advice broke off.

By which advice informed and fortified
As he professed himself — as bound by birth
To hear God's voice in primogeniture —   80
Paolo, who kept his mother company
In her domain Subiaco, straightway dared
His whole enormity of enterprise
And, falling on her, stabbed the lady dead;
Whose death demonstrated her innocence,

And happened, — by the way, — since Jesus Christ
Died to save man, just sixteen hundred years.
Costanza was of aspect beautiful
Exceedingly, and seemed, altho' in age
Sixty about, to far surpass her peers   90
The coëtaneous dames, in youth and grace.

Done the misdeed, its author takes to flight,
Foiling thereby the justice of the world :
Not God's however, — God, be sure, knows well
The way to clutch a culprit.   Witness here !
The present sinner, when he leasts expects,
Snug-cornered somewhere i' the Basilicate,
Stumbles upon his death by violence.
A man of blood assaults a man of blood
And slays him somehow.   This was afterward :   100
Enough, he promptly met with his deserts,
And, ending thus, permits we end with him,
And push forthwith to this important point —
His matricide fell out, of all the days,
Precisely when the law-procedure closed
Respecting Count Francesco Cenci's death
Chargeable on his daughter, sons and wife.
" Thus patricide was matched with matricide,"
A poet not inelegantly rhymed :
Nay, fratricide — those Princes Massimi ! —   110
Which so disturbed the spirit of the Pope
That all the likelihood Rome entertained
Of Beatrice's pardon vanished straight,
And she endured the piteous death.

                        Now see
The sequel — what effect commandment had
For strict inquiry into this last case,
When Cardinal Aldobrandini (great
His efficacy — nephew to the Pope)
Was bidden crush — ay, tho' his very hand
Got soil i' the act — crime spawning everywhere !   120
Because, when all endeavour had been used
To catch the aforesaid Paolo, all in vain —
"Make perquisition" quoth our Eminence,
" Throughout his now deserted domicile ! .
Ransack the palace, roof and floor, to find
If haply any scrap of writing, hid
In nook or corner, may convict — who knows? —
Brother Onofrio of intelligence
With brother Paolo, as in brotherhood
Is but too likely : crime spawns everywhere ! "   130

And, every cranny searched accordingly,
There comes to light — O lynx-eyed Cardinal!—
Onofrio's unconsidered writing-scrap,
The letter in reply to Paolo's prayer,
The word of counsel that — things proving so,
Paolo should act the proper knightly part,
And do as was incumbent on a son,
A brother — and a man of birth, be sure!

Whereat immediately the officers
Proceeded to arrest Onofrio — found   140
At football, child's play, unaware of harm,
Safe with his friends, the Orsini, at their seat
Monte Giordano; as he left the house
He came upon the watch in wait for him
Set by the Barigel, — was caught and caged.

News of which capture being, that same hour,
Conveyed to Rome, forthwith our Eminence
Commands Taverna, Governor and Judge,
To have the process in especial care,
Be, first to last, not only president   150
In person, but inquisitor as well,
Nor trust the by-work to a substitute :
Bids him not, squeamish, keep the bench, but scrub
The floor of Justice, so to speak, — go try
His best in prison with the criminal ;
Promising, as reward for by-work done
Fairly on all-fours, that, success obtained
And crime avowed, or such connivency
With crime as should procure a decent death —
Himself will humbly beg — which means, procure —   160
The Hat and Purple from his relative
The Pope, and so repay a diligence
Which, meritorious in the Cenci-case,
Mounts plainly here to Purple and the Hat !

Whereupon did my lord the Governor
So masterfully exercise the task
Enjoined him, that he, day by day, and week
By week, and month by month, from first to last
Toiled for the prize : now, punctual at his place,
Played Judge, and now, assiduous at his post,   170
Inquisitor — pressed cushion and scoured plank,
Early and late.   Noon's fervour and night's chill,
Naught moved whom morn would, purpling, make amends!
So that observers laughed as, many a day,
He left home, in July when day is flame,

Posted to Tordinona-prison, plunged
Into a vault where daylong night is ice,
There passed his eight hours on a stretch, content,
Examining Onofrio: all the stress
Of all examination steadily   180
Converging into one pin-point, — he pushed
Tentative now of head and now of heart.
As when the nuthatch taps and tries the nut
This side and that side till the kernel sound, —
So did he press the sole and single point
— What was the very meaning of the phrase
" *Do as beseems an honoured cavalier ?* "

Which one persistent question-torture, — plied
Day by day, week by week, and month by month,
Morn, noon and night, — fatigued away a mind   190
Grown imbecile by darkness, solitude,
And one vivacious memory gnawing there
As when a corpse is coffined with a snake :
— Fatigued Onofrio into what might seem
Admission that perchance his judgment groped
So blindly, feeling for an issue — aught
With semblance of an issue from the toils
Cast of a sudden round feet late so free,
He possibly might have envisaged, scarce
Recoiled from — even were the issue death   200
— Even her death whose life was death and worse!
Always provided that the charge of crime,
Each jot and tittle of the charge were true.
In such a sense, belike, he might advise
His brother to expurgate crime with . . . well,
With blood, if blood must follow on " *the course
Taken as might beseem a cavalier*."

Whereupon process ended, and report
Was made without a minute of delay
To Clement, who, because of those two crimes   210
O' the Massimi and Cenci flagrant late,
Must needs impatiently desire result.

Result obtained, he bade the Governor
Summon the Congregation and despatch.
Summons made, sentence passed accordingly
— Death by beheading.   When his death-decree
Was intimated to Onofrio, all
Man could do — that did he to save himself.
'T was much, the having gained for his defence
The Advocate o' the Poor, with natural help   220

Of many noble friendly persons fain
To disengage a man of family,
So young too, from his grim entanglement :
But Cardinal Aldobrandini ruled
There must be no diversion of the law.
Justice is justice, and the magistrate
Bears not the sword in vain.   Who sins must die.

So, the Marchese had his head cut off
With Rome to see, a concourse infinite ;
In Place Saint Angelo beside the Bridge :   230
Where, demonstrating magnanimity
Adequate to his birth and breed, — poor boy ! —
He made the people the accustomed speech,
Exhorted them to true faith, honest works,
And special good behaviour as regards
A parent of no matter what the sex,
Bidding each son take warning from himself.
Truly, it was considered in the boy
Stark staring lunacy, no less, to snap
So plain a bait, be hooked and hauled a-shore   240
By such an angler as the Cardinal!
Why make confession of his privity
To Paolo's enterprise?   Mere sealing lips —
Or, better, saying "When I counselled him
' To do as might beseem a cavalier,'
What could I mean but *' Hide our parent's shame*
As Christian ought, by aid of Holy Church!
Bury it in a convent — ay, beneath
Enough dotation to prevent its ghost
From troubling earth!' "   Mere saying thus, — 't is plain,   250
Not only were his life the recompense,
But he had manifestly proved himself
True Christian, and in lieu of punishment
Got praise of all men.   So the populace.

Anyhow, when the Pope made promise good
(That of Aldobrandini, near and dear)
And gave Taverna, who had toiled so much,
A Cardinal's equipment, some such word
As this from mouth to ear went saucily :
"Taverna's cap is dyed in what he drew   260
From Santa Croce's veins! "   So joked the world.

I add : Onofrio left one child behind,
A daughter named Valeria, dowered with grace
Abundantly of soul and body, doomed
To life the shorter for her father's fate.

By death of her, the Marquisate returned
To that Orsini House from whence it came:
Oriolo having passed as donative
To Santa Croce from their ancestors.

And no word more? By all means! Would you know   270
The authoritative answer, when folk urged
"What made Aldobrandini, hound-like staunch,
Hunt out of life a harmless simpleton?"
The answer was — "Hatred implacable,
By reason they were rivals in their love."
The Cardinal's desire was to a dame
Whose favour was Onofrio's. Pricked with pride,
The simpleton must ostentatiously
Display a ring, the Cardinal's love-gift,
Given to Onofrio as the lady's gage;   280
Which ring on finger, as he put forth hand
To draw a tapestry, the Cardinal
Saw and knew, gift and owner, old and young;
Whereon a fury entered him — the fire
He quenched with what coul_ quench fire only — blood.
Nay, more: "there want not who affirm to boot,
The unwise boy, a certain festal eve,
Feigned ignorance of who the wight might be
That pressed too closely on him with a crowd.
He struck the Cardinal a blow: and then,   290
To put a face upon the incident,
Dared next day, smug as ever, go pay court
I' the Cardinal's antechamber. Mark and mend,
Ye youth, by this example how may greed
Vainglorious operate in worldly souls!"

So ends the chronicler, beginning with
"God's justice, tardy tho' it prove perchance,
Rests never till it reach delinquency."
Ay, or how otherwise had come to pass
That Victor rules, this present year, in Rome?   300

PORPHYRIA'S LOVER.

I.

THE rain set early in to-night,
    The sullen wind was soon awake,
It tore the elm-tops down for spite,
    And did its worst to vex the lake:
I listened with heart fit to break.

s

II.

When glided in Porphyria ; straight
　　She shut the cold out and the storm,
And kneeled and made the cheerless grate
　　Blaze up, and all the cottage warm ;
Which done, she rose, and from her form　　　　**10**

III.

Withdrew the dripping cloak and shawl,
　　And laid her soiled gloves by, untied
Her hat and let the damp hair fall,
　　And, last, she sat down by my side
And called me.　When no voice replied,

IV.

She put my arm about her waist,
　　And made her smooth white shoulder bare,
And all her yellow hair displaced,
　　And, stooping, made my cheek lie there,
And spread, o'er all, her yellow hair,　　　　**20**

V.

Murmuring how she loved me — she
　　Too weak, for all her heart's endeavour,
To set its struggling passion free
　　From pride, and vainer ties dissever,
And give herself to me for ever.

VI.

But passion sometimes would prevail,
　　Nor could to-night's gay feast restrain
A sudden thought of one so pale
　　For love of her, and all in vain :
So, she was come thro' wind and rain.　　　　**30**

VII.

Be sure I looked up at her eyes
　　Happy and proud ; at last I knew
Porphyria worshiped me ; surprise
　　Made my heart swell, and still it grew
While I debated what to do.

VIII.

That moment she was mine, mine, fair,
　　Perfectly pure and good : I found

A thing to do, and all her hair
  In one long yellow string I wound
Three times her little throat around,   40

IX.

And strangled her.   No pain felt she;
  I am quite sure she felt no pain.
As a shut bud that holds a bee,
  I warily oped her lids : again
Laughed the blue eyes without a stain.

X.

And I untightened next the tress
  About her neck ; her cheek once more
Blushed bright beneath my burning kiss :
  I propped her head up as before.
Only, this time my shoulder bore   50

XI.

Her head, which droops upon it still :
  The smiling rosy little head,
So glad it has its utmost will,
  That all it scorned at once is fled,
And I, its love, am gained instead !

XII.

Porphyria's love : she guessed not how
  Her darling one wish would be heard.
And thus we sit together now.
  And all night long we have not stirred,
And yet God has not said a word !   60

FILIPPO BALDINUCCI ON THE PRIVILEGE OF BURIAL

A Reminiscence of A.D. 1676.

I.

NO, boy, we must not (so began
  My Uncle — he 's with God long since
A-petting me, the good old man!)
We must not (and he seemed to wince,

And lost that laugh whereto had grown
　　His chuckle at my piece of news,
How cleverly I aimed my stone)
　　I fear we must not pelt the Jews!

II.

When I was young, indeed, — ah, faith
　　Was young and strong in Florence too!　　　10
We Christians never dreamed of scathe
　　Because we cursed or kicked the crew.
But now — well, well!　The olive-crops
　　Weighed double then, and Arno's pranks
Would always spare religious shops
　　Whenever he o'erflowed his banks!

III.

I 'll tell you (and his eye regained
　　Its twinkle) tell you something choice!
Something may help you keep unstained
　　Your honest zeal to stop the voice　　　20
Of unbelief with stone-throw — spite
　　Of laws, which modern fools enact,
That we must suffer Jews in sight
　　Go wholly unmolested!　　Fact!

IV.

There was, then, in my youth, and yet
　　Is, by our San Frediano, just
Below the Blessed Olivet,
　　A wayside ground wherein they thrust
Their dead, — these Jews, — the more our shame!
　　Except that, so they will but die,　　　30
Christians perchance incur no blame
　　In giving hogs a hoist to stye.

V.

There, anyhow, Jews stow away
　　Their dead ; and, — such their insolence, —
Slink at odd times to sing and pray
　　As Christians do — all make-pretence ! —
Which wickedness they perpetrate
　　Because they think no Christians see.
They reckoned here, at any rate,
　　Without their host : ha, ha! he, he!　　　40

VI.

For, what should join their plot of ground
  But a good Farmer's Christian field?
The Jews had hedged their corner round
  With bramble-bush to keep concealed
Their doings: for the public road
  Ran betwixt this their ground and that
The Farmer's, where he ploughed and sowed,
  Grew corn for barn and grapes for vat.

VII.

So, properly to guard his store
  And gall the unbelievers too,   50
He builds a shrine and, what is more,
  Procures a painter whom I knew,
One Buti (he 's with God) to paint
  A holy picture there — no less
Than Virgin Mary free from taint
  Borne to the sky by angels: yes!

VIII.

Which shrine he fixed, — who says him nay? —
  A-facing with its picture-side
Not as you 'd think, the public way,
  But just where sought these hounds to hide   60
Their carrion from that very truth
  Of Mary's triumph: not a hound
Could act his mummeries uncouth
  But Mary shamed the pack all round!

IX.

Now, if it was amusing, judge!
  — To see the company arrive,
Each Jew intent to end his trudge
  And take his pleasure (tho' alive)
With all his Jewish kith and kin
  Below ground, have his venom out,   70
Sharpen his wits for next day's sin,
  Curse Christians, and so home, no doubt!

X.

Whereas, each phiz upturned beholds
  Mary, I warrant, soaring brave!
And in a trice, beneath the folds
  Of filthy garb which gowns each knave,

Down drops it — there to hide grimace,
  Contortion of the mouth and nose
At finding Mary in the place
  They 'd keep for Pilate, I suppose !   80

XI.

At last, they will not brook — not they! —
  Longer such outrage on their tribe :
So, in some hole and corner, lay
  Their heads together — how to bribe
The meritorious Farmer's self
  To straight undo his work, restore
Their chance to meet, and muse on pelf —
  Pretending sorrow, as before!

XII.

Forthwith, a posse, if you please,
  Of Rabbi This and Rabbi That   90
Almost go down upon their knees
  To get him lay the picture flat.
The spokesman, eighty years of age,
  Gray as a badger, with a goat's
— Not only beard but bleat, 'gins wage
  War with our Mary. Thus he dotes : —

XIII.

"Friends, grant a grace ! How Hebrews toil
  Thro' life in Florence — why relate
To those who lay the burden, spoil
  Our paths of peace ? We bear our fate   100
But when with life the long toil ends,
  Why must you — the expression craves
Pardon, but truth compels me, friends ! —
  Why must you plague us in our graves?

XIV.

"Thoughtlessly plague, I would believe !
  For how can you — the lords of ease
By nurture, birthright — e'en conceive
  Our luxury to lie with trees
And turf, — the cricket and the bird
  Left for our last companionship :   110
No harsh deed, no unkindly word,
  No frowning brow nor scornful lip!

XV.

" Death's luxury, we now rehearse
 While, living thro' your streets we fare
And take your hatred : nothing worse
 Have we, once dead and safe, to bear!
So we refresh our souls, fulfil
 Our works, our daily tasks ; and thus
Gather you grain — earth's harvest — still
 The wheat for you, the straw for us.   **120**

XVI.

" ' What flouting in a face, what harm,
 In just a lady borne from bier
By boys' heads, wings for leg and arm?'
 You question. Friends, the harm is here —
That just when our last sigh is heaved,
 And we would fain thank God and you
For labour done and peace achieved,
 Back comes the Past in full review!

XVII.

" At sight of just that simple flag,
 Starts the foe-feeling serpent-like   **130**
From slumber. Leave it lulled, nor drag —
 Tho' fangless — forth, what needs must strike
When stricken sore, tho' stroke be vain
 Against the mailed oppressor! Give
Play to our fancy that we gain
 Life's rights when once we cease to live!

XVIII.

" Thus much to courtesy, to kind,
 To conscience! Now to Florence folk!
There 's core beneath this apple-rind,
 Beneath this white-of-egg there 's yolk! **140**
Beneath this prayer to courtesy,
 Kind, conscience — there 's a sum to pouch!
How many ducats down will buy
 Our shame's removal, sirs? Avouch!

XIX.

" Removal, not destruction, sirs!
 Just turn your picture! Let it front
The public path! Or memory errs,
 Or that same public path is wont

To witness many a chance befall
　　Of lust, theft, bloodshed — sins enough,   **150**
Wherein our Hebrew part is small.
　　Convert yourselves!"— he cut up rough.

XX.

Look you, how soon a service paid
　　Religion yields the servant fruit!
A prompt reply our Farmer made
　　So following : "Sirs, to grant your suit
Involves much danger! How? Transpose
　　Our Lady? Stop the chastisement,
All for your good, herself bestows?
　　What wonder if I grudge consent?   **160**

XXI.

" — Yet grant it : since, what cash I take
　　Is so much saved from wicked use.
We know you! And, for Mary's sake,
　　A hundred ducats shall induce
Concession to your prayer. One day
　　Suffices : Master Buti's brush
Turns Mary round the other way,
　　And deluges your side with slush.

XXII.

" Down with the ducats therefore!" Dump,
　　Dump, dump it falls, each counted piece,   **170**
Hard gold.   Then out of door they stump,
　　These dogs, each brisk as with new lease
Of life, I warrant, — glad he 'll die
　　Henceforward just as he may choose,
Be buried and in clover lie!
　　Well said Esaias — "stiff-necked Jews!"

XXIII.

Off posts without a minute's loss
　　Our Farmer, once the cash in poke,
And summons Buti — ere its gloss
　　Have time to fade from off the joke —   **180**
To chop and change his work, undo
　　The done side, make the side, now blank,
Recipient of our Lady — who,
　　Displaced thus, had these dogs to thank!

XXIV.

Now, boy, you 're hardly to instruct
   In technicalities of Art!
My nephew's childhood sure has sucked
   Along with mother's-milk some part
Of painter's-practice — learned, at least,
   How expeditiously is plied 190
A work in fresco — never ceased
   When once begun — a day, each side.

XXV.

So, Buti — he 's with God — begins :
   First covers up the shrine all round
With hoarding ; then, as like as twins,
   Paints, t' other side the burial-ground,
New Mary, every point the same ;
   Next, sluices over, as agreed,
The old ; and last — but, spoil the game
   By telling you? Not I, indeed! 200

XXVI.

Well, ere the week was half at end,
   Out came the object of this zeal,
This fine alacrity to spend
   Hard money for mere dead men's weal!
How think you? That old spokesman Jew
   Was High Priest, and he had a wife
As old, and she was dying too,
   And wished to end in peace her life!

XXVII.

And he must humour dying whims,
   And soothe her with the idle hope 210
They 'd say their prayers and sing their hymns
   As if her husband were the Pope!
And she did die — believing just
   This privilege was purchased! Dead
In comfort thro' her foolish trust!
   " Stiff-necked ones," well Esaias said!

XXVIII.

So, Sabbath morning, out of gate
   And on to way, what sees our arch
Good Farmer? Why, they hoist their freight —
   The corpse — on shoulder, and so, march! 220

"Now for it, Buti!"   In the nick
  Of time 't is pully-hauly, hence
With hoarding!   O'er the wayside quick
  There 's Mary plain in evidence!

XXIX.

And here 's the convoy halting : right!
  O they are bent on howling psalms
And growling prayers, when opposite!
  And yet they glance, for all their qualms,
Approve that promptitude of his,
  The Farmer's — duly at his post   230
To take due thanks from every phiz,
  Sour smirk — nay, surly smile almost!

XXX.

Then earthward drops each brow again ;
  The solemn task 's resumed ; they reach
Their holy field — the unholy train :
  Enter its precinct, all and each,
Wrapt somehow in their godless rites ;
  Till, rites at end, up-waking, lo
They lift their faces!   What delights
  The mourners as they turn to go ?   240

XXXI.

Ha, ha ! he, he! On just the side
  They drew their purse-strings to make quit
Of Mary, — Christ the Crucified
  Fronted them now — these biters bit!
Never was such a hiss and snort,
  Such screwing nose and shooting lip!
Their purchase — honey in report —
  Proved gall and verjuice at first sip!

XXXII.

Out they break, on they bustle, where,
  A-top of wall, the Farmer waits   250
With Buti : never fun so rare !
  The Farmer has the best : he rates
The rascal, as the old High Priest
  Takes on himself to sermonize —
Nay, sneer "We Jews supposed, at least,
  Theft was a crime in Christian eyes!"

XXXIII.

" Theft ? " cries the Farmer, " Eat your words !
   Show me what constitutes a breach
Of faith in aught was said or heard !
   I promised you in plainest speech   260
I 'd take the thing you count disgrace
   And put it here — and here 't is put !
Did you suppose I 'd leave the place
   Blank therefore, just your rage to glut?

XXXIV.

" I guess you dared not stipulate
   For such a damned impertinence !
So, quick, my graybeard, out of gate
   And in at Ghetto !   Haste you hence !
As long as I have house and land,
   To spite you irreligious chaps   270
Here shall the Crucifixion stand —
   Unless you down with cash, perhaps ! "

XXXV.

So snickered he and Buti both.
   The Jews said nothing, interchanged
A glance or two, renewed their oath
   To keep ears stopped and hearts estranged
From grace, for all our Church can do.
   Then off they scuttle : sullen jog
Homewards, against our Church to brew
   Fresh mischief in their synagogue.   280

XXXVI.

But next day — see what happened, boy !
   See why I bid you have a care
How you pelt Jews !   The knaves employ
   Such methods of revenge, forbear
No outrage on our faith, when free
   To wreak their malice !   Here they took
So base a method — plague o' me
   If I record it in my Book!

XXXVII.

For, next day, while the Farmer sat
   Laughing with Buti, in his shop,   290
At their successful joke, — rat-tat, —
   Door opens, and they 're like to drop

Down to the floor as in there stalks
  A six-feet-high herculean-built
Young he-Jew with a beard that baulks
  Description.   " Help ere blood be spilt! "

XXXVIII.

— Screamed Buti : for he recognized
  Whom but the son, no less no more,
Of that High Priest his work surprised
  So pleasantly the day before !   300
Son of the mother, then, whereof
  The bier he lent a shoulder to,
And made the moans about, dared scoff
  At sober Christian grief — the Jew!

XXXIX.

" Sirs, I salute you !   Never rise !
  No apprehension ! "   (Buti, white
And trembling like a tub of size,
  Had tried to smuggle out of sight
The picture's self — the thing in oils,
  You know, from which a fresco 's dashed   310
Which courage speeds while caution spoils)
  " Stay and be praised sir, unabashed!

XL.

" Praised, — ay, and paid too : for I come
  To buy that very work of yours.
My poor abode, which boasts — well, some
  Few specimens of Art, secures
Haply, a masterpiece indeed
  If I should find my humble means
Suffice the outlay.   So, proceed!
  Propose — ere prudence intervenes! "   320

XLI.

On Buti, cowering like a child,
  These words descended from aloft,
In tones so ominously mild,
  With smile terrifically soft
To that degree — could Buti dare
  (Poor fellow) use his brains, think twice?
He asked, thus taken unaware,
  No more than just the proper price !

XLII.

" Done ! " cries the monster.   " I disburse
   Forthwith your moderate demand.   **330**
Count on my custom — if no worse
   Your future work be, understand,
Than this I carry off !   No aid !
   My arm, sir, lacks nor bone nor thews :
The burden 's easy, and we 're made,
   Easy or hard, to bear — we Jews ! "

XLIII.

Crossing himself at such escape,
   Buti by turns the money eyes
And, timidly, the stalwart shape
   Now moving doorwards ; but, more wise,   **340**
The Farmer, — who, tho' dumb, this while
   Had watched advantage — straight conceived
A reason for that tone and smile
   So mild and soft !   The Jew — believed !

XLIV.

Mary in triumph borne to deck
   A Hebrew household !   Pictured where
No one was used to bend the neck
   In praise or bow the knee in prayer !
Borne to that domicile by whom ?
   The son of the High Priest !   Thro' what ?   **350**
An insult done his mother's tomb !
   Saul changed to Paul — the case came pat !

XLV.

" Stay, dog-Jew . . . gentle sir, that is !
   Resolve me !   Can it be, she crowned, —
Mary, by miracle, — Oh bliss ! —
   My present to your burial-ground ?
Certain, a ray of light has burst
   Your veil of darkness !   Had you else,
Only for Mary's sake, unpursed
   So much hard money ?   Tell — oh, tell 's ! "   **360**

XLVI.

Round — like a serpent that we took
   For worm and trod on — turns his bulk
About the Jew.   First dreadful look
   Sends Buti in a trice to skulk

Out of sight somewhere, safe — alack!
    But our good Farmer faith made bold:
And firm (with Florence at his back)
    He stood, while gruff the gutturals rolled —

XLVII.

" Ay, sir, a miracle was worked,
    By quite another power, I trow,   370
Than ever yet in canvas lurked,
    Or you would scarcely face me now!
A certain impulse did suggest
    A certain grasp with this right-hand,
Which probably had put to rest
    Our quarrel, — thus your throat once spanned!

XLVIII.

" But I remembered me, subdued
    That impulse, and you face me still!
And soon a philosophic mood
    Succeeding (hear it, if you will!)   380
Has altogether changed my views
    Concerning Art.   Blind prejudice!
Well may you Christians tax us Jews
    With scrupulosity too nice!

XLIX.

" For, don't I see, — let's issue join! —
    Whenever I'm allowed pollute
(I — and my little bag of coin)
    Some Christian palace of repute, —
Don't I see stuck up everywhere
    Abundant proof that cultured taste   390
Has Beauty for its only care,
    And upon Truth no thought to waste?

L.

" ' Jew, since it must be, take in pledge
    Of payment ' — so a Cardinal
Has sighed to me as if a wedge
    Entered his heart — ' this best of all
My treasures!'   Leda, Ganymede
    Or Antiope: swan, eagle, ape,
(Or what's the beast of what's the breed)
    And Jupiter in every shape!   400

LI.

"Whereat if I presume to ask
  'But, Eminence, tho' Titian's whisk
Of brush have well performed its task,
  How comes it these false godships frisk
In presence of — what yonder frame
  Pretends to image? Surely, odd
It seems, you let confront The Name
  Each beast the heathen called his god!'

LII.

"Benignant smiles me pity straight
  The Cardinal. ''T is Truth, we prize!   410
Art 's the sole question in debate!
  These subjects are so many lies.
We treat them with a proper scorn
  When we turn lies — called gods forsooth —
To lies' fit use, now Christ is born.
  Drawing and colouring are Truth.

LIII.

"'Think you I honour lies so much
  As scruple to parade the charms
Of Leda — Titian, every touch —
  Because the thing within her arms   420
Means Jupiter who had the praise
  And prayer of a benighted world?
He would have mine too, if, in days
  Of light, I kept the canvas furled!'

LIV.

"So ending, with some easy gibe.
  What power has logic! I, at once,
Acknowledged error in our tribe
  So squeamish that, when friends ensconce
A pretty picture in its niche
  To do us honour, deck our graves,   430
We fret and fume and have an itch
  To strangle folk — ungrateful knaves!

LV.

"No, sir! Be sure that — what 's its style,
  Your picture? — shall possess ungrudged
A place among my rank and file
  Of Ledas and what not — be judged

Just as a picture! — and (because
　I fear me much I scarce have bought
A Titian) Master Buti's flaws
　Found there, will have the laugh flaws ought!"　　44c

LVI.

So, with a scowl, it darkens door —
　This bulk — no longer!　Buti makes
Prompt glad re-entry; there 's a score
　Of oaths, as the good Farmer wakes
From what must needs have been a trance,
　Or he had struck (he swears) to ground
The bold bad mouth that dared advance
　Such doctrine the reverse of sound!

LVII.

Was magic here?　Most like!　For, since,
　Somehow our city's faith grows still　　　　450
More and more lukewarm, and our Prince
　Or loses heart or wants the will
To check increase of cold.　'T is " Live
　And let live!　Languidly repress
The Dissident!　In short, — contrive
　Christians must bear with Jews : no less! "

LVIII.

The end seems, any Israelite
　Wants any picture, — pishes, poohs,
Purchases, hangs it full in sight
　In any chamber he may choose!　　　　　　460
In Christ's crown, one more thorn we rue !
　In Mary's bosom, one more sword!
No, boy, you must not pelt a Jew!
　O Lord, how long?　How long, O Lord?

———◦∘◦———

SOLILOQUY OF THE SPANISH CLOISTER.

I.

G R–R–R — there go, my heart's abhorrence!
　　Water your damned flower-pots, do!
If hate killed men, Brother Lawrence,
　God's blood, would not mine kill you!

What? your myrtle-bush wants trimming?
　　Oh, that rose has prior claims —
Needs its leaden vase filled brimming?
　　Hell dry you up with its flames!

II.

At the meal we sit together:
　　Salve tibi! I must hear　　　　　　　　　10
Wise talk of the kind of weather,
　　Sort of season, time of year:
Not a plenteous cork-crop: scarcely
　　Dare we hope oak-galls, I doubt:
What's the Latin name for "parsley"?
　　What's the Greek name for Swine's Snout?

III.

Whew! We 'll have our platter burnished,
　　Laid with care on our own shelf!
With a fire-new spoon we 're furnished,
　　And a goblet for ourself,　　　　　　　　20
Rinsed like something sacrificial
　　Ere 't is fit to touch our chaps —
Marked with L for our initial!
　　(He-he! There his lily snaps!)

IV.

Saint, forsooth! While brown Dolores
　　Squats outside the Convent bank
WIth Sanchicha, telling stories,
　　Steeping tresses in the tank,
Blue-black, lustrous, thick like horse hairs,
　　— Can 't I see his dead eye glow,　　　　30
Bright as 't were a Barbary corsair's?
　　(That is, if he 'd let it show!)

V.

When he finishes refection,
　　Knife and fork he never lays
Cross-wise, to my recollection,
　　As do I, in Jesu's praise.
I the Trinity illustrate,
　　Drinking watered orange-pulp —
In three sips the Arian frustrate;
　　While he drains his at one gulp.　　　　40

T

VI.

Oh, those melons? If he 's able
  We 're to have a feast: so nice!
One goes to the Abbot's table,
  All of us get each a slice.
How go on your flowers? None double?
  Not one fruit-sort can you spy?
Strange! — And I, too, at such trouble
  Keep them close-nipped on the sly!

VII.

There 's a great text in Galatians
  Once you trip on it, entails   50
Twenty-nine distinct damnations
  One sure, if another fails:
If I trip him just a-dying,
  Sure of heaven as sure can be,
Spin him round and send him flying
  Off to hell, a Manichee?

VIII.

Or, my scrofulous French novel
  On gray paper with blunt type!
Simply glance at it, you grovel
  Hand and foot in Belial's gripe: 60
If I double down its pages
  At the woeful sixteenth print,
When he gathers his greengages,
  Ope a sieve and slip it in 't?

IX.

Or, there 's Satan! — one might venture
  Pledge one's soul to him, yet leave
Such a flaw in the indenture
  As he 'd miss, till, past retrieve,
Blasted lay that rose-acacia
  We 're so proud of! *Hy, Zy, Hine . . .*   70
'St, there 's Vespers! *Plena gratià*
  Ave, Virgo! Gr-r-r — you swine!

THE HERETIC'S TRAGEDY.

A MIDDLE-AGE INTERLUDE.

ROSA MUNDI; SEU, FULCITE ME FLORIBUS. A CONCEIT OF MASTER GYS-
BRECHT, CANON-REGULAR OF SAINT JODOCUS-BY-THE-BAR, YPRES CITY.
CANTUQUE, *Virgilius.* AND HATH OFTEN BEEN SUNG AT HOCKTIDE
AND FESTIVALS. GAVISUS ERAM, *Jessides.*

(It would seem to be a glimpse from the burning of Jacques du Bourg-
Molay, at Paris, A.D. 1314; as distorted by the refraction from Flemish brain
to brain during the course of a couple of centuries.)

I.

PREADMONISHETH THE ABBOT DEODAET.

THE Lord, we look to once for all,
    Is the Lord we should look at, all at once:
He knows not to vary, saith St. Paul,
    Nor the shadow of turning, for the nonce.
See him no other than as he is!
    Give both the infinitudes their due —
Infinite mercy, but, I wis,
    As infinite a justice too.

                              [*Organ: plagal-cadence.*]

    As infinite a justice too.

II.

ONE SINGETH.

John, Master of the Temple of God,   10
    Falling to sin the Unknown Sin,
What he bought of Emperor Aldabrod,
    He sold it to Sultan Saladin:
Till, caught by Pope Clement, a-buzzing there,
    Hornet-prince of the mad wasps' hive,
And clipt of his wings in Paris square,
    They bring him now to be burned alive.
        [*And wanteth there grace of lute or clavicithern,
            ye shall say to confirm him who singeth —*
    We bring John now to be burned alive.

III.

In the midst is a goodly gallows built;
    'Twixt fork and fork, a stake is stuck;   20

But first they set divers tumbrils a-tilt,
  Make a trench all round with the city muck ;
Inside they pile log upon log, good store ;
  Fagots no few, blocks great and small,
Reach a man's mid-thigh, no less, no more, —
  For they mean he should roast in the sight of all.

CHORUS.

We mean he should roast in the sight of all.

IV.

Good sappy bavins that kindle forthwith ;
  Billets that blaze substantial and slow ;
Pine-stump split deftly, dry as pith ;   30
  Larch-heart that chars to a chalk-white glow :
Then up they hoist me John in a chafe,
  Sling him fast like a hog to scorch,
Spit in his face, then leap back safe,
  Sing "Laudes" and bid clap-to the torch.

CHORUS.

Laus Deo — who bids clap-to the torch.

V.

John of the Temple, whose fame so bragged,
  Is burning alive in Paris square !
How can he curse, if his mouth is gagged ?
  Or wriggle his neck, with a collar there ?   40
Or heave his chest, which a band goes round ?
  Or threat with his fist, since his arms are spliced ?
Or kick with his feet, now his legs are bound ?
  — Thinks John, I will call upon Jesus Christ.
                    [*Here one crosseth himself.*

VI.

Jesus Christ — John had bought and sold,
  Jesus Christ — John had eaten and drunk ;
To him, the Flesh meant silver and gold.
  (*Salvâ reverentiâ nunc.*)
Now it was, " Saviour, bountiful lamb,
  I have roasted thee Turks, tho' men roast me !
See thy servant, the plight wherein I am !   50
  Art thou a saviour ?   Save thou me ! "

CHORUS.

'T is John the mocker cries, " Save thou me! "

VII.

Who maketh God's menace an idle word?
— Saith, it no more means what it proclaims,
Than a damsel's threat to her wanton bird? —
For she too prattles of ugly names.
— Saith, he knoweth but one thing, — what he knows?
That God is good and the rest is breath ;
Why else is the same styled Sharon's rose?
Once a rose, ever a rose, he saith. 60

CHORUS.

O, John shall yet find a rose, he saith!

VIII.

Alack, there be roses and roses, John!
Some, honied of taste like your leman's tongue :
Some, bitter ; for why? (roast gaily on!)
Their tree struck root in devil's dung.
When Paul once reasoned of righteousness
And of temperance and of judgment to come,
Good Felix trembled, he could no less :
John, snickering, crook'd his wicked thumb.

CHORUS.

What cometh to John of the wicked thumb? 70

IX.

Ha, ha, John plucketh now at his rose
To rid himself of a sorrow at heart!
Lo, — petal on petal, fierce rays unclose ;
Anther on anther, sharp spikes outstart ;
And with blood for dew, the bosom boils ;
And a gust of sulphur is all its smell ;
And lo, he is horribly in the toils
Of a coal-black giant flower of hell!

CHORUS.

What maketh heaven, That maketh he..

x.

So, as John called now, thro' the fire amain,   80
 On the Name, he had cursed with, all his life —
To the Person, he bought and sold again —
 For the Face, with his daily buffets rife —
Feature by feature It took its place :
 And his voice, like a mad dog's choking bark,
At the steady whole of the Judge's face —
 Died.   Forth John's soul flared into the dark.

SUBJOINETH THE ABBOT DEODAET.

God help all poor souls lost in the dark!

    —◦◦—

HOLY–CROSS DAY.

ON WHICH THE JEWS WERE FORCED TO ATTEND AN ANNUAL CHRIS-
TIAN SERMON IN ROME.

["Now was come about Holy-Cross Day, and now must my lord preach his first sermon to the Jews : as it was of old cared for in the merciful bowels of the Church, that, so to speak, a crumb at least from her conspicuous table here in Rome, should be, though but once yearly, cast to the famishing dogs, under-trampled and bespitten-upon beneath the feet of the guests.   And a moving sight in truth, this, of so many of the besotted blind restif and ready-to-perish Hebrews ! now maternally brought — nay, (for He saith, 'Compel them to come in') haled, as it were, by the head and hair, and against their obstinate hearts, to partake of the heavenly grace.   What awakening, what striving with tears, what working of a yeasty conscience !   Nor was my lord wanting to himself on so apt an occasion ; witness the abundance of conversions which did incontinently reward him : though not to my lord be altogether the glory." —*Diary by the Bishop's Secretary*, 1600.]

What the Jews really said, on thus being driven to church, was rather to this effect : —

I.

FEE, faw, fum! bubble and squeak!
 Blessedest Thursday 's the fat of the week.
Rumble and tumble, sleek and rough,
Stinking and savoury, smug and gruff,
Take the church-road, for the bell's due chime
Gives us the summons — 't is sermon-time!

II.

Boh, here 's Barnabas!   Job, that 's you?
Up stumps Solomon — bustling too?
Shame, man! greedy beyond your years
To handsel the bishop's shaving-shears?   10
Fair play 's a jewel!   Leave friends in the lurch?
Stand on a line ere you start for the church!

III.

Higgledy, piggledy, packed we lie,
Rats in a hamper, swine in a stye,
Wasps in a bottle, frogs in a sieve,
Worms in a carcass, fleas in a sleeve.
Hist! square shoulders, settle your thumbs
And buzz for the bishop — here he comes.

IV.

Bow, wow, wow — a bone for the dog!
I liken his Grace to an acorned hog.   20
What, a boy at his side, with the bloom of a lass,
To help and handle my lord's hour-glass!
Didst ever behold so lithe a chine?
His cheek hath laps like a fresh-singed swine.

V.

Aaron 's asleep — shove hip to haunch,
Or somebody deal him a dig in the paunch!
Look at the purse with the tassel and knob,
And the gown with the angel and thingumbob!
What 's he at, quotha? reading his text!
Now you 've his curtsey — and what comes next?   30

VI.

See to our converts — you doomed black dozen —
No stealing away — nor cog nor cozen!
You five, that were thieves, deserve it fairly;
You seven, that were beggars, will live less sparely;
You took your turn and dipped in the hat,
Got fortune — and fortune gets you; mind that!

VII.

Give your first groan — compunction 's at work;
And soft! from a Jew you mount to a Turk.
Lo, Micah, — the selfsame beard on chin

He was four times already converted in!
Here 's a knife, clip quick — it 's a sign of grace —
Or he ruins us all with his hanging-face.

VIII.

Whom now is the bishop a-leering at?
I know a point where his text falls pat.
I 'll tell him to-morrow, a word just now
Went to my heart and made me vow
I meddle no more with the worst of trades:
Let somebody else pay his serenades!

IX.

Groan altogether now, whee—hee—hee!
It 's a-work, it 's a-work, ah, woe is me!
It began, when a herd of us, picked and placed,
Were spurred thro' the Corso, stripped to the waist;
Jew brutes, with sweat and blood well spent
To usher in worthily Christian Lent.

X.

It grew, when the hangman entered our bounds,
Yelled, pricked us out to his church like hounds:
It got to a pitch, when the hand indeed
Which gutted my purse, would throttle my creed:
And it overflows, when, to even the odd,
Men I helped to their sins help me to their God.

XI.

But now, while the scapegoats leave our flock,
And the rest sit silent and count the clock,
Since forced to muse the appointed time
On these precious facts and truths sublime, —
Let us fitly employ it, under our breath,
In saying Ben Ezra's Song of Death.

XII.

For Rabbi Ben Ezra, the night he died,
Called sons and sons' sons to his side,
And spoke, "This world has been harsh and strange;
Something is wrong: there needeth a change.
But what, or where? at the last or first?
In one point only we sinned, at worst.

40

50

60

70

XIII.

" The Lord will have mercy on Jacob yet,
And again in his border see Israel set.
When Judah beholds Jerusalem,
The stranger-seed shall be joined to them :
To Jacob's House shall the Gentiles cleave,
So the Prophet saith and his sons believe.

XIV.

" Ay, the children of the chosen race
Shall carry and bring them to their place : 80
In the land of the Lord shall lead the same,
Bondsmen and handmaids. Who shall blame,
When the slaves enslave, the oppressed ones o'er
The oppressor triumph for evermore ?

XV.

" God spoke, and gave us the word to keep :
Bade never fold the hands nor sleep
'Mid a faithless world, — at watch and ward,
Till Christ at the end relieve our guard.
By his servant Moses the watch was set :
Tho' near upon cock-crow, we keep it yet. 90

XVI.

" Thou! if thou wast he, who at mid-watch came,
By the starlight, naming a dubious name!
And if, too heavy with sleep — too rash
With fear — O thou, if that martyr-gash
Fell on thee coming to take thine own,
And we gave the Cross, when we owed the Throne —

XVII.

" Thou art the Judge. We are bruisèd thus.
But, the Judgment over, join sides with us!
Thine too is the cause! and not more thine
Than ours, is the work of these dogs and swine, 100
Whose life laughs thro' and spits at their creed,
Who maintain thee in word, and defy thee in deed!

XVIII.

" We withstood Christ then? Be mindful how
At least we withstand Barabbas now!
Was our outrage sore? But the worst we spared,

To have called these — Christians, had we dared!
Let defiance to them pay mistrust of thee,
And Rome make amends for Calvary!

XIX.

" By the torture, prolonged from age to age,
By the infamy, Israel's heritage,   110
By the Ghetto's plague, by the garb's disgrace,
By the badge of shame, by the felon's place,
By the branding-tool, the bloody whip,
And the summons to Christian fellowship, —

XX.

" We boast our proof that at least the Jew
Would wrest Christ's name from the Devil's crew.
Thy face took never so deep a shade
But we fought them in it, God our aid!
A trophy to bear, as we march, thy band
South, East, and on to the Pleasant Land! "   120

[*Pope Gregory XVI abolished this bad business of the
Sermon. — R. B.*]

———◆———

AMPHIBIAN.

I.

THE fancy I had to-day,
    Fancy which turned a fear!
I swam far out in the bay,
    Since waves laughed warm and clear.

II.

I lay and looked at the sun,
    The noon-sun looked at me :
Between us two, no one
    Live creature, that I could see.

III.

Yes!   There came floating by
    Me, who lay floating too,   10
Such a strange butterfly!
    Creature as dear as new :

IV.

Because the membraned wings
    So wonderful, so wide,
So sun-suffused, were things
    Like soul and naught beside.

V.

A handbreadth over head!
    All of the sea my own,
It owned the sky instead;
    Both of us were alone.   20

VI.

I never shall join its flight,
    For, naught buoys flesh in air.
If it touch the sea — good night!
    Death sure and swift waits there.

VII.

Can the insect feel the better
    For watching the uncouth play
Of limbs that slip the fetter,
    Pretend as they were not clay?

VIII.

Undoubtedly I rejoice
    That the air comports so well   30
With a creature which had the choice
    Of the land once.   Who can tell?

IX.

What if a certain soul
    Which early slipped its sheath,
And has for its home the whole
    Of heaven, thus look beneath,

X.

Thus watch one who, in the world,
    Both lives and likes life's way,
Nor wishes the wings unfurled
    That sleep in the worm, they say?   40

XI.

But sometimes when the weather
    Is blue, and warm waves tempt
To free oneself of tether,
    And try a life exempt

XII.

From worldly noise and dust,
    In the sphere which overbrims
With passion and thought, — why, just
    Unable to fly, one swims!

XIII.

By passion and thought upborne,
    One smiles to oneself — " They fare   50
Scarce better, they need not scorn
    Our sea, who live in the air! "

XIV.

Emancipate thro' passion
    And thought, with sea for sky,
We substitute, in a fashion,
    For heaven — poetry:

XV.

Which sea, to all intent,
    Gives flesh such noon-disport
As a finer element
    Affords the spirit-sort.   60

XVI.

Whatever they are, we seem:
    Imagine the thing they know;
All deeds they do, we dream;
    Can heaven be else but so?

XVII.

And meantime, yonder streak
    Meets the horizon's verge:
That is the land, to seek
    If we tire or dread the surge;

XVIII.

Land the solid and safe —
  To welcome again (confess!)   70
When, high and dry, we chafe
  The body, and don the dress.

XIX.

Does she look, pity, wonder
  At one who mimics flight,
Swims — heaven above, sea under,
  Yet always earth in sight ?

———◦◦◦———

ST. MARTIN'S SUMMER.

I.

NO protesting, dearest !
  Hardly kisses even !
  Don't we both know how it ends ?
How the greenest leaf turns serest ?
  Bluest outbreak — blankest heaven ?
    Lovers — friends ?

II.

You would build a mansion,
  I would weave a bower
    — Want the heart for enterprise.
Walls admit of no expansion :   10
  Trellis-work may haply flower
    Twice the size.

III.

What makes glad Life's Winter ?
  New buds, old blooms after.
    Sad the sighing "How suspect
Beams would ere mid-Autumn splinter,
  Rooftree scarce support a rafter,
    Walls lie wrecked ? "

IV.

You are young, my princess !
  I am hardly older :   20

Yet — I steal a glance behind !
Dare I tell you what convinces
  Timid me that you, if bolder,
    Bold — are blind?

v.

Where we plan our dwelling
  Glooms a graveyard surely !
    Headstone, footstone moss may drape, —
Name, date, violets hide from spelling, —
  But, tho' corpses rot obscurely,
    Ghosts escape.   30

vi.

Ghosts! O breathing Beauty,
  Give my frank word pardon!
    What if I — somehow, somewhere —
Pledged my soul to endless duty
  Many a time and oft?   Be hard on
    Love — laid there?

vii.

Nay, blame grief that 's fickle,
  Time that proves a traitor,
    Chance, change, all that purpose warps, —
Death who spares to thrust the sickle,   40
  Laid Love low, thro' flowers which later
    Shroud the corpse!

viii.

And you, my winsome lady,
  Whisper with like frankness!
    Lies nothing buried long ago ?
Are yon — which shimmer mid the shady
  Where moss and violet run to rankness —
    Tombs or no ?

ix.

Who taxes you with murder?
  My hands are clean — or nearly !   50
    Love being mortal needs must pass.
Repentance ? Nothing were absurder.
  Enough : we felt Love's loss severely ;
    Tho' now — alas !

x.

Love's corpse lies quiet therefore,
  Only Love's ghost plays truant,
    And warns us have in wholesome **awe**
Durable mansionry; that 's wherefore
  I weave but trellis work, pursuant
    — Life, to law.   60

xi.

The solid, not the fragile,
  Tempts rain and hail and thunder.
    If bower stand firm at Autumn's close,
Beyond my hope, — why, boughs were agile;
  If bower fall flat, we scarce need wonder
    Wreathing — rose!

xii.

So, truce to the protesting,
  So, muffled be the kisses!
    For, would we but avow the **truth**,
Sober is genuine joy.   No jesting!   70
  Ask else Penelope, Ulysses —
    Old in youth!

xiii.

For why should ghosts feel angered?
  Let all their interference
    Be faint march-music in the air!
"Up!   Join the rear of us the vanguard!
  Up, lovers, dead to all appearance,
    Laggard pair!"

xiv.

The while you clasp me closer,
  The while I press you deeper,   80
    As safe we chuckle, — under breath,
Yet all the slyer, the jocoser, —
  "So, life can boast its day, like leap-year,
    Stolen from death!"

xv.

Ah me — the sudden terror!
  Hence quick — avaunt, avoid me,
    You cheat, the ghostly flesh-disguised!

Nay, all the ghosts in one!   Strange error!
   So, 't was Death's self that clipped and coyed me,
      Loved — and lied!   90

XVI.

Ay, dead loves are the potent!
   Like any cloud they used you,
      Mere semblance you, but substance they!
Build we no mansion, weave we no tent!
   Mere flesh — their spirit interfused you!
      Hence, I say!

XVII.

All theirs, none yours the glamour!
   Theirs each low word that won me,
      Soft look that found me Love's, and left
What else but you — the tears and clamour   100
   That 's all your very own!   Undone me —
      Ghost bereft!

JAMES LEE'S WIFE.

I.

JAMES LEE'S WIFE SPEAKS AT THE WINDOW.

I.

AH, Love, but a day,
      And the world has changed!
The sun 's away,
   And the bird estranged;
The wind has dropped,
   And the sky 's deranged:
Summer has stopped.

II.

Look in my eyes!
   Wilt thou change too?
Should I fear surprise?   10
   Shall I find aught new
In the old and dear,
   In the good and true,
With the changing year?

III.

Thou art a man,
　But I am thy love.
For the lake, its swan;
　For the dell, its dove;
And for thee — (oh, haste!)
　Me, to bend above,
Me, to hold embraced.　　　　20

II.

BY THE FIRESIDE.

I.

Is all our fire of shipwreck wood,
　Oak and pine?
Oh, for the ills half-understood,
　The dim dead woe
　Long ago
Befallen this bitter coast of France!
Well, poor sailors took their chance;
　I take mine.

II.

A ruddy shaft our fire must shoot
　O'er the sea;　　　　　　　10
Do sailors eye the casement — mute,
　Drenched and stark,
　From their bark —
And envy, gnash their teeth for hate
O' the warm safe house and happy freight
　— Thee and me?

III.

God help you, sailors, at your need!
　Spare the curse!
For some ships, safe in port indeed,
　Rot and rust,　　　　　　　20
　Run to dust,
All thro' worms i' the wood, which crept,
Gnawed our hearts out while we slept:
　That is worse.

U

IV.

Who lived here before us two?
  Old-world pairs.
Did a woman ever — would I knew! —
  Watch the man
  With whom began
Love's voyage, full-sail, — (now, gnash your teeth!)   30
When planks start, open hell beneath
  Unawares?

———

III.

IN THE DOORWAY.

I.

The swallow has set her six young on the rail,
  And looks seaward :
The water 's in stripes like a snake, olive-pale
  To the leeward, —
On the weather-side, black, spotted white with the wind.
"Good fortune departs, and disaster 's behind,"
Hark, the wind with its wants and its infinite wail!

II.

Our fig-tree, that leaned for the saltness, has furled
  Her five fingers,
Each leaf like a hand opened wide to the world   10
  Where there lingers
No glint of the gold, Summer sent for her sake :
How the vines writhe in rows, each impaled on its stake!
My heart shrivels up and my spirit shrinks curled.

III.

Yet here are we two ; we have love, house enough,
  With the field there,
This house of four rooms, that field red and rough,
  Tho' it yield there,
For the rabbit that robs, scarce a blade or a bent ;
If a magpie alight now, it seems an event ;   20
And they both will be gone at November's rebuff.

IV.

But why must cold spread? but wherefore bring change
  To the spirit,

God meant should mate his with an infinite range,
  And inherit
His power to put life in the darkness and cold?
Oh, live and love worthily, bear and be bold!
Whom Summer made friends of, let Winter estrange!

IV.

ALONG THE BEACH.

I.

I WILL be quiet and talk with you,
  And reason why you are wrong.
You wanted my love — is that much true?
And so I did love, so I do:
  What has come of it all along?

II.

I took you — how could I otherwise?
  For a world to me, and more;
For all, love greatens and glorifies
Till God 's a-glow, to the loving eyes,
  In what was mere earth before.   10

III.

Yés, earth — yes, mere ignoble earth!
  Now do I mis-state, mistake?
Do I wrong your weakness and call it worth?
Expect all harvest, dread no dearth,
  Seal my sense up for your sake?

IV.

Oh, Love, Love, no, Love! not so indeed!
  You were just weak earth, I knew:
With much in you waste, with many a weed
And plenty of passions run to seed,
  But a little good grain too.   20

V.

And such as you were, I took you for mine:
  Did not you find me yours,
To watch the olive and wait the vine,

And wonder when rivers of oil and wine
　Would flow, as the Book assures?

VI.

Well, and if none of these good things came,
　What did the failure prove?
The man was my whole world, all the same,
With his flowers to praise or his weeds to blame,
　And, either or both, to love.　　　　　　　30

VII.

Yet this turns now to a fault — there! there!
　That I do love, watch too long,
And wait too well, and weary and wear;
And 't is all an old story, and my despair
　Fit subject for some new song:

VIII.

" How the light, light love, he has wings to fly
　At suspicion of a bond:
My wisdom has bidden your pleasure good-bye,
Which will turn up next in a laughing eye,
　And why should you look beyond?"　　　40

V.

ON THE CLIFF.

I.

I LEANED on the turf,
I looked at a rock
Left dry by the surf;
For the turf, to call it grass were to mock:
Dead to the roots, so deep was done
The work of the summer sun.

II.

And the rock lay flat
As an anvil's face:
No iron like that!
Baked dry: of a weed, of a shell, no trace:　　10
Sunshine outside, but ice at the core,
Death's altar by the lone shore.

III.

On the turf, sprang gay
With his films of blue,
No cricket, I 'll say,
But a war-horse, barded and chanfroned too.
The gift of a quixote-mage to his knight,
Real fairy, with wings all right.

IV.

On the rock, they scorch
Like a drop of fire
From a brandished torch,
Fall two red fans of a butterfly: 20
No turf, no rock, — in their ugly stead,
See, wonderful blue and red!

V.

Is it not so
With the minds of men?
The level and low,
The burnt and bare, in themselves; but then
With such a blue and red grace, not theirs,
Love settling unawares!   30

———

VI.

READING A BOOK, UNDER THE CLIFF.

I.

" STILL ailing, Wind?   Wilt be appeased or no?
   Which needs the other's office, thou or I?
Dost want to be disburthened of a woe,
   And can, in truth, my voice untie
Its links, and let it go?

II.

" Art thou a dumb wronged thing that would be righted,
   Entrusting thus thy cause to me?   Forbear!
No tongue can mend such pleadings; faith, requited
   With falsehood, — Love, at last aware
Of scorn, — hopes, early blighted, —   10

III.

"We have them; but I know not any tone
    So fit as thine to falter forth a sorrow:
Dost think men would go mad without a moan,
    If they knew any way to borrow
A pathos like thine own?

IV.

"Which sigh wouldst mock, of all the sighs? The one
    So long escaping from lips starved and blue,
That lasts while on her pallet-bed the nun
    Stretches her length; her foot comes through
The straw she shivers on;   20

V.

"You had not thought she was so tall: and spent,
    Her shrunk lids open, her lean fingers shut
Close, close, their sharp and livid nails indent
    The clammy palm; then all is mute:
That way, the spirit went.

VI.

"Or wouldst thou rather that I understand
    Thy will to help me? — like the dog I found
Once, pacing sad this solitary strand,
    Who would not take my food, poor hound,
But whined and licked my hand."   30

VII.

All this, and more, comes from some young man's pride
    Of power to see, — in failure and mistake,
Relinquishment, disgrace, on every side, —
    Merely examples for his sake,
Helps to his path untried:

VIII.

Instances he must — simply recognize?
    Oh, more than so! — must, with a learner's zeal,
Make doubly prominent, twice emphasize,
    By added touches that reveal
The god in babe's disguise.   40

IX.

Oh, he knows what defeat means, and the rest!
    Himself the undefeated that shall be:

Failure, disgrace, he flings them you to test, —
   His triumph, in eternity
Too plainly manifest!

X.

Whence, judge if he learn forthwith what the wind
   Means in its moaning — by the happy prompt
Instinctive way of youth, I mean; for kind
   Calm years, exacting their accompt
Of pain, mature the mind: 50

XI.

And some midsummer morning, at the lull
   Just about daybreak, as he looks across
A sparkling foreign country, wonderful
   To the sea's edge for gloom and gloss,
Next minute must annul, —

XII.

Then, when the wind begins among the vines,
   So low, so low, what shall it say but this?
"Here is the change beginning, here the lines
   Circumscribe beauty, set to bliss
The limit time assigns."   60

XIII.

Nothing can be as it has been before;
   Better, so call it, only not the same.
To draw one beauty into our hearts' core
   And keep it changeless! such our claim;
So answered, — Never more!

XIV.

Simple? Why this is the old woe o' the world;
   Tune, to whose rise and fall we live and die.
Rise with it, then! Rejoice that man is hurled
   From change to change unceasingly,
His soul's wings never furled!   70

XV.

That's a new question; still replies the fact,
   Nothing endures: the wind moans, saying so;
We moan in acquiescence: there's life's pact,
   Perhaps probation — do *I* know?
God does: endure his act!

XVI.

Only, for man, how bitter not to grave
  On his soul's hands' palms one fair good wise thing
Just as he grasped it !   For himself, death's wave ;
While time first washes — ah, the sting ! —
O'er all he 'd sink to save.   80

———

VII.

AMONG THE ROCKS.

I.

Oh, good gigantic smile o' the brown old earth,
  This autumn morning!   How he sets his bones
To bask i' the sun, and thrusts out knees and feet
For the ripple to run over in its mirth ;
  Listening the while, where on the heap of stones
The white breast of the sea-lark twitters sweet.

II.

That is the doctrine, simple, ancient, true ;
  Such is life's trial, as old earth smiles and knows.
If you loved only what were worth your love,
Love were clear gain, and wholly well for you :   10
  Make the low nature better by your throes!
Give earth yourself, go up for gain above!

———

VIII.

BESIDE THE DRAWING-BOARD.

I.

"As like as a Hand to another Hand!"
  Whoever said that foolish thing,
Could not have studied to understand
  The counsels of God in fashioning,
Out of the infinite love of his heart,
This Hand, whose beauty I praise, apart
From the world of wonder left to praise,

If I tried to learn the other ways
Of love in its skill, or love in its power.
  " As like as a Hand to another Hand : "   10
  Who said that, never took his stand,
Found and followed, like me, an hour,
The beauty in this, — how free, how fine
To fear, almost, — of the limit-line !
As I looked at this, and learned and drew,
  Drew and learned, and looked again,
While fast the happy minutes flew,
  Its beauty mounted into my brain,
  And a fancy seized me ; I was fain
To efface my work, begin anew,   20
Kiss what before I only drew ;
Ay, laying the red chalk 'twixt my lips,
  With soul to help if the mere lips failed,
  I kissed all right where the drawing ailed,
Kissed fast the grace that somehow slips
Still from one's soulless finger-tips.

II.

'T is a clay cast, the perfect thing,
  From Hand live once, dead long ago :
Princess-like it wears the ring
  To fancy's eye, by which we know   30
That here at length a master found
  His match, a proud lone soul its mate,
As soaring genius sank to ground,
  And pencil could not emulate
The beauty in this, — how free, how fine
To fear almost ! — of the limit-line.
Long ago the god, like me
The worm, learned, each in our degree :
Looked and loved, learned and drew,
  Drew and learned and loved again,   40
While fast the happy minutes flew,
  Till beauty mounted into his brain
And on the finger which outvied
  His art he placed the ring that 's there,
Still by fancy's eye descried,
  In token of a marriage rare :
For him on earth, his arts despair,
For him in heaven, his soul's fit bride.

III.

Little girl with the poor coarse hand
  I turned from to a cold clay cast —   50

I have my lesson, understand
   The worth of flesh and blood at last!
Nothing but beauty in a Hand?
   Because he could not change the hue,
   Mend the lines and make them true
To this which met his soul's demand, —
   Would Da Vinci turn from you?
I hear him laugh my woes to scorn —
"The fool forsooth is all forlorn
Because the beauty, she thinks best,   60
Lived long ago or was never born, —
Because no beauty bears the test
In this rough peasant Hand!   Confessed!
'Art is null and study void!'
So sayest thou?   So said not I,
Who threw the faulty pencil by,
And years instead of hours employed,
Learning the veritable use
Of flesh and bone and nerve beneath
Lines and hue of the outer sheath,   70
If haply I might reproduce
One motive of the powers profuse
Flesh and bone and nerve that make
The poorest coarsest human hand
An object worthy to be scanned
A whole life long for their sole sake.
Shall earth and the cramped moment-space
Yield the heavenly crowning grace?
Now the parts and then the whole!
Who art thou, with stinted soul   80
And stunted body, thus to cry
'I love, — shall that be life's strait dole?
I must live beloved or die!'
This peasant hand that spins the wool
And bakes the bread, why lives it on,
Poor and coarse with beauty gone, —
What use survives the beauty?"   Fool!

Go, little girl with the poor coarse hand!
I have my lesson, shall understand.   90

IX.

ON DECK.

I.

THERE is nothing to remember in me,
　　Nothing I ever said with a grace,
Nothing I did that you care to see,
　　Nothing I was that deserves a place
In your mind, now I leave you, set you free.

II.

Conceded!　In turn, concede to me,
　　Such things have been as a mutual flame.
Your soul 's locked fast ; but, love for a key,
　　You might let it loose, till I grew the same
In your eyes, as in mine you stand : strange plea!　　10

III.

For then, then, what would it matter to me
　　That I was the harsh, ill-favoured one?
We both should be like as pea and pea ;
　　It was ever so since the world begun :
So, let me proceed with my reverie.

IV.

How strange it were if you had all me,
　　As I have all you in my heart and brain,
You, whose least word brought gloom or glee,
　　Who never lifted the hand in vain
Will hold mine yet, from over the sea!　　20

V.

Strange, if a face, when you thought of me,
　　Rose like your own face present now,
With eyes as dear in their due degree,
　　Much such a mouth, and as bright a brow,
Till you saw yourself, while you cried " 'T is She!"

VI.

Well, you may, you must, set down to me
　　Love that was life, life that was love ;
A tenure of breath at your lips' decree,
　　A passion to stand as your thoughts approve,
A rapture to fall where your foot might be.　　30

VII.

But did one touch of such love for me
   Come in a word or a look of yours,
Whose words and looks will, circling, flee
   Round me and round while life endures,—
Could I fancy " As I feel, thus feels He ; "

VIII.

Why, fade you might to a thing like me,
   And your hair grow these coarse hanks of hair,
Your skin, this bark of a gnarled tree,—
   You might turn myself !— should I know or care,   40
When I should be dead of joy, James Lee?

RESPECTABILITY.

I.

DEAR, had the world in its caprice
   Deigned to proclaim "I know you both,
Have recognized your plighted troth,
Am sponsor for you : live in peace !"
How many precious months and years
   Of youth had passed, that speed so fast,
   Before we found it out at last,
The world, and what it fears?

II.

How much of priceless life were spent
   With men that every virtue decks,   10
   And women models of their sex,
Society's true ornament,—
Ere we dared wander, nights like this,
   Thro' wind and rain, and watch the Seine,
   And feel the Boulevard break again
To warmth and light and bliss?

III.

I know! the world proscribes not love ;
   Allows my finger to caress
   Your lips' contour and downiness,
Provided it supply a glove.   20

The world's good word!— the Institute!
  Guizot receives Montalembert!
  Eh ? Down the court three lampions flare:
Put forward your best foot!

---•◆•---

DÎS ALITER VISUM ; OR, LE BYRON DE NOS JOURS.

I.

STOP, let me have the truth of that!
  Is that all true ? I say, the day
Ten years ago when both of us
  Met on a morning, friends — as thus
We meet this evening, friends or what ?—

II.

Did you — because I took your arm
  And sillily smiled, "A mass of brass
That sea looks, blazing underneath !"
  While up the cliff-road edged with heath,
We took the turns nor came to harm —   10

III.

Did you consider " Now makes twice
  That I have seen her, walked and talked
With this poor pretty thoughtful thing,
  Whose worth I weigh: she tries to sing;
Draws, hopes in time the eye grows nice ;

IV.

" Reads verse and thinks she understands ;
  Loves all, at any rate, that 's great,
Good, beautiful ; but much as we
  Down at the bath-house love the sea,
Who breathe its salt and bruise its sands :   20

V.

"While . . . do but follow the fishing-gull
  That flaps and floats from wave to cave!
There 's the sea-lover, fair my friend!
  What then? Be patient, mark and mend!
Had you the making of your skull? "

VI.

And did you, when we faced the church
  With spire and sad slate roof, aloof
From human fellowship so far,
  Where a few graveyard crosses are,
And garlands for the swallows' perch, —   30

VII.

Did you determine, as we stepped
  O'er the lone stone fence, " Let me get
Her for myself, and what 's the earth
  With all its art, verse, music, worth —
Compared with love, found, gained, and kept ?

VIII.

" Schumann 's our music-maker now ;
  Has his march-movement youth and mouth?
Ingres 's the modern man that paints ;
  Which will lean on me, of his saints?
Heine for songs ; for kisses, how? "   40

IX.

And did you, when we entered, reached
  The votive frigate, soft aloft
Riding on air this hundred years,
  Safe-smiling at old hopes and fears, —
Did you draw profit while she preached?

X.

Resolving, " Fools we wise men grow :
  Yes, I could easily blurt out curt
Some question that might find reply
  As prompt in her stopped lips, dropped eye
And rush of red to cheek and brow :   50

XI.

" Thus were a match made, sure and fast,
  'Mid the blue weed-flowers round the mound
Where, issuing, we shall stand and stay
  For one more look at baths and bay,
Sands, sea-gulls, and the old church last —

XII.

" A match 'twixt me, bent, wigged and lamed,
   Famous, however, for verse and worse,
Sure of the Fortieth spare Arm-chair
   When gout and glory seat me there,
So, one whose love-freaks pass unblamed, —   60

XIII.

" And this young beauty, round and sound
   As a mountain-apple, youth and truth
With loves and doves, at all events
   With money in the Three per Cents ;
Whose choice of me would seem profound : —

XIV.

" She might take me as I take her.
   Perfect the hour would pass, alas !
Climb high, love high, what matter?   Still,
   Feet, feelings, must descend the hill :
An hour's perfection can't recur.   70

XV.

" Then follows Paris and full time
   For both to reason : ' Thus with us,'
She 'll sigh, ' Thus girls give body and soul
   At first word, think they gain the goal,
When 't is the starting-place they climb !

XVI.

" ' My friend makes verse and gets renown ;
   Have they all fifty years, his peers ?
He knows the world, firm, quiet and gay ;
   Boys will become as much one day :
They 're fools ; he cheats, with beard less brown.   80

XVII.

" ' For boys say, *Love me or I die !*
   He did not say, *The truth is, youth
I want, who am old and know too much ;
   I 'd catch youth : lend me sight and touch !
Drop heart's blood where life's wheels grate dry !* '

XVIII.

" While I should make rejoinder " — (then
    It was, no doubt, you ceased that least
Light pressure of my arm in yours)
    I can conceive of cheaper cures
For a yawning-fit o'er books and men.   90

XIX.

" ' What ?   All I am, was, and might be,
    All, books taught, art brought, life's whole strife,
Painful results since precious, just
    Were fitly exchanged, in wise disgust,
For two cheeks freshened by youth and sea?

XX.

" ' All for a nosegay! — what came first ;
    With fields in flower, untried each side ;
I rally, need my books and men,
    And find a nosegay :' drop it, then,
No match yet made for best or worst! "   100

XXI.

That ended me.   You judged the porch
    We left by, Norman ; took our look
At sea and sky ; wondered so few
    Find out the place for air and view ;
Remarked the sun began to scorch ;

XXII.

Descended, soon regained the baths,
    And then, good-bye !   Years ten since then :
Ten years !   We meet : you tell me, now,
    By a window-seat for that cliff-brow,
On carpet-stripes for those sand-paths.   110

XXIII.

Now I may speak : you fool, for all
    Your lore !   Who made things plain in vain ?
What was the sea for ?   What, the gray
    Sad church, that solitary day,
Crosses and graves and swallows' call ?

XXIV.

Was there naught better than to enjoy?
  No feat which, done, would make time break
And let us pent-up creatures through
  Into eternity, our due?
No forcing earth teach heaven's employ?   120

XXV.

No wise beginning, here and now,
  What cannot grow complete (earth's feat)
And heaven must finish, there and then?
  No tasting earth's true food for men,
Its sweet in sad, its sad in sweet?

XXVI.

No grasping at love, gaining a share
  O' the sole spark from God's life at strife
With death, so, sure of range above
  The limits here?   For us and love,
Failure; but, when God fails, despair.   130

XXVII.

This you call wisdom?   Thus you add
  Good unto good again, in vain?
You loved, with body worn and weak;
  I loved, with faculties to seek:
Were both loves worthless since ill-clad?

XXVIII.

Let the mere star-fish in his vault
  Crawl in a wash of weed, indeed,
Rose-jacynth to the finger-tips:
  He, whole in body and soul, outstrips
Man, found with either in default.   140

XXIX.

But what 's whole, can increase no more,
  Is dwarfed and dies, since here 's its sphere.
The devil laughed at you in his sleeve!
  You knew not?   That I well believe;
Or you had saved two souls: nay, four.

x

For Stephanie sprained last night her wrist,
    Ankle or something. "Pooh," cry you?
At any rate she danced, all say,
    Vilely; her vogue has had its day.
Here comes my husband from his whist.   150

CONFESSIONS.

I.

WHAT is he buzzing in my ears?
    "Now that I come to die,
Do I view the world as a vale of tears?"
    Ah, reverend sir, not I!

II.

What I viewed there once, what I view again
    Where the physic bottles stand
On the table's edge,—is a suburb lane,
    With a wall to my bedside hand.

III.

That lane sloped, much as the bottles do,
    From a house you could descry   10
O'er the garden-wall: is the curtain blue
    Or green to a healthy eye?

IV.

To mine, it serves for the old June weather
    Blue above lane and wall;
And that farthest bottle labeled "Ether"
    Is the house o'er-topping all.

V.

At a terrace, somewhere near the stopper,
    There watched for me, one June,
A girl: I know, sir, it's improper,
    My poor mind's out of tune.   20

VI.

Only, there was a way . . . you crept
　Close by the side, to dodge
Eyes in the house, two eyes except:
　They styled their house " The Lodge."

VII.

What right had a lounger up their lane?
　But, by creeping very close,
With the good wall's help, — their eyes might strain
　And stretch themselves to Oes,

VIII.

Yet never catch her and me together,
　As she left the attic, there,
By the rim of the bottle labeled " Ether,"　　　30
　And stole from stair to stair,

IX.

And stood by the rose-wreathed gate.　Alas,
　We loved, sir — used to meet:
How sad and bad and mad it was —
　But then, how it was sweet!

THE HOUSEHOLDER.

I.

SAVAGE I was sitting in my house, late, lone:
　Dreary, weary with the long day's work:
Head of me, heart of me, stupid as a stone:
　Tongue-tied now, now blaspheming like a Turk;
When, in a moment, just a knock, call, cry,
　Half a pang and all a rapture, there again were we! —
" What, and is it really you again? " quoth I:
　" I again, what else did you expect? " quoth She.

II.

" Never mind, hie away from this old house —
　Every crumbling brick embrowned with sin and shame!　　**10**

Quick, in its corners ere certain shapes arouse!
  Let them — every devil of the night — lay claim,
Make and mend, or rap and rend, for me! Goodbye!
  God be their guard from disturbance at their glee,
Till, crash, comes down the carcass in a heap!" quoth I:
  "Nay, but there's a decency required!" quoth She.

III.

"Ah, but if you knew how time has dragged, days, nights!
  All the neighbour-talk with man and maid — such men!
All the fuss and trouble of street-sounds, window-sights:
  All the worry of flapping door and echoing roof: and then, 20
All the fancies . . . Who were they had leave, dared try
  Darker arts that almost struck despair in me?
If you knew but how I dwelt down here!" quoth I:
  "And was I so better off up there?" quoth She.

IV.

"Help and get it over! *Re-united to his wife*
  (How draw up the paper lets the parish-people know?)
Lies M. or N., departed from this life,
  Day the this or that, month and year the so and so,
What i' the way of final flourish? Prose, verse? Try!
  Affliction sore, long time he bore, or, what is it to be? 30
Till God did please to grant him ease. Do end!" quoth I:
  "I end with — Love is all and Death is naught!" quoth She.

TRAY.

SING me a hero! Quench my thirst
  Of soul, ye bards!
               Quoth Bard the first:
"Sir Olaf, the good knight, did don
His helm and eke his habergeon. . ."
Sir Olaf and his bard——!

"That sin-scathed brow" (quoth Bard the second),
"That eye wide ope as tho' Fate beckoned
My hero to some steep, beneath
Which precipice smiled tempting Death . . ."
You too without your host have reckoned!   10

" A beggar-child " (let 's hear this third!)
" Sat on a quay's edge : like a bird
Sang to herself at careless play,
And fell into the stream.   ' Dismay!
Help, you the standers-by! '   None stirred.

" Bystanders reason, think of wives
And children ere they risk their lives.
Over the balustrade has bounced
A mere instinctive dog, and pounced
Plumb on the prize.   ' How well he dives!   20

" ' Up he comes with the child, see, tight
In mouth, alive too, clutched from quite
A depth of ten feet — twelve, I bet!
Good dog !   What, off again?   There 's yet
Another child to save?   All right!

" ' How strange we saw no other fall!
It 's instinct in the animal.
Good dog!   But he 's a long while under :
If he got drowned I should not wonder —
Strong current, that against the wall!   30

" ' Here he comes, holds in mouth this time
— What may the thing be?   Well, that 's prime!
Now, did you ever?   Reason reigns
In man alone, since all Tray's pains
Have fished — the child's doll from the slime!'

" And so, amid the laughter gay,
Trotted my hero off, — old Tray, —
Till somebody, prerogatived
With reason, reasoned : ' Why he dived,
His brain would show us, I should say.   40

" ' John, go and catch — or, if needs be,
Purchase that animal for me!
By vivisection, at expense
Of half-an-hour and eighteen pence,
How brain secretes dog's soul, we 'll see!' "

CAVALIER TUNES.

I.

MARCHING ALONG.

I.

KENTISH Sir Byng stood for his King,
　　Bidding the crop-headed Parliament swing:
And, pressing a troop unable to stoop
And see the rogues flourish and honest folk droop,
Marched them along, fifty-score strong,
Great-hearted gentlemen, singing this song.

II.

God for King Charles!　Pym and such carles
To the Devil that prompts 'em their treasonous parles!
Cavaliers, up!　Lips from the cup,
Hands from the pasty, nor bite take nor sup　　　10
Till you 're —
　　　　(Chorus) Marching along, fifty-score strong,
　　　　　　Great-hearted gentlemen, singing this song.

III.

Hampden to hell, and his obsequies' knell
Serve Hazelrig, Fiennes, and young Harry as well!
England, good cheer!　Rupert is near!
Kentish and loyalists, keep we not here,
　　　　(Chorus) Marching along, fifty-score strong,
　　　　　　Great-hearted gentlemen, singing this song?

IV.

Then, God for King Charles!　Pym and his snarls
To the Devil that pricks on such pestilent carles!　　　20
Hold by the right, you double your might;
So, onward to Nottingham, fresh for the fight,
　　　　(Chorus) March we along, fifty-score strong,
　　　　　　Great-hearted gentlemen, singing this song!

II.

GIVE A ROUSE.

I.

KING CHARLES, and who 'll do him right now?
King Charles, and who 's ripe for fight now?
Give a rouse: here 's, in hell's despite now,
King Charles!

II.

Who gave me the goods that went since?
Who raised me the house that sank once?
Who helped me to gold I spent since?
Who found me in wine you drank once?

> (*Chorus*) *King Charles, and who 'll do him right now?*
> *King Charles, and who 's ripe for fight now?* 10
> *Give a rouse: here 's, in hell's despite now,*
> *King Charles!*

III.

To whom used my boy George quaff else,
By the old fool's side that begot him?
For whom did he cheer and laugh else,
While Noll's damned troopers shot him?

> (*Chorus*) *King Charles, and who 'll do him right now?*
> *King Charles, and who 's ripe for fight now?*
> *Give a rouse: here 's, in hell's despite now,*
> *King Charles!*   20

III.

BOOT AND SADDLE.

I.

BOOT, saddle, to horse, and away!
Rescue my castle before the hot day
Brightens to blue from its silvery gray,

> (*Chorus*) *Boot, saddle, to horse, and away!*

II.

Ride past the suburbs, asleep as you 'd say;
Many 's the friend there, will listen and pray
" God's luck to gallants that strike up the lay —
     (*Chorus*) *" Boot, saddle, to horse, and away!"*

III.

Forty miles off, like a roebuck at bay,
Flouts Castle Brancepeth the Roundheads' array: 10
Who laughs, " Good fellows ere this, by my fay,
     (*Chorus*) *" Boot, saddle, to horse, and away!"*

IV.

Who? My wife Gertrude; that, honest and gay,
Laughs when you talk of surrendering, " Nay!
I 've better counsellors; what counsel they?
     (*Chorus*) *" Boot, saddle, to horse, and away!"*

BEFORE.

I.

LET them fight it out, friend! things have gone too far.
  God must judge the couple: leave them as they are
— Whichever one 's the guiltless, to his glory,
And whichever one the guilt 's with, to my story!

II.

Why, you would not bid men, sunk in such a slough,
Strike no arm out further, stick and stink as now,
Leaving right and wrong to settle the embroilment,
Heaven with snaky hell, in torture and entoilment?

III.

Who 's the culprit of them? How must he conceive
God — the queen he caps to, laughing in his sleeve,   10
" 'T is but decent to profess oneself beneath her:
Still, one must not be too much in earnest, either!"

IV.

Better sin the whole sin, sure that God observes;
Then go live his life out! Life will try his nerves,

When the sky, which noticed all, makes no disclosure,
And the earth keeps up her terrible composure.

V.

Let him pace at pleasure, past the walls of rose,
Pluck their fruits when grape-trees graze him as he goes!
For he 'gins to guess the purpose of the garden,
With the sly mute thing, beside there, for a warden.   20

VI.

What 's the leopard-dog-thing, constant at his side,
A leer and lie in every eye of its obsequious hide?
When will come an end to all the mock obeisance,
And the price appear that pays for the misfeasance?

VII.

So much for the culprit.   Who 's the martyred man?
Let him bear one stroke more, for be sure he can!
He that strove thus evil's lump with good to leaven,
Let him give his blood at last and get his heaven!

VIII.

All or nothing, stake it!   Trusts he God or no?
Thus far and no farther? farther? be it so!   30
Now, enough of your chicane of prudent pauses,
Sage provisos, sub-intents and saving-clauses!

IX.

Ah, "Forgive" you bid him?   While God's champion lives,
Wrong shall be resisted: dead, why, he forgives.
But you must not end my friend ere you begin him;
Evil stands not crowned on earth, while breath is in him.

X.

Once more — Will the wronger, at this last of all,
Dare to say, "I did wrong," rising in his fall?
No? — Let go, then!   Both the fighters to their places!
While I count three, step you back as many paces!   40

AFTER.

TAKE the cloak from his face, and at first
   Let the corpse do its worst!

How he lies in his rights of a man!
   Death has done all death can:
And, absorbed in the new life he leads,
   He recks not, he heeds
Nor his wrong nor my vengeance; both strike
   On his senses alike,
And are lost in the solemn and strange
   Surprise of the change.   10

Ha, what avails death to erase
   His offence, my disgrace?
I would we were boys as of old
   In the field, by the fold:
His outrage, God's patience, man's scorn
   Were so easily borne!

I stand here now, he lies in his place:
   Cover the face!

HERVÉ RIEL.

I.

ON the sea and at the Hogue, sixteen hundred ninety two,
   Did the English fight the French, — woe to France!
And, the thirty-first of May, helter-skelter thro' the blue,
Like a crowd of frightened porpoises a shoal of sharks pursue,
   Came crowding ship on ship to St. Malo on the Rance,
With the English fleet in view.

II.

'T was the squadron that escaped, with the victor in full chase;
   First and foremost of the drove, in his great ship, Damfreville;
     Close on him fled, great and small,
     Twenty-two good ships in all;   10
And they signaled to the place
" Help the winners of a race!
   Get us guidance, give us harbour, take us quick — or, quicker still,
Here 's the English can and will!"

III.

Then the pilots of the place put out brisk and leapt on board;
   "Why, what hope or chance have ships like these to pass?" laughed
      they:
"Rocks to starboard, rocks to port, all the passage scarred and scored,
Shall the '*Formidable*' here with her twelve and eighty guns
   Think to make the river-mouth by the single narrow way,
Trust to enter where 't is ticklish for a craft of twenty tons,   20
     And with flow at full beside?
     Now 't is slackest ebb of tide.
   Reach the mooring?   Rather say,
While rock stands or water runs,
Not a ship will leave the bay!"

IV.

Then was called a council straight.
Brief and bitter the debate:
"Here 's the English at our heels; would you have them take in tow
All that 's left us of the fleet, linked together stern and bow,
For a prize to Plymouth Sound?   30
Better run the ships aground!"
   (Ended Damfreville his speech).
Not a minute more to wait!
   "Let the Captains all and each
   Shove ashore, then blow up, burn the vessels on the beach!
France must undergo her fate.

V.

"Give the word!"   But no such word
Was ever spoke or heard;
   For up stood, for out stepped, for in struck amid all these
— A Captain? A Lieutenant? A Mate — first, second, third?   40
   No such man of mark, and meet
   With his betters to compete!
But a simple Breton sailor pressed by Tourville for the fleet,
A poor coasting-pilot he, Hervé Riel the Croisickese.

VI.

And, "What mockery or malice have we here?" cries Hervé Riel:
   "Are you mad, you Malouins?   Are you cowards, fools, or rogues?
Talk to me of rocks and shoals, me who took the soundings, tell
On my fingers every bank, every shallow, every swell
   'Twixt the offing here and Grève where the river disembogues?
Are you bought by English gold?   Is it love the lying 's for?   50
     Morn and eve, night and day,
     Have I piloted your bay,

Entered free and anchored fast at the foot of Solidor.
    Burn the fleet and ruin France?   That were worse than fifty Hogues!
        Sirs, they know I speak the truth!   Sirs, believe me there 's a way!
Only let me lead the line,
    Have the biggest ship to steer,
    Get this '*Formidable*' clear,
Make the others follow mine,
And I lead them, most and least, by a passage I know well,   60
    Right to Solidor past Grève,
        And there lay them safe and sound;
    And if one ship misbehave,
        — Keel so much as grate the ground,
Why, I 've nothing but my life, — here 's my head!" cries Hervé Riel.

VII.

Not a minute more to wait.
" Steer us in, then, small and great!
    Take the helm, lead the line, save the squadron!" cried its chief.
Captains, give the sailor place!
    He is Admiral, in brief.   70
Still the north-wind, by God's grace!
See the noble fellow's face
As the big ship, with a bound,
Clears the entry like a hound,
Keeps the passage as its inch of way were the wide sea's profound!
    See, safe thro' shoal and rock,
    How they follow in a flock,
Not a ship that misbehaves, not a keel that grates the ground,
    Not a spar that comes to grief!
The peril, see, is past,   80
All are harboured to the last,
And just as Hervé Riel hollas "Anchor!" — sure as fate
Up the English come, too late!

VIII.

So, the storm subsides to calm:
    They see the green trees wave
    On the heights o'erlooking Grève.
Hearts that bled are stanched with balm.
" Just our rapture to enhance,
    Let the English rake the bay,
Gnash their teeth and glare askance   90
    As they cannonade away!
'Neath rampired Solidor pleasant riding on the Rance!"
How hope succeeds despair on each Captain's countenance!
Out burst all with one accord,
    "This is Paradise for Hell!

Let France, let France's King
    Thank the man that did the thing ! "
What a shout, and all one word,
    "Hervé Riel ! "
As he stepped in front once more,   100
    Not a symptom of surprise
    In the frank blue Breton eyes,
Just the same man as before.

IX.

Then said Damfreville, " My friend,
I must speak out at the end,
    Tho' I find the speaking hard.
Praise is deeper than the lips :
You have saved the King his ships,
    You must name your own reward.
'Faith our sun was near eclipse !   110
Demand whate'er you will,
France remains your debtor still.
Ask to heart's content and have ! or my name 's not Damfreville."

X.

Then a beam of fun outbroke
On the bearded mouth that spoke,
As the honest heart laughed through
Those frank eyes of Breton blue :
"Since I needs must say my say,
    Since on board the duty 's done,
    And from Malo Roads to Croisic Point, what is it but a run? —   120
Since 't is ask and have, I may —
    Since the others go ashore —
Come !   A good whole holiday !
    Leave to go and see my wife, whom I call the Belle Aurore ! "
That he asked and that he got, — nothing more.

XI.

Name and deed alike are lost :
Not a pillar nor a post
    In his Croisic keeps alive the feat as it befell ;
Not a head in white and black
On a single fishing smack,   130
In memory of the man but for whom had gone to wrack
    All that France saved from the fight whence England bore the bell.
Go to Paris : rank on rank
    Search the heroes flung pell-mell
On the Louvre, face and flank !

You shall look long enough ere you come to Hervé Riel.
So, for better and for worse,
Hervé Riel, accept my verse!
In my verse, Hervé Riel, do thou once more
Save the squadron, honour France, love thy wife the Belle Aurore! 140

———◆◆◆———

IN A BALCONY.

CONSTANCE *and* NORBERT.

Nor. Now!
   Con.   Not now!
   Nor.   Give me them again, those hands —
Put them upon my forehead, how it throbs!
Press them before my eyes, the fire comes through!
You cruelest, you dearest in the world,
Let me! The Queen must grant whate'er I ask —
How can I gain you and not ask the Queen?
There she stays waiting for me, here stand you;
Some time or other this was to be asked:
Now is the one time — what I ask, I gain:
Let me ask now, Love!
   Con.   Do, and ruin us!   10
   Nor. Let it be now, Love! All my soul breaks forth.
How I do love you! Give my love its way!
A man can have but one life and one death,
One heaven, one hell. Let me fulfil my fate —
Grant me my heaven now! Let me know you mine,
Prove you mine, write my name upon your brow,
Hold you and have you, and then die away,
If God please, with completion in my soul.
   Con. I am not yours then? How content this man!
I am not his — who change into himself,   20
Have passed into his heart and beat its beats,
Who give my hands to him, my eyes, my hair,
Give all that was of me away to him —
So well, that now, my spirit turned his own,
Takes part with him against the woman here,
Bids him not stumble at so mere a straw
As caring that the world be cognizant
How he loves her and how she worships him.
You have this woman, not as yet that world.
Go on, I bid, nor stop to care for me   30
By saving what I cease to care about,
The courtly name and pride of circumstance —

The name you 'll pick up and be cumbered with
Just for the poor parade's sake, nothing more ;
Just that the world may slip from under you —
Just that the world may cry " So much for him —
The man predestined to the heap of crowns :
There goes his chance of winning one, at least ! "
    Nor. The world !
    Con.   You love it ! Love me quite as well,
And see if I shall pray for this in vain !   40
Why must you ponder what it knows or thinks ?
    Nor. You pray for — what, in vain ?
    Con.   Oh my heart's heart,
How I do love you, Norbert ! That is right :
But listen, or I take my hands away !
You say, " let it be now : " you would go now
And tell the Queen, perhaps six steps from us,
You love me — so you do, thank God !
    Nor.   Thank God !
    Con. Yes, Norbert, — but you fain would tell your love,
And, what succeeds the telling, ask of her
My hand. Now take this rose and look at it,   50
Listening to me. You are the minister,
The Queen's first favourite, nor without a cause.
To-night completes your wonderful year's-work
(This palace-feast is held to celebrate)
Made memorable by her life's success,
The junction of two crowns, on her sole head,
Her house had only dreamed of anciently :
That this mere dream is grown a stable truth,
To-night's feast makes authentic. Whose the praise ?
Whose genius, patience, energy, achieved   60
What turned the many heads and broke the hearts ?
You are the fate, your minute 's in the heaven.
Next comes the Queen's turn. " Name your own reward ! "
With leave to clench the past, chain the to-come,
Put out an arm and touch and take the sun
And fix it ever full-faced on your earth,
Possess yourself supremely of her life, —
You choose the single thing she will not grant ;
Nay, very declaration of which choice
Will turn the scale and neutralize your work :   70
At best she will forgive you, if she can.
You think I 'll let you choose — her cousin's hand ?
    Nor. Wait. First, do you retain your old belief
The Queen is generous, — nay, is just ?
    Con.   There, there !
So men make women love them, while they know
No more of women's hearts than . . . look you here,

You that are just and generous beside,
Make it your own case!   For example now,
I 'll say — I let you kiss me, hold my hands —
Why? do you know why?   I 'll instruct you, then —   80
The kiss, because you have a name at court,
This hand and this, that you may shut in each
A jewel, if you please to pick up such.
That 's horrible?   Apply it to the Queen —
Suppose I am the Queen to whom you speak.
" I was a nameless man ; you needed me :
Why did I proffer you my aid? there stood
A certain pretty cousin at your side.
Why did I make such common cause with you?
Access to her had not been easy else.   90
You give my labour here abundant praise?
'Faith, labour, which she overlooked, grew play.
How shall your gratitude discharge itself?
Give me her hand ! "
    Nor.   And still I urge the same.
Is the Queen just? just — generous or no!
    Con. Yes, just.   You love a rose ; no harm in that :
But was it for the rose's sake or mine
You put it in your bosom? mine, you said —
Then, mine you still must say or else be false.
You told the Queen you served her for herself ;   100
If so, to serve her was to serve yourself,
She thinks, for all your unbelieving face!
I know her.   In the hall, six steps from us,
One sees the twenty pictures ; there 's a life
Better than life, and yet no life at all.
Conceive her born in such a magic dome,
Pictures all round her! why, she sees the world,
Can recognize its given things and facts,
The fight of giants or the feast of gods,
Sages in senate, beauties at the bath,   110
Chases and battles, the whole earth's display,
Landscape and sea-piece, down to flowers and fruit —
And who shall question that she knows them all,
In better semblance than the things outside?
Yet bring into the silent gallery
Some live thing to contrast in breath and blood,
Some lion, with the painted lion there —
You think she 'll understand composedly?
— Say, " that 's his fellow in the hunting-piece
Yonder, I 've turned to praise a hundred times? "   120
Not so.   Her knowledge of our actual earth,
Its hopes and fears, concerns and sympathies,
Must be too far, too mediate, too unreal.

The real exists for us outside, not her:
How should it, with that life in these four walls,
That father and that mother, first to last
No father and no mother — friends, a heap,
Lovers, no lack — a husband in due time,
And every one of them alike a lie!
Things painted by a Rubens out of naught   130
Into what kindness, friendship, love should be;
All better, all more grandiose than the life,
Only no life; mere cloth and surface-paint,
You feel, while you admire. How should she feel?
Yet now that she has stood thus fifty years
The sole spectator in that gallery,
You think to bring this warm real struggling love
In to her of a sudden, and suppose
She 'll keep her state untroubled? Here 's the truth:
She 'll apprehend truth's value at a glance,   140
Prefer it to the pictured loyalty?
You only have to say " So men are made,
For this they act; the thing has many names,
But this the right one: and now, Queen, be just!"
Your life slips back; you lose her at the word:
You do not even for amends gain me.
He will not understand! oh, Norbert, Norbert,
Do you not understand?
      Nor.   The Queen 's the Queen:
I am myself — no picture, but alive
In every nerve and every muscle, here   150
At the palace-window o'er the people's street,
As she in the gallery where the pictures glow:
The good of life is precious to us both.
She can not love; what do I want with rule?
When first I saw your face a year ago
I knew my life's good, my soul heard one voice —
" The woman yonder, there 's no use of life
But just to obtain her! heap earth's woes in one
And bear them — make a pile of all earth's joys
And spurn them, as they help or help not this;   160
Only, obtain her!" — How was it to be?
I found you were the cousin of the Queen;
I must then serve the Queen to get to you.
No other way. Suppose there had been one,
And I, by saying prayers to some white star
With promise of my body and my soul,
Might gain you, — should I pray the star or no?
Instead, there was the Queen to serve! I served,
Helped, did what other servants failed to do.
Neither she sought nor I declared my end.   170

Y

Her good is hers, my recompense be mine,
I therefore name you as that recompense.
She dreamed that such a thing could never be?
Let her wake now.   She thinks there was more cause
In love of power, high fame, pure loyalty?
Perhaps she fancies men wear out their lives
Chasing such shades.   Then, I 've a fancy too;
I worked because I want you with my soul:
I therefore ask your hand.   Let it be now!
   Con.   Had I not loved you from the very first,   180
Were I not yours, could we not steal out thus
So wickedly, so wildly, and so well,
You might become impatient.   What 's conceived
Of us without here, by the folks within?
Where are you now? immersed in cares of state —
Where am I now? — intent on festal robes —
We two, embracing under death's spread hand!
What was this thought for, what that scruple of yours
Which broke the council up? — to bring about
One minute's meeting in the corridor!   190
And then the sudden sleights, strange secrecies,
Complots inscrutable, deep telegraphs,
Long-planned chance-meetings, hazards of a look,
"Does she know? does she not know? saved or lost?"
A year of this compression's ecstasy
All goes for nothing! you would give this up
For the old way, the open way, the world's,
His way who beats, and his who sells his wife!
What tempts you? — their notorious happiness,
Makes you ashamed of ours?   The best you 'll gain   200
Will be — the Queen grants all that you require,
Concedes the cousin, rids herself of you
And me at once, and gives us ample leave
To live like our five hundred happy friends.
The world will show us with officious hand
Our chamber-entry and stand sentinel,
Where we so oft have stolen across its traps!
Get the world's warrant, ring the falcon's feet,
And make it duty to be bold and swift,
Which long ago was nature.   Have it so!   210
We never hawked by rights till flung from fist?
Oh, the man's thought; no woman 's such a fool.
   Nor.   Yes, the man's thought and my thought, which is more —
One made to love you, let the world take note!
Have I done worthy work? be love's the praise,
Tho' hampered by restrictions, barred against
By set forms, blinded by forced secrecies!
Set free my love, and see what love can do

Shown in my life — what work will spring from that!
The world is used to have its business done   220
On other grounds, find great effects produced
For power's sake, fame's sake, motives in men's mouth!
So, good: but let my low ground shame their high!
Truth is the strong thing.   Let man's life be true!
And love's the truth of mine.   Time prove the rest!
I choose to wear you stamped all over me,
Your name upon my forehead and my breast,
You, from the sword's blade to the ribbon's edge,
That men may see, all over, you in me —
That pale loves may die out of their pretence   230
In face of mine, shames thrown on love fall off.
Permit this, Constance!   Love has been so long
Subdued in me, eating me through and through,
That now 't is all of me and must have way.
Think of my work, that chaos of intrigues,
Those hopes and fears, surprises and delays,
That long endeavour, earnest, patient, slow,
Trembling at last to its assured result —
Then think of this revulsion!   I resume
Life after death, (it is no less than life,   240
After such long unlovely labouring days)
And liberate to beauty life's great need
O' the beautiful, which, while it prompted work,
Suppressed itself erewhile.   This eve 's the time,
This eve intense with yon first trembling star
We seem to pant and reach; scarce aught between
The earth that rises and the heaven that bends;
All nature self-abandoned, every tree
Flung as it will, pursuing its own thoughts
And fixed so, every flower and every weed,   250
No pride, no shame, no victory, no defeat;
All under God, each measured by itself
These statues round us stand abrupt, distinct,
The strong in strength, the weak in weakness fixed,
The Muse for ever wedded to her lyre,
Nymph to her fawn, and Silence to her rose:
See God's approval on his universe!
Let us do so — aspire to live as these
In harmony with truth, ourselves being true!
Take the first way, and let the second come!   260
My first is to possess myself of you;
The music sets the march-step — forward, then!
And there 's the Queen, I go to claim you of,
The world to witness, wonder and applaud.
Our flower of life breaks open.   No delay!
    Con. And so shall we be ruined, both of us

Norbert, I know her to the skin and bone :
You do not know her, were not born to it,
To feel what she can see or can not see.
Love, she is generous, — ay, despite your smile,   270
Generous as you are : for, in that thin frame
Pain-twisted, punctured through and through with cares,
There lived a lavish soul until it starved
Debarred of healthy food.   Look to the soul —
Pity that, stoop to that, ere you begin
(The true man's-way) on justice and your rights,
Exactions and acquittance of the past !
Begin so — see what justice she will deal !
We women hate a debt as men a gift.
Suppose her some poor keeper of a school   280
Whose business is to sit thro' summer months
And dole out children leave to go and play,
Herself superior to such lightness — she
In the arm-chair's state and pædagogic pomp,
To the life, the laughter, sun and youth outside :
We wonder such a face looks black on us?
I do not bid you wake her tenderness,
(That were vain truly — none is left to wake)
But, let her think her justice is engaged
To take the shape of tenderness, and mark   290
If she 'll not coldly pay its warmest debt !
Does she love me, I ask you? not a whit :
Yet, thinking that her justice was engaged
To help a kinswoman, she took me up —
Did more on that bare ground than other loves
Would do on greater argument.   For me,
I have no equivalent of such cold kind
To pay her with, but love alone to give
If I give anything.   I give her love :
I feel I ought to help her, and I will.   300
So, for her sake, as yours, I tell you twice
That women hate a debt as men a gift.
If I were you, I could obtain this grace —
Could lay the whole I did to love's account
Nor yet be very false as courtiers go —
Declaring my success was recompense ;
It would be so, in fact : what were it else?
And then, once loose her generosity, —
Oh, how I see it ! — then, were I but you
To turn it, let it seem to move itself,   310
And make it offer what I really take,
Accepting just, in the poor cousin's hand,
Her value as the next thing to the Queen's —
Since none love Queens directly, none dare that,

And a thing's shadow or a name's mere echo
Suffices those who miss the name and thing!
You pick up just a ribbon she has worn,
To keep in proof how near her breath you came.
Say, I 'm so near I seem a piece of her —
Ask for me that way — (oh, you understand)   320
You 'd find the same gift yielded with a grace,
Which, if you make the least show to extort . . .
— You 'll see! and when you have ruined both of us,
Dissertate on the Queen's ingratitude!

   Nor. Then, if I turn it that way, you consent?
'T is not my way; I have more hope in truth:
Still, if you won't have truth — why, this indeed,
Were scarcely false, as I 'd express the sense.
Will you remain here?

   Con.   O best heart of mine,
How I have loved you! then, you take my way?   330
Are mine as you have been her minister,
Work out my thought, give it effect for me,
Paint plain my poor conceit and make it serve?
I owe that withered woman everything —
Life, fortune, you, remember! Take my part —
Help me to pay her! Stand upon your rights?
You, with my rose, my hands, my heart on you?
Your rights are mine — you have no rights but mine.

   Nor. Remain here. How you know me!

   Con.   Ah, but still——

    [*He breaks from her: she remains. Dance-music from
      within.*

Enter the QUEEN.

   Queen. Constance? She is here as he said. Speak quick! 340
Is it so? Is it true or false? One word!

   Con. True.

   Queen.   Mercifullest Mother, thanks to thee!

   Con. Madam?

   Queen.   I love you, Constance, from my soul.
Now say once more, with any words you will,
'T is true, all true, as true as that I speak.

   Con. Why should you doubt it?

   Queen.   Ah, why doubt? why doubt?
Dear, make me see it! Do you see it so?
None see themselves; another sees them best.
You say "why doubt it?" — you see him and me.
It is because the Mother has such grace   350
That if we had but faith — wherein we fail —
Whate'er we yearn for would be granted us;

Yet still we let our whims prescribe despair,
Our fancies thwart and cramp our will and power,
And while accepting life, abjure its use.
Constance, I had abjured the hope of love
And being loved, as truly as yon palm
The hope of seeing Egypt from that plot.
    Con. Heaven!
    Queen.   But it was so, Constance, it was so!
Men say — or do men say it? fancies say —   360
"Stop here, your life is set, you are grown old.
Too late — no love for you, too late for love —
Leave love to girls. Be queen: let Constance love!"
One takes the hint — half meets it like a child,
Ashamed at any feelings that oppose.
"Oh love, true, never think of love again!
I am a queen: I rule, not love forsooth."
So it goes on; so a face grows like this,
Hair like this hair, poor arms as lean as these,
Till, — nay, it does not end so, I thank God!   370
    Con. I can not understand —
    Queen.   The happier you!
Constance, I know not how it is with men:
For women (I am a woman now like you)
There is no good of life but love — but love!
What else looks good, is some shade flung from love;
Love gilds it, gives it worth. Be warned by me,
Never you cheat yourself one instant! Love,
Give love, ask only love, and leave the rest!
O Constance, how I love you!
    Con.   I love you.
    Queen. I do believe that all is come thro' you.   380
I took you to my heart to keep it warm
When the last chance of love seemed dead in me;
I thought your fresh youth warmed my withered heart.
Oh, I am very old now, am I not?
Not so! it is true and it shall be true!
    Con. Tell it me: let me judge if true or false.
    Queen. Ah, but I fear you! you will look at me
And say, "she's old, she's grown unlovely quite
Who ne'er was beauteous: men want beauty still."
Well, so I feared — the curse! so I felt sure.   390
    Con. Be calm. And now you feel not sure, you say?
    Queen. Constance, he came, — the coming was not strange —
Do not I stand and see men come and go?
I turned a half-look from my pedestal
Where I grow marble — "one young man the more!
He will love some one; that is naught to me:
What would he with my marble stateliness?"

Yet this seemed somewhat worse than heretofore;
The man more gracious, youthful, like a god,
And I still older, with less flesh to change —   400
We two those dear extremes that long to touch.
It seemed still harder when he first began
To labour at those state-affairs, absorbed
The old way for the old end — interest.
Oh, to live with a thousand beating hearts
Around you, swift eyes, serviceable hands,
Professing they 've no care but for your cause,
Thought but to help you, love but for yourself,
And you the marble statue all the time
They praise and point at as preferred to life,   410
Yet leave for the first breathing woman's smile,
First dancer's, gipsy's or street baladine's!
Why, how I have ground my teeth to hear men's speech
Stifled for fear it should alarm my ear,
Their gait subdued lest step should startle me,
Their eyes declined, such queendom to respect,
Their hands alert, such treasure to preserve,
While not a man of them broke rank and spoke,
Wrote me a vulgar letter all of love,
Or caught my hand and pressed it like a hand!   420
There have been moments, if the sentinel
Lowering his halbert to salute the queen,
Had flung it brutally and clasped my knees,
I would have stooped and kissed him with my soul.
   Con. Who could have comprehended?
   Queen.   Ay, who — who?
Why, no one, Constance, but this one who did.
Not they, not you, not I.   Even now perhaps
It comes too late — would you but tell the truth.
   Con. I wait to tell it.
   Queen.   Well, you see, he came,
Outfaced the others, did a work this year   430
Exceeds in value all was ever done,
You know — it is not I who say it — all
Say it.   And so (a second pang and worse)
I grew aware not only of what he did,
But why so wondrously.   Oh, never work
Like his was done for work's ignoble sake —
Souls need a finer aim to light and lure!
I felt, I saw, he loved — loved somebody.
And Constance, my dear Constance, do you know,
I did believe this while 't was you he loved.   440
   Con. Me, madam?
   Queen.   It did seem to me, your face
Met him where'er he looked: and whom but you

Was such a man to love? It seemed to me,
You saw he loved you, and approved his love,
And both of you were in intelligence.
You could not loiter in that garden, step
Into this balcony, but I straight was stung
And forced to understand.   It seemed so true,
So right, so beautiful, so like you both,
That all this work should have been done by him   450
Not for the vulgar hope of recompense,
But that at last — suppose, some night like this —
Borne on to claim his due reward of me,
He might say, " Give her hand and pay me so."
And I (O Constance, you shall love me now!)
I thought, surmounting all the bitterness,
— " And he shall have it.   I will make her blest,
My flower of youth, my woman's self that was,
My happiest woman's self that might have been!
These two shall have their joy and leave me here."   460
Yes — yes!

   Con.   Thanks!

   Queen.   And the word was on my lips
When he burst in upon me.   I looked to hear
A mere calm statement of his just desire
For payment of his labour.   When — O heaven,
How can I tell you? lightning on my eyes
And thunder in my ears proved that first word
Which told 't was love of me, of me, did all —
He loved me — from the first step to the last,
Loved me!

   Con.   You hardly saw, scarce heard him speak
Of love : what if you should mistake?

   Queen.   No, no —   470
No mistake!   Ha, there shall be no mistake!
He had not dared to hint the love he felt —
You were my reflex — (how I understood!)
He said you were the ribbon I had worn,
He kissed my hand, he looked into my eyes,
And love, love came at end of every phrase.
Love is begun ; this much is come to pass :
The rest is easy.   Constance, I am yours!
I will learn, I will place my life on you,
Teach me but how to keep what I have won!   480
Am I so old?   This hair was early gray ;
But joy ere now has brought hair brown again,
And joy will bring the cheek's red back, I feel.
I could sing once too ; that was in my youth.
Still, when men paint me, they declare me . . . yes,
Beautiful — for the last French painter did!

I know they flatter somewhat; you are frank —
I trust you.   How I loved you from the first!
Some queens would hardly seek a cousin out
And set her by their side to take the eye: 490
I must have felt that good would come from you.
I am not generous — like him — like you!
But he is not your lover after all:
It was not you he looked at.   Saw you him?
You have not been mistaking words or looks?
He said you were the reflex of myself.
And yet he is not such a paragon
To you, to younger women who may choose
Among a thousand Norberts.   Speak the truth!
You know you never named his name to me —   500
You know, I can not give him up — ah God,
Not up now, even to you!
    Con.   Then calm yourself.
    Queen. See, I am old — look here, you happy girl!
I will not play the fool, deceive — ah whom?
'T is all gone: put your cheek beside my cheek
And, what a contrast does the moon behold!
But then I set my life upon one chance,
The last chance and the best — am *I* not left,
My soul, myself?   All women love great men
If young or old; it is in all the tales: 510
Young beauties love old poets who can love —
Why should not he, the poems in my soul,
The passionate faith, the pride of sacrifice,
Life-long, death-long?   I throw them at his feet.
Who cares to see the fountain's very shape,
And whether it be a Triton's or a Nymph's
That pours the foam, makes rainbows all around?
You could not praise indeed the empty conch;
But I 'll pour floods of love and hide myself.
How I will love him!   Can not men love love?   520
Who was a queen and loved a poet once
Humpbacked, a dwarf? ah, women can do that!
Well, but men too; at least, they tell you so.
They love so many women in their youth,
And even in age they all love whom they please;
And yet the best of them confide to friends
That 't is not beauty makes the lasting love —
They spend a day with such and tire the next:
They like soul, — well then, they like phantasy,
Novelty even.   Let us confess the truth,   530
Horrible tho' it be, that prejudice,
Prescription . . . curses! they will love a queen
They will, they do: and will not, does not — he?

Con. How can he? You are wedded; 't is a name
We know, but still a bond. Your rank remains,
His rank remains. How can he, nobly souled
As you believe and I incline to think,
Aspire to be your favourite, shame and all?
    Queen. Hear her! There, there now — could she love like me?
What did I say of smooth-cheeked youth and grace?   540
See all it does or could do! so, youth loves!
Oh, tell him, Constance, you could never do
What I will — you, it was not born in! I
Will drive these difficulties far and fast
As yonder mists curdling before the moon.
I 'll use my light too, gloriously retrieve
My youth from its enforced calamity,
Dissolve that hateful marriage, and be his,
His own in the eyes alike of God and man.
    Con. You will do — dare do . . . pause on what you say!   550
    Queen. Hear her! I thank you, sweet, for that surprise.
You have the fair face: for the soul, see mine!
I have the strong soul: let me teach you, here.
I think I have borne enough and long enough,
And patiently enough, the world remarks,
To have my own way now, unblamed by all.
It does so happen (I rejoice for it)
This most unhoped-for issue cuts the knot.
There 's not a better way of settling claims
Than this: God sends the accident express: 560
And were it for my subjects' good, no more,
'T were best thus ordered. I am thankful now,
Mute, passive, acquiescent. I receive,
And bless God simply, or should almost fear
To walk so smoothly to my ends at last.
Why, how I baffle obstacles, spurn fate!
How strong I am! Could Norbert see me now!
    Con. Let me consider! It is all too strange.
    Queen. You, Constance, learn of me; do you, like me!
You are young, beautiful: my own, best girl,   570
You will have many lovers, and love one —
Light hair, not hair like Norbert's, to suit yours,
Taller than he is, since yourself are tall.
Love him, like me! Give all away to him;
Think never of yourself; throw by your pride,
Hope, fear, — your own good as you saw it once,
And love him simply for his very self.
Remember, I (and what am I to you?)
Would give up all for one, leave throne, lose life,
Do all but just unlove him! He loves me.   580
    Con. He shall.

Queen.   You, step inside my inmost heart!
Give me your own heart : let us have one heart!
I 'll come to you for counsel ; " this he says,
This he does ; what should this amount to, pray?
Beseech you, change it into current coin!
Is that worth kisses?   Shall I please him there?"
And then we 'll speak in turn of you — what else?
Your love, according to your beauty's worth,
For you shall have some noble love, all gold :
Whom choose you? we will get him at your choice.   590
— Constance, I leave you.   Just a minute since,
I felt as I must die or be alone
Breathing my soul into an ear like yours :
Now, I would face the world with my new life,
Wear my new crown.   I 'll walk around the rooms,
And then come back and tell you how it feels.
How soon a smile of God can change the world!
How we are made for happiness — how work
Grows play, adversity a winning fight!
True I have lost so many years : what then?   600
Many remain : God has been very good.
You, stay here!   'T is as different from dreams,
From the mind's cold calm estimate of bliss,
As these stone statues from the flesh and blood.
The comfort thou hast caused mankind, God's moon!
      [*She goes out, leaving* CONSTANCE.   *Dance-music from
      within.*

NORBERT *enters.*

Nor.   Well? we have but one minute and one word!
Con.   I am yours, Norbert!
Nor.   Yes, mine.
Con.   Not till now!
You were mine.   Now I give myself to you.
Nor.   Constance?
Con.   Your own!   I know the thriftier way
Of giving — haply, 't is the wiser way   610
Meaning to give a treasure, I might dole
Coin after coin out (each, as that were all,
With a new largess still at each despair)
And force you keep in sight the deed, preserve
Exhaustless till the end my part and yours,
My giving and your taking ; both our joys
Dying together.   Is it the wiser way?
I choose the simpler ; I give all at once.
Know, what you have to trust to, trade upon!
Use it, abuse it, — anything but think   620

Hereafter, " Had I known she loved me so,
And what my means, I might have thriven with it."
This is your means.   I give you all myself.
   Nor. I take you and thank God.
   Con.   Look on thro' years!
We can not kiss, a second day like this ;
Else were this earth no earth.
   Nor.   With this day's heat
We shall go on thro' years of cold.
   Con.   So, best!
— I try to see those years — I think I see.
You walk quick and new warmth comes ; you look back
And lay all to the first glow — not sit down   630
For ever brooding on a day like this
While seeing embers whiten and love die.
Yes, love lives best in its effect ; and mine,
Full in its own life, yearns to live in yours.
   Nor. Just so.   I take and know you all at once.
Your soul is disengaged so easily,
Your face is there, I know you ; give me time,
Let me be proud and think you shall know me.
My soul is slower : in a life I roll
The minute out whereto you condense yours —   640
The whole slow circle round you I must move,
To be just you.   I look to a long life
To decompose this minute, prove its worth.
'T is the sparks' long succession one by one
Shall show you, in the end, what fire was crammed
In that mere stone you struck : how could you know,
If it lay ever unproved in your sight,
As now my heart lies ? your own warmth would hide
Its coldness, were it cold.
   Con.   But how prove, how ?
   Nor. Prove in my life, you ask ?
   Con.   Quick, Norbert — how ?   650
   Nor. That 's easy told.   I count life just a stuff
To try the soul's strength on, educe the man.
Who keeps one end in view makes all things serve.
As with the body — he who hurls a lance
Or heaps up stone on stone, shows strength alike,
So must I seize and task all means to prove
And show this soul of mine, you crown as yours,
And justify us both.
   Con.   Could you write books,
Paint pictures!   One sits down in poverty
And writes or paints, with pity for the rich.   660
   Nor. And loves one's painting, and one's writing, then,
And not one's mistress!   All is best, believe

And we best as no other than we are.
We live, and they experiment on life —
Those poets, painters, all who stand aloof
To overlook the farther.   Let us be
The thing they look at!   I might take your face
And write of it and paint it — to what end?
For whom? what pale dictatress in the air
Feeds, smiling sadly, her fine ghost-like form   670
With earth's real blood and breath, the beauteous life
She makes despised for ever?   You are mine,
Made for me, not for others in the world,
Nor yet for that which I should call my art,
The cold calm power to see how fair you look.
I come to you; I leave you not, to write
Or paint.   You are, I am: let Rubens there
Paint us!
    Con.   So, best!
    Nor.   I understand your soul.
You live, and rightly sympathize with life,
With action, power, success.   This way is straight;   680
And time were short beside, to let me change
The craft my childhood learnt: my craft shall serve.
Men set me here to subjugate, enclose,
Manure their barren lives, and force thence fruit
First for themselves, and afterward for me
In the due tithe ; the task of some one soul,
Thro' ways of work appointed by the world.
I am not bid create — men see no star
Transfiguring my brow to warrant that —
But find and bind and bring to bear their wills.   690
So I began : to-night sees how I end.
What if it see, too, power's first outbreak here
Amid the warmth, surprise and sympathy,
And instincts of the heart that teach the head?
What if the people have discerned at length
The dawn of the next nature, novel brain
Whose will they venture in the place of theirs,
Whose work, they trust, shall find them as novel ways
To untried heights which yet he only sees?
I felt it when you kissed me.   See this Queen,   700
This people — in our phrase, this mass of men,
See how the mass lies passive to my hand
Now that my hand is plastic, with you by
To make the muscles iron!   Oh, an end
Shall crown this issue as this crowns the first!
My will be on this people! then, the strain,
The grappling of the potter with his clay,
The long uncertain struggle, — the success

And consummation of the spirit-work,
Some vase shaped to the curl of the god's lip,   710
While rounded fair for human sense to see
The Graces in a dance men recognize
With turbulent applause and laughs of heart!
So triumph ever shall renew itself;
Ever shall end in efforts higher yet,
Ever begin . . .
    Con.   I ever helping?
    Nor.   Thus!
          [*As he embraces her, the* QUEEN *enters.*
  Con. Hist, madam!   So have I performed my part.
You see your gratitude's true decency,
Norbert?   A little slow in seeing it!
Begin, to end the sooner!   What's a kiss?   720
    Nor. Constance?
    Con.   Why, must I teach it you again?
You want a witness to your dulness, sir?
What was I saying these ten minutes long?
Then I repeat — when some young handsome man
Like you has acted out a part like yours,
Is pleased to fall in love with one beyond,
So very far beyond him, as he says —
So hopelessly in love that but to speak
Would prove him mad, — he thinks judiciously,
And makes some insignificant good soul,   730
Like me, his friend, adviser, confidant,
And very stalking-horse to cover him
In following after what he dares not face —
When his end's gained — (sir, do you understand?)
When she, he dares not face, has loved him first,
— May I not say so, madam? — tops his hope,
And overpasses so his wildest dream,
With glad consent of all, and most of her
The confidant who brought the same about —
Why, in the moment when such joy explodes,   740
I do hold that the merest gentleman
Will not start rudely from the stalking-horse,
Dismiss it with a " There, enough of you!"
Forget it, show his back unmannerly;
But like a liberal heart will rather turn
And say, " A tingling time of hope was ours;
Betwixt the fears and falterings, we two lived
A chanceful time in waiting for the prize:
The confidant, the Constance, served not ill.
And tho' I shall forget her in due time,   750
Her use being answered now, as reason bids,
Nay as herself bids from her heart of hearts, —

Still, she has rights, the first thanks go to her,
The first good praise goes to the prosperous tool,
And the first — which is the last — rewarding kiss."
 Nor. Constance, it is a dream — ah, see, you smile!
 Con. So, now his part being properly performed,
Madam, I turn to you and finish mine
As duly; I do justice in my turn.
Yes, madam, he has loved you — long and well;   760
He could not hope to tell you so — 't was I
Who served to prove your soul accessible,
I led his thoughts on, drew them to their place
When they had wandered else into despair,
And kept love constant toward its natural aim.
Enough, my part is played; you stoop half-way
And meet us royally and spare our fears:
'T is like yourself. He thanks you, so do I.
Take him — with my full heart! my work is praised
By what comes of it. Be you happy, both!   770
Yourself — the only one on earth who can —
Do all for him, much more than a mere heart
Which tho' warm is not useful in its warmth
As the silk vesture of a queen! fold that
Around him gently, tenderly. For him —
For him, — he knows his own part!
 Nor.   Have you done?
I take the jest at last. Should I speak now?
Was yours the wager, Constance, foolish child,
Or did you but accept it? Well — at least
You lose by it.
 Con.   Nay, madam, 't is your turn!   780
Restrain him still from speech a little more,
And make him happier as more confident!
Pity him, madam, he is timid yet!
Mark, Norbert! Do not shrink now! Here I yield
My whole right in you to the Queen, observe!
With her go put in practice the great schemes
You teem with, follow the career else closed —
Be all you can not be except by her!
Behold her! — Madam, say for pity's sake
Anything — frankly say you love him! Else   790
He 'll not believe it: there 's more earnest in
His fear than you conceive: I know the man!
 Nor. I know the woman somewhat, and confess
I thought she had jested better: she begins
To overcharge her part. I gravely wait
Your pleasure, madam: where is my reward?
 Queen. Norbert, this wild girl (whom I recognize
Scarce more than you do, in her fancy-fit,

Eccentric speech and variable mirth,   800
Not very wise perhaps and somewhat bold,
Yet suitable, the whole night's work being strange)
— May still be right: I may do well to speak
And make authentic what appears a dream
To even myself.   For, what she says, is true.
Yes, Norbert — what you spoke just now of love,
Devotion, stirred no novel sense in me,
But justified a warmth felt long before.
Yes, from the first — I loved you, I shall say:
Strange! but I do grow stronger, now 't is said.
Your courage helps mine: you did well to speak   810
To-night, the night that crowns your twelvemonths' toil:
But still I had not waited to discern
Your heart so long, believe me!   From the first
The source of so much zeal was almost plain,
In absence even of your own words just now
Which hazarded the truth.   'T is very strange,
But takes a happy ending — in your love
Which mine meets: be it so! as you chose me,
So I choose you.
    Nor.   And worthily you choose.
I will not be unworthy your esteem,   820
No, madam.   I do love you; I will meet
Your nature, now I know it.   This was well.
I see, — you dare and you are justified:
But none had ventured such experiment,
Less versed than you in nobleness of heart,
Less confident of finding such in me.
I joy that thus you test me ere you grant
The dearest richest beauteousest and best
Of women to my arms: 't is like yourself.
So — back again into my part's set words —   830
Devotion to the uttermost is yours,
But no, you can not, madam, even you,
Create in me the love our Constance does.
Or — something truer to the tragic phrase —
Not yon magnolia-bell superb with scent
Invites a certain insect — that 's myself —
But the small eye-flower nearer to the ground.
I take this lady.
    Con.   Stay — not hers, the trap —
Stay, Norbert — that mistake were worst of all!
He is too cunning, madam!   It was I,   840
I, Norbert, who . . .
    Nor.   You, was it, Constance?   Then,
But for the grace of this divinest hour
Which gives me you, I might not pardon here!

I am the Queen's; she only knows my brain:
She may experiment upon my heart
And I instruct her too by the result.
But you, Sweet, you who know me, who so long
Have told my heart-beats over, held my life
In those white hands of yours, — it is not well!
   Con. Tush! I have said it, did I not say it all? 850
The life, for her — the heart-beats, for her sake!
   Nor. Enough! my cheek grows red, I think. Your test?
There 's not the meanest woman in the world,
Not she I least could love in all the world,
Whom, did she love me, had love proved itself,
I dare insult as you insult me now.
Constance, I could say, if it must be said,
" Take back the soul you offer, I keep mine!"
But — " Take the soul still quivering on your hand,
The soul so offered, which I can not use, 860
And, please you, give it to some playful friend,
For — what 's the trifle he requites me with?"
— I, tempt a woman, to amuse a man,
That two may mock her heart if it súccumb?
No: fearing God and standing 'neath His heaven,
I would not dare insult a woman so,
Were she the meanest woman in the world,
And he, I cared to please, ten emperors!
   Con. Norbert!
   Nor.   I love once as I live but once.
What case is this to think or talk about? 870
I love you. Would it mend the case at all
If such a step as this killed love in me?
Your part were done: account to God for it!
But mine — could murdered love get up again,
And kneel to whom you please to designate,
And make you mirth? It is too horrible.
You did not know this, Constance? now you know
That body and soul have each one life, but one;
And here 's my love, here, living, at your feet.
   Con. See the Queen! Norbert — this one more last word — 880
If thus you have taken jest for earnest — thus
Loved me in earnest. . . .
   Nor.   Ah, no jest holds here!
Where is the laughter in which jests break up,
And what this horror that grows palpable?
Madam — why grasp you thus the balcony?
Have I done ill? Have I not spoken truth?
How could I other? Was it not your test,
To try me, what my love for Constance meant?
Madam, your royal soul itself approves,

   z

The first, that I should choose thus! so one takes
A beggar, — asks him, what would buy his child?
And then approves the expected laugh of scorn
Returned as something noble from the rags.
Speak, Constance, I 'm the beggar! Ha, what 's this?
You two glare each at each like panthers now.
Constance, the world fades : only you stand there!
You did not, in to-night's wild whirl of things,
Sell me — your soul of souls, for any price?
No — no — 't is easy to believe in you!
Was it your love's mad trial to o'ertop   900
Mine by this vain self-sacrifice? well, still —
Tho' I might curse, I love you.   I am love
And can not change : love's self is at your feet!

> > > > > > [*The* QUEEN *goes out.*

    Con. Feel my heart ; let it die against your own!
    Nor. Against my own.   Explain not ; let this be!
This is life's height.
    Con.   Yours, yours, yours!
    Nor.   You and I —
Why care by what meanders we are here
I' the centre of the labyrinth?   Men have died
Trying to find this place, which we have found.
    Con. Found, found!
    Nor.   Sweet, never fear what she can do!   910
We are past harm now.
    Con.   On the breast of God.
I thought of men — as if you were a man.
Tempting him with a crown!
    Nor.   This must end here :
It is too perfect.
    Con.   There 's the music stopped.
What measured heavy tread?   It is one blaze
About me and within me.
    Nor.   Oh, some death
Will run its sudden finger round this spark
And sever us from the rest!
    Con.   And so do well.
Now the doors open.
    Nor.   'T is the guard comes.
    Con.   Kiss!

OLD PICTURES IN FLORENCE.

I.

THE morn when first it thunders in March,
    The eel in the pond gives a leap, they say.
As I leaned and looked over the aloed arch
    Of the villa-gate, this warm March day,
No flash snapped, no dumb thunder rolled
    In the valley beneath where, white and wide
And washed by the morning water-gold,
    Florence lay out on the mountain-side.

II.

River and bridge and street and square
    Lay mine, as much at my beck and call,   10
Thro' the live translucent bath of air,
    As the sights in a magic crystal ball.
And of all I saw and of all I praised,
    The most to praise and the best to see
Was the startling bell-tower Giotto raised:
    But why did it more than startle me?

III.

Giotto, how, with that soul of yours,
    Could you play me false who loved you so?
Some slights if a certain heart endures
    Yet it feels, I would have your fellows know!   20
I' faith, I perceive not why I should care
    To break a silence that suits them best,
But the thing grows somewhat hard to bear
    When I find a Giotto join the rest.

IV.

On the arch where olives overhead
    Print the blue sky with twig and leaf,
(That sharp-curled leaf which they never shed)
    'Twixt the aloes, I used to lean in chief,
And mark thro' the winter afternoons,
    By a gift God grants me now and then,   30
In the mild decline of those suns like moons,
    Who walked in Florence, besides her men.

V.

They might chirp and chaffer, come and go
    For pleasure or profit, her men alive —

My business was hardly with them, I trow,
   But with empty cells of the human hive;
— With the chapter-room, the cloister-porch,
   The church's apsis, aisle or nave,
Its crypt, one fingers along with a torch,
   Its face set full for the sun to shave.   40

VI.

Wherever a fresco peels and drops,
   Wherever an outline weakens and wanes
Till the latest life in the painting stops,
   Stands One whom each fainter pulse-tick pains:
One, wishful each scrap should clutch the brick,
   Each tinge not wholly escape the plaster,
— A lion who dies of an ass's kick,
   The wronged great soul of an ancient Master.

VII.

For oh, this world and the wrong it does!
   They are safe in heaven with their backs to it,   50
The Michaels and Rafaels, you hum and buzz
   Round the works of, you of the little wit!
Do their eyes contract to the earth's old scope,
   Now that they see God face to face,
And have all attained to be poets, I hope?
   'T is their holiday now, in any case.

VIII.

Much they reck of your praise and you!
   But the wronged great souls — can they be quit
Of a world where their work is all to do,
   Where you style them, you of the little wit,   60
Old Master This and Early the Other,
   Not dreaming that Old and New are fellows:
A younger succeeds to an elder brother,
   Da Vincis derive in good time from Dellos.

IX.

And here where your praise might yield returns,
   And a handsome word or two give help,
Here, after your kind, the mastiff girns
   And the puppy pack of poodles yelp.
What, not a word for Stefano there,
   Of brow once prominent and starry,   70
Called Nature's Ape and the world's despair
   For his peerless painting? (See Vasari.)

X.

There stands the Master.   Study, my friends,
　What a man's work comes to!   So he plans it,
Performs it, perfects it, makes amends
　For the toiling and moiling, and then, *sic transit!*
Happier the thrifty blind-folk labour,
　With upturned eye while the hand is busy,
Not sidling a glance at the coin of their neighbour!
　'T is looking downward that makes one dizzy.　　80

XI.

" If you knew their work you would deal your dole."
　May I take upon me to instruct you?
When Greek Art ran and reached the goal,
　Thus much had the world to boast *in fructu* —
The Truth of Man, as by God first spoken,
　Which the actual generations garble,
Was re-uttered, and Soul (which Limbs betoken)
　And Limbs (Soul informs) made new in marble.

XII.

So, you saw yourself as you wished you were,
　As you might have been, as you can not be;　　90
Earth here, rebuked by Olympus there:
　And grew content in your poor degree
With your little power, by those statues' godhead,
　And your little scope, by their eyes' full sway,
And your little grace, by their grace embodied,
　And your little date, by their forms that stay.

XIII.

You would fain be kinglier, say, than I am?
　Even so, you will not sit like Theseus.
You would prove a model?   The Son of Priam
　Has yet the advantage in arms' and knees' use.　　100
You 're wroth — can you slay your snake like Apollo?
　You 're grieved — still Niobe 's the grander!
You live — there 's the Racers' frieze to follow:
　You die — there 's the dying Alexander.

XIV.

So, testing your weakness by their strength,
　Your meagre charms by their rounded beauty,
Measured by Art in your breadth and length,
　You learned — to submit is a mortal's duty.

— When I say " you " 't is the common soul,
  The collective, I mean : the race of Man   110
That receives life in parts to live in a whole
  And grow here according to God's clear plan.

XV.

Growth came when, looking your last on them all,
  You turned your eyes inwardly one fine day
And cried with a start — What if we so small
  Be greater and grander the while than they?
Are they perfect of lineament, perfect of stature?
  In both, of such lower types are we
Precisely because of our wider nature ;
  For time, theirs — ours, for eternity.   120

XVI.

To-day's brief passion limits their range ;
  It seethes with the morrow for us and more.
They are perfect — how else? they shall never change :
  We are faulty — why not? we have time in store.
The Artificer's hand is not arrested
  With us ; we are rough-hewn, no-wise polished.
They stand for our copy, and, once invested
  With all they can teach, we shall see them abolished.

XVII.

'T is a life-long toil till our lump be leaven —
  The better! What 's come to perfection perishes.   130
Things learned on earth, we shall practise in heaven :
  Works done least rapidly, Art most cherishes.
Thyself shalt afford the example, Giotto!
  Thy one work, not to decrease or diminish,
Done at a stroke, was just (was it not?) " O!"
  Thy great Campanile is still to finish.

XVIII.

Is it true that we are now, and shall be hereafter,
  But what and where depend on life's minute?
Hails heavenly cheer or infernal laughter
  Our first step out of the gulf or in it?   140
Shall Man, such step within his endeavour,
  Man's face, have no more play and action
Than joy which is crystallized for ever,
  Or grief, an eternal petrifaction?

XIX.

On which I conclude, that the early painters,
  To cries of "Greek Art and what more wish you?" —
Replied, "To become now self-acquainters,
  And paint man, man, whatever the issue !
Make new hopes shine thro' the flesh they fray,
  New fears aggrandize the rags and tatters :   150
To bring the invisible full into play !
  Let the visible go to the dogs — what matters?"

XX.

Give these, I exhort you, their guerdon and glory
  For daring so much, before they well did it.
The first of the new, in our race's story,
  Beats the last of the old ; 't is no idle quiddit.
The worthies began a revolution,
  Which if on earth you intend to acknowledge,
Why, honour them now! (ends my allocution)
  Nor confer your degree when the folk leave college.   160

XXI.

There 's a fancy some lean to and others hate —
  That, when this life is ended, begins
New work for the soul in another state,
  Where it strives and gets weary, loses and wins :
Where the strong and the weak, this world's congeries,
  Repeat in large what they practised in small,
Through life after life in unlimited series ;
  Only the scale 's to be changed, that 's all.

XXII.

Yet I hardly know. When a soul has seen
  By the means of Evil that Good is best,   170
And, thro' earth and its noise, what is heaven's serene, —
  When our faith in the same has stood the test —
Why, the child grown man, you burn the rod,
  The uses of labour are surely done ;
There remaineth a rest for the people of God :
  And I have had troubles enough, for one.

XXIII.

But at any rate I have loved the season
  Of Art's spring-birth so dim and dewy :
My sculptor is Nicolo the Pisan,
  My painter — who but Cimabue?   180

Nor ever was man of them all indeed,
   From these to Ghiberti and Ghirlandajo,
Could say that he missed my critic-meed.
   So, now to my special grievance — heigh ho !

XXIV.

Their ghosts still stand, as I said before,
   Watching each fresco flaked and rasped,
Blocked up, knocked out, or whitewashed o'er :
   — No getting again what the Church has grasped !
The works on the wall must take their chance ;
   " Works never conceded to England's thick clime ! "   190
(I hope they prefer their inheritance
   Of a bucketful of Italian quick-lime.)

XXV.

When they go at length, with such a shaking
   Of heads o'er the old delusion, sadly
Each master his way thro' the black streets taking,
   Where many a lost work breathes tho' badly —
Why don't they bethink them of who has merited?
   Why not reveal, while their pictures dree
Such doom, how a captive might be out-ferreted?
   Why is it they never remember me?   200

XXVI.

Not that I expect the great Bigordi,
   Nor Sandro to hear me, chivalric, bellicose ;
Nor the wronged Lippino ; and not a word I
   Say of a scrap of Frà Angelico's :
But are you too fine, Taddeo Gaddi,
   To grant me a taste of your intonaco,
Some Jerome that seeks the heaven with a sad eye?
   Not a churlish saint, Lorenzo Monaco?

XXVII.

Could not the ghost with the close red cap,
   My Pollajolo, the twice a craftsman,   210
Save me a sample, give me the hap
   Of a muscular Christ that shows the draughtsman?
No Virgin by him the somewhat petty,
   Of finical touch and tempera crumbly —
Could not Alesso Baldovinetti
   Contribute so much, I ask him humbly?

XXVIII.

Margheritone of Arezzo,
  With the grave-clothes garb and swaddling barret
(Why purse up mouth and beak in a pet so,
  You bald old saturnine poll-clawed parrot?)   220
Not a poor glimmering Crucifixion,
  Where in the foreground kneels the donor?
If such remain, as is my conviction,
  The hoarding it does you but little honour.

XXIX.

They pass; for them the panels may thrill,
  The tempera grow alive and tinglish;
Their pictures are left to the mercies still
  Of dealers and stealers, Jews and the English,
Who, seeing mere money's worth in their prize,
  Will sell it to somebody calm as Zeno   230
At naked High Art, and in ecstacies
  Before some clay-cold vile Carlino!

XXX.

No matter for these! But Giotto, you,
  Have you allowed, as the town-tongues babble it, —
Oh, never! it shall not be counted true —
  That a certain precious little tablet
Which Buonarroti eyed like a lover,
  Was buried so long in oblivion's womb
And, left for another than I to discover,
  Turns up at last! and to whom? — to whom?   240

XXXI.

I, that have haunted the dim San Spirito,
  (Or was it rather the Ognissanti?)
Patient on altar-step planting a weary toe!
  Nay, I shall have it yet! *Detur amanti!*
My Koh-i-noor — or (if that 's a platitude)
  Jewel of Giamschid, the Persian Sofi's eye;
So, in anticipative gratitude,
  What if I take up my hope and prophesy?

XXXII.

When the hour grows ripe, and a certain dotard
  Is pitched, no parcel that needs invoicing,   250
To the worst side of the Mont St. Gothard,
  We shall begin by way of rejoicing;

None of that shooting the sky (blank cartridge),
  Nor a civic guard, all plumes and lacquer,
Hunting Radetzky's soul like a partridge
  Over Morello with squib and cracker.

XXXIII.

This time we 'll shoot better game and bag 'em hot —
  No mere display at the stone of Dante,
But a kind of sober Witanagemot
  (Ex: "Casa Guidi," *quod videas ante*)   260
Shall ponder, once Freedom restored to Florence,
  How Art may return that departed with her.
Go, hated house, go each trace of the Loraine's,
  And bring us the days of Orgagna hither!

XXXIV.

How we shall prologize, how we shall perorate,
  Utter fit things upon art and history,
Feel truth at blood-heat and falsehood at zero rate,
  Make of the want of the age no mystery;
Contrast the fructuous and sterile eras,
  Show — monarchy ever its uncouth cub licks   270
Out of the bear's shape into Chimæra's,
  While Pure Art's birth is still the republic's!

XXXV.

Then one shall propose in a speech (curt Tuscan,
  Expurgate and sober, with scarcely an "*issimo*"),
To end now our half-told tale of Cambuscan,
  And turn the bell-tower's *alt* to *altissimo*:
And, fine as the beak of a young beccaccia,
  The Campanile, the Duomo's fit ally,
Shall soar up in gold full fifty braccia,
  Completing Florence, as Florence, Italy.   280

XXXVI.

Shall I be alive that morning the scaffold
  Is broken away, and the long-pent fire,
Like the golden hope of the world, unbaffled
  Springs from its sleep, and up goes the spire
While, "God and the People" plain for its motto,
  Thence the new tricolour flaps at the sky?
At least to foresee that glory of Giotto
  And Florence together, the first am I!

NOTE. — The space left here tempts to a word on the line about Apollo the snake-slayer, which my friend Professor Colvin condemns, believing that the God of the Belvedere grasps no bow, but the Ægis, as described in the 15th Iliad. Surely the text represents that portentous object (θοῦριν, δεινὴν, ἀμφι-δάσειαν, ἀριπρεπέ' — μαρμαρέην) as "shaken violently" or "held immovably" by both hands, not a single one and that the left hand:

> ἀλλὰ σύ γ' ἐν χείρεσσι λάβ' αἰγίδα θυσανόεσσαν
> τὴν μάλ' ἐπισσείων φοβέειν ἥρωας Ἀχαιούς,

and so on, τὴν ἄρ' ὅ γ' ἐν χείρεσσιν ἔχων — χερσὶν ἔχ' ἀτρέμα κ.τ.λ. More-over, while he shook it he "shouted enormously," σεῖσ', ἐπὶ δ' αὐτὸς ἄϋσε μάλα μέγα, which the statue does not. Presently when Teukros, on the other side, plies the bow, it is τόξον ἔχων ἐν χειρὶ παλίντονον. Besides, by the act of discharging an arrow, the right arm and hand are thrown back as we see: a quite gratuitous and theatrical display in the case supposed. The conjecture of Flaxman that the statue was suggested by the bronze Apollon Alexikakos of Kalamis, mentioned by Pausanias, remains probable, — though the "hard-ness" which Cicero considers to distinguish the artist's workmanship from that of Muron is not by any means apparent in our marble copy, if it be one. — Feb. 16, 1880.

BISHOP BLOUGRAM'S APOLOGY.

NO more wine? then we'll push back chairs and talk.
   A final glass for me, tho': cool, i' faith!
We ought to have our Abbey back, you see.
It's different, preaching in basilicas,
And doing duty in some masterpiece
Like this of brother Pugin's, bless his heart!
I doubt if they're half baked, those chalk rosettes,
Ciphers and stucco-twiddlings everywhere;
It's just like breathing in a lime-kiln: eh?
These hot long ceremonies of our Church
Cost us a little — oh, they pay the price,
You take me — amply pay it! Now, we'll talk!

So, you despise me, Mr. Gigadibs.
No deprecation, — nay, I beg you, sir!
Beside 't is our engagement: don't you know
I promised, if you 'd watch a dinner out,
We 'd see truth dawn together? — truth that peeps
Over the glasses' edge when dinner 's done,
And body gets its sop and holds its noise
And leaves soul free a little. Now 's the time:
Truth's break of day! You do despise me then.
And if I say, "despise me," — never fear!

I know you do not in a certain sense —
Not in my arm-chair, for example : here,
I well imagine you respect my place
(*Status, entourage*, worldly circumstance)
Quite to its value — very much indeed :
— Are up to the protesting eyes of you
In pride at being seated here for once —
You 'll turn it to such capital account !   30
When somebody, thro' years and years to come,
Hints of the bishop, — names me — that 's enough :
" Blougram?   I knew him " — (into it you slide)
Dined with him once, a Corpus Christi Day,
All alone, we two ; he 's a clever man :
And after dinner, — why, the wine you know, —
Oh, there was wine, and good ! — what with the wine . . .
'Faith, we began upon all sorts of talk !
He 's no bad fellow, Blougram ; he had seen
Something of mine he relished, some review :   40
He 's quite above their humbug in his heart,
Half-said as much, indeed — the thing 's his trade.
I warrant, Blougram 's sceptical at times :
How otherwise?   I liked him, I confess!"
Che, che, my dear sir, as we say at Rome,
Don't you protest now!   It 's fair give and take ;
You have had your turn and spoken your home-truths :
The hand 's mine now, and here you follow suit.

        Thus much conceded, still the first fact stays —
You do despise me ; your ideal of life   50
Is not the bishop's : you would not be I.
You would like better to be Goethe, now,
Or Buonaparte, or, bless me, lower still,
Count D'Orsay, — so you did what you preferred,
Spoke as you thought, and, as you can not help,
Believed or disbelieved, no matter what,
So long as on that point, whate'er it was,
You loosed your mind, were whole and sole yourself.
— That, my ideal never can include,
Upon that element of truth and worth   60
Never be based! for say they make me Pope —
(They can't — suppose it for our argument!)
Why, there I 'm at my tether's end, I 've reached
My height, and not a height which pleases you :
An unbelieving Pope won't do, you say.
It 's like those eerie stories nurses tell,
Of how some actor on a stage played Death,
With pasteboard crown, sham orb and tinselled dart,
And called himself the monarch of the world ;

Then, going in the tire-room afterward,   70
Because the play was done, to shift himself,
Got touched upon the sleeve familiarly,
The moment he had shut the closet door,
By Death himself.   Thus God might touch a Pope
At unawares, ask what his baubles mean,
And whose part he presumed to play just now
Best be yourself, imperial, plain and true!

So, drawing comfortable breath again,
You weigh and find, whatever more or less
I boast of my ideal realized,   80
Is nothing in the balance when opposed
To your ideal, your grand simple life,
Of which you will not realize one jot.
I am much, you are nothing; you would be all,
I would be merely much: you beat me there.

No, friend, you do not beat me: harken why!
The common problem, yours, mine, every one's,
Is — not to fancy what were fair in life
Provided it could be, — but, finding first
What may be, then find how to make it fair   90
Up to our means: a very different thing !
No abstract intellectual plan of life
Quite irrespective of life's plainest laws,
But one, a man, who is man and nothing more,
May lead within a world which (by your leave)
Is Rome or London, not Fool's-paradise.
Embellish Rome, idealize away,
Make paradise of London if you can,
You 're welcome, nay, you 're wise.

                          A simile !
We mortals cross the ocean of this world   100
Each in his average cabin of a life ;
The best 's not big, the worst yields elbow-room.
Now for our six months' voyage — how prepare?
You come on shipboard with a landsman's list
Of things he calls convenient : so they are !
An India screen is pretty furniture,
A piano-forte is a fine resource,
All Balzac's novels occupy one shelf,
The new edition fifty volumes long ;
And little Greek books, with the funny type   110
They get up well at Leipsic, fill the next :
Go on! slabbed marble, what a bath it makes!

And Parma's pride, the Jerome, let us add !
'T were pleasant could Correggio's fleeting glow
Hang full in face of one where'er one roams,
Since he more than the others brings with him
Italy's self, — the marvellous Modenese ! —
Yet was not on your list before, perhaps.
— Alas, friend, here 's the agent . . . is 't the name?
The captain, or whoever 's master here —　　　　　120
You see him screw his face up ; what 's his cry
Ere you set foot on shipboard? "Six feet square !"
If you won't understand what six feet mean,
Compute and purchase stores accordingly —
And if, in pique because he overhauls
Your Jerome, piano, bath, you come on board
Bare — why, you cut a figure at the first
While sympathetic landsmen see you off ;
Not afterward, when long ere half seas over,
You peep up from your utterly naked boards　　　130
Into some snug and well-appointed berth,
Like mine for instance (try the cooler jug —
Put back the other, but don't jog the ice !)
And mortified you mutter "Well and good ;
He sits enjoying his sea-furniture ;
'T is stout and proper, and there 's store of it :
Tho' I 've the better notion, all agree,
Of fitting rooms up.　Hang the carpenter,
Neat ship-shape fixings and contrivances —
I would have brought my Jerome, frame and all !"　140
And meantime you bring nothing : never mind —
You 've proved your artist-nature : what you don't
You might bring, so despise me, as I say.

Now come, let 's backward to the starting-place.
See my way : we 're two college friends, suppose.
Prepare together for our voyage, then ;
Each note and check the other in his work, —
Here 's mine, a bishop's outfit ; criticize!
What 's wrong? why won't you be a bishop too?

Why first, you don't believe, you don't and can't,　150
(Not stately, that is, and fixedly
And absolutely and exclusively)
In any revelation called divine.
No dogmas nail your faith ; and what remains
But say so, like the honest man you are?
First, therefore, overhaul theology !
Nay, I too, not a fool, you please to think,
Must find believing every whit as hard :

And if I do not frankly say as much,
The ugly consequence is clear enough.   160

Now wait, my friend : well, I do not believe —
If you 'll accept no faith that is not fixed,
Absolute and exclusive, as you say.
You 're wrong — I mean to prove it in due time.
Meanwhile, I know where difficulties lie
I could not, can not solve, nor ever shall,
So give up hope accordingly to solve —
(To you, and over the wine).   Our dogmas then
With both of us, tho' in unlike degree,
Missing full credence — overboard with them!   170
I mean to meet you on your own premise :
Good, there go mine in company with yours!

And now what are we? unbelievers both,
Calm and complete, determinately fixed
To-day, to-morrow and for ever, pray?
You 'll guarantee me that?   Not so, I think!
In no wise! all we 've gained is, that belief,
As unbelief before, shakes us by fits,
Confounds us like its predecessor.   Where 's
The gain? how can we guard our unbelief,   180
Make it bear fruit to us? — the problem here.
Just when we are safest, there 's a sunset-touch,
A fancy from a flower-bell, some one's death,
A chorus-ending from Euripides, —
And that 's enough for fifty hopes and fears
As old and new at once as nature's self,
To rap and knock and enter in our soul,
Take hands and dance there, a fantastic ring,
Round the ancient idol, on his base again, —
The grand Perhaps!   We look on helplessly.   190
There the old misgivings, crooked questions are —
This good God, — what he could do, if he would,
Would, if he could — then must have done long since :
If so, when, where and how? some way must be, —
Once feel about, and soon or late you hit
Some sense, in which it might be, after all.
Why not " The Way, the Truth, the Life? "

                                — That way
Over the mountain, which who stands upon
Is apt to doubt if it be meant for a road ;
While, if he views it from the waste itself,   200
Up goes the line there, plain from base to brow,
Not vague, mistakeable! what 's a break or two

Seen from the unbroken desert either side?'
And then (to bring in fresh philosophy)
What if the breaks themselves should prove at last
The most consummate of contrivances
To train a man's eye, teach him what is faith?
And so we stumble at truth's very test!
All we have gained then by our unbelief
Is a life of doubt diversified by faith,   210
For one of faith diversified by doubt:
We called the chess-board white, — we call it black.

  "Well," you rejoin, "the end 's no worse, at least;
We 've reason for both colours on the board:
Why not confess then, where I drop the faith
And you the doubt, that I 'm as right as you?"

  Because, friend, in the next place, this being so,
And both things even, — faith and unbelief
Left to a man's choice, — we 'll proceed a step,
Returning to our image, which I like.   220

  A man's choice, yes — but a cabin passenger's —
The man made for the special life o' the world —
Do you forget him? I remember though!
Consult our ship's conditions and you find
One and but one choice suitable to all;
The choice, that you unluckily prefer,
Turning things topsy-turvy — they or it
Going to the ground.   Belief or unbelief
Bears upon life, determines its whole course,
Begins at its beginning.   See the world   230
Such as it is, — you made it not, nor I;
I mean to take it as it is, — and you,
Not so you 'll take it, — tho' you get naught else.
I know the special kind of life I like,
What suits the most my idiosyncrasy,
Brings out the best of me and bears me fruit
In power, peace, pleasantness and length of days.
I find that positive belief does this
For me, and unbelief, no whit of this.
— For you, it does, however? — that, we 'll try!   240
'T is clear, I can not lead my life, at least,
Induce the world to let me peaceably,
Without declaring at the outset, "Friends,
I absolutely and peremptorily
Believe!" — I say, faith is my waking life:
One sleeps, indeed, and dreams at intervals,
We know, but waking 's the main point with us

And my provision 's for life's waking part.
Accordingly, I use heart, head and hand
All day, I build, scheme, study, and make friends: 250
And when night overtakes me, down I lie,
Sleep, dream a little, and get done with it,
The sooner the better, to begin afresh.
What 's midnight doubt before the dayspring's faith?
You, the philosopher, that disbelieve,
That recognize the night, give dreams their weight —
To be consistent you should keep your bed,
Abstain from healthy acts that prove you man,
For fear you drowse perhaps at unawares!
And certainly at night you 'll sleep and dream,   260
Live thro' the day and bustle as you please,
And so you live to sleep as I to wake,
To unbelieve as I to still believe?
Well, and the common sense o' the world calls you
Bed-ridden, — and its good things come to me.
Its estimation, which is half the fight,
That 's the first-cabin comfort I secure:
The next . . . but you perceive with half an eye!
Come, come, it 's best believing, if we may;
You can't but own that!

            Next, concede again,   270
If once we choose belief, on all accounts
We can't be too decisive in our faith,
Conclusive and exclusive in its terms,
To suit the world which gives us the good things.
In every man's career are certain points
Whereon he dares not be indifferent;
The world detects him clearly, if he dare,
As baffled at the game, and losing life.
He may care little, or he may care much
For riches, honour, pleasure, work, repose,   280
Since various theories of life and life's
Success are extant which might easily
Comport with either estimate of these;
And whoso chooses wealth or poverty,
Labour or quiet, is not judged a fool
Because his fellow would choose otherwise:
We let him choose upon his own account
So long as he 's consistent with his choice.
But certain points, left wholly to himself,
When once a man has arbitrated on,   290
We say he must succeed there or go hang.
Thus, he should wed the woman he loves most
Or needs most, whatsoe'er the love or need —

2 A

For he can't wed twice.   Then, he must avouch,
Or follow, at the least, sufficiently,
The form of faith his conscience holds the best,
Whate'er the process of conviction was:
For nothing can compensate his mistake
On such a point, the man himself being judge:
He can not wed twice, nor twice lose his soul.   300

Well now, there's one great form of Christian faith
I happened to be born in — which to teach
Was given me as I grew up, on all hands,
As best and readiest means of living by;
The same on examination being proved
The most pronounced moreover, fixed, precise
And absolute form of faith in the whole world —
Accordingly, most potent of all forms
For working on the world.   Observe, my friend!
Such as you know me, I am free to say,   310
In these hard latter days which hamper one,
Myself — by no immoderate exercise
Of intellect and learning, but the tact
To let external forces work for me,
— Bid the street's stones be bread and they are bread;
Bid Peter's creed, or rather, Hildebrand's,
Exalt me o'er my fellows in the world
And make my life an ease and joy and pride;
It does so, — which for me's a great point gained,
Who have a soul and body that exact   320
A comfortable care in many ways.
There's power in me and will to dominate
Which I must exercise, they hurt me else:
In many ways I need mankind's respect,
Obedience, and the love that's born of fear:
While at the same time, there's a taste I have,
A toy of soul, a titillating thing,
Refuses to digest these dainties crude.
The naked life is gross till clothed upon:
I must take what men offer, with a grace   330
As tho' I would not, could I help it, take!
An uniform I wear tho' over-rich —
Something imposed on me, no choice of mine;
No fancy-dress worn for pure fancy's sake
And despicable therefore! now folk kneel
And kiss my hand — of course the Church's hand.
Thus I am made, thus life is best for me,
And thus that it should be I have procured;
And thus it could not be another way.
I venture to imagine.

You 'll reply,   340
So far my choice, no doubt, is a success ;
But were I made of better elements,
With nobler instincts, purer tastes, like you,
I hardly would account the thing success
'Tho' it did all for me I say.

But, friend,
We speak of what is ; not of what might be,
And how 't were better if 't were otherwise.
I am the man you see here plain enough :
Grant I 'm a beast, why, beasts must lead beasts' lives!
Suppose I own at once to tail and claws ;   350
The tailless man exceeds me : but being tailed
I 'll lash out lion fashion, and leave apes
To dock their stump and dress their haunches up.
My business is not to remake myself,
But make the absolute best of what God made.
Or — our first simile — tho' you prove me doomed
To a viler berth still, to the steerage-hole,
The sheep-pen or the pig-stye, I should strive
To make what use of each were possible ;
And, as this cabin gets upholstery,   360
That hutch should rustle with sufficient straw.

But, friend, I don't acknowledge quite so fast
I fail of all your manhood's lofty tastes
Enumerated so complacently,
On the mere ground that you forsooth can find
In this particular life I choose to lead
No fit provision for them. Can you not?
Say you, my fault is I address myself
To grosser estimators than should judge?
And that 's no way of holding up the soul,   370
Which, nobler, needs men's praise perhaps, yet knows
One wise man's verdict outweighs all the fools' —
Would like the two, but, forced to choose, takes that.
I pine among my million imbeciles
(You think) aware some dozen men of sense
Eye me and know me, whether I believe
In the last winking Virgin, as I vow,
And am a fool, or disbelieve in her
And am a knave, — approve in neither case,
Withhold their voices though I look their way :   380
Like Verdi when, at his worst opera's end
(The thing they gave at Florence — what 's its name?)
While the mad houseful's plaudits near out-bang
His orchestra of salt-box, tongs and bones,

He looks thro' all the roaring and the wreaths
Where sits Rossini patient in his stall.

    Nay, friend, I meet you with an answer here —
That even your prime men who appraise their kind
Are men still, catch a wheel within a wheel,
See more in a truth than the truth's simple self,   390
Confuse themselves.   You see lads walk the street
Sixty the minute ; what 's to note in that ?
You see one lad o'erstride a chimney-stack ;
Him you must watch — he 's sure to fall, yet stands !
Our interest 's on the dangerous edge of things.
The honest thief, the tender murderer,
The superstitious atheist, demirep
That loves and saves her soul in new French books —
We watch while these in equilibrium keep
The giddy line midway : one step aside,   400
They 're classed and done with. I, then, keep the line
Before your sages, — just the men to shrink
From the gross weights, coarse scales and labels broad
You offer their refinement. Fool or knave ?
Why needs a bishop be a fool or knave
When there 's a thousand diamond weights between ?
So, I enlist them. Your picked twelve, you 'll find
Profess themselves indignant, scandalized
At thus being held unable to explain
How a superior man who disbelieves   410
May not believe as well : that 's Schelling's way !
It 's thro' my coming in the tail of time,
Nicking the minute with a happy tact.
Had I been born three hundred years ago
They 'd say, "What 's strange ? Blougram of course believes ; "
And, seventy years since, "disbelieves of course."
But now, "He may believe ; and yet, and yet
How can he ? " All eyes turn with interest.
Whereas, step off the line on either side —
You, for example, clever to a fault,   420
The rough and ready man who write apace,
Read somewhat seldomer, think perhaps even less —
You disbelieve ! Who wonders and who cares ?
Lord So-and-so — his coat bedropped with wax,
All Peter's chains about his waist, his back
Brave with the needlework of Noodledom —
Believes ! Again, who wonders and who cares ?
But I, the man of sense and learning too,
The able to think yet act, the this, the that,
I, to believe at this late time of day !   430
Enough ; you see, I need not fear contempt.

— Except it 's yours!   Admire me as these may,
You don't.   But whom at least do you admire?
Present your own perfection, your ideal,
Your pattern man for a minute — oh, make haste!
Is it Napoleon you would have us grow?
Concede the means; allow his head and hand
(A large concession, clever as you are)
Good!   In our common primal element
Of unbelief (we can't believe, you know — 440
We 're still at that admission, recollect!)
Where do you find — apart from, towering o'er
The secondary temporary aims
Which satisfy the gross taste you despise —
Where do you find his star? — his crazy trust —
God knows thro' what or in what? it 's alive
And shines and leads him, and that 's all we want.
Have we aught in our sober night shall point
Such ends as his were, and direct the means
Of working out our purpose straight as his, 450
Nor bring a moment's trouble on success
With after-care to justify the same?
— Be a Napoleon and yet disbelieve —
Why, the man 's mad, friend, take his light away.
What 's the vague good o' the world, for which you dare
With comfort to yourself blow millions up?
We neither of us see it! we do see
The blown-up millions — spatter of their brains
And writhing of their bowels and so forth,
In that bewildering entanglement 460
Of horrible eventualities
Past calculation to the end of time!
Can I mistake for some clear word of God
(Which were my ample warrant for it all)
His puff of hazy instinct, idle talk,
"The State, that 's I," quack-nonsense about crowns
And (when one beats the man to his last hold)
A vague idea of setting things to rights,
Policing people efficaciously,
More to their profit, most of all to his own; 470
The whole to end that dismallest of ends
By an Austrian marriage, cant to us the Church,
And resurrection of the old régime?
Would I, who hope to live a dozen years,
Fight Austerlitz for reasons such and such?
No: for, concede me but the merest chance
Doubt may be wrong — there 's judgment, life to come!
With just that chance, I dare not.   Doubt proves right?
This present life is all? — you offer me

Its dozen noisy years, without a chance   480
That wedding an arch-duchess, wearing lace,
And getting called by divers new-coined names,
Will drive off ugly thoughts and let me dine,
Sleep, read and chat in quiet as I like!
Therefore I will not.

     Take another case :
Fit up the cabin yet another way.
What say you to the poets? shall we write
Hamlet, Othello — make the world our own,
Without a risk to run of either sort?
I can't! — to put the strongest reason first.   490
" But try," you urge, " the trying shall suffice ;
The aim, if reached or not, makes great the life :
Try to be Shakespeare, leave the rest to fate! "
Spare my self-knowledge — there 's no fooling me!
If I prefer remaining my poor self,
I say so not in self-dispraise but praise,
If I 'm a Shakespeare, let the well alone!
Why should I try to be what now I am?
If I 'm no Shakespeare, as too probable, —
His power and consciousness and self-delight   500
And all we want in common, shall I find —
Trying for ever? while on points of taste
Wherewith, to speak it humbly, he and I
Are dowered alike — I 'll ask you, I or he,
Which in our two lives realizes most?
Much, he imagined : somewhat, I possess.
He had the imagination ; stick to that!
Let him say, " In the face of my soul's works
Your world is worthless and I touch it not
Lest I should wrong them " — I 'll withdraw my plea   510
But does he say so? look upon his life!
Himself, who only can, gives judgment there.
He leaves his towers and gorgeous palaces
To build the trimmest house in Stratford town ;
Saves money, spends it, owns the worth of things,
Giulio Romano's pictures, Dowland's lute ;
Enjoys a show, respects the puppets, too,
And none more, had he seen its entry once,
Than " Pandulph, of fair Milan cardinal."
Why then should I who play that personage,   520
The very Pandulph Shakespeare's fancy made,
Be told that had the poet chanced to start
From where I stand now (some degree like mine
Being just the goal he ran his race to reach)
He would have run the whole race back, forsooth,

And left being Pandulph, to begin write plays?
Ah, the earth's best can be but the earth's best!
Did Shakespeare live, he could but sit at home
And get himself in dreams the Vatican,
Greek busts, Venetian paintings, Roman walls,   530
And English books, none equal to his own,
Which I read, bound in gold (he never did).
— Terni's fall, Naples' bay and Gothard's top —
Eh, friend? I could not fancy one of these;
But, as I pour this claret, there they are:
I 've gained them — crossed St. Gothard last July
With ten mules to the carriage and a bed
Slung inside; is my hap the worse for that?
We want the same things, Shakespeare and myself,
And what I want, I have: he, gifted more,   540
Could fancy he too had them when he liked,
But not so thoroughly that, if fate allowed,
He would not have them also in my sense.
We play one game; I send the ball aloft
No less adroitly that of fifty strokes
Scarce five go o'er the wall so wide and high
Which sends them back to me: I wish and get.
He struck balls higher and with better skill,
But at a poor fence level with his head,
And hit — his Stratford house, a coat of arms,   550
Successful dealings in his grain and wool, —
While I receive heaven's incense in my nose
And style myself the cousin of Queen Bess.
Ask him, if this life 's all, who wins the game?

    Believe — and our whole argument breaks up.
Enthusiasm 's the best thing, I repeat;
Only, we can't command it; fire and life
Are all, dead matter 's nothing, we agree:
And be it a mad dream or God's very breath,
The fact 's the same, — belief's fire, once in us,   560
Makes of all else mere stuff to show itself:
We penetrate our life with such a glow
As fire lends wood and iron — this turns steel,
That burns to ash — all 's one, fire proves its power
For good or ill, since men call flare success.
But paint a fire, it will not therefore burn.
Light one in me, I 'll find it food enough!
Why, to be Luther — that 's a life to lead,
Incomparably better than my own.
He comes, reclaims God's earth for God, he says,   570
Sets up God's rule again by simple means,
Re-opens a shut book, and all is done.

He flared out in the flaring of mankind ;
Such Luther's luck was : how shall such be mine?
If he succeeded, nothing 's left to do :
And if he did not altogether — well,
Strauss is the next advance.   All Strauss should be
I might be also.   But to what result?
He looks upon no future : Luther did.
What can I gain on the denying side?   580
Ice makes no conflagration.   State the facts,
Read the text right, emancipate the world —
The emancipated world enjoys itself
With scarce a thank-you : Blougram told it first
It could not owe a farthing, — not to him
More than Saint Paul! 't would press its pay, you think?
Then add there 's still that plaguy hundredth chance
Strauss may be wrong.   And so a risk is run —
For what gain? not for Luther's, who secured
A real heaven in his heart throughout his life,   590
Supposing death a little altered things.

   " Ay, but since really you lack faith," you cry,
" You run the same risk really on all sides,
In cool indifference as bold unbelief.
As well be Strauss as swing 'twixt Paul and him.
It 's not worth having, such imperfect faith,
No more available to do faith's work
Than unbelief like mine.   Whole faith, or none! "

   Softly, my friend!   I must dispute that point.
Once own the use of faith, I 'll find you faith.   600
We 're back on Christian ground.   You call for faith :
I show you doubt, to prove that faith exists.
The more of doubt, the stronger faith, I say,
If faith o'ercomes doubt.   How I know it does?
By life and man's free will, God gave for that!
To mould life as we choose it, shows our choice :
That 's our one act, the previous work 's His own.
You criticize the soul? it reared this tree —
This broad life and whatever fruit it bears!
What matter tho' I doubt at every pore,   610
Head-doubts, heart-doubts, doubts at my fingers' ends,
Doubts in the trivial work of every day,
Doubts at the very bases of my soul
In the grand moments when she probes herself—
If finally I have a life to show,
The thing I did, brought out in evidence
Against the thing done to me underground
By hell and all its brood, for aught I know?
I say, whence sprang this? shows it faith or doubt?

All 's doubt in me ; where 's break of faith in this?   620
It is the idea, the feeling and the love,
God means mankind should strive for and show forth
Whatever be the process to that end, —
And not historic knowledge, logic sound,
And metaphysical acumen, sure!
" What think ye of Christ," friend? when all 's done and said,
Like you this Christianity or not?
It may be false, but will you wish it true?
Has it your vote to be so if it can?
Trust you an instinct silenced long ago   630
That will break silence and enjoin you love
What mortified philosophy is hoarse,
And all in vain, with bidding you despise?
If you desire faith — then you 've faith enough :
What else seeks God — nay, what else seek ourselves?
You form a notion of me, we 'll suppose,
On hearsay ; it 's a favourable one :
" But still," (you add) " there was no such good man,
Because of contradiction in the facts.
One proves, for instance, he was born in Rome,   640
This Blougram ; yet throughout the tales of him
I see he figures as an Englishman."
Well, the two things are reconcileable.
But would I rather you discovered that,
Subjoining — " Still, what matter tho' they be?
Blougram concerns me naught, born here or there."

    Pure faith, indeed? you know not what you ask!
Naked belief in God the Omnipotent,
Omniscient, Omnipresent, sears too much
The sense of conscious creatures to be borne.   650
It were the seeing Him, no flesh shall dare.
Some think, Creation 's meant to show Him forth :
I say it 's meant to hide Him all it can,
And that 's what all the blessed evil 's for.
Its use in Time is to environ us,
Our breath, our drop of dew, with shield enough
Against that sight till we can bear its stress.
Under a vertical sun, the exposed brain
And lidless eye and disemprisoned heart
Less certainly would wither up at once   660
Than mind, confronted with the truth of Him.
But time and earth case-harden us to live ;
The feeblest sense is trusted most ; the child
Feels God a moment, ichors o'er the place,
Plays on and grows to be a man like us.
With me, faith means perpetual unbelief

Kept quiet like the snake 'neath Michael's foot
Who stands calm just because he feels it writhe.
Or, if that's too ambitious, — here's my box —
I need the excitation of a pinch   670
Threatening the torpor of the inside-nose
Nigh on the imminent sneeze that never comes.
"Leave it in peace!" advise the simple folk:
Make it aware of peace by itching-fits,
Say I — let doubt occasion still more faith!

    You'll say, once all believed, man, woman, child,
In that dear middle-age these noodles praise.
How you'd exult if I could put you back
Six hundred years, blot out cosmogony,
Geology, ethnology, what not,   680
(Greek endings, each the little passing-bell
That signifies some faith's about to die)
And set you square with Genesis again, —
When such a traveler told you his last news,
He saw the ark a-top of Ararat
But did not climb there since 't was getting dusk
And robber-bands infest the mountain's foot!
How should you feel, I ask, in such an age,
How act?   As other people felt and did;
With soul more blank than this decanter's knob,   690
Believe — and yet lie, kill, rob, fornicate
Full in belief's face, like the beast you'd be!

    No, when the fight begins within himself,
A man's worth something. God stoops o'er his head,
Satan looks up between his feet — both tug —
He's left, himself, i' the middle: the soul wakes
And grows.   Prolong that battle thro' his life!
Never leave growing till the life to come!
Here we've got callous to the Virgin's winks
That used to puzzle people wholesomely: 700
Men have outgrown the shame of being fools.
What are the laws of nature, not to bend
If the Church bid them? — brother Newman asks.
Up with the Immaculate Conception, then —
On to the rack with faith! — is my advice.
Will not that hurry us upon our knees,
Knocking our breasts, "It can't be — yet it shall!
Who am I, the worm, to argue with my Pope?
Low things confound the high things!" and so forth.
That's better than acquitting God with grace,   710
As some folk do.   He's tried — no case is proved,
Philosophy is lenient — He may go!

You 'll say, the old system 's not so obsolete
But men believe still : ay, but who and where?
King Bomba's lazzaroni foster yet
The sacred flame, so Antonelli writes ;
But even of these, what ragamuffin-saint
Believes God watches him continually,
As he believes in fire that it will burn,
Or rain that it will drench him?   Break fire's law,   720
Sin against rain, altho' the penalty
Be just a singe or soaking?   "No," he smiles ;
" Those laws are laws that can enforce themselves."

The sum of all is — yes, my doubt is great,
My faith still greater, then my faith 's enough.
I have read much, thought much, experienced much,
Yet would die rather than avow my fear
The Naples' liquefaction may be false,
When set to happen by the palace-clock
According to the clouds or dinner-time.   730
I hear you recommend, I might at least
Eliminate, decrassify my faith
Since I adopt it ; keeping what I must
And leaving what I can — such points as this.
I won't — that is, I can't throw one away.
Supposing there 's no truth in what I hold
About the need of trial to man's faith,
Still, when you bid me purify the same,
To such a process I discern no end.
Clearing off one excrescence to see two,   740
There 's ever a next in size, now grown as big,
That meets the knife : I cut and cut again!
First cut the Liquefaction, what comes last
But Fichte's clever cut at God himself?
Experimentalize on sacred things!
I trust nor hand nor eye nor heart nor brain
To stop betimes : they all get drunk alike.
The first step, I am master not to take.

You 'd find the cutting-process to your taste
As much as leaving growths of lies unpruned,   750
Nor see more danger in it, — you retort.
Your taste 's worth mine ; but my taste proves more wise
When we consider that the steadfast hold
On the extreme end of the chain of faith
Gives all the advantage, makes the difference
With the rough purblind mass we seek to rule :
We are their lords, or they are free of us,
Just as we tighten or relax our hold.

So, other matters equal, we'll revert
To the first problem — which, if solved my way   760
And thrown into the balance, turns the scale —
How we may lead a comfortable life,
How suit our luggage to the cabin's size.

Of course you are remarking all this time
How narrowly and grossly I view life,
Respect the creature-comforts, care to rule
The masses, and regard complacently
" The cabin," in our old phrase.   Well, I do.
I act for, talk for, live for this world now,
As this world prizes action, life and talk :   770
No prejudice to what next world may prove,
Whose new laws and requirements, my best pledge
To observe then, is that I observe these now,
Shall do hereafter what I do meanwhile.
Let us concede (gratuitously though)
Next life relieves the soul of body, yields
Pure spiritual enjoyment : well, my friend,
Why lose this life i' the meantime, since its use
May be to make the next life more intense?

Do you know, I have often had a dream   780
(Work it up in your next month's article)
Of man's poor spirit in its progress, still
Losing true life for ever and a day
Thro' ever trying to be and ever being —
In the evolution of successive spheres —
Before its actual sphere and place of life,
Halfway into the next, which having reached,
It shoots with corresponding foolery
Halfway into the next still, on and off !
As when a traveler, bound from North to South,   790
Scouts fur in Russia ; what 's its use in France?
In France spurns flannel ; where 's its need in Spain ?
In Spain drops cloth, too cumbrous for Algiers!
Linen goes next, and last the skin itself,
A superfluity at Timbuctoo.
When, thro' his journey, was the fool at ease?
I 'm at ease now, friend ; worldly in this world,
I take and like its way of life ; I think
My brothers, who administer the means,
Live better for my comfort — that 's good too ;   800
And God, if He pronounce upon such life,
Approves my service, which is better still.
If He keep silence, — why, for you or me
Or that brute beast pulled-up in to-day's " Times,"
What odds is 't, save to ourselves, what life we lead?

You meet me at this issue : you declare, —
All special-pleading done with, truth is truth,
And justifies itself by undreamed ways.
You don't fear but it 's better, if we doubt,
To say so, act up to our truth perceived   810
However feebly. Do then, — act away!
'T is there I 'm on the watch for you.   How one acts
Is, both of us agree, our chief concern :
And how you 'll act is what I fain would see
If, like the candid person you appear,
You dare to make the most of your life's scheme
As I of mine, live up to its full law
Since there 's no higher law that counterchecks.
Put natural religion to the test
You 've just demolished the revealed with — quick,   820
Down to the root of all that checks your will,
All prohibition to lie, kill and thieve
Or even to be an atheistic priest!
Suppose a pricking to incontinence —
Philosophers deduce you chastity
Or shame, from just the fact that at the first
Whoso embraced a woman in the field
Threw club down and forewent his brains beside,
So, stood a ready victim in the reach
Of any brother-savage, club in hand ;   830
Hence saw the use of going out of sight
In wood or cave to prosecute his loves :
I read this in a French book t' other day.
Does law so analyzed coerce you much?
Oh, men spin clouds of fuzz where matters end,
But you who reach where the first thread begins,
You 'll soon cut that! — which means you can, but won't,
Thro' certain instincts, blind, unreasoned-out,
You dare not set aside, you can't tell why,
But there they are, and so you let them rule.   840
Then, friend, you seem as much a slave as I,
A liar, conscious coward and hypocrite,
Without the good the slave expects to get,
In case he has a master after all!
You own your instincts? why, what else do I,
Who want, am made for, and must have a God
Ere I can be aught, do aught? — no mere name
Want, but the true thing with what proves its truth,
To wit, a relation from that thing to me,
Touching from head to foot — which touch I feel,   850
And with it take the rest, this life of ours!
I live my life here ; yours you dare not live.

— Not as I state it, who (you please subjoin)
Disfigure such a life and call it names,
While, to your mind, remains another way
For simple men : knowledge and power have rights,
But ignorance and weakness have rights too.
There needs no crucial effort to find truth
If here or there or anywhere about :
We ought to turn each side, try hard and see,   860
And if we can't, be glad we 've earned at least
The right, by one laborious proof the more,
To graze in peace earth's pleasant pasturage.
Men are not angels, neither are they brutes :
Something we may see, all we can not see.
What need of lying ? I say, I see all,
And swear to each detail the most minute
In what I think a Pan's face — you, mere cloud :
I swear I hear him speak and see him wink,
For fear, if once I drop the emphasis,   870
Mankind may doubt there 's any cloud at all.
You take the simple life — ready to see,
Willing to see (for no cloud 's worth a face) —
And leaving quiet what no strength can move,
And which, who bids you move? who has the right?
I bid you ; but you are God's sheep, not mine :
"*Pastor est tui Dominus.*"   You find
In this the pleasant pasture of our life
Much you may eat without the least offence,
Much you don't eat because your maw objects,   880
Much you would eat but that your fellow-flock
Open great eyes at you and even butt,
And thereupon you like your mates so well
You can not please yourself, offending them ;
Tho' when they seem exorbitantly sheep,
You weigh your pleasure with their butts and bleats
And strike the balance.   Sometimes certain fears
Restrain you, real checks since you find them so ;
Sometimes you please yourself and nothing checks :
And thus you graze thro' life with not one lie,   890
And like it best.

                    But do you, in truth's name?
If so, you beat — which means you are not I —
Who needs must make earth mine and feed my fill
Not simply unbutted at, unbickered with,
But motioned to the velvet of the sward
By those obsequious wethers' very selves.
Look at me, sir ; my age is double yours :
At yours, I knew beforehand, so enjoyed,

What now I should be — as, permit the word,
I pretty well imagine your whole range   900
And stretch of tether twenty years to come.
We both have minds and bodies much alike:
In truth's name, don't you want my bishopric,
My daily bread, my influence and my state?
You're young. I'm old; you must be old one day;
Will you find then, as I do hour by hour,
Women their lovers kneel to, who cut curls
From your fat lap-dog's ear to grace a brooch —
Dukes, who petition just to kiss your ring —
With much beside you know or may conceive?   910
Suppose we die to-night: well, here am I,
Such were my gains, life bore this fruit to me,
While writing all the same my articles
On music, poetry, the fictile vase
Found at Albano, chess, Anacreon's Greek.
But you — the highest honour in your life,
The thing you'll crown yourself with, all your days,
Is — dining here and drinking this last glass
I pour you out in sign of amity
Before we part for ever.   Of your power   920
And social influence, worldly worth in short,
Judge what's my estimation by the fact —
I do not condescend to enjoin, beseech,
Hint secrecy on one of all these words!
You're shrewd and know that should you publish one
The world would brand the lie — my enemies first,
Who'd sneer — " the bishop's an arch-hypocrite
And knave perhaps, but not so frank a fool."
Whereas I should not dare for both my ears
Breathe one such syllable, smile one such smile,   930
Before the chaplain who reflects myself —
My shade's so much more potent than your flesh.
What's your reward, self-abnegating friend?
Stood you confessed of those exceptional
And privileged great natures that dwarf mine —
A zealot with a mad ideal in reach,
A poet just about to print his ode,
A statesman with a scheme to stop this war,
An artist whose religion is his art —
I should have nothing to object: such men   940
Carry the fire, all things grow warm to them,
Their drugget's worth my purple, they beat me.
But you, — you're just as little those as I —
You, Gigadibs, who, thirty years of age,
Write stately for Blackwood's Magazine,
Believe you see two points in Hamlet's soul

Unseized by the Germans yet — which view you 'll print —
Meantime the best you have to show being still
That lively lightsome article we took
Almost for the true Dickens, — what 's its name?   950
" The Slum and Cellar, or Whitechapel life
Limned after dark!" it made me laugh, I know,
And pleased a month, a .d brought you in ten pounds.
— Success I recognize a id compliment,
And therefore give you, if you choose, three words
(The card and pencil-scratch is quite enough)
Which whether here, in Dublin or New York,
Will get you, prompt as at my eyebrow's wink,
Such terms as never you aspired to get
In all our own reviews and some not ours.   960
Go write your lively sketches! be the first
" Blougram, or The Eccentric Confidence " —
Or better simply say, " The Outward-bound."
Why, men as soon would throw it in my teeth
As copy and quote the infamy chalked broad
About me on the church-door opposite.
You will not wait for that experience though,
I fancy, howsoever you decide,
To discontinue — not detesting, not
Defaming, but at least — despising me!   970

Over his wine so smiled and talked his hour
Sylvester Blougram, styled *in partibus*
Episcopus, *nec non* — (the deuce knows what
It 's changed to by our novel hierarchy)
With Gigadibs the literary man,
Who played with spoons, explored his plate's design,
And ranged the olive-stones about its edge,
While the great bishop rolled him out a mind
Long crumpled, till creased consciousness lay smooth.

For Blougram, he believed, say, half he spoke.   980
The other portion, as he shaped it thus
For argumentatory purposes,
He felt his foe was foolish to dispute.
Some arbitrary accidental thoughts
That crossed his mind, amusing because new,
He chose to represent as fixtures there,
Invariable convictions (such they seemed
Beside his interlocutor's loose cards
Flung daily down, and not the same way twice)
While certain hell-deep instincts, man's weak tongue   990
Is never bold to utter in their truth

Because styled hell-deep ('t is an old mistake
To place hell at the bottom of the earth)
He ignored these, — not having in readiness
Their nomenclature and philosophy :
He said true things, but called them by wrong names.
"On the whole," he thought, "I justify myself
On every point where cavillers like this
Oppugn my life : he tries one kind of fence,
I close, he 's worsted, that 's enough for him.   1000
He 's on the ground : if ground should break away
I take my stand on, there 's a firmer yet
Beneath it, both of us may sink and reach.
His ground was over mine and broke the first :
So, let him sit with me this many a year!"

   He did not sit five minutes.   Just a week
Sufficed his sudden healthy vehemence.
Something had struck him in the "Outward-bound"
Another way than Blougram's purpose was :
And having bought, not cabin-furniture   1010
But settler's-implements (enough for three)
And started for Australia — there, I hope,
By this time he has tested his first plough,
And studied his last chapter of St. John.

— ◦◦◦ —

MR. SLUDGE, "THE MEDIUM."

NOW, don't, sir!   Don't expose me!   Just this once!
   This was the first and only time, I 'll swear,—
Look at me, — see, I kneel, — the only time,
I swear, I ever cheated, — yes, by the soul
Of Her who hears — (your sainted mother, sir!)
All, except this last accident, was truth —
This little kind of slip! — and even this,
It was your own wine, sir, the good champagne,
(I took it for Catawba, you 're so kind)
Which put the folly in my head!

                "Get up?"   10
You still inflict on me that terrible face?
You show no mercy? — Not for Her dear sake,
The sainted spirit's, whose soft breath even now
Blows on my cheek — (don't you feel something, sir?)
You 'll tell?

2 B

           Go tell, then! Who the devil cares
What such a rowdy chooses to . . .

                            Aie — aie — aie!
Please, sir! your thumbs are thro' my windpipe, sir!
Ch — ch!

             Well, sir, I hope you 've done it now
Oh Lord! I little thought, sir, yesterday,
When your departed mother spoke those words   20
Of peace thro' me, and moved you, sir, so much,
You gave me — (very kind it was of you)
These shirt-studs — (better take them back again,
Please, sir) — yes, little did I think so soon
A trifle of trick, all thro' a glass too much
Of his own champagne, would change my best of friends
Into an angry gentleman!

                   Though, 't was wrong.
I don't contest the point; your anger 's just:
Whatever put such folly in my head,
I know 't was wicked of me. There 's a thick   30
Dusk undeveloped spirit (I 've observed)
Owes me a grudge — a negro's, I should say,
Or else an Irish emigrant's; yourself
Explained the case so well last Sunday, sir,
When we had summoned Franklin to clear up
A point about those shares i' the telegraph:
Ay, and he swore . . or might it be Tom Paine? .
Thumping the table close by where I crouched,
He 'd do me soon a mischief: that 's come true!
Why, now your face clears! I was sure it would!   40
Then, this one time . . don't take your hand away,
Thro' yours I surely kiss your mother's hand . .
You 'll promise to forgive me? — or, at least,
Tell nobody of this? Consider, sir!
What harm can mercy do? Would but the shade
Of the venerable dead-one just vouchsafe
A rap or tip! What bit of paper 's here?
Suppose we take a pencil, let her write,
Make the least sign, she urges on her child
Forgiveness? There now! Eh? Oh! 'T was your foot, 50
And not a natural creak, sir?

                  Answer, then!
Once, twice, thrice . . . see, I 'm waiting to say " thrice!"
All to no use? No sort of hope for me?
It 's all to post to Greeley's newspaper?

What? If I told you all about the tricks?
Upon my soul! — the whole truth, and naught else,
And how there 's been some falsehood — for your part,
Will you engage to pay my passage out,
And hold your tongue until I 'm safe on board?
England 's the place, not Boston — no offence!   60
I see what makes you hesitate: don't fear!
I mean to change my trade and cheat no more,
Yes, this time really it 's upon my soul!
Be my salvation! — under Heaven, of course.
I 'll tell some queer things. Sixty V's must do.
A trifle, though, to start with! We 'll refer
The question to this table?

                        How you 're changed!
Then split the difference; thirty more, we 'll say.
Ay, but you leave my presents! Else I 'll swear
'T was all thro' those: you wanted yours again,   70
So, picked a quarrel with me, to get them back!
Tread on a worm, it turns, sir! If I turn,
Your fault! 'T is you 'll have forced me! Who 's obliged
To give up life yet try no self-defence?
At all events, I 'll run the risk. Eh?

                                Done!
May I sit, sir? This dear old table, now!
Please, sir, a parting egg-nogg and cigar!
I 've been so happy with you! Nice stuffed chairs,
And sympathetic sideboards; what an end
To all the instructive evenings! (It 's alight.)   80
Well, nothing lasts, as Bacon came and said.
Here goes, — but keep your temper, or I 'll scream!

Fol-lol-the-rido-liddle-iddle-ol!
You see, sir, it 's your own fault more than mine;
It 's all your fault, you curious gentlefolk!
You 're prigs, — excuse me, — like to look so spry
So clever, while you cling by half a claw
To the perch whereon you puff yourselves at roost,
Such piece of self-conceit as serves for perch
Because you chose it, so it must be safe.   90
Oh, otherwise you 're sharp enough! You spy
Who slips, who slides, who holds by help of wing,
Wanting real foothold, — who can't keep upright
On the other perch, your neighbour chose, not you:
There 's no outwitting you respecting him!
For instance, men love money — that, you know —

And what men do to gain it : well, suppose
A poor lad, say a help's son in your house,
Listening at keyholes, hears the company
Talk grand of dollars, V-notes, and so forth,   100
How hard they are to get, how good to hold,
How much they buy, — if, suddenly, in pops he —
" *I* 've got a V-note! " — what do you say to him?
What 's your first word which follows your last kick?
" Where did you steal it, rascal? "   That 's because
He finds you, fain would fool you, off your perch,
Not on the special piece of nonsense, sir,
Elected your parade-ground : let him try
Lies to the end of the list, — " He picked it up.
His cousin died and left it him by will,   110
The President flung it to him, riding by,
An actress trucked it for a curl of his hair,
He dreamed of luck and found his shoe enriched,
He dug up clay, and out of clay made gold " —
How would you treat such possibilities?
Would not you, prompt, investigate the case
With cow-hide?   " Lies, lies, lies," you 'd shout : and
          why?
Which of the stories might not prove mere truth?
This last, perhaps, that clay was turned to coin!
Let 's see, now, give him me to speak for him!   120
How many of your rare philosophers,
In plaguy books I 've had to dip into,
Believed gold could be made thus, saw it made
And made it?   Oh, with such philosophers
You 're on your best behaviour!   While the lad —
With him, in a trice, you settle likelihoods,
Nor doubt a moment how he got his prize :
In his case, you hear, judge and execute,
All in a breath : so would most men of sense.

But let the same lad hear you talk as grand   130
At the same keyhole, you and company,
Of signs and wonders, the invisible world ;
How wisdom scouts our vulgar unbelief
More than our vulgarest credulity ;
How good men have desired to see a ghost,
What Johnson used to say, what Wesley did,
Mother Goose thought, and fiddle-diddle-dee : —
If he break in with, " Sir, *I* saw a ghost! "
Ah, the ways change!   He finds you perched and prim ;
It 's a conceit of yours that ghosts may be :   140
There 's no talk now of cow-hide.   " Tell it out!
Don't fear us!   Take your time and recollect!

Sit down first ; try a glass of wine, my boy!
And, David, (is not that your Christian name?)
Of all things, should this happen twice — it may —
Be sure, while fresh in mind, you let us know! "
Does the boy blunder, blurt out this, blab that,
Break down in the other, as beginners will?
All's candour, all's considerateness — " No haste!
Pause and collect yourself !   We understand!   150
That's the bad memory, or the natural shock,
Or the unexplained *phenomena !* "

                                    Egad,
The boy takes heart of grace ; finds, never fear,
The readiest way to ope your own heart wide,
Show — what I call your peacock-perch, pet post
To strut, and spread the tail, and squawk upon!
" Just as you thought, much as you might expect!
There be more things in heaven and earth, Horatio," . .
And so on.   Shall not David take the hint,
Grow bolder, stroke you down at quickened rate?   160
If he ruffle a feather, it's " Gently, patiently!
Manifestations are so weak at first!
Doubting, moreover, kills them, cuts all short,
Cures with a vengeance! "

                          There, sir, that's your style!
You and your boy — such pains bestowed on him,
Or any headpiece of the average worth,
To teach, say, Greek, would perfect him apace,
Make him a Person (" Porson? " thank you, sir!)
Much more, proficient in the art of lies.
You never leave the lesson!   Fire alight,   170
Catch you permitting it to die!   You 've friends ;
There's no withholding knowledge, — least from those
Apt to look elsewhere for their souls' supply :
Why should not you parade your lawful prize?
Who finds a picture, digs a medal up,
Hits on a first edition, — he henceforth
Gives it his name, grows notable : how much more
Who ferrets out a " medium "?   " David 's yours,
You highly-favoured man?   Then, pity souls
Less privileged!   Allow us share your luck! "   180
So, David holds the circle, rules the roast,
Narrates the vision, peeps in the glass ball,
Sets-to the spirit-writing, hears the raps,
As the case may be.

              Now mark!   To be precise —
Tho' I say, " lies " all these, at this first stage,
'T is just for science' sake : I call such grubs
By the name of what they 'll turn to, dragonflies.
Strictly, it 's what good people style untruth ;
But yet, so far, not quite the full-grown thing :
It 's fancying, fable-making, nonsense-work —   190
What never meant to be so very bad —
The knack of story-telling, brightening up
Each dull old bit of fact that drops its shine.
One does see somewhat when one shuts one's eyes,
If only spots and streaks ; tables do tip
In the oddest way of themselves : and pens, good Lord,
Who knows if you drive them or they drive you?
'T is but a foot in the water and out again ;
Not that duck-under which decides your dive.
Note this, for it 's important : listen why.   200

I 'll prove, you push on David till he dives
And ends the shivering.   Here 's your circle, now :
Two-thirds of them, with heads like you their host,
Turn up their eyes, and cry, as you expect,
" Lord, who 'd have thought it ! "   But there 's always one
Looks wise, compassionately smiles, submits
" Of your veracity no kind of doubt,
But — do you feel so certain of that boy's?
Really, I wonder!   I confess myself
More chary of my faith!"   That 's galling, sir!   210
What, he the investigator, he the sage,
When all 's done?   Then, you just have shut your eyes,
Opened your mouth, and gulped down David whole,
You!   Terrible were such catastrophe!
So, evidence is redoubled, doubled again,
And doubled besides ; once more, " He heard, we heard,
You and they heard, your mother and your wife,
Your children and the stranger in your gates :
Did they or did they not? "   So much for him,
The black sheep, guest without the wedding-garb,   220
The doubting Thomas!   Now 's your turn to crow :
"He 's kind to think you such a fool : Sludge cheats?
Leave you alone to take precautions ! "

                                 Straight
The rest join chorus.   Thomas stands abashed,
Sips silent some such beverage as this,
Considers if it be harder, shutting eyes
And gulping David in good fellowship,
Than going elsewhere, getting, in exchange,

With no egg-nogg to lubricate the food,
Some just as tough a morsel.   Over the way,   230
Holds Captain Sparks his court : is it better there?
Have not you hunting-stories, scalping-scenes,
And Mexican War exploits to swallow plump
If you 'd be free o' the stove-side, rocking-chair,
And trio of affable daughters?

                           Doubt succumbs!
Victory!   All your circle 's yours again!
Out of the clubbing of submissive wits,
David's performance rounds, each chink gets patched,
Every protrusion of a point 's filed fine,
All 's fit to set a-rolling round the world,   240
And then return to David finally,
Lies seven-feet thick about his first half-inch.
Here 's a choice birth o' the supernatural,
Poor David 's pledged to!   You 've employed no tool
That laws exclaim at, save the devil's own,
Yet screwed him into henceforth gulling you
To the top o' your bent, — all out of one half-lie!

You hold, if there 's one half or a hundredth part
Of a lie, that 's his fault, — his be the penalty!
I dare say!   You 'd prove firmer in his place?   250
You 'd find the courage, — that first flurry over,
That mild bit of romancing-work at end, —
To interpose with "It gets serious, this ;
Must stop here.   Sir, I saw no ghost at all.
Inform your friends I made . . well, fools of them,
And found you ready made.   I 've lived in clover
These three weeks : take it out in kicks of me!"
I doubt it.   Ask your conscience!   Let me know,
Twelve months hence, with how few embellishments
You 've told almighty Boston of this passage   260
Of arms between us, your first taste o' the foil
From Sludge who could not fence, sir!   Sludge, your boy!
I lied, sir, — there!   I got up from my gorge.
On offal in the gutter, and preferred
Your canvas-backs : I took their carver's size,
Measured his modicum of intelligence,
Tickled him on the cockles of his heart
With a raven feather, and next week found myself
Sweet and clean, dining daintily, dizened smart,
Set on a stool buttressed by ladies' knees,   270
Every soft smiler calling me her pet,
Encouraging my story to uncoil
And creep out from its hole, inch after inch,

"How last night, I no sooner snug in bed,
Tucked up, just as they left me, — than came raps!
While a light whisked" . . "Shaped somewhat like a star?"
"Well, like some sort of stars, ma'am," — "So we thought!
And any voice? Not yet? Try hard, next time,
If you can't hear a voice; we think you may;
At least, the Pennsylvanian 'mediums' did."   280
Oh, next time comes the voice! "Just as we hoped!"
Are not the hopers proud now, pleased, profuse
O' the natural acknowledgment?

                          Of course!
So, off we push, illy-oh-yo, trim the boat,
On we sweep with a cataract ahead,
We 're midway to the Horse-shoe : stop, who can,
The dance of bubbles gay about our prow!
Experiences become worth waiting for,
Spirits now speak up, tell their inmost mind,
And compliment the " medium " properly,   290
Concern themselves about his Sunday coat,
See rings on his hand with pleasure. Ask yourself
How you 'd receive a course of treats like these!
Why, take the quietest hack and stall him up,
Cram him with corn a month, then out with him
Among his mates on a bright April morn,
With the turf to tread; see if you find or no
A caper in him, if he bucks or bolts!
Much more a youth whose fancies sprout as rank
As toadstool-clump from melon-bed. 'T is soon,   300
" Sirrah, you spirit, come, go, fetch and carry,
Read, write, rap, rub-a-dub, and hang yourself! "
I 'm spared all further trouble; all 's arranged;
Your circle does my business; I may rave
Like an epileptic dervish in the books,
Foam, fling myself flat, rend my clothes to shreds;
No matter: lovers, friends and countrymen
Will lay down spiritual laws, read wrong things right
By the rule o' reverse. If Francis Verulam
Styles himself Bacon, spells the name beside   310
With a *y* and a *k*, says he drew breath in York,
Gave up the ghost in Wales when Cromwell reigned,
(As, sir, we somewhat fear he was apt to say,
Before I found the useful book that knows)
Why, what harm 's done? The circle smiles apace,
" It was not Bacon, after all, you see!
We understand; the trick 's but natural:
Such spirits' individuality
Is hard to put in evidence: they incline

To gibe and jeer, these undeveloped sorts.   320
You see, their world 's much like a jail broke loose,
While this of ours remains shut, bolted, barred,
With a single window to it.   Sludge, our friend,
Serves as this window, whether thin or thick,
Or stained or stainless ; he 's the medium-pane
Thro' which, to see us and be seen, they peep :
They crowd each other, hustle for a chance,
Tread on their neighbour's kibes, play tricks enough!
Does Bacon, tired of waiting swerve aside?
Up in his place jumps Barnum — ' I 'm your man,   330
I 'll answer you for Bacon!' Try once me   !"

Or else it 's — "What 's a 'medium?' He 's a means,
Good, bad, indifferent, still the only means
Spirits can speak by ; he may misconceive,
Stutter and stammer, — he 's their Sludge and drudge,
Take him or leave him ; they must hold their peace,
Or else, put up with having knowledge strained
To half-expression thro' his ignorance.
Suppose, the spirit Beethoven wants to shed
New music he 's brimful of ; why, he turns   340
The handle of this organ, grinds with Sludge,
And what he poured in at the mouth o' the mill
As a Thirty-third Sonata, (fancy now!)
Comes from the hopper as brand-new Sludge, naught else,
The Shakers' Hymn in G, with a natural F,
Or the ' Stars and Stripes ' set to consecutive fourths."

Sir, where 's the scrape you did not help me through,
You that are wise?   And for the fools, the folk
Who came to see, — the guests, (observe that word!)
Pray do you find guests criticize your wine,   350
Your furniture, your grammar, or your nose?
Then, why your " medium?"   What 's the difference?
Prove your madeira red-ink and gamboge, —
Your Sludge, a cheat — then somebody 's a goose
For vaunting both as genuine.   "Guests!"   Don't fear!
They 'll make a wry face, nor too much of that,
And leave you in your glory.

                    " No, sometimes
They doubt and say as much!"   Ay, doubt they do!
And what 's the consequence?   "Of course they doubt "—
(You triumph) "that explains the hitch at once!   360
Doubt posed our 'medium,' puddled his pure mind ;
He gave them back their rubbish : pitch chaff in,
Could flour come out o' the honest mill?"   So, prompt

Applaud the faithful : cases flock in point,
"How, when a mocker willed a 'medium' once
Should name a spirit James whose name was George,
'James' cried the 'medium' — 't was the test of truth !"
In short, a hit proves much, a miss proves more.
Does this convince?   The better : does it fail?
Time for the double-shotted broadside, then —   370
The grand means, last resource.   Look black and big!
"You style us idiots, therefore — why stop short?
Accomplices in rascality : this we hear
In our own house, from our invited guest
Found brave enough to outrage a poor boy
Exposed by our good faith!   Have you been heard?
Now, then, hear us ; one man 's not quite worth twelve.
You see a cheat?   Here 's some twelve see an ass :
Excuse me if I calculate : good day!"
Out slinks the sceptic, all the laughs explode,   380
Sludge waves his hat in triumph!

                     Or — he don't.
There 's something in real truth (explain who can!)
One casts a wistful eye at, like the horse
Who mopes beneath stuffed hay-racks and won't munch
Because he spies a corn-bag : hang that truth,
It spoils all dainties proffered in its place!
I 've felt at times when, cockered, cossetted
And coddled by the aforesaid company,
Bidden enjoy their bullying, — never fear,
But o'er their shoulders spit at the flying man, —   390
I 've felt a child ; only, a fractious child
That, dandled soft by nurse, aunt, grandmother,
Who keep him from the kennel, sun and wind,
Good fun and wholesome mud, — enjoined be sweet,
And comely and superior, — eyes askance
The ragged sons o' the gutter at their game,
Fain would be down with them i' the thick o' the filth,
Making dirt-pies, laughing free, speaking plain,
And calling granny the gray old cat she is.
I 've felt a spite, I say, at you, at them,   400
Huggings and humbug — gnashed my teeth to mark
A decent dog pass!   It 's too bad, I say,
Ruining a soul so!

              But what 's "so," what 's fixed,
Where may one stop?   Nowhere!   The cheating 's nursed
Out of the lying, softly and surely spun
To just your length, sir!   I 'd stop soon enough :
But you 're for progress.   "All old, nothing new?

Only the usual talking thro' the mouth,
Or writing by the hand?   I own, I thought
This would develop, grow demonstrable,   410
Make doubt absurd, give figures we might see,
Flowers we might touch.   There's no one doubts you, Sludge!
You dream the dreams, you see the spiritual sights,
The speeches come in your head, beyond dispute.
Still, for the sceptics' sake, to stop all mouths,
We want some outward manifestation! — well,
The Pennsylvanians gained such; why not Sludge?
He may improve with time!"

                              Ay, that he may!
He sees his lot: there's no avoiding fate.
'T is a trifle at first.   " Eh, David?   Did you hear?   420
You jogged the table, your foot caused the squeak,
This time you're . . . joking, are you not, my boy?"
"N-n-no!" — and I'm done for, bought and sold henceforth.
The old good easy jog-trot way, the . . . eh?
The . . . n t so very false, as falsehood goes,
The spinning out and drawing fine, you know, —
Really mere novel-writing of a sort,
Acting, or improvising, make believe,
Surely not downright cheatery, — any how,
'T is done with and my lot cast; Cheat 's my name: 430
The fatal dash of brandy in your tea
Has settled what you'll have the souchong's smack:
The caddy gives way to the dram-bottle.

Then, it's so cruel easy!   Oh, those tricks
That can't be tricks, those feats by sleight of hand,
Clearly no common conjuror's! — no, indeed!
A conjuror?   Choose me any craft i' the world
A man puts hand to; and with six months' pains
I'll play you twenty tricks miraculous
To people untaught the trade.   Have you seen glass blown, 440
Pipes pierced?   Why, just this biscuit that I chip,
Did you ever watch a baker toss one flat
To the oven?   Try and do it!   Take my word,
Practise but half as much, while limbs are lithe,
To turn, shove, tilt a table, crack your joints,
Manage your feet, dispose your hands aright,
Work wires that twitch the curtains, play the glove
At end o' your slipper, — then put out the lights
And . . . there, there, all you want you'll get, I hope!
I found it slip, easy as an old shoe.   450

Now, lights on table again!   I 've done my part,
You take my place while I give thanks and rest.
"Well, Judge Humgruffin, what 's your verdict, sir?
You, hardest head in the United States, —
Did you detect a cheat here?   Wait!   Let 's see!
Just an experiment first, for candour's sake!
I 'll try and cheat you, Judge!   The table tilts :
Is it I that move it?   Write!   I 'll press your hand :
Cry when I push, or guide your pencil, Judge!"
Sludge still triumphant!   "That a rap, indeed?   460
That, the real writing?   Very like a whale!
Then, if, sir, you — a most distinguished man,
And, were the Judge not here, I 'd say, . . no matter!
Well, sir, if you fail, you can't take us in, —
There 's little fear that Sludge will!"

                                        Won't he ma'am?
But what if our distinguished host, like Sludge,
Bade God bear witness that he played no trick,
While you believed that what produced the raps
Was just a certain child who died, you know,
And whose last breath you thought your lips had felt?   470
Eh?   That 's a capital point, ma'am : Sludge begins
At your entreaty with your dearest dead,
The little voice set lisping once again,
The tiny hand made feel for yours once more,
The poor lost image brought back, plain as dreams,
Which image, if a word had chanced recall,
The customary cloud would cross your eyes,
Your heart return the old tick, pay its pang!
A right mood for investigation, this!
One 's at one's ease with Saul and Jonathan,   480
Pompey and Cæsar : but one's own lost child . . .
I wonder, when you heard the first clod drop
From the spadeful at the grave-side, felt you free
To investigate who twitched your funeral scarf
Or brushed your flounces?   Then, it came of course
You should be stunned and stupid ; then, (how else?)
Your breath stopped with your blood, your brain struck work.
But now, such causes fail of such effects,
All 's changed, — the little voice begins afresh,
Yet you, calm, consequent, can test and try,   490
And touch the truth.   "Tests?   Did n't the creature tell
Its nurse's name, and say it lived six years,
And rode a rocking-horse?   Enough of tests!
Sludge never could learn that!"

                              He could not, eh?
You compliment him.   "Could not?"   Speak for yourself!

I 'd like to know the man I ever saw
Once, — never mind where, how, why, when, — once saw,
Of whom I do not keep some matter in mind
He 'd swear I " could not " know, sagacious soul!
What? Do you live in this world's blow of blacks,   500
Palaver, gossipry, a single hour
Nor find one smut has settled on your nose,
Of a smut's worth, no more, no less? — one fact
Out of the drift of facts, whereby you learn
What someone was, somewhere, somewhen, somewhy?
You don't tell folk — " See what has stuck to me!
Judge Humgruffin, our most distinguished man,
Your uncle was a tailor, and your wife
Thought to have married Miggs, missed him, hit you! " —
Do you, sir, tho' you see him twice a-week?   510
" No," you reply, " what use retailing it?
Why should I ? " But, you see, one day you *should*,
Because one day there 's much use, — when this fact
Brings you the Judge upon both gouty knees
Before the supernatural ; proves that Sludge
Knows, as you say, a thing he " could not " know :
Will not Sludge thenceforth keep an outstretched face
The way the wind drives?

                      " Could not ! " Look you now,
I 'll tell you a story! There 's a whiskered chap,
A foreigner, that teaches music here   520
And gets his bread, — knowing no better way.
He says, the fellow who informed of him
And made him fly his country and fall West,
Was a hunchback cobbler, sat, stitched soles and sang,
In some outlandish place, the city Rome,
In a cellar by their Broadway, all day long ;
Never asked questions, stopped to listen or look,
Nor lifted nose from lapstone ; let the world
Roll round his three-legged stool, and news run in
The ears he hardly seemed to keep pricked up.   530
Well, that man went on Sundays, touched his pay
And took his praise from government, you see ;
For something like two dollars every week,
He 'd engage tell you some one little thing
Of some one man, which led to many more,
(Because one truth leads right to the world's end)
And make you that man's master — when he dined
And on what dish, where walked to keep his health
And to what street. His trade was, throwing thus
His sense out, like an ant-eater's long tongue,   540
Soft, innocent, warm, moist, impassible,

And when 't was crusted o'er with creatures — slick,
Their juice enriched his palate.　"Could not Sludge!"

I 'll go yet a step further, and maintain,
Once the imposture plunged its proper depth
I' the rotten of your natures, all of you, —
(If one 's not mad nor drunk, and hardly then)
It 's impossible to cheat — that 's, be found out!
Go tell your brotherhood this first slip of mine,
All to-day's tale, how you detected Sludge, 550
Behaved unpleasantly, till he was fain confess,
And so has come to grief!　You 'll find, I think,
Why Sludge still snaps his fingers in your face.
There now, you 've told them!　What 's their prompt reply?
"Sir, did that youth confess he had cheated me,
I 'd disbelieve him.　He may cheat at times;
That 's in the 'medium'-nature, thus they 're made,
Vain and vindictive, cowards, prone to scratch.
And so all cats are; still a cat 's the beast
You coax the strange electric sparks from out, 560
By rubbing back its fur; not so a dog,
Nor lion, nor lamb: 't is the cat's nature, sir!
Why not the dog's?　Ask God, who made them beasts!
D' ye think the sound, the nicely-balanced man
(Like me " — aside) — "like you yourself," — (aloud)
" — He 's stuff to make a 'medium'?　Bless your soul,
'T is these hysteric, hybrid half-and-halfs,
Equivocal, worthless vermin yield the fire!
We take such as we find them, 'ware their tricks,
Wanting their service.　Sir, Sludge took in you — 570
How, I can't say, not being there to watch:
He was tried, was tempted by your easiness, —
He did not take in me!"

　　　　　　　Thank you for Sludge!
I 'm to be grateful to such patrons, eh,
When what you hear 's my best word? 'T is a challenge:
" Snap at all strangers, half-tamed prairie-dog,
So you cower duly at your keeper's beck!
Cat, show what claws were made for, muffling them
Only to me!　Cheat others if you can,
Me, if you dare!"　And, my wise sir, I dared — 580
Did cheat you first, made you cheat others next,
And had the help o' your vaunted manliness
To bully the incredulous.　You used me?
Have not I used you, taken full revenge,
Persuaded folk they knew not their own name,
And straight they 'd own the error!　Who was the fool
When, to an awe-struck wide-eyed open-mouthed

Circle of sages, Sludge would introduce
Milton composing baby-rhymes, and Locke ·
Reasoning in gibberish, Homer writing Greek   590
In naughts and crosses, Asaph setting psalms
To crotchet and quaver?   I 've made a spirit squeak
In sham voice for a minute, then outbroke
Bold in my own, defying the imbeciles —
Have copied some ghost's pothooks, half a page,
Then ended with my own scrawl undisguised.
" All right!   The ghost was merely using Sludge,
Suiting itself from his imperfect stock!"
Don't talk of gratitude to me!   For what?
For being treated as a showman's ape,   600
Encouraged to be wicked and make sport,
Fret or sulk, grin or whimper, any mood
So long as the ape be in it and no man —
Because a nut pays every mood alike.
Curse your superior, superintending sort,
Who, since you hate smoke, send up boys that climb
To cure your chimney, bid a "medium" lie
To sweep you truth down!   Curse your women too,
Your insolent wives and daughters, that fire up
Or faint away if a male hand squeeze theirs,   610
Yet, to encourage Sludge, may play with Sludge
As only a "medium," only the kind of thing
They must humour, fondle . . oh, to misconceive
Were too preposterous!   But I 've paid them out!
They 've had their wish — called for the naked truth,
And in she tripped, sat down and bade them stare :
They had to blush a little and forgive!
" The fact is, children talk so ; in next world
All our conventions are reversed, — perhaps
Made light of : something like old prints, my dear!   620
The Judge has one, he brought from Italy,
A metropolis in the background, — o'er a bridge,
A team of trotting roadsters, — cheerful groups
Of wayside travelers, peasants at their work,
And, full in front, quite unconcerned, why not?
Three nymphs conversing with a cavalier,
And never a rag among them : ' fine,' folk cry —
And heavenly manners seem not much unlike!
Let Sludge go on ; we 'll fancy it 's in print!"
If such as came for wool, sir, went home shorn,   630
Where is the wrong I did them?   'T was their choice :
They tried the adventure, ran the risk, tossed up
And lost, as some one 's sure to do in games.
They fancied I was made to lose, — smoked glass
Useful to spy the sun through, spare their eyes :

And had I proved a red-hot iron plate
They thought to pierce, and, for their pains, grew blind,
Whose were the fault but theirs?   While, as things go,
Their loss amounts to gain, the more 's the shame!
They 've had their peep into the spirit-world,   640
And all this world may know it.   They 've fed fat
Their self-conceit which else had starved: what chance
Save this, of cackling o'er a golden egg
And compassing distinction from the flock,
Friends of a feather?   Well, they paid for it,
And not prodigiously; the price o' the play,
Not counting certain pleasant interludes,
Was scarce a vulgar play's worth.   When you buy
The actor's talent, do you dare propose
For his soul beside?   Whereas, my soul you buy!   650
Sludge acts Macbeth, obliged to be Macbeth,
Or you 'll not hear his first word!   Just go through
That slight formality, swear himself 's the Thane,
And thenceforth he may strut and fret his hour,
Spout, spawl, or spin his target, no one cares!
Why had n't I leave to play tricks, Sludge as Sludge?
Enough of it all!   I 've wiped out scores with you —
Vented your fustian, let myself be streaked
Like tom-fool with your ochre and carmine,
Worn patchwork your respectable fingers sewed   660
To metamorphose somebody, — yes, I 've earned
My wages, swallowed down my bread of shame,
And shake the crumbs off — where but in your face?

As for religion — why, I served it, sir!
I 'll stick to that!   With my *phenomena*
I laid the atheist sprawling on his back,
Propped up Saint Paul, or, at least, Swedenborg!
In fact, it 's just the proper way to baulk
These troublesome fellows: liars, one and all,
Are not these sceptics?   Well, to baffle them,   670
No use in being squeamish: lie yourself!
Erect your buttress just as wide o' the line,
Your side, as they build up the wall on theirs;
Where both meet, midway in a point, is truth,
High overhead: so, take your room, pile bricks,
Lie!   Oh, there 's titillation in all shame!
What snow may lose in white, snow gains in rose!
Miss Stokes turns — Rahab, — nor a bad exchange!
Glory be on her, for the good she wrought,
Breeding belief anew 'neath ribs of death,   680
Brow-beating now the unabashed before,
Ridding us of their whole life's gathered straws

By a live coal from the altar! Why, of old,
Great men spent years and years in writing books
To prove we 've souls, and hardly proved it then :
Miss Stokes with her live coal, for you and me!
Surely, to this good issue, all was fair —
Not only fondling Sludge, but, even suppose
He let escape some spice of knavery, — well,
In wisely being blind to it! Don't you praise   690
Nelson for setting spy-glass to blind eye
And saying . . what was it — that he could not see
The signal he was bothered with? Ay, indeed!

I 'll go beyond : there 's a real love of a lie,
Liars find ready-made for lies they make,
As hand for glove, or tongue for sugar-plum.
At best, 't is never pure and full belief;
Those furthest in the quagmire, — don't suppose
They strayed there with no warning, got no chance
Of a filth-speck in their face, which they clenched teeth,   700
Bent brow against! Be sure they had their doubts,
And fears, and fairest challenges to try
The floor o' the seeming solid sand! But no!
Their faith was pledged, acquaintance too apprised,
All but the last step ventured, kerchiefs waved,
And Sludge called "pet : " 't was easier marching on
To the promised land ; join those who, Thursday next,
Meant to meet Shakespeare : better follow Sludge —
Prudent, oh sure! — on the alert, how else?
But making for the mid-bog, all the same!   710
To hear your outcries, one would think I caught
Miss Stokes by the scruff o' the neck, and pitched her flat,
Foolish-face-foremost! Hear these simpletons,
That 's all I beg, before my work 's begun,
Before I 've touched them with my finger-tip!
Thus they await me (do but listen, now!
It 's reasoning, this is, — I can't imitate
The baby voice, though) " In so many tales
Must be some truth, truth tho' a pin-point big,
Yet, some : a single man 's deceived, perhaps —   720
Hardly, a thousand : to suppose one cheat
Can gull all these, were more miraculous far
Than aught we should confess a miracle" —
And so on. Then the Judge sums up — (it 's rare)
Bids you respect the authorities that leap
To the judgment-seat at once, — why, don't you note
The limpid nature, the unblemished life,
The spotless honour, indisputable sense
Of the first upstart with his story? What —

2 C

Outrage a boy on whom you ne'er till now   730
Set eyes, because he finds raps trouble him?

Fools, these are : ay, and how of their opposites
Who never did, at bottom of their hearts,
Believe for a moment? — Men emasculate,
Blank of belief, who played, as eunuchs use,
With superstition safely, — cold of blood,
Who saw what made for them i' the mystery,
Took their occasion, and supported Sludge
— As proselytes? No, thank you, far too shrewd!
— But promisers of fair play, encouragers   740
O' the claimant ; who in candour needs must hoist
Sludge up on Mars' Hill, get speech out of Sludge
To carry off, criticize, and cant about!
Did n't Athens treat Saint Paul so? — at any rate,
It 's "a new thing," philosophy fumbles at.
Then there 's the other picker out of pearl
From dung heaps, — ay, your literary man,
Who draws on his kid gloves to deal with Sludge
Daintily and discreetly, — shakes a dust
O' the doctrine, flavours thence, he well knows how,   750
The narrative or the novel, — half-believes,
All for the book's sake, and the public's stare,
And the cash that 's God's sole solid in this world!
Look at him! Try to be too bold, too gross
For the master! Not you! He 's the man for muck ;
Shovel it forth, full-splash, he 'll smooth your brown
Into artistic richness, never fear!
Find him the crude stuff ; when you recognize
Your lie again, you 'll doff your hat to it,
Dressed out for company! "For company,"   760
I say, since there 's the relish of success :
Let all pay due respect, call the lie truth,
Save the soft silent smirking gentleman
Who ushered in the stranger : you must sigh
"How melancholy, he, the only one
Fails to perceive the bearing of the truth
Himself gave birth to!" — There 's the triumph's smack!
That man would choose to see the whole world roll
I' the slime o' the slough, so he might touch the tip
Of his brush with what I call the best of browns —   770
Tint ghost-tales, spirit-stories, past the power
Of the outworn umber and bistre!

                                             Yet I think
There 's a more hateful form of foolery —
The social sage's, Solomon of saloons

And philosophic diner-out, the fibble
Who wants a doctrine for a chopping-block
To try the edge of his faculty upon,
Prove how much common-sense he 'll hack and hew
I' the critical minute 'twixt the soup and fish!
These were my patrons : these and the like of them   780
Who, rising in my soul now, sicken it, —
These I have injured! Gratitude to these?
The gratitude, forsooth, of a prostitute
To the greenhorn and the bully — friends of hers,
From the wag that wants the queer jokes for his club,
To the snuff-box-decorator, honest man,
Who just was at his wits' end where to find
So genial a Pasiphae! All and each
Pay, compliment, protect from the police,
And how she hates them for their pains, like me!   790
So much for my remorse at thanklessness
Toward a deserving public!

                              But, for God?
Ay, that 's a question! Well, sir, since you press —
(How you do tease the whole thing out of me!
I don't mean you, you know, when I say, "them :"
Hate you, indeed! But that Miss Stokes, that Judge!
Enough, enough — with sugar : thank you, sir!)
Now for it, then! Will you believe me, though?
You 've heard what I confess ; I don't unsay
A single word : I cheated when I could,   800
Rapped with my toe-joints, set sham hands at work,
Wrote down names weak in sympathetic ink,
Rubbed odic lights with ends of phosphor-match,
And all the rest ; believe that: believe this,
By the same token, though it seem to set
The crooked straight again, unsay the said,
Stick up what I 've knocked down ; I can't help that,
It 's truth! I somehow vomit truth to-day.
This trade of mine — I don't know, can't be sure
But there was something in it, tricks and all!   810
Really, I want to light up my own mind.
They were tricks, — true, but what I mean to add
Is also true. First, — don't it strike you, sir?
Go back to the beginning, — the first fact
We 're taught is, there 's a world beside this world,
With spirits, not mankind, for tenantry ;
That much within that world once sojourned here,
That all upon this world will visit there,
And therefore that we, bodily here below,
Must have exactly such an interest   820

In learning what may be the ways o' the world
Above us, as the disembodied folk
Have (by all analogic likelihood)
In watching how things go in the old home
With us, their sons, successors, and what not.
Oh yes, with added powers probably,
Fit for the novel state, — old loves grown pure,
Old interests understood aright, — they watch!
Eyes to see, ears to hear, and hands to help,
Proportionate to advancement : they 're ahead,   830
That 's all — do what we do, but noblier done —
Use plate, whereas we eat our meals off delf
(To use a figure).

                     Concede that, and I ask
Next — what may be the mode of intercourse
Between us men here, and those once-men there?
First comes the Bible's speech ; then, history
With the supernatural element, — you know —
All that we sucked in with our mothers' milk,
Grew up with, got inside of us at last.
Till it 's found bone of bone and flesh of flesh.   840
See now, we start with the miraculous,
And know it used to be, at all events :
What 's the first step we take, and can't but take,
In arguing from the known to the obscure?
Why this : "What was before, may be to-day.
Since Samuel's ghost appeared to Saul, of course
My brother's spirit may appear to me."
Go tell your teacher that! What 's his reply?
What brings a shade of doubt for the first time
O'er his brow late so luminous with faith?   850
"Such things have been," says he, "and there 's no doubt
Such things may be : but I advise mistrust
Of eyes, ears, stomach, and more than all, your brain,
Unless it be of your great-grandmother,
Whenever they propose a ghost to you!"
The end is, there 's a composition struck ;
'T is settled, we 've some way of intercourse
Just as in Saul's time ; only, different :
How, when and where, precisely, — find it out!
I want to know, then, what 's so natural   860
As that a person born into this world
And seized on by such teaching, should begin
With firm expectancy and a frank look-out
For his own allotment, his especial share
I' the secret, — his particular ghost, in fine?
I mean, a person born to look that way,

Since natures differ: take the painter-sort,
One man lives fifty years in ignorance
Whether grass be green or red, — "No kind of eye
For colour," say you; while another picks   870
And puts away even pebbles, when a child,
Because of bluish spots and pinky veins —
"Give him forthwith a paint-box!"   Just the same
Was I born . . . "medium," you won't let me say, —
Well, seer of the supernatural
Everywhen, everyhow and everywhere, —
Will that do?

          I and all such boys of course
Started with the same stock of Bible-truth;
Only, — what in the rest you style their sense,
Instinct, blind reasoning but imperative,   880
This, betimes, taught them the old world had one law
And ours another: "New world, new laws," cried they:
"None but old laws, seen everywhere at work,"
Cried I, and by their help explained my life
The Jews' way, still a working way to me.
Ghosts made the noises, fairies waved the lights,
Or Santa Claus slid down on New Year's Eve
And stuffed with cakes the stocking at my bed,
Changed the worn shoes, rubbed clean the fingered slate
O' the sum that came to grief the day before.   890

This could not last long: soon enough I found
Who had worked wonders thus, and to what end:
But did I find all easy, like my mates?
Henceforth no supernatural any more?
Not a whit: what projects the billiard-balls?
"A cue," you answer: "Yes, a cue," said I;
"But what hand, off the cushion, moved the cue?
What unseen agency, outside the world,
Prompted its puppets to do this and that,
Put cakes and shoes and slates into their mind,   900
These mothers and aunts, nay even schoolmasters?"
Thus high I sprang, and there have settled since.
Just so I reason, in sober earnest still,
About the greater god-sends, what you call
The serious gains and losses of my life.
What do I know or care about your world
Which either is or seems to be?   This snap
O' my fingers, sir!   My care is for myself;
Myself am whole and sole reality
Inside a raree-show and a market-mob   910
Gathered about it: that 's the use of things.

'T is easy saying they serve vast purposes,
Advantage their grand selves : be it true or false,
Each thing may have two uses.   What 's a star?
A world, or a world's sun : does n't it serve
As taper also, time-piece, weather-glass,
And almanac?   Are stars not set for signs
When we should shear our sheep, sow corn, prune trees?
The Bible says so.

    Well, I add one use
To all the acknowledged uses, and declare   920
If I spy Charles's Wain at twelve to-night,
It warns me, " Go, nor lose another day,
And have your hair cut, Sludge! "   You laugh : and why?
Were such a sign too hard for God to give?
No : but Sludge seems too little for such grace :
Thank you, sir!   So you think, so does not Sludge!
When you and good men gape at Providence,
Go into history and bid us mark
Not merely powder-plots prevented, crowns
Kept on kings' heads by miracle enough,   930
But private mercies — oh, you 've told me, sir,
Of such interpositions!   How yourself
Once, missing on a memorable day
Your handkerchief — just setting out, you know, —
You must return to fetch it, lost the train,
And saved your precious self from what befell
The thirty-three whom Providence forgot.
You tell, and ask me what I think of this?
Well, sir, I think, then, since you needs must know,
What matter had you and Boston city to boot   940
Sailed skyward, like burnt onion-peelings?   Much
To you, no doubt : for me — undoubtedly
The cutting of my hair concerns me more,
Because, however sad the truth may seem,
Sludge is of all-importance to himself.
You set apart that day in every year
For special thanksgiving, were a heathen else :
Well, I who can not boast the like escape,
Suppose I said " I don't thank Providence
For my part, owing it no gratitude? "   950
" Nay, but you owe as much " — you 'd tutor me,
" You, every man alive, for blessings gained
In every hour o' the day, could you but know!
I saw my crowning mercy : all have such,
Could they but see! "   Well sir, why don't they see?
" Because they won't look — or perhaps, they can't."
Then, sir, suppose I can, and will, and do

Look, microscopically as is right,
Into each hour with its infinitude
Of influences at work to profit Sludge?   960
For that 's the case: I 've sharpened up my sight
To spy a providence in the fire's going out,
The kettle's boiling, the dime's sticking fast
Despite the hole i' the pocket. Call such facts
Fancies, too petty a work for Providence,
And those same thanks which you exact from me,
Prove too prodigious payment; thanks for what,
If nothing guards and guides us little men?
No, no, sir! You must put away your pride,
Resolved to let Sludge into partnership!   970
I live by signs and omens: looked at the roof
Where the pigeons settle — " If the further bird,
The white, takes wing first, I 'll confess when thrashed;
Not, if the blue does " — so I said to myself
Last week, lest you should take me by surprise:
Off flapped the white, — and I 'm confessing, sir!
Perhaps 't is Providence's whim and way
With only me, i' the world: how can you tell?
" Because unlikely!" Was it likelier, now,
That this our one out of all worlds beside,   980
The what-d'you-call-'em millions, should be just
Precisely chosen to make Adam for,
And the rest o' the tale? Yet the tale 's true, you know:
Such undeserving clod was graced so once;
Why not graced likewise undeserving Sludge?
Are we merit-mongers, flaunt we filthy rags?
All you can bring against my privilege
Is, that another way was taken with you, —
Which I don't question. It 's pure grace, my luck:
I 'm broken to the way of nods and winks,   990
And need no formal summoning. You 've a help;
Holloa his name or whistle, clap your hands,
Stamp with your foot or pull the bell: all 's one,
He understands you want him, here he comes.
Just so, I come at the knocking: you, sir, wait
The tongue o' the bell, nor stir before you catch
Reason's clear tingle, nature's clapper brisk,
Or that traditional peal was wont to cheer
Your mother's face turned heavenward: short of these
There 's no authentic intimation, eh?   1000
Well, when you hear, you 'll answer them, start up
And stride into the presence, top of toe,
And there find Sludge beforehand, Sludge that sprang
At noise o' the knuckle on the partition-wall!
I think myself the more religious man.

Religion 's all or nothing ; it 's no mere smile
O' contentment, sigh of aspiration, sir —
No quality o' the finelier-tempered clay
Like its whiteness or its lightness ; rather, stuff
O' the very stuff, life of life, and self of self.   1010
I tell you, men won't notice ; when they do,
They 'll understand.   I notice nothing else :
I 'm eyes, ears, mouth of me, one gaze and gape,
Nothing eludes me, everything 's a hint,
Handle and help.   It 's all absurd, and yet
There 's something in it all, I know : how much?
No answer !   What does that prove ?   Man 's still man,
Still meant for a poor blundering piece of work
When all 's done ; but, if somewhat 's done, like this,
Or not done, is the case the same ?   Suppose   1020
I blunder in my guess at the true sense
O' the knuckle-summons, nine times out of ten, —
What if the tenth guess happen to be right ?
If the tenth shovel-load of powdered quartz
Yield me the nugget ?   I gather, crush, sift all,
Pass o'er the failure, pounce on the success.
To give you a notion, now — (let who wins, laugh !)
When first I see a man, what do I first ?
Why, count the letters which make up his name,
And as their number chances, even or odd,   1030
Arrive at my conclusion, trim my course :
Hiram H. Horsefall is your honoured name,
And have n't I found a patron, sir, in you?
"Shall I cheat this stranger ? "   I take apple-pips,
Stick one in either *canthus* of my eye,
And if the left drops first — (your left, sir, stuck)
I 'm warned, I let the trick alone this time.
You, sir, who smile, superior to such trash,
You judge of character by other rules :
Don't your rules sometimes fail you?   Pray, what rule   1040
Have you judged Sludge by hitherto?

                          Oh, be sure,
You, everybody blunders, just as I,
In simpler things than these by far !   For see :
I knew two farmers, — one, a wiseacre
Who studied seasons, rummaged almanacs,
Quoted the dew-point, registered the frost,
And then declared, for outcome of his pains,
Next summer must be dampish : 't was a drought.
His neighbour prophesied such drought would fall,
Saved hay and corn, made cent. per cent. thereby,   1050
And proved a sage indeed : how came his lore?

Because one brindled heifer, late in March,
Stiffened her tail of evenings, and somehow
He got into his head that drought was meant!
I don't expect all men can do as much :
Such kissing goes by favour.   You must take
A certain turn of mind for this, — a twist
I' the flesh, as well.   Be lazily alive,
Open-mouthed, like my friend the ant-eater,
Letting all nature's loosely-guarded motes   1060
Settle and, slick, be swallowed!   Think yourself
The one i' the world, the one for whom the world
Was made, expect it tickling at your mouth!
Then will the swarm of busy buzzing flies,
Clouds of coincidence, break egg-shell, thrive,
Breed, multiply, and bring you food enough.

   I can't pretend to mind your smiling, sir!
Oh, what you mean is this!   Such intimate way,
Close converse, frank exchange of offices,
Strict sympathy of the immeasurably great   1070
With the infinitely small, betokened here
By a course of signs and omens, raps and sparks, —
How does it suit the dread traditional text
O' the "Great and Terrible Name?"   Shall the Heaven
        of Heavens
Stoop to such child's play?

                              Please sir, go with me
A moment, and I'll try to answer you.
The "*Magnum et terribile*" (is that right?)
Well, folk began with this in the early day ;
And all the acts they recognized in proof
Were thunders, lightnings, earthquakes, whirlwinds, dealt   1080
Indisputably on men whose death they caused.
There, and there only, folk saw Providence
At work, — and seeing it, 't was right enough
All heads should tremble, hands wring hands amain,
And knees knock hard together at the breath
O' the Name's first letter ; why, the Jews, I'm told,
Won't write it down, no, to this very hour,
Nor speak aloud : you know best if 't be so.
Each ague-fit of fear at end, they crept
(Because somehow people once born must live)   1090
Out of the sound, sight, swing and sway o' the Name,
Into a corner, the dark rest of the world
And safe space where as yet no fear had reached ;
'T was there they looked about them, breathed again,
And felt indeed at home, as we might say.

The current o' common things, the daily life,
This had their due contempt; no Name pursued
Man from the mountain-top where fires abide,
To his particular mouse-hole at its foot
Where he ate, drank, digested, lived in short.   1100
Such was man's vulgar business, far too small
To be worth thunder: "small," folk kept on, "small,"
With much complacency in those great days!
A mote of sand, you know, a blade of grass —
What was so despicable as mere grass.
Except perhaps the life o' the worm or fly
Which fed there?   These were "small" and men were
      great.
Well, sir, the old way 's altered somewhat since,
And the world wears another aspect now:
Somebody turns our spyglass round, or else   1110
Puts a new lens in it: grass, worm, fly grow big:
We find great things are made of little things,
And little things go lessening till at last
Comes God behind them.   Talk of mountains now?
We talk of mould that heaps the mountain, mites
That throng the mould, and God that makes the mites.
The Name comes close behind a stomach-cyst,
The simplest of creations, just a sac
That 's mouth, heart, legs and belly at once, yet lives
And feels, and could do neither, we conclude,   1120
If simplified still further one degree:
The small becomes the dreadful and immense!
Lightning, forsooth?   No word more upon that!
A tin-foil bottle, a strip of greasy silk,
With a bit of wire and knob of brass, and there 's
Your dollar's worth of lightning!   But the cyst —
The life of the least of the little things?

                              No, no!
Preachers and teachers try another tack,
Come near the truth this time: they put aside
Thunder and lightning: " That 's mistake," they cry,   1130
" Thunderbolts fall for neither fright nor sport,
But do appreciable good, like tides,
Changes o' the wind, and other natural facts —
' Good ' meaning good to man, his body or soul.
Mediate, immediate, all things minister
To man, — that 's settled: be our future text
' We are His children! ' "   So, they now harangue
About the intention, the contrivance, all
That keeps up an incessant play of love, —
See the Bridgewater book.

Amen to it!   1140

Well, sir, I put this question : I 'm a child?
I lose no time, but take you at your word :
How shall I act a child's part properly?
Your sainted mother, sir, — used you to live
With such a thought as this a-worrying you?
" She has it in her power to throttle me,
Or stab or poison : she may turn me out,
Or lock me in, — nor stop at this to-day,
But cut me off to-morrow from the estate
I look for "— (long may you enjoy it, sir!)   1150
" In brief, she may unchild the child I am."
You never had such crotchets?   Nor have I!
Who, frank confessing childship from the first,
Can not both fear and take my ease at once,
So, don't fear, — know what might be, well enough
But know too, child-like, that it will not be,
At least in my case, mine, the son and heir
O' the kingdom, as yourself proclaim my style.
But do you fancy I stop short at this?
Wonder if suit and service, son and heir   1160
Needs must expect, I dare pretend to find?
If, looking for signs proper to such an one,
I straight perceive them irresistible?
Concede that homage is a son's plain right,
And, never mind the nods and raps and winks,
'T is the pure obvious supernatural
Steps forward, does its duty : why, of course!
I have presentiments : my dreams come true :
I fancy a friend stands whistling all in white
Blithe as a boblink, and he 's dead I learn.   1170
I take dislike to a dog my favourite long,
And sell him ; he goes mad next week and snaps.
I guess that stranger will turn up to-day
I have not seen these three years ; there 's his knock.
I wager " sixty peaches on that tree!"—
That I pick up a dollar in my walk,
That your wife's brother's cousin's name was George —
And win on all points.   Oh, you wince at this?
You 'd fain distinguish between gift and gift,
Washington's oracle and Sludge's itch   1180
O' the elbow when at whist he ought to trump?
With Sludge it 's too absurd?   *Fine, draw the line
Somewhere, but, sir, your somewhere is not mine!*

Bless us, I 'm turning poet!   It 's time to end.
How you have drawn me out, sir!   All I ask
Is — am I heir or not heir?   If I 'm he,

Then, sir, remember, that same personage
(To judge by what we read i' the newspaper)
Requires, beside one nobleman in gold
To carry up and down his coronet,   1190
Another servant, probably a duke,
To hold egg-nogg in readiness : why want
Attendance, sir, when helps in his father's house
Abound, I 'd like to know?

                    Enough of talk!
My fault is that I tell too plain a truth.
Why, which of those who say they disbelieve,
Your clever people, but has dreamed his dream,
Caught his coincidence, stumbled on his fact
He can't explain, (he 'll tell you smilingly)
Which he 's too much of a philosopher   1200
To count as supernatural, indeed,
So calls a puzzle and problem, proud of it?
— Bidding you still be on your guard, you know,
Because one fact don't make a system stand,
Nor prove this an occasional escape
Of spirit beneath the matter : that 's the way!
Just so wild Indians picked up, piece by piece,
The fact in California, the fine gold
That underlay the gravel — hoarded these,
But never made a system stand, nor dug!   1210
So wise men hold out in each hollowed palm
A handful of experience, sparkling fact
They can't explain ; and since their rest of life
Is all explainable, what proof in this?
Whereas I take the fact, the grain of gold,
And fling away the dirty rest of life,
And add this grain to the grain each fool has found
O' the million other such philosophers, —
Till I see gold, all gold and only gold,
Truth questionless tho' unexplainable,   1220
And the miraculous proved the commonplace!
The other fools believed in mud, no doubt —
Failed to know gold they saw : was that so strange?
Are all men born to play Bach's fiddle-fugues,
"Time" with the foil in carte, jump their own height,
Cut the mutton with the broadsword, skate a five,
Make the red hazard with the cue, clip nails
While swimming, in five minutes row a mile,
Pull themselves three feet up with the left arm,
Do sums of fifty figures in their head,   1230
And so on, by the scores of instances?
The Sludge with luck, who sees the spiritual facts

His fellows strive and fail to see, may rank
With these, and share the advantage.

                              Ay, but share
The drawback!   Think it over by yourself;
I have not heart, sir, and the fire 's gone gray.
Defect somewhere compensates for success,
Everyone knows that.   Oh, we 're equals, sir!
The big-legged fellow has a little arm
And a less brain, tho' big legs win the race.   1240
Do you suppose I 'scape the common lot?
Say, I was born with flesh so sensitive,
Soul so alert, that, practice helping both,
I guess what 's going on outside the veil,
Just as a prisoned crane feels pairing-time
In the islands where his kind are, so must fall
To capering by himself some shiny night,
As if your back-yard were a plot of spice —
Thus am I 'ware o' the spirit-world: while you,
Blind as a beetle that way, — for amends,   1250
Why, you can double fist and floor me, sir!
Ride that hot hardmouthed horrid horse of yours,
Laugh while it lightens, play with the great dog,
Speak your mind tho' it vex some friend to hear,
Never brag, never bluster, never blush, —
In short, you 've pluck, when I 'm a coward — there!
I know it, I can't help it, — folly or no,
I 'm paralyzed, my hand 's no more a hand,
Nor my head a head, in danger: you can smile
And change the pipe in your cheek. Your gift 's not mine.   1260
Would you swap for mine? No! but you 'd add my gift
To yours: I dare say! I too sigh at times,
Wish I were stouter, could tell truth nor flinch,
Kept cool when threatened, did not mind so much
Being dressed gaily, making strangers stare,
Eating nice things; when I 'd amuse myself,
I shut my eyes and fancy in my brain,
I 'm — now the President, now, Jenny Lind,
Now, Emerson, now, the Benicia Boy —
With all the civilized world a-wondering   1270
And worshiping.   I know it 's folly and worse;
I feel such tricks sap, honeycomb the soul:
But I can't cure myself, — despond, despair,
And then, hey, presto, there 's a turn o' the wheel,
Under comes uppermost, fate makes full amends;
Sludge knows and sees and hears a hundred things
You all are blind to, — I 've my taste of truth,
Likewise my touch of falsehood, — vice no doubt,
But you 've your vices also: I 'm content.

What, sir?   You won't shake hands?   "Because I   1280
      cheat!
You 've found me out in cheating!"   That 's enough
To make an apostle swear!   Why, when I cheat,
Mean to cheat, do cheat, and am caught in the act,
Are you, or rather, am I sure o' the fact?
(There 's verse again, but I 'm inspired somehow.)
Well then I 'm not sure!   I may be, perhaps,
Free as a babe from cheating: how it began,
My gift, — no matter; what 't is got to be
In the end now, that 's the question; answer that!
Had I seen, perhaps, what hand was holding mine,   1290
Leading me whither, I had died of fright,
So, I was made believe I led myself.
If I should lay a six-inch plank from roof
To roof, you would not cross the street, one step,
Even at your mother's summons: but, being shrewd,
If I paste paper on each side the plank
And swear 't is solid pavement, why, you 'll cross
Humming a tune the while, in ignorance
Beacon Street stretches a hundred feet below:
I walked thus, took the paper-cheat for stone.   1300
Some impulse made me set a thing o' the move
Which, started once, ran really by itself;
Beer flows thus, suck the siphon; toss the kite,
It takes the wind and floats of its own force.
Don't let truth's lump rot stagnant for the lack
Of a timely helpful lie to leaven it!
Put a chalk-egg beneath the clucking hen,
She 'll lay a real one, laudably deceived,
Daily for weeks to come.   I 've told my lie,
And seen truth follow, marvels none of mine;   1310
All was not cheating, sir, I 'm positive!
I don't know if I move your hand sometimes
When the spontaneous writing spreads so far,
If my knee lifts the table all that height,
Why the inkstand don't fall off the desk a-tilt,
Why the accordion plays a prettier waltz
Than I can pick out on the piano-forte,
Why I speak so much more than I intend,
Describe so many things I never saw.
I tell you, sir, in one sense, I believe   1320
Nothing at all, — that everybody can,
Will, and does cheat: but in another sense
I 'm ready to believe my very self —
That every cheat 's inspired, and every lie
Quick with a germ of truth.

                                  You ask perhaps
Why I should condescend to trick at all
If I know a way without it?   This is why!
There 's a strange secret sweet self-sacrifice
In any desecration of one's soul
To a worthy end, — is n't it Herodotus   1330
(I wish I could read Latin!) who describes
The single gift o' the land's virginity,
Demanded in those old Egyptian rites,
(I 've but a hazy notion — help me, sir!)
For one purpose in the world, one day in a life,
One hour in a day — thereafter, purity,
And a veil thrown o'er the past for evermore!
Well now they understood a many things
Down by Nile city, or wherever it was!
I 've always vowed, after the minute's lie,   1340
And the end's gain, — truth should be mine henceforth.
This goes to the root o' the matter, sir, — this plain
Plump fact: accept it and unlock with it
The wards of many a puzzle!

                                  Or, finally,
Why should I set so fine a gloss on things?
What need I care?   I cheat in self-defence,
And there 's my answer to a world of cheats!
Cheat?   To be sure, sir!   What 's the world worth else?
Who takes it as he finds, and thanks his stars?
Don't it want trimming, turning, furbishing up   1350
And polishing over?   Your so-styled great men,
Do they accept one truth as truth is found,
Or try their skill at tinkering?   What 's your world?
Here are you born, who are, I 'll say at once,
Of the luckiest kind whether in head and heart,
Body and soul, or all that helps them both.
Well, now, look back : what faculty of yours
Came to its full, had ample justice done
By growing when rain fell, biding its time,
Solidifying growth when earth was dead,   1360
Spiring up, broadening wide, in seasons due?
Never!   You shot up and frost nipped you off,
Settled to sleep when sunshine bade you sprout;
One faculty thwarted its fellow : at the end,
All you boast is, " I had proved a topping tree
In other climes " — yet this was the right clime
Had you foreknown the seasons.   Young, you 've force
Wasted like well-streams : old, — oh, then indeed,
Behold a labyrinth of hydraulic pipes
Thro' which you 'd play off wondrous waterwork;   1370

Only, no water 's left to feed their play.
Young, — you 've a hope, an aim, a love ; it 's tossed
And crossed and lost : you struggle on, some spark
Shut in your heart against the puffs around,
Thro' cold and pain ; these in due time subside :
Now then for age's triumph, the hoarded light
You mean to loose on the altered face of things, —
Up with it on the tripod! It 's extinct.
Spend your life's remnant asking — which was best,
Light smothered up that never peeped forth once,   1380
Or the cold cresset with full leave to shine?
Well, accept this too, — seek the fruit of it
Not in enjoyment, proved a dream on earth,
But knowledge, useful for a second chance,
Another life, — you 've lost this world, you 've gained
Its knowledge for the next. — What knowledge, sir,
Except that you know nothing?   Nay, you doubt
Whether 't were better have made you man or brute,
If aught be true, if good and evil clash.
No foul, no fair, no inside, no outside,   1390
There 's your world!

               Give it me! I slap it brisk
With harlequin's pasteboard sceptre : what 's it now?
Changed like a rock-flat, rough with rusty weed,
At first wash-over o' the returning wave!
All the dry dead impracticable stuff
Starts into life and light again ; this world
Pervaded by the influx from the next. :
I cheat, and what 's the happy consequence?
You find full justice straightway dealt you out,
Each want supplied, each ignorance set at ease,   1400
Each folly fooled.   No life-long labour now
As the price of worse than nothing!   No mere film
Holding you chained in iron, as it seems,
Against the outstretch of your very arms
And legs i' the sunshine moralists forbid!
What would you have?   Just speak and, there, you see!
You 're supplemented, made a whole at last :
Bacon advises, Shakespeare writes you songs,
And Mary Queen of Scots embraces you.
Thus it goes on, not quite like life perhaps,   1410
But so near, that the very difference piques,
Shows that e'en better than this best will be —
This passing entertainment in a hut
Whose bare walls take your taste since, one stage more,
And you arrive at the palace : all half real,
And you, to suit it, less than real beside,

In a dream, lethargic kind of death in life,
That helps the interchange of natures, flesh
Transfused by souls, and such souls!   Oh, 't is choice!
And if at whiles the bubble, blown too thin,   1420
Seem nigh on bursting, — if you nearly see
The real world thro' the false, — what *do* you see?
Is the old so ruined?   You find you 're in a flock
O' the youthful, earnest, passionate — genius, beauty,
Rank and wealth also, if you care for these :
And all depose their natural rights, hail you,
(That 's me, sir) as their mate and yoke-fellow.
Participate in Sludgehood — nay, grow mine,
I veritably possess them — banish doubt,
And reticence and modesty alike!   1430
Why, here 's the Golden Age, old Paradise
Or new Eutopia!   Here 's true life indeed,
And the world well won now, mine for the first time!

And all this might be, may be, and with good help
Of a little lying shall be : so, Sludge lies!
Why, he 's at worst your poet who sings how Greeks
That never were, in Troy which never was,
Did this or the other impossible great thing!
He 's Lowell — it 's a world (you smile applause)
Of his own invention — wondrous Longfellow,   1440
Surprising Hawthorne!   Sludge does more than they,
And acts the books they write : the more his praise!

But why do I mount to poets?   Take plain prose —
Dealers in common sense, set these at work,
What can they do without their helpful lies?
Each states the law and fact and face o' the thing
Just as he 'd have them, finds what he thinks fit,
Is blind to what missuits him, just records
What makes his case out, quite ignores the rest.
It 's a History of the World, the Lizard Age,   1450
The Early Indians, the Old Country War,
Jerome Napoleon, whatsoever you please,
All as the author wants it.   Such a scribe
You pay and praise for putting life in stones,
Fire into fog, making the past your world.
There 's plenty of " How did you contrive to grasp
The thread which led you thro' this labyrinth?
How build such solid fabric out of air?
How on so slight foundation found this tale,
Biography, narrative?" or, in other words,   1460
"How many lies did it require to make
The portly truth you here present us with?"
    2 D

"Oh," quoth the penman, purring at your praise,
" 'T is fancy all; no particle of fact:
I was poor and threadbare when I wrote that book
' Bliss in the Golden City.'   I, at Thebes?
We writers paint out of our heads, you see!"
"— Ah, the more wonderful the gift in you,
The more creativeness and godlike craft!"
But I, do I present you with my piece,   1470
It 's "What, Sludge?   When my sainted mother spoke
The verses Lady Jane Grey last composed
About the rosy bower in the seventh heaven
Where she and Queen Elizabeth keep house, —
You made the raps?   'T was your invention that?
Cur, slave and devil!"— eight fingers and two thumbs
Stuck in my throat!

          Well, if the marks seem gone,
'T is because stiffish cock-tail, taken in time,
Is better for a bruise than arnica.
There, sir!   I bear no malice: 't is n't in me.   1480
I know I acted wrongly: still, I've tried
What I could say in my excuse, — to show
The devil 's not all devil . . . I don't pretend
He 's angel, much less such a gentleman
As you, sir!   And I've lost you, lost myself,
Lost all-l-l-l- . . . .

          No — are you in earnest, sir?
O, yours, sir, is an angel's part!   I know
What prejudice prompts, and what 's the common course
Men take to soothe their ruffled self-conceit:
Only you rise superior to it all!   1490
No, sir, it don't hurt much; it 's speaking long
That makes me choke a little: the marks will go!
What?   Twenty V-notes more, and outfit too,
And not a word to Greeley?   One — one kiss
O' the hand that saves me?   You 'll not let me speak,
I well know, and I 've lost the right, too true!
But I must say, sir, if She hears (she does)
Your sainted . . . Well, sir, — be it so!   That 's, I think,
My bed-room candle.   Good-night!   Bl-l-less you, sir!

————

R-r-r, you brute-beast and blackguard!   Cowardly scamp!   1500
I only wish I dared burn down the house
And spoil your sniggering!   Oh, what, you 're the man?
You 're satisfied at last?   You 've found out Sludge?
We 'll see that presently: my turn, sir, next!

I too can tell my story : brute, — do you hear? —
You throttled your sainted mother, that old hag,
In just such a fit of passion : no, it was . . .
To get this house of hers, and many a note
Like these . . . I 'll pocket them, however . . . five,
Ten, fifteen . . . ay, you gave her throat the twist,   1510
Or else you poisoned her ! Confound the cuss !
Where was my head? I ought to have prophesied
He 'll die in a year and join her : that 's the way.

I don't know where my head is : what had I done?
How did it all go? I said he poisoned her,
And hoped he 'd have grace given him to repent ;
Whereon he picked this quarrel, bullied me
And called me cheat : I thrashed him, — who could help?
He howled for mercy, prayed me on his knees
To cut and run and save him from disgrace :   1520
I do so, and once off, he slanders me.
An end of him ! Begin elsewhere anew !
Boston 's a hole, the herring-pond is wide,
V-notes are something, liberty still more.
Beside, is he the only fool in the world?

———◦◦◦———

THE BOY AND THE ANGEL.

MORNING, evening, noon and night,
  "Praise God!" sang Theocrite.

Then to his poor trade he turned,
Whereby the daily meal was earned.

Hard he laboured, long and well ;
O'er his work the boy's curls fell.

But ever, at each period,
He stopped and sang, "Praise God!"

Then back again his curls he threw,
And cheerful turned to work anew.   10

Said Blaise, the listening monk, "Well done ;
I doubt not thou art heard, my son :

" As well as if thy voice to-day
Were praising God, the Pope's great way.

" This Easter Day, the Pope at Rome
Praises God from Peter's dome."

Said Theocrite, "Would God that I
Might praise Him, that great way, and die!"

Night passed, day shone,
And Theocrite was gone.   20

With God a day endures alway,
A thousand years are but a day,

God said in heaven, "Nor day nor night
Now brings the voice of my delight."

Then Gabriel, like a rainbow's birth,
Spread his wings and sank to earth;

Entered, in flesh, the empty cell,
Lived there, and played the craftsman well;

And morning, evening, noon and night,
Praised God in place of Theocrite.   30

And from a boy, to youth he grew:
The man put off the stripling's hue:

The man matured and fell away
Into the season of decay:

And ever o'er the trade he bent,
And ever lived on earth content.

(He did God's will; to him, all one
If on the earth or in the sun.)

God said, " A praise is in mine ear;
There is no doubt in it, no fear: 40

" So sing old worlds, and so
New worlds that from my footstool go.

" Clearer loves sound other ways:
I miss my little human praise."

Then forth sprang Gabriel's wings, off fell
The flesh disguise, remained the cell.

'T was Easter Day: he flew to Rome,
And paused above Saint Peter's dome.

In the tiring-room close by
The great outer gallery,   50

With his holy vestments dight,
Stood the new Pope, Theocrite:

And all his past career
Came back upon him clear,

Since when, a boy, he plied his trade,
Till on his life the sickness weighed;

And in his cell, when death drew near,
An angel in a dream brought cheer:

And rising from the sickness drear,
He grew a priest, and now stood here.   60

To the East with praise he turned,
And on his sight the angel burned.

"I bore thee from thy craftsman's cell,
And set thee here; I did not well.

"Vainly I left my angel-sphere,
Vain was thy dream of many a year.

"Thy voice's praise seemed weak; it dropped —
Creation's chorus stopped!

"Go back and praise again
The early way, while I remain.   70

"With that weak voice of our disdain,
Take up creation's pausing strain.

"Back to the cell and poor employ:
Resume the craftsman and the boy!"

Theocrite grew old at home;
A new Pope dwelt in Peter's dome.

One vanished as the other died:
They sought God side by side.

A DEATH IN THE DESERT.

[SUPPOSED of Pamphylax the Antiochene:
　It is a parchment, of my rolls the fifth,
Hath three skins glued together, is all Greek,
And goeth from *Epsilon* down to *Mu*:
Lies second in the surnamed Chosen Chest,
Stained and conserved with juice of terebinth,
Covered with cloth of hair, and lettered *Xi*,
From Xanthus, my wife's uncle, now at peace:
Mu and *Epsilon* stand for my own name,
I may not write it, but I make a cross　　　　　　10
To show I wait His coming, with the rest,
And leave off here: beginneth Pamphylax.]

I said, "If one should wet his lips with wine,
And slip the broadest plantain-leaf we find,
Or else the lappet of a linen robe,
Into the water-vessel, lay it right,
And cool his forehead just above the eyes,
The while a brother, kneeling either side,
Should chafe each hand and try to make it warm, —
He is not so far gone but he might speak."　　　20

This did not happen in the outer cave,
Nor in the secret chamber of the rock,
Where, sixty days since the decree was out,
We had him, bedded on a camel-skin,
And waited for his dying all the while;
But in the midmost grotto: since noon's light
Reached there a little, and we would not lose
The last of what might happen on his face.

I at the head, and Xanthus at the feet,
With Valens and the Boy, had lifted him,　　　30
And brought him from the chamber in the depths,
And laid him in the light where we might see:
For certain smiles began about his mouth,
And his lids moved, presageful of the end.

Beyond, and half way up the mouth o' the cave,
The Bactrian convert, having his desire,
Kept watch, and made pretence to graze a goat
That gave us milk, on rags of various herb,
Plantain and quitch, the rocks' shade keeps alive:
So that if any thief or soldier passed,　　　　40
(Because the persecution was aware)

Yielding the goat up promptly with his life,
Such man might pass on, joyful at a prize,
Nor care to pry into the cool o' the cave.
Outside was all noon and the burning blue.

" Here is wine," answered Xanthus, — dropped a drop ;
I stooped and placed the lap of cloth aright,
Then chafed his right hand, and the Boy his left :
But Valens had bethought him, and produced
And broke a ball of nard, and made perfume.   50
Only, he did — not so much wake, as — turn
And smile a little, as a sleeper does
If any dear one call him, touch his face —
And smiles and loves, but will not be disturbed.

Then Xanthus said a prayer, but still he slept :
It is the Xanthus that escaped to Rome,
Was burned, and could not write the chronicle.

Then the Boy sprang up from his knees, and ran,
Stung by the splendour of a sudden thought,
And fetched the seventh plate of graven lead   60
Out of the secret chamber, found a place,
Pressing with finger on the deeper dints,
And spoke, as 't were his mouth proclaiming first,
" I am the Resurrection and the Life."

Whereat he opened his eyes wide at once,
And sat up of himself, and looked at us ;
And thenceforth nobody pronounced a word :
Only, outside, the Bactrian cried his cry
Like the lone desert-bird that wears the ruff,
As signal we were safe, from time to time.   70

First he said, " If a friend declared to me,
This my son Valens, this my other son,
Were James and Peter, — nay, declared as well
This lad was very John, — I could believe!
— Could, for a moment, doubtlessly believe :
So is myself withdrawn into my depths,
The soul retreated from the perished brain
Whence it was wont to feel and use the world
Thro' these dull members, done with long ago.
Yet I myself remain ; I feel myself :   80
And there is nothing lost.   Let be, awhile!"

[This is the doctrine he was wont to teach,
How divers persons witness in each man,
Three souls which make up one soul : first, to wit,

A soul of each and all the bodily parts,
Seated therein, which works, and is what Does,
And has the use of earth, and ends the man
Downward: but tending upward for advice,
Grows into, and again is grown into
By the next soul, which, seated in the brain,   90
Useth the first with its collected use,
And feeleth, thinketh, willeth, — is what Knows:
Which, duly tending upward in its turn,
Grows into, and again is grown into
By the last soul, that uses both the first,
Subsisting whether they assist or no,
And, constituting man's self, is what Is —
And leans upon the former, makes it play,
As that played off the first: and, tending up,
Holds, is upheld by, God, and ends the man   100
Upward in that dread point of intercourse,
Nor needs a place, for it returns to Him,
What Does, what Knows, what Is; three souls, one man.
I give the glossa of Theotypas.]

And then, "A stick, once fire from end to end;
Now, ashes save the tip that holds a spark!
Yet, blow the spark, it runs back, spreads itself
A little where the fire was: thus I urge
The soul that served me, till it task once more
What ashes of my brain have kept their shape,   110
And these make effort on the last o' the flesh,
Trying to taste again the truth of things — "
(He smiled) — "their very superficial truth;
As that ye are my sons, that it is long
Since James and Peter had release by death,
And I am only he, your brother John,
Who saw and heard, and could remember all.
Remember all!   It is not much to say.
What if the truth broke on me from above
As once and ofttimes?   Such might hap again: 120
Doubtlessly He might stand in presence here,
With head wool-white, eyes, flame, and feet like brass,
The sword and the seven stars, as I have seen —
I who now shudder only and surmise
' How did your brother bear that sight and live?'

"If I live yet, it is for good, more love
Thro' me to men: be naught but ashes here
That keep awhile my semblance, who was John, —
Still, when they scatter, there is left on earth
No one alive who knew (consider this!)   130

—Saw with his eyes and handled with his hands
That which was from the first, the Word of Life.
How will it be when none more saith, 'I saw?'

" Such ever was love's way: to rise, it stoops.
Since I, whom Christ's mouth taught, was bidden teach,
I went, for many years, about the world,
Saying 'It was so; so I heard and saw.'
Speaking as the case asked: and men believed.
Afterward came the message to myself
In Patmos isle; I was not bidden teach,   140
But simply listen, take a book and write,
Nor set down other than the given word,
With nothing left to my arbitrament
To choose or change: I wrote, and men believed.
Then, for my time grew brief, no message more,
No call to write again, I found a way,
And, reasoning from my knowledge, merely taught
Men should, for love's sake, in love's strength, believe;
Or I would pen a letter to a friend
And urge the same as friend, nor less nor more: 150
Friends said I reasoned rightly, and believed.
But at the last, why, I seemed left alive
Like a sea-jelly weak on Patmos strand,
To tell dry sea-beach gazers how I fared
When there was mid-sea, and the mighty things;
Left to repeat, 'I saw, I heard, I knew,'
And go all over the old ground again,
With Antichrist already in the world,
And many Antichrists, who answered prompt
'Am I not Jasper as thyself art John?   160
Nay, young, whereas thro' age thou mayest forget:
Wherefore, explain, or how shall we believe?'
I never thought to call down fire on such,
Or, as in wonderful and early days,
Pick up the scorpion, tread the serpent dumb;
But patient stated much of the Lord's life
Forgotten or misdelivered, and let it work:
Since much that at the first, in deed and word,
Lay simply and sufficiently exposed,
Had grown (or else my soul was grown to match,   170
Fed thro' such years, familiar with such light,
Guarded and guided still to see and speak)
Of new significance and fresh result;
What first were guessed as points, I now knew stars,
And named them in the Gospel I have writ.
For men said, 'It is getting long ago:'
'Where is the promise of His coming?'—asked

These young ones in their strength, as loth to wait,
Of me who, when their sires were born, was old.
I, for I loved them, answered, joyfully,   180
Since I was there, and helpful in my age;
And, in the main, I think such men believed.
Finally, thus endeavouring, I fell sick,
Ye brought me here, and I supposed the end,
And went to sleep with one thought that, at least,
Tho' the whole earth should lie in wickedness,
We had the truth, might leave the rest to God.
Yet now I wake in such decrepitude
As I had slidden down and fallen afar,
Past even the presence of my former self,   190
Grasping the while for stay at facts which snap,
Till I am found away from my own world,
Feeling for foot-hold thro' a blank profound,
Along with unborn people in strange lands,
Who say — I hear said or conceive they say —
'Was John at all, and did he say he saw?
Assure us, ere we ask what he might see!'

"And how shall I assure them?   Can they share
— They, who have flesh, a veil of youth and strength
About each spirit, that needs must bide its time,   200
Living and learning still as years assist
Which wear the thickness thin, and let man see —
With me who hardly am withheld at all,
But shudderingly, scarce a shred between,
Lie bare to the universal prick of light?
Is it for nothing we grow old and weak,
We whom God loves?   When pain ends, gain ends too.
To me, that story — ay, that Life and Death
Of which I wrote 'it was' — to me, it is;
— Is, here and now: I apprehend naught else.   210
Is not God now i' the world His power first made?
Is not His love at issue still with sin,
Visibly when a wrong is done on earth?
Love, wrong, and pain, what see I else around?
Yea, and the Resurrection and Uprise
To the right hand of the throne — what is it beside,
When such truth, breaking bounds, o'erfloods my soul,
And, as I saw the sin and death, even so
See I the need yet transiency of both,
The good and glory consummated thence?   220
I saw the Power; I see the Love, once weak,
Resume the Power: and in this word 'I see,'
Lo, there is recognized the Spirit of both
That moving o'er the spirit of man, unblinds

His eye and bids him look.   These are, I see;
But ye, the children, His beloved ones too,
Ye need, — as I should use an optic glass
I wondered at erewhile, somewhere i' the world,
It had been given a crafty smith to make ;
A tube, he turned on objects brought too close,   230
Lying confusedly insubordinate
For the unassisted eye to master once :
Look thro' his tube, at distance now they lay,
Become succinct, distinct, so small, so clear!
Just thus, ye needs must apprehend what truth
I see, reduced to plain historic fact,
Diminished into clearness, proved a point
And far away : ye would withdraw your sense
From out eternity, strain it upon time,
Then stand before that fact, that Life and Death,   240
Stay there at gaze, till it dispart, dispread,
As tho' a star should open out, all sides,
Grow the world on you, as it is my world.

" For life, with all it yields of joy and woe,
And hope and fear, — believe the aged friend, —
Is just our chance o' the prize of learning love,
How love might be, hath been indeed, and is ;
And that we hold thenceforth to the uttermost
Such prize despite the envy of the world,
And, having gained truth, keep truth : that is all.   250
But see the double way wherein we are led,
How the soul learns diversely from the flesh!
With flesh, that hath so little time to stay,
And yields mere basement for the soul's emprise,
Expect prompt teaching.   Helpful was the light,
And warmth was cherishing and food was choice
To every man's flesh, thousand years ago,
As now to yours and mine ; the body sprang
At once to the height, and stayed : but the soul, — no!
Since sages who, this noontide, meditate   260
In Rome or Athens, may descry some point
Of the eternal power, hid yestereve :
And, as thereby the power's whole mass extends,
So much extends the æther floating o'er
The love that tops the might, the Christ in God.
Then, as new lessons shall be learned in these
Till earth's work stop and useless time run out,
So duly, daily, needs provision be
For keeping the soul's prowess possible,
Building new barriers as the old decay,   270
Saving us from evasion of life's proof,

Putting the question ever, 'Does God love,
And will ye hold that truth against the world?'
Ye know there needs no second proof with good
Gained for our flesh from any earthly source:
We might go freezing, ages, — give us fire,
Thereafter we judge fire at its full worth,
And guard it safe thro' every chance, ye know!
That fable of Prometheus and his theft,
How mortals gained Jove's fiery flower, grows old   280
(I have been used to hear the pagans own)
And out of mind; but fire, howe'er its birth,
Here is it, precious to the sophist now
Who laughs the myth of Æschylus to scorn,
As precious to those satyrs of his play,
Who touched it in gay wonder at the thing.
While were it so with the soul, — this gift of truth
Once grasped, were this our soul's gain safe, and sure
To prosper as the body's gain is wont, —
Why, man's probation would conclude, his earth   290
Crumble; for he both reasons and decides,
Weighs first, then chooses: will he give up fire
For gold or purple once he knows its worth?
Could he give Christ up were His worth as plain?
Therefore, I say, to test man, the proofs shift,
Nor may he grasp that fact like other fact,
And straightway in his life acknowledge it,
As, say, the indubitable bliss of fire.
Sigh ye, 'It had been easier once than now?'
To give you answer I am left alive;   300
Look at me who was present from the first!
Ye know what things I saw; then came a test,
My first, befitting me who so had seen:
'Forsake the Christ thou sawest transfigured, Him
Who trod the sea and brought the dead to life?
What should wring this from thee!'—ye laugh and ask.
What wrung it?   Even a torchlight and a noise,
The sudden Roman faces, violent hands,
And fear of what the Jews might do!   Just that,
And it is written, 'I forsook and fled;'   310
There was my trial, and it ended thus.
Ay, but my soul had gained its truth, could grow:
Another year or two, — what little child,
What tender woman that had seen no least
Of all my sights, but barely heard them told,
Who did not clasp the cross with a light laugh,
Or wrap the burning robe round, thanking God?
Well, was truth safe for ever, then?   Not so,
Already had begun the silent work

Whereby truth, deadened of its absolute blaze, 320
Might need love's eye to pierce the o'erstretched doubt.
Teachers were busy, whispering ' All is true
As the aged ones report ; but youth can reach
Where age gropes dimly, weak with stir and strain,
And the full doctrine slumbers till to-day.'
Thus, what the Roman's lowered spear was found,
A bar to me who touched and handled truth,
Now proved the glozing of some new shrewd tongue,
This Ebion, this Cerinthus or their mates,
Till imminent was the outcry ' Save our Christ!' 330
Whereon I stated much of the Lord's life
Forgotten or misdelivered, and let it work.
Such work done, as it will be, what comes next?
What do I hear say, or conceive men say,
'Was John at all, and did he say he saw?
Assure us, ere we ask what he might see!'

"Is this indeed a burthen for late days,
And may I help to bear it with you all,
Using my weakness which becomes your strength?
For if a babe were born inside this grot, 340
Grew to a boy here, heard us praise the sun,
Yet had but yon sole glimmer in light's place,—
One loving him and wishful he should learn,
Would much rejoice himself was blinded first
Month by month here, so made to understand
How eyes, born darkling, apprehend amiss :
I think I could explain to such a child
There was more glow outside than gleams he caught,
Ay, nor need urge ' I saw it, so believe!'
It is a heavy burthen you shall bear 350
In latter days, new lands, or old grown strange,
Left without me, which must be very soon.
What is the doubt, my brothers? Quick with it!
I see you stand conversing, each new face,
Either in fields, of yellow summer eves,
On islets yet unnamed amid the sea ;
Or pace for shelter 'neath a portico
Out of the crowd in some enormous town
Where now the larks sing in a solitude ;
Or muse upon blank heaps of stone and sand 360
Idly conjectured to be Ephesus ;
And no one asks his fellow any more
'Where is the promise of His coming?' but
'Was he revealed in any of His lives,
As Power, as Love, as Influencing Soul?'

" Quick, for time presses, tell the whole mind out,
And let us ask and answer and be saved!
My book speaks on, because it can not pass;
One listens quietly, nor scoffs but pleads
'Here is a tale of things done ages since;   370
What truth was ever told the second day?
Wonders, that would prove doctrine, go for naught.
Remains the doctrine, love; well, we must love,
And what we love most, power and love in one,
Let us acknowledge on the record here,
Accepting these in Christ: must Christ then be?
Has He been? Did not we ourselves make Him?
Our mind receives but what it holds, no more.
First of the love, then; we acknowledge Christ —
A proof we comprehend His love, a proof   380
We had such love already in ourselves,
Knew first what else we should not recognize.
'T is mere projection from man's inmost mind,
And, what he loves, thus falls reflected back,
Becomes accounted somewhat out of him;
He throws it up in air, it drops down earth's,
With shape, name, story added, man's old way.
How prove you Christ came otherwise at least?
Next try the power: He made and rules the world:
Certes there is a world once made, now ruled,   390
Unless things have been ever as we see.
Our sires declared a charioteer's yoked steeds
Brought the sun up the east and down the west,
Which only of itself now rises, sets,
As if a hand impelled it and a will, —
Thus they long thought, they who had will and hands:
But the new question's whisper is distinct,
Wherefore must all force needs be like ourselves?
We have the hands, the will; what made and drives
The sun is force, is law, is named, not known,   400
While will and love we do know; marks of these,
Eye-witnesses attest, so books declare —
As that, to punish or reward our race,
The sun at undue times arose or set
Or else stood still: what do not men affirm?
But earth requires as urgently reward
Or punishment to-day as years ago,
And none expects the sun will interpose:
Therefore it was mere passion and mistake,
Or erring zeal for right, which changed the truth.   410
Go back, far, farther, to the birth of things;
Ever the will, the intelligence, the love,
Man's! — which he gives, supposing he but finds,

As late he gave head, body, hands and feet,
To help these in what forms he called his gods.
First, Jove's brow, Juno's eyes were swept away,
But Jove's wrath, Juno's pride continued long!
At last, will, power, and love discarded these,
So law in turn discards power, love, and will.
What proveth God is otherwise at least?   420
All else, projection from the mind of man!'

" Nay, do not give me wine, for I am strong,
But place my gospel where I put my hands.

" I say that man was made to grow, not stop;
That help, he needed once, and needs no more,
Having grown but an inch by, is withdrawn:
For he hath new deeds, and new helps to these.
This imports solely, man should mount on each
New height in view; the help whereby he mounts,
The ladder-rung his foot has left, may fall,   430
Since all things suffer change save God the Truth.
Man apprehends Him newly at each stage
Whereat earth's ladder drops, its service done;
And nothing shall prove twice what once was proved.
You stick a garden-plot with ordered twigs
To show inside lie germs of herbs unborn,
And check the careless step would spoil their birth;
But when herbs wave, the guardian twigs may go,
Since should ye doubt of virtues, question kinds,
It is no longer for old twigs ye look,   440
Which proved once underneath lay store of seed,
But to the herb's self, by what light ye boast,
For what fruit's signs are.   This book's fruit is plain,
Nor miracles need prove it any more.
Doth the fruit show?   Then miracles bade 'ware
At first of root and stem, saved both till now
From trampling ox, rough boar and wanton goat.
What?   Was man made a wheelwork to wind up,
And be discharged, and straight wound up anew?
No! — grown, his growth lasts; taught, he ne'er forgets   450
May learn a thousand things, not twice the same.

" This might be pagan teaching: now hear mine.

" I say, that as the babe, you feed awhile,
Becomes a boy and fit to feed himself,
So, minds at first must be spoon-fed with truth:
When they can eat, babe's nurture is withdrawn.
I fed the babe whether it would or no:
I bid the boy or feed himself or starve.

I cried once, 'That ye may believe in Christ,
Behold this blind man shall receive his sight!'   460
I cry now, 'Urgest thou, *for I am shrewd*
And smile at stories how John's word could cure—
Repeat that miracle and take my faith?'
I say, that miracle was duly wrought
When, save for it, no faith was possible.
Whether a change were wrought i' the shows o' the
          world,
Whether the change came from our minds which see
Of shows o' the world so much as and no more
Than God wills for His purpose,—(what do I
See now, suppose you, there where you see rock   470
Round us?)—I know not; such was the effect,
So faith grew, making void more miracles
Because too much: they would compel, not help.
I say, the acknowledgment of God in Christ
Accepted by thy reason, solves for thee
All questions in the earth and out of it,
And has so far advanced thee to be wise.
Wouldst thou unprove this to re-prove the proved?
In life's mere minute, with power to use that proof,
Leave knowledge and revert to how it sprung?   480
Thou hast it; use it and forthwith, or die!

"For I say, this is death and the sole death,
When a man's loss comes to him from his gain,
Darkness from light, from knowledge ignorance,
And lack of love from love made manifest;
A lamp's death when, replete with oil, it chokes;
A stomach's when, surcharged with food, it starves.
With ignorance was surety of a cure,
When man, appalled at nature, questioned first
'What if there lurk a might behind this might?'   490
He needed satisfaction God could give,
And did give, as ye have the written word:
But when he finds might still redouble might,
Yet asks, 'Since all is might, what use of will?'
—Will, the one source of might,—he being man
With a man's will and a man's might, to teach
In little how the two combine in large,—
That man has turned round on himself and stands:
Which in the course of nature is, to die.

"And when man questioned, 'What if there be love   500
Behind the will and might, as real as they?'—
He needed satisfaction God could give,
And did give, as ye have the written word:

But when, beholding that love everywhere,
He reasons, ' Since such love is everywhere,
And since ourselves can love and would be loved,
We ourselves make the love, and Christ was not,' —
How shall ye help this man who knows himself,
That he must love and would be loved again,
Yet, owning his own love that proveth Christ,   510
Rejecteth Christ thro' very need of Him?
The lamp o'erswims with oil, the stomach flags
Loaded with nurture, and that man's soul dies.

" If he rejoin, ' But this was all the while
A trick ; the fault was, first of all, in thee,
Thy story of the places, names and dates,
Where, when and how the ultimate truth had rise,
— Thy prior truth, at last discovered none,
Whence now the second suffers detriment.
What good of giving knowledge if, because   520
O' the manner of the gift, its profit fail?
And why refuse what modicum of help
Had stopped the after-doubt, impossible
I' the face of truth — truth absolute, uniform?
Why must I hit of this and miss of that,
Distinguish just as I be weak or strong,
And not ask of thee and have answer prompt,
Was this once, was it not once? — then and now
And evermore, plain truth from man to man.
Is John's procedure just the heathen bard's?   530
Put question of his famous play again
How for the ephemerals' sake, Jove's fire was filched,
And carried in a cane and brought to earth :
The fact is in the fable, cry the wise,
Mortals obtained the boon, so much is fact,
Tho' fire be spirit and produced on earth.
As with the Titan's, so now with thy tale :
Why breed in us perplexity, mistake,
Nor tell the whole truth in the proper words?

" I answer, Have ye yet to argue out   540
The very primal thesis, plainest law,
— Man is not God but hath God's end to serve,
A master to obey, a course to take,
Somewhat to cast off, somewhat to become?
Grant this, then man must pass from old to new,
From vain to real, from mistake to fact,
From what once seemed good, to what now proves best :
How could man have progression otherwise?
Before the point was mooted ' What is God?'

2 E

No savage man inquired 'What am myself?'   550
Much less replied, 'First, last, and best of things.'
Man takes that title now if he believes
Might can exist with neither will nor love,
In God's case — what he names now Nature's Law —
While in himself he recognizes love
No less than might and will: and rightly takes.
Since if man prove the sole existent thing
Where these combine, whatever their degree,
However weak the might or will or love,
So they be found there, put in evidence, —   560
He is as surely higher in the scale
Than any might with neither love nor will,
As life, apparent in the poorest midge,
(When the faint dust-speck flits, ye guess its wing)
Is marvellous beyond dead Atlas' self —
Given to the nobler midge for resting-place!
Thus, man proves best and highest — God, in fine,
And thus the victory leads but to defeat,
The gain to loss, best rise to the worst fall,
His life becomes impossible, which is death.   570

"But if, appealing thence, he cower, avouch
He is mere man, and in humility
Neither may know God nor mistake himself;
I point to the immediate consequence
And say, by such confession straight he falls
Into man's place, a thing nor God nor beast,
Made to know that he can know and not more:
Lower than God who knows all and can all,
Higher than beasts which know and can so far
As each beast's limit, perfect to an end,   580
Nor conscious that they know, nor craving more;
While man knows partly but conceives beside,
Creeps ever on from fancies to the fact,
And in this striving, this converting air
Into a solid he may grasp and use,
Finds progress, man's distinctive mark alone,
Not God's, and not the beasts': God is, they are,
Man partly is and wholly hopes to be.
Such progress could no more attend his soul
Were all it struggles after found at first   590
And guesses changed to knowledge absolute,
Than motion wait his body, were all else
Than it the solid earth on every side,
Where now thro' space he moves from rest to rest.
Man, therefore, thus conditioned, must expect
He could not, what he knows now, know at first;

What he considers that he knows to-day,
Come but to-morrow, he will find misknown;
Getting increase of knowledge, since he learns
Because he lives, which is to be a man, 600
Set to instruct himself by his past self:
First, like the brute, obliged by facts to learn,
Next, as man may, obliged by his own mind,
Bent, habit, nature, knowledge turned to law.
God's gift was that man should conceive of truth
And yearn to gain it, catching at mistake,
As midway help till he reach fact indeed.
The statuary ere he mould a shape
Boasts a like gift, the shape's idea, and next
The aspiration to produce the same; 610
So, taking clay, he calls his shape thereout,
Cries ever, 'Now I have the thing I see:'
Yet all the while goes changing what was wrought,
From falsehood like the truth, to truth itself.
How were it had he cried 'I see no face,
No breast, no feet i' the ineffectual clay?'
Rather commend him that he clapped his hands,
And laughed 'It is my shape and lives again!'
Enjoyed the falsehood, touched it on to truth,
Until yourselves applaud the flesh indeed 620
In what is still flesh-imitating clay.
Right in you, right in him, such way be man's!
God only makes the live shape at a jet.
Will ye renounce this pact of creatureship?
The pattern on the Mount subsists no more,
Seemed awhile, then returned to nothingness;
But copies, Moses strove to make thereby,
Serve still and are replaced as time requires:
By these, make newest vessels, reach the type!
If ye demur, this judgment on your head, 630
Never to reach the ultimate, angels' law,
Indulging every instinct of the soul
There where law, life, joy, impulse are one thing!

"Such is the burthen of the latest time.
I have survived to hear it with my ears,
Answer it with my lips: does this suffice?
For if there be a further woe than such,
Wherein my brothers struggling need a hand,
So long as any pulse is left in mine,
May I be absent even longer yet, 640
Plucking the blind ones back from the abyss,
Tho' I should tarry a new hundred years!"

But he was dead: 't was about noon, the day
Somewhat declining: we five buried him
That eve, and then, dividing, went five ways,
And I, disguised, returned to Ephesus.

By this, the cave's mouth must be filled with sand.
Valens is lost, I know not of his trace;
The Bactrian was but a wild childish man,
And could not write nor speak, but only loved: 650
So, lest the memory of this go quite,
Seeing that I to-morrow fight the beasts,
I tell the same to Phœbas, whom believe!
For many look again to find that face,
Beloved John's to whom I ministered,
Somewhere in life about the world; they err:
Either mistaking what was darkly spoke
At ending of his book, as he relates,
Or misconceiving somewhat of this speech
Scattered from mouth to mouth, as I suppose.   660
Believe ye will not see him any more
About the world with his divine regard!
For all was as I say, and now the man
Lies as he lay once, breast to breast with God.

―――――

[Cerinthus read and mused; one added this:

"If Christ, as thou affirmest, be of men
Mere man, the first and best but nothing more,—
Account Him, for reward of what He was,
Now and forever, wretchedest of all.
For see; Himself conceived of life as love,   670
Conceived of love as what must enter in,
Fill up, make one with His each soul He loved:
Thus much for man's joy, all men's joy for Him.
Well, He is gone, thou sayest, to fit reward.
But by this time are many souls set free,
And very many still retained alive:
Nay, should His coming be delayed awhile,
Say, ten years longer (twelve years, some compute)
See if, for every finger of thy hands,
There be not found, that day the world shall end,   680
Hundreds of souls, each holding by Christ's word
That He will grow incorporate with all,
With me as Pamphylax, with him as John,
Groom for each bride!   Can a mere man do this?
Yet Christ saith, this He lived and died to do.

Call Christ, then, the illimitable God,
Or lost!"

But 't was Cerinthus that is lost.]

———◦∘◦———

FEARS AND SCRUPLES.

I.

HERE'S my case.   Of old I used to love him,
   This same unseen friend, before I knew:
Dream there was none like him, none above him, —
   Wake to hope and trust my dream was true.

II.

Loved I not his letters full of beauty?
   Not his actions famous far and wide?
Absent, he would know I vowed him duty,
   Present, he would find me at his side.

III.

Pleasant fancy! for I had but letters,
   Only knew of actions by hearsay:
He himself was busied with my betters;
   What of that?   My turn must come some day.

IV.

"Some day" proving — no day!   Here 's the puzzle.
   Passed and passed my turn is.   Why complain?
He 's so busied!   If I could but muzzle
   People's foolish mouths that give me pain!

V.

"Letters?" (hear them!)   "You a judge of writing?
   Ask the experts! — How they shake the head
O'er these characters, your friend's inditing —
   Call them forgery from A to Z!

VI.

"Actions?   Where 's your certain proof" (they bother)
   "He, of all you find so great and good,
He, he only, claims this, that, the other
   Action — claimed by men, a multitude?"

VII.

I can simply wish I might refute you,
  Wish my friend would, — by a word, a wink, —
Bid me stop that foolish mouth, — you brute you!
  He keeps absent, — why, I can not think.

VIII.

Never mind! Tho' foolishness may flout me,
  One thing 's sure enough : 't is neither frost,   30
No, nor fire, shall freeze or burn from out me
  Thanks for truth — tho' falsehood, gained — tho' lost

IX.

All my days, I 'll go the softlier, sadlier,
  For that dream's sake!   How forget the thrill
Thro' and thro' me as I thought " The gladlier
  Lives my friend because I love him still!"

X.

Ah, but there 's a menace some one utters!
  "What and if your friend at home play tricks?
Peep at hide-and-seek behind the shutters?
  Mean your eyes should pierce thro' solid bricks?   40

XI.

"What and if he, frowning, wake you, dreamy?
  Lay on you the blame that bricks — conceal?
Say '*At least I saw who did not see me,*
  Does see now, and presently shall feel'?"

XII.

"Why, that makes your friend a monster!" say you :
  "Had his house no window?   At first nod,
Would you not have hailed him?"   Hush, I pray you!
  What if this friend happen to be — God?

———•◦•———

ARTEMIS PROLOGIZES.

I AM a goddess of the ambrosial courts,
  And save by Here, Queen of Pride, surpassed
By none whose temples whiten this the world.
Thro' heaven I roll my lucid moon along;

I shed in hell o'er my pale people peace;
On earth I, caring for the creatures, guard
Each pregnant yellow wolf and fox-bitch sleek,
And every feathered mother's callow brood,
And all that love green haunts and loneliness.
Of men, the chaste adore me, hanging crowns   10
Of poppies red to blackness, bell and stem,
Upon my image at Athenai here;
And this dead youth, Asclepios bends above,
Was dearest to me.   He, my buskined step
To follow thro' the wild-wood leafy ways,
And chase the panting stag, or swift with darts
Stop the swift ounce, or lay the leopard low.
Neglected homage to another god:
Whence Aphrodite, by no midnight smoke
Of tapers lulled, in jealousy despatched   20
A noisome lust that, as the gadbee stings,
Possessed his stepdame Phaidra for himself
The son of Theseus her great absent spouse.
Hippolutos exclaiming in his rage
Against the fury of the Queen, she judged
Life insupportable; and, pricked at heart
An Amazonian stranger's race should dare
To scorn her, perished by the murderous cord:
Yet, ere she perished, blasted in a scroll
The fame of him her swerving made not swerve.   30
And Theseus read, returning, and believed,
And exiled, in the blindness of his wrath,
The man without a crime who, last as first,
Loyal, divulged not to his sire the truth.
Now Theseus from Poseidon had obtained
That of his wishes should be granted three,
And one he imprecated straight—"Alive
May ne'er Hippolutos reach other lands!"
Poseidon heard, ai ai!   And scarce the prince
Had stepped into the fixed boots of the car   40
That give the feet stay against the strength
Of the Henetian horses, and around
His body flung the rein, and urged their speed
Along the rocks and shingles of the shore,
When from the gaping wave a monster flung
His obscene body in the coursers' path.
These, mad with terror, as the sea-bull sprawled
Wallowing about their feet, lost care of him
That reared them; and the master-chariot-pole
Snapping beneath their plunges like a reed,   50
Hippolutos, whose feet were trammeled fast,
Was yet dragged forward by the circling rein

Which either hand directed; nor they quenched
The frenzy of their flight before each trace,
Wheel-spoke and splinter of the woeful car,
Each boulder-stone, sharp stub and spiny shell,
Huge fish-bone wrecked and wreathed amid the sands
On that detested beach, was bright with blood
And morsels of his flesh : then fell the steeds
Head-foremost, crashing in their mooned fronts,   60
Shivering with sweat, each white eye horror-fixed.
His people, who had witnessed all afar,
Bore back the ruins of Hippolutos.
But when his sire, too swoln with pride, rejoiced
(Indomitable as a man foredoomed)
That vast Poseidon had fulfilled his prayer,
I, in a flood of glory visible,
Stood o'er my dying votary and, deed
By deed, revealed, as all took place, the truth.
Then Theseus lay the woefullest of men,   70
And worthily; but ere the death-veils hid
His face, the murdered prince full pardon breathed
To his rash sire.   Whereat Athenai wails.

So I, who ne'er forsake my votaries,
Lest in the cross-way none the honey-cake
Should tender, nor pour out the dog's hot life;
Lest at my fane the priests disconsolate
Should dress my image with some faded poor
Few crowns, made favours of, nor dare object
Such slackness to my worshipers who turn   80
Elsewhere the trusting heart and loaded hand,
As they had climbed Olumpos to report
Of Artemis and nowhere found her throne —
I interposed : and, this eventful night, —
(While round the funeral pyre the populace
Stood with fierce light on their black robes which bound
Each sobbing head, while yet their hair they clipped
O'er the dead body of their withered prince,
And, in his palace, Theseus prostrated
On the cold hearth, his brow cold as the slab   90
'T was bruised on, groaned away the heavy grief—
As the pyre fell, and down the cross-logs crashed
Sending a crowd of sparkles thro' the night,
And the gay fire, elate with mastery,
Towered like a serpent o'er the clotted jars
Of wine, dissolving oils and frankincense,
And splendid gums like gold), — my potency
Conveyed the perished man to my retreat
In the thrice-venerable forest here.

And this white-bearded sage who squeezes now   100
The berried plant, is Phoibos' son of fame,
Asclepios, whom my radiant brother taught
The doctrine of each herb and flower and root,
To know their secret'st virtue and express
The saving soul of all: who so has soothed
With lavers the torn brow and murdered cheeks,
Composed the hair and brought its gloss again,
And called the red bloom to the pale skin back,
And laid the strips and jagged ends of flesh
Even once more, and slacked the sinew's knot   110
Of every tortured limb — that now he lies
As if mere sleep possessed him underneath
These interwoven oaks and pines. Oh cheer,
Divine presenter of the healing rod,
Thy snake, with ardent throat and lulling eye,
Twines his lithe spires around! I say, much cheer!
Proceed thou with thy wisest pharmacies!
And ye, white crowd of woodland sister-nymphs,
Ply as the sage directs, these buds and leaves
That strew the turf around the twain! While I   120
Await, in fitting silence, the event.

PHEIDIPPIDES.

χαίρετε, νικῶμεν.

FIRST I salute this soil of the blessed, river and rock!
   Gods of my birthplace, dæmons and heroes, honour to all!
Then I name thee, claim thee for our patron, co-equal in praise
— Ay, with Zeus the Defender, with Her of the ægis and spear!
Also, ye of the bow and the buskin, praised be your peer,
Now, henceforth and forever, — O latest to whom I upraise
Hand and heart and voice! For Athens, leave pasture and flock!
Present to help, potent to save, Pan — patron I call!

Archons of Athens, topped by the tettix, see, I return!
See, 't is myself here standing alive, no spectre that speaks!   10
Crowned with the myrtle, did you command me, Athens and you,
" Run, Pheidippides, run and race, reach Sparta for aid!
Persia has come, we are here, where is She?" Your command I
   obeyed,
Ran and raced: like stubble, some field which a fire runs through,
Was the space between city and city: two days, two nights did I burn
Over the hills, under the dales, down pits and up peaks.

Into their midst I broke: breath served but for "Persia has come.
Persia bids Athens proffer slaves'-tribute, water and earth;
Razed to the ground is Eretria — but Athens, shall Athens sink,
Drop into dust and die — the flower of Hellas utterly die,   20
Die with the wide world spitting at Sparta, the stupid, the stander-by?
Answer me quick, what help, what hand do you stretch o'er destruction's
    brink?
How, — when?   No care for my limbs! — there 's lightning in all and
    some —
Fresh and fit your message to bear, once lips give it birth!"

O my Athens — Sparta love thee?   Did Sparta respond?
Every face of her leered in a furrow of envy, mistrust,
Malice, — each eye of her gave me its glitter of gratified hate!
Gravely they turned to take counsel, to cast for excuses.   I stood
Quivering, — the limbs of me fretting as fire frets, an inch from dry
    wood:
"Persia has come, Athens asks aid, and still they debate?   30
Thunder, thou Zeus!   Athene, are Spartans a quarry beyond
Swing of thy spear?   Phoibos and Artemis, clang them ' Ye must'!"

No bolt launched from Olumpos!   Lo, their answer at last!
"Has Persia come, — does Athens ask aid, — may Sparta befriend?
Nowise precipitate judgment — too weighty the issue at stake!
Count we no time lost time which lags thro' respect to the Gods!
Ponder that precept of old, 'No warfare, whatever the odds
In your favour, so long as the moon, half-orbed, is unable to take
Full-circle her state in the sky!'   Already she rounds to it fast:
Athens must wait, patient as we — who judgment suspend."   40

Athens, — except for that sparkle, — thy name, I had mouldered to ash!
That sent a blaze thro' my blood; off, off and away was I back,
— Not one word to waste, one look to lose on the false and the vile!
Yet "O Gods of my land!" I cried, as each hillock and plain,
Wood and stream, I knew, I named, rushing past them again,
"Have ye kept faith, proved mindful of honours we paid you erewhile?
Vain was the filleted victim, the fulsome libation!   Too rash
Love in its choice, paid you so largely service so slack!

"Oak and olive and bay, — I bid you cease to enwreathe
Brows made bold by your leaf!   Fade at the Persian's foot,   50
You that, our patrons were pledged, should never adorn a slave!
Rather I hail thee, Parnes, — trust to thy wild waste tract!
Treeless, herbless, lifeless mountain!   What matter if slacked
My speed may hardly be, for homage to crag and to cave
No deity deigns to drape with verdure? — at least I can breathe,
Fear in thee no fraud from the blind, no lie from the mute!"

Such my cry as, rapid, I ran over Parnes' ridge;
Gully and gap I clambered and cleared till, sudden, a bar
Jutted, a stoppage of stone against me, blocking the way.
Right! for I minded the hollow to traverse, the fissure across: 60
"Where I could enter, there I depart by!   Night in the fosse?
Athens to aid?   Tho' the dive were thro' Erebos, thus I obey —
Out of the day dive, into the day as bravely arise!   No bridge
Better!" — when — ha! what was it I came on, of wonders that are?

There, in the cool of a cleft, sat he — majestical Pan!
Ivy drooped wanton, kissed his head, moss cushioned his hoof;
All the great God was good in the eyes grave-kindly — the curl
Carved on the bearded cheek, amused at a mortal's awe
As, under the human trunk, the goat-thighs grand I saw.
"Halt, Pheidippides!" — halt I did, my brain of a whirl: 70
"Hither to me!   Why pale in my presence?" he gracious began:
"How is it, — Athens, only in Hellas, holds me aloof?

"Athens, she only, rears me no fane, makes me no feast!
Wherefore?   Than I what godship to Athens more helpful of old?
Ay, and still, and forever her friend!   Test Pan, trust me!
Go, bid Athens take heart, laugh Persia to scorn, have faith
In the temples and tombs!   Go, say to Athens, 'The Goat-God
    saith:
When Persia — so much as strews not the soil — is cast in the sea,
Then praise Pan who fought in the ranks with your most and least,
Goat-thigh to greaved-thigh, made one cause with the free and the
    bold!' 80

"Say Pan saith: 'Let this, foreshowing the place, be the pledge!'"
(Gay, the liberal hand held out this herbage I bear
— Fennel, — I grasped it a-tremble with dew — whatever it bode),
"While, as for thee . . ."   But enough!   He was gone.   If I ran
    hitherto —
Be sure that the rest of my journey, I ran no longer, but flew.
Parnes to Athens — earth no more, the air was my road;
Here am I back.   Praise Pan, we stand no more on the razor's
    edge!
Pan for Athens, Pan for me!   I too have a guerdon rare!

Then spoke Miltiades.   "And thee, best runner of Greece,
Whose limbs did duty indeed, — what gift is promised thyself? 90
Tell it us straightway, — Athens the mother demands of her son!"
Rosily blushed the youth: he paused: but, lifting at length
His eyes from the ground, it seemed as he gathered the rest of his
    strength

Into the utterance — "Pan spoke thus : 'For what thou hast done
Count on a worthy reward! Henceforth be allowed thee release
From the racer's toil, no vulgar reward in praise or in pelf !'

"I am bold to believe, Pan means reward the most to my mind!
Fight I shall, with our foremost, wherever this fennel may grow, —
Pound — Pan helping us — Persia to dust, and, under the deep,
Whelm her away forever ; and then, — no Athens to save, —   100
Marry a certain maid, I know keeps faith to the brave, —
Hie to my house and home : and, when my children shall creep
Close to my knees, — recount how the God was awful yet kind,
Promised their sire reward to the full — rewarding him — so!"

Unforeseeing one! Yes, he fought on the Marathon day :
So, when Persia was dust, all cried "To Akropolis!
Run, Pheidippides, one race more! the meed is thy due!
'Athens is saved, thank Pan,' go shout!" He flung down his shield,
Ran like fire once more : and the space 'twixt the Fennel-field
And Athens was stubble again, a field which a fire runs through,   110
Till in he broke : "Rejoice, we conquer!" Like wine thro' clay,
Joy in his blood bursting his heart, he died — the bliss!

So, to this day, when friend meets friend, the word of salute
Is still "Rejoice!" — his word which brought rejoicing indeed.
So is Pheidippides happy forever, — the noble strong man
Who could race like a god, bear the face of a god, whom a god loved so
       well,
He saw the land saved he had helped to save, and was suffered to tell
Such tidings, yet never decline, but, gloriously as he began,
So to end gloriously — once to shout, thereafter be mute :
"Athens is saved!" — Pheidippides dies in the shout for his meed.   120

THE PATRIOT.

AN OLD STORY.

I.

IT was roses, roses, all the way,
   With myrtle mixed in my path like mad :
The house-roofs seemed to heave and sway,
   The church-spires flamed, such flags they had,
A year ago on this very day.

II.

The air broke into a mist with bells,
　The old walls rocked with the crowd and cries.
Had I said, "Good folk, mere noise repels—
　But give me your sun from yonder skies!"
They had answered "And afterward, what else?"　　10

III.

Alack, it was I who leaped at the sun
　To give it my loving friends to keep!
Naught man could do, have I left undone:
　And you see my harvest, what I reap
This very day, now a year is run.

IV.

There's nobody on the house-tops now—
　Just a palsied few at the windows set;
For the best of the sight is, all allow,
　At the Shambles' Gate—or, better yet,
By the very scaffold's foot, I trow.　　20

V.

I go in the rain, and, more than needs,
　A rope cuts both my wrists behind;
And I think, by the feel, my forehead bleeds,
　For they fling, whoever has a mind,
Stones at me for my year's misdeeds.

VI.

Thus I entered, and thus I go!
　In triumphs, people have dropped down dead.
"Paid by the world, what dost thou owe
　Me?"—God might question; now instead,
'T is God shall repay: I am safer so.　　30

———◦•◦———

POPULARITY.

I.

STAND still, true poet that you are!
　I know you; let me try and draw you.
Some night you'll fail us: when afar
　You rise, remember one man saw you,
Knew you, and named a star!

II.

My star, God's glow-worm!   Why extend
    That loving hand of his which leads you,
Yet locks you safe from end to end
    Of this dark world, unless he needs you,
Just saves your light to spend?   10

III.

His clenched hand shall unclose at last,
    I know, and let out all the beauty:
My poet holds the future fast,
    Accepts the coming ages' duty,
Their present for this past.

IV.

That day, the earth's feast-master's brow
    Shall clear, to God the chalice raising:
"Others give best at first, but thou
    For ever set'st our table praising,
Keep'st the good wine till now!"   20

V.

Meantime, I 'll draw you as you stand,
    With few or none to watch and wonder:
I 'll say — a fisher, on the sand
    By Tyre the old, with ocean-plunder,
A netful, brought to land.

VI.

Who has not heard how Tyrian shells
    Enclosed the blue, that dye of dyes
Whereof one drop worked miracles,
    And coloured like Astarte's eyes
Raw silk the merchant sells?   30

VII.

And each bystander of them all
    Could criticize, and quote tradition
How depths of blue sublimed some pall
    — To get which, pricked a king's ambition;
Worth sceptre, crown and ball.

VIII.

Yet there 's the dye, in that rough mesh,
  The sea has only just o'er-whispered!
Live whelks, each lip's beard dripping fresh,
  As if they still the water's lisp heard
Thro' foam the rock-weeds thresh. 40

IX.

Enough to furnish Solomon
  Such hangings for his cedar-house,
That, when gold-robed he took the throne
  In that abyss of blue, the Spouse
Might swear his presence shone

X.

Most like the centre-spike of gold
  Which burns deep in the blue-bell's womb
What time, with ardours manifold,
  The bee goes singing to her groom,
Drunken and overbold. 50

XI.

Mere conchs! not fit for warp or woof!
  Till cunning come to pound and squeeze
And clarify, — refine to proof
  The liquor filtered by degrees,
While the world stands aloof.

XII.

And there 's the extract, flasked and fine,
  And priced and saleable at last!
And Hobbs, Nobbs, Stokes and Nokes combine
  To paint the future from the past,
Put blue into their line. 60

XIII.

Hobbs hints blue, — straight he turtle eats:
  Nobbs prints blue, — claret crowns his cup:
Nokes outdares Stokes in azure feats, —
  Both gorge.   Who fished the murex up?
What porridge had John Keats?

PISGAH–SIGHTS. 1.

I.

OVER the ball of it,
 Peering and prying,
How I see all of it,
 Life there, outlying!
Roughness and smoothness,
 Shine and defilement,
Grace and uncouthness;
 One reconcilement.

II.

Orbed as appointed,
 Sister with brother
Joins, ne'er disjointed
 One from the other.
All 's lend-and-borrow;
 Good, see, wants evil,
Jcy demands sorrow,
 Angel weds devil!

10

III.

" Which things must — *why* be?"
 Vain our endeavour!
So shall things aye be
 As they were ever.
" Such things should *so* be!"
 Sage our desistence!
Rough-smooth let globe be,
 Mixed — man's existence!

20

IV.

Man — wise and foolish,
 Lover and scorner,
Docile and mulish —
 Keep each his corner!
Honey yet gall of it!
 There 's the life lying,
And I see all of it,
 Only, I 'm dying!

30

PISGAH-SIGHTS. 2.

I.

COULD I but live again,
 Twice my life over,
Would I once strive again?
 Would not I cover
Quietly all of it —
 Greed and ambition —
So, from the pall of it,
 Pass to fruition?

II.

"Soft!" I'd say, "Soul mine!
 Three-score and ten years,   10
Let the blind mole mine
 Digging out deniers!
Let the dazed hawk soar,
 Claim the sun's rights too!
Turf 't is thy walk 's o'er,
 Foliage thy flight 's to."

III.

Only a learner,
 Quick one or slow one,
Just a discerner,
 I would teach no one.   20
I am earth's native:
 No re-arranging it!
I be creative,
 Chopping and changing it?

IV.

March, men, my fellows!
 Those who, above me,
(Distance so mellows)
 Fancy you love me:
Those who, below me,
 (Distance makes great so)   30
Free to forego me,
 Fancy you hate so'

V.

Praising, reviling,
  Worst head and best head,
Past me defiling,
  Never arrested,
Wanters, abounders,
  March, in gay mixture,
Men, my surrounders!
  I am the fixture!   40

VI.

So shall I fear thee,
  Mightiness yonder!
Mock-sun — more near thee,
  What is to wonder?
So shall I love thee,
  Down in the dark, — lest
Glowworm I prove thee,
  Star that now sparklest!

———◦◦———

PISGAH–SIGHTS. 3.

I.

GOOD, to forgive :
  Best, to forget!
Living, we fret ;
Dying, we live.
Fretless and free,
  Soul, clap thy pinion!
  Earth have dominion,
Body, o'er thee!

II.

Wander at will,
  Day after day, —
  Wander away,
Wandering still —
Soul that canst soar!
  Body may slumber :
  Body shall cumber
Soul-flight no more.   10

III.

Waft of soul's wing!
    What lies above?
    Sunshine and Love,
Skyblue and Spring!   20
Body hides — where?
    Ferns of all feather,
    Mosses and heather,
Yours be the care!

AT THE "MERMAID."

The figure that thou here seest . . Tut!
Was it for gentle Shakespeare put?
                B. JONSON. (*Adapted.*)

I.

I — " NEXT Poet?"   No, my hearties,
    I nor am nor fain would be!
Choose your chiefs and pick your parties,
    Not one soul revolt to me!
I, forsooth, sow song-sedition?
    I, a schism in verse provoke?
I, blown up by bard's ambition,
    Burst — your bubble-king?   You joke.

II.

Come, be grave!   The sherris mantling
    Still about each mouth, mayhap,   10
Breeds you insight — just a scantling —
    Brings me truth out — just a scrap.
Look and tell me!   Written, spoken,
    Here 's my life-long work : and where
— Where 's your warrant or my token
    I 'm the dead king's son and heir?

III.

Here 's my work : does work discover —
    What was rest from work — my life?
Did I live man's hater, lover?
    Leave the world at peace, at strife?   20

Call earth ugliness or beauty?
　　See things there in large or small?
Use to pay its Lord my duty?
　　Use to own a lord at all?

IV.

Blank of such a record, truly,
　　Here 's the work I hand, this scroll,
Yours to take or leave; as duly,
　　Mine remains the unproffered soul.
So much, no whit more, my debtors —
　　How should one like me lay claim　　　　30
To that largess elders, betters
　　Sell you cheap their souls for — fame?

V.

Which of you did I enable
　　Once to slip inside my breast,
There to catalogue and label
　　What I like least, what love best,
Hope and fear, believe and doubt of,
　　Seek and shun, respect — deride?
Who has right to make a rout of
　　Rarities he found inside?　　　　40

VI.

Rarities or, as he 'd rather,
　　Rubbish such as stocks his own:
Need and greed (O strange) the Father
　　Fashioned not for him alone!
Whence — the comfort set a-strutting,
　　Whence — the outcry "Haste, behold!
Bard's breast open wide, past shutting,
　　Shows what brass we took for gold!"

VII.

Friends, I doubt not he 'd display you
　　Brass — myself call orichalc, —　　　　50
Furnish much amusement; pray you
　　Therefore, be content I balk
Him and you, and bar my portal!
　　Here 's my work outside; opine
What 's inside me mean and mortal!
　　Take your pleasure, leave me mine!

VIII.

Which is — not to buy your laurel
  As last king did, nothing loth.
Tale adorned and pointed moral
  Gained him praise and pity both.   60
Out rushed sighs and groans by dozens,
  Forth by scores oaths, curses flew:
Proving you were cater-cousins,
  Kith and kindred, king and you!

IX.

Whereas do I ne'er so little
  (Thanks to sherris) leave ajar
Bosom's gate — no jot nor tittle
  Grow we nearer than we are.
Sinning, sorrowing, despairing,
  Body-ruined, spirit-wrecked, —   70
Should I give my woes an airing, —
  Where 's one plague that claims respect?

X.

Have you found your life distasteful?
  My life did and does smack sweet.
Was your youth of pleasure wasteful?
  Mine I saved and hold complete.
Do your joys with age diminish?
  When mine fail me, I 'll complain.
Must in death your daylight finish?
  My sun sets to rise again.   80

XI.

What, like you, he proved — your Pilgrim —
  This our world of wilderness,
Earth still gray and heaven still grim,
  Not a hand there his might press,
Not a heart his own might throb to,
  Men all rogues and women — say,
Dolls which boys' heads duck and bob to,
  Grown folk drop or throw away?

XII.

My experience being other,
  How should I contribute verse   90
Worthy of your king and brother?
  Balaam-like I bless, not curse.

I find earth not gray but rosy,
　　Heaven not grim but fair of hue.
Do I stoop?　I pluck a posy.
　　Do I stand and stare?　All 's blue.

XIII.

Doubtless I am pushed and shoved by
　　Rogues and fools enough : the more
Good luck mine, I love, am loved by
　　Some few honest to the core.　　　　　　　100
Scan the near high, scout the far low!
　　"But the low come close : " what then?
Simpletons?　My match is Marlowe;
　　Sciolists?　My mate is Ben.

XIV.

Womankind — "the cat-like nature,
　　False and fickle, vain and weak " —
What of this sad nomenclature
　　Suits my tongue, if I must speak?
Does the sex invite, repulse so,
　　Tempt, betray, by fits and starts?　　　　　110
So becalm but to convulse so,
　　Decking heads and breaking hearts?

XV.

Well may you blaspheme at fortune!
　　I "threw Venus " (Ben, expound!)
Never did I need importune
　　Her, of all the Olympian round.
Blessings on my benefactress!
　　Cursings suit — for aught I know —
Those who twitched her by the back tress,
　　Tugged and thought to turn her — so!　　　120

XVI.

Therefore, since no leg to stand on
　　Thus I 'm left with, — joy or grief
Be the issue, — I abandon
　　Hope or care you name me Chief!
Chief and king and Lord's anointed,
　　I? — who never once have wished
Death before the day appointed :
　　Lived and liked, not poohed and pished!

XVII.

" Ah, but so I shall not enter,
    Scroll in hand, the common heart —   130
Stopped at surface : since at centre
    Song should reach *Welt-schmerz*, world smart ! "
" Enter in the heart ? " Its shelly
    Cuirass guard mine, fore and aft !
Such song " enters in the belly
    And is cast out in the draught. "

XVIII.

Back then to our sherris-brewage !
    " Kingship " quotha ? I shall wait —
Waive the present time : some new age . . .
    But let fools anticipate !   140
Meanwhile greet me — " friend, good fellow,
    Gentle Will," my merry men !
As for making Envy yellow
    With " Next Poet " — (Manners, Ben !)

———— ⋈ ————

HOUSE.

I.

SHALL I sonnet-sing you about myself?
    Do I live in a house you would like to see?
Is it scant of gear, has it store of pelf?
    " Unlock my heart with a sonnet-key ? "

II.

Invite the world, as my betters have done?
    " Take notice : this building remains on view,
Its suites of reception every one,
    Its private apartment and bedroom too ;

III.

" For a ticket, apply to the Publisher."
    No : thanking the public, I must decline.   10
A peep thro' my window, if folk prefer ;
    But, please you, no foot over threshold of mine !

IV.

I have mixed with a crowd and heard free talk
 In a foreign land where an earthquake chanced,
And a house stood gaping, naught to balk
 Man's eye wherever he gazed or glanced.

V.

The whole of the frontage shaven sheer,
 The inside gaped : exposed to day,
Right and wrong and common and queer,
 Bare, as the palm of your hand, it lay.   20

VI.

The owner?   Oh, he had been crushed, no doubt
 " Odd tables and chairs for a man of wealth!
What a parcel of musty old books about!
 He smoke̊d, — no wonder he lost his health!

VII.

" I doubt if he bathed before he dressed.
 A brasier? — the pagan, he burned perfumes!
You see it is proved, what the neighbours guessed :
 His wife and himself had separate rooms."

VIII.

Friends, the goodman of the house at least
 Kept house to himself till an earthquake came :   30
'T is the fall of its frontage permits you feast
 On the inside arrangement you praise or blame.

IX.

Outside should suffice for evidence :
 And whoso desires to penetrate
Deeper, must dive by the spirit-sense —
 No optics like yours, at any rate!

X.

Hoity toity!   A street to explore,
 Your house the exception!   ' *With this same key
Shakespeare unlocked his heart*,' once more!"
 Did Shakespeare?   If so, the less Shakespeare he!   40

SHOP.

I.

SO, friend, your shop was all your house!
   Its front, astonishing the street,
Invited view from man and mouse
   To what diversity of treat
   Behind its glass — the single sheet!

II.

What gimcracks, genuine Japanese :
   Gape-jaw and goggle-eye, the frog ;
Dragons, owls, monkeys, beetles, geese ;
   Some crush-nosed, human-hearted dog :
   Queer names, too, such a catalogue!   10

III.

I thought "And he who owns the wealth
   Which blocks the window's vastitude,
— Ah, could I peep at him by stealth
   Behind his ware, pass shop, intrude
   On house itself, what scenes were viewed!

IV.

If wide and showy thus the shop,
   What must the habitation prove?
The true house with no name a-top —
   The mansion, distant one remove,
   Once get him off his traffic groove!   20

V.

Pictures he likes, or books perhaps ;
   And as for buying most and best,
Commend me to these City chaps!
   Or else he 's social, takes his rest
   On Sundays, with a Lord for guest.

VI.

Some suburb-palace, parked about
   And gated grandly, built last year :
The four-mile walk to keep off gout ;
   Or big seat sold by bankrupt peer :
   But then he takes the rail, that 's clear.   30

VII.

Or, stop!   I wager, taste selects
  Some out o' the way, some all-unknown
Retreat: the neighbourhood suspects
  Little that he who rambles lone
  Makes Rothschild tremble on his throne!

VIII.

Nowise!   Nor Mayfair residence
  Fit to receive and entertain, —
Nor Hampstead villa's kind defence
  From noise and crowd, from dust and drain, —
  Nor country-box was soul's domain!   40

IX.

Nowise!   At back of all that spread
  Of merchandize, woe 's me, I find
A hole i' the wall where, heels by head,
  The owner couched, his ware behind,
  — In cupboard suited to his mind.

X.

For why?   He saw no use of life
  But, while he drove a roaring trade,
To chuckle "Customers are rife!"
  To chafe " So much hard cash outlaid
  Yet zero in my profits made!   50

XI.

" This novelty costs pains, but — takes?
  Cumbers my counter!   Stock no more!
This article, no such great shakes,
  Fizzes like wild fire?   Underscore
  The cheap thing — thousands to the fore!"

XII.

'T was lodging best to live most nigh
  (Cramp, coffinlike as crib might be)
Receipt of Custom ; ear and eye
  Wanted no outworld : " Hear and see
  The bustle in the shop!" quoth he.   60

XIII.

My fancy of a merchant-prince
    Was different.   Thro' his wares we groped
Our darkling way to — not to mince
    The matter — no black den where moped
    The master if we interloped!

XIV.

Shop was shop only: household-stuff?
    What did he want with comforts there?
" Walls, ceiling, floor, stay blank and rough,
    So goods on sale show rich and rare!
    ' Sell and scud home,' be shop's affair! "   70

XV.

What might he deal in?   Gems, suppose!
    Since somehow business must be done
At cost of trouble, — see, he throws
    You choice of jewels, every one
    Good, better, best, star, moon and sun!

XVI.

Which lies within your power of purse?
    This ruby that would tip aright
Solomon's sceptre?   Oh, your nurse
    Wants simply coral, the delight
    Of teething baby, — stuff to bite!   80

XVII.

Howe'er your choice fell, straight you took
    Your purchase, prompt your money rang
On counter, — scarce the man forsook
    His study of the " Times," just swang
    Till-ward his hand that stopped the clang, —

XVIII.

Then off made buyer with a prize,
    Then seller to his " Times " returned,
And so did day wear, wear, till eyes
    Brightened apace, for rest was earned:
    He locked door long ere candle burned.   90

XIX.

And whither went he?   Ask himself,
   Not me!   To change of scene, I think.
Once sold the ware and pursed the pelf,
   Chaffer was scarce his meat and drink,
   Nor all his music — money-chink.

XX.

Because a man has shop to mind
   In time and place, since flesh must live,
Needs spirit lack all life behind,
   All stray thoughts, fancies fugitive,
   All loves except what trade can give?   100

XXI.

I want to know a butcher paints,
   A baker rhymes for his pursuit,
Candlestick-maker much acquaints
   His soul with song, or, haply mute,
   Blows out his brains upon the flute!

XXII.

But — shop each day and all day long!
   Friend, your good angel slept, your star
Suffered eclipse, fate did you wrong!
   From where these sorts of treasures are,
   There should our hearts be — Christ, how far!   110

—◦◦—

A TALE.

I.

WHAT a pretty tale you told me
   Once upon a time
— Said you found it somewhere (scold me!)
   Was it prose or was it rhyme,
Greek or Latin?   Greek, you said,
While your shoulder propped my head.

II.

Anyhow there 's no forgetting
   This much if no more,

That a poet (pray, no petting!)
 Yes, a bard, sir, famed of yore,
Went where suchlike used to go,
Singing for a prize, you know.

III.

Well, he had to sing, nor merely
 Sing but play the lyre;
Playing was important clearly
 Quite as singing: I desire,
Sir, you keep the fact in mind
For a purpose that's behind.

IV.

There stood he, while deep attention
 Held the judges round,
— Judges able, I should mention,
 To detect the slightest sound
Sung or played amiss: such ears
Had old judges, it appears!

V.

None the less he sang out boldly,
 Played in time and tune,
Till the judges, weighing coldly
 Each note's worth, seemed, late or soon,
Sure to smile "In vain one tries
Picking faults out: take the prize!"

VI.

When, a mischief! Were they seven
 Strings the lyre possessed?
Oh, and afterwards eleven,
 Thank you! Well, sir, — who had guessed
Such ill luck in store? — it happed
One of those same seven strings snapped.

VII.

All was lost, then! No! a cricket
 (What "cicada"? Pooh!)
— Some mad thing that left its thicket
 For mere love of music — flew
With its little heart on fire,
Lighted on the crippled lyre.

10

20

30

40

VIII.

So that when (Ah joy!) our singer
　　For his truant string
Feels with disconcerted finger,
　　What does cricket else but fling
Fiery heart forth, sound the note
Wanted by the throbbing throat?

IX.

Ay and, ever to the ending,
　　Cricket chirps at need,
Executes the hand's intending,
　　Promptly, perfectly, — indeed
Saves the singer from defeat
With her chirrup low and sweet.

50

X.

Till, at ending, all the judges
　　Cry with one assent
"Take the prize — a prize who grudges
　　Such a voice and instrument?
Why, we took your lyre for harp,
So it shrilled us forth F sharp!"

60

XI.

Did the conqueror spurn the creature,
　　Once its service done?
That's no such uncommon feature
　　In the case when Music's son
Finds his Lotte's power too spent
For aiding soul-development.

XII.

No! This other, on returning
　　Homeward, prize in hand,
Satisfied his bosom's yearning:
　　(Sir, I hope you understand!)
— Said "Some record there must be
Of this cricket's help to me!"

70

XIII.

So, he made himself a statue:
　　Marble stood, life-size;

On the lyre, he pointed at you,
    Perched his partner in the prize;
Never more apart you found
Her, he throned, from him, she crowned.

XIV.

That 's the tale: its application?
    Somebody I know   80
Hopes one day for reputation
    Thro' his poetry that 's — Oh,
All so learned and so wise
And deserving of a prize!

XV.

If he gains one, will some ticket,
    When his statue 's built,
Tell the gazer " 'T was a cricket
    Helped my crippled lyre, whose lilt
Sweet and low, when strength usurped
Softness' place i' the scale, she chirped?   90

XVI.

" For as victory was nighest,
    While I sang and played, —
With my lyre at lowest, highest,
    Right alike, — one string that made
' Love' sound soft was snapt in twain,
Never to be heard again, —

XVII.

" Had not a kind cricket fluttered,
    Perched upon the place
Vacant left, and duly uttered
    ' Love, Love, Love,' whene'er the bass   100
Asked the treble to atone
For its somewhat sombre drone."

XVIII.

But you don't know music! Wherefore
    Keep on casting pearls
To a — poet? All I care for
    Is — to tell him that a girl's
" Love " comes aptly in when gruff
Grows his singing. (There, enough!)

ADDITIONAL SELECTIONS FROM BROWN-
ING'S LATEST WORKS, 1880–1889.

———∘⋅∘⋅∘∘———

ECHETLOS.

HERE is a story shall stir you! Stand up, Greeks dead and gone,
Who breasted, beat Barbarians, stemmed Persia rolling on,
Did the deed and saved the world, for the day was Marathon!

No man but did his manliest, kept rank and fought away
In his tribe and file : up, back, out, down — was the spear-arm play :
Like a wind-whipt branchy wood, all spear-arms a-swing that day!

But one man kept no rank, and his sole arm plied no spear,
As a flashing came and went, and a form i' the van, the rear,
Brightened the battle up, for he blazed now there, now here.

Nor helmed nor shielded he! but, a goat-skin all his wear,   10
Like a tiller of the soil, with a clown's limbs broad and bare,
Went he ploughing on and on : he pushed with a ploughman's share.

Did the weak mid-line give way, as tunnies on whom the shark
Precipitates his bulk?   Did the right-wing halt when, stark
On his heap of slain lay stretched Kallimachos Polemarch?

Did the steady phalanx falter?   To the rescue, at the need,
The clown was ploughing Persia, clearing Greek earth of weed,
As he routed thro' the Sakian and rooted up the Mede.

But the deed done, battle won, — nowhere to be descried
On the meadow, by the stream, at the marsh, — look far and wide   20
From the foot of the mountain, no, to the last blood-plashed sea-side, —

Not anywhere on view blazed the large limbs thonged and brown,
Shearing and clearing still with the share before which — down
To the dust went Persia's pomp, as he ploughed for Greece, that clown!

How spake the Oracle?   "Care for no name at all!
Say but just this: 'We praise one helpful whom we call
The Holder of the Ploughshare.'   The great deed ne'er grows small."

Not the great name!   Sing — woe for the great name Míltiadés
And its end at Paros isle!   Woe for Themistokles
— Satrap in Sardis court!   Name not the clown like these!   30

TOUCH HIM NE'ER SO LIGHTLY.

SONG.

"TOUCH him ne'er so lightly, into song he broke:
     Soil so quick-receptive, — not one feather-seed,
Not one flower-dust fell but straight its fall awoke
Vitalizing virtue: song would song succeed
Sudden as spontaneous — prove a poet-soul!"

                                                    Indeed?
Rock's the song-soil rather, surface hard and bare:
Sun and dew their mildness, storm and frost their rage
Vainly both expend, — few flowers awaken there:
Quiet in its cleft broods — what the after-age
Knows and names a pine, a nation's heritage.   10

WANTING IS — WHAT?

WANTING is — what?
          Summer redundant,
     Blueness abundant,
          — Where is the blot?
Beamy the world, yet a blank all the same,
     — Framework which waits for a picture to frame:
What of the leafage, what of the flower?
Roses embowering with naught they embower!
Come then, complete incompletion, O comer,
Pant thro' the blueness, perfect the summer!   10
               Breathe but one breath
               Rose-beauty above,
               And all that was death
               Grows life, grows love,
                    Grows love!

NEVER THE TIME AND THE PLACE.

NEVER the time and the place
　　And the loved one all together!
This path — how soft to pace!
　　This May — what magic weather!
Where is the loved one's face?
In a dream that loved one's face meets mine,
　　But the house is narrow, the place is bleak
Where, outside, rain and wind combine
　　With a furtive ear, if I strive to speak,
　　With a hostile eye at my flushing cheek,　　　10
With a malice that marks each word, each sign!
O enemy sly and serpentine,
　　Uncoil thee from the waking man!
　　　　Do I hold the Past
　　　　Thus firm and fast
　　Yet doubt if the Future hold I can?
This path so soft to pace shall lead
Thro' the magic of May to herself indeed!
Or narrow if needs the house must be,
Outside are the storms and strangers: we —　　20
Oh, close, safe, warm sleep I and she,
— I and she!

* * *

ROUND US THE WILD CREATURES.

ROUND us the wild creatures, overhead the trees,
　　Underfoot the moss-tracks, — life and love with these!
I to wear a fawn-skin, thou to dress in flowers:
All the long lone summer-day that greenwood life of ours!

Rich-pavilioned, rather, — still the world without, —
Inside — gold-roofed silk-walled silence round about!
Queen it thou on purple, — I, at watch and ward
Couched beneath the columns, gaze, thy slave, love's guard!

So, for us no world?　Let throngs press thee to me!
Up and down amid men, heart by heart fare we!　　　10
Welcome squalid vesture, harsh voice, hateful face!
God is soul, souls I and thou: with souls should souls have place.

ASK NOT ONE LEAST WORD OF PRAISE.

ASK not one least word of praise!
   Words declare your eyes are bright?
What then meant that summer day's
Silence spent in one long gaze?
   Was my silence wrong or right?

Words of praise were all to seek!
   Face of you and form of you,
Did they find the praise so weak
When my lips just touched your cheek —
   Touch which let my soul come through?   10

EPILOGUE TO "FERISHTAH'S FANCIES."

OH, Love — no, Love! All the noise below, Love,
   Groanings all and moanings — none of Life I lose!
All of Life 's a cry just of weariness and woe, Love —
   " Hear at least, thou happy one!" How can I, Love, but choose?

Only, when I do hear, sudden circle round me
   — Much as when the moon's might frees a space from cloud —
Iridescent splendours : gloom — would else confound me —
   Barriered off and banished far — bright-edged the blackest shroud!

Thronging through the cloud-rift, whose are they, the faces
   Faint revealed yet sure divined, the famous ones of old?   10
" What " — they smile — " our names, our deeds so soon erases
   Time upon his tablet where Life's glory lies enrolled?

" Was it for mere fool's-play, make-believe, and mumming,
   So we battled it like men, not boy-like sulked or whined?
Each of us heard clang God's ' Come!' and each was coming:
   Soldiers all, to forward-face, not sneaks to lag behind!

" How of the field's fortune? That concerned our Leader!
   Led, we struck our stroke nor cared for doings left and right:
Each as on his sole head, failer or succeeder,
   Lay the blame or lit the praise : no care for cowards: fight!"   20

Then the cloud-rift broadens, spanning earth that 's under,
   Wide our world displays its worth, man's strife, and strife's success :

All the good and beauty, wonder crowning wonder,
    Till my heart and soul applaud perfection, nothing less.

Only, at heart's utmost joy and triumph, terror
    Sudden turns the blood to ice : a chill wind disencharms
All the late enchantment!   What if all be error —
    If the halo irised round my head were, Love, thine arms?

Palazzo Giustinian-Recanati,
    VENICE, *Dec.* 1, 1883.

———◦◦———

THE NAMES.

SHAKESPEARE! — to such name's sounding, what succeeds
    Fitly as silence?   Falter forth the spell, —
    Act follows word, the speaker knows full well,
Nor tampers with its magic more than needs.
Two names there are : That which the Hebrew reads
    With his soul only : if from lips it fell,
    Echo, back thundered by earth, heaven, and hell,
Would own "Thou didst create us!"   Naught impedes
We voice the other name, man's most of might,
    Awesomely, lovingly : let awe and love   10
Mutely await their working, leave to sight
    All of the issue as — below — above —
Shakespeare's creation rises : one remove,
Tho' dread — this finite from that infinite.

March 12, 1884.

———◦◦———

WHY I AM A LIBERAL.

"WHY?"   Because all I haply can and do,
    All that I am now, all I hope to be, —
    Whence comes it save from fortune setting free
Body and soul the purpose to pursue,
God traced for both?   If fetters, not a few,
    Of prejudice, convention, fall from me,
    These shall I bid men — each in his degree
Also God-guided — bear, and gayly too?

    But little do or can the best of us :
That little is achieved thro' Liberty.   10
    Who then dares hold, emancipated thus,
His fellow shall continue bound? not I,
    Who live, love, labour freely, nor discuss
A brother's right to freedom.   That is "Why."

PROLOGUE TO "ASOLANDO."

" THE Poet's age is sad : for why ?
  In youth, the natural world could show
No common object but his eye
  At once involved with alien glow —
His own soul's iris-bow.

" And now a flower is just a flower :
  Man, bird, beast are but beast, bird, man —
Simply themselves, uncinct by dower
  Of dyes which, when life's day began,
Round each in glory ran."   10

Friend, did you need an optic glass,
  Which were your choice ?   A lens to drape
In ruby, emerald, chrysopras,
  Each object — or reveal its shape
Clear outlined, past escape,

The naked very thing ? — so clear
  That, when you had the chance to gaze,
You found its inmost self appear
  Thro' outer seeming — truth ablaze,
Not falsehood's fancy-haze ?   20

How many a year, my Asolo,
  Since — one step just from sea to land —
I found you, loved yet feared you so —
  For natural objects seemed to stand
Palpably fire-clothed !   No —

No mastery of mine o'er these !
  Terror with beauty, like the Bush
Burning but unconsumed.   Bend knees,
  Drop eyes to earthward !   Language ?   Tush !
Silence 't is awe decrees.   30

And now ?   The lambent flame is — where ?
  Lost from the naked world : earth, sky,
Hill, vale, tree, flower, — Italia's rare
  O'er-running beauty crowds the eye —
But flame ?   The Bush is bare.

Hill, vale, tree, flower, — they stand distinct,
  Nature to know and name.   What then ?

A Voice spoke thence which straight unlinked
  Fancy from fact : see, all 's in ken :
Has once my eyelid winked?   40

No, for the purged ear apprehends
  Earth's import, not the eye late dazed :
The Voice said " Call my works thy friends!
  At Nature dost thou shrink amazed?
God is it who transcends."

Asolo, *Sept.* 6, 1889.

--- ◆ ---

ROSNY.

WOE, he went galloping into the war,
        Clara, Clara!
Let us two dream : shall he 'scape with a scar?
  Scarcely disfigurement, rather a grace
Making for manhood which nowise we mar :
  See, while I kiss it, the flush on his face —
        Rosny, Rosny!

Light does he laugh : "With your love in my soul " —
        (Clara, Clara!)
"How could I other than — sound, safe and whole —   10
  Cleave who opposed me asunder, yet stand
Scatheless beside you, as, touching love's goal,
  Who won the race kneels, craves reward at your hand —
        Rosny, Rosny?"

Ay, but if certain who envied should see!
        Clara, Clara,
Certain who simper : "The hero for me
  Hardly of life were so chary as miss
Death — death and fame — that 's love's guerdon when she
  Boasts, proud bereaved one, her choice fell on this   20
        Rosny, Rosny!"

So, — go on dreaming, — he lies mid a heap
        (Clara, Clara,)
Of the slain by his hand : what is death but a sleep?
  Dead, with my portrait displayed on his breast :
Love wrought his undoing : "No prudence could keep
  The love-maddened wretch from his fate." That is best,
        Rosny, Rosny!

POETICS.

" SO say the foolish! "   Say the foolish so, Love?
   " Flower she is, my rose " — or else " My very swan is she " —
Or perhaps " Yon maid-moon, blessing earth below, Love,
   That art thou!" — to them, belike : no such vain words from me.

" Hush, rose, blush! no balm like breath," I chide it :
   " Bend thy neck its best, swan, — hers the whiter curve! "
Be the moon the moon : my Love I place beside it :
   What is she?   Her human self, — no lower word will serve.

SUMMUM BONUM.

ALL the breath and the bloom of the year in the bag of one bee :
   All the wonder and wealth of the mine in the heart of one gem :
In the core of one pearl all the shade and the shine of the sea :
   Breath and bloom, shade and shine, — wonder, wealth, and — how
     far above them —
       Truth, that 's brighter than gem,
       Trust, that 's purer than pearl, —
Brightest truth, purest trust in the universe — all were for me
       In the kiss of one girl.

MUCKLE–MOUTH MEG.

FROWNED the Laird on the Lord : " So, red-handed I catch thee?
   Death-doomed by our Law of the Border!
We 've a gallows outside and a chiel to dispatch thee :
   Who trespasses — hangs : all 's in order."

He met frown with smile, did the young English gallant :
   Then the Laird's dame : " Nay, Husband, I beg!
He 's comely : be merciful!   Grace for the callant
   — If he marries our Muckle-mouth Meg! "

" No mile-wide-mouthed monster of yours do I marry :
   Grant rather the gallows! " laughed he.   10
" Foul fare kith and kin of you — why do you tarry? "
   " To tame your fierce temper! " quoth she.

"Shove him quick in the Hole, shut him fast for a week:
    Cold, darkness and hunger work wonders:
Who lion-like roars now, mouse-fashion will squeak,
    And 'it rains' soon succeed to 'it thunders.'"

A week did he bide in the cold and the dark
    — Not hunger: for duly at morning
In flitted a lass, and a voice like a lark
    Chirped "Muckle-mouth Meg still ye 're scorning?   20

"Go hang, but here 's parritch to hearten ye first!"
    "Did Meg's muckle-mouth boast within some
Such music as yours, mine should match it or burst:
    No frog-jaws!   So tell folk, my Winsome!"

Soon week came to end, and, from Hole's door set wide,
    Out he marched, and there waited the lassie:
"Yon gallows, or Muckle-mouth Meg for a bride!
    Consider!   Sky 's blue and turf 's grassy:

"Life 's sweet: shall I say ye wed Muckle-mouth Meg?"
    "Not I," quoth the stout heart: "too eerie   30
The mouth that can swallow a bubblyjock's egg:
    Shall I let it munch mine?   Never, Dearie!"

"Not Muckle-mouth Meg?   Wow, the obstinate man!
    Perhaps he would rather wed me!"
"Ay, would he — with just for a dowry your can!"
    "I 'm Muckle-mouth Meg," chirruped she.

"Then so — so — so — so —" as he kissed her apace —
    "Will I widen thee out till thou turnest
From Margaret Minnikin-mou', by God's grace,
    To Muckle-mouth Meg in good earnest!"   40

——◦◦◦——

EPILOGUE TO "ASOLANDO."

A T the midnight in the silence of the sleep-time,
    When you set your fancies free,
Will they pass to where — by death, fools think, imprisoned —
Low he lies who once so loved you, whom you loved so,
        — Pity me?

Oh to love so, be so loved, yet so mistaken!
 What had I on earth to do
With the slothful, with the mawkish, the unmanly?
Like the aimless, helpless, hopeless, did I drivel
   — Being — who?   10

One who never turned his back but marched breast forward,
 Never doubted clouds would break,
Never dreamed, tho' right were worsted, wrong would triumph,
 Held we fall to rise, are baffled to fight better,
   Sleep to wake.

No, at noonday in the bustle of man's work-time
 Greet the unseen with a cheer!
Bid him forward, breast and back as either should be,
 " Strive and thrive! " cry " Speed, — fight on, fare ever
   There as here! "   20

THE END.

NOTES.

———◦◇◦———

P. 1. My Star. A love lyric, showing how the soul of the loved one reveals itself fully to the sympathetic insight of the lover alone, who, having this revelation, cares nothing if the choice of others be more distinguished. — 4. *Angled spar.* A prism of Iceland spar has the property of polarizing or dividing a ray of light into two parts. Suppose this polarized ray be passed through a plate of Iceland spar, at a certain angle, and a second prism of Iceland spar be rotated in front of it, different colors will be given out, complementary tints being ninety degrees apart, and four times during the rotation the light will vanish completely. Some such experiment as this was probably in the poet's mind when he made the comparison with the angled spar. It is said that this poem refers to Mrs. Browning, and serves here as an inscription to her; having been placed first by Browning himself in this volume of selections intended to accompany a like volume of selections from her poetry. ('Men and Women,' 1855. Set to music by Helen A. Clarke, in *Poet-lore*, July, 1889.)

P. 1. A Face. The poet, in sketching how he would like to have painted the portrait of a certain beautiful woman, gives a vivid likeness of her, though his descriptions are all indirect. — 3. *Tuscan's early art.* The early Tuscan painters were still under the influence of the Byzantine school of painting, one of the marked features of which was the constant use of gold backgrounds. Cimabue, who was the first of the Tuscans to break away from the conventions of the Byzantine school, frequently used gold backgrounds. — 14. *Correggio loves to mass,* etc. This is a true bit of criticism upon Correggio's style, which is especially remarkable for its chiaroscuro. "He knew how to anatomize light and shade in endless gradation." His angels, grouped in brilliant depths of sky, might well wonder at the solitary head on the pale gold ground. ('Dramatis Personæ,' 1864.)

P. 2. My Last Duchess puts in the mouth of a Duke of Ferrara, a typical husband and art patron of the Renaissance, a description of his last wife, whose happy nature and universal kindliness were a perpetual affront to his exacting self-predominance, and whose suppression, by his command, has made the vacancy he is now, therefore, in his interview with the envoy for a new match, taking every precaution to fill more acceptably. — 3. *Fra Pandolf,* and 56. *Claus of Innsbruck,* are imaginary. ('Bells and Pomegranates, No. 3 — Dramatic Lyrics,' 1842. There entitled 'Italy,' with a companion piece, 'France,' retitled respectively 'My Last Duchess, Ferrara,' and 'Count Gismond, Aix in Provence,' in 'Poems,' Vol. II., 1849.)

P. 3. Song from Pippa Passes. Sung by the little girl, Pippa, and founded upon a story — as the lines in the poem following the song explain — told of Caterina

Cornaro, how once a certain page pined for the love of her so far above him that it was entirely beyond his power to do her service. — 6. *Kate the Queen.* Caterina, born in Venice about 1454, daughter of Marco Cornaro, a wealthy and noble citizen. She married James Lusignan, King of Cyprus, after having been adopted by the Venetian Senate as a daughter of the republic. After the King's death she became Queen of Cyprus, but her reign was much troubled by other claimants to the throne. Venice, at first giving her its protection, finally forced her to abdicate, and took possession of Cyprus. Her abdication was attended with great ceremony; and everywhere, on her journey from Cyprus to Venice, she was received with acclamation. Upon her arrival at Venice, the Doge and Senate received her with great honor, and assigned her, for a dwelling, the Chateau-fort of Asolo, in the province of Trévise. At Asolo, Caterina formed a little court, "wielded her little sceptre for her people's good, and won their love by gentleness and grace." Died in Venice, 1510. See H. F. Brown, 'Venetian Studies.' ('Bells and Pomegranates,' No. 1, 1841.)

P. 4. **Cristina** expresses the eternal character of the love awakened by a look, and the lover's sense of the worth of love to the soul as the supreme gain of life. Though Cristina's half of the rapture be quenched in worldly honors, his remains forever blent with hers to his spiritual enrichment. Cristina, daughter of Francis I. of Naples, born 1806, was handsome and a coquette, married Ferdinand VII., King of Spain, 1829; became regent on his death, 1833, till her daughter Isabel II. took the throne, 1843. ('Bells and Pomegranates, No. 3 — Dramatic Lyrics,' 1842. First appeared under the main title 'Queen Worship,' with 'Rudel and the Lady of Tripoli' preceding it, 1842.)

P. 5. **Count Gismond: Aix in Provence** illustrates in the person of the woman who relates to a friend an episode of her own life, the power of innate purity to raise up for her a defender when caught in the toils woven by the unsuspected envy and hypocrisy of her cousins and Count Gauthier, who attempt to bring dishonor upon her, on her birthday, with the seeming intention of honoring her. Her faith that the trial by combat between Gauthier and Gismond must end in Gismond's victory and her vindication reflects most truly, as Arthur Symons has pointed out, the mediæval atmosphere of chivalrous France. — 124. *Tercel*, a male falcon. ('Bells and Pomegranates, No. 3 — Dramatic Lyrics,' 1842. See Notes, **P.** 2.

P. 9. **Eurydice to Orpheus** gives speech to the yearning expressed in Eurydice's face, in the picture, which tempts them both to let the past go and to defy the future for the sake of the instant's satisfaction of their love. Orpheus descending to Hades so worked upon Persephone, Queen of the Dead, by the magic of his music, that she gave him his wife Eurydice on condition that he should not turn to look at her till they reached the upper world, else he would "all his long toils forfeit" for that look. (Royal Academy Catalogue, 1864. Included in 'Poetical Works,' Vol. VI. — 'Dramatis Personæ,' 1868.)

P. 9. **The Glove** gives a transcript from Court life, in Paris, under Francis I. In making Ronsard the mouthpiece for a deeper observation of the meaning of the incident he is supposed to witness and describe than Marot and the rest saw, characteristic differences between these two poets of the time are brought out, the genuineness of courtly love and chivalry is tested, and to the original story of the glove is added a new view of the lady's character; a sketch of her humbler and truer lover, and their happiness; and a pendent scene showing the courtier De Lorges, having won a beauty for his wife, in the ignominious position of assisting the king to enjoy her favors and of submitting to pleasantries upon his discomfiture.

The original story as told by Poullain de St. Croix in his *Essais Historiques sur Paris* ran thus: " One day whilst Francis I. amused himself with looking at a combat between his lions, a lady having let her glove drop, said to De Lorges, ' If you would have me believe that you love me as much as you swear you do, go and bring back my glove.' De Lorges went down, picked up the glove from amidst the ferocious beasts, returned, and threw it in the lady's face ; and in spite of all her advances and cajoleries would never look at her again." Schiller running across this anecdote of St. Croix, in 1797, as he writes Goethe, wrote a poem on it which adds nothing to the story. Leigh Hunt's ' The Glove and the Lions ' adds some traits. It characterizes the lady as shallow and vain, with smiles and eyes " which always seem'd the same." She calculates since " king, ladies, lovers, all look on " that " the occasion is divine " to drop her glove and " prove his love, then look at him and smile " ; and after De Lorges has returned and thrown the glove, " but not with love, right in the lady's face," Hunt makes the king rise and swear " rightly done ! No love, quoth he, but vanity, sets love a task like that ! " This is the material Browning worked on ; he makes use of this speech of the king's, but remodels the lady's character wholly, and gives her an appreciative lover, and also a keen-eyed young poet to tell her story afresh and to reveal through his criticism the narrowness of the Court and the Court poets. — 12. *Naso,* Ovid. Love of the classics and curiosity as to human nature were both characteristic of Peter Ronsard (1524–1585), at one time page to Francis I., the most erudite and original of French mediæval poets. — 45. *Clement Marot* (1496–1544), Court poet to Francis I. His nature and verse were simpler than Ronsard's, and he belonged more peculiarly to his own day. — 48. *Versifies David.* Marot was suspected of Protestant leanings which occasioned his imprisonment twice and put him in need of the protection Francis and his sister gave him. Among his works were sixty-five epistles addressed to grandees, attesting his courtiership, and the paraphrase of forty-nine of the Psalms to which Ronsard alludes. — 50. *Illum Juda,* etc. That lion of the tribe of Judah. — 89. *Venienti,* etc. Meet the coming disease ; that is, if evil be anticipated, don't wait till it seizes you, but dare to assure yourself and then forestall it as the lady did. — 190. *Theorbo.* An old Italian stringed instrument such as pages used. (' Bells and Pomegranates, No. 7 — Dramatic Romances and Lyrics,' 1845.)

P. 14. Song reflects the mood of a lover who in his own infatuation imagines every one else must see his mistress as he sees her and praise her as he thinks she should be praised, though the intensity of his emotion prevents him from doing it himself. (' Bells and Pomegranates, No. 7 — Dramatic Romances and Lyrics,' 1845. Set to music by E. C. Gregory. London: Novello, Ewer, and Co.)

P. 14. A Serenade at the Villa reflects the mood of the speaker as he calls to mind the scene of his serenade the night before, when, in spite of the thunderous, sultry night, and the deadness of nature, he ventured to go forth and sing his devotion to his lady. He wonders whether the lady recognized that here was a friend who would serve her with the utmost devotion to life's end, or whether, as something warns him, she considered the music merely an annoyance that only added to the discomfort of an already unbearable night — an impression evidently due to the inhospitable blackness of her windows and to his excited imagination reflected in the unfriendliness of the grass in grudging him place to stand and the gate's grinding its teeth as he passed through. (' Men and Women,' 1855.)

P. 16. Youth and Art. In this half-humorous soliloquy a woman regrets the foolishness that made herself and a young artist choose worldly ease and comfort instead of confessing to each other their love and casting in their lot together, thus gaining the true happiness that only once was within their grasp. — 8. *Gibson,* John

(1790–1866), sculptor, well known by his 'Tinted Venus.' — 12. *Grisi*, Giulietta (born in Milan, 1812), a celebrated opera singer. — 58. *bals-parés*, dress balls. ('Dramatis Personæ,' 1864.)

P. 19. The Flight of the Duchess. A story of the triumph of a free and loving life over a cold and conventional one. The duke's huntsman frees his mind to his friend as to his part in the escape of the gladsome, ardent young duchess from the blighting yoke of a husband whose life consisted in imitating defunct mediæval customs. An old gipsy is the agency that awakens her to the joy and freedom of love. Her mystic chant and charm claim the duchess as the true heir of gipsy blood, thrill her with life, half-hypnotize the huntsman, too, and transform the gipsy crone herself into an Eastern queen. He helps them off, and looks for no better future, when the duke's death releases him, than to travel to the land of the gipsies and hear the last news of his lady.

The poem grew from the fancies aroused in the poet's heart by the snatch of a woman's song he overheard when a boy, — "Following the Queen of the Gipsies, O!" (First nine sections, *Hood's Magazine*, April, 1845; whole in 'Bells and Pomegranates,' No. 7, 1845.)

P. 39. Song from Pippa Passes. Little song sung by Pippa expressing trust in God because of the beautiful spring morning. (See Notes, **P. 3.**)

P. 39. How they brought the Good News from Ghent to Aix describes the gallop of three horses with their riders from Ghent at midnight to Aix at midday. Two of the horses falling dead by the way, the good steed Roland is left alone to reach the goal and save Aix.

In answer to inquiries Browning wrote: "There is no sort of historical foundation about 'Good News from Ghent.' I wrote it under the bulwark of a vessel off the African coast, after I had been at sea long enough to appreciate even the fancy of a gallop on the back of a certain good horse 'York,' then in my stable at home. It was written in pencil on the flyleaf of Bartoli's 'Simboli,' I remember."

It has, however, been pointed out by several commentators that the poem may be said to have a sort of historical background, as such an incident might easily have grown out of the event of the "Pacification of Ghent," a treaty of union entered into by Holland, Zealand, and the southern Netherlands, headed by William of Orange, and directed against the tyrannical power of Philip II. of Spain. (See Motley's 'Rise of the United Netherlands,' Vol. VIII.)

"The 'horse without peer' might possibly have galloped the ninety-odd miles between Ghent and Aix, but the feat would be a marvellous one. — 10. *Pique*. The pommel of the saddle. We state this on authority of an army officer, although the meaning is in none of the dictionaries. — 14. *Lokeren*. A town twelve miles from Ghent, in a direction a little north of east. — 15. *Boom*. Sixteen miles due east from Lokeren. — 16. *Düffeld*, or Duffel, is about twelve miles east of Boom, and a few miles north of Mechlin. — 17. *Mecheln*. The contracted form of *Mechelen*, the Flemish form of *Mechlin* (French, *Malines*). The *church steeple* is the lofty (324 feet) though unfinished tower of the Cathedral of St. Rombold. Like many of the great Belgian churches, it is noted for its chimes. — 18. *Aerschot*. All the eds. spell the name *Aershot;* but the *sch* is pronounced like *sk*. The town is fifteen miles from Duffel. — 31. *Hasselt*. The capital of the province of Limbourg. It is about twenty-four miles from Aerschot, and almost eighty from Ghent by the route described. Dirck had, indeed, 'galloped bravely.' — 38. *Looz*. This town is seven or eight miles due *south* from Hasselt, and *Tongres* is also out of the direct road to Aix-la-Chapelle. We should expect the riders to take the route *via* Maastricht. By rail it is forty-one miles from Hasselt to Aix, and the highway cannot be much less. — 41. *Dalhem.* Apparently some village near Aix. It cannot be the frontier-town Dalheim, for that lies too far to the north. The *dome-spire* is probably the cupola of the ' octagon ' of the cathedral, built by Charlemagne and containing his tomb." — *Rolfe and Hersey's Notes.*

('Bells and Pomegranates, No. 7 — Dramatic Romances and Lyrics,' 1845. Set to Music by "Yolande," London : Boosey ; and by Miss H. V. Ormerod, London : Forsyth Bros.)

P. 41. Song from ' Paracelsus.' Sung by Paracelsus (Part IV.), half in mockery, of his dead dreams on their funeral pyre. (1835.)

P. 42. Through the Metidja to Abd-el-Kadr describes the ride of an Arab insurgent through the Algerian plain called the Metidja to rejoin his chief, Abd-el-Kadr. The leap of his blood quickens his insight, makes him proud of his loyalty to his leader, defiant of witnesses, exultant over the visions he has of the French who came boasting to the desert, to remain there slain, their dead bodies seeming to be uncovered by the shifting sands he leaves behind him as he rides past on his unspurred horse towards the fate he refuses to pry into, content to accept death when Mohammed pleases. — *Abd-el-Kadr* (" servant of God "), born 1807, united the Arab tribes to resist the French invasions of their country, made himself recognized as the Emir of Mascara, and forced the French to offer terms of peace. War breaking out again, and the French being again defeated, a larger force was sent into Algeria. The incident of the poem follows the seizure of the emir's camp, in 1842, by the Duc d'Aumale, when several thousand prisoners were taken, Abd-el-Kadr himself escaping with difficulty and collecting the Arabs for renewed resistance. He was forced later to give himself up, and was imprisoned at Pau until 1852, when Louis Napoleon freed him on condition that he did not return to Algeria. He died in 1883. — 38. *The Prophet and the Bride.* The prophet is of course Mohammed.

('Bells and Pomegranates, No. 3 — Dramatic Lyrics,' 1842.)

P. 43. Incident of the French Camp. A story of modest heroism. The incident related is said by Mrs. Orr to be a true one of the siege of Ratisbon by Napoleon in 1809 — except that the real hero was a man. — 1. *Ratisbon* (German Regensburg) : an ancient city of Bavaria on the right bank of the Danube, has endured seventeen sieges since the tenth century, the last one being that of Napoleon, 1809. — 11. *Lannes,* Duke of Montebello, one of Napoleon's generals. ('Bells and Pomegranates, No. 3 — Dramatic Lyrics,' 1842. With 'Soliloquy in a Spanish Cloister,' under the title ' Camp and Cloister : I. Camp [French], II. Cloister [Spanish],' entitled as at present, ' Poems,' Vol. II., 1849.)

P. 44. The Lost Leader sings with undaunted spirit the sad desertion of the people's cause by one who had been one of its leaders. Asked if he referred to Wordsworth, Browning wrote, in 1875 : —

" I can only answer, with something of shame and contrition, that I undoubtedly had Wordsworth in my mind — but simply as a model ; you know an artist takes one or two striking traits in the features of his ' model,' and uses them to start his fancy on a flight which may end far enough from the good man or woman who happens to be sitting for nose and eye. I thought of the great Poet's abandonment of liberalism at an unlucky juncture, and no repaying consequence that I could ever see. But, once call my fancy-portrait *Wordsworth* — and how much more ought one to say ! "

Wordsworth, liberal in his youth, grew conservative with advancing years, opposed Catholic Emancipation, the Reform Bill, and educational progress. ('Bells and Pomegranates, No. 7 — Dramatic Romances and Lyrics,' 1845.)

P. 45. In a Gondola is a lyric dialogue between two Venetian lovers who have stolen away in a gondola spite of "the three," "Himself"—perhaps a husband—and "Paul" and "Gian," her brothers, whose vengeance discovers them at the end, but not before their love and danger have moved them to weave a series of lyrical fancies and led them to a climax of emotion which makes Life so deep a joy that Death is of no account.

"The first stanza was written," writes Browning, "to illustrate Maclise's picture, for which he was anxious to get some line or two. I had not seen it, but from Forster's description, gave it to him in his room, impromptu. . . . When I did see it I thought the serenade too jolly, somewhat, for the notion I got from Forster, and I took up the subject in my own way."—113. *Lido's graves.* Jewish tombs were there.—127. *Guidecca*, a canal of Venice.—155. *lory*, a kind of parrot.—186. *Schidone's eager Duke.* An imaginary painting by Bartolommeo Schidone of Modena (1560-1616).—188. *Haste-thee-Luke*, the English form of the nickname, *Luca-fà-presto*, given Luca Giordano (1632-1705), a Neapolitan painter, on account of his constantly being goaded on in his work by his penurious and avaricious father. —190. *Castelfranco*, the Venetian painter, Giorgione, called Castelfranco, because born there, 1478, died 1511.—193. *Tizian* (1477-1516). The pictures are all imaginary but suggestive of the style of each of these artists.

P. 51. A Lovers' Quarrel is a lover's protest against any severance of the union in whose endless pleasures his memory revels. His sudden word that unwittingly struck discord into their happy world must be too slight to blot out the love that amassed them such memories and experiences of each other. ('Men and Women,' 1855. Set to music by E. C. Gregory. London: Novello, Ewer, and Co.)—123. *Minor third.* See 'Toccata of Galuppi.'

P. 56. Earth's Immortalities. A two-fold lyric singing Time's power over Fame and Love. The touch of Time upon a poet's grave symbolizes the one, his deafness to the human outcry against old age and the progress of the seasons typifies the other. ('Bells and Pomegranates, No. 7—Dramatic Romances and Lyrics,' 1845. Appeared first as I. and II. without the sub-titles which were added in 1849.)

P. 56. The Last Ride Together. The rapture of a rejected lover in the one more last ride which he asks for and obtains, discovers for him the all-sufficing glory of love in itself. Soldiership, statesmanship, art are disproportionate in their results; love can be its own reward, yes, heaven itself. ('Men and Women,' 1855.)

P. 59. Mesmerism. With a continuous tension of will, whose unbroken concentration impregnates the very structure of the poem, a mesmerist describes the processes of the act by which he summons shape and soul of the woman he desires, and then reverent perception of the sacredness of the soul awes him from trespassing upon another's individuality. ('Men and Women,' 1855.)

P. 64. By the Fireside. A mature man's anticipated reminiscence in old age of the scene and the crowning moment of a ripe and perfect love. The initial insight and force to seize the vital moment, fusing the physical and spiritual elements of love and testing the soul and exalting it to the highest potency, is attributed to the "perfect wife," whose "great brow" and "spirit-small hand" clearly refer to Mrs. Browning and give the situation of the poem an autobiographical implication. The scene is placed in a little mountain gorge near the baths of Lucca, where the Brownings passed the summer in 1849 and in 1853. "We have taken a sort of eagle's nest in this place," writes Mrs. Browning, "the highest house of the highest of the three villages which are called the Bagni di Lucca, and which lie at the heart of a hundred mountains sung to continually by a rushing mountain stream. The sound of the river and of the cicale is all the sound we hear. . . . The silence is full of joy and consolation. . . . I find myself able to climb the hills with Robert, and help him to lose himself in the forests." (' Men and Women,' 1855.)

P. 72. Any Wife to any Husband. Another expression of the wife's superior perception of the unity of the physical and spiritual in love, and the psychical value of constancy. Destined to die first she protests against the husband's wronging their genuine love and his own spiritual dignity by indulging in cheaper attractions he would only put up with in her absence, and she does not dare to prophesy his loyalty with unwavering trust. (' Men and Women,' 1855.)

P. 76. In a Year. A woman's lyric, unconsciously dramatizing her own and her fickle lover's character, and at last through a truer estimate of the worth of his heart getting her own glimpse of the Divine quality residing in constancy. (' Men and Women,' 1855.)

P. 79. Song from 'James Lee.' (See ' James Lee's Wife,' Notes, P. 288.)

P. 79. A Woman's Last Word implies a dramatic situation, — a resistance of soul and intellect against overmastery, and gives lyrical expression to the pathetic outcome of the struggle, — the self-surrender of a fond heart. (' Men and Women,' 1855. Set to music by Leslie Johnson. London : Browning Society.)

P. 81. Meeting at Night and Parting at Morning. Supplementary pictures of a love-tryst, one giving the lover's impressions in turning at night towards isolation with the loved one, the other of the return to the larger needs and uses of the world at sunrise. Whether the man speaks throughout, or in the second part the woman speaks, are open questions. (' Bells and Pomegranates, No. 7 — Dramatic Romances and Lyrics,' 1845. Originally called ' Night' and ' Morning.' Titled as at present in ' Poems,' 1849.)

P. 81. Women and Roses. A dreamy glimpse of the actual woman animating the past, present, and future ideals of woman which are typified in the poet's fancy by the three roses faded, blooming, and just budded, on a rose-tree sent by a friend to Mrs. Browning. He seeks in vain to appropriate the dearest of these ideals. His only hold upon them is through his knowledge of the real womanhood of the woman akin to them who is closest to him. They circle their particular rose on his real rose-tree. (Written in Paris, in 1852. ' Men and Women,' 1855.)

P. 83. Misconceptions sings the lover's flitting moment of joy in a love fully answering his own ere undeceived like the spray which the bird clung to, he learns that the queen, like the bird, had but casually used his help in order to pass on to a happiness beyond him. (' Men and Women,' 1855. Set to music by E. C. Gregory. London : Novello, Ewer, and Co.)

P. 83. A Pretty Woman is a light sketch of a typical pretty woman whose brains and heart are rudimentary, and of the typical treatment she receives from men, who make her their peculiar prize for their cleverness or valor, " a word's sake or a sword's sake." The " Conclusion " to try is, — why crush her for lack of qualities debarred her, or lavish devotion upon her fruitlessly. Rather appreciate her beauty by leaving it unsullied, as its own excuse for being. The Oriental treatment of pretty women is dexterously intimated in the craftsman's way to grace a rose. (' Men and Women,' 1855.)

P. 86. A Light Woman is the story of a dramatic situation brought about by the speaker's intermeddling to save his less sophisticated friend from a light woman's toils. He deflects her interest and wins her heart, and this is the ironical outcome : his friendly, dispassionate act makes him seem to his friend a disloyal passion's slave ; his scorn of the light woman teaches him her genuineness and proves himself lighter than she ; his futile assumption of the god manœuvering souls makes

2 H

the whole story dramatically imply, in a way dear to Browning's heart, the sacredness and worth of each individuality. ('Men and Women,' 1855.)

P. 88. Love in a Life, and **Life in a Love** are lyrical expressions, the first of the search for love as an uncertain, undiscovered ideal, the other of the pursuit of love as an ideal that is sure and discovered, the first consisting in the attempt to gain a love within a life, the other in the spending of a life in love's attainment. ('Men and Women,' 1855.)

P. 89. The Laboratory presents as an episode in the course of a ball the scene and agents of a jealous woman's preparation to poison her rival, the social and scientific conditions of the feudal period being illustrated by this glimpse of a laboratory dim with arsenic fumes, of the fierce, chattering little lady peering through her protecting glass mask, and the morose old alchemist including a kiss in his pay. (*Hood's Magazine*, June, 1844. 'Bells and Pomegranates, No. 7 — Dramatic Romances and Lyrics,' 1845, appearing with 'The Confessional' under the general title 'France and Spain.')

P. 91. Gold Hair. A quizzical story playing with the pious naïvetés of a guide-book legend. It tells how a reputed girl-saint of good family in Brittany valued the gold of this life spite of heaven and the grave, and, managing to hide her money in her beautiful gold hair before she died, remained in men's praise as a model of sanctity, and was only detected as a miser years afterwards when her skull was found in her coffin wedged in with her dear gold coins. The sophistical moral suggested is that such a marvellous and damning mixture of good and evil in the human heart as this story lays bare warrants the doctrine of Original Sin and supplies a reason for sticking to the Christian faith, despite Bishop Colenso and the 'Essays and Reviews.' — 143. *Essays and Reviews*. A collection of seven dissertations by Dr. Temple of Rugby, Professor Jowett of Oxford, and other English churchmen, on theological topics, all bearing on the advantage to religion and morality derivable from a freer scrutiny of the Bible, the character of its facts, and the nature of its authority as a sacred book. It was a shock to many and it excited much discussion, initiating in England what is now known as the Higher Criticism of the Bible. — 145. *Colenso*. Bishop of Natal, South Africa — whose examination of the Bible was instigated by the questions of a Zulu native — published in 1862 the first volume of his work on the Pentateuch, which added fuel to the debate stirred up by the 'Essays and Reviews.' (Written in Normandy and printed as a leaflet. 'Dramatis Personæ,' 1864.)

P. 96. The Statue and the Bust creates the characters and the situation, and dramatically represents a story which is based on a Florentine tradition that Duke Ferdinand I. placed his equestrian statue in the Piazza dell' Annuziata so that he might gaze forever towards the old Riccardi palace, where a lady he loved was imprisoned by her jealous husband. The bride and her ducal lover are seen exchanging their first looks, through which they perceive the genuineness of their love; and the temporizing of each is presented, through which, for the sake of petty conveniences, they submit to be thwarted by the wary husband, and to have the end they count supreme delayed until love and youth have gone, and the best left them is the artificial gaze interchanged by a bronze statue in the square and a clay face at the window. The closing stanzas point the moral against the palsy of the will whose strenuous exercise is life's main gift. — 1. *There's a palace in Florence* refers to the old Riccardi palace, now the Palazzo Antinori, in the square of the Annuziata, where the statue still stands. — 33. *The pile which the mighty shadow makes* refers to another palace in the Via Larga where the duke (*not* the lady) lived, and which is to-day known as the Riccardi Palace. Cooke's 'Browning Guide Book' and Berdoe's 'Browning Cyclopædia' both confuse the two, attributing error to Browning in spite of his letter about it. This confusion was cleared up by Harriet Ford (*Poet-lore*, Dec., 1891, Vol. III., p. 648, 'Browning right about the Riccardi Palace.') — 36. *Because of a crime*, etc. refers to the destroying of the liberties of the Florentine republic by Cosimo dei Medici and his grandson, Lorenzo, who lived in the then Medici (now Riccardi) Palace, whose darkening of the street with its bulk symbolizes the crime which took the light from Florence. — 94. *Arno bowers*. The palace by the Arno, the river flowing through Florence. — 95. *Petraja*, a Florentine suburb. — 69. *Robbia's craft*. The Robbia family were skilled in shaping the bisque known as Della Robbia ware which was long one of the Florentine manufactures, and traces of which, when Browning wrote, still adorned the outer cornice of the palace. — 202. *John of Douay*, sculptor, 1524–1608. The statue is one of his finest works. — 237. *De te, fabula!* Concerning thee, this fable! ('Men and Women,' 1855.)

P. 103. Love among the Ruins. A lover, meditating, draws a contrast showing how the ruined spot where he and the beloved one meet — "The single little turret that remains on the plains" from which kings were once wont to look forth — is more glorified by the perfect love existing between them than it has ever been in the past when the ancient city stood there with all its pomp of triumph and war, its folly and noise and sin. The poem was written in Rome in the winter of 1853–54 when Robert and Mrs. Browning were staying there. — 21. *hundred-gated circuit of a wall*. The poet perhaps had in mind Homer's description of Thebes as the "hundred-gated" city. Rome never had more than twenty (or possibly a few over twenty) gates. Homer's epithet evidently applied to the gates of the temples, as Thebes was not a walled city. ('Men and Women,' 1855.)

P. 105. Time's Revenges. An author soliloquizes in his garret over the fact that he possesses a friend who loves him and would do anything in his power to serve him, but for whom he cares almost nothing. At the same time he himself loves a woman to such distraction that he counts himself crowned with love's best crown while sacrificing his soul, his body, his peace, and his fame in brooding on his love, while she could calmly decree that he should roast at a slow fire if it would compass her frivolously ambitious designs. Thus his indifference to his friend is avenged by the indifference the lady shows toward him. — 46. *the Florentine*, Dante. Used here, seemingly, as a symbol of the highest attainments in poesy, his (the speaker's) reverence for which is so great that he would rather put his cheek under his lady's foot than that poetry should suffer any indignity at his hands; yet in spite of all the possibilities open to him through his enthusiasm for poetry, he prefers wasting his entire energies upon one unworthy of him. ('Bells and Pomegranates, No. 7 — Dramatic Romances and Lyrics,' 1845.)

P. 107. Waring. In recounting the sudden disappearance from among his friends of a man proud and sensitive, who with fine powers of intellect yet incurred somewhat of disdain because of his failure to accomplish anything permanent, expression is given to the deep regret experienced by his friends now that he has left them, his absence having brought them to a truer realization of his worth. If only Waring would come back, the speaker, at least, would give him the sympathy and encouragement he craved instead of playing with his sensibilities as he had done. Conjectures are indulged in as to Waring's whereabouts. The speaker prefers to think of him as back in London preparing to astonish the world with some great masterpiece in art, music, or literature. Another speaker surprises all by telling how he had seen the "last of Waring" in a momentary meeting at Trieste, but the first speaker is certain that the star of Waring is destined to rise again above their horizon. — 1. *Waring.* Alfred Domett (born at Camberwell Grove, Surrey, May 20, 1811), a friend of Browning's, distinguished as a poet and as a Colonial statesman and ruler. His first volume of poems was published in 1832. Some verses of his in *Blackwood's*, 1837, attracted much attention to him as a rising young poet. In 1841 he was called to the bar, and in 1842 went out to New Zealand among the earliest settlers. There he lived for thirty years, filling several important official positions. His unceremonious departure for New Zealand with no leave-takings was the occasion of Browning's poem, which is said by Mrs. Orr to give a lifelike sketch of Domett's character. His "star" did, however, rise again for his English friends, for he returned to London in 1871. The year following saw the publication of his 'Ranolf and Amohia,' a New Zealand poem, in the course of which he characterizes Browning as "Subtlest Asserter of the Soul in Song." He met Browning again in London, and was one of the vice-presidents of the London Browning Society. Died Nov. 12, 1877. — 15. *I left his arm that night myself.* Geo. W. Cooke points out that in his 'Living Authors of England' Thomas Powell describes this incident, the 'young author' mentioned being himself: —

"We have a vivid recollection of the last time we saw him. It was at an evening party, a few days before he sailed from England; his intimate friend, Mr. Browning, was also present. It happened that the latter was introduced that evening for the first time to a young author who had just then appeared in the literary world. This, consequently, prevented the two friends from conversation, and they parted from each other without the slightest idea on Mr. Browning's part that he was seeing his old friend Domett for the last time. Some days after, when he found that Domett had sailed, he expressed in strong terms to the writer of this sketch the self-reproach he felt at having preferred the conversation of a stranger to that of his old associate."

— 54. *Monstr'-inform'-ingens-horrend-ous*, a slight transposition of part of a line in Virgil describing Polyphemus, "*Monstrum horrendum informe ingens*," a monster horrid, misshapen, huge. — 55. *Demoniaco-seraphic.* These two lines form a compound of adjectives humorously used by Browning to express the inferiority of the writers he praised to Waring. — 99. *Ichabod*, "Ichabod, the glory is departed," 1 Samuel iv. 21. — 122. *lambwhite maiden.* Iphigenia, who was borne away to Taurus by Diana, when her father, Agamemnon, was about to sacrifice her to obtain favorable winds for his expedition to Troy. — 152. *Caldara Polidore*, a celebrated painter, born in Milan, 1492, went to Rome and was employed by Raphael to paint the friezes in the Vatican, was murdered by a servant in Messina, 1543. — 155. *Purcell.* An eminent English musician, composer of church music, operas, songs, and instrumental music (1658–1695). *Rosy Bowers.* One of Purcell's most celebrated songs. "'From Rosie Bowers' is said to have been set in his last sickness, at which time he seems to have realized the poetical fable of the Swan and to have sung more sweetly as he approached nearer his dissolution, for it seems to us as if no one of his productions was so elevated, so pleasing, so expressive, and throughout so perfect as this." (Rees's Cyclopædia, 1819.) — 190. *Garrick*, David. An English actor, celebrated especially for his Shakespearian parts (1716–1779). — 193. *Junius*, the assumed name of a political writer who in 1769 began to issue in London a series of famous letters which opposed the ministry in power and denounced several eminent persons with severe invective and pungent sarcasm. — 195. *Some Chatterton shall have the luck of calling Rowley into life.* The chief claim to celebrity of Thomas Chatterton (1752–1770) is the real or pretended discovery of poems said to have been written in the fifteenth century by Thomas Rowley, a priest of Bristol, and found in Radcliffe church, of which Chatterton's ancestors had been sextons for many years. They are now generally considered Chatterton's own. ('Bells and Pomegranates, No. 3 — Dramatic Lyrics,' 1842.)

P. 113. Home Thoughts from Abroad. Expresses the longing for home of one who when spring comes remembers the joyous, dainty beauties of the English spring. The gaudy melon flower at hand, symbolic of the rankness of a southern spring, is dull in comparison with the gay buttercups that little children love. ('Bells and Pomegranates, No. 7 — Dramatic Romances and Lyrics,' 1845.)

P. 113. The Italian in England. An Italian patriot who has taken part in an unsuccessful revolt against Austrian dominance, reflects upon the incidents of his escape and flight from Italy to the end that if he ever should have a thought beyond the welfare of Italy, he would wish first for the discomfiture of his enemies and then to go and see once more the noble woman who at the risk of her own life helped him to escape. — Though there is no exact historical incident upon which this poem is founded, it has a historical background. The Charles referred to (lines 8, 11, 20, 116, 125) is Charles Albert, Prince of Carignano, of the younger branch of the house of Savoy. His having played with the patriot in his youth, as the poem says, is quite possible, for Charles was brought up as a simple citizen in a public school, and one of his chief friends was Alberta Nota, a writer of liberal principles, whom he made his secretary. As indicated in the poem, Charles at first declared himself in sympathy, though in a somewhat lukewarm manner, with the rising led by Santa Rosa against Austrian domination in 1823, and upon the abdication of Victor Emanuel he became regent of Turin. But when the king Charles Felix issued a denunciation against the new government, Charles Albert succumbed to the king's threats and left his friends in the lurch. Later the Austrians marched into the country, Santa Rosa was forced to retreat from Turin, and, with his friends, he who might well have been the very patriot of the poem, was obliged to fly from Italy. — 19. *Metternich.* The distinguished Austrian diplomatist and determined enemy of Austrian independence. — 76. *Tenebræ*, darkness. "The office of matins and lauds, for the three last days in Holy Week. Fifteen lighted candles are placed on a triangular stand, and at the conclusion of each psalm one is put out till a single candle is left at the top of the triangle. The extinction of the other candles is said to figure the growing darkness of the world at the time of the Crucifixion. The last candle (which is not extinguished, but hidden behind the altar for a few moments) represents Christ, over whom Death could not prevail" (Dr. Berdoe). ('Bells and Pomegranates, No. 7 — Dramatic Romances and Lyrics,' 1845.)

P. 117. The Englishman in Italy. A graphic, humorous picture of peasant life on the plain of Sorrento is here presented by an Englishman, who tells his memories of various scenes grown familiar to his foreign eyes in order to keep a little peasant girl amused during the gloom of the Scirocco, just as he is preoccupying himself in Italy, while in his own England another sort of tempest is abroad and men are actually debating in parliament the use of abolishing the gloom of a human Scirocco, namely, the misery caused by the corn-laws. — 3. *Scirocco.* A fierce hot wind from Africa crossing the Mediterranean in autumn. — 100. *Isles of the Siren.* The three islands off the coast, one and one half miles from Crapolla, supposed to be those described in the Odyssey (Bk. xii. and xxiii.) where the sirens sang, and referred to by Virgil in Æneid v. 1125. — 125. *Feast of the Rosary.* The anniversary of the battle of Lepanto, where the Turkish fleet was destroyed by the Catholic powers of Europe, and for which victory our Lady of the Rosary receives annual thanks. — 145. *Corn-laws.* In October, 1845, Sir Robert Peel, England's prime minister, asked his cabinet to concur with him in relieving the people from the duty on corn or grain-stuffs, repealing the law passed by the parliament of 1815 in the interest of land-holders. It excited the stormy opposition to which the poem refers, resulting, however, in the passing of Peel's bill in June, 1846.— 186. *Calvano.* Browning is not sure he used the right name for the great mountain opposite Sorrento. ('Bells and Pomegranates, No. 7 — Dramatic Romances and Lyrics,' 1845.)

P. 120. Up at a Villa—Down in the City. A humorous portraiture of a pleasure-loving Italian nobleman who contrasts the boredom of life in the country with the excitements of town-life, and sighs over the expense of the city which condemns him to his rustic villa.— 52. *Seven Swords.* Figurative of the Seven Sorrows of Our Lady, and contrasting naïvely with the pink gauze and spangles. —56. *Tax on salt . . . oil pays passing the gate.* Italy's system of revenue included a tax on salt, and the *octroi*, or town dues, must be paid on all provisions entering the city-gates. ('Men and Women,' 1855.)

P. 123. Pictor Ignotus is a reverie characteristic of a monastic painter of the Renaissance who recognizes, in the genius of a youth whose pictures are praised, a gift akin to his own, but which he has never so exercised, spite of the joy such free human expression and recognition of his power would have given him, because he could not bear to submit his art to worldly contact. So, he has chosen to sink his name in unknown service to the Church, and to devote his fancy to pure and beautiful, but cold and monotonous, repetitions of sacred themes. His gentle regret that his own pictures will moulder unvisited is half wonderment that the youth can endure the sullying of his work by secular fame. ('Bells and Pomegranates, No. 7 — Dramatic Romances and Lyrics,' 1845.)

P. 124. Fra Lippo Lippi is a dramatic monologue which incidentally conveys the whole story of the occurrence the poem starts from — the seizure of Fra Lippo by the City Guards, past midnight, in an equivocal neighborhood — and the lively talk that arose thereupon; outlines the character and past life of the artist-monk and the subordinate personalities of the group of officers; and makes all this cohere towards the presentation of Fra Lippo as a type of the more realistic and secular artist of the Renaissance who valued flesh, and protested against the ascetic spirit which strove to isolate the soul. The poem's presentation of Fra Lippo (1412–1469) breathes life into the passages from Vasari's Lives which it follows thus : — *Vasari :* "The Carmelite Monk Fra Filippo di Tommaso Lippi was born in a bye street . . . behind the Convent." *Browning :* 7. "The Carmine's very Cloister." *Vasari :* "Cosimo de Medici, wishing him to execute a work in his own palace, shut him up, that he might not waste his time in running about; but having endured this confinement for two days he made ropes with the sheets of his bed . . . let himself down from a window . . . and for several days gave himself up to his amusements." *Brng.:* 15. "Lodging with a friend . . . Cosimo of the Medici," etc. 47. "Three weeks shut within my mew, etc., . . . Into shreds it went," etc. [Browning apologizes a little for the Frate by making the confinement three weeks instead of two days, and giving him only one night's revelry.] *Vasari :* "By the death of his father he was left a friendless orphan at the age of two years . . . for some time under the care of Mona Lapaccia, his aunt, who brought him up with very great difficulty till his eighth year, when, being no longer able to support the burden, she placed him in the Convent of the Carmelites . . . Placed with others under the care of a master to . . . see what could be done with him; in place of studying he never did anything but daub his books with caricatures, whereupon the prior determined to give him . . . opportunity for learning to draw. The chapel, then newly painted by Masaccio,

. . . he frequented, and practising there . . . surpassed all the others . . . while still very young painted a picture in the cloister . . . with others in fresco . . . among these John the Baptist." *Brng.:* 81. "I was a baby when my mother died," etc.; 129. "I drew men's faces on my copy books," etc.; 136. "Nay, quoth the Prior," etc.; 196. "Herodias I would say," etc. *Vasari:* "For the nuns of Sant' Ambrogio he painted a most beautiful picture." [The Virgin crowned with angels and saints, now in Florence at the Belle Arti. Vasari says by means of it he became known to Cosimo. Browning on the other hand crowns his poem with Lippo's description of this picture as an expiation for his pranks.] *Brng.:* 345. "I shall paint a piece . . . Something in Sant' Ambrogio's," etc. — 23. *pilchards,* a kind of fish. — 53. *Flower o' the broom.* Of the many varieties of folk-songs in Italy that which furnished Browning with a model for Lippo's songs is called a *stornello.* The name is variously derived. Some take it as merely short for *ritornello,* others derive it from *a storno,* to sing against each other, because the peasants sing them at their work, and as one ends a song, another caps it with a fresh one, and so on. These *stornelli* consist of three lines. The first usually contains the name of a flower which sets the rhyme, and is five syllables long. Then the love theme is told in two lines of eleven syllables each, agreeing by rhyme, assonance, or repetition with the first, —

> " Flower of the fern !
> Wherever you pass by, the grass springs green
> And blooms or ever summer doth return."

The last two lines lose a syllable in the translation.

The address to the flower usually has no connection with the sentiment expressed in the lines following, a very evident example of which are these, —

> " Flower of the broom bough !
> If you want a husband make you one of dough,
> Dress him up and put him in the window for a show."

In some cases, salt, pepper, lemons, and even cigars are used in the first line instead of flowers. The first line may be looked upon as a burden set at the beginning instead of, as is more familiar to us, at the end. There are also *stornelli* formed of three lines of eleven syllables without any burden.

Browning has made Lippo's songs of only two lines, but he has strictly followed the rule of making the first line, containing the address to the flower, of five syllables. The Tuscany versions of two of the songs used by Browning are as follows : —

> " Flower of the pine !
> Call me not ever happy heart again,
> But call me heavy heart, O comrades mine."

> " Flower of the broom !
> Unwed thy mother keeps thee not to lose
> That flower from the window of the room."

68. *Saint Laurence.* The church of San Lorenzo. — 121. *The Eight.* The magistrates of Florence. — 130. *antiphonary,* the Roman Service-Book, containing all that is sung in the choir — the antiphones, responses, etc.; it was compiled by Gregory the Great. — 131. *Joined arms and legs to the long music-notes.* The musical notation of Lippo's day was entirely different from ours, the notes being square and oblong

and rather less suited for arms and legs than the present rounded notes.—139. *Camaldolese.* Monks of Camaldoli. *Preaching Friars.* The Dominicans.— 189. *Giotto.* The painter, sculptor, and architect (1266-1337).—235. *Brother Angelico.* Fra Angelico, Giovanni da Fiesole (1387-1455), of the monastic school, who was said to paint on his knees.—236. *Brother Lorenzo.* Lorenzo Monaca of the same school.—276. *Guidi.* Tommaso Guidi, or Masaccio, nick-named "Hulking Tom" (1401-1429). [Vasari makes him Lippo's predecessor. Browning followed the best knowledge of his time in making him, instead, Lippo's pupil. Vasari is now thought to be right.]—323. *A Saint Laurence at Prato.* Near Florence, where Lippi painted many saints. [Vasari speaks of a St. Stephen painted there in the same realistic manner as Browning's St. Laurence, whose martyrdom of broiling to death on a gridiron affords Lippo's powers a livelier effect.] The legend of this saint makes his fortitude such that he bade his perse-cutors turn him over, as he was "done on one side."—346. *Sant' Ambrogio.* St. Ambrose Church in Florence.—377. *Iste perfecit opus.* This one completed the work. (Written at Rome in the winter of 1853-1854. 'Men and Women,' 1855.)

P. 133. Andrea del Sarto. The interaction and interdependence of Andrea del Sarto's own nature upon his choice of a wife and the character of his art are revealed in this monologue, along with the personalities of both Andrea and Lucrezia, the degrading influence of their relationship, and the main incidents of their lives, the whole serving to illustrate the picture on which the poem is based. The gray tone that silvers the picture pervades the poem with an air of helpless, resigned melancholy, and sets forth the fatal quality of facile craftsmanship joined with a flaccid spirit. Mr. John Kenyon, Mrs. Browning's cousin, asked Browning to get him a copy of the picture of Andrea and his wife in the Pitti Palace. Brown-ing, being unable to find one, wrote this poem describing it, instead. Andrea, (1486-1531), because his father was a tailor, was called del Sarto, also, *il pittore senza errori,* "the faultless painter." Vasari's Life of him supplied the poet with material as follows:—*Brng.:* 1. "Do not let us quarrel any more," etc. *Vasari:* "He destroyed his own peace and estranged his friends by marrying Lucrezia di Baccio del Fede, a cap-maker's widow who ensnared him before her husband's death, and who delighted in trapping the hearts of men . . . he soon became jealous and found that he had fallen into the hands of an artful woman who made him do as she pleased in all things . . . but although Andrea lived in . . . torment he yet accounted it a high pleasure." *Brng.:* 60. "I can do with my pencil . . . easily, too, . . . what many dream of," etc. 82. "This low-pulsed forthright crafts-man's hand," etc. *Vasari:* "Art and nature combined to show all that may be done in painting when design, coloring, and invention unite in the same person. Had this master possessed a somewhat bolder and more elevated mind . . . he would have been without an equal. But there was a certain timidity of mind, a sort of diffidence and want of force in his nature, which rendered it impossible that . . . ardor and animation, which are proper to the more exalted character, should ever appear in him . . . His figures are well drawn . . . free from errors . . . the coloring exquisite." *Brng.:* 98. "All is silver gray, placid and perfect," etc. *Vasari:* "Andrea understood the management of light and shade most perfectly, causing the objects depicted to take their due degree of prominence or to retire within the shadows." *Brng.:* 76. "Some one says." 184. "Said Agnolo . . . to Raphael." 189. "Friend, there's a certain sorry little scrub," etc. *Vasari:* "If he had remained in Rome when he went thither to see the works of Raffaello and Michelagnolo . . . would eventually have attained the power of imparting a more elevated character and increased force to his figures . . . nay, there are not wanting those who affirm he would . . . have surpassed all the artists of his time . . . Raffaello and other young artists whom he perceived to possess great power . . . deprived Andrea, timid as he was, of courage to make trial of himself." Michael Angelo's remark to Raphael is given thus by Bocchi, ' Bellezze di Firenze,' " There is a bit of a mannikin in Florence who, if he chanced to be employed in great undertakings as you have happened to be, would compel you to look well about you." *Brng.:* 149. "That Francis . . . that long festal year at Fontainebleau," etc. *Vasari:* " Two pictures he had sent into France, obtaining much admiration from King Francis . . . that monarch was told he might prevail upon Andrea to visit France . . . the king therefore gave orders that a sum of money should be paid to Andrea for the expenses of the journey . . . his arrival was marked by proofs of liberality and courtesy . . . his labors rendering him so acceptable to the king and the whole court, his departure from his native country appeared . . . to have conducted him from wretchedness to felicity . . . But one day . . . came to him certain letters from Florence written to him by his wife . . . with bitter complaints . . . Moved by all this he resolved to resume his chain . . . Taking the money which the king confided to him for the purchase of pictures and statues . . . he set off . . . having sworn on the gospels to return in a few months. Arrived in Florence, he lived joyously with his wife for some time, making presents to her father and sisters, but doing nothing for his own parents, who died in poverty and misery. When the period specified by the king had come . . . he found himself at the end not only of his own money but . . . of that of the king . . . remained in Florence, therefore, procuring a livelihood . . . as he best might." ('Men and Women,' 1855.)

P. 138. The Bishop Orders his Tomb. This half-delirious pleading of the dying prelate for a tomb which shall gratify his luxurious artistic tastes and personal rivalries, in presenting dramatically the special scene of the worldly old bishop's petulant struggle against his failing power, and his collapse, finally, beneath the will of his so-called nephews, also sets forth to the life a characteristic gross form of the Renaissance spirit encumbered with Pagan survivals, fleshly appetites, and selfish monopolizings which hampered its development. — " It is nearly all that I said of the Central Renaissance, — its worldliness, inconsistency, pride, hypocrisy, ignorance of itself, love of art, of luxury, and of good Latin — in thirty pages of the ' Stones of Venice,' put into as many lines, Browning's being also the antecedent work." (Ruskin.) The church of St. Praxed was rich in mosaics, its chapel St. Zeno being called *Orto del Paradiso,* or the Garden of Paradise, and so, although the bishop and his tomb there are entirely imaginations of Browning, it supplies an appropriate setting for the poetic scene. — 31. *Onion stone.* For the Italian *cipollino,* a kind of greenish-white marble splitting into coats like an onion, *cipolla,* hence so called. — 41. *Olive-frail,* a basket made of rushes, used for packing olives. — 42. *Lapis lazuli,* a bright blue stone. — 48. *God the father's globe.* In the group of the Trinity adorning the altar of St. Ignatius at the church of Il Gesù in Rome. — 58. *Some tripod, thyrsus.* The first an emblem of the Delphic oracle, the second, of Bacchic orgy. — 77. *Tully's.* Marcus Tullius Cicero. — 79. *Ulpian.* A Roman jurist (170–228 A.D.). — 99. *Elucescebat.* Wrongly formed from the verb *eluceo, eluxi, elucere,* to be illustrious. — 102. *Else I give the Pope my villas.* Perhaps a threat founded on the custom of Julius II. and other popes, according to Burckhardt, of enlarging their power " by making themselves heirs of the cardinals and clergy . . . Hence the splendor of the tombs of the prelates . . . a part of the plunder being in this way saved from the hands of the Pope." — 108. *A Visor and a Term.* A mask, and a bust springing from a square pillar, representing the

Roman god Term who presided over boundaries. (*Hood's Magazine*, March, 1845, as 'The Tomb at St. Praxed's,' so also in 'Bells and Pomegranates, No. 7 — Dramatic Romances and Lyrics.' Classed under ' Men and Women,' and entitled as at present, in ' Poetical Works,' 1863.

P. 141. A Toccata of Galuppi's. Here is shown the power of music to call up a vision of the times which gave it birth. It has lost all possibility of direct personal appeal, because it is not the outcome of an age marked by deep and universal feeling, and its very coldness makes more vivid the picture of soulless frivolity of the Venice of the composer's day. To his contemporaries it spoke only of death, and so to the poet it not only reflects its own age, but is in its deadness a lasting monument of the "dust and ashes" into which the shallow life of Venice vanished. — 1. *Galuppi Baldassare* (1706–1785). An Italian musician, famous in his day, an industrious composer of whose seventy operas none have survived. He lived and worked in London from 1741 to 1744 ; also in Russia at the court of the Empress Catherine II. till 1768, when he left Russia and became organist of St. Mark's, Venice. When he died he left fifty thousand lire to the poor of that city. — 6. *St. Mark's.* The great cathedral of Venice named for St. Mark, because it is said that the body of that evangelist was brought to Venice and enshrined there. *Where the Doges used to wed the sea with rings.* " The ceremony of wedding the Adriatic was instituted in 1174 by Pope Alexander III., who gave the Doge a gold ring from his own finger in token of the victory achieved by the Venetian fleet at Istria over Frederick Barbarossa, in defense of the Pope's quarrel. When his Holiness gave the ring, he desired the Doge to throw a similar Ring into the sea annually, in commemoration of the event" (Brewer). — 8. *Shylock's bridge.* Probably the Rialto bridge, by which they show Shylock's house. — 18. *Toccatas.* The name toccata is derived from the Italian *toccari*, to touch. It is a piece in which a certain passage or figure is repeated over and over again either in the strict or the free style. *Clavichord*, a keyed and stringed instrument, one of the forerunners of the modern piano. The technical musical allusions in the poem are all to be found in the 7th, 8th, and 9th stanzas. The *lesser thirds* (10) are minor thirds (intervals containing three semitones), and are of common occurrence, but the diminished sixth (10) is an interval rarely used. Ordinarily a *diminished sixth* (seven semitones), exactly the same interval as a perfect fifth, instead of giving a plaintive, mournful, or minor impression, would suggest a feeling of rest and satisfaction. There is one way, however, in which it can be used, — as a suspension, in which the root of the chord on the *lowered* super-tonic of the scale is suspended from above into the chord with added seventh on the super-tonic, making a diminished sixth between the root of the first and the third of the second chord. The effect of this progression is most dismal, and possibly Browning had it in mind. *Suspensions* (19) are notes which are held over from one chord into another, and must be made according to certain strict musical rules. This holding over of a note always produces a dissonance, and must be followed by a concord, — in other words, a *solution.* Sevenths are very important dissonances in music, and a *commiserating seventh* (20) is most likely the variety called a minor seventh. Being a somewhat less mournful interval than the lesser thirds and the diminished sixths, whether real or imaginary, yet not so final as " those solutions" which seem to put an end to all uncertainty, and therefore to life, they arouse in the listeners to Galuppi's playing a hope that life may last, although in a sort of dissonantal, Wagnerian fashion. The "commiserating sevenths" are closely connected with the "dominant's persistence" (24). The dominant chord in music is the chord written on the fifth degree of the scale, and it almost always has a seventh added to it, and

In a large percentage of cases is followed by the tonic, the chord on the first degree of the scale. Now, in fugue form a theme is first presented in the tonic key, then the same theme is repeated in the dominant key, the latter being called the answer; after some development of the theme the fugue comes to what is called an episode, after which the theme is presented first, in the dominant. "Hark! the dominant's persistence" alludes to this musical fact; but according to rule this dominant must be answered in the tonic an octave above the first presentation of the theme, and "So an octave struck the answer." Thus the inexorable solution comes in after the dominant's persistence. Although life seemed possible with commiserating sevenths, the tonic, a resistless fate, strikes the answer that all must end. The use of these terms belonging to the fugue form indicate that this particular Toccata was strict rather than free in form. ('Men and Women,' 1855.)

P. 143. **How it Strikes a Contemporary** is a portrait of the Poet as the unpoetic gossiping public of his day see him. It is humorously colored in every detail by the alien point of view of one who suspects without understanding either the greatness of the poet's spiritual personality and mission, nor the nature of his life, which is withdrawn from that of the commonalty yet spent in clear-sighted universal sympathies and kindly mediation between Humanity and its God. ('Men and Women,' 1855.)

P. 146. **Protus** sets in contrast the representations by artist and annalist of the two busts and the two lives of Protus, the baby emperor of Byzantium, born in the purple, gently nurtured and cherished, yet fated to obscurity, and of John, the blacksmith's bastard, predestined to usurp his throne and save the empire with his harder hand. ('Men and Women,' 1855.)

P. 147. **Master Hugues of Saxe-Gotha.** After wrestling with the unmanageable difficulties of a mountainous fugue, likening it to a wordy quarrel over a simple proposition and seeking for the soul of meaning that inspired Master Hugues when he wrote it, the organist finally decides to regard it as a symbol of life which, with its play and interplay of human action and thought, ends by obscuring God's truth. Though Hugues may have had no discoverable moral in writing his fugue, the organist draws the moral that truth shines ever above though it is not always grasped. — 2. *Hugues,* an imaginary person. — 4. *Mountainous fugues.* A fugue is a composition in parts, the construction of which requires great skill, for it is necessary to start with a theme in the first part that can be repeated in all the other parts and yet harmonize with itself. First the theme or subject is presented in a single part in the tonic key, and is repeated in the second part a fifth higher while the first part continues in counterpoint against it. Then the subject is repeated again at the octave, and then at the fifth and so on. As the fugue progresses, the themes are developed and the intertwisting of parts grows more and more complex. The laws which govern the harmonizing of the parts together are called laws of counterpoint and form one of the most difficult branches of the art of composition (see note on 'A Toccata'). The fugue described in this poem would seem to be one of those mathematical productions of the fifteenth and sixteenth centuries, when music in the hands of the learned musicians had become little more than an affair of the head. Only with the advent of John Sebastian Bach (1685–1750) did the fugue become a thing of beauty. The fact that the poet has made Hugues from Saxe-Gotha has led to the conclusion that a Bach fugue is meant, because Bach was born in Saxe-Gotha, but the turning of the organist to Palestrina (140) as a relief from the gorgon counterpoint of Hugues, would indicate that the poet was thinking of the fugues that preceded Palestrina rather than those of Bach, which belong about a hundred years later than Palestrina (1524–1594).

when German music had come under the influence of the Italian style, founded by Palestrina, who freed music from the excesses of the current contrapuntal complications. — 26. *Aloys and Jurien and Just.* Sacristan's assistants. — 39. *Claviers.* The keyboard of the organ. — 44. *two great breves.* The longest note in music, formerly square in shape. — 80. *O Danaides, O Sieve!* The Danaides were the daughters of Danaus, who were condemned for their crimes to pour water forever through a sieve. — 88. *Escobar,* of Mendoza, a Spanish casuist, the general tendency of whose writings was to find excuses for human frailties (Dr. Berdoe). — 86. *Est fuga, volvitur rota* = it is a flight, the wheel rolls itself round. — 92. *Risposting.* A term in fencing equivalent here to making a repartee. — 100. *Ticken,* ticking. — 136. *Meâ poenâ,* at my risk of punishment. — 140. *Mode Palestrina,* in the style of Palestrina. ('Men and Women,' 1855.)

P. 152. Abt Vogler (after he has been extemporizing upon the musical instrument of his invention). The musician rises into a state of exaltation through the wonder of his own musical gift, the outcome of which seems to him more entirely creative than that of any other art, because the form is evolved from the subjective consciousness and not imitated from nature, as it is, more or less, in the other arts. While they are obedient to laws, the composer's inspiration is a revelation of the divine will, and being such is eternal in its essence. From this he reasons that all good is of the same nature, and, though only partial now, is destined to persist and form a perfect whole in the future. Evil is simply the discord that enhances the beauty of the coming concord, and is destined to be resolved in it, is, indeed, the evidence in its aspect of failure that perfection is assured in the future. — *Abt Vogler.* George Joseph Vogler, born Würzburg, Bavaria, June 15, 1749; educated for the church, but his musical talent, which showed itself at an early age, was also developed; ordained priest in Rome, 1773, and opened a school of music in Mannheim, 1775. At Stockholm, founded a second school of music, and became famous for his performances on an instrument which he had invented, called the Orchestrion, a compact organ, in which, four keyboards of five octaves each, and a pedal board of thirty-six keys, with swell complete, were packed into a cube of nine feet; travelled all over Europe with his organ, his performances being received with enthusiasm; opened a third school of music at Darmstadt, where Weber and Meyerbeer became his pupils. Here he died May 6, 1814. His "Missa Pastoricia" is performed every Christmas at the Hof Kapelle, Vienna. (See Grove's 'Dictionary of Music and Musicians.') — *Solomon willed.* Jewish and Moslem legends gave Solomon sovereignty over the demons and powers of nature which he owed to the possession of a seal on which the "most great name of God was engraved" (Lane, 'Arabian Nights'). — 7. *ineffable name,* the unspeakable name of God. Mysterious names of the deity occur in other religions besides the Jewish. — 23. *Rome's dome.* It has been customary to illuminate the dome of St. Peter's on Easter Sunday and other important festivals. — 35. *Protoplast.* The thing first modelled from which copies are imitated. — 52. *Out of three sounds he frames not a fourth sound but a star,* etc. If you were to mix three colors together the result would be a fourth color in which the individuality of the first three colors would be sunk, but if you mix three sounds together in a chord the result will not be a fourth sound, but a wonderful harmony of all three, partaking of the individuality of each, and this is done by combining tones chosen from nature's chaos of sounds through the creative power of the artist. — 91. *common chord,* consists of the fundamental, with a major (four semitones), or minor (three semitones) third, and a perfect fifth (seven semitones) over it. — 93. *ninth,* if major, contains an octave and two semitones; if minor, an octave and one semitone. These last lines of the poem, stripped of their symbolic meaning, may be taken as an exact explanation of a simple harmonic modulation. Suppose Abt Vogler when he " feels for the common chord" to have struck the chord of C major in its first inversion, *i.e.* the third, E, in the bass, the fifth, G, at the top; now, " sliding by semitones," that is, playing in succession chords with the upper note a semitone lower, he would come to the chord A, E, C, which is the (minor) tonic chord of the scale of A, the relative minor of C, and so he would thus " *sink* to the minor." Now he blunts the fifth of this chord E, to E♭, which thus becomes a minor ninth over the root D, the whole chord being D, F♯, A, C, E♭, and, as he explains, he stands on alien ground because he has modulated away from the key of C, but, instead of following this dominant by its natural solution, its own tonic, which would be G, B, D, he treats it as if it were what is called a supertonic harmony. So, after pausing on this chord to survey a while the heights he rolled from into the deep, he suddenly modulates back to C. He has dared and done, his resting place is found — the C major of this life. This is the progression : —

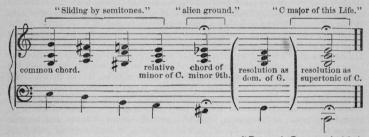

(' Dramatis Personæ,' 1864.)

P. 155. Two in the Campagna. A sense of elusiveness pervades this poem. The perpetual failure of the mind to realize thought, of the heart to realize the ideal in an earthly passion, leads the yearning human soul towards an infinite which transcends finite power. The Campagna, "Rome's Ghost," comprises an area round Rome nearly co-extensive with ancient Latium. It is populous with ruined cities and crumbling tombs; a malarial desert in summer; in May, the time of the poem, a rich unbroken pasturage. (' Men and Women,' 1855.)

P. 157. "De Gustibus — " for tastes — " De Gustibus non disputandum " — there is no accounting. Illustrative of likings inherent in each person, perhaps persistent in each ghost; for the tree-lover, rusticity, and a congenial train of English sights and sounds and scenes of youthful love-making, from which the ghostly self must stay in shadow; for the speaker, if he gets loose from his grave, scenes rich in complex human associations, Italy, the old-world life, the sea, and the stir of civic events. (' Men and Women,' 1855.)

P. 158. The Guardian Angel describes Guercino's picture through the feeling it awakens in the poet — the craving to take the child's place in it and be nurtured of the angel in the serenity of prayer. The poet, however, would not look towards heaven as the child does, but gaze contentedly upon the gracious guardian face, and view the world again afterwards, too, but with new eyes. So he now links with his translation of the picture into song thoughts of his own angel (his wife), his friend Alfred (Domett), and the artist's fame. — "A Picture at Fano," *L'Angelo Custode*, in the church of St. Augustine by the Bolognese artist Giovanni Francesco

Barbieri, called Guercino (1590–1666)." — 55. "Wairoa." A river in New Zea-
land, the country Domett went to. See 'Waring.' (Written at Ancona, 1847.
'Men and Women,' 1855.)

P. 160. Evelyn Hope expresses a lover's faith in the potency of love to reward
love, overcoming Death and Time, and making itself understood, at last, by the
young girl who dies unconscious of the secret he shuts within the keeping of her
cold hand. ('Men and Women,' 1855.)

P. 162. Memorabilia renders homage to Shelley by signalizing the moment
when an unappreciative person's remembrance of him was made known, like a
moor blank of interest save for the space where the sign of an eagle's flight was
found and prized. — "The eagle feather," says Professor Corson, "causes an iso-
lated flash of association with the poet of the atmosphere, the winds, and the
clouds, 'The meteoric poet of air and sea.'" (Written on the Campagna, winter
of 1853–1854. 'Men and Women,' 1855.)

P. 162. Apparent Failure saves the Morgue in a double sense; for it was
written to preserve the famous little building from destruction, and it seeks to make
its gloomy purpose less hopeless, retrieving three poor wretches whose death and
doom seemed sealed there from the imputation of utter failure.

Seven years since : In the summer of 1856 Browning was in Paris. — *The Bap-
tism of your Prince :* Louis Napoleon, only child of Napoleon III. and Empress
Eugénie, born March 16, 1856. — *The Congress :* The Paris Congress of the Euro-
pean Powers on Italy's unity and freedom, Prince Gortschakoff representing
Russia, Count Cavour, then prime minister of Piedmont, speaking for Italy,
Count Buol, Austrian foreign minister, 1852–1859, objecting. — *Petrarch's Vaucluse :*
a fountain in Vaucluse, in southern France, the source of the Sorgues. In the
village of Vaucluse Petrarch lived for a time. ('Dramatis Personæ,' 1864.)

P. 164. Prospice, meaning "look forward," anticipates Death as the climax
and fruition of Life, — the best and last occasion for the assertion of the spirit's
mastery, — the gateway to the rapture of the Soul's reunion with its supplementary
Soul. (Written in the autumn following Mrs. Browning's death, 1861. 'Dramatis
Personæ,' 1864. Set to music by C. V. Stanford. London : Stanley, Lucas &
Webber.)

P. 165. Childe Roland symbolizes the Conquest of Despair by Fealty to the
Ideal. Browning emphatically disclaimed any precise allegorical intention in this
poem. He acknowledged only an ideal purport in which the significance of the
whole, as suggesting a vision of life and the saving power of constancy, had its
due place. Certain picturesque materials which had made their impressions on
the poet's mind contributed towards the building up of this realistic fantasy : a
tower he saw in the Carrara Mountains ; a painting which caught his eye later in
Paris ; the figure of a horse in the tapestry in his own drawing-room, — welded
together with the remembrance of the line cited from "King Lear," iii. 4. 187,
which last, it should be remembered, has a background of ballads and legend
cycles of which a man like Browning was not unaware. For allegorical schemes
of the Poem see Nettleship's 'Essays and Thoughts,' and *The Critic*, Apr. 24,
1886 ; for an antidote to these, *The Critic*, May 8, 1886 ; an orthodox view, *Poet-
lore*, Nov., 1890 : for interpretations touching on the ballad sources, London Brown-
ing Society Papers, Part iii., p. 21, and *Poet-lore*, Aug.–Sept., 1892. (Written at
Paris in one day, Jan. 3, 1852. 'Men and Women,' 1855.)

P. 171. A Grammarian's Funeral is an elegy of a typical pioneer scholar of
the Renaissance period, sung by the leader of the chorus of disciples, and inter-
spersed with parenthetical directions to them, while they all bear the body of their

master to its appropriate burial-place on the highest mountain-peak. A humorous sense of disproportion in the labors of devoted scholarship to its results heightens their exaltation of the dead humanist's indomitable trust in the supremacy of the immaterial. — 86. *Calculus*, the stone. — 88. *Tussis*, a cough. — 95. *Hydroptic*, dropsical. — 129. *Hoti*, the Greek particle ˝Οτι, conjunction, that. — 130. *Oun*, Greek particle Οὖν, then, now then. — 131. *Enclitic ds.* Greek Δε, concerning which Browning wrote to the Editor of *The News*, London, Nov. 21, 1874:

"In a clever article you speak of 'the doctrine of the enclitic *De*'—'which, with all deference to Mr. Browning, in point of fact, does not exist.' No, not to Mr. Browning: but pray defer to Herr Buttmann, whose fifth list of 'enclitics' ends 'with the inseparable *De*,'—or to Curtius, whose fifth list ends also with *De* (meaning '*towards*' and as a demonstrative appendage).' That this is not to be confounded with the accentuated '*De*, meaning but,' was the 'Doctrine' which the Grammarian bequeathed to those capable of receiving it." ('Men and Women,' 1855.)

P. 174. Cleon expresses the approach of Greek thought at the time of Christ towards the idea of immortality as made known by Cleon, a Greek poet writing in reply to a Greek patron whose princely gifts and letter asking comment on the philosophical significance of death have just reached him. The important conclusions reached by Cleon in his answer are that the composite mind is greater than the minds of the past, because it is capable of accomplishing much in many lines of activity, and of sympathizing with each of those simple great minds that had reached the highest possible perfection "at one point." It is, indeed, the necessary next step in development, though all classes of mind fit into the perfected mosaic of life, no one achievement blotting out any other. This soul and mind development he deduces from the physical development he sees about him. But since with the growth of human consciousness and the increase of knowledge comes greater capability to the soul for joy while the failure of physical powers shuts off the possibility of realizing joy, it would have been better had man been left with nothing higher than mere sense like the brutes. Dismissing the idea of immortality through one's works as unsatisfactory to the individual, he finally concludes that a long and happy life is all there is to be hoped for, since, had the future life which he has sometimes dared to hope for been possible, Zeus would long before have revealed it. He dismisses the preaching of one Paulus as untenable.

As certain of your own poets also have said (Acts xvii. 28). Cleon is supposed to be one of the Greek poets or thinkers to whom St. Paul alludes in this line. (Mrs. Orr.)

1. *Sprinkled isles*, probably the Sporades, so named because they were scattered, and in opposition to the Cyclades which formed a circle around Delos. — 51. *phare*, light-house. The French authority, Allard, says that though there is no mention in classical writings of any light-house in Greece proper, it is probable that there was one at the port of Athens as well as at other points in Greece. There were certainly several along both shores of the Hellespont, besides the famous father of all light-houses, on the island of Pharos, near Alexandria. Hence the French name for light-house, *phare*. — 53. *Poecile*. The portico at Athens painted with battle pictures by Polygnotus the Thasian. — *Combined the moods*. In Greek music the scales were called moods or modes, and were subject to great variation in the arrangement of tones and semitones. — 340. *To one called Paulus; we have heard his fame*. Paul in his mission to the Gentiles touched at several of the islands of the Ægean Sea. ('Men and Women,' 1855.)

P. 182. Instans Tyrannus is a despot's confession of one of his own experiences which showed him the inviolability of the weakest man who is in the right and who can call the spiritual force of good to his aid against the utmost violence or cunning. — " Instans Tyrannus," or the threatening tyrant, suggested by Horace, third Ode in Book III. : —

> " Justum et tenacem proposti virum,
> Non civium ardor prava jubentium,
> Non vultus instantis tyranni," etc.

[The just man tenacious of purpose is not to be turned aside by the heat of the populace nor the brow of the threatening tyrant.]   (' Men and Women,' 1855.)

P. 184. An Epistle gives the observations and opinions of Karshish, the Arab physician, writing to Abib his master upon meeting with Lazarus after he has been raised from the dead.   Well versed in Eastern medical lore, he tries to explain the extraordinary phenomenon according to his knowledge.   He attributes Lazarus' version of the miracle to mania induced by trance, and the means used by the Nazarene physician to awaken him, and strengthens his view by describing the strange state of mind in which he finds Lazarus — like a child with no appreciation of the relative values of things.   Through his renewal of life he had caught a glimpse of it from the infinite point of view, and lives now only with the desire to please God.   His sole active quality is a great love for all humanity ; his impatience manifests itself only at sin and ignorance, and is quickly curbed.   Karshish, not able to realize this new plane of vision in which had been revealed to Lazarus the equal worth of all things in the divine plan, is incapable of understanding Lazarus, but in spite of his attempt to make light of the case, he is deeply impressed by the character of Lazarus, and has besides a hardly acknowledged desire to believe in this revelation, told of by Lazarus, of God as Love.   Professor Corson says of this poem, " It may be said to polarize the idea, so often presented in Browning's poetry, that doubt is a condition of the vitality of faith." — 17. *Snake-stone*, a name given to any substance used as a remedy for snake-bites, for example, some are of chalk, some of animal charcoal, and some of vegetable substances. — 45. *There's a spider here.*   Dr. H. C. McCook, a specialist on spiders, says in regard to this : " The habits of the aranead here described point very clearly to some one of the Wandering group, which stalk their prey in the open field or in divers lurking places, and are distinguished by this habit from the other great group, known as the Sedentary spiders, because they sit or hang upon their webs and capture their prey by means of silken snares.   The next line is not determinative of the species, for there is a great number of spiders, any one of which might be described as ' Sprinkled with mottles on an ash-gray back.'   We have a little Saltigrade or Jumping spider, known as the Zebra spider (*Epiblemum scenicum*), which is found in Europe, and I believe also in Syria.   One often sees this species and its con-geners upon the ledges of rocks, the edges of tombstones, the walls of buildings, and like situations, hunting their prey, which they secure by jumping upon them. So common is the Zebra spider, that I might think that Browning referred to it, if I were not in doubt whether he would express the stripes of white upon its ash-gray abdomen by the word ' mottles.'   However, there are other spiders belonging to the same tribe (Saltigrades) that really are mottled.

" There are also spiders, known as the Lycosids or Wolf spiders or Ground spiders, which are often of an ash-gray color, and marked with little whitish spots after the manner of Browning's Syrian species.   Perhaps the poet had one of these in mind, at least he accurately describes their manner of seeking prey.   The next line is an interrupted one, ' Take five and drop them. . . .'   Take five what ?   Five of these ash-gray mottled spiders ?   Certainly.   But what can be meant by the expression, ' drop them ' ? This opens up to us a strange chapter in human superstition. It was long a prevalent idea that the spider in various forms possessed some occult power of healing, and men administered it internally or applied it externally as a cure for many diseases. Pliny gives a number of such remedies. A certain spider applied in a piece of cloth, or another one (' a white spider with very elongated thin legs ') beaten up in oil, is said by this ancient writer upon Natural History to form an ointment for the eyes. Similarly, ' the thick pulp of a spider's body, mixed with the oil of roses, is used for the ears.' Sir Matthew Lister, who was indeed the father of English araneology, is quoted in Dr. James's Medical Dictionary as using the distilled water of boiled black spiders as an excellent cure for wounds. " (In *Poet-lore*, Nov., 1889.) — 55. *gum-tragacanth*, yielded by the leguminous shrub, Astragalus tragacantha. — 60. *Zoar*, the only one that was spared of the five cities of the plain (Gen. xiv. 2). — 177. *Greek fire*, used by the Byzantine Greeks in warfare, first against the Saracens at the siege of Constantinople in 673 A.D. Therefore an anachronism in this poem. Liquid fire was, however, known to the ancients, as Assyrian bas-reliefs testify. Greek fire was made possibly of naphtha, saltpetre, and sulphur, and was thrown upon the enemy from copper tubes; or pledgets of tow were dipped in it and attached to arrows. — 281. *Blue-flowering borage* (Borago officinalis). The ancients deemed this plant one of the four " cordial flowers," for cheering the spirits, the others being the rose, violet, and alkanet. Pliny says it produces very exhilarating effects. (' Men and Women,' 1855.)

P. 191. Caliban upon Setebos gives the ruminations of a typical undeveloped mind as to the nature of God, which is influenced by his observations of the capriciousness of nature, his fear of its threatening aspects, his hatred of his master's cruelty to him, and his own undeveloped nature. Yet even at this low stage of development a reaching toward something better is evidenced in Caliban's supposition that behind Setebos is a power which he calls the Quiet, indifferent to the affairs of man, but so far superior to Setebos as not to be actively antagonistic to man. Browning has taken Shakespeare's Caliban as a fit subject out of which to evolve the sort of anthropomorphic reasoning he wished to portray. Shakespeare possibly got his hint for Caliban from an old book of travels, ' Purchas his Pilgrimage,' in which a strange brute-man is described (see also Dr. Furness' Variorum 'Tempest'). — 4. *While he kicks.* The third person used by Caliban is characteristic of an early phase in language development. — 24. *Setebos.* In Eden's ' History of Travayle ' there is a description of giants that inhabited Patagonia, two of whom were captured by Captain Magellan, and finding themselves caught " cryed upon theye greate deuyll Setebos to helpe them." (See Variorum ' Tempest'). (' Dramatis Personæ,' 1864.)

P. 198. Saul — founded on the passage in 1 Samuel xvi. 14–23, where Saul is described as being troubled with an evil spirit which David drives away by playing the harp — puts into David's mouth the account of his ministry to Saul's great need by means of his music which, working upon the memory and emotions of Saul, at last arouses him from his lethargy. First, he sings to him the simpler tunes to the Brutes, then the help-tunes for great epochs in human life. Leading up to the tunes of human aspiration, he sings first of the great joys of life, and then centres his song upon the greatness of Saul's life especially. Seeing that Saul is now fully aroused but not comforted, David sings another song showing that Saul's true greatness does not lie in his mortal life, but in the far-reaching effect of his great deeds. Then, through the intense and self-sacrificing love with which David is inspired for Saul, the prophetic revelation of God as an incarnation of love in

2 I

Christ is borne in upon him. Yearning to give Saul greater comfort, even the assurance of a future resurrection of life, the Truth comes to him. In nature God has been revealed to him as the Almighty; in his own love God is revealed to him as love, infinitely strong in his power to love and able to accomplish what David only desires to accomplish, but infinitely weak in his power to be loved, through which weakness he shall become incarnate and be the salvation of mankind. — 1. *Abner*, the son of Ner, captain of Saul's host (1 Samuel xxvi. 5). — 36. *"And I first played the tune."* Prof. Albert S. Cook suggests that Browning obtained his hints for these tunes from Longus's romance of ' Daphnis and Chloe.' The first is found on pp. 303-4 (Smith's Translation, Bohn Ed.), "He ran through all variations of pastoral melody, he played the tune which the oxen obey, and which attracts the goats, — that in which the sheep delight," etc.; pp. 332-4, ". . . standing under the shade of a beech-tree, he took his pipe from his scrip and breathed into it very gently. The goats stood still, merely lifting up their heads. Next he played the pasture tune, upon which they all put down their heads and began to graze. Now he produced some notes soft and sweet in tone; at once his herd lay down. After this he piped in a sharp key, and they ran off to the wood, as if a wolf were in sight." In answer to the question as to whether there is any historical foundation for David's songs, Rabbi Charles Fleischer of Boston replied in a letter to the editors : " I believe that David's songs in Browning's poem ' Saul' are the inspired melodies of our nineteenth century David rather than the songs of Israel's poetic shepherd-king. . . . While, then, I believe that these melodies in ' Saul' were not current among the Jews of old, I know that they would serve well to express beliefs and ideals characteristic of the best minds among the Jews of to-day." — 45. *Jerboa*, a small jumping rodent, called also a jumping hare. — 65. *male-sapphires*, superior. The ancient sapphire was the same as our lapis-lazuli. — 203. *Hebron*, the most southern of the three cities of refuge west of Jordan. — 204. *Kidron*, a brook in Jerusalem. (' Bells and Pomegranates, No. 7 — Dramatic Romances and Lyrics,' 1845, the first nine stanzas. ' Men and Women,' 1855, the completed poem.)

P. 207. Rabbi Ben Ezra gives expression to a religious philosophy which recognizes the perfectness of the divine plan in which love plays an equal part with power. Therefore, doubts and rebuffs are welcomed as the divine means for perfecting the soul's growth and shaping it for the glorification of the divine. The very failure of man in the flesh showing his infinite possibilities of growth removes him forever from the brute, perfect on its plane, and gives assurance both of God, and of man's tendency Godwards, from which follows the certainty of God and the enduringness of the human soul. Old age is joyously accepted as the vantage ground from which life can be viewed and the truth in regard to its struggles discerned.

Rabbi Ben Ezra, or Ibn Ezra, was a mediæval Jewish writer and thinker, born in Toledo near the end of the eleventh century. His real name is said to be Abraham ben Meir ben Ezra. He was poor, but studied hard and travelled in Africa, the Holy Land, Persia, India, Italy, France, and England, but during all his wanderings he kept busy writing and gained much fame as a theologian, philosopher, physician, astronomer, mathematician, and poet. Dr. Berdoe quotes Mr. A. J. Campbell to the effect that the distinctive features of the Rabbi of the poem and the philosophy put into his mouth are drawn from the writings of the real Rabbi. Dr. M. Friedländer has written five volumes of exposition on the writings of Ibn Ezra, published for the Society of Hebrew Literature by Trübner and Co. (Died 1167 or 1168.) — 26. *Potter's wheel*, borrowed from Isaiah lxiv. 8, and Jeremiah xviii. 2-6. (' Dramatis Personæ,' 1864.)

P. 213. Epilogue. First Speaker, as David, gives symbolically the point of view of one who believes in special revelation of religious truths. Second Speaker, as Renan, shows disillusionment as to special revelation along with regret for the lost ideal and hopelessness in consequence of it. Third Speaker, the poet, restores the lost ideal, not through the reinstating of a special revelation but through the recognition of the revelation that comes to every human being in feeling and knowledge. — 1. "*On the first of the Feast of Feasts*," refers of course to the dedication of Solomon's Temple, 1 Kings viii. and ix. ; 2 Chronicles v. and vi. — Renan, born at Tréguier, Cotes-du-Nord, France, 1823. Distinguished for his ' Life of Christ,' from which he banished all supernatural elements. (' Dramatis Personæ,' 1864.)

P. 217. A Wall expresses the speaker's pleasure in looking at a dead wall clothed with vines, and makes the impression it presents of mysterious life pulsating over an inert surface symbolical of spiritual force stirring behind matter, and of the special kindred soul whose indwelling spirit has power to transfuse the external shows of life that bar him away from her, rallying his faith in " the subtle thing that's spirit" and calling him to a reunion despite material obstacles and worldly interventions. — This lyric seems to have been chosen by Browning to stand as the Prologue of his Second Series of Selections (1880), as ' My Star ' was of the First Series, because it refers to Mrs. Browning, and would serve as a sort of dedicatory verse. (Prologue to ' Pacchiarotto,' 1876, first titled 'A Wall ' in present Selections, 1880.)

P. 218. Apparitions symbolizes in three different poetical figures the power of love to change the whole aspect of life, with the added thought in the last stanza that love is a revelation of the divine. (Proem to ' Two Poets of Croisic,' with ' La Saisiaz,' 1878. Set to music by F. Tetaldi ; pub. by London Browning Society ; by E. C. Gregory, London: Novello, Ewer and Co. ; by Helen A. Clarke, in *Poet-lore*, May, 1890, Boston : Poet-lore Co.)

P. 218 and 219. 'Natural Magic' and **Magical Nature** are supplementary lyrics, both emblematical of the power of spirit over fact, but, the first, expressive more particularly of the inexplicable power of one personality over another's life and circumstances, and the second of the equally wonderful power of a soul over the conditions of its own existence. ('Pacchiarotto, with Other Poems,' 1876.)

P. 219. Garden Fancies. I. ' The Flower's Name ' gives the reveries of a would-be lover as he walks through a garden he had lately visited, recalling every little act of the girl who accompanied him and feeling the subtle influence of her presence in the flower she pointed out to him, especially the one with the soft meandering Spanish name which he would have stay forever as it was when she touched it. II. ' Sibrandus Schafnaburgensis ' shows how different the mood induced by a pedantic old book from that by a charming girl. She glorifies nature, but nature's only use in this poem is to bury out of sight the tiresome old pedant and torment him with its romping and frisking, while the hero of the occasion forgets both in ministering to his material welfare, and to his frivolous mental mood with Rabelais. In a sober moment he repents of his unkindness to the pedant, and gives him at least space on his book-shelf if not his admiration. 10. *Arbute*, probably arbutus, an ornamental shrub of the Heath family, often planted in gardens. — *Laurustine*, Viburnum Tinus, an evergreen shrub of the Honeysuckle family. — 19. *Pont-levis*, drawbridge. — 38. *De profundis accentibus lætis cantate*, sing from the depths with joyful tones. (*Hood's Magazine*, July, 1844, ' Bells and Pomegranates, No. 7,' 1845.)

P. 223. In Three Days is a lover's song of expectant joy in reunion ; his eagerness that makes the three days seem long contends with his anticipation of happiness that makes the three days seem short; and fear of change and chance is but a trifle that his perfect faith over-rides. ('Men and Women,' 1855.)

P. 224. The Lost Mistress is the farewell of a lover who seeks, with a good grace, to suppress his love to the level of that mere friendship whose privileges he must resign, but whose tenderness he transcends. ('Bells and Pomegranates, No. 7 — Dramatic Romances and Lyrics,' 1845.)

P. 225. One way of Love is a "way" so pure and unselfish that though the lover's passion is unrequited he can still see others win heaven without feeling envy. ('Men and Women,' 1855.)

P. 225. Rudel to the Lady of Tripoli. Rudel symbolizes his love as the aspiration of the sunflower that longs only to become like the sun, so losing a flower's true grace, while the sun does not even perceive the flower. He imagines himself as a pilgrim revealing to the Lady of Tripoli by means of this symbol the entire sinking of self in his love for her. Even men's praise of his songs are no more to him than the bees which bask on a sunflower are to it.

Rudel was a Provençal troubadour, and lived in the twelfth century. The Crusaders, returning from the East, spread abroad wonderful reports of the beauty, learning, and wit of the Countess of Tripoli, a small duchy on the Mediterranean, north of Palestine. Rudel, although never having seen her, fell in love with her and composed songs in honor of her beauty, and finally set out to the East in pilgrim's garb. On his way he was taken ill, but lived to reach the port of Tripoli. The countess, being told of his arrival, went on board the vessel. When Rudel heard she was coming he revived, said she had restored him to life by her coming, and that he was willing to die, having seen her. He died in her arms; she gave him a rich and honorable burial in a sepulchre of porphyry on which were engraved verses in Arabic. ('Bells and Pomegranates, No. 3 — Dramatic Lyrics,' 1842; appeared as I. under the general title of 'Queen Worship,' 'Cristina' being II.)

P. 226. Numpholeptos is an expression of womanhood as ideally conceived and actually restricted by man. Under the image of a man caught by a nymph (*Numpho-leptos*) and ensnared to undertake a series of quests colored by the unnatural broken light emanating from this unreal feminity, in the vain hope of gaining a genuine human love from her in return, an implication is given of what ideal womanhood is for man and what actual womanhood could be. The symbol is, therefore, not explicable completely by any one or all ideals of womanhood as related to man. The type presented is complex, unreal, and yet historical, implying associations with the Pagan notions of the nymphs from whom the poem derives its name — the primitive Zeus-begotten daughters of nature; with the passive woman of the Renaissance or of Chivalry, who called on men for ceaseless love and service; with the exalted woman-visions, more or less founded on actual Beatrices and Lauras by the Dantes and Petrarchs; with the divination of what woman has it actually in herself to be when she possesses knowledge and purity as a natural consequence of free individual life, obtaining them not by inheritance and imagination but by achievement. Replying to an inquiry as to the purport of 'Numpholeptos' Browning wrote: —

"An allegory of an impossible ideal object of love, accepted conventionally as such by a man, who, all the while, cannot quite blind himself to the demonstrable fact that the possessor of knowledge and purity obtained without the natural consequences of obtaining them by achievement — not inheritance, — such a being is imaginary, not real, a nymph and no woman: and only such an one would be ignorant of and surprised at the results of a lover's endeavour to emulate the qualities which the beloved is entitled to consider as pre-existent to earthly experience, and independent of its inevitable results.

"I had no particular woman in my mind; certainly never intended to personify wisdom, philosophy, or any other abstraction; and the orb, raying colour out of whiteness, was altogether a fancy of my own. The 'seven-spirits' are in the Apocalypse, also in Coleridge and Byron: a common image." (' Pacchiarotto,' 1876.)

P. 230. **Appearances** symbolizes by means of two illustrative incidents how unimportant externals are in comparison with the life beneath them. (' Pacchiarotto, with Other Poems,' 1876.)

P. 230. **The worst of it** is addressed mentally by a husband to a wife who has been false to him after having given him a year's perfect happiness. Love of her has been so much to him that staunch apology for her rights of choice, and loyal resentment of the imputation of evil she will suffer in the world through having broken his bonds, contend with his own pain, and his secret fear that her womanhood must sustain some real taint, without in the least marring the quality of his own fidelity or altering his obedient renunciation of any right over her. (' Dramatis Personæ,' 1864.)

P. 234. **Too Late** presents a series of moods of a man who first realizes the full force of his love when the woman he loved is dead. He blames himself now for not having been more determined in his suit. He waited to tell his love until she should sufficiently encourage him with a glance; when she marries some one else, he blames no one, but calmly thinks that Time will give her to him. Either his love will reach out toward her round the obstacle of her husband, or else a miracle will sweep the obstruction entirely away. Now Edith is dead there is no hope. It isn't worth while to vent his rage on the past, nor upon the husband whom he represents as a person very inferior to himself, a poet, who rhymed rubbish that nobody read — and incapable of loving Edith. All that is left to him is to get what satisfaction he can by living with his back to the world, kneeling in the imagined presence of Edith, and perfecting in spirit the courtship once planned. — 138. *Summus Jus*, utmost justice. (' Dramatis Personæ,' 1864.)

P. 237. **Bifurcation** presents a case of conflict between love and duty, in the guise of two epitaphs imagined by the lover, which sum up two life-histories: the one of the woman who chooses for herself the smoother and safer path of duty, contenting her heart with bidding her lover to be constant, and to await with her the pleasure of a future life where they need not make a choice between good things, but have both easily; the other of the man, left perforce by her decision upon the rougher road, to proceed against ceaseless pains and hindrances, content only in a faith that does not dissever love from duty nor count the cost of enduring actual imperfection for its sake; both lives, thus set forth, calling for a nice decision as to which person was sinner, which was saint. (' Pacchiarotto, with Other Poems,' 1876.)

P. 238. **A Likeness,** in giving two instances of the unsympathetic regard which the uninitiated will bestow upon a likeness deeply cherished by its owner, and a third instance in which a friend being too appreciative, the possessor of the likeness feels it no longer peculiarly his own, and half pleased, half vexed, would as soon toss it to his friend as only a duplicate after all, illustrates: first, how the person to whose sympathies an object has especially appealed, is secretly grieved by others' lack of appreciation; and second, the irritation aroused through the loss of the sense of peculiar possession occasioned by the full appreciation of another. — 19. *Tipton Slasher*. An English boxer. — 20. *Rarey*. The famous horse tamer whose method of subduing the most vicious brutes consisted in firmness and genlleness. — 22. *Sayers*. The English prize-fighting champion. — 55. *Festina lentè*, hasten slowly. — 61. *Volpato*. An eminent designer and engraver, born at Bassano in 1738; died 1803. ('Dramatis Personæ,' 1864.)

P. 240. May and Death. A natural outbreak of irritation at the return of May, with its renewed joys and poignant memories of old associations cut short by Death, the first pang of it, starting the wish that all Spring's joys had died with the friend, softening, for the sake of other such pairs of friends, to the longing to reserve as sacred to the dead merely one little plant whose red-splashed leaf seems to betoken his own bleeding sorrow. — The "poem was a personal utterance," Mrs. Orr says, incited by the death of a dearly loved relative. — 13. *One plant*. The Spotted Persicaria or *Polygonum Persicaria*, whose leaves have purple stains varying in size and brightness according to the nature of the soil where it grows. ('The Keepsake,' 1857, included in 'Dramatis Personæ,' 1864.)

P. 241. A Forgiveness presents a conflict between two proud souls, who love each other, but who do not fully understand each other's natures, resulting in crime and repentance on the woman's part, and in self-justified crime on the man's part. The incidents of the story come out in the husband's confession to a priest. The wife, jealous of her husband's attention to state affairs, thinks to teach him her worth in arousing his jealousy by an intrigue with another man, whom she avows to her husband she loves. Scorn at her utter contemptibleness is the result, and though all sympathy is over between them, everything appears to go on smoothly in the eyes of the world. At the end of three years the wife feels that unless she confesses to her husband the truth, that she had loved him and him alone, she will die, and gain the peace she does not deserve. She chooses, therefore, to live, and confessing to him, asks only that she may be allowed to go and burn her life out to ashes. In learning the truth, the husband's scorn is raised to hate. He requires her to write down her confession. She evidently fearing that this change in his attitude means that he now thinks her, according to his code, worthy of death, hopes that her blood for ink will suffice, to which he acquiesces equivocally, while handing her the poisoned weapon that kills her. In her death he tells her, hate is quenched in vengeance, and that dead he pardons her. The final stanza unexpectedly increases the dramatic intensity of the scene by revealing the fact that the confession has been made to the man with whom his wife had intrigued, and who can no longer escape the husband's vengeance. Mary Wilson says of this poem, "Nothing could more effectively express the stoic Spaniard, his code and ideal, than the measured punctiliousness, the gradation from contempt to hatred, the self-command, the unhasting, unresting vindictiveness, and the exquisite torture devised for his enemy." — 99. *Which changed for me a barber's basin straight into Mambrino's helm*. Mambrino was a Moorish king, in the romantic poems of Bojardo and Ariosto, who was the possessor of an enchanted golden helmet, which rendered the wearer invulnerable. The allusion is to an episode in the 'Adventures of Don Quixote,' when the crazy knight thought he had found the golden helmet in what proved to be nothing but a copper basin, highly polished, which a barber on his way to bleed a patient had put on his head to protect a new hat during a shower. Don Quixote exclaims to Sancho, "Seest thou not yon knight coming toward us on a dapple-grey steed with a helmet of gold on his head? . . . If I mistake not there cometh one toward us who carries on his head Mambrino's helmet, concerning which thou mayest remember I swore the oath" (chap. xxi.). — 201. *arquebus* or harquebus, the earliest form of hand gun, resembling the modern musket, first used about 1476. — 249. *Arms of Eastern workmanship*. Browning had in his possession just such a collection of arms. ('Pacchiarotto,' 1876.)

P. 251. Cenciaja is a note throwing light on the passage in Shelley's tragedy ot 'The Cenci,' act v. sc. 4, wherein Cardinal Camillo reports the Pope's decision that Beatrice and her brother must die. Browning's poetic commentary on this supplies an account of the historic occurrences connected with Paolo Santa Croce's matricide which determined the Pope's decision in the then pending Cenci case, and incidentally reveals the secret motives which instigated Cardinal Aldobrandini and Judge Taverna to secure the condemnation of Paolo's innocent brother Onofrio; the whole serving in Browning's hands to reinforce Shelley's picture of the time and to illustrate with grim irony how unerring "God's justice" has been when left in men's hands. Of the historic basis of the poem, Browning writes: "I got the facts from a contemporaneous account I found in a MS. volume containing the 'Relations' of the Cenci affair — with other memorials of Italian crime — lent me by Sir J. Simeon; who published the Cenci Narrative, with notes, in the series of the Philobiblon Society. It was a better copy of the 'Relation' than that used by Shelley, differing at least in a few particulars. I believe I have seen somewhere that the translation was made by Mrs. Shelley — the note appended to an omitted passage seems a womanly performance." Of the Title and Motto he writes : "'Aia' is generally an accumulative yet depreciative termination: 'Cenciaja'—a bundle of rags—a trifle. The proverb means 'every poor creature will be pressing into the company of his betters,' and I used it to deprecate the notion that I intended anything of the kind." ('Pacchiarotto, with Other Poems,' 1876.)

P. 257. Porphyria's Lover relates how, by strangling Porphyria with her own yellow hair, the lover seized and preserved the moment of perfect love when, pure and good, Porphyria left the world she could not forego for his sake, and came to him, for once conquered by her love. A latent misgiving as to his action is intimated in the closing line of the poem.

Remarking upon the fact that Browning removed the original title, 'Madhouse Cells,' which headed this poem, and 'Johannes Agricola in Meditation,' Mrs. Orr says : "Such a crime might be committed in a momentary aberration, or even intense excitement of feeling. It is characterized here by a matter-of-fact simplicity, which is its sign of madness. The distinction, however, is subtle; and we can easily guess why this and its companion poem did not retain their title. A madness which is fit for dramatic treatment is not sufficiently removed from sanity. (Fox's *Monthly Repository*, over the signature "Z," 1836. Reprinted as II. 'Madhouse Cells.' 'Bells and Pomegranates, No. 3— Dramatic Lyrics, 1842.')

P. 259. Filippo Baldinucci is an old man's racy account of an incident of the seventeenth century, recalled to mind by his relish of his nephew's disorderliness in pelting Jews. The boy's prejudices, appearing as a faint reflex of the Christian trick his uncle narrates, are thus dramatically shown to be a heritage from an elder generation, and already growing out of date. The religious tolerance embodied in current laws, on the other hand, falling in line with the larger view of all religions evinced, in the sequel of the old man's story, by the burly young Jew, serves to vindicate and avenge the persecuted and to set forth in a humorous, satirical light the childishness of the piety of the persecutors. The first part of the old man's story is given, as an actual occurrence in the life of the painter Lodovico Buti (1624–1696), in a passage in Filippo Baldinucci's 'Notices of Painters' (*'Notizie dei Professori del Disegno da Cimabue in quà,'* 1629–1670, published 1681–1728). The Rabbi who remonstrated is there told: "'Your bargain has been fulfilled to the letter, and what else do you want? It is my opinion that you are very presumptuous, that with your sordid money you wished to buy my patron's liberty." The story then closes, thus : "Then the Rabbis dispersed discontentedly, but tacitly acknowledging they were wrong. They said no more about it and no longer tried with their ill-gotten riches to control the piety of good Christians." The sequel, as told in stanzas xxxvii to lvi, is of Browning's own devising, and of course is not to be found in Baldinucci's book, so the poet cleverly accounts for this in stanza xxxvi by making Filippo declare, " plague o' me if I record it in my book! " The initial situation of the boy and his uncle is, also, Browning's own dramatic setting of the occurrence. — 176. *Esaias: " stiff-necked Jews*." Isaiah xlviii. 4 : " Thy neck is an iron sinew." — 397. *Leda, Ganymede, Antiope*, refers to three of the many loves of Jupiter for whom he abandoned his godlike aspect and assumed for the sake of Leda, the wife of Tyndarus, King of Sparta, the form of a swan ; for Ganymede, the fair Trojan boy, the form of an eagle ; for Antiope, the daughter of Asopus, the river-god, the form of a satyr. — 402. *Titian*. The great Venetian painter, 1477–1576. (' Pacchiarotto, with Other Poems,' 1876.)

P. 272. **Soliloquy of the Spanish Cloister** gives the ill-natured attitude of mind of a monk, jealous of a brother monk, whom he hates because of his genial nature and goodness, his simple interest in natural life, and his neglect of those narrow-minded superstitious forms upon the observance of which the ill-natured monk especially congratulates himself. — 10. *Salve tibi*. Hail to thee. — 39. *Arian*. One who adheres to the doctrines of Arius, a presbyter of the Church in the fourth century, who held Christ to be a created being, inferior to God the Father in nature and dignity, though the first and noblest of created beings. — 49. *There's a great text in Galatians*. Dr. Berdoe writes : " The great *text* I take to be the tenth verse of the third chapter : ' For as many as are of the works of the law are under the curse : for it is written, " Cursed is every one that continueth not in all things which are written in the book of the law to do them." ' ' It is written,' — that is to say in the Book of Deuteronomy, xxviii. 15–68, wherein are set forth at length the curses for disobedience. Those arithmetically minded commentators on this poem, who have been disappointed in finding only some seventeen works of the flesh in Galatians v. 19–21, will find an abundant opportunity for their discrimination in the chapter of Deuteronomy to which I refer. The question to settle is ' the twenty-nine distinct damnations.' St. James says in his epistle (ii. 10) that ' he who offends against the law in one point is guilty of all.' It, therefore, the envious monk could induce his brother to trust to his works instead of to his faith, he would fall under the condemnation of the law, as explained by St. Paul in his epistle." — 56. *Manichee*, a follower of Manes, a Persian, who tried to combine the Oriental philosophy with Christianity, and maintained that there are two supreme principles — light, the author of all good, and darkness, the author of all evil. — 71. *Plene gratiâ, Ave, Virgo!* Full of grace, Hail, Virgin. Evidently a slight change of *Ave Maria gratia plena*, demanded by the exigencies of rhyme and metre. (' Bells and Pomegranates, No. 3 — Dramatic Lyrics,' 1842. See Notes, **P. 43**.)

P. 275. **The Heretic's Tragedy** is an Interlude imagined in the manner of the Middle Ages and typically representing this period of human development in its quaint piety and prejudice, its childish delight in cruelty, and its cumulative legend-making during the course of two centuries as reflected through the Flemish nature. It is supposed to be sung by an abbot, a choir-singer, and a chorus, in celebration of the burning of Jacques du Bourg-Molay, last Grand Master of the wealthy and powerful secular order of Knights Templars, which came into rivalry with the Church after the Crusades and was finally suppressed by Philip IV. of France and Pope Clement V., Molay's burning at Paris in 1314 being a final scene in their discomfiture and the Church's triumph. — 8. *Plagal-cadence*. A closing progression of chords in which the sub-dominant or chord on the fourth degree of the scale precedes the tonic or chord on the first degree of the scale. The name arises from the modes used in early church music called Plagal Modes, which were a transposition of the authentic modes beginning on the fourth degree of the authentic modes. — 12. *Bought of Aldabrod*, etc. Clement's arraignment of Jacques or John being that the riches won piously by the order during the Crusades, he had not scrupled to sell again to Saladin, the Sultan, who is portrayed by Scott in 'The Talisman.' — 14. *Pope Clement*. The fifth Clement, 1305–1314. — 18. *clavicithern*, a cithern with keys like a harpsichord. — 35. *Sing "Laudes."* Sing the seven Psalms of praise making up the service of the church called Lauds. — 47. *Salvâ*, etc. The bidding to greet here with a reverence, according to custom, the Host, or Christ's flesh, which had been mentioned. — 59. *Sharon's rose.* Solomon's Song ii. 1. ('Men and Women,' 1855.)

P. 278. Holy-Cross Day reflects the attitude of the corrupt mediæval Christians and Jews toward each other. The prose preceding the poem gives the point of view of an imaginary Bishop's Secretary, who congratulates himself upon the good work the Church is doing in forcing its doctrine on the Jews in the Holy-Cross Day sermon, and effecting many conversions. The poem shows that the Jews regard this solicitude on the part of the Christians with hatred and scorn, and that their conversions are in derision of their would-be converters. The sarcasm of the speaker reaches a pinnacle of bitterness when he accuses the Christian bishops of being men he had helped to their sins and who now help him to their God. From scorn toward such followers of Christ, he passes, in the contemplation of Rabbi Ben Ezra's death song, to a defence of Christ against these followers who profess but do not act his precepts, and a hope that if the Jews were mistaken in not accepting Christ, the tortures they now suffer will be received as expiation for their sin.

Holy-Cross Day is September 14. The discovery of the true cross by St. Helen inaugurated the festival, celebrated both by Latins and Greeks as early as the fifth or sixth centuries, under the title of the Exaltation of the Cross and later in commemoration of the alleged miraculous appearance of the Cross to Constantine in the sky at midday. Though the particular incidents of the poem are not historical, it is a fact (see Milman's 'History of the Jews') that, by a Papal Bull issued by Gregory XIII. in 1584, all Jews above the age of twelve years were compelled to listen every week to a sermon from a Christian priest. — 52. *Corso*, a street in Rome. — 67. *Rabbi Ben Ezra*. See Notes, P. 207. — 111. *Ghetto*, the Jew's quarter. Pope Paul IV. first shut the Jews up in the Ghetto and prohibited them from leaving it after sunset. ('Men and Women,' 1855.)

P. 282. Amphibian is a fancy suggested by the contrast between a creature whose realm is merely the air and man whose realm of earth can be exchanged at times, as in swimming, for an amphibious life, dependent partly on water, partly on air, and which images a similar contrast between the life of a man on earth and that of an unbodied soul beyond death, whose spiritual realm is approached by the man through his ability to disport himself in the corresponding realm of thought and passion, which is poetry. (Prologue to 'Fifine at the Fair,' 1872.)

P. 285. St. Martin's Summer argues that old loves though buried come forth in ghostly shape to haunt the new love, and remind it that it may not be enduring; therefore it is better not to protest too much, not to consider it as durable masonry, which tempts destruction, but rather as a light trellis that may either bend with circumstances, or else fall flat without causing much dismay. But even this concession to the ghosts fails to reduce their interference to "faint march-music." While the new love is congratulating itself upon having found a safe basis, the ghosts assert themselves, proving that they are more real than the new love which, in fact, receives all its glamour through the interfusion of their spirit, and the conclusion is that tears and clamor are the sole portion of the new love, and in the discovery of this the lover is even bereft of the comfort of ghosts of old love.

St. Martin's Summer. From October 9 to November 11. Also called Martinmas and Martelmas, because the feast of St. Martin is kept on November 11. The feast of St. Luke being on October 18, it is also called St. Luke's Summer. It corresponds with our Indian Summer. —71. When Penelope and Ulysses meet after their long separation, in the last book of the ' Odyssey,' she, as soon as she is convinced that it is indeed her husband, throws her arms about his neck and weeps. ('Pacchiarotto, with Other Poems,' 1876.)

P. 288. James Lee's Wife. A cycle of love-lyrics, each representing a scene in the growth of a husband's estrangement as reflected in the mood of the constant wife. In I., which represents her as having turned to look out upon the world, descrying in the face of nature a change ominous to her of a change in their love, the mood is one of vague dread and forecast. In II., seated by the fireside, whose security and cheer kindle sinister suggestions of wreck by sea and land, the mood is one of poignant foreboding. In III., the outer world again calling her attention to the stormy and decrepit aspects of the waning year, the mood is one of remonstrance against the overpowering of the light of the inner life by the law of change which masters the external world. In IV., the home being left behind, the walk and talk along the beach reveal husband and wife on the brink of alienation. Alike irksome to him are her loving idealization and criticism of him, and the mood which here leads her to anatomize his love, is one of clear recognition of the estrangement. In V., on the cliff, left alone and aloft, her mood is one of brooding over the meaning of love, finding appropriate images for her thoughts and feelings in dry turf and cold rock, dreary in spite of sunshine, but which the cricket and butterfly visit with color, even as love with its resplendent grace dowers the low mind with a sudden winged glory. In VI., turning for distraction to a book, she reads a fanciful poem of the wind as a voice of human woes. Her impatience with the young poet for his easy assumption of defeat by imagination instead of experience, leads her to put her own actual experience into imaginative shape, transitoriness, she typifies in the flitting beauty of the dawn, making its perpetual call upon the spiritual faculty of man, and urging him onward ceaselessly. Then recognizing this insight into the use of change as a step further on, her mood turns again to the contemplation of the human piteousness of perpetual change. In VII., at the sea's edge, among its rocks, the mood that finds expression is one of spiritual aspiration as the fruit of suffering. The autumn of the "brown old earth" diffusing cheer, though weighted with experience, seems to her fancy the embodiment of her insight that the love which is disappointed of its satisfaction on the natural plane of life must seek through that disappointment a finer spiritual fruition. In VIII., beside the drawing-board, pursuing in art the impulse she has just received to seek the significance of love on a higher impersonal plane, the hand whose beauty she is learning, through her faulty drawing, to love becomes to her one of God's many exemplifications of love in skill or in power. Her perception of its beauty as beyond the human power, even of a Da Vinci to outvie, leads her to understand a Da Vinci's interest in the actual as well as in the beautiful. The crude peasant hand in its structure and uses, showing God's power, is as worthy of study as the perfect hand that shows God's skill. The mood expressed is one of rapid insight through analogies of art and experience, which imply that her bemoaning her love for lack of the ideal perfection she craved is like her scorn of the peasant hand for lack of the beauty of the cast. The use that survives the beauty, and the use that survives the failure of her ideal, remain. In IX., on deck, taking her way in the world apart from her husband, the estrangement fully grown to the separation she accepts, the final mood is one of utter belief in the power of love. Had his love been as supreme as hers no fault in look or thought would have mattered. (The young poet's poem, in part VI., was printed as ' Lines,' signed " Z," in the *Monthly Repository*, 1836. As ' James Lee,' ' Dramatis Personæ,' 1864, entitled as at present in ' Poetical Works,' 1868. Set to music by E. C. Gregory, London : Novello, Ewer, and Co. Part I., ' Oh, Love but a Day ! ' by Cécile Hartog, London : Boosey and Co., and under title of ' Wilt thou change too ? ' by Ethel Harraden, London : C. Jeffreys.)

P. 300. **Respectability.** Two lovers wandering in Paris at night declare that had they belonged to respectable society, many months and years would have been wasted before they found out the hollowness of social conventions and dared to break them, and enjoy the pleasure of personal freedom. An illustration of the falseness of convention is furnished by their coming upon the Institute where Guizot, hating Montalembert because of their opposite views, will yet receive him with pretended courtesy, and they in the flare of the lights must also make a pretence of respectability. — 22. *Guizot*, the celebrated French writer and politician. He adopted the principles of the Constitutional Royalists. (Born at Nimes, 1787 ; died 1874.) — *Montalembert*, also celebrated as a writer and politician, and a champion of Catholicism united to democracy. (Born in London, 1810, his mother being a Scotch lady and his father, a peer of France ; died 1870.) (' Men and Women,' 1855.)

P. 301. **Dis Aliter Visum.** A woman's arraignment of a man's worldly-wise decision against yielding to the impulse to express the love he felt for her. Her keen recollection of their last meeting, and her ironical reproach of him, because their present meeting reveals each entangled in a degrading companionship, find outlet in the shape of an undercurrent of thought addressed to him under cover of an apparently light manner, suited to a casual meeting of friends. The situation before and after the ten dividing years that have passed is made clear ; and not less so her conclusion, that his wise caution was unwise and cowardly from the larger point of view, thwarting to their soul-development thenceforth, and involving two others, moreover, in their spiritual blight. The double title emphasizes the moral motive of the poem : *Dis Aliter Visum*, " The gods see otherwise," words used by Virgil, 'Æneid,' ii. 579, after describing the last vain resistance of the Greeks by the Trojans. — *Le Byron de nos jours*. " The modern Byron," that is, the lover who excites passion, but does not indulge love. — *Schumann*, Robert, musical composer and critic, 1810–1856. — *Ingres*, Jean August, painter, 1780–1867. — *Heine*, Heinrich, lyrical poet, 1800–1856. — *Votive frigate*. The model of a vessel hanging in the church, the pious (votive) offering, presumably, of one whom the saints had aided to make a safe voyage. — *Sure of the fortieth spare arm-chair*. Sure of being elected to fill the first vacancy in membership of forty of the French Academy. (' Dramatis Personæ,' 1864.)

P. 306. **Confessions.** A dying man confessing to a priest refuses to be overcome by a sense of the world's badness, but dwells instead upon the sweetness of love as he tells of his stolen interviews with a girl he loved, illustrating with his medicine bottles and the curtain, which from their arrangement call up a vision in all its details of the scene where the lovers used to meet. (' Dramatis Personæ,' 1864.)

P. 307. **The Householder** is a symbolical poem, humorously and dramatically prefiguring a scene of re-union between any husband, dominant in his house of flesh and marriage custom, who has had enough of the experimentation accorded husbands, and any wife, whose less fleshly and more protected experience has not been less wearing than his. The wife sums up the outcome of the discipline that has developed both, with the statement of the Ideal that has been their guiding star in the evolution of a better marriage, — " Love is all and Death is nought." (Epilogue to ' Fifine at the Fair,' 1872.)

P. 308. Tray. The speaker, thirsting for a song of heroism to stir his soul, dismisses those offered by two Bards, one of the heroism of war, the other of moral heroism, and gives the preference to the story of a brave dog who rescued a beggar child from drowning. With graphic touches, the scene of the rescue is placed before the reader, while the teller of the story hints that the instinct of the dog to save life, without regard to persons or consequences, is more worthy of admiration than the human reason which calculates so much upon consequences that it does nothing, and is even so blind to the moral aspect of the dog's act that it thinks by vivisection to discover the cause of the instinct. (' Dramatic Idyls,' 1879.)

P. 310. Cavalier Tunes. Three rousing songs rendering to the life the stalwart and confident temper of the uprising for King Charles against the Parliament. — 7. *Pym*, John (1584–1643), leader of the Parliament party in every important movement, from the impeachments of Buckingham and Strafford, to the proceedings against their Royal Master himself. — 14. *Hampden*, John (1594–1643), advocate for the people against the king's right to exact the ship-money tax. He took up arms in the civil war, falling in the engagement of Chalgrove Field against Prince Rupert. — 15. *Hazelrig*, Sir Arthur, introduced Pym's bill of attainder against Strafford, and was one of the five members Charles tried to impeach in 1642. Died in the Tower, 1661. *Fiennes*, Nathaniel (1608–1669), a rigid Presbyterian and leading member of Parliament, in special favor with Cromwell. *Young Harry*, son of the Secretary of State to Charles I., Sir Henry Vane the elder, held views opposed to his father's, and distinguished himself as a Liberal. Beheaded in 1662 on a charge of high treason. — 16. *Rupert*, Prince Robert, of Bavaria (1619–1682), son of Elizabeth, daughter of James I. He embraced the cause of his uncle, Charles I., and went to England at the beginning of the civil war, proving himself a brave but imprudent soldier.— II. 16. *Noll's damned troopers*. Oliver Cromwell's own company of horse, noted for their discipline and valor. (' Bells and Pomegranates, No. 3 — Dramatic Lyrics,' 1842, III., originally entitled, ' My Wife Gertrude,' as now in ' Poems,' 1849. Set to music by C. V. Stanford.)

P 312. Before and After. ' Before ' is an argument on the part of a third person in favor of two men fighting out a quarrel, on the grounds that the one in the wrong will never acknowledge his guilt, and the wronged one will not forgive as long as there is wrong to be resisted ; while if the guilty man lives, life with its ever recurrent reminders of his deed will be constant torment for him, and thus he will be fitly punished, and if the guiltless man dies, he will but have borne one stroke more in the cause of truth and will win heaven. ' After ' reflects the feelings of the man who survives after the quarrel — the wronged man, who realizes when it is too late, that death avails nought to erase either offence or disgrace. If only their old days of friendship could be recalled how easily all might be borne. (' Men and Women,' 1855.)

P. 314. Hervé Riel. A ballad of the Breton hero who piloted the French ships into harbor and saved them from the English, and being urged to name his own reward asked leave to go and see his wife. " Written in 1867, published 1871, in the *Cornhill*, because Browning desired to give a subscription to the Fund on behalf of the French after the siege of Paris by the Germans in 1870–71. He sent the £100 given by Mr. Smith for the poem to that fund. When the poem appeared, the facts of the story were denied at St. Malo; but on the reports to the French Admiralty of the time being looked up, they were found to be correct. Browning was mistaken, however, in stating that Hervé Riel was granted but one day's holiday in which to see his wife, " La Belle Aurore," — that is, if the *Notes sur le Croisic* (par Caillo Jeune) are correct : " Ce brave homme ne demanda pour récompense d'un service aussi signalé, qu'un congé absolu pour rejoindre sa femme, qu'il nommait la Belle Aurore." This fact was brought to the poet's notice by Dr. Furnivall, to whom he writes : " Where do you find that the holiday of Hervé Riel was for more than a day — his whole life-time ? If it is to be found, I have strangely overlooked it." That he *had* " overlooked it" is evident from the following letter : —

" . . . You are undoubtedly right, and I have mistaken the meaning of the phrase — I suppose through thinking that, if the coasting-pilot's business ended with reaching land, he might claim as a right to be let go : otherwise, an absolute discharge seems to approach in importance a substantial reward. Still — truth above all things." (*Poet-lore*, Feb. 1896.) — 1. *at the Hogue*. " Cap la Hougue." — 2. *The English*, etc. Louis XIV. had sent an expedition against England to restore James II. to the throne, when the English and Dutch fleets fell upon them and the French retired. — 5. *St. Malo*. An island in the mouth of the Rance River.— 30. *Plymouth Sound*. The harbor of the Devonshire English naval station. — 43. *Tourville*. The French naval leader. — 46. *Malouins*. Inhabitants of St. Malo.— 50. *Grève*. The dangerous sands left bare by the ebbing tide. — 53. *Solidor*. The fort defending the bay of St. Michel. (' Pacchiarotto with other Poems,' 1876.)

P. 318. In a Balcony presents in three dramatic scenes a crisis in the lives of three human beings, ending tragically for two of them. The dramatic motive is the conflict between truth on the part of Norbert, and dissembling policy on the part of Constance, who winning her way loses all she thought to have gained and more, while had Norbert's straightforward course been followed, all would have been gained for both. As it is, Constance, misunderstanding the true nature, both of the Queen and of Norbert, tries to convince Norbert that if he should now ask her hand of the Queen, — from whom he has just won such high favor on account of his services, that he might aspire to ask of her anything, even to the sharing of her crown — the revulsion of feeling will be so great upon the discovery that all was for the sake of Constance and not primarily for her, that not only will she not grant his request, but his own future prospects will be ruined. Rather than this, Constance would have their love remain unannounced, but he will not consent to anything less than a frank avowal to all the world of his love, and is ready to rely on the justice of the Queen to grant him the reward he chooses. Against his better judgment, he finally submits to follow the advice of Constance so far as to flatter the Queen by insinuating that he asks for Constance, because she is as near as he dare approach to the Queen. When Constance learns that the Queen has mistaken Norbert's dissembling for an avowal of love to herself, that she is overwhelmed with joy, and how great her sufferings have been through the starving of her affections, with sympathies roused and with fears for the consequences if the Queen finds out the mistake, she tries to force Norbert, whose character she still fails fully to comprehend, into actually giving himself to the Queen. Norbert now shows himself the champion of truth at any cost, but too late. The Queen is undeceived, but cannot forgive the deception. Constance, at last, learns to know Norbert as he really is, and her love reaches a height worthy of his. — 130. *Rubens* (1577–1640), the greatest of the Flemish school of painters. (' Men and Women,' 1855.)

P. 339. Old Pictures in Florence is a plea for the catholic appreciation of all exponents and schools of art as related parts in the whole plan of man's soul-growth, and, especially, for the due praise of those early painters whose decaying work is still unapprehended, yet who were the pioneers in the development of the perfected art of the great Italian Masters. This is expressed in the course of the spontaneous soliloquy of a genuine art-critic whose picture-collecting is a labor of love. His delight in Giotto's bell-tower, aspiring above the beauty of Florence on a certain warm March morning, provokes these thoughts, also the reproaches he sportively addresses to the ghosts of the artists he is so alone in understanding that they have not helped him to ferret out their lost art treasures. Even his adored, great Giotto has let another discover a " certain precious little tablet " he will not yet give up hoping to secure, and in anticipation of which he closes his musings with a prophecy of Florence freed from the Austrian yoke, celebrating her liberty by no noisy demonstration, but by sympathetically correlating the historic evolutions of art and life, attributing the fruitful periods to the Republic, the sterile to Monarchy, and carrying on the unfinished work of Giotto to a new pinnacle of glory. — 15. *Bell-tower Giotto raised.* The Campanile of Santa Maria in Florence, founded 1334, from designs and models of Giotto's which were his last public work. — 64. *Da Vincis derive from Dellos.* Leonardo da Vinci (1452–1519) representing the fullest scope of artistic power; Niccolo Dello, who painted cassoni, in the style of the bird-painter Uccelli, with careful perspective, representing the power of art in little. — 69. *Stefano,* a pupil of Giotto's, called the " Ape of Nature " for his improved color and softness. — 97. *Sit like Theseus.* As represented in the sculptures from the Parthenon now in the British Museum. — 98. *Son of Priam.* The Paris of the Ægina sculptures, kneeling and drawing a bow, now in the Munich Glyptothek. — 101. *Slay your snake like Apollo.* See Browning's own note. — 102. *Niobe's the grander.* The sculptured Niobe mourning for her children, now in the Uffizi, Florence. — 103. *Racers' frieze.* From the Parthenon. — 104. *Dying Alexander.* The sculptured head, so called, now in Florence. — 134. *Thy one work . . . done at a stroke.* When the envoy of Benedict IX., visiting Giotto, asked for a drawing to carry as a proof of his skill to that Pope, Giotto took a sheet of paper and a brushful of red paint, and resting his elbow on his hip, to form a sort of compass, with one turn of his hand drew a circle so perfect that it was a marvel to behold, whence the proverb " rounder than the O of Giotto." — 179. *Nicolo* (1207–1278) and *Cimabue* (1240–1302), Giotto's teacher, pioneers both of a more natural art. — 182. *Ghiberti,* Lorenzo (1381–1455), and *Ghirlandajo* or Domenico Bigordi, *the great Bigordi,* line 201 (1449–1494). — 198. *Dree.* Endure, Anglo Saxon *dreógan.* — 202. *Sandro.* Filipepi or Botticelli, 1457–1515. — 203. *Lippino* (1460–1505), son of Fra Lippo Lippi, " wronged " because his work was credited to others. — 203. *Angelico* (1387–1455), greatest of monastic painters. — 204. *Gaddi* (1300–1366), Giotto's pupil who carried out his plans for erecting the bell-tower. — 205. *intonaco.* Rough plaster cast. — 207. *Monaco* (about 1410), a monastic painter. — 210. *Pollajolo* (1430–1498), first artist to study anatomy. — 215. *Baldovinetti* (1422–1499), distinguished for his minuteness. — 217. *Margheritone* (1236–1313), among the first to show some departure from the Byzantine manner. Crucifix painting was his specialty. His sour expression refers to mixed disdain and despair excited in him by Giotto's innovations, which made him take to his death-bed in vexation. The epithet " poll-clawed parrot " applied to him by Browning seems to be a reminiscence from Shakespeare : 2 Henry IV. ii. 4, 282. The pictures described in stanzas twenty-seven and twenty-eight, Browning possessed. — 230. *Calm as Zeno.* The first stoic philosopher. — 232. *Carlino*, Carlo Dolci (1616–1686), whose pictures were smoothed into lifelessness. — 236. *A certain tablet.* This, Browning wrote Dr. Corson, "was a famous 'Last Supper' mentioned by Vasari, gone astray long ago from the Church of S. Spirito: it turned up, according to report, in some obscure corner, while I was in Florence, and was at once acquired by some stranger. I saw it, genuine or no, a work of great beauty." — 242. *Ognissanti.* All Saints Church. — 244. *Detur Amanti.* Let it be given to the loving one. — 245. *Kohinoor.* The celebrated diamond, "Mountain of light," presented to Queen Victoria in 1850; the *Jewel of Giamschid*, its only rival, belonging to the king of Persia. — 249. *A certain dotard.* Joseph Wenzel Radetzky (1766–1858), governor of Italy for the Austrians. For the allusions in stanza thirty-three, see, as Browning suggests, Mrs. Browning's 'Casa Guidi Windows,' Part I. — 260. *Quod videas ante,* "which you may have seen before."— 264. *Orgagna,* Andrea (1315–1376), an artist who derived from Giotto yet without imitation. — 271. *Chimæra.* A three-headed monster, "one indeed," says Hesiod, "of a grim-visaged lion, one of a goat, and another of a serpent," — an unnatural birth. — 275. *Half-told tale.* Chaucer's unfinished story of Cambuscan in the 'Squire's Tale.' — 277. *Beccaccia.* Woodcock. — 279. *Fifty braccia,* etc. The Campanile, as Giotto planned it, was to have been crowned by a spire fifty braccia (cubits) high. ('Men and Women,' 1855.)

P. 347. Bishop Blougram's Apology is made over the wine after dinner, to defend himself from the criticisms of a doubting young literary man, who despises him because he considers that he cannot be true to his convictions in conforming to the doctrines of the Catholic Church. He builds up his defence from the proposition that the problem of life is not to conceive ideals which cannot be realized, but to find what is and make it as fair as possible. The bishop admits his unbelief, but being free to choose either belief or unbelief, since neither can be proved wholly true, chooses belief as his guiding principle, because he finds it the best for making his own life and that of others happy and comfortable in this world. Once having chosen faith on this ground, the more absolute the form of faith, the more potent the results; besides, the bishop has that desire of domination in his nature, which the authorization of the Church makes safer for him. To Gigadibs' objection that were his nature nobler, he would not count this success, he replies he is as God made him, and can but make the best of himself as he is. To the objection that he addresses himself to grosser estimators than he ought, he replies that all the world is interested in the fact that a man of his sense and learning, too, still believes at this late hour. He points out the impossibility of his following an ideal like Napoleon's, for conceding the merest chance that doubt may be wrong, and judgment to follow this life, he would not dare to slaughter men as Napoleon had for such slight ends. As for Shakespeare's ideal, he can't write plays like his if he wanted to, but he has realized things in his life which Shakespeare only imagined, and which he presumes Shakespeare would not have scorned to have realized in *his* life, judging from his fulfilled ambition to be a gentleman of property at Stratford. He admits, however, that enthusiasm in belief, such as Luther's, would be far preferable to his own way of living, and after this, enthusiasm in unbelief, which he might have if it were not for that plaguy chance that doubt may be wrong. Gigadibs interposes that the risk is as great for cool indifference as for bold doubt. Blougram disputes that point by declaring that doubts prove faith, and that man's free will preferring to have faith true to having doubt true tips the balance in favor of faith and shows that man's instinct or aspiration is toward belief, that unquestioning belief, such as that of the Past, has no moral effect on man, but faith which knows itself through doubt is a moral spur. Thus the arguments from expediency, instinct, and consciousness, all bear on the side of faith and convince the bishop that it is safer to keep his faith intact from his doubts. He then proves that Gigadibs, with all his assumption of superiority in his frankness of unbelief, is in about the same position as himself, since the moral law which he follows has no surer foundation than the religious law the bishop follows, both founded upon instinct. The bishop closes as he began, with the consciousness that rewards for his way of living are of a substantial nature, while Gigadibs has nothing to show for his frankness, and does not hesitate to say that Gigadibs will consider his conversation with the bishop the greatest honor ever conferred upon him. The poet adds some lines, somewhat apologetic for the bishop, intimating that his arguments were suited to the calibre of his critic, and that with a profounder critic he would have made a more serious defence. Speaking of a review of this poem by Cardinal Wiseman, Browning says in a letter to a friend, printed in *Poet-lore*, May, 1896, " The most curious notice I ever had was from Cardinal Wiseman on *Blougram* — *i.e.*, himself. It was in the *Rambler*, a Catholic journal of those days, and certified to be his by Father Prout, who said nobody else would have dared put it in." This review praises the poem for its " fertility of illustration and felicity of argument," and says that " though utterly mistaken in the very groundwork of religion, though starting from the most unworthy notions of the work of a Catholic bishop, and defending a self-indulgence every honest man must feel to be disgraceful, [it] is yet in its way triumphant." — 10. *Brother Pugin* (1810–1852), an eminent English architect, who, becoming a Catholic, designed many cathedrals for the Catholic Church. — 34. *Corpus Christi Day*, Thursday after Trinity Sunday, when the Feast of the Sacrament of the Altar is celebrated. — 45. *Che*, what. — 54. *Count D'Orsay* (1798–1852), a clever Frenchman, distinguished as a man of fashion, and for his drawings of horses. — 113. *Parma's pride, the Jerome ;* 114. *Correggio ;* 117. *Modenese.* In the Ducal academy at Parma, one of the most important paintings is the St. Jerome by Correggio. He was born in the territory of Modena, Italy. — 184. *A chorus-ending from Euripides.* The Greek dramatist, Euripides (480 B.C.–406 B.C.), frequently ended his choruses with this thought — sometimes with slight variations in expression : " The Gods perform many things contrary to our expectations, and those things which we looked for are not accomplished; but God hath brought to pass things unthought of." — 316. *Hildebrand* (Gregory VII., 1073–85), claimed the temporal power of the Popes and the authority of the Papacy over sovereigns. — 411. *Schelling*, distinguished German philosopher (1775–1854). — 516. *Giulio Romano* (1492–1546), Italian painter, referred to in ' Winter's Tale,' v. ii. *Dowland*, English musician, praised for his lute playing in a sonnet in ' The Passionate Pilgrim,' attributed to Shakespeare. — 588. *Strauss* (1808–74), one of the Tübingen philosophers, author of a Rationalistic ' Life of Jesus.' — 715. *King Bomba*, means King Puffcheek, King Liar, King Knave, a sobriquet given to Ferdinand II., late king of the Two Sicilies. *Lazzaroni*, Naples beggars, named from Lazarus. — 716. *Antonelli*, Cardinal, secretary of Pope Pius IX. — 728. *Naples liquefaction.* The supposed miracle of the liquefaction of the blood of St. Januarius the Martyr. A small quantity of it is preserved in a crystal reliquary in the great church at Naples, and when brought into the presence of the head of the saint it melts. — 744. *Fichte* (1762–1814), celebrated German metaphysician. He defined God as the " moral order of the universe." — 877. *Pastor est tui Dominus*, the Lord is your shepherd. — 915. *Anacreon*, Greek lyric poet of the sixth century B.C. — 972. *In partibus, Episcopus*, etc. " In countries where the Roman Catholic faith is not regularly established, as it was not in England before the time of Cardinal Wiseman, there were no bishops of sees in the kingdom itself, but they took their titles from heathen lands " (Dr. Berdoe). ('Men and Women,' 1855.)

P. 369. Mr. Sludge the Medium is a humorous monologue conveying an American medium's defence to his patron who has caught him in cheating, followed by a short soliloquy conveying his unequivocal self-exposure. The whole presents dramatically the conditions and nature, both of spiritualism and the belief in spiritualism, current in the middle part of the nineteenth century, illustrating the credulity of the public and the self-deception of the medium. Hawthorne, in his 'French and Italian Note-books,' June 9, 1858, writes : " Browning and his wife had both been present at a spiritual session held by Mr. Home [the American medium, David D. Home], and had seen and felt the unearthly hands, one of which had placed a laurel wreath on Mrs. Browning's head. Browning, however, avowed his belief that these hands were affixed to the feet of Mr. Home, who lay extended in his chair, with his legs stretched far under the table. The marvellousness . . . melted strangely away in his hearty gripe, and at the sharp touch of his logic." — 168. *Porson*, Richard (1759–1808), the celebrated sc' olar, professor of Greek and librarian of the London Institution. — 346. *Hymn in G with natural F*, etc. Impossible music, of course, since the scale of G requires F sharp, and a piece set in *consecutive fourths* would be cacophony. — 788. *Pasiphæ*. Wife of Minos, and according to the Greek myth enamoured of a bull. — 921. *Charles's Wain*. The constellation of the Great Bear. — 1140. *Bridgewater Book*. The Bridgewater treatises were written to meet the thesis set by the Earl of Bridgewater, " On the Power, Wisdom, and Goodness of God as manifested in Creation," for which purpose he bequeathed £8000, in 1829, to the Royal Society. (' Dramatis Personæ,' 1864.)

P. 403. The Boy and the Angel. An imaginary legend illustrating the worth of humble, human love to God, who missed in the praise of the Pope, Theocrite, and of the Angel Gabriel, the precious human quality in the song of the poor boy, Theocrite. (*Hood's Magazine*, August, 1844, rewritten with five new couplets added in 'Bells and Pomegranates, No. 7 — Dramatic Romances and Lyrics,' 1845. In the ' Poetical Works' of 1868, a fresh verse was added.)

P. 406. A Death in the Desert is a supposed MS. account of St. John's dying testimony to the truth of the revelation of God made man through Christ. John's own spiritual faith transcends the idea of evidence as dependent upon witness or memory of signs and wonders. He has been nourished on such external evidence to the end that his faith now rests upon internal evidence, — has become one with the desires and aspirations of his soul. Foreseeing future scrutiny of the superficial truth of fact, he meets these doubts by declaring that there must be development in the nature of the evidence which shall appeal to developing man ; and that man's progress is dependent on his finding a developing internal warrant for faith in Absolute Love and Power, the good for man of proof, consisting merely in its capacity to educe his faith, not to enable him to dispense with the need of it. So, when man can perceive will and love in man, before assumed to be altogether God's, instead of requiring conviction from the sort of proof that satisfied less developed man, let him exert his faith in the essential truth, acknowledging its action as a result of old processes outgrown because assimilated, and not disproved because in essence true. Pamphylax, Xanthus, Valeus, Theotypas, and narrative and gloss are all imagined by Browning, the Revelation and Gospel of St. John being the main sources feeding the inspiration of the poem. — 6. *Terebinth*. The turpentine tree. — 23. *The decree*. Some decree ordering the persecution of the Christians, perhaps Domitian's. — 50. *Ball of nard*. Spikenard, giving an aromatic odor. — 279. *Prometheus*. The Titan who stole fire from Olympos and brought it to man, defying Zeus who had refused it. Æschylus founded his ' Prometheus Bound' upon the myth, and possibly in the two other parts of this

2 K

Trilogy which have not come down to us, his satyrs may have *touched it in gay wonder* as Browning imagines. — 329. *This Ebion, this Cerinthus.* Ebion is said to have been a pupil of Cerinthus, but may not have been a real person. Cerinthus was a contemporary of John, or nearly so, who held the Ebionite heresy that the Christ part only resided in Jesus, who was merely human, and that this divine part was not crucified, having flown away before. (' Dramatis Personæ,' 1864.)

P. 421. **Fears and Scruples** gives expression to the doubts which beset one who formerly believed implicitly in God (symbolized as an Unseen Friend), but whose belief has been shaken by the criticisms of others, whom he wishes he might refute with a word; but God makes no direct revelations to him, so he concludes that though his belief is not capable of absolute proof he will be thankful for the truth manifest in the ideal. Even this position is assaulted by a menace from some one who suggests that perhaps God is simply trying man's faith by not revealing himself, and will blame man for not gaining a knowledge of him through all obstructions. But that God would be a monster, who refused to accept love because it had not attained perfect knowledge of him, for is not man ready to love him fully revealed as he already loves his manifestations? The only answer to this is that God is God — something higher not lower than man. In a letter to Mr. Wm. G. Kingsland, Browning thus interpreted the poem : —

" I think that the point I wanted to illustrate in the poem you mention was this : Where there is a genuine love of the ' letters ' and ' actions ' of the invisible ' friend,' — however these may be disadvantaged by an inability to meet the objections to their authenticity or historical value urged by ' experts ' who assume the privilege of learning over ignorance, — it would indeed be a wrong to the wisdom and goodness of the ' friend ' if he were supposed capable of overlooking the actual ' love ' and only considering the ' ignorance ' which, failing to in any degree affect ' love ' is really the highest evidence that ' love ' exists. So I *meant*, whether the result be clear or no. . . ." (' Pacchiarotto, with Other Poems,' 1876.)

P. 422. **Artemis Prologizes** represents the goddess Artemis awaiting the revival of the youth Hippolytus, whom she has carried to her woods and given to Asclepios to heal. It is a fragment meant to introduce an unwritten work and carry on the story related by Euripides in ' Hippolytus.' (' Bells and Pomegranates, No. 3 — Dramatic Lyrics,' 1842.)

P. 425. **Pheidippides is** founded on a historical legend told by the Greek historian Herodotus, the dry bones of which Browning has clothed with life. Instead of a sketch of bare events, Pheidippides himself is made to relate to the archons of Athens his own experiences and emotions as he went on his errand to Sparta for aid to Athens, and on his way back met the great god Pan, who promised Athens aid. The incident of Pan's offering him a worthy reward, and of his last run to Athens to announce the victory of Marathon, is added by the poet.

" And first, before they left the city, the generals sent off to Sparta a herald, one Pheidippides, who was by birth an Athenian, and by birth and practice a trained runner. This man, according to the account which he gave to the Athenians on his return, when he was near Mount Parthenium, above Tegea, fell in with the god Pan, who called him by his name, and bade him ask the Athenians ' wherefore they neglected him so entirely, when he was kindly disposed towards them, and had often helped them in times past, and would do so again in time to come ? ' The Athenians, entirely believing in the truth of this report, as soon as their affairs were once more in good order, set up a temple to Pan under the Acropolis, and, in return for the message which I have recorded, established in his honor yearly sacrifices and a torch-race.

" On the occasion of which we speak, when Pheidippides was sent by the

Athenian generals, and, according to his own account saw Pan on his journey, he reached Sparta on the very next day after quitting the city of Athens. Upon his arrival he went before the rulers, and said to them : —

" ' Men of Lacedæmon, the Athenians beseech you to hasten to their aid, and not allow that state, which is the most ancient in all Greece, to be enslaved by the barbarians. Eretria, look you, is already carried away captive, and Greece weakened by the loss of no mean city.'

" Thus did Pheidippides deliver the message committed to him. And the Spartans wished to help the Athenians, but were unable to give them any present succor, as they did not like to break their established law. It was the ninth day of the first decade, and they could not march out of Sparta on the ninth, when the moon had not reached the full. So they waited for the full of the moon." (Herodotus, translated by Rawlinson VI.)

— Χαίρετε νικῶμεν. Rejoice; we conquer! — 4. *Her of the ægis and spear!* Athene (Minerva), who was represented with a shield and spear. — 5. *Ye of the bow,* etc. Artemis (Diana). — 8. *Pan,* the god of woods and fields, of flocks and shepherds. He dwelt in caves, wandered on the mountains and in valleys, played with nymphs, and so on. He was represented as having the horns and hoofs of a goat, which caused many to be frightened at his appearance, hence the word ' panic.' It is said he won the fight at Marathon by causing a panic among the Persians. — 9. Tettix, a grasshopper. Golden grasshoppers were worn by the Athenians to signify that they were the descendants of the original inhabitants of the country, these insects being supposed to spring from the ground. — 18. *Persia bids Athens proffer slaves'-tribute.* Darius (493 B.C.) sent heralds into all parts of Greece to require, according to the custom of the Persians when they wished to exact submission, earth and water. — 19. Eretria was one of the principal cities of the Island of Eubœa. — 20. *Hellas,* Greece. — 31. *Phoibos,* an epithet of Apollo. — 33. *Olumpos,* Greek spelling of Olympus, the home of the gods. — 47. *Filetted victim.* It was the custom to adorn sacrificial victims with ribbons and wreaths. *Fulsome,* rich, liberal. — 52. *Parnes,* an error, these mountains being in the north of Attica, outside the route of Pheidippides. — 62. *Erebos,* the mysterious darkness under earth. — 89. *Miltiades* (died 489), the Greek general who commanded the Athenians at the battle of Marathon, fought 490 B.C. — 106. *Akropolis,* the citadel of Athens. — 109. *Fennel field,* in Greek, *Marathon ;* and Pan meant when he gave Pheidippides the bunch of fennel to signify the place where the victory would be won. (' Dramatic Idyls,' First Series, 1879.)

P. 428. The Patriot is a hero's story of the reward and punishment dealt him for his services by his people within one year. To act regardless of praise or blame, save God's, seems safer. (' Men and Women,' 1855.)

P. 429. Popularity draws in symbolical language the portrait of a poet whose genius the world has not yet recognized, but who holds in his hands the appreciation of the future ; a poet whose inspirations come direct from his own soul, like the fisherman catching fresh netfuls of Tyrian shells. The critics, learned in the poetic inspirations of the past, do not recognize the same thing when it is caught afresh, though there is enough of the marvellous blue dye (poetic inspiration) to furnish forth beauties never before imagined. " Mere genius in the rough ! " they say, not fit to be called art until refined and extracted to but a semblance of its original force by the crowd of imitating poets, who straightway become popular, while he who was their inspiration probably died of starvation. — 24. *Tyre,* ancient city of Phœnicia, with great harbors and splendid buildings. — 26. *Tyrian shells,* the genera *Murex* and *Purpura* have a gland called the " adrectal gland," which secretes a colorless liquid. It turns purple upon exposure to the atmosphere, and was discovered first by the Phœnicians and used as a dye. — 42. *Solomon;* 43. *Cedar House.* 1 Kings vii. — 64. *What porridge had John Keats,* refers, of course, to the lack of contemporary appreciation from which Keats suffered. ('Men and Women,' 1855.)

P. 432. Pisgah Sights. Views over the whole of life from the heights of ripe experience. I. Perceives the reconciliation and relation of all its elements, — unity. II. Perceives the value of imperfection, the uselessness of reformation, — relativity. III. Is a fancy of the soul, disengaged by death from the body, disporting itself in freedom, while the body finds pleasures native to it on earth. At the close of the life of Moses, the Lord caused him to view the land he was not to enter, from "the top of Pisgah." Deut. xxxiv. (I. and II. in 'Pacchiarotto, with Other Poems,' 1876. III. the Prologue to 'La Saisiaz,' 1878, placed by Browning as the third 'Pisgah Sight' in these 'Selections,' 1880.)

P. 435. At the Mermaid puts into the mouth of Shakespeare the refutation of the supposition that his life is to be discovered in his plays. He disclaims any desire to be considered "next Poet" on the ground that he has revealed his soul to the public. Such a poet he depicts in contrast to himself — one, a pessimist, seeing no good in the world, with a mind self-centred upon his own woes; the other, the optimist, seeing good everywhere in the world, regarding his personal woes of no account. The world will object that unless he lays bare his own soul, he cannot hope to touch the heart of humanity. Very well, he will wait for recognition in the future, in the meantime content to be friend and good fellow. *The Mermaid,* a tavern in Cheapside, the favorite resort of the great Elizabethan dramatists and poets. The motto of the poem is adapted from Ben Jonson's lines: "To the Reader," opposite the portrait of Shakespeare, in the First Folio edition: "This figure that thou hére seest put, It was for gentle Shakespeare cut." — 50. *Orichalc,* a mixed metal, something like bronze. — 114. *Threw Venus,* the most successful throw of the dice, double sixes, was called "Venus" by the Romans. ('Pacchiarotto, with Other Poems,' 1876.)

P. 439. House deprecates the assumption of the public, that the private and personal affairs of a poet be open to it. The indelicacy is illustrated by an accidental exposure of a house-interior, and the comments of the curious crowd. As Shakespeare's high example, as alleged in his sonnets, it is doubtful, since he must then have abandoned his characteristic dramatic bent. — 38. *With this same key,* etc. A quotation from Wordsworth's Sonnet, beginning, "Scorn not the Sonnet." ('Pacchiarotto, with Other Poems,' 1876.)

P. 441. Shop is a picturesque presentation of the thought that one's life should not be lived merely for the sake of worldly success, and that if sordid interests are necessary to ensure the existence of the body, the mind and soul should not be allowed to suffer for want of spiritual food. ('Pacchiarotto, with Other Poems,' 1876.)

P. 444. A Tale illustrates the power of love to round out the broken harmonies of life and art, by a Greek tale supposed to be told to a poet by a young girl of a Greek poet, whose lyre-string, snapping at a critical moment, was supplied to perfection by the voice of a cricket, which lighted on the crippled lyre "for mere love of music." — 4. *Was it prose or was it rhyme?* The tale appears in the Greek Anthology in both prose and verse, and is quoted by Strabo from Timæus, and by others. The version Browning used is given in Mackail's 'Select Epigrams from Greek Anthology,' as follows: —

"The strife was of the lyre, and Parthis stood up against me; but when the Locrian shell sounded under the plectrum, a lyre-string rang and snapped jarringly; but ere ever the tune halted in its fair harmonies, a delicate trilling grasshopper seated itself on the lyre and took up the note of the last string, and turned the rustic sound that till then was vocal in the groves to the strain of our touch upon the lyre; and, therefore, Eunomus does honor, blessed son of Leto, to thy grass-hopper, seating the singer in brass upon his harp."

—65. *His Lotte's power too spent*, etc. An allusion to Goethe's elusive manner with young women when affairs pushed him to a choice between marriage and a career, as in Fredrika's case. Charlotte Buff, on whom the Lotte of 'Werther' was modelled, was not really one of these, but, as Goethe says, he bestowed on this Lotte "the qualities of several lovely women." (Epilogue to 'The Two Poets of Croisic,' 1878.)

P. 448. Echetlos illustrates the superior worth of a great deed, in contrast with that of a great name, since a deed can never grow less, while a great name may, as in the case of Miltiades and Themistocles. The poem is developed from a legend of the battle of Marathon told in Pausanias' 'Description of Greece' (Book I., Chap. 32), as follows: "And it chanced, as they say in the battle, that a man of rustic appearance and dress appeared, who slew many of the Persians with a ploughshare, and vanished after the fight: and when the Athenians made enquiry of the oracle, the god gave no other answer, but bade them honor the god *Echet-læus*," that is, the wielder of the ploughshare. — 3. *Marathon*, see Notes, P. 425. — 12. *Kallimachos, Polemarch.* Polemarch was the name given to the archon (or ruler, of which there were nine in Athens) who had charge of military affairs; Kallimichos held that office at the time of the battle of Marathon, and was among the brave Greeks who fell. — 18. *Sakian*. The *Sakæ* were Scythian tribes border-ing on the Bactrians and Sogdians of the East, a part of whom had submitted to pay tribute to Persia. — 28. *Woe for the great name Miltiades.* After the battle of Marathon, Miltiades incurred the displeasure of the Athenians by the failure of his siege of the Island of Paros, which, it was found, he had undertaken in order to avenge a personal spite. He was indicted and sentenced to pay a fine, but died shortly afterwards of a hurt received at Paros. — 29. *Themistocles* (about 514 B.C. to 449 B.C.), chief archon of Athens. Long prominent for his services both in war and peace, he was at last accused of bribery and ostracized; later, of treason, when he fled from Greece to Artaxerxes, in Persia, who treated him with much favor. (' Dramatic Idyls,' Second Series, 1880.)

P. 449. Touch him ne'er so lightly. A lyrical picture of the contrast between the popular notion of the poet's work, as quick-rooted and easy growing, like an annual in a flower garden, and its actual nature, strenuous and persistent in char-acter and nurtured by obstacle, like a slow-growing pine tree. How truly Brown-ing rated the popular opinion of a poet was shown by the criticism that greeted this song, as if he had drawn a contrast between all other poets and himself. In copying the poem in the autograph album of a young American girl in Venice, October, 1880, he added the following comment, which explains his intention : —

> " Thus I wrote in London, musing on my betters,
> Poets dead and gone; and lo, the critics cried,
> ' Out on such a boast!' as if I dreamed that fetters
> Binding Dante bind up — me ! as if true pride
> Were not also humble !
>   So I smiled and sighed
> As I oped your book in Venice this bright morning,
> Sweet new friend of mine ! and felt the clay or sand,
> Whatso'er my soil be, break — for praise or scorning —
> Out in grateful fancies — weeds ; but weeds expand
> Almost into flowers, held by such a kindly hand."

(Epilogue to ' Dramatic Idyls,' Second Series, 1880.)

P. 449. Wanting is What? may simply express that no beauty is perfect without its complement, love; or it may refer more particularly to Divine love, without which life is incomplete. The latter interpretation is rendered probable on account of the use of the term, " O comer," line 9, which the Rev. J. Sharpe points out is one of the titles of the Messiah in the New Testament. " ὁ ἐρχόμενος," the Future One, He who shall come (Mat. xi. 3; xxi. 9; Luke vii. 19, 20; John xii. 13; vi. 14; xi. 27). (Prologue to ' Jocoseria,' 1883.)

P. 450. Never the Time and the Place. A song of longing for a loved Presence, lacking under friendly conditions of time and place, and only to be supplied now under unfriendly conditions in a dream and within the grave, yet towards which the love whose power the lover's Past has known shall be able to guide his Future. (' Jocoseria,' 1883.)

P. 450. Round us the Wild Creatures. A lyric illustrating the thought that two who love each other should let their love expand into a love for humanity, and should live in and for the world, not selfishly for each other alone. (' Ferishtah's Fancies,' 1884.)

P. 451. Ask not one least word of praise, sings the inadequacy of speech and the intelligence of sense to impart the emotions of the soul. (' Ferishtah's Fancies,' 1884.)

P. 451. Epilogue to Ferishtah's Fancies expresses a doubt as to whether an optimistic view of life is not after all but the illumination shed over it by love. (1884.)

P. 452. The Names. This sonnet, contrasting the potency mixed with love associated with Shakespeare's name, as representing the utmost of finite creative might, with the unmixed awe associated with the name of the Infinite Creator, is based upon the fact that the Hebrews regard the Sacred Name as unspeakable, substituting Adonai for Jahwé in reading. (Written for the book of the Shaksperian Show, held in London, May 29–31, 1884, to pay off the debt on the Woman's Hospital.)

P. 452. Why I am a Liberal? Because, answers the poet, freedom is the necessary condition for development. Therefore, he wishes for all others the same opportunities as he himself has had for that development. This poem was written in answer to the question, Why I am a Liberal? sent out by Cassell and Co. to English men of letters. It was published by them, together with the other replies, in a volume edited by Andrew Reid in 1885.

P. 453. Prologue to ' Asolando ' exalts the clear sobriety of sight that comes with age to the poet, divesting nature of the alien, falsifying vari-color that made her seem divine, and reporting her works truly as akin to man, God alone transcending both nature and humanity. (' Asolando,' published Dec. 12, 1889, the day of the poet's death : date given on the title-page, however, is 1890.)

P. 454. Rosny. A girl, whose lover has gone to the war, holds dreamy converse with herself, her mind divided between a mood in which she pictures her pride in him, returned with an honorable scar on his face, while he declares that with her love in his soul he could not do other than conquer his foes and return to her safe ; and a mood in which she pictures him dead on the battlefield, driven to his fate by her love, and finds it better that it should be so, since certain envious ones might sneer that they would hardly be proud of a hero who returned from the war safe. — 2. *Clara, Clara.* This refrain throughout the poem makes it particularly difficult of interpretation. It has been suggested that Clara is a rival whom the speaker addresses. It seems rather to the editors of the present volume to be the speaker's grief-stricken address to herself, showing the conflict between her love and ambition, and the realization that if her lover falls it will be because her ideal of heroism has driven him to his fate. (' Asolando,' 1889.)

P. 455. Poetics illustrates the deficiency of metaphors conventionally drawn from the inanimate, or the lower animal world, to celebrate fitly the beauty of human love. ('Asolando,' 1889.)

P. 455. Summum Bonum. In a moment of love, which is the highest good, is contained all the beauty and truth of the universe. ('Asolando,' 1889.)

P. 455. Mucklemouth Meg. A lively ballad describing an actual foray over the border of a young English lord, William Scott of the House of Harden; his seizure by the Scotch laird, Sir Gideon Murray of Elibank; the intervention of the Dame should he marry wide-mouthed Meg; his contumacy, confinement, and happy release by the misnamed Meg. ('Asolando,' 1889.)

P. 456. Epilogue to 'Asolando' deprecates the thought that those who love the poet should pity him in death, and so, mistake the whole tenor of his life with its strenuous hopefulness in the face of all difficulties, and its joyous faith in a future of soul development. ('Asolando,' 1889.)

BIBLIOGRAPHY.

———•◦•———

1833. Pauline: A Fragment of a Confession.
1835. Paracelsus.
1837. Strafford: A Historical Tragedy.
1840. Sordello.
1841. Bells and Pomegranates. No. I. Pippa Passes.
1842. Bells and Pomegranates. No. II. King Victor and King Charles.
1842. Bells and Pomegranates. No. III. Dramatic Lyrics.

CONTENTS.

Cavalier Tunes:
   (1) Marching Along.
   (2) Give a Rouse.
   (3) My Wife Gertrude.
Italy and France.
Camp and Cloister.
In a Gondola.
Artemis Prologizes.
Waring.
Queen-Worship:
   (1) Rudel and the Lady of Tripoli.
   (2) Cristina.
Madhouse Cells.
Through the Metidja to Abd-el-Kadr. 1842.
The Pied Piper of Hamelin.
1843. Bells and Pomegranates. No. IV. The Return of the Druses. A Tragedy in Five Acts.
1843. Bells and Pomegranates. No. V. A Blot in the 'Scutcheon. A Tragedy in Three Acts.

1844. Bells and Pomegranates. No. VI. Colombe's Birthday. A Play in Five Acts.
1845. Bells and Pomegranates. No. VII. Dramatic Romances and Lyrics.

CONTENTS.

" How they brought the Good News from Ghent to Aix."
Pictor Ignotus.
Italy in England.
England in Italy.
The Lost Leader.
The Lost Mistress.
Home Thoughts from Abroad.
The Tomb at St. Praxed's.
Garden Fancies:
   (1) The Flower's Name.
   (2) Sibrandus Schafnaburgensis.
France and Spain:
   (1) The Laboratory.
   (2) The Confessional.
The Flight of the Duchess.
Earth's Immortalities.
Song: " Nay, but you, who do not love her."
The Boy and the Angel.
Night and Morning.
Claret and Tokay.
Saul.
Time's Revenges.
The Glove.

504

1846. Bells and Pomegranates. No. VIII. and last. Luria: and A Soul's Tragedy.

1849. Poems: A New Edition in Two Volumes.

1850. Christmas-Eve and Easter-Day.

1852. Letters of Percy Bysshe Shelley. With an Introductory Essay by Robert Browning.

1854. Two Poems by Elizabeth Barrett and Robert Browning. [The Twins.]

1855. Cleon.

1855. The Statue and the Bust.

1855. Men and Women. In two vols.

CONTENTS. I.

Love among the Ruins.
A Lovers' Quarrel.
Evelyn Hope.
Up at a Villa — Down in the City. (As Distinguished by an Italian Person of Quality.)
A Woman's Last Word.
Fra Lippo Lippi.
A Toccata of Galuppi's.
By the Fireside.
Any Wife to Any Husband.
An Epistle containing the Strange Medical Experience of Karshish, the Arab Physician.
Mesmerism.
A Serenade at the Villa.
My Star.
Instans Tyrannus.
A Pretty Woman.
"Childe Roland to the Dark Tower came."
Respectability.
A Light Woman.
The Statue and the Bust.
Love in a Life.
Life in a Love.
How it strikes a Contemporary.
The Last Ride Together.
The Patriot — An Old Story.
Master Hugues of Saxe-Gotha.
Bishop Blougram's Apology.
Memorabilia.

CONTENTS. II.

1855. Andrea del Sarto. (Called "The Faultless Painter.")
Before.
After.
In Three Days.
In a Year.
Old Pictures in Florence.
In a Balcony. First Part.
In a Balcony. Second Part.
In a Balcony. Third Part.
Saul.
"De Gustibus —"
Women and Roses.
Protus.
Holy-Cross Day. (On which the Jews were forced to attend an Annual Christian Sermon in Rome.)
The Guardian-Angel: A Picture at Fano.
Cleon.
The Twins.
Popularity.
The Heretic's Tragedy: A Middle-Age Interlude.
Two in the Campagna.
A Grammarian's Funeral.
One Way of Love.
Another Way of Love.
"Transcendentalism:" A Poem in Twelve Books.
Misconceptions.
One Word More. To E. B. B.

1863. The Poetical Works of Robert Browning. Third Edition.

1863. Selections from the Poetical Works of Robert Browning. Three volumes.

1864. Gold Hair: A Legend of Pornic.

1864. Dramatis Personæ.

CONTENTS.

James Lee.
Gold Hair: A Legend of Pornic.
The Worst of it.
Dîs Aliter Visum; or, Le Byron de Nos Jours.

1864. Too Late.
 Abt Vogler.
 Rabbi ben Ezra.
 A Death in the Desert.
 Caliban upon Setebos ; or Natural
   Theology in the Island.
 Confessions.
 May and Death.
 Prospice.
 Youth and Art.
 A Face.
 A Likeness.
 Mr. Sludge, " The Medium."
 Apparent Failure.
 Epilogue.
1865. A Selection from the Works of
   Robert Browning.
1868. The Poetical Works of Robert
   Browning. Six volumes.
1868. The Ring and the Book.
1871. Balaustion's Adventure : Includ-
   ing a Transcript from Euripides.
1871. Prince Hohenstiel-Schwangau,
   Saviour of Society.
1872. Fifine at the Fair.
1872. Selections from the Poetical
   Works.
1873. Red Cotton Night-Cap Country ;
   or, Turf and Towers.
1875. Aristophanes' Apology : Includ-
   ing a Transcript from Euripides,
   being the Last Adventure of
   Balaustion.
1875. The Inn Album.
1876. Pacchiarotto, and how he worked
   in Distemper : with Other
   Poems.

CONTENTS.

Prologue.
Of Pacchiarotto, and how he
   worked in Distemper.
At the " Mermaid."
House.
Shop.
Pisgah-Sights (1).
Pisgah-Sights (2).
Fears and Scruples.
Natural Magic.

1876. Magical Nature.
 Bifurcation.
 Numpholeptos.
 Appearances.
 St. Martin's Summer.
 Hervé Riel.
 A Forgiveness.
 Cenciaja.
 Filippo Baldinucci on the Privi
   lege of Burial.
 Epilogue.
1877. The Agamemnon of Æschylus.
1878. La Saisiaz.
1878. The Two Poets of Croisic.
1879. Dramatic Idyls.

CONTENTS.

Martin Relph.
Pheidippides.
Halbert and Hob.
Ivàn Ivànovitch.
Tray.
Ned Bratts.

1880. Dramatic Idyls : Second Series.

CONTENTS.

Proem.
Echetlos.
Clive.
Muléykeh.
Pietro of Abano.
Doctor ——.
Pan and Luna.
Epilogue.

1880. Selections from the Poetical
   Works of Robert Browning :
   Second Series.
1883. Jocoseria.

CONTENTS.

Wanting is — what ?
Donald.
Solomon and Balkis.
Cristina and Monaldeschi.
Mary Wollstonecraft and Fuseli.
Adam, Lilith, and Eve.
Ixion.
Jochanan Hakkadosh.
Never the Time and the Place.

1883. Pambo.
1884. Ferishtah's Fancies.

CONTENTS.

Prologue.
The Eagle.
The Melon-Seller.
Shah Abbas.
The Family.
The Sun.
Mihrab Shah.
A Camel-Driver.
Two Camels.
Cherries.
Plot-Culture.
A Pillar at Sebzevar.
A Bean-Stripe: Also Apple-Eat-
      ing.
Epilogue.

1887. Parleyings with Certain People of
      Importance in their Day, to wit:
      Bernard de Mandeville, Daniel
      Bartoli, Christopher Smart,
      George Bubb Dodington, Fran-
      cis Furini, Gerard de Lairesse,
      and Charles Avison. Intro-
      duced by a Dialogue between
      Apollo and the Fates; con-
      cluded by another between
      John Fust and his Friends.

1888-9. The Poetical Works of Robert
      Browning. Sixteen volumes.

1890 [1889]. Asolando: Fancies and
      Facts.

CONTENTS.

1890. Prologue.
      Rosny.
      Dubiety.
      Now.
      Humility.
      Poetics.
      Summum Bonum.
      A Pearl, a Girl.
      Speculative.
      White Witchcraft.
      Bad Dreams, I.
      Bad Dreams, II.
      Bad Dreams, III.
      Bad Dreams, IV.
      Inapprehensiveness.
      Which?
      The Cardinal and the Dog.
      The Pope and the Net.
      The Bean-Feast.
      Muckle-mouth Meg.
      Arcades Ambo.
      The Lady and the Painter.
      Ponte dell' Angelo, Venice.
      Beatrice Signorini.
      Flute Music, with an Accompani-
          ment.
      " Imperante Augusto natusest — "
      Development.
      Rephan.
      Reverie.
      Epilogue.

INDEX TO POEMS.

	PAGE			PAGE	
	Poems	Notes		Poems	Notes
Abt Vogler	152	476	Fireside, By the	64	464
After	314	492	Flight of the Duchess, The	19	462
Amphibian	282	489	Forgiveness, A	241	486
Andrea del Sarto	133	472	Fra Lippo Lippi	124	470
Any Wife to Any Husband	72	465	French Camp, Incident of the	43	463
Apparent Failure	162	478	Garden Fancies	219	483
Apparitions	218	483	Gismond, Count	5	460
Appearances	230	485	Glove, The	9	460
Artemis Prologizes	422	498	Gold Hair	91	466
Ask not One Least Word of Praise	451	502	Gondola, In a	45	464
"Asolando," Epilogue to	456	503	Grammarian's Funeral, A	171	478
"Asolando," Prologue to	453	502	Guardian-Angel, The	158	477
Balcony, In a	318	493	Heretic's Tragedy, The	275	488
Before	312	492	Hervé Riel	314	492
Bifurcation	237	485	Holy-Cross Day	278	489
Bishop Blougram's Apology	347	495	Home Thoughts from Abroad	113	469
Bishop orders his Tomb at Saint Praxed's Church, The	138	473	House	439	500
			Householder, The	307	491
Boy and the Angel, The	403	497	How it strikes a Contemporary	143	475
Caliban upon Setebos	191	481	"How they brought the Good News from Ghent to Aix"	39	462
Cavalier Tunes	310	492			
Cenciaja	251	487	In a Gondola	45	464
"Childe Roland to the Dark Tower came"	165	478	Instans Tyrannus	182	479
			Italian in England, The	113	469
Cleon	174	479	"James Lee's Wife," Song from	79	465
Confessions	306	491	James Lee's Wife	288	490
Count Gismond	5	460	Laboratory, The	89	466
Cristina	4	460	Last Ride together, The	56	464
Death in the Desert, A	407	497	Liberal, Why I am a	452	502
"De Gustibus—"	157	477	Life in a Love	88	466
Dis Aliter Visum; or, Le Byron de Nos Jours	301	491	Light Woman, A	86	465
			Likeness, A	238	485
Earth's Immortalities	56	464	Lost Leader, The	44	463
Echetlos	448	501	Lost Mistress, The	224	484
Englishman in Italy, The	117	469	Love among the Ruins	103	467
Epilogue	213	483	Love in a Life	88	466
Epilogue to "Asolando"	456	503	Lovers' Quarrel, A	51	464
Epilogue to "Ferishtah's Fancies"	451	502	Magical Nature	219	483
Epistle, An	184	480	Master Hugues of Saxe-Gotha	147	475
Eurydice to Orpheus	9	460	May and Death	240	486
Evelyn Hope	160	478	Meeting at Night	81	465
Face, A	1	459	Memorabilia	162	478
Fears and Scruples	421	498	"Mermaid," At the	435	500
"Ferishtah's Fancies," Epilogue to	451	502	Mesmerism	59	464
			Metidja to Abd-el-Kadr, Through the	42	463
Filippo Baldinucci on the Privilege of Burial	259	487	Misconceptions	83	465

	PAGE			PAGE	
	Poems	Notes		Poems	Notes
Mr. Sludge, " The Medium "	369	497	Rudel to the Lady of Tripoli	225	484
Muckle-Mouth Meg	455	503	Saul	198	481
My Last Duchess	2	459	Serenade at the Villa, A	14	461
My Star	1	459	Shop	441	500
Names, The	452	502	Soliloquy of the Spanish Cloister	272	488
Natural Magic	218	483	Song	14	461
Never the Time and the Place	450	502	Song from " James Lee's Wife "	79	465
Numpholeptos	226	484	Song from " Paracelsus "	41	463
Old Pictures in Florence	339	494	Song from " Pippa Passes "	3, 39, 459,	462
One Way of Love	225	484	Spanish Cloister, Soliloquy of the	272	488
" Paracelsus," Song from	41	463	Statue and the Bust, The	96	466
Parting at Morning	81	465	St. Martin's Summer	285	489
Patriot, The	428	499	Summum Bonum	455	503
Pictor Ignotus	123	470	Tale, A	444	500
" Pippa Passes," Song from	3, 39, 459,	462	Three Days, In	223	483
Pisgah Sights. 1	432	500	Time's Revenges	105	467
Pisgah Sights. 2	433	500	Toccata of Galuppi's, A	141	474
Pisgah Sights. 3	434	500	Too Late	234	485
Pheidippides	425	498	Touch him ne'er so Lightly	449	501
Poetics	455	503	Tray	309	492
Popularity	429	499	Two in the Campagna	155	477
Porphyria's Lover	257	487	Up at a Villa — Down in the City.	120	470
Pretty Woman, A	83	465	Wall, A	217	483
Privilege of Burial, Filippo Baldi-			Wanting is — What?	449	502
nucci on the	259	487	Waring	107	467
Prologue to "Asolando "	453	502	Why I am a Liberal	452	502
Prospice	164	478	Woman's Last Word, A	79	465
Protus	146	475	Women and Roses	81	465
Rabbi Ben Ezra	207	482	Worst of it, The	230	485
Respectability	300	491	Year, In a	76	465
Rosny	454	502	Youth and Art	17	461
Round us the Wild Creatures	450	502			

INDEX TO FIRST LINES.

	PAGE
Ah, did you once see Shelley plain	162
Ah, Love, but a day	288
All I believed is true	59
All I can say is — I saw it	218
All June I bound the rose in sheaves	225
All 's over, then: does truth sound bitter	224
All that I know	1
All the health and the bloom of the year in the bag of one bee	455
Among these latter busts we count by scores	146
And so you found that poor room dull	230
As I ride, as I ride	42
Ask not one least word of praise	451
At the midnight in the silence of the sleep-time	456
Beautiful Evelyn Hope is dead	160
But do not let us quarrel any more	133
But give them me, the mouth, the eyes, the brow	9
Christ God who savest man, save most	5
Cleon the poet, (from the sprinkled isles	174
Could I but live again	433
Dear and great Angel, wouldst thou only leave	158
Dear, had the world in its caprice	300
Escape me	88
Fear death? to feel the fog in my throat	164
Fee, faw, fum! bubble and squeak	278
First I salute this soil of the blessed, river and rock	425
Flower — I never fancied, jewel — I profess you	219
Fortù, Fortù, my beloved one, sit here by my side	117
Frowned the Laird on the Lord: "So red-handed I catch thee	455
Give her but a least excuse to love me	3
Good to forgive	434
Grow old along with me	207
Gr-r-r — there go, my heart's abhorrence	272
Had I but plenty of money, money enough and to spare	120
Heap cassia, sandal-buds and stripes	41
"Heigho," yawned one day King Francis	9
Here is a story shall stir you! Stand up, Greeks dead and gone	448
Here's my case. Of old I used to love him	421
Here's the garden she walked across	219
Here was I with my arm and heart	234
Hist, but a word, fair and soft	149
How well I know what I mean to do	64
I am a goddess of the ambrosial courts	422
I am indeed the personage you know	241
I am poor brother Lippo, by your leave	124
I could have painted pictures like that youth's	123
I dream of a red-rose tree	81
If one could have that little head of hers	1
I know a Mount, the gracious Sun perceives	225
I — "next Poet?" No, my hearties	435
I only knew one poet in my life	143
I said — Then, dearest, since 't is so	56
I send my heart up to thee, all my heart	45
I sprang to the stirrup, and Joris, and he	39
It once might have been, once only	16
It was roses, roses, all the way	428
I 've a Friend, over the sea	105
I wish that when you died last May	240
I wonder do you feel to-day	155
Just for a handful of silver he left us	44
Karshish, the picker-up of learning's crumbs	184
Kentish Sir Byng stood for his King	310
Let 's contend no more, Love	79
Let them fight it out, friend! things have gone too far	312
Let us begin and carry up this corpse	171
May I print, Shelley, how it came to pass	251
Morning, evening, noon, and night	403
My first thought was, he lied in every word	165
My love, this is the bitterest, that thou	72
Nay but you, who do not love her	14
Never any more	76
Never the time and the place	450
No, boy, we must not (so began	259
No, for I 'll save it! Seven years since	162
No more wine! then we 'll push back chairs and talk	347
No protesting, dearest	285
Now	318
Now, don't, sir! Don't expose me! Just this once	369
Now that I, tying thy glass mask tightly	89
Of the million or two, more or less	182

PAGE

Oh, Galuppi, Baldassare, this is very sad to find 141
Oh, good gigantic smile o' the brown old earth 79
Oh, Love — no, Love! All the noise below, Love 451
Oh, the beautiful girl, too white . . 91
Oh, to be in England now that April's there 113
Oh, what a dawn of day . . . 51
On the first of the Feast of Feasts . 213
On the sea, and at the Hogue, sixteen hundred ninety-two . . . 314
O the old wall here! How could I pass 217
Over the ball of it 432
Room after room 88
Round the cape of a sudden came the sea 81
Round us the wild creatures, overhead the trees 450
Said Abner, "At last thou art come! Ere I tell, ere thou speak . . . 198
Savage I was sitting in my house, late, lone 307
See, as the prettiest graves will do in time 56
Shakespeare! — to such name's sounding what succeeds 452
Shall I sonnet-sing you about myself 439
She should never have looked at me if she meant I should not love her . . 4
Sing me a hero. Quench my thirst . 308
So far as our story approaches the end . 86
So, friend, your shop was all your house 441
So I shall see her in three days . . 223
Some people hang portraits up . . 238
"So say the foolish!" Say the foolish so, Love 455
Stand still, true poet that you are . . 429
Still you stand, still you listen, still you smile 226

PAGE

Stop, let me have the truth of that . 301
Such a starved bank of moss . . 218
[Supposed of Pamphylax the Antiochene 406
Take the cloak from his face and at first 314
That fawn-skin-dappled hair of hers . 83
That second time they hunted me . . 113
That's my last Duchess painted on the wall 2
That was I, you heard last night . . 14
The fancy I had to-day . . . 282
The gray sea and the long black land . 81
The Lord we look to once for all . 275
The morn when first it thunders in March 339
The Poet's age is sad: for why . . 453
The rain set early in to-night . . 257
There's a palace in Florence, the world knows well 96
The year's at the spring . . . 39
This is a spray the Bird clung to . . 83
Touch him ne'er so lightly, into song he broke 449
Vanity, saith the preacher, vanity . 138
Wanting is — What 449
We were two lovers; let me lie by her . 237
What a pretty tale you told me . . 444
What is he buzzing in my ears . . 306
What's become of Waring . . . 107
Where the quiet-coloured end of evening smiles 103
"Why?" Because all I haply can and do 452
['Will sprawl, now that the heat of day is best 191
Woe, he went galloping into the war . 454
Would it were I had been false, not you . 230
Would that the structure brave, the manifold music I build 152
Your ghost will walk, you lover of trees 157
You know, we French stormed Ratisbon 43
You're my friend 19